Foundations
of Education

an introduction to the
Foundations of EDUCATION
Second Edition

Allan C. Ornstein
Loyola University

Daniel U. Levine
University of Missouri, Kansas City

HOUGHTON MIFFLIN COMPANY   **BOSTON**

Dallas   Geneva, Illinois   Hopewell, New Jersey   Palo Alto   London

The future belongs to the children and youth.
To Stacey and Joel, from Allan
To Jennifer and Bruce, from Daniel

Printed in the U.S.A.

Library of Congress Catalog Card Number: 80-50974

ISBN: 0-395-30690-6

FOREWORD

Try as hard as we may to prevent changes, things do not remain the same in either form or substance. Nevertheless, certain issues and problems persist through time and, like those of other domains such as economics and politics, the issues and problems of education continue to revolve about continuing themes.

Among school personnel, there continue to be questions about the purpose of schools, how they should be financed and controlled, what they should teach, and how those subjects should be taught. Then there are the broader issues of how these educational institutions should be related to community life and how they should respond to the various issues and conflicts that, from time to time, arise in the community—issues related to social classes, racial and ethnic groups, and economic and political interests. Furthermore, students have become concerned about their own rights and privileges within the school itself—and these have sometimes become matters of litigation. The increasing traffic in drugs and alcoholic beverages has placed upon the school not only more serious discipline problems but also new problems of moral and character education. The relationships and interrelationships between all of these issues and problems are treated in this second edition in the context of the emerging social, economic, and political fabric of American society.

This new edition, as was true of the first, treats these matters of educational concern in a fundamental and thorough manner. It provides not only data about current problems but also gives a firm historical and philosophical orientation for the student to understand issues in the context of continuing social evolution. The treatment of this material is based not only on historical and philosophical concepts and principles but also on hard and current data, a unique feature of this text.

As a student, you will find here a lucid and substantial treatment of the issues you will confront in classroom discussion, no matter what position you may hold. You will find in the pages of this volume, the knowledge you will need as you work in schools, in teacher organizations, and in communities, and as you engage parents, teachers, students, and community members in a common effort to shape the school system of this nation for our time.

B. Othanel Smith
Advisory Editor

PREFACE

An Introduction to the Foundations of Education is an overview of the foundations of education intended for introductory courses. It is meant to interest both those students who want to teach and new teachers, as well as citizens who are directly or indirectly concerned about educational issues and policies in this country. This overview has proven to be the most appropriate form for beginning students in education. It provides education majors with a foundation on which to build their later professional curriculum and noneducation majors with a broad background of educational ideas. It also gives students a frame of reference for understanding the important problems and aspects of the past, present, and future in the field of education. Finally, it fosters students' interests in teaching and helps them to make an early decision about a teaching career.

This new edition includes a number of major changes. It was written with the collaboration of Daniel Levine, a well-known social and urban foundations educator. That, alone, has provided fresh insight for the text. In addition, the psychological foundations section of the first edition has been omitted. Four new chapters were written and all others have been updated and revised.

The book is divided into four major parts. Part One, "Understanding the Teaching Profession," comprises four chapters and sets the stage for a discussion of the dynamics of teaching and the teaching profession. Two new chapters of importance have been written for this part. Chapter 1 has added sections on job satisfaction, stress and coping, and teacher burnout. Chapter 2 contains new data on teacher centers and the early field experiences of teachers, as well as on licensing procedures and teacher reciprocity. Chapter 3 is new and examines teacher organizations, collective bargaining, and teacher professionalism. Chapter 4 is also new and discusses the relationship of teacher behavior and student outcomes, classroom management and student discipline, and teacher competency.

Part Two, "Historical and Philosophical Foundations," examines the roots of American education and traces the present through the past. The historical and philosophical roots of education do not change rapidly. However, Chapter 5 raises some new questions about Greek, Roman, and Renaissance education, and Chapter 6 discusses some additional pioneers of education—John Locke, Booker T. Washington, W.E.B. DuBois—along with influential educators such as Ivan Illich and John Holt. Chapter 7 has a new discussion on historiographical education topics, particularly the celebrationist, liberal, and revisionist interpretations of education. Chapter 8 adds a new section on Thomism.

Part Three, "Social Foundations," focuses on socialization, social class, minority status, peer group influences, and educational achievement. Chapter 9 now details sex roles and sex differences, as well as the achievements of women. Socializing agents—the family, peer group, school, and mass media (including television)—are presented, too. In Chapter 10, new sections on social class, minority status, affirmative action, educational deprivation, environment vs. heredity, equal educational opportunity, and the difference school make are included. Chapter 11 views extracurricular activities and student responsibilities as a complement to the first edition's discussion of student rights.

Part Four, "Schools in a Changing Society," deals with schools as a social institution within society that serves the needs of all students. There are two new chapters in this section. In Chapter 12, the discussion of instructional objectives and the aims of education for the 1970s has been expanded, and there is an added section on gifted and talented students. Chapter 13 includes new information on present and future curricular trends. Chapter 14 now discusses alternative schools, magnet schools, and school reform in general. The final two chapters of the book are also new. In Chapter 15, there is a comprehensive discussion of three important aspects of school organization: desegregation, decentralization and compensatory education. Chapter 16 examines the trends and issues affecting education for the 1980s. These include multicultural education, education for the handicapped, mastery learning, minimum competency testing, school finances, the role of the courts and the federal government, and educational futurism.

In short, this book has had a major revision in order to improve and update the content—so as to make it most meaningful for students.

The purpose of the book remains the same as in the first edition: to offer a body of information on the various foundations of education with a broad, interdisciplinary view of education. The scope of topics has been organized to give students ready access to important ideas and issues and influential educational thinkers and theories of the past, present, and future. It summarizes and synthesizes the important concepts and research findings of education in a practical way; controversial data are not shunned.

To give the greatest value to the book, study questions and activities are provided at the end of each chapter, along with introductory overviews and suggested readings for each part. Marginal notes also appear throughout the text material to help orient and inform the reader. Finally, to maximize the value of the book, as in the case of the previous edition, an instructor's manual has been provided.

In presenting the material, both authors have utilized their past experiences as public school teachers, as well as their present college-level experiences in teaching the foundations of education course. Gerald Guteck, as in the first edition, contributed the material for Part Two.

The authors wish to thank the following reviewers for their help in preparing this edition: David Mielke of Appalachian State University, Austin Groden of the University Hospitals of Cleveland, Charles L. Foxworth of Louisiana Tech University, and Charles E. Skipper of Miami University of Ohio. We particularly want to thank Project Editor Robyn Greenberg for her assistance and patience in all stages of manuscript preparation, and Louise Waller, Sponsoring Editor, who initiated and guided the development of this second edition.

Allan C. Ornstein
Daniel U. Levine

CONTENTS

PART ONE
UNDERSTANDING
THE TEACHING
PROFESSION

No one can be a genuine teacher who has not made a real attempt to understand the nature of the teaching profession. To be effective, teachers must gain insight into the various relationships and trends that influence their work. They must also be aware of the issues that directly affect their status as professionals, and how these concerns change through time. In Part One, we take a look at the climate in which teachers operate today, observe how this climate affects both the act of teaching and the profession, and examine what teachers are doing to shape their future.

Chapter 1 is devoted to the situation of the teacher—reasons for becoming a teacher, the economic position and prestige of teachers, and the demand for teachers. We deal with the basic decision to teach, we analyze salaries to teachers and supply-demand curves, and we review the current and prospective job market for teachers.

In the second chapter, the discussion shifts to issues related to teacher preparation. Three questions arise: What is the appropriate mix of general or liberal education, specialization, and professional education courses needed to prepare effective teachers? Do we know how to train effective teachers for the world of the classroom? What are the trends in teacher preparation programs?

The third chapter is concerned with teaching as a profession. After presenting information on the two major teacher organizations (the National Education Association and the American Federation of Teachers), we inquire whether teaching is fully a profession and discuss recent trends toward increased professionalization.

Chapter 4 deals with teacher effectiveness and evaluation. What is a "good" teacher? Can teachers be held accountable for effective teaching? These questions are investigated by examining research on teacher behavior as well as proposals that have been made to introduce accountability in elementary and secondary schools.

Our portrayal of the teaching profession as we enter the 1980s may be viewed as either discouraging or encouraging. On the one hand, there is evidence

that teachers' salaries and prestige are not as high as
those of some other professions, and that problems
and pressures in the schools can make the teaching
job troublesome for persons who do not handle stress
well. Teacher salaries have improved over the past
two decades, but inflation has eliminated much of
this gain in recent years. In addition, there is a general oversupply of instructors, which limits the job
market for many prospective teachers. On the other
hand, teachers are much better organized than they
were in the past, and teaching has become more of a
profession. As in previous eras, teachers enter the
field because it provides an opportunity to perform
an important and personally rewarding service to
society. Much has been learned about effective
teaching and instruction. Later parts of this book
will show that progress can and is being made
toward improving elementary and secondary schools
in the face of enormous challenges posed by a rapidly
changing society.

CHAPTER 1
MOTIVATION AND STATUS OF THE TEACHER

Focusing questions

What are the advantages and disadvantages of becoming a teacher?

What is satisfying and dissatisfying in the job of teaching?

How does teachers' prestige compare to other occupations?

What do beginning teachers earn? How does this compare with other occupations?

What are the employment trends for teachers?

What jobs other than teaching in elementary and secondary schools are open to persons trained as teachers?

Anyone who is considering becoming a teacher should have some understanding about the situation of the teacher. Why do people become teachers? If given a chance to do it all over again, would they still choose teaching? To what degree do teachers enjoy the respect of the American public? What level and range of salaries do they earn? Are teachers still underpaid? What are the supply-demand trends for the profession? These are some of the important concerns of the teaching profession that will be explored in this chapter.

The American people and the teachers of the country are natural partners; the people depend on teachers to educate their children and the teachers are paid by the citizenry through taxes. While the public must recognize the impact of the teaching profession on their lives, teachers must be aware of their responsibilities as members of the profession. Together, the public and teaching profession can work to improve education, and, through education, to enhance the general welfare of the country.

Natural partnership between citizens and teachers

WHY TEACH? The teaching profession should attract the keenest minds, the finest personalities, and the most humane people. This, of course, does not always happen. Generally, those who enter the profession are "average" people with "average" abilities. Many come from working-class and low-income backgrounds and envision teaching as a means of upward mobility. Women tend to decide earlier in life than men to go into teaching. One reason, perhaps, is that until very recently, a wider range of professional choices was open to men. Another reason is that women seem to achieve more status in teaching than do men. Parents often encourage their daughters to become teachers but rarely express similar feelings to their sons. As a result, females comprised 66 percent and males comprised 34 percent of the public school teachers in 1979. More than 80 percent of the elementary teachers and 45 percent of the secondary teachers were females. More men are gradually entering the profession, however. Between 1955 and 1979, male teachers increased by 5 percent; more important, the younger male group (under 40 years) today is considerably larger than the older group.[1]

Teachers are "average" people

MOTIVATION There are many motives, both positive and negative, for choosing a career in teaching. Those who are thinking of entering the teaching profession—and even those who are already teaching—should ask themselves why they have made, or are about to make, this choice. On the positive side their motives may include (1) a love of

Reasons for entering the profession

1 *Digest of Education Statistics, 1979* (Washington, D.C.: U.S. Government Printing Office, 1979), p. 54, Table 49; National Education Association, *Teacher Supply and Demand in Public Schools, 1978* (Washington, D.C.: NEA, 1979), p. 4.

children, (2) a desire to impart knowledge, (3) an interest in and excitement about teaching, and (4) a desire to perform a valuable service to society. Negative reasons may be (1) job security and pension, (2) relatively short working days and long vacations, (3) the difficulty of preparing for another field, causing a switch to education, and (4) need for income while preparing for another profession.[2] Also, there may be some persons who are undecided on which profession to enter, and teaching may seem to them at least a viable possibility.

For the prospective (or beginning) teacher, an awareness of the importance of the decision to enter the teaching field is essential. Your reasons, both conscious and unconscious, for choosing teaching as a career will undoubtedly affect your attitude and behavior with your students if you eventually become (or are already) a teacher. Precise analysis of your feelings is hard to come by, but it might be beneficial to discuss them in class. Ignoring what may appear to be negative motives, denying that they exist, or feeling guilty about them is not the best procedure. Pure dedication and love of teaching and children seem to be fables from the past, when the profession was imbued with the image of the schoolmarm and Mr. Chips. Whatever your reasons for wanting to become a teacher, you might consider the following reasons given by others already teaching.

The
schoolmarm
and Mr. Chips

A nationwide stratified sample of 1,533 teachers taken in 1971 by the National Education Association listed the major reasons they decided to enter the profession. The main reason is a *desire to work with young people*. This was indicated by almost 72 percent of the respondents as one of their three major reasons and was the *only* reason on the list of a majority of the teachers. Next highest response was the *value of education to society* with 37 percent. Predictably, a much larger percentage of secondary than elementary school teachers were drawn to teaching because of their *interest in a subject-matter field*. It was mentioned by 57 percent of the secondary teachers, compared to 14 percent of the elementary teachers.[3]

A desire to
work with
young people

Career choices are also likely to be related to sex, age, and level of teaching (elementary or secondary). More of the older teachers are women, and their responses as a group reflect the attitudes of an older generation of teachers. The desire to work with young people and the value of education in society are top-ranking reasons that are evenly distributed for both sexes and all age groups. Interest in a subject-matter field is a reason for almost 20 percent more men than women. A similar study was conducted

Differences by
sex, age, and
teaching level

2   Allan C. Ornstein and W. Eugene Hedley, *Educational Foundations: Ideas and Issues* (Columbus, Ohio: Merrill, 1973); Allan C. Ornstein and Harry L. Miller, *Looking Into Teaching* (Chicago: Rand McNally, 1980).

3   National Education Association, *Status of American Public School Teachers, 1970-71* (Washington, D.C.: NEA, 1972), p. 159, Appendix C.

Teachers have the desire to perform a service of value to society and have positive feelings about the young people they are able to help.

in 1976 by the NEA with almost identical results.[4] Another study of 2,200 student teachers also found that the main reason for entering teaching was the desire to work with children. This study confirmed the conclusion that potential teachers see teaching as fulfilling, important, and challenging.[5]

COMMITMENT   Table 1.1 shows the results of a question asked of the same 1971 respondents: would they become teachers if they had the choice to make over again? As many as 45 percent are *certain* and 30 percent are *probably certain* that they would teach again. A much smaller proportion of the men than women (one-third compared with one-half) are certain they would teach again. This is not surprising in view of the wider range of career opportunities open to men in the past, coupled with the low salaries of teachers. Older teachers are consistently more likely to choose teaching again, illustrating the interaction effect between sex and age. Another interpretation of the data is that with recent expan-

More career opportunities for men

4 National Education Association, *Status of the American Public School Teacher, 1975–76* (Washington, D.C.: NEA, 1976).

5 Sam S. Yarger, Kenneth Howey, and Bruce Joyce, "Reflections on Preservice Preparation: Impressions of the National Survey," *Journal of Teacher Education* (November–December 1977), pp. 34–37.

TABLE 1.1
WILLINGNESS TO TEACH AGAIN BY
SEX AND AGE

	TOTAL	SEX		AGE			
		MEN	WOMEN	LESS THAN 30	30–39	40–49	50 OR MORE
Certainly would teach	44.9	33.0	56.6	41.4	41.4	47.1	53.0
Probably would teach	29.5	27.8	26.9	34.2	27.1	28.1	26.2
Chances are about even	13.0	16.9	9.5	12.8	17.4	11.4	10.1
Probably would not teach	8.9	16.1	5.7	8.6	12.1	9.5	5.5
Certainly would not teach	3.7	6.2	1.3	3.1	3.2	3.8	5.2

Note: Data in percentages.

Source: National Education Association, *Status of American Public School Teachers, 1970-71* (Washington, D.C.: NEA, 1972), p. 54, Table 36.

sion of job opportunities for women, younger female teachers are more likely to have considered other options, whereas older ones may never really have considered anything but teaching as a career.

Data reported in 1979 continued to indicate that most teachers are happy with their career choice. These data were collected between 1973 and 1979 as part of the National Study of Schooling, directed by John Goodlad. Information was collected from 1,334 elementary and secondary teachers. In response to the question, "If you had to do it over again, would you choose education as a profession?" 77 percent of the elementary teachers and 66 percent of the secondary teachers gave an affirmative response.[6] The overall percentage of respondents giving a positive answer (69 percent for elementary and secondary combined) was close to the 74 percent of respondents in the NEA survey (Table 1.1) who said they "certainly" or "probably" would decide to teach again. However, the most recent study on this issue indicated that only two-thirds of teachers asked this question in 1979 said they would go into teaching if they had the option of starting college again.[7]

Yet with all this seeming dedication and strong urge to teach, other data strongly suggest a relatively low commitment to the profession. One out of three persons trained to teach never do, and a significant percentage

Choosing education as a profession

High commitment

Low commitment

6 Mary M. Bentzen, Richard C. Williams, and Paul Heckman, "A Study of Schooling: Adult Experiences in Schools," *Phi Delta Kappan* (February 1980), pp. 394-97.

7 Willard H. McGuire, "Teacher Burnout," *Today's Education* (November-December 1979), p. 5.

of persons who enter teaching drop out after two years.[8] Ronald Corwin contends that the reasons are a reflection of the relative ease of achieving certification. Rather than recruiting more teachers, we need to restrict the number of teachers by raising standards; thus the quality and retention rate may be increased. B. O. Smith points out that there is little individual investment in preparation for teaching. Not many people who have prepared to practice medicine, law, or engineering fail to follow their profession; they would most likely consider it a waste of knowledge and training. Apparently those who prepare to teach but never enter the classroom do not feel this sense of waste. Smith goes on to advocate more and higher-quality pedagogy; thus the investment in education would be greater and fewer people might look at teaching as a transient occupation. Interestingly, neither author connects teacher turnover and insufficient commitment with traditional low salaries and the large number of women who leave to raise a family. Both of these historical trends are changing; salaries (as we shall see below) are improving and there is a growing acceptance in the working world for women to combine marriage and a career. Also, a good many who trained to teach would like to teach but today are unable to find jobs.

Need for raising standards

Combining marriage and a teaching career

PROS AND CONS OF TEACHING

Having examined some reasons for becoming a teacher, as well as the degree of commitment among teachers, we now turn to some advantages and disadvantages of the profession. Movies like "To Sir With Love" and the recent crop of television programs using a school setting do not really portray what teaching is about. Life is not as simple, and neither is teaching; nor are problems as quickly and easily resolved as the entertainment industry would have us believe. What do *you* feel are the advantages and disadvantages of teaching? Why? Are you sure? What can be done to improve teaching? To help facilitate your discussion, let us consider what other students taking the first course in education have to say about the advantages and disadvantages of teaching.

Not like the movies

The results shown in Table 1.2 compare the rank order of the lists of advantages and disadvantages compiled by 228 beginning students of education at the University of Montana in 1964-65 with those of 178 beginning students of education at four universities in the Chicago area ten years later. The lists differ—reflecting both geographic location and more probably the changing status of the profession. Although the main

8 Ronald G. Corwin, *A Sociology of Education* (New York: Appleton–Century–Crofts, 1965); B. O. Smith, *Teachers for the Real World* (Washington, D.C.: American Association of Colleges for Teacher Education, 1969); Smith, *A Design for a School of Pedagogy* (Washington, D.C.: U.S. Government Printing Office, 1980).

TABLE 1.2
RANK ORDER OF ADVANTAGES
AND DISADVANTAGES OF
TEACHING AS A CAREER BY
BEGINNING STUDENTS OF
EDUCATION, 1964-65 AND 1975-76

1964-65	1975-76
ADVANTAGES	
1. Teacher performs valuable service to society	1. Chance to help young people
2. Teacher works with young people	2. Teaching is a rewarding career
3. Teaching can lead to other careers	3. A chance to improve society
4. General teacher shortage	4. Long (summer and winter) vacations
5. Develops character of teacher	5. Job security
6. Pleasant working environment	6. Good pay
7. Opportunity for leadership	7. Opportunity for advancement
8. Long summer vacations	8. High prestige
9. Opportunity for advancement	9. Teaching can lead to other careers
10. Job security	10. Time to pursue other interests
11. Acquisition of culture	11. Working with knowledgeable colleagues
12. High prestige	12. Fulfilling career
DISADVANTAGES	
1. Personal freedom restricted	1. Oversupply of teachers in most fields
2. Low salaries	2. Difficulty of finding a job
3. Imbalance in supply and demand in some fields	3. Discipline problems
4. Freedom to teach is restricted	4. Difficult working conditions
5. Teachers are overworked	5. Difficulty in working with parents or community residents
6. Certification requirements are unrealistic	6. Low prestige
7. Oversupply of teachers in desirable locations	7. Low salaries (at the present)
8. Low prestige	8. Teachers are overworked
9. Many disciplinary problems	9. Restriction on personal freedom
10. Job insecurity	10. Long hours
	11. Low salaries (in the future)
	12. Bureaucratic red tape

Note: Survey conducted for purposes of this text includes 1975-76 data from students of four universities in Chicago: Chicago State University, Loyola University, Roosevelt University, and University of Illinois—Circle Campus.

Source: Charles E. Hood, "Why 226 University Students Selected Teaching as a Career," *Clearing House* (December 1965), p. 228.

advantages listed by both groups are idealistic, the later group lists more practical problems relating to job status.

The *general shortage* of teachers was the fourth ranking advantage in 1964–65; by 1975–76, the oversupply of teachers was considered a major disadvantage. Imbalance in *supply and demand* ranked as the third most important disadvantage in the earlier survey; ten years later it was considered to be the number-one problem and the wording on oversupply changed from *some* to *most* teaching fields. This item was followed by the closely related one of the difficulties of *finding a teaching job*. While *pay* and *prestige* had increased over the ten-year period, the later respondents also indicated concern for future salaries. This probably reflected the growing inflation of the period combined with shrinking educational budgets. *Personal freedom* in teaching was perceived as the major problem in school year 1964–65; this was ranked much lower ten years later—in part reflecting attitudinal changes of society and possibly the more cosmopolitan ideas and freedoms of a large city locale. *Discipline problems* were considered more of a disadvantage in 1975–76, perhaps due to the increase in school violence and the fact that many respondents expected to teach in the city schools. While the contemporary respondents ranked *working with young people* high on their list of advantages, they also expressed concern about their *relations with parents and community residents*. This may be attributable to the growing stress on human relations and working with people, as well as concerns over racial tension and the demand for community control and teacher accountability in many city schools.

Supply and demand

Pay and prestige

The perceived disadvantages that loomed large in the eyes of those considering (and already) teaching as a career should be of concern to you as a future teacher. Perceived problems—whether real or imaginary—can be discussed, and in some cases a closer examination of them will alleviate some of the anxieties. Indeed, you might ask yourself how closely the above list of disadvantages and advantages corresponds to your own attitudes about teaching—and possibly what other items might have been included.

Your own attitudes about teaching

SATISFACTION AND DISSATISFACTION WITH THE JOB

The previously mentioned study of schooling[9] asked teachers to report whether they were satisfied or dissatisfied with their jobs. Respondents were asked to react to the item, "I usually look forward to each working day at this school." Seventy-eight percent of the 1,334 teachers in the study agreed with the statement.

Responses varied somewhat, however, in accordance with the economic status of the community in which teachers worked: 83 percent of

9   Bentzen, Williams, and Heckman, "A Study of Schooling."

the teachers in high-income communities agreed with the statement, as compared with 73 percent in low-income communities. Level of schooling also made a difference: 83 percent of the elementary teachers agreed, as compared with 79 percent of the junior high teachers and 74 percent of the senior high teachers.

The study also examined reasons why teachers were dissatisfied in their jobs. This was done by asking the question, "Hypothetically, which one of the following reasons would most likely cause you to leave your present position?" Reasons given in order of frequency were as follows: personal frustration or lack of satisfaction with my own job performance, more money, obtain a higher-status job, difficult student population or related reasons, personal conflict with the administration, severe staff conflict, and inadequate plant and physical materials. These results make it clear that dissatisfaction centers on displeasure with one's own performance or chances to do a good job and on unhappiness with pay and status as a public school teacher. Another recent (1979) survey of more than 10,000 elementary school teachers reveals that as many as 88 percent of the respondents were proud of the job they were doing and confident in their worth as teachers. Some 77 percent of the respondents said they teach because they enjoy it. Next choice was "It is what I do best." Major reasons for dissatisfaction were large class size, too much paperwork, no administrative support, unruly students, and children with minimal cognitive skills.[10]

STRESS AND COPING   Like other occupations, teaching has its difficult and stressful moments. This conclusion was underscored in a 1979 study conducted for the American Academy of Family Physicians. The Academy surveyed six different groups as part of a study on lifestyle and health care in differing occupations: business executives, physicians, farmers, garment workers, secretaries, and teachers. Included in the study were 501 teachers.

One of the questions asked was, "How stressful is your work environment?" Sixty-three percent of the teachers answered "usually" or "always," as compared with 81 percent of the executives, 65 percent of the physicians, 38 percent of the farmers, 44 percent of the garment workers, and 61 percent of the secretaries. It should not be inferred, however, that stress is necessarily a negative job characteristic. Challenging jobs are bound to involve a significant amount of stress, and many people feel that challenge is desirable as long as stress is manageable. Thus, although 81 percent of executives said their jobs were usually or always stressful, 93 percent said they liked their work. Conversely, although only 44 percent

10 "The American Elementary Teacher Today," *Instructor* (January 1980), pp. 24-26.

of the garment workers said their jobs usually or always involved stress, only 75 percent said they liked their jobs.[11]

Respondents in this study also were asked "Which of the following do you do to cope with stress?" and were given a list of 12 activities in which people frequently engage to reduce their stress level. The three activities selected most frequently by the teachers were: "talk to friend," "exercise," and "eat." None of the other activities, including "smoke cigarettes," "alcohol," and "talk to therapists," were mentioned by more than 17 percent of the teachers.

Another group of researchers have found that teachers, especially those who are under 35 and single, tend to frequent certain designated local bars to unwind and release job-related tensions. Conversations and stories told at these bars or lounges focus on their students, supervisors, and school in general. Teachers view these places as warm, informal, and characterized by ease and leisurely conversations in contrast to stressful conditions that exist in school.[12]

TEACHER BURNOUT Evidence that accumulated in the latter part of the 1970s indicated that elementary and secondary teaching has become more stressful than in earlier periods, and that greater stress is causing a "burnout" reaction among many teachers. One definition of *burnout* makes it simply synonymous with "physical, emotional, and attitudinal exhaustion."[13] A more elaborate definition distinguishes three degrees of burnout:

Exhaustion

> *First-degree burn (mild):* Short-lived bouts of irritability, fatigue, worry, frustration.

> *Second-degree (moderate):* Same as mild but lasts for two weeks or more.

> *Third-degree burn (severe):* Physical ailments occur such as ulcers, chronic back pain, migraine headaches, and so on.[14]

Authorities on burnout believe that it disproportionately strikes persons in the "helping" professions such as counselors, social workers,

11 Research and Forecasts, *A Report on Lifestyles/Personal Health Care in Different Occupations* (Kansas City, Mo.: The American Academy of Family Physicians, 1979).

12 Arthur Blumberg and David J. Kleinke, "Factors Associated with Frequenting a Teacher Bar." Paper presented at the Annual Meeting of the American Educational Research Association, Boston, April 1980; Sandra Mehlenbacher and Earl Mehlenbacher, "A Participant Observation Study of Teachers in a Bar on Friday Afternoon." Paper presented at the Annual Meeting of the American Educational Research Association, Boston, April 1980.

13 Robert Scrivens, "The Big Click," *Today's Education* (November–December 1979), pp. 34–36.

14 "Teacher Burnout," *Instructor* (January 1979), p. 57.

parole officers, and teachers.[15] Willard McGuire, 1980 President of the
NEA, has summarized the situation with respect to teacher burnout:

> A major new malady has afflicted the teaching profession and
> threatens to reach epidemic proportions if it isn't checked soon. It
> has already stricken thousands of sensitive, thoughtful, and dedi-
> cated teachers—teachers who are abandoning the profession. Addi-
> tional thousands may join their peers, for they fear for their
> physical and mental health.
>   What is the malady? It is teacher burnout—a condition that
> results from stress, tension, and anxiety in its victims. It is caused
> by many horrendous problems that plague teachers and that they
> receive little help in dealing with.[16]

**Teachers are
abandoning
the profession**

Burnout of teachers has been attributed to a wide variety of causes,
including public criticism of the quality of education, school financing
problems, classroom violence, involuntary transfers, disciplinary conflicts, administrative hassles, "mid-life crises," declining student test
scores and academic pressures, and constant demands for innovation and
improvement in the classroom.[17] Although the balance of these and other
factors clearly varies from one case of burnout to another, the pressures
on teachers seem to have been growing to the extent that burnout has
become a matter of national concern.

**National
concern**

   Burnout appears to be taking place in all types of school districts, but
it probably is most frequent in big cities, where student behavior and
school finance problems tend to be most severe. Thus, some teachers in
ghetto schools (where most of the annual 70,000 teacher assaults by students take place) are said to be suffering from the World War I "combat
neurosis," a syndrome characterized by insomnia, high blood pressure,
anxiety, depression, or—in a few cases—psychotic collapse. A survey of
Chicago public school teachers indicated that 57 percent claimed to have
suffered from physical and/or mental problems as a direct result of their
jobs.[18]

   Alarming as much of the violence and other stress-producing conditions are, a positive approach is possible and necessary. Counselors point

15   "Teacher Burnout," *Instructor;* Jerry Edelwich and Archie Brodsky, *Burnout: Stages of
Disillusionment in the Helping Professions* (New York: Human Sciences Press, 1980).

16   Willard H. McGuire, "Teacher Burnout," *Today's Education* (November–December 1979),
p. 5.

17   Scrivens, "The Big Click"; "Teacher Burnout: A National Issue Says NEA Panel," *NEA
Reporter* (October 1979), p. 7; Irene R. Mazer and Marjorie Griffin, "Perceived and Experienced
Stress in a Medium-Sized Local School District." Paper presented at the Annual Meeting of the
American Educational Research Association, Boston, April 1980.

18   Debbie Walsh, "Classroom Stress and Teacher Burnout," *Phi Delta Kappan* (December
1979), p. 253.

out that exercise, rest, hobbies, meditation or other relaxation techniques, efficient scheduling of personal affairs, and vacations can help individuals cope with high-stress jobs.[19] Recommendations for avoiding burnout also advise teachers to participate in professional renewal activities, separate their jobs from home life, and try to maintain flexibility and an open-minded attitude toward change.[20] Activities or projects undertaken by professional organizations and school districts to help teachers avoid burnout include an effort in Chicago to train volunteers to conduct rap sessions for teachers, a program of counseling and possible leaves of absence for stress victims sponsored by the Tucson Education Association, and Prevention and Management of Educational Stress workshops conducted by the Northwest Staff Development Center in Wayne County, Michigan.[21] The NEA has initiated several national projects, including its Instruction and Professional Development Program, to train hundreds of teachers in techniques for improving classroom management and discipline.[22]

STATUS OF TEACHERS

Prestige, salaries, and supply of teachers are all interrelated factors. Their relative positions are major concerns for future and present teachers. Generally, when the supply of members of a given profession is scarce, demand and salaries increase; when the salaries of a profession are high, professional status is high; when salaries are low, so is professional status.

THE PRESTIGE FACTOR

Prestige refers to the estimation an individual or group occupies in the eyes of others in a social system; it connotes that individual's or group's status within the society. A few studies of social status and occupational ratings are available that shed some light on the social status of teachers. Perhaps the most well-known studies of occupational prestige are those conducted by the National Opinion Research Center (NORC), affiliated with the University of Chicago. In 1947 NORC asked 2,290 persons throughout the country to rank 88 occupations.[23] The study showed that school teachers

19   "What Can You Do About Teacher Stress?" *NEA Reporter* (October 1979), p. 10.

20   "Teacher Burnout," *Instructor.*

21   "Teacher Burnout," *Instructor;* "Tucson Teachers Initiate Stress Counseling Program," *NEA Reporter* (October 1979), p. 60; Dennis Sparks, "A Teacher Center Tackles the Issue," *Today's Education* (November–December 1979), pp. 37–39.

22   McGuire, "Teacher Burnout."

23   C. C. North and Paul K. Hatt, "Jobs and Occupation: A Popular Evaluation," *Opinion News* (September 1, 1947), pp. 3–13; Richard Centers, "Social Class, Occupation, and Imputed Values," *American Journal of Sociology* (May 1953), pp. 543–55.

ranked 37th in prestige and college professors outranked others in the teaching profession. A related study of 90 occupations with similar populations was conducted by NORC in 1964, making comparisons possible.[24] In the later study teachers ranked 29.5, showing a slight occupational rank increase of 7.5 points. Since most other professional occupations also tended to show gains in prestige, however, the new status of teachers must be qualified on a comparative basis. In a 1970 survey of 650 people about prestige ratings of more than 500 overlapping occupational titles, the highest mean score was 81.5 for physicians and surgeons and the lowest was 9.3 for a shoe shiner.[25] Elementary school teachers were rated 60.1 and secondary school teachers were rated 63.1—both above the 90th percentile. About the same level of prestige for teachers also was reported in a 1977 summary of research on occupational status.[26]

Income and prestige are related

Although a combination of factors determines prestige, in our society income is related to prestige. As teacher salaries have increased, the occupational rating of teaching has also risen. It is still evident, however, that teachers do not receive salaries in keeping with the ratings they receive on occupational status scales.

Inasmuch as the public determines teacher income, what the public does adds or detracts from the prestige of the teacher. The amount of money spent for schools and the income of teachers must be judged in terms of the local community's ability to spend. A poor community may pay low teacher salaries but it usually spends a relatively larger proportion of its total funds for schools than the national average expenditures. Thus, a poor community may actually place a high value on teaching. While the above ratings give a national picture of comparative ranks, such a scale does not reveal the level of public acceptance of education and teacher prestige in a specific school system.

Teacher prestige varies by community

In a summary of a number of other occupational studies, we find that teachers score higher as credit risks than do judges, ministers, lawyers, and others who rate higher on the occupational prestige scale.[27] Within the profession, college teachers, school administrators, and high school teachers—positions predominantly filled by men—have a higher position on the prestige scale than teachers in elementary schools. The implications are that the teaching profession establishes levels of stratification within its own group.

Stratification within the teaching profession

24 Robert W. Hodge, Paul M. Siegel, and Peter H. Rossi, "Occupational Prestige in the United States, 1925-63", *American Journal of Sociology* (November 1964), pp. 286-302.

25 Paul M. Siegel, "Prestige in the American Occupational Structure." Unpublished Ph.D. dissertation, Department of Sociology, University of Chicago, 1971.

26 Donald J. Trieman, *Occupational Prestige in Comparative Perspective* (New York: Academic Press, 1977).

27 James M. Hughes, *Education in America,* 3rd ed. (New York: Harper & Row, 1970).

PAY SCALES AND
TRENDS
There is a wealth of literature on how little teachers earn. While this was unquestionably characteristic of the past, there has been some improvement in salaries. The 1955-56 mean salary paid to teachers was $4,156; by 1979-80 this had risen to $16,001,[28] or nearly four times the earlier figure. The most rapid gains came between school year 1967-68, when the average teacher earned $7,630, and 1970-71, when the average teacher was earning $9,165. From 1970-71 until 1979-80, average teacher salaries did not increase more than $1,000 per year, despite rapid inflation.[29] Yet it is not uncommon for some teachers to have salary ranges between $25,000 and $30,000, and there are opportunities to work in after-school programs and/or summers for supplementary income, and to advance to administrative positions with salary ranges from $25,000 to $100,000.

**Salary as
high as
$25,000-30,000**

Current dollars and real income But there is another side to the picture. Between 1968 and 1978 teachers have had no real gain in purchasing power and have been hit hard in terms of real income drop. While average salaries of teachers approximately doubled between 1968 and 1978, the rate of inflation has been moving at a more accelerated pace. From this point of view, long-term teacher salary gains have not been encouraging. Between 1968 and 1978 annual salaries for teachers increased from $7,630 to $14,836, but in terms of the purchasing power of 1977-78 dollars, the increase was only from $14,047 ($7,630 adjusted to the 1978 value of the dollar) to $14,836—almost as if no progress had been made.[30] Of course, similar trends have been experienced across virtually all occupations; the average worker actually lost ground during this ten-year period. Although precise data are not yet available, inflation from 1978 to 1980 was even greater, thus actually reducing the purchasing power of teachers' salaries. Based on estimates of 1980 teacher salaries compared with annual inflation rates, it appears that teacher salaries declined in purchasing power at a rate of nearly 2 percent a year between 1970 and 1980. Furthermore, if recent trends continue, it is estimated that the average teacher's salary will decline from 77 percent of a standard budget (U.S. Department of Labor estimate of the amount of money a family of four needs to live comfortably) in 1980 to 53 percent of a standard budget in 1990.[31]

**A decline in
purchasing
power**

28 National Education Association, *Estimates of School Statistics, 1979-80* (Washington, D.C.: NEA, 1980).

29 National Education Association, *Economic Status of the Teaching Profession, 1972-73,* Research Report 1973-R3 (Washington, D.C.: NEA, 1973), p. 26, Table 21, p. 30, Table 25; National Education Association, *Estimates of School Statistics, 1979-80,* p. 32, Table 7.

30 *Digest of Education Statistics, 1979,* pp. 57-58, Tables 53-54.

31 Allan C. Ornstein, "Teacher Salaries: Past, Present, Future," *Phi Delta Kappan* (June 1980), pp. 677-79.

Teachers have taken notice of an increasing number of workers in other occupations covered by escalator clauses tied to the rate of inflation. By the end of 1975, 8.5 million union workers in private and public industry were covered by such clauses.[32] There is now talk among teacher organizations about using price-cost formulas to avoid the annual friction of collective negotiations; these formulas could be based on important consumer goods and services as in the manner already developed by the Department of Labor to figure out the nation's consumer price index, or to the living costs of a particular city or state.[33]

Salary differentials   Teaching pay varies considerably among and within states.[34] Table 1.3 shows 1979–80 average salaries paid to teachers among states. The range for that year was almost $14,000, from $11,900 in Mississippi to $26,173 in Alaska. Average yearly salaries in the three highest-paying states (Alaska, Hawaii, and New York) were 75–100 percent higher than in the three lowest-paying states (Mississippi, South Dakota, and Arkansas).

Salaries vary
among states

Table 1.3 also shows regional salaries. Regional differences in mean salaries are less acute than state differences, because we are dealing with a larger number of school systems. The Great Lakes region ($16,624) comes closest to the 1979–80 average ($16,001). The Southeast ($13,819) is the lowest paid region, while the Far West ($18,678) is the highest paid region. The difference between the lowest and highest paid regions was $4,860. Of course, comparative living costs must be considered. For example, Alaska's figure must be reduced about 30 percent and Hawaii's must be reduced about 15 percent to correct for differences in purchasing power; on the other hand, the Southeast (with the exception of Atlanta, Nashville, and a few cities in Florida such as Daytona, Miami, and Orlando) has the lowest living costs.

Salary differences within states are wide, especially where mean state pay scales are high. For example, in Niles, Illinois, the average salary in 1979–80 was $10,000 more than for other Illinois teachers. In southern states where the mean salaries are low the range is narrower, but there are still considerable differences. In Georgia, for example, if you put down your roots in Cobb County your maximum salary in 1980 was $5,000 lower than for Atlanta teachers.

The greatest variation in salaries is based on years of experience and education. Teachers with more years of experience and more education earn more than those with less of either. Thus the salary range among

Experience
and education

32   John Zalusky, "Cost of Living Causes: Inflation Fighters," *American Federationist* (March 1976), pp. 1–6.

33   James N. Fox, "Cost-of-Living Adjustments: Right Intent, Wrong Technique," *Phi Delta Kappan* (April 1975), pp. 548–50; Anthony M. Cresswell and Michael J. Murphy, *Teachers, Unions and Collective Bargaining* (Berkeley, Calif.: McCutchan, 1979).

34   Ornstein, "Teacher Salaries."

TABLE 1.3
AVERAGE SALARY OF PUBLIC
CLASSROOM TEACHERS BY REGIONS
AND STATES, 1979-80

STATE	SALARY	STATE	SALARY
50 States and D.C.	$16,001		
New England	16,296	Plains	$14,601
Connecticut	16,344	Iowa	15,030
Maine	13,100	Kansas	14,016
Massachusetts	17,500	Minnesota	16,751
New Hampshire	12,550	Missouri	13,725
Rhode Island	17,896	Nebraska	13,519
Vermont	12,430	North Dakota	13,148
Mideast (Incl. D.C.)	17,987	South Dakota	12,220
Delaware	16,157	Southwest	14,076
Maryland	17,580	Arizona	15,835
New Jersey	17,075	New Mexico	13,915
New York	19,200	Oklahoma	13,210
Pennsylvania	16,760	Texas	14,000
Southeast	13,819	Rocky Mountains	15,226
Alabama	13,520	Colorado	15,950
Arkansas	12,419	Idaho	13,615
Florida	14,570	Montana	14,680
Georgia	14,027	Utah	14,965
Kentucky	14,480	Wyoming	16,030
Louisiana	13,770	Far West	18,678
Mississippi	11,900	California	19,090
North Carolina	14,355	Nevada	16,390
South Carolina	13,000	Oregon	16,245
Tennessee	13,668	Washington	18,745
Virginia	14,025	Alaska	26,173
West Virginia	13,642	Hawaii	19,750
Great Lakes	16,624		
Illinois	17,399		
Indiana	15,078		
Michigan	18,840		
Ohio	15,187		
Wisconsin	15,930		

Source: National Education Association, *Estimates of School Statistics, 1979-80* (Washington D.C.: NEA, 1979), p. 32, Table 7.

teachers in Chicago in 1979 was $12,750 for new teachers with a bachelor's degree to $27,100 for experienced teachers with a doctor's degree. Equivalent figures for Detroit were $12,884 and $25,132, respectively.[35]

A good yardstick of the economic position of an occupational group is to compare salaries with other groups of workers having similar years of education. While Table 1.4 shows that beginning teacher salaries have

35 Richard A. Musemeche and James W. Firnberg, "Which Factors Affect Teachers' Salaries?" *School Business Affairs* (January 1979), pp. 24-25, 40.

TABLE 1.4
MEAN SALARIES OF BEGINNING
TEACHERS AND OTHER GRADUATES
WITH BACHELOR'S DEGREES IN FOUR
SELECTED OCCUPATIONS 1965-66 TO
1979-80

	1965/1966	1970/1971	1975/1976	1979/1980
Teachers	$4,925	$ 6,850	$ 8,611	$10,750
Engineering	7,584/8,112	10,476/10,620	12,744/13,848	18,528
Accounting	6,732/7,128	10,080/10,140	11,888/12,144	14,784
Sales/marketing	6,276/6,744	8,580/8,904	10,344/11,856	15,072
Business administration	6,240/6,576	8,124/8,340	9,768/10,116	13,440

Note: Teacher salaries in this table are reported on by the school year; other salaries are reported on an annual basis.

Source: Frank S. Endicott, *Trends in Employment of College and University Graduates in Business and Industry,* Annual Reports (Evanston, Ill.: Northwestern University, 1965, 1966, 1970, 1971, 1975, 1976, 1979, 1980); National Education Association, *Economic Status of the Teaching Profession, 1972-73,* (Washington, D.C.: NEA, 1973), p. 35, Table 32; National Education Association, *Prices, Budgets, Salaries, and Income* (Washington, D.C.: NEA, 1980), pp. 24-26, Tables 20-22.

risen about 55 percent between 1970 and 1979, the table also presents data on beginning salaries for four other occupational groups (usually entered, like teachers, at the bachelor's degree level) that have consistently started at an annual average salary higher than teachers; moreover, the gap between these four groups and teachers has steadily widened since 1965.

    We should note that while the median family income in the United States for 1979 was $8,240, the average teacher salary was $16,001.[36] Moreover, of some 2.4 million persons employed as public school teachers more than 1.5 million are women. Where the teacher is a married woman (and about two-thirds of the female teachers *are* married) we can assume their spouses earn similar or higher salaries.[37] Thus their combined incomes are likely to put a great many teachers in the top five percentiles in the country, having family incomes of $40,000 or more. (This point is rarely mentioned by professional journals for obvious reasons of self-interest.)

Beginning salaries

Married female teachers and family income

SUPPLY AND DEMAND   The beginning of the 1969-70 school year marked the nation's recovery from what had been considered a chronic disease—the teacher shortage. Due to

36 National Education Association, *Prices, Budgets, Salaries, and Income* (Washington, D.C.: NEA, 1980), pp. 13, 27, Tables 9, 23.

37 National Education Association, *Highlights of Public School Teachers, 1975-76* (Washington, D.C.: NEA, 1976), pp. 1-3; Allan C. Ornstein, *Education and Social Inquiry* (Itasca, Ill.: Peacock, 1970), p. 226, Figure 6.1.

a cumulative effect over previous years, the nation's total teaching force has been steadily expanding while the number of new openings has been declining. If present trends persist, we can expect a growing number of teacher education graduates to find themselves on waiting lists without immediate prospects of a position. Several reasons can be cited for the change in the job situation for teachers.

Reasons for oversupply

1. The teaching profession is no longer underprivileged. Strongly organized, teachers now have a voice. Recent militancy among teachers, combined with higher educational aspirations among American parents, has helped bolster salaries. Only in a few rural areas do truly substandard pay scales still remain, and even this is quickly coming to an end.

2. A teaching career now offers additional pay inducements. For those who want to add to their salaries, there are afternoon teaching positions, as well as recreational and athletic jobs, often in the teachers' own schools. Various part-time neighborhood and community posts are sometimes available. Summer school work or other employment during the summer is still another common method of earning extra income. The majority of teachers report that they have additional income from summer or part-time school year employment, up from 51 percent in 1961 to 57 percent in 1971.[38] By 1976/80 it was estimated that the annual additional income for teachers averaged close to $3,000.

Supplementary income

3. The population trends have changed. During the 1950s and until the mid-1960s the schools were bursting at the seams with record enrollments that had their beginning in the post-World War II baby boom. These high birthrate groups had to rely on teachers born during the low birthrates of the Great Depression years. The Depression babies entered teaching during the early 1950s—a trickle of teachers for a flood of students. The situation is reversing. The birthrate started to level off around 1963, first affecting the elementary schools in the early 1970s and affecting the secondary schools in the late 1970s. Yet the postwar babies are streaming out of college, many available for teaching careers. (In 1969 it was reported that there were 16,000 "excess" beginning teachers; thereafter, the annual oversupply of teachers has been steadily increasing.) By 1974, the number of surplus beginning teachers was more than 60,000, with several additional thousands no longer even applying for jobs.[39]

Many teacher education graduates

38 National Education Association, *Status of American Public School Teachers, 1970–71*, p. 75, Tables 47, 48; *The New York Times* (August 5, 1973), sect. 4, p. 7.

39 "Trends in Teacher Supply and Demand in Public Schools, 1973–76," *NEA Research Memo* (June 1973), pp. 2–3; Stanley M. Elam, "A Somber Economic Picture for Teachers, *Phi Delta Kappan* (November 1974), p. 170.

Data for 1978 indicated that there were 146,000 new teachers seeking work but that teaching jobs were available for only 74,450.[40]

4. A departure from traditional turnover patterns of male and female teachers has occurred since 1961. Men, it had long been shown, tended to leave teaching either for more lucrative employment outside education or for positions in education administration. Women, on the other hand, tended to occupy themselves with teaching before and after marrying and raising their families. Signs of change are becoming evident. A greater number of teachers are remaining in the profession, in part because of higher pay scales and in part because of the recent trend among women of combining marriage with a career. In addition, the increase of women in college and in the work force has been dramatic in the 1970s, and a great many choose teaching as a career.

Less teacher turnover

Estimates of the oversupply of new teachers by 1986 range from as low as 150,000 to as high as 500,000, with the bulk of the oversupply at the secondary level.[41] In the midst of such gloomy predictions, hope is indicated by the projections of those who contend that the supply-demand curve will start reversing in the mid-1980s, first at the elementary level and followed by the secondary level some eight years later—producing another large shortage of teachers around 1995.[42] (In fact, serious shortages of teachers already have begun to appear in some areas of the country.[43]) The exact path of all these projections will depend on the number of college graduates preparing to teach, the rate of teacher turnover and retirement, student enrollments and class size, and the size of families yet unborn. Subject area also makes a difference: despite the general oversupply of teachers, shortages in some fields and specializations (see page 24) still exist.[44]

Projected reversal of trend

Undersupply of money   A major point raised by many educators is that there are not enough teachers on the job to meet the real needs of the schools and to achieve quality education for all students. The problem

40   National Education Association, *Teacher Supply and Demand in Public Schools, 1978* (Washington, D.C.: NEA, 1979).

41   *Projections of Education Statistics to 1986-87* (Washington, D.C.: U.S. Government Printing Office, 1978), pp. 64–65, Table 21; Timothy Weaver, "Projecting Teacher Needs and Professional Staffing Patterns for the Mid-1980s." Paper presented at the Annual Meeting of the American Educational Research Association, Boston, April 1980, pp. 16–17, Table 8.

42   Cyril G. Sargeant, "Fewer Pupils, Surplus Space: The Problem of School Shrinkage," *Phi Delta Kappan* (January 1975), pp. 352–57; Robert L. Jacobson, "Job Market for Teachers: Better Times Ahead?" *Chronicle of Higher Education* (February 26, 1979), p. 7.

43   Arni T. Dunathan, "Midwest Schools Face Shortage of Good Teachers," *Phi Delta Kappan* (October 1979), pp. 121–22; "Texas Experiences a 'Critical' Teacher Shortage," *Phi Delta Kappan* (January 1980), p. 307.

44   National Education Association, *Teacher Supply and Demand in Public Schools, with Population Trends and Their Indications for Schools, 1976-77* (Washington, D.C.: NEA, 1977); Ornstein and Miller, *Looking into Teaching;* Weaver, "Projecting Teacher Needs and Professional Staffing Patterns."

is not an *oversupply of teachers*, but an *undersupply of money* needed to reduce class sizes, expand course offerings, hire special personnel, and enlarge the coverage of special programs to serve the needs of students. The executive director of the American Association of State Colleges and Universities asked:

> How can we talk of a teacher surplus when perhaps half our communities are without kindergartens; . . . when according to a recent study at Harvard, almost half of the adult population 25 years and over is functionally illiterate; . . . when in our high schools we have less than one counselor for every 500 students; when our rural and urban areas are woefully inadequate in meeting the special educational needs of our underprivileged children? There is no teacher surplus. There is an educational deficit which . . . we now have an opportunity to correct.[45]

Some educators are now advocating a system of lifelong education so that an individual would have more than one chance to succeed.[46] Why should a person who made the mistake of dropping out of school at an early age not be given a second chance—or a third—to return to school? Such a system of education would start at the prekindergarten age, the most important years for potential cognitive growth and development. It would include new programs for mature adults who wish to retool and who desire better employment opportunities and for senior citizens who seek new interests and leisure-oriented activities. Such a program would obviously generate the need for thousands of additional teachers; it would drastically change the present supply-demand curve.

Unfortunately, money is the problem in all of the above examples. It is easy to talk about spending someone else's money; but talk to the average taxpayer and you get a different slant on things; talk to someone who has no children and is already paying $1,000 or more in taxes (most of which is earmarked for schools) just for a home; talk to parents who have to pay for their children's college education while their taxes permit other children to attend college at no cost and even to receive financial aid. Their sentiments represent the kind of public reaction that teachers will have to face as they seek higher wages, smaller class size, and special programs.

Teachers will be struggling against these trends mainly through collective bargaining and, in the political arena, through more involvement in electing pro-education legislators and in activating allies among parents and citizens who are interested in improving educational quality.

45 "Too Many Teachers?" *Changing Times* (October 1970), p. 44.
46 Albert Shanker, "Teacher 'Oversupply' or 'Underutilization'," *New York Times* (August 18, 1974), sect. 4, p. 9; Simon Beagle, "Educare '75," *American Teacher* (January 1975), p. 11.

But the idea of having more teachers for fewer students, or of creating new jobs by providing services to children that should have been provided all along, will not gain easy acceptability. In fact, the trend is to cut teaching positions because of declining enrollments and to reduce service in order to trim budget deficits.

Trimming
school budgets

Coping with the teacher market   Although most state departments of education take a *laissez-faire* approach to the production of teachers, there is growing sentiment to advise colleges to deemphasize teacher education programs and to counsel incoming freshmen students about the reality of the teacher market. As early as 1973, eight states (Colorado, Illinois, Iowa, Maryland, Minnesota, Oklahoma, Pennsylvania, and Utah) already had imposed some type of quota on teacher education programs and/or established new criteria for accepting (actually limiting) teacher candidates. Five states were also involved in manpower planning, and another five states were anticipating such plans, to try to predict the teacher labor market on a statewide basis and to implement appropriate policy.[47]

Limiting
teacher
candidates

That many college students are aware of the supply-demand curve and declining teacher education enrollments is clearly evidenced throughout the nation. In 1968, just prior to the decline in the teacher market, 23.5 percent of all college freshmen opted for a probable career in teaching. Since 1973 the annual percentages have been less than 10 percent (8.8 percent in 1973; 6.5 percent in 1975; 6 percent in 1978) and there seem to be no indications of a quick reversal.[48] These changes in freshmen career attitudes are dramatic, to the extent that an overreaction may be taking place and the supply-demand curve may be modified sooner than anticipated.

Changes in
freshmen
career
attitudes

Prospective teachers should be aware that these supply-demand trends are not national in scope. In selected areas, however, such as the Southeast, South Central, Southwest, and Far West (the sunbelt area), the percentage of teachers not finding jobs was less than 15 percent during the mid- and late 1970s.[49] These areas are expected to continue to grow until at least the mid-1980s. Moreover, in almost all 50 states there are regional pockets, such as the outer suburban ring of the metropolitan sprawl and the rural areas, where demand is still evident and where there are still projected estimates of increasing student enrollments. And there are also a few subject areas in which demand, while it may not be greater than supply, is still strong and the great majority of teachers can find

47   Evelyn Zerfoss and Leo J. Shapiro, *The Supply and Demand of Teachers and Teaching*, Study Commission on Undergraduate Education and the Education of Teachers (Lincoln, Neb.: University of Nebraska, 1973).
48   *The American Freshmen: National Norms*, Annual Reports (Washington, D.C.: American Council on Education, 1968, 1975); Jacobson, "Job Market for Teachers."
49   U.S. Department of Labor, *Occupational Outlook Handbook, 1978–79* (Washington, D.C.: U.S. Government Printing Office, 1979).

jobs. At the elementary level, these include art, music, physical education, remedial reading, and special education. At the secondary level, these include (to a lesser degree) agriculture, mathematics, music, vocational and industrial education, and special education. Bilingual and bicultural teachers at both levels are in vogue in many urban centers, too.[50] But how long these demographic trends will continue, and how long the demand for teachers in these special subject areas will last are difficult to assess.

OTHER CAREER OPTIONS   Unless the federal government figures out a better way to utilize teachers, or unless local communities are willing to shift teachers temporarily into alternative areas of instruction (adult education, for instance, which seems to be a growth market), education students should maintain flexibility and think of related jobs or teaching in organizations other than public schools. A few of these options are:

Related educational jobs

1. Adult education centers
2. Colleges and universities
3. Consulting and research agencies
4. Educational consortia and regional centers
5. State departments of education
6. Federal agencies
7. Community organizations
8. Social service organizations
9. Guidance and vocational agencies
10. Chambers of commerce
11. Travel agencies
12. Religious organizations
13. Camping organizations
14. Boy and Girl Scout organizations
15. Private and public foundations
16. Museums
17. Hospitals (training and evaluation centers)
18. Labor organizations
19. Business and industry (training and development departments)
20. Military organizations

Among the more positive responses to the supply-demand gap in teaching has been a movement to help teacher education students prepare for careers other than in schools or classrooms. In conjunction with programs leading directly to a teaching certificate, some colleges and universities are offering interdisciplinary majors that blend the liberal arts with an educational-studies major to prepare students for a broad range of education-related careers. These new career programs frequently eliminate

Combining liberal arts and education

50 Ornstein and Miller, Looking into Teaching; National Education Association, *Teacher Supply and Demand in Public Schools, 1978.*

the practical teaching methods courses and substitute courses of study that can lead to one of several fields of work or to the career options just listed.

General employment trends   It should also be noted that a considerable amount of educating is being done by other sectors of the economy, especially in the field of health science, labor, business and industry, and civil service. Only a few years ago, there was an apparent oversupply of lawyers, but they began to find new positions for themselves by extending legal services into other fields, such as sports, agriculture, schools, and community and social organizations. These areas had never been previously considered as job opportunities. It is possible that a large number of teachers, along with counselors and school psychologists, will in the future find positions for themselves in occupations just now being considered.

On the other hand, the number of job offerings is not growing as rapidly as the increasing number of students expected to graduate from college. This is only partly due to the recession years of the 1970s. Another cause is increased college enrollment and the subsequent growing number of graduates. For example, the proportion of Americans with four or more years of college has increased sixfold from 1940 to 1978.[51] Coincident with this increase in college graduates seeking work, the growth of most sectors of the economy that use a large number of educated personnel has leveled off and even declined in some areas. Future trends both in the job market and in the numbers of college graduates indicate that the latter may exceed demand by more than 10 percent by 1985. In other words, barring an unforeseen drop in bachelor's degree recipients, the job deficit for college graduates is expected to increase to 140,000 per year between 1980 and 1985.[52]

While the overall projections show an oversupply—and, hence, underemployment of college graduates—the prospects differ greatly among various fields. Teachers will have considerable difficulty getting placed, but accountants, engineers, and workers in the health field will be in demand.[53] The whole country will probably face not only an underutilization of teachers but also an overall underutilization of college-trained personnel. Indeed, the nation may wind up with an overeducated, unemployed, or underemployed intellectual proletariat. Jobs that were once available without educational credentials are already being redefined to require such credentials, and individuals may not perform well in jobs

Expanding the educational sector

Recession and job curtailment

Oversupply of college graduates

---

51 *Progress of Education in the United States of America 1976-77 and 1977-78* (Washington, D.C.: U.S. Government Printing Office, 1979), p. 109, Table 19.

52 Michael E. Kraft and Mark Schneider, *Population Policy Analysis* (Lexington, Mass.: Heath, 1978); *Occupational Manpower and Training Needs, 1979* (Washington, D.C.: U.S. Government Printing Office, 1980), p. 42, Table 38.

53 Brigitte Berger, "The Coming Age of People Work," *Change* (May 1976), pp. 24-30; Jarl Bentssen, "The Shape of Work to Come," *Change* (July 1979), pp. 16-21.

they feel are not suited to a liberally educated person. The price will also be paid by those who do not go to college, predominantly the children of the working class, whose opportunities and mobility are already restricted. We can also expect many male white job seekers to be caught in a tightening employment vise, while opportunities for women and racial minorities expand as a result of affirmative action programs.

SUMMING UP

1. The teaching profession has far more members than any other profession. Its instructional membership (including college professors) is more than three million, two million more than the next largest profession—nursing.

2. The reasons for entering the teaching profession are many, although the research tends to indicate that most people enter the profession to help young children and provide a valuable service to society.

3. Although the prestige ot the profession is well above average, because of its great numbers it cannot be as selective as some other professions. Within the profession, the prestige of classroom teachers is the lowest, and elementary school teachers traditionally have had less status than secondary school teachers. This is in part related to the fact that most teachers are women—reflecting the norms of society.

4. Despite a twofold increase in teacher salaries between 1970 and 1980, the purchasing power or real income of teachers declined. Nationwide, average teacher salaries were $16,001 in the 1979–80 school year—and as low as $11,900 in Mississippi to as high as $26,173 in Alaska.

5. There are several advantages and disadvantages related to teaching; more and more, the major disadvantage seems to be the problem of finding a job. Difficulties in obtaining a teaching job reflect a larger national problem, namely an increasing oversupply of college graduates.

DISCUSSION QUESTIONS

1. Why are you thinking of becoming a teacher? Give some of your reasons. How do your reasons compare with those in the chapter? Which of the reasons given by members of the class appear worthwhile? Which seem selfishly motivated?

2. What do you see as some of the advantages and disadvantages of teaching as a career? How do your responses compare with the items listed in Table 1.2?

3. What are the major causes of teacher burnout? How can teachers cope with and reduce stress and burnout?

4. Why are teaching positions now difficult to obtain?

5. What jobs other than teaching in elementary or secondary schools may be open to persons with a teaching certificate? What additional preparation would be needed to obtain such jobs?

THINGS TO DO

1. Arrange to visit a school, especially a classroom, to observe a teacher and a classroom situation firsthand. Report back to the class and discuss what you saw. (Ask your professor to make advance arrangements with the school principal.)

2. Develop a questionnaire dealing with possible reasons for becoming a teacher. Administer the questionnaire, tabulate responses, and report back to the class.

3. Obtain salary schedules for several school systems in the area. Compare salaries in terms of beginning and maximum levels, the number of increments before reaching maximum, and the amount of increment for each year of teaching experience and for educational preparation.

4. Speak to an administrator from the certification or personnel office of the state department of education on employment opportunities. Have this person examine population shifts, geographical areas, levels of teaching, and fields of specialization.

5. Interview people who work in fields such as adult education, management consulting, and research. What opportunities do they think will be available for persons with a teaching degree?

CHAPTER 2
THE EDUCATION
OF TEACHERS

Focusing questions

What is the proper mix of courses in arts and science, in a subject area, and in education for the prospective teacher?

What effect do college open admission policies have on the kinds of people who become teachers?

Should teachers be screened on the basis of mental health?

Should teachers exercise greater influence than they do now on teacher training and certification requirements?

Will school-based teacher training replace our present college-based teacher training?

What is competency-based teacher education? Can it improve teacher education?

What are the most important recent trends in teacher education?

During the colonial period, and well into the early nineteenth century, an individual who wanted to become a teacher usually went before a local minister or a board of trustees associated with a religious institution to be certified. A high school or college diploma was not considered a necessary prerequisite. If you could read, write, and spell, and if you were of good moral character, you could teach school. By the 1820s future teachers began attending normal schools to prepare for teaching, although formal certification procedures still were not required. These teaching institutions did not grant a degree; rather, they offered a number of courses that prepared the candidate for teaching. Today, the nation's colleges and universities are exclusively responsible for training teachers. By 1967 all states required the bachelor's degree or five years of college work for entrance to high school teaching; forty-seven states required a four-year degree for entrance to elementary teaching.

The pattern that has evolved for preparing teachers will be examined in the first part of this chapter. Teacher education represents a formal process for making the teaching profession truly professional. Stiffening entry requirements, improving education courses and certification practices, and possibly requiring competency-based education are related avenues leading to the same goal. Competency-based preparation has become an important characteristic of teacher training at many colleges and universities. Other trends in teacher education also are discussed in the second half of this chapter.

PREPARATION OF TEACHERS

The preparation of teachers consists of three components: (1) liberal education, (2) specialized subject field, and (3) professional education. Briefly, the purpose of a *liberal* education is to liberate the mind, to provide knowledge of self and culture worthy of a citizen in a free society. A liberal program combines the arts and sciences and seeks to give the student a broad cultural background. The *specialized subject* field consists of a cluster of courses in a specific subject area and provides the prospective teacher with in-depth preparation for his or her chosen teaching field. In most colleges and universities this part of the program is described as the student's "major" or "minor." Whereas secondary teachers are typically certified in one subject field, and for this reason usually take a greater amount of work in one or two areas, most elementary teachers are responsible for all subject fields. Elementary teachers may specialize, however, in areas such as music, art, physical education, foreign language, and reading. *Professional education* refers to educational courses designed to provide professional orientation and training in the art of teaching. Typical liberal and specialized subject courses will enroll students with diverse interests and

Liberal education

Specialization

Professional education

Professional training of teachers is both practical and reality-oriented, but centers mainly on the status of teachers in the society.

occupational goals; professional courses will enroll those who are interested in the career goal of teaching.[1]

Almost all educators agree that the preparation of good teachers rests upon these three components. The relative emphasis that each area should receive, however, provokes strong arguments among educators. That is to say: How much time should the education student devote to liberal or general education, to specialization or subject-matter field, and to professional or education courses?

LIBERAL OR
PEDAGOGICAL
EMPHASIS

The major conflict is rooted in the disagreements between professors of arts and sciences and professors of education. According to a noted American historian, efforts to introduce pedagogical courses into liberal arts colleges go back to the latter half of the nineteenth

**Disagreements
between
professors**

1 See B. J. Chandler, Daniel Powell, and William R. Hazard, *Education and the New Teacher* (New York: Dodd, Mead, 1971); Kevin Ryan and James M. Cooper, *Those Who Can, Teach,* 2nd ed. (Boston: Houghton Mifflin, 1975); Allan C. Ornstein and Harry L. Miller, *Looking Into Teaching* (Chicago: Rand McNally, 1980).

century when Horace Mann and Henry Barnard began their crusade for the professionalization of education.[2] These efforts have intensified throughout the twentieth century. So bitter has been the argument and so strong has been the resistance of the liberal arts colleges, that what resulted was the development of separate institutions to provide for the preparation of teachers. Thus, the normal school, which later became the teachers college, evolved separately and the rift between the arts and science faculties and the professional education faculties persisted. The split even persists where an arts and science curriculum and education courses have been taught on the same college campus.

James Conant, the most influential educator of the second half of the twentieth century, who has also had experience with both faculties, characterized this quarrel "as a power struggle among professors, which has come to involve parents, alumni, legislators, and trustees." Early in his career, as a professor of chemistry, he held the view that there "was no excuse for the existence of people who sought to teach others how to teach." He claimed to have developed his skills as a teacher "without benefit of professors of education" and saw no reason "why others could not do likewise, including those who wished to teach in the [public schools]." When he became president of Harvard University in the 1930s, the presiding officer of *all* the faculties, he sought a reconciliation between the warring groups—education versus arts and science. He was cautioned by a friend that "a shotgun would be needed to carry the wedding off." As the years went on, Conant noted some improvement between the two Harvard faculties as well as among other universities across the country. But the quarrel is by no means ended. As one dean of education remarked: "The boys have at least agreed to check their hatchets with their hats at the Faculty Club coatroom when they lunch together."[3]

Conant made it clear that no single type of institution was providing a superior educational program for teachers. The belief that "liberal arts" colleges provide a better education than do teachers colleges rests on the notion that courses in education in teachers colleges displace general arts and science courses, as well as subject specialization courses. He wrote, "My investigations have convinced me that this is simply not the case." The time devoted to education courses that displace elective courses "also give way in a 'liberal arts' college to courses that prepare students for certification."[4] What Conant failed to point out, however, is that while this may be true today, it was not always the case. Students at teachers colleges tended to take many additional educational courses at the expense of the

Conflict
between
faculties

2   Merle E. Curti, *The Social Ideas of American Educators* (New York: Scribner's, 1935).
3   James B. Conant, *The Education of American Teachers* (New York: McGraw-Hill, 1963), pp. 1-3.
4   Ibid., p. 77.

general arts and science program offered at traditional arts and science colleges.

Some of you might ask what this has to do with the present course in education—or who is teaching it. It is indeed one of the tragedies of American higher education that liberal arts/science and teacher education faculties traditionally have neither been able to communicate effectively, nor even to have a tolerant understanding of each others' goals. The squabble over what courses should be taught and who should teach them persists today, albeit on a less overt basis. In many colleges and universities, professors of education still have less prestige than other faculty members. A conflict over the number of required educational courses, which faculty should teach courses such as the history of education, the philosophy of education, or the psychology of education, and which part of the university should be in charge of certification continues on some campuses. Recently, however, substantial progress has been made toward achieving agreement on these issues.[5]

Who should teach education courses?

Fewer education courses   In the last twenty years there has been a substantial reduction in the number of education courses required for certification, as well as a decrease in education courses taken in place of general and specialized courses in the arts and sciences. For example, in a tabulation of 1,600 transcripts of students from thirty-two colleges of education in the late 1950s it was found that 22 percent of the total program of secondary teachers and more than 41 percent of the time of elementary teachers normally was devoted to education courses (required and elective). The percentages were even higher among those attending teachers colleges. More than 25 percent of the secondary teacher education program and 45 percent of the elementary program was allocated in this way. Some schools had required as many as 69 credits in education.[6]

How many education courses suffice?

Today most colleges of education require 18 educational semester credits (or about 12 percent of the total program) for secondary teachers and 24 credits (or about 20 percent) for elementary teachers. Of course there are some that encourage or require more than this number of credits, or even courses beyond state certification requirements.[7] The introduction of these education courses varies considerably. Some colleges and universities distribute them throughout the four-year program, while a few cluster these courses during the last year, and others have im-

5 Harry S. Broudy, *The Real World of the Public Schools* (New York: Harcourt Brace Jovanovich 1972); M. L. Cushman, *The Governance of Teacher Education* (Berkeley, Calif.: McCutchan, 1977).

6 See James D. Koerner, *The Miseducation of American Teachers* (Boston: Houghton Mifflin, 1963).

7 *Standards for State Approval of Teacher Education*, 6th ed. (Salt Lake City: National Association of State Directors of Teacher Education and Certification, 1976); T. M. Stinnett, *A Manual on Standards and Developments Affecting School Personnel in the United States*, 1973 ed. (Washington D.C.: National Commission on Teacher Education and Professional Standards, National Education Association, 1974).

plemented a fifth-year component consisting of subject-field and professional courses.

WHO SHOULD
TEACH?

The question of standards arises for both college students and teacher education candidates who are admitted, allowed to continue, and given degrees. If requirements for college entrance and graduation change, it is assumed that requirements for teaching will change in the same direction, although not at the same level. For example, several different authors present data showing that while there is a great deal of talk about upgrading the teaching profession, the minimum level of scholastic aptitude to be required of entry candidates for teaching has consistently been below the college mean.[8] All these observers conclude that the level of academic aptitude of the student body from which potential teachers are drawn must be raised. Conant goes so far as to suggest that potential teachers be recruited from only the top 30 percent in terms of school graduating class on a national (not individual high school) basis.

Upgrading academic standards

Several years ago as many as 25 percent of the education majors scored less than 110 (the mean of college students) on various scholastic aptitude tests. It was also found that the median IQ for 26,000 high school seniors (including those not going to college) was higher than the median of the candidates for education majors.[9] Results of selective service qualifying tests for officers' school show that college men entering the teaching profession score lower as a group than college men entering other professions. While 33 percent of engineering majors passed the examination, only 25 percent of education majors passed—the lowest score of any professional group.[10]

Low achievement and IQ scores

Data compiled by Graduate Record Examinations suggest that the situation may be unchanged. The distribution of GRE scores for candidates in sixteen major fields of study shows that teacher education majors in 1975–76 had verbal scores lower than every other group except two. Verbal scores of education majors were 25 points below the national average, and their quantitative scores were 51 points below the national average.[11]

Declining test scores The average scores of high school students on the Scholastic Aptitude Test (SAT) are even more dismal; they have been

8 Daniel S. Arnold et al., *Quality Control in Teacher Education: Some Policy Issues* (Washington, D.C.: American Association of Colleges for Teacher Education, 1977); Conant, *Education of American Teachers;* Ronald G. Corwin, *A Sociology of Education* (New York: Appleton-Century-Crofts, 1965); Koerner, *The Miseducation of American Teachers.*

9 William S. Leonard and Ben D. Wood, *The Student and His Knowledge* (New York: Carnegie Foundation for the Advancement of Teaching, 1938).

10 Dael Wolfe, *America's Resources of Specialized Talent* (New York: Harper & Row, 1954).

11 Timothy Weaver, "Educators in Supply and Demand: Effects of Quality," *School Review* (August 1979), pp. 552–93; Weaver, "Supply and Demand Effects and Professional Education." Unpublished paper, Boston University School of Education, 1979.

falling nearly every year since 1962. The average scores have declined from 478 in 1962 to 427 in 1979 on the verbal section and from 502 to 467 on the math section.[12] The SAT is based on a 200–800 scale. Students who check teaching as a preferred occupational choice have consistently averaged 10 to 20 points lower than the average on the test.

**SAT scores
decline**

Math abilities of 9 year olds, 13 year olds, 17 year olds, and young adults (26–35) have shown a marked decline in the first report of the National Assessment of Educational Progress (NAEP). More than 50 percent of our 17-year old population enter college, but only 10 percent can correctly calculate a taxi fare; only 1 percent can balance a checkbook.[13] Students' writing is marked by more awkwardness, run-on sentences, and spelling errors. Essays of 17 year olds dropped from 5.12 to 4.85 on a scale of 1 to 8, and the percentage of students writing papers ranked 4 or better declined from 85 percent to 78 percent. In particular, the poor writers were worse, and there were more of them.[14] The NAEP patterns of change in science from 1969 to 1973 show similar declines, with the greatest drops occurring for 17 year olds, in part because those students who normally would have dropped out are remaining in school and being pushed from one grade to another.[15]

Are the tests becoming more difficult? Or do we have different students entering college—those who five or ten years ago would not have considered going to college because they lacked traditional skills. Most observers agree that the decline is real; the percentage of high and average scoring students has remained fairly constant for both the SAT and NAEP, but the percentage of low scoring students has dramatically increased over the last ten years.

**Larger
percentage of
low achievers**

Increasingly each year thousands of students enter college seriously deficient in the ability to write clearly, read at grade level, and perform simple mathematical calculations.[16] In fact, the available data strongly suggest we are admitting students into college who are performing at less than an eighth-grade level—as low as fifth-grade level.[17] The rise of open

**Fifth-grade
reading levels**

12   "SAT and Math Scores Drop; Back-to-Basics Gets Some Blame," *Education USA* (September 17, 1979), pp. 17–18.

13   *Changes in Mathematical Achievement, 1973–78* (Denver, Colo.: Education Commission of the States, 1979); *National Assessment of Educational Progress: Math Fundamentals* (Washington, D.C.: U.S. Government Printing Office, 1975).

14   *National Assessment of Educational Progress: Writing National Results* (Washington, D.C.: U.S. Government Printing Office, 1975).

15   J. Stanley Ahman, "National Achievement Profiles in Ten Learning Areas," *Educational Studies* (Winter 1979), pp. 351–64.

16   Thomas C. Wheeler, *The Great American Writing Block: Causes and Cures of the New Illiteracy* (New York: Viking, 1979).

17   Theodore L. Gross, *Academic Turmoil: The Reality and Promise of Open Education* (New York: Doubleday, 1979); Louis G. Heller, *The Death of the American University* (New York: Arlington House, 1974); Jeffrey M. Katz, "What Price CUNY?" *Change* (June 1976), pp. 45–47; Thomas Sowell, *Black Education: Myths and Tragedies* (New York: McKay, 1973); Weaver, *Educators in Supply and Demand.*

admission and open access policies among many institutions of higher learning and the equalitarian push toward equal educational opportunity for all students stem from a philosophy that declares that everyone has a right to a college education.

Effect of declining test scores on teaching   A number of questions arise out of this discussion to which you might give some thought. Why is there a grade inflation in most colleges when student achievement levels are declining? What effect will these academic trends have on the kinds of people that become teachers? Should colleges of education hold the line or change their entrance standards? And since we can no longer guarantee academic outcomes, what happens to the worth of a college degree? And to the quality of our teachers?

Grade inflation

Now we have an oversupply of teachers. This fact now makes it feasible to raise academic requirements for entrance to the teaching profession. Unfortunately, college enrollment trends indicate more and more students with below-average skills are entering college and many of these students express a preference toward teaching. Indeed, there are data which already suggest that many teachers cannot tell good prose from bad, and can neither write nor speak properly; some are even illiterate.[18]

Teacher quality declining

Teacher quality is also bound to be affected by the recent view of the courts that tests as a prerequisite for employment cannot be used unless it can be proved that a body of knowledge or skills exists as a condition for performing the job and that the test is demonstrably instrumental to the job. These decisions also relate to the issue of affirmative action programs for minorities, in terms of hiring already qualified or "qualifiable" personnel. At present, the courts have upheld the use of the National Teacher Examination, but this test, based on multiple-choice questions, is relatively easy. It does not test one's ability to add, write, read, or speak properly.

What about the teacher's mental health?   Most teacher education programs do not have a selection process that takes into account the mental health of candidates, although the importance of this factor in evaluating people who will be dealing with children is obvious. Rather than measuring attitudes and values, and utilizing personality ratings, professors of education often ask candidates, "Why do you want to teach?" This is a safe question to ask, whereas delving into personality can lead to complications, even potential law suits. For example, in one survey fewer than 10 of 464 institutions reported the use of personality

18 Bernard Bard, "College for All: Dream or Disaster?" *Phi Beta Kappan* (May 1972), pp. 55-58; *Chicago Daily News* (March 26, 1976) sect. 4, p. 29; Lance M. Gentile and Merna McMillan, "Some of Our Student Teachers Can't Read Either," *Journal of Reading* (November 1977), pp. 145-48; Robert P. Hilldrup, "What Are You Doing About Your Illiterate Teachers?" *American School Board Journal* (April 1978) pp. 26-30; Robert Z. Zais, "Prospective Teachers' Reading Scores: A Cause for Concern," *Phi Delta Kappan* (May 1978), p. 635.

inventories of any kind as part of the selection process.[19] Whether these inventories at the few colleges cited are used to screen out questionable or potentially unfit candidates, or whether they are merely used as another source of information to be filed in the candidate's portfolio, is difficult to say.

Generally, mental health studies indicate that most teachers are well adjusted and exert a positive influence on children. Yet there are some teachers who, in their daily contacts with students, eventually do psychological damage.[20] For example, one study suggests that nearly 10 percent of classroom teachers are "maladjusted" and that "more than four and a half million students are exposed each year to seriously maladjusted teachers."[21] To be fair to teachers, available data suggest that as much as 10 percent of the general population has mental disorders of some type. As a group, "teachers . . . are about as well adjusted as any other professional group."[22]

Most teachers are well-adjusted

But, of course, teachers are working with children, and those who suffer from a psychiatric disorder or even a mild mental illness may do grave and irreparable harm to the young students with whom they have daily contact. Moreover, the teachers' behavior may go unnoticed, "because they do not resort to physical abuse that is illegal," but instead may resort to psychological abuse "by shouting, sarcasm, humiliation, temper tantrums, nagging and belittling."[23] Although the use of these behaviors as a means of control or punishment has been universally condemned from the mental hygiene standpoint, a visit to almost any school will probably reveal that these psychologically abusive practices are used by some teachers.

Psychologically abusive practices

To date, teachers are admitted into programs mainly on the basis of academic scores, and they must be certified in subject matter and education content. There are no psychological examinations to screen them for mental stability at the point of entry into the teacher education programs or at the point of certification. Furthermore, few professors of education are willing to make a statement to the effect that someone "appears to be psychologically unfit for teaching," nor do they seem willing to single out an individual for a psychological examination. Nonetheless, with the sup-

Psychological screening

19 Martin Haberman, "Guidelines for the Selection of Students into Programs of Teacher Education," Association of Teacher Educators and Educational Research Information Center and ERIC; *Clearinghouse on Teacher Education* (May 1972), pp. 12–17.

20 Dean F. Miller and Jan Wiltse, "Mental Health and the Teacher," *Journal of School Health* (September 1979), pp. 374–77; John Mackiel, "Positive Mental Health for Teachers," *Clearing House* (March 1979), pp. 307–10.

21 Myron Brenton, "Troubled Teachers Whose Behavior Disturbs Our Kids," *Today's Health* (November 1971), p. 19.

22 Louis Kaplan, *Education and Mental Health* (New York: Harper & Row, 1971), p. 402.

23 Samuel Brodbelt, "Teachers' Mental Health: Whose Responsibility?" *Phi Delta Kappan* (December 1973), p. 268.

ply of teachers rapidly increasing, it might be possible to apply stringent mental health standards for teacher candidates.

CERTIFICATION Part of the problem concerning the prep-
REQUIREMENTS aration of teachers is that the decision-
making structure is so diffuse. In addition to variations within states, each state has its own procedures. The situation can be summarized as follows: From state to state the power to determine requirements for teacher certification is divided among legislatures, state departments of education, superintendents of public instruction, and boards of education. Whatever these requirements, the programs of teacher education must respect them in preparing prospective teachers. Content, sequence, and the number of educational courses vary even within states, because some colleges and universities establish supplementary requirements or course work beyond minimum requirements.

There is tremendous variation in the extent to which the require- **Academic** ments are spelled out by state authorities. The number of semester or **requirements** quarter hours needed to teach an academic subject varies with the field as **vary by state** well as the state. In Nebraska, for example, a prospective teacher of art needs only 12 semester hours to qualify for a certificate to teach art; in Connecticut a prospective art teacher needs 40 semester hours. In Georgia a prospective teacher of English needs 6 semester hours to qualify for a certificate to teach English; in New York the counterpart English teacher needs a minimum of 36 semester hours. Georgia also permits a minimum of 6 mathematical semester hours for authorization to teach in this subject, compared to Missouri, which requires a minimum of 30 semester hours.[24] In some states, such as Hawaii, Minnesota, Nevada, North Dakota, Pennsylvania, and Vermont, the number of semester hours required to teach academic subjects is not indicated. Rather, the state requires that the teacher have a ''major'' in the subject field or an ''approved curriculum,'' and the hours required in that field are left to the training institutions—suggesting a difference within states. And across the country it is usually the responsibility of the teacher preparation institution to decide what courses in the subject field will be used to meet the semester requirements.

The requirements for professional education also vary. Nebraska's **Professional** minimum requirements are 18 semester hours for elementary teachers, **education** while Mississippi's minimum requirements are 36 semester hours. The **requirements** elementary certification requirements for the other states vary within this **differ, too** range, with 24 as the mode or most frequent number. New York requires a minimum of 12 semester hours for secondary teachers, while Tennessee

24 *Standards for State Approval of Teacher Education;* Stinnett, *A Manual on Standards Affecting School Personnel.*

requires 24 semester hours. The secondary certification requirements for
the other states fall within this range, with 18 as the mode. There are two
states that require an additional 30 semester hours of graduate credit for
their elementary and/or secondary teachers, and six other states that accept an approved program as required by the preparing institution.[25] Despite the state regulation requiring a certain number of professional
semester requirements, the training institution usually decides which
courses will in fact be used to meet requirements and whether additional
course work will be required at the given institution. The result is a proliferation of required educational courses at the expense of liberal education
and of the field of specialization.

Even when course titles are similar, there are often wide differences
in the content, the intellectual level of instruction, and the competencies
required. This is true for both academic and professional courses. The
result is that state requirements and teacher training institutions do not
guarantee that teachers know how to teach or even know their subject
matter.

**No guarantee
that teachers
can teach**

How do we end this confusion? Perhaps the practitioners, as in other
professions, will soon exercise a greater role in shaping programs for
their own training and certification. One of the characteristics of a profession is that its practitioners control entry to its practice. Teacher training
institutions could maintain their autonomy and have considerable freedom to develop their own programs, but they would still have to guarantee
a minimum level of competency for their students—and work out these
levels with teacher organizations or state departments of education. On
the other hand, a recent suggestion would turn over all teacher preparation, selection, and placement to community groups and to consumers of
education (parents and/or student groups). This movement would divest
professional educators of what little responsibility and authority they now
have over teacher training, licensing standards, and certification.[26]

**Greater
teacher control**

*RECIPROCITY
OF TEACHER
CERTIFICATES*
Differences in the certification requirements of the individual states have traditionally stifled the free movement of
teachers throughout the country. For example, a teacher certified to teach
in New York might not meet the requirements for teaching in Oregon.
Even where reciprocity exists, and this trend is increasing, as indicated
below, differences in supply and demand, salaries, and tenure provisions
hamper interstate movement.

25 Ibid.

26 *Teacher Education in the United States: The Responsibility Gap*, Study Commission on
Undergraduate Education and the Education of Teachers (Lincoln, Neb.: University of Nebraska
Press, 1976).

Such organizations as the American Association of Colleges for Teacher Education, Association for Student Teaching, the National Commission on Teacher Education and Professional Standards, and the National Council for Accreditation of Teacher Education (NCATE) have concerned themselves with this problem. The advantages of free interstate movement for teachers have been enumerated by these organizations and include (1) a means of nationally balancing teacher supply and demand, (2) improved opportunities and mobility for teachers, (3) less inbreeding and provincialism in local school systems, (4) increased professionalism and higher morale among teachers, and (5) a means of balancing minimum standards of preparation among states.[27] With varying degrees of success, reciprocity compacts were established between some states as early as 1900. More recently, the trend toward certifying teachers on the basis of completing institutionally approved programs by the National Council for Accreditation of Teacher Education, rather than specific state department requirements, has given rise to new regional and interstate arrangements; in effect, the program, not the credential, is now the basis for reciprocity. As a result, persons graduating from approved programs leading to certification in one state are automatically eligible for similar certification in other states participating in the agreement.[28] As of 1977, 31 states and the District of Columbia had adopted reciprocity of basic teaching credentials.[29]

Advantages of interstate movement

31 states have reciprocity agreements

While reciprocity officially exists for the basic credential, the states do not encourage it; furthermore, with the existing oversupply of teachers, interest in reciprocity among participating states has declined.

In the future, it appears that NCATE accreditation will be the chief basis of reciprocity and that future graduates of institutions holding such accreditation will not experience as much difficulty in moving from one state to another as teachers have in the past.[30]

COMPETENCY-BASED TEACHER EDUCATION Teacher education and certification based on measured competencies or performance (CBTE) is being discussed and introduced nationwide as a recent movement for improving education and certification of teachers. It combines (1) the former U.S. Office of Education's (USOE) investment in Teacher Corps projects, Triple T (Training for Teachers of Teachers) projects, and model elementary programs that have been funded to improve teacher education with (2) trends in

27 *Standards for the Accreditation of Teacher Education* (Washington, D.C.: National Council for Accreditation of Teacher Education, 1977); *Twenty-Third Annual List, 1976-77* (Washington, D.C.: National Council for Accreditation of Teacher Education, 1977).

28 Robert W. Richey, *Planning for Teaching*, 6th ed. (New York: McGraw-Hill, 1979).

29 *Twenty-Third Annual List, 1976-77.*

30 Ibid.

minicourses, micro-teaching, and computer-assisted instruction. All these programs have focused on instruction tailored to specific student outcomes based on explicit objectives and performance tests.

The emphasis on CBTE leads away from talking *about* teaching to a more direct approach: What can the prospective teacher (or, the practicing teacher) *do* in a simulated or actual teaching situation? Rather than describing what one might do in a particular situation, or selecting the best answer from a list of alternatives, the candidate must do a particular task. The task coincides with the act of teaching. In this connection, CBTE advocates seek to create a list of competencies, almost like a portfolio of the candidate, describing his or her special teaching skills and capabilities.

One of the most penetrating and influential analyses of the issues involved in CBTE is found in the USOE's 1972 task force report.[31] The report indicates that traditional educational programs unintentionally break up the acts of teaching into smaller units via courses, lectures, reading lists, and demonstrations when training teachers. CBTE does it deliberately and formally to make the parts of the whole more explicit and significant, as well as to provide opportunity for the prospective teacher to practice under real or simulated classroom conditions. Minimum levels of competency or performance are required for prospective teachers, and these minimum levels must correspond with acceptable patterns of teacher behavior.

A nationwide survey taken in 1972 among the fifty state superintendents of public instruction indicates that ten states already had mandated competency-based education and certification programs, although definitions and characteristics of the program varied.[32] By 1979, 31 states had mandated some form of competency-based teacher education.[33]

Another nationwide survey indicates that in 1975, 228 teacher training institutions (52 percent) were operating competency-based programs as compared to 125 institutions (16 percent) in 1973. On a full-scale basis 47 institutions reported involvement in CBTE in 1975, compared to only 10 in 1973.[34] Three years later 87 percent of teacher training institutions had developed or were developing some form of competency-based

Simulated teaching and specific tasks

Minimum levels of performance

CBTE in 31 states

31 Kay P. Torsher, *The Mastery Approach to Competency-Based Education* (New York: Academic Press, 1977); Benjamin Rosner, *The Power of Competency-Based Teacher Education*, Task Force 1972 Committee on National Program Priorities in Teacher Education (Washington, D.C.: U.S. Government Printing Office, 1972).

32 Alfred P. Wilson and William W. Curtis, "The States Mandate Performance-Based Teacher Education," *Phi Delta Kappan* (October 1972), pp. 76–77.

33 William P. Gorth, "The NIE Minimum Competency Study: Review and Analysis of State and Local Minimum Competency Testing Programs." Paper presented at the Annual Meeting of the American Educational Research Association, Boston, April 1980; *The State of Teacher Education, 1977* (Washington, D.C.: U.S. Government Printing Office, 1978).

34 Douglass C. Westbrook and Walter Sandefur, "Involvement of ACCTE Institutions in CBTE Programs," *Phi Delta Kappan* (December 1975), pp. 276–78.

teacher education.[35] Conclusion: teacher training institutions are moving toward some CBTE model (although the models vary).

It is probable that many institutions that indicated they have a competency-based teacher program really have basically traditional programs that are either more field oriented or are divided into modularized components. Others may have responded affirmatively because they were convinced that they have always trained competent teachers. Also, there is a tendency to attach differing meanings to the concept. Nevertheless, with so many institutions exploring alternative approaches to teacher education, it seems safe to assume that there is growing dissatisfaction with present approaches.

Different meanings to CBTE

Problems with CBTE　　In general, CBTE should be considered a viable alternative in the overdue reform of teacher education; it is certainly a growing movement with accelerated risks and problems. A few of the issues, major problems, and related questions that have been raised are outlined below.[36]

1. CBTE means different things to different people. If this issue is not resolved shortly, there will be more and more institutions proclaiming they are offering such a program, while they are actually proceeding in another direction. If this is not solved, can the real promise of the movement be realized?

2. CBTE may further fragment teacher education. Although it deliberately breaks down the acts of teaching and training, there is a point where it may become excessive. For example, at one time the Michigan State University elementary education model identified as many as 2,700 modules. Are all of these components necessary or appropriate?

Fragmenting teacher education

3. Questions of reliability and validity, associated with the competency units, need to be studied. The past history of the research on teacher behavior and demonstrations of teacher effectiveness is not encouraging. There are, indeed, a host of other technical measurement questions about behavioral objectives, micro-teaching and

Measurement problems

35　Kenneth Howey, Sam Yarger, and Bruce Joyce, "Reflections on Preservice Preparation: Impressions from the National Survey. Part III: Institutions and Programs," *Journal of Teacher Education* (January–February 1978), pp. 38–40.

36　Robert O. Brinkerhoff, "Competency Assessment: A Perspective and an Approach," *Journal of Teacher Education* (March–April 1978), pp. 21-24: Stanley M. Elam, *Performance-Based Teacher Education: What Is the State of the Art?* (Washington, D.C.: American Association of Colleges for Teacher Education, 1972); W. Robert Houston, *Exploring Competency-Based Education* (Berkeley, Calif.: McCutchan, 1974); W. James Popham, "Measurement Concomitants of Competency-Oriented Instruction." Paper presented at the Annual Meeting of the American Educational Research Association, Boston, April 1980; Sam J. Yarger and Bruce R. Joyce, "Going Beyond the Data: Reconstructing Teacher Education," *Journal of Teacher Education* (November–December 1977), pp. 21-25.

simulated tests that still need to be answered. If standardized tests of achievement are under attack for being "culturally biased," will competency-based tests (which are more difficult to develop and where we have limited experience) fall under the same gun?

4. Many teachers and professors of education lack sufficient knowledge in the areas of tests and measurements, and empirical research procedures. Their beliefs about teaching frequently are based on a nonanalytical and nonresearch orientation, on traditional principles, subjective ideas, and anecdotes. If the educational community does not fully understand or utilize research procedures, can CBTE be fully realized as it is intended?

5. How shall the information regarding a prospective teacher's competency be translated into certification units and communicated to licensing authorities? Questions of how to match student credits with degree requirements and faculty credits and work-load definitions have not been answered adequately. What makes CBTE exercises 1–10, or any number of exercises, equivalent to the content tested under the traditional methods course at your college?

Translating competencies into credits

6. In theory it is possible for teaching candidates who have taken no education courses, and perhaps even people without college degrees, to argue that they should be certified to teach if they can demonstrate competence during trial periods as classroom teachers. Recall the old adage: "Those who can, do; those who can't, teach." What relationship do education courses have to teacher effectiveness?

No education courses

To make CBTE programs operational, it is necessary to identify appropriate competencies, assess these competencies accurately, define good teaching while accommodating for different teaching styles and roles, develop and prepare instructional materials, switch to an analytical and research focus in teacher education, and train educators to manage these programs. Can all these things be accomplished? Our track record in education is not impressive; it suggests that we will have trouble accomplishing these prerequisite tasks.

TRENDS IN TEACHER EDUCATION

Earlier in this chapter we described the competency-based teacher education approach and noted that CBTE has become a central part of teacher education programs at many colleges and universities. One purpose of the CBTE approach, as emphasized by its advocates, is to make teacher education more practical and reality oriented. That is, the emphasis is on providing future teachers with concrete skills they will need in the classroom and on determining whether they can use these

Practical training

skills successfully in practice. Other types of efforts also are being made to increase the "reality orientation" of teacher education programs, notably by reducing the separation between professional coursework and clinical experience in the schools, and by providing early and continuous exposure to the actual teaching situation. In addition, advances in knowledge, media, and communications have made it possible to use instructional technology more extensively in improving the preparation of future teachers.

SCHOOL-BASED One of the ways in which teacher trainers
EDUCATION CENTERS have attempted to make teacher prepara-
tion more realistic and practical is by conducting a significant part of the training at cooperating elementary or secondary schools specifically designated to provide preservice preparation. Much of the training that previously was provided at the college or university campus is now provided at school-based teacher education centers, which generally have office space for college faculty, special equipment for use in teacher training, and outstanding teachers to serve as supervisors and models for future teachers.

Moving from college classrooms to school centers

The growth of school-based teacher education centers has been documented in the National Survey of the Preservice Preparation of Teachers. Whereas in 1968 only 22 percent of higher education teacher training institutions had established centers for this purpose either on or off campus, by 1975 36 percent of such institutions had done so. The vast majority of these centers were at elementary or secondary schools in local school districts. The trend toward establishment of such centers was particularly evident among public colleges and universities: 64 percent of the public higher education institutions had established a teacher education center of some kind, and about half of these centers were located in local school districts.[37]

EARLY FIELD Another way in which teacher education
EXPERIENCE programs have become more practical is
by requiring or encouraging future teachers to spend a significant amount of time in elementary or secondary schools shortly after they enter the preparation program. This trend was identified in a 1977 study of teacher training programs, which found that students in about one-fourth of the programs have classroom experience as early as the freshman year.[38] In many cases professional courses in subjects like introduction to education, educational psychology, or teaching methods are closely coor-

Early field experiences

---

37 *The State of Teacher Education, 1977.*
38 Howey, Yarger, and Joyce, "Reflections on Preservice Preparation: Impressions from the National Survey."

dinated with classroom observation, teacher aide assignments, or other field experiences in local schools. In general, institutions that require early and continuous field experience have constructed a sequence of assignments such that students move from observation to service as a teacher's aide to relatively full-scale teaching responsibility such as the traditional "practice" teaching semester.

According to the National Survey of the Preservice Preparation of Teachers, early field experience for prospective teachers is being provided using a variety of arrangements. In some teacher training programs, a future teacher may serve an hour or two a day as a teaching assistant in the classroom, but the bulk of the training program still takes place at the college campus. At the other extreme, most or even all of the professional coursework is provided at an elementary or secondary school site by college or university personnel. Whichever arrangement is followed, the survey found a gradual progression from relatively unsupervised contact and observation during the first year or two to actual teaching during the final year. Thus the data show that during the 1975–76 academic year, 76 percent of the field experience of college freshmen enrolled in teacher education programs was spent in unsupervised contact and observation, as compared with seniors, who devoted 63 percent of their field experience time to actual teaching and only 2 percent to unsupervised contact and observation.[39]

Increased supervision of field experiences

INSTRUCTIONAL TECHNOLOGY AND ANALYSIS

The term *instructional technology* can have a large number of referents, including physical materials such as computers or videotapes and systematized intellectual resources such as comprehensive sets of learning skills or objectives. The National Survey of the Preservice Preparation of Teachers examined the use of instructional technology in teacher education programs and concluded that several kinds of technologies became more prevalent in the 1970s.

The most noticeable increase in utilization of instructional technology occurred with respect to *techniques for the analysis of classroom interaction*. This term refers to a variety of techniques and instruments for the systematic measurement and analysis of classroom interactions between teachers and pupils.[40] Teacher trainers hope that systematic analysis of this kind will help prospective teachers learn to establish and maintain a constructive classroom environment when they become teachers. The use of interaction analysis techniques spread from 10 percent of teacher training institutions in 1968 to 71 percent in 1975.[41]

Measurement and analysis of classroom interactions

39 *The State of Teacher Education, 1977.*
40 Interaction analysis is further described in Chapter 4 of this text.
41 *The State of Teacher Education, 1977.*

A second type of technology that was widely adopted in teacher training programs during the 1970s involved utilization of classification systems known as taxonomies to analyze educational goals and objectives. The most commonly used taxonomy of objectives, the analysis of cognitive and affective behaviors and goals, was developed by Benjamin Bloom and his colleagues.[42] The psychomotor taxonomy, also in use, is gaining in popularity.[43] The national survey found that 52 percent of teacher training institutions were using the cognitive and/or affective taxonomy in 1975, as compared with only 16 percent in 1968.[44]

Taxonomies of educational objectives

The national survey also found that several well-known instructional technologies either did not become more widely adopted or actually declined in use during the 1970s. For example, use of videotapes or other equipment for simulations, in which trainees actually teach a class and then are critiqued in order to improve their performance, was reported at 61 percent of teacher training institutions in 1973; by 1975 only 32 percent were using simulations. Decline in the use of the simulation approach was attributed mainly to its relatively high cost. Similarly, micro-teaching techniques, in which future teachers work with a small group of pupils in teaching a practice lesson devoted to a specific learning objective and then analyze their performance (usually on videotape), also declined from 77 percent of the institutions surveyed in 1973 to 39 percent in 1975.[45] While the use of simulation and micro-teaching was declining, however, the use of interaction analysis and the taxonomy was increasing, according to the survey.

Decline in simulation and micro-teaching techniques

SUMMING UP

1. The preservice preparation of teachers rests upon a three-fold set of components: liberal education, specialized subject matter, and professional studies. These areas are interrelated and each is considered important for the proper education of teachers.

2. Educators do not agree upon the amount of time to be devoted by prospective teachers to each of the three areas. As a result, the liberal arts/science-education controversy has developed.

3. Requirements for teacher certification vary among states and institutions of higher learning. Prospective teachers must be ac-

---

42 Benjamin S. Bloom, et al., *Taxonomy of Educational Objectives, Handbook I: Cognitive Domain* (New York: McKay, 1956); David R. Krathwohl, Benjamin S. Bloom, and Bertram Masia, *Taxonomy of Educational Objectives, Handbook II: Affective Domain* (New York: McKay, 1964).

43 Anita J. Harlow, *Taxonomy of the Psychomotor Domain: A Guide for Developing Behavioral Objectives* (New York: McKay, 1972). See Chapter 13 of this text for a description of the taxonomies.

44 *The State of Teacher Education, 1977.*

45 Ibid.

quainted with the certification requirements in the state or states in which they wish to teach.

4. Unquestionably, teacher education and certification need to be improved. In addition to raising academic standards and creating some uniformity among the states, there is a growing demand for the introduction of competency- or performance-based teacher education and certification.

5. In general, teacher education is becoming more practical and reality oriented. Trends in this direction include the establishment of school-based centers for preparing future teachers and provision of early field experience in elementary and secondary classrooms.

6. In addition, techniques for teacher-pupil interaction analysis, taxonomies specifying a comprehensive set of learning goals and behaviors, and other forms of instructional technology are being used to improve the preparation of future teachers.

DISCUSSION QUESTIONS

1. Why do you suppose professors of arts and science and professors of education do not always see eye to eye on the education of teachers?

2. What are some of the possible reasons for the declining SAT scores of college students? What impact does this have on who enters the teaching profession?

3. What kinds of education courses should be required for teacher preparation?

4. What are the merits of and problems with competency-based education?

5. Do you believe the trends identified as taking place in teacher education are desirable? Why or why not?

THINGS TO DO

1. Obtain information on teacher certification requirements in your state by level (elementary, secondary) and subject area (elementary art, secondary art, reading, English, etc.). Contrast the data with (a) the information presented in this chapter, and (b) the requirements established by your own college or university.

2. Examine a professional journal most closely related to your prospective area of teaching (level and subject area). Discuss the value of the journal.

3. Contact several teacher training institutions in your region to determine whether or how they have changed their preparation program during the past five years.

4. Draw up an optimal program for preparing teachers. What balance should it have between liberal arts, subject matter, and professional studies?

5. Survey nearby states to determine whether they have reciprocity agreements with your state. What courses or subjects would you have to take to acquire a certificate in another state?

CHAPTER 3
THE TEACHING
PROFESSION

Focusing questions

What are the essential differences between the NEA and the AFT?

Can these differences be reconciled?

In what ways is teaching not fully a profession?

What are the trends toward teaching becoming a more full-fledged profession?

Until the twentieth century, teachers had relatively little preparation for their job and relatively little voice in determining the conditions of their employment. Teacher training consisted of one or two years and sometimes less at a normal school or teachers college, and teachers had to follow strict rules and regulations concerning their behavior outside the school. Unorganized and isolated from one another in small schools and school districts, teachers could be summarily dismissed by a board of education. Many were told they could not teach any material that someone in the community might find objectionable.

Times have changed. Today, teachers are well organized, mostly as part of the National Education Association or the American Federation of Teachers, and they aspire to be professional persons with expert knowledge concerning the content and methods of instruction in their particular subject fields. In addition, teachers generally have gained greater rights to be judged mainly on the basis of their performance rather than on the basis of their behavior outside the school and to participate in making decisions about the conditions in which they work. The first part of this chapter describes how teacher organizations have grown in power and prominence, and the second half discusses the ways in which teachers are striving for full professional status.

TEACHER ORGANIZATIONS

The benefits received by teachers have been the result of a hard and long uphill climb. "The good old days" may have benefited school administrators, school board members, or the power brokers of the community, but they were terrible for teachers. Today's working conditions still need to be improved, but they sharply contrast with the rewards and restrictions teachers (mainly women) once endured. Here are the details of what is reputed to be a Wisconsin teacher's contract for 1922, calling for a salary of $75 a month.

Restrictions on teachers

Miss———agrees:

1. Not to get married. This contract becomes null and void immediately if the teacher marries.

2. Not to keep company with men.

3. To be home between the hours of 8 P.M. and 6 A.M. unless in attendance at a school function.

4. Not to loiter downtown in ice-cream parlors.

5. Not to leave town at any time without the permission of the chairman of the Trustees.

6. Not to smoke cigarettes.

7. Not to drink beer, wine, or whiskey.

8. Not to ride in a carriage or automobile with any man except her brother or father.

9. Not to dress in bright colors.

10. Not to dye her hair.

11. Not to wear less than two petticoats.

12. Not to wear dresses shorter than two inches above the ankles.

13. To keep the schoolroom clean:
   a. To sweep the classroom floor at least once daily.
   b. To scrub the classroom floor at least once weekly.
   c. To clean the blackboard at least once daily.
   d. To start the fire at 7 A.M. so that the room will be warm at 8 A.M. when the children arrive.

14. Not to wear face powder, mascara or to paint the lips.[1]

Consider these requirements in the context of the times: the status of women, the image of teachers, and what Small Town, U.S.A. was like. Those were the days of the Model T Ford, the protest marches of Susan B. Anthony, the growing pains of labor, the "muckrakers," and Sinclair Lewis's *Main Street* and *Babbitt*.

Consider the times

Obviously, the conditions described above no longer exist and to a large extent the growth of teacher organizations and teacher militancy have played a role in improving the conditions of teaching. Although there are more than 300 teacher organizations in the country, the National Education Association (NEA) and the American Federation of Teachers (AFT) are the two most important organizations. These two organizations usually are considered rivals, competing for members, recognition, and power. Although some educators believe that perpetuation of this division is healthy and a form of professional competition, others view this as detrimental to the teaching profession—a splitting of power and waste of resources.

NEA and AFT are rivals

NATIONAL EDUCATION ASSOCIATION The NEA, originally founded in 1857 by 43 educators, is a complex, multifaceted organization involved in many areas of education on local, state, and national levels. The NEA, unlike the AFT, includes both teachers and administrators. As shown in Table 3.1, membership grew from 2,332 in 1900[2] to an estimated 1.8 million in 1980. Among these members approximately 50,000 were students, 75,000 were college

1.8 million members

1 *Chicago Tribune* (September 28, 1975), sect. 1, p. 3.
2 *NEA Handbook, 1977-78* (Washington, D.C.: National Education Association, 1977).

TABLE 3.1
MEMBERSHIP OF THE NEA BY
DECADES

YEAR	MEMBERSHIP
1857[a]	43
1870	170
1880	354
1890	5,474
1900	2,322
1910	6,909
1920	22,850
1930	216,188
1940	203,429
1950	453,797
1960	713,994
1970	1,100,000
1975	1,500,000
1980[b]	1,800,000

Note: a = Year organization was
founded.
b = Estimated membership.

Source: Adapted from Allan C. Ornstein,
Education and Social Inquiry (Itasca,
Ill.: Peacock, 1978), p. 311; T. M.
Stinnett and Raymond E. Cleveland,
"The Politics and Rise of Teacher
Organizations," in A. C. Ornstein and
S. I. Miller, eds., *Policy Issues in
Education* (Lexington, Mass.: Heath,
1976), p. 90.

professors, 275,000 were administrators and 1.4 million were teachers.
This figure comprises more than half of the nation's 2.4 million teachers.
The membership, disproportionately suburban and rural, is served by a
large network of affiliates in every state, Puerto Rico, and the District of
Columbia and by an Overseas Educational Association. There are more
than 7,000 local affiliate groups. In sheer numbers, the NEA represents
the second largest lobbying force in the country, outnumbering all other
public employee organizations, and among unions trailing only the
Teamsters. Its combined annual budget is over $250 million, and there is
an average of about 4,000 members in every congressional district. The
state affiliates are usually among the most influential education lobbies in
the state legislatures.[3]

**Strength in
rural and
suburban areas**

3 Anthony M. Cresswell and Michael J. Murphy, *Teachers, Unions, and Collective Bargaining* (Berkeley, Calif.: McCutchan, 1976); Allan C. Ornstein and Harry L. Miller, *Looking
Into Teaching* (Chicago: Rand McNally, 1980).

*Times have changed and teachers are becoming increasingly
aware of their professionalism, as the movement toward
militancy increases.*

The NEA is composed of several departments, national affiliates,
associated organizations, commissions, committees, councils, and divisions. The departments serve general interests, such as the Association of
Classroom Teachers (ACT), and the national affiliates represent separate
disciplines, such as art teachers, mathematics teachers, and science
teachers, and have considerable influence among many secondary school
teachers who identify themselves by the subject they teach. The influential
Association for Supervision and Curriculum Development (ASCD), consisting of 37,500 members, is also affiliated with the NEA. Other special-
interest groups that are loosely affiliated with the NEA include the American Library Association (ALA) and the National Association of Secondary
School Principals (NASSP). The commissions, committees, and councils
conduct investigations, recommend standards, and support programs.

A wide range of services is offered by the NEA. The Research Division, organized in 1922, conducts annual research studies on the status of the profession; it also publishes the *NEA Research Bulletin*. The major publication of the NEA is *Today's Education*, previously called the *NEA Journal*. In addition, the association's departments and councils publish monthly or quarterly journals. For example, the American Association of School Administrators (AASA) publishes the *School Administrator;* the Department of Elementary School Principals (DESP) publishes the *Elementary School Principal;* NASSP puts out the *Bulletin of the National Association of Secondary School Principals*. The national councils for the various subject fields—mathematics, science, English, social studies, modern language, speech, home economics, business education, art, etc.—also publish professional journals. In addition, most of the 50 state affiliates publish a monthly magazine.

*Today's
Education*

The NEA and teacher strikes   Until the mid-1960s, the NEA relied on sanctions as the most aggressive measure against a school board. It condemned the AFT for its strike tactics, which it considered illegal and unprofessional. The sanctions basically involved one or more of four steps: (1) a factual study and report of the conditions in a specific school system; (2) widespread publicity on teachers' dissatisfaction with existing conditions; (3) a warning to NEA members that accepting a position in the system would be considered unethical; and (4) messages to college and university placement agencies asking them not to recommend teachers to the system. (Steps 3 and 4 were rarely put into practice.)

The NEA did an about-face in its position largely for two reasons: the success of the AFT strike tactic and the growing demand by its own members that it assume greater responsibility for improving their occupational status. The NEA's transition from a relatively antimilitant position to a more aggressive organization culminated in the following resolution passed at its annual convention in 1968:

**Becoming
more militant**

> The NEA recognizes that under conditions of severe stress causing deterioration of the educational program, and when good-faith attempts at resolution have been rejected, strikes have occurred and may occur in the future. In such instances, the NEA will offer all of the services at its command to the affiliate concerned to help resolve the impasse.[4]

The resolution focused its major attention on preventing unnecessary strikes and stressed that every effort should be made to avoid the strikes. Nevertheless, it did recognize the strike tactic as legitimate if

4 National Education Association Annual Meeting, Dallas, Texas, 1968. Resolution 68–19, reprinted in the *NEA Handbook, 1968–69* (Washington, D.C.: NEA, 1969), pp. 82–83.

TABLE 3.2
MEMBERSHIP OF THE AFT BY
DECADES

YEAR	MEMBERSHIP
1918[a]	1,500
1920	10,000
1930	7,000
1940	30,000
1950	41,000
1960	59,000
1970	205,000
1975	450,000
1980[b]	600,000

Note: a = Year the organization
         was founded.
      b = Estimated membership.

Source: Adapted from Ornstein, *Educa-
tion and Social Inquiry*, p. 311: T. M.
Stinnett and Raymond E. Cleveland,
"The Politics and Rise of Teacher
Organizations," p. 93.

other actions had failed to rectify the situation.[5] Whereas only 50 percent
of the teachers surveyed by the NEA in 1965 supported the right to strike,
by 1970 as many as 90 percent supported some type of group action, and
75 percent approved the strike tactic.[6] This change within the NEA is not
only the crucial element in understanding the power struggle with the
AFT, but is also a key event in the possible merger of the two organizations.

AMERICAN
FEDERATION
OF TEACHERS

The AFT was formed in 1918. It is affiliated with the AFL–CIO and is open to
classroom teachers only. Current mem-
bership is nearly 600,000, organized in some five hundred locals concen- **600,000**
trated in large and medium-sized cities. As shown in Table 3.2, most of its **members**
membership increase has taken place within the last twenty years. Among

5 National Education Association, *Formal Grievance Procedures for Public School
Teachers 1965-66*, Research Report 1967-R10 (Washington, D.C.: NEA, 1967).

6 Ronald G. Corwin, "The New Teaching Profession" in K. Ryan, ed., *Teacher Education*,
National Society for the Study of Education, Part II (Chicago: University of Chicago Press,
1975), pp. 230-64: "Teacher Strikes," *Today's Education* (November 1969), p. 10.

its 600,000 members are some 25,000 paraprofessionals, 75,000 municipal workers who are not teachers, 100,000 college professors, and
400,000 teachers.[7]

The national governing body of the AFT is the Annual Convention,
representing local affiliates according to a proportional formula. The
Executive Council assumes the leadership between the annual conventions. Unlike the NEA affiliates, the AFT locals tend to be militant in
philosophy and more eager to collectively bargain over economic matters
and working conditions, although many of the NEA state affiliates have
become more aggressive since the 1968 national resolution.

The AFT has not, in the past, been involved with research and publication to the extent of the NEA, but the union does publish a professional
magazine, *Changing Education*, a *Consortium Yearbook*, and a monthly
newspaper, *American Teacher*. In addition, the local affiliates put out a
newsletter. Unlike the NEA, the AFT members are usually required to join
the local, state (twenty-two in all), and national organizations simultaneously. Also, the NEA dues policy emphasizes local support, whereas the
AFT dues are mainly channeled to the national level.

*American
Teacher*

The AFT remained quite small until criticism of the schools mounted
in the post-Sputnik era. The membership breakthrough for the union
came when AFT leaders made a policy decision to concentrate on the New
York City school system. In 1961 the union group defeated the organization supporting the NEA, and the United Federation of Teachers (UFT) was
chosen to represent New York City teachers. Following its victory, the
UFT engaged in a number of strikes in New York City over the next decade—for improved working conditions, salary increases, health benefits,
pensions, and teacher rights. Success in New York City led to a series of
victories over the NEA in several other large cities for the right to represent teachers. The AFT became the dominant teacher organization in
many large urban centers where unions have traditionally flourished,
where militant tactics such as collective bargaining and strikes have been
a common occurrence, and where teachers in general perceived a need for
a powerful organization to represent them. In rural and suburban areas,
where union tactics have typically received less support, the NEA remained dominant.

**Strength in
urban areas**

The AFT and teacher strikes   Albert Shanker, president of the
AFT, stated the union's view on the right to strike and the school boards'
"right to manage" as follows:

> If school boards are not merely curious about why teachers are
> angry, but genuinely want to re-establish good relations with
> teachers, they will need first to eliminate all vestige of paternalism

**Vestiges of
paternalism**

7   Ornstein and Miller, *Looking Into Teaching.*

from their dealings with teachers and the unions of which teachers are members.

School boards also will need to give strong direction to their agents—both district-level and building-level administrators—to behave as educational managers and statesmen, rather than as guardians of a collection of unmanageable child-adults (which is how teachers sometimes are treated by school administrators).[8]

An education writer, commenting on the success of the AFT in teacher strikes, points out:

> Strikes . . . have given the AFT's growth a snow-balling effect, advancing its image as a militant fighter for teachers' rights, destroying the picture of the teacher as a silent partner in the educational process. Nothing kills the Mr. Chips fantasy faster than a picture of striking teachers being loaded into police vans. . . . [9]

Annual strike figures have averaged about 150 since 1970; only once **Strike figures** between 1970 and 1980 did the annual figure drop below 100 and in 1976 a record was established—203 strikes. This trend continued in the late 1970s: in 1979, a new record of more than 210 strikes was established.[10] The major reasons involve general wage changes, union organization and security, working conditions, and job security. With high levels of teacher unemployment throughout the nation, strikes over job security might be expected to increase in number. Generally, the growth and outcome of teacher work stoppages and strikes can be assessed in terms of the change in teacher power—from relative impotence prior to the 1960s to increased recognition of teacher organizations as the official bargaining representative of their members around issues once considered the prerogatives of school boards and school administrators.[11]

THE POSSIBILITY Without question there has been intense *OF A MERGER* organizational rivalry between the NEA and AFT for years. These two organizations have competed for members and for exclusive local rights to represent teachers. Prior to the 1960s any thought of merging seemed highly unlikely. The NEA has historically viewed itself as a professional association, not a union. It shunned collec- **Professionalism** tive bargaining, strikes, and other militant tactics. It vehemently criti- **vs. unionism**

8 Albert Shanker, "Why Teachers Are Angry," *American School Board Journal* (January 1975), p. 23.

9 Peter Janssen, "The Union Response to Academic Mass Production," *Saturday Review* (October 21, 1967), p. 65.

10 "It's Agreed: This Should Be a Record Year for Strikes," *Phi Delta Kappan* (February 1980), p. 444.

11 "Teachers Will Be Using Bargaining, Books, and Ballots to Get What They Want from You This Year," *American School Board Journal* (September 1979), pp. 21-24.

cized the AFT for its labor affiliation and maintained that this relationship was detrimental to the professional image. For its part, the AFT criticized the NEA's more conciliatory tactics as unrealistic, and argued that union affiliation provided political and economic "clout." Even more important was its criticism of the NEA for admitting and even encouraging administrators to join.

The AFT argument was that the NEA was "management-oriented," and that so long as administrators were in the organization, and so long as these individuals wielded power, the NEA could not make adequate progress toward securing a professional level of income and status for teachers. The NEA countered that the organization was concerned with the interests of teachers, and that it was good professional practice to include both teachers and administrators. Attacks and counterattacks at both organizations are found in the literature of the 1950s and 1960s.

It has become evident, however, that some of these issues no longer divide the organizations as they did in the past. The collective bargaining and strike issues have undergone a policy change by the NEA. Also, a number of teacher negotiation statutes and state administrative agency decisions have settled the issue over administrative membership basically along the lines advocated by the AFT. In many cases, state legislation permits and even mandates the inclusion of administrative personnel in a teacher bargaining unit. But the NEA local affiliates have come to realize that this creates too many practical problems for all parties concerned.

Following the example of the Michigan Education Association in 1966, when administrators withdrew from the association, many other school principals and superintendents in other parts of the country have pulled out of the local and/or state affiliates. The issue of administrative membership is being discussed at various organizational levels. In some school districts, the issue is seen as pertaining to local organizations; it is argued that administrators can and should retain membership in state and national teacher organizations. In other places, it is accepted that administrative personnel should not be regular members of the local and state units, but that they should continue as members of the national NEA. Compounding the problem even more is the fact that school administrators, mostly in the big cities, have organized into unions and separate bargaining associations with more than 1,800 local units as of 1979. Although the AFT has refused to become affiliated with them, its parent organization, the AFL–CIO, has granted these administrative units a charter.[12]

Administrative membership

Administrators unionize

---

12   Bruce S. Cooper, "Collective Bargaining for School Administrators Four Years Later." *Phi Delta Kappan* (October 1979), pp. 130–31; Cooper, "Unionism in Education: Its Implications for Political and Organizational Theory," Paper presented at the Annual Meeting of the American Educational Research Association, Boston, April 1980.

Further roadblocks   The AFT's affiliation with the AFL-CIO still remains an important roadblock. Some NEA officials maintain that a merger of the two organizations within the AFL-CIO would cause a large part of NEA's membership to break away and form a more conservative group.[13] Affiliation with the AFL-CIO is less important to most rank-and-file AFT members than to some AFT leaders who see derived benefits and support from a larger union affiliation. Although NEA leaders still spend time at national conventions criticizing organized labor, and AFT leaders still insist that they will not drop national affiliation with the union, there is discussion of various plans to overcome the obstacle at the local level.

AFL-CIO
affiliation

Recently rivalry between the NEA and AFT has intensified over enrolling professors into their organizations. The desire among professors to organize is linked to financial stringencies and hiring and tenure problems plaguing the colleges and universities; henceforth, we can expect large membership gains within the NEA and AFT—and also greater rivalry.

Membership of
professors

College and university teachers have been somewhat slow to seek organized labor's support, but the picture seems to be changing now. In a recent survey, Everett Ladd and Seymour Lipset found that three-fourths of all professors, a majority at every type of institution of higher learning, said that they would vote for collective bargaining and a pro-union agent if an election were held at their institution. As many as 76 percent in each of two surveys credited collective bargaining with bringing higher salaries and improved benefits.[14]

Despite the higher percentage of professors who now endorse collective bargaining and unionization, a considerably smaller percentage actually have voted to be represented by such agents. Perhaps the reasons for the gap are that the professors cannot agree on what organizations should represent them and that there is rivalry not only among the organizations but also among professors themselves. In addition, inertia must be overcome if college professors are to join militant organizations.

Differing positions on affirmative action also divide the NEA and AFT. The NEA has adopted a policy of guaranteeing that a percentage of all its administrative committees be from minority groups; it has taken the position that any merger must include guarantees of quotas, and the AFT leadership has rejected this position. Furthermore, the NEA and AFT took opposing sides in the 1978 U.S. Supreme Court decision regarding Alan

Affirmative
action

13   Marshall O. Donley, *The Future of Teacher Power in America* (Bloomington, Ind.: *Phi Delta Kappan*, 1977); Martha Gottron, "NEA Pushes for Teachers' Rights," *Change* (February 1975), pp. 17–20.

14   *Chronicle of Higher Education* (March 13, 1978), p. 14; Everett Ladd and Seymour M. Lipset, "Faculty Support for Unionization," *Education Digest* (May 1978), pp. 56–58.

Bakke.[15] Beyond that, the NEA leadership is diffuse and lacking in well-known leaders who can deliver votes on a controversial issue; moreover, until 1973 the national president was elected for a one-year term only, which in effect created a lame-duck presiding officer who lacked sufficient power to effect a merger. The term of the president has now been extended to two years with eligibility for re-election. Although this change should help to facilitate merger discussion, the 1974 election of Albert Shanker to the presidency of the AFT has hindered talks because of his uncompromising stand on many educational and labor issues. Then, too, there is no guarantee that both organizations can assure membership acceptance. Finally, there is the major problem of who gets which jobs and how much decision-making power in a merged organization.

Presiding officers

Pro-merger factors The movement toward merger has been enhanced by the recognition by the NEA and AFT of the need to elect pro-teacher and pro-education political representatives at the local, state, and federal levels. Both organizations are now spending millions of dollars annually and encouraging their teachers to volunteer time in election contests. The NEA, in particular, has been successful in this approach; about 75 percent of the candidates whom it has supported in recent years have won election.[16] Behind these successes is the fact that in states where the NEA and AFT decide to support selected candidates, they usually throw their muscle behind the same candidates—illustrating that their political views are compatible.

Political activism

Both the NEA and AFT advocate a federal law guaranteeing collective bargaining. As of 1979, as many as 32 states had laws providing some form of collective bargaining, although they varied considerably.[17] It makes little sense to have more than 30 different state laws on collective negotiations—and 20 states with no laws. No doubt more states will adopt collective negotiation laws, but the NEA and AFT would prefer a uniform, federal law to safeguard their rights to strike and, more important, to guarantee their benefits on retirement, sick leave, seniority and tenure, holidays, work days and work year, leave benefits (personal, military, maternity, etc.) and other protections and benefits now provided to public-sector employees by statute.

Guaranteeing collective negotiation

In an era of teacher retrenchment, the NEA and AFT are also in basic agreement on securing unemployment benefits for teachers (only eight states currently provide them), enlarging the demand for teachers by ex-

---

15 "Bakke: Pro and Con: The National Education Association and American Federation of Teachers *Amicus Curiae* Brief," *Phi Delta Kappan* (March 1978), pp. 477-555.

16 Cresswell and Murphy, *Teachers, Unions, and Collective Bargaining*; T. M. Stinnett and Raymond E. Cleveland, "The Politics and Rise of Teacher Organizations," in A. C. Ornstein and S. Miller, eds. *Policy Issues in Education* (Lexington, Mass.: Heath, 1976), pp. 83-94.

17 Myron Lieberman, "Eggs That I Have Laid: Teacher Bargaining Reconsidered," *Phi Delta Kappan* (February 1979), pp. 415-19.

tending free public education to all children and youth from prekindergarten to grade 14, convincing the public of the proved value of smaller classes, increasing fringe benefits that are tax-free, increasing teacher pay and implementing cost-of-living adjustments, increasing teacher retirement benefits, and stepping up teacher militancy to resist possible cutbacks.

Questions concerning tenure laws, accountability, the growing antiteacher mood of the public, school budget cutbacks, as well as teacher unemployment, may force teachers to conclude that the best way to combat the dangers facing them is to end the organizational rivalry and move toward greater unity. To be sure, there are immense political and economic advantages to be gained by such a merger—with members of their families in every voting district in the nation. As many as 3.5 million teachers, paraprofessionals, and miscellaneous educators from state and federal departments and nonprofit and foundation organizations would provide enormous potential power unavailable to the present two separate organizations. The nearly one million teachers who presently do not belong to either organization would probably join the united "super" teacher organization.

Antiteacher mood

IS TEACHING A PROFESSION?

Whether teaching can be considered a profession in the fullest sense has been an issue of great concern to educators for many decades. A number of educators have tried to identify the ideal characteristics of professions and, by rating teaching on these, to determine whether teaching is a profession. Table 3.3 lists the characteristics of a profession as defined by three educators in ten-year intervals since the 1950s. Not only is there considerable overlap among these evaluations, but also the general conclusions are similar: Teaching is not a profession in the fullest sense; it does not possess some of the characteristics professions are supposed to possess; and in some ways it may be viewed as a semiprofession or a vocation in the process of achieving these characteristics. If readers were asked whether the teaching profession is marked by the characteristics listed in Table 3.3, it is probable that some would answer yes, some no, and others would be ambivalent. The general conclusion follows that teaching is partially but not entirely a true profession at present.

Viewed as a semiprofession

Of the 13 characteristics of a profession listed in Table 3.3, perhaps the four most important are: (1) defined body of knowledge beyond that grasped by laymen, (2) control over licensing standards and/or entry requirements, (3) autonomy in making decisions about selected spheres of work, and (4) high prestige and economic standing. The following discussion of these characteristics clearly indicates that the teaching profession

Knowledge, control, autonomy, and prestige

TABLE 3.3
CHARACTERISTICS
OF A PROFESSION

Characteristic	Lieberman (1956)	Corwin (1965)	Ornstein (1976)
1. A sense of public service.	X		
2. A defined body of knowledge beyond that grasped by laymen.		X	X
3. Application of research and theory to practice (to human problems).	X	X	X
4. A lengthy period of specialized training.	X	X	
5. Control over licensing standards and/or entry requirements.		X	X
6. Autonomy in making decisions about selected spheres of work.	X	X	X
7. An acceptance of responsibility for judgments made and acts performed related to services rendered.	X		
8. Commitment to work and client; an emphasis upon service to be rendered.	X		X
9. Administrators facilitate work of professionals; administrators' functions are considered secondary and their work is considered undesirable.			X
10. A self-governing organization comprised of members of the profession.	X		
11. Professional associations and/or elite groups provide recognition for individual achievements.			X
12. There is a code of ethics to help clarify ambiguous matters or doubtful points related to services rendered.	X	X	X
13. High prestige and economic standing.		X	X

Note: X denotes an author's designation of a profession, with implications for teachers.

Sources: Myron Lieberman, *Education as a Profession* (Englewood Cliffs, N.J.: Prentice-Hall 1956); Ronald G. Corwin, *Sociology of Education* (New York: Appleton-Century-Crofts, 1965); Allan C. Ornstein, *Teaching in a New Era* (Champaign, Ill.: Stipes, 1976).

does not possess them all. Although no profession has achieved the ideal state, teaching seems to lag behind many others, such as law and medicine.

A DEFINED BODY
OF KNOWLEDGE
All professions have a monopoly on certain knowledge that separates their members from the general public and allows for exercise of control over the vocation. Members of a profession have mastered a body of knowledge that establishes their expertise and protects the public from quacks, untrained amateurs, and special-interest groups. There is, however, no agreed-upon specialized body of knowledge that is "education" or "teaching." Whereas the behavioral sciences, physical sciences, and health fields can be guided by extensive rules of procedure and established methodologies, education lacks a well-defined body of knowledge that is applicable to the real world of teaching,[18] or that has been validated and agreed upon by most authorities. One result is that the content of teacher education courses varies from state to state and among teacher training institutions within states.

No agreed-upon knowledge

Moreover, it is estimated that many teachers working in the secondary schools are teaching out of license; in other words, teachers of English did not major in English in college, nor are they certified to teach English. This problem is especially acute in the areas of science and mathematics teaching, although it has declined with the recent surplus of teachers.

Teaching out of license

Whether teachers possess a defined body of knowledge is also determined by training standards. Despite state regulations requiring a certain number of education courses, minimal requirements and content vary among states. As late as 1946 only 15 states required a bachelor's degree for elementary teachers;[19] in 1976 only three states required that its teachers hold a master's degree.[20] In 1975 as many as 40 percent of the 1,350 colleges involved in training teachers were not accredited by the national accrediting agency.[21]

Non-accredited training institutions

To develop and gain acknowledgment of a specialized body of knowledge and to upgrade weak teacher training institutions, teachers must acquire decision-making influence. Teacher organizations have the potential power and leadership to work with interested parties, such as teacher

18   Dan C. Lortie, *Schoolteacher: A Sociological Study* (Chicago: University of Chicago Press, 1975).

19   Ronald G. Corwin, *Sociology of Education* (New York: Appleton-Century-Crofts, 1965).

20   Allan C. Ornstein, "Characteristics of a Profession," *Illinois School Journal* (Winter 1976–77), pp. 12–21.

21   Egon G. Guba and David Clark, "Selected Demographic Data about Teacher Education Institutions," Paper presented at the First Annual Conference on Teacher Education, Indiana University, Indianapolis, November 1975; Allan C. Ornstein, "Educational Poverty in the Midst of Educational Abundance: Status and Policy Implications of Teacher/Supply Demand," *Educational Researcher* (April 1976), pp. 13–16.

training colleges and school districts, to develop exemplary models. Teacher training institutions that do not cooperate might not be allowed to send their student teachers to work in nearby school systems, and their graduates might not be licensed to teach in the schools.

CONTROL OVER REQUIREMENTS FOR ENTRY, LICENSING Whereas most professions have uniform standards and requirements to ensure minimum competencies, this is not the case in the teaching profession. The problem concerns both the types of individuals who enter teacher education programs and the skills held by those who emerge from the programs and are certified to teach.

No minimum competencies

As mentioned in Chapter 2, students who enter teacher training programs have lower aptitude scores than students in most other fields, and there are no widely accepted tests used to determine whether the graduate of a teacher training program is adequately or inadequately prepared to be a teacher. In addition, there is wide variation in the certification requirements for teaching in various states.

Whatever they may think about these differing requirements, teachers do not have much say on these matters. The outcome is that teacher mobility is limited from state to state by the different licensing procedures. Most people, including teachers themselves, reject teacher regulation of licensing requirements because they are publicly employed. From an educator's point of view, however, the exercise of professional autonomy would be enhanced if teachers could establish licensing laws, or if certification standards were functionally recognized by states. It is in the public interest to place control of professional standards and requirements partly in the hands of educators rather than to continue to leave such decisions entirely to laymen who know little about teaching.

Different licensing procedures

AUTONOMY IN DECIDING ABOUT SPHERES OF WORK In a profession every member of the group, but not outsiders, is assumed to be qualified to make professional judgments on the nature of the work involved. Professionals usually establish laws of exclusive jurisdiction in a given area of competence, and custom and tradition are relied on to maintain effective control over matters relating to work and dealing with clients. Indeed, lay control is considered the natural enemy of professions; it limits the power of the professional and opens the door to outside interference.

Lay control vs. professional control

Teachers accept the assumption that local and state officials have the right to decide on the subjects, instructional materials, and books to be used. While they sometimes question the wisdom of the community in exercising such rights, the legitimacy of these rights is rarely questioned. At best, teachers are permitted minimal input in curriculum decisions, and they are vulnerable when they seek to introduce textbooks or discussions considered controversial by pressure groups.

The problem is that teachers believe that the democratic process gives the public the right to tell them which books to use and what content to teach. Teachers may be challenged by almost any parent or taxpayer; the community may dictate what they will teach and how, even in opposition to the teachers' professional judgments. Taxpayers are said to "reasonably" claim a share in decision making, since they foot the bill and provide the clients.

The physician and lawyer also provide services that their clients pay for, yet no one expects the client or the public to prescribe drugs or write the clauses in a contract. When the client interferes with the decisions of the practicing physician or lawyer, the professional-client relationship ends. This protects clients from being victimized by their own lack of knowledge, while it safeguards the professional from the unreasonable judgments of the lay public. Professionals recognize the obligation to serve their clients, but not at their own expense. There is a point in the professional-client relationship when the professional's self-interest and autonomy suffer—when service to the client is governed by the whims of the client or other laymen. Peter Blau and W. Richard Scott observe that "professional service . . . requires that the [professional] maintain independence of judgment and not permit the clients' *wishes* as distinguished from their *interests* to influence his decisions." The professional has the knowledge and expertise to make judgments, "and the client is not qualified to evaluate the services he needs." Professionals who permit their clients to tell them what to do "fail to provide optimum service."[22]

Guarding against client interference

Professional independence

The same kind of reasoning does not hold true with teachers. They can be told what to do by parents and other citizens, principals, superintendents, and school board members. Although school officials realize they no longer have "the sole right of management," since collective bargaining has resulted in new arrangements between teachers and administrators, most people still believe that teachers are public servants and therefore accountable to the people and to the school officials who are hired, elected, or appointed by the people. While it is true teachers must not lose sight of the welfare of their clients or those who are in the position to make decisions for the public, they should not completely surrender the power to determine the nature of the service they render. To err in the first direction is to become rigid and despotic; to err in the second direction is to become subservient and impotent.

Teacher accountability

Professional autonomy does not mean the total absence of any control over professionals. On the contrary, it means that controls requiring

22   Peter Blau and W. Richard Scott, *Formal Organizations* (San Francisco: Chandler, 1965), pp. 51–52.

technical competencies are exercised by people who possess such competencies; it calls for the development of controls related to the work of members of the profession. This can be enhanced by initiating collective negotiations that define areas in which teachers can make use of their experiences and competencies, by increasing teacher representation on school boards at the local level and teaching licensing and governing boards at the state level, and by helping to elect political candidates to office who are pro-teacher and pro-education.[23]

State
governing
boards

PRESTIGE AND ECONOMIC STANDING

As pointed out in Chapter 1, teachers have registered major gains in salary and status during the past 50 years. In some ways, these gains have been dramatic: in 1930 the average teacher earned $1,420; in 1950, $3,126; in 1980, $16,001. Much of this increase was due to inflation, but real gains also were registered, especially between 1960 and 1970, the period corresponding with the growth of teacher militancy. During this period salaries for teachers rose 44 percent and prices rose 28 percent.[24] Since 1970, however, teacher salary increases have not kept up with inflation.

Real salary
gains

Though teachers' salary gains since 1930 have been greater than those of the average worker in industry, teacher pay remains lower than that of the average college graduate.[25] In addition, teachers still earn far less than lawyers, business executives, and some other professionals with similar levels of formal education. Of course, there is no realistic salary comparison between teachers with a master's or doctor's degree and physicians, lawyers, dentists, or top business executives. Although levels of formal education are nearly similar, earnings of the latter group approach $100,000 per year, with some earning as much as $500,000; these groups also have traditionally high occupational ratings.

Lower salaries
than other
college
graduates

The fact is that while the prestige and income standards of teachers have risen relative to their past station, they have risen only slightly more than for the average worker, while declining in comparison to other professions and groups with similar levels of education. The *status-consistency hypothesis* holds that a group tends to compare its achievements (prestige and salary) with other groups and will strive to bring its

23 John Ralph Pisapia, "Trilateral Practices and the Public Sector Bargaining Model," *Phi Delta Kappan* (February 1979), pp. 424-27; Leonard L. Gregory, "Unintended Consequences of Public School Negotiations," *School Business Affairs* (January 1979), pp. 26-27; "Women, Educators Gain Ground in Statehouses," *U.S. News and World Report* (December 17, 1979), p. 74.

24 Allan C. Ornstein, *Education and Social Inquiry*, (Itasca, Ill.: Peacock, 1978).

25 Frank S. Endicott, *Trends in Employment of College and University Graduates in Business and Industry* (Evanston, Ill.: Northwestern University, 1980).

rewards up to a level with people who have similar jobs, even similar years of education.[26] If this is true, we can expect teachers to make comparisons with other professional groups, to remain dissatisfied, and to express this dissatisfaction through militancy; in fact, this has been one of the major reasons for teacher militancy since the mid-1960s.

Overall, one can conclude that while the status of the teacher has improved, teachers' income and prestige still lag far behind those of many other professions. Teaching is still not fully a profession in terms of its economic standing and occupational prestige.

TRENDS TOWARD PROFESSIONALISM

It was pointed out above that teaching probably should not be considered a fully professionalized occupation in terms of the major criteria for classification as a profession. We also noted, however, that the status of the teacher has been improving and that collective bargaining can enhance teachers' capacity to make decisions about their work in the classroom. Several major aspects of a long-range trend toward the professionalization of teaching can also be seen.

PROFESSIONAL PRACTICE COMMISSIONS

It is not likely that educators will be given complete autonomy in setting standards for professional practice, but teachers have been gaining a greater role in setting professional standards than they formerly had. Gains in this direction are illustrated by developments in several states, particularly Oregon, California, Michigan, and South Carolina. Teacher Standards and Practices Commissions have been established in these states in which teachers comprise a majority or plurality and set standards for the preparation of teachers and maintenance of minimal competence in professional practice. These commissions also have placed a few teachers on probation, suspended certificates, and reprimanded teachers for unprofessional or illegal behavior. It is anticipated that these powers will be used more frequently in the future, and that educators thus will begin doing what they long have said they wanted to do: clean their own house and eliminate those who do not meet minimal professional standards.[27]

26 Ronald G. Corwin, *Militant Professionalism: A Study of Militant Conflict in High Schools* (New York: Appleton-Century-Crofts, 1970).

27 Peter L. LaPresti, "California: The Impact of the Commission for Teacher Preparation and Licensing," *Phi Delta Kappan* (May 1977), pp. 674-77; Russell B. Vlaanderen, "State Review: Focus on Certification, Teacher Education, and Governance," *Legislative Review* (October 1979), pp. 4-5; James M. Wallace, "The Making of a Profession: An Oregon Case Study," *Phi Delta Kappan* (May 1977), pp. 671-73.

*THE SCOPE
OF COLLECTIVE
BARGAINING*   By 1980, teachers had won the right to have their representatives formally bargain with their employers in most of the United States. The extent and nature of collective bargaining varied from negotiations conducted in the absence of a law allowing or forbidding it to full-scale contract bargaining backed by the right to strike. Knowledgeable observers feel that further development of teachers' collective bargaining power will depend partly on congressional action to extend bargaining rights to all public employees. There is considerable uncertainty, however, regarding the position of teacher organizations on specific proposals for federal legislation, the willingness of Congress to pass additional legislation, and constitutional limitations concerning its power to extend bargaining rights to state employees.[28]

Congressional action to extend bargaining rights

In some ways collective bargaining may be considered a nonprofessional or even an antiprofessional activity. In many professions such as law, medicine, and the ministry, few professionals work in organizations in which terms of employment are determined by collective bargaining. From another point of view, however, collective bargaining can significantly enhance professionalization of teaching, because it can give teachers greater authority in determining the conditions of their work and their effectiveness as teachers. The trend in collective bargaining has been to include more and more concerns other than the fundamental salary issue. Collective bargaining in the 1970s often was concerned with problems and issues, such as class size, grouping of students in classes, instructional materials, testing, classroom discipline and management, teacher-supervisory relations, and community relations.[29]

Bargaining issues

TEACHER CENTERS   Another way in which teachers are achieving greater professional status is by exercising more control over their own affairs involves the important area of staff development. To stay up to date in their preparation and to acquire new professional skills for application in the classroom, teachers traditionally have participated in various kinds of in-service training. In general, most of this training has been provided on college campuses, frequently to meet school district requirements for additional college credit for continuing certification. Many observers have viewed this kind of in-service training as constituting basically a ''cafeteria of courses and workshops'' with no relationship ''to job roles and student needs.''[30]

28 Donley, *The Future of Teacher Power in America.*

29 Thomas J. Flygare, *Collective Bargaining in the Public Schools* (Bloomington, Ind.: *Phi Delta Kappan*, 1977).

30 Arnold M. Gallegos, ''Politics and Realities of Staff Development,'' *Educational Leadership* (January–February 1980), p. 21; Bruce Joyce, ''The Ecology of Staff Development,'' Paper presented at the Annual Meeting of the American Educational Research Association, Boston, April 1980.

In the past few years, however, a growing percentage of teachers' in-service training opportunities have been provided by teacher centers that are governed partly by teachers themselves. They are intended to make staff development more relevant to teachers' actual training needs and more useful in terms of applicability in the classroom. As used here, the teacher center refers to an in-service training center; it differs from the education center described in Chapter 2, which focuses on preservice training. This movement to establish teacher centers may represent a significant advance toward teachers' participation in making decisions that have important implications for their professional performance.

Partially governed by teachers

Teacher centers have existed for years in the form of exchange centers where teachers can obtain ideas about new instructional practices and talk with colleagues about how to apply appropriate methods in their classrooms. Centers of this kind have provided valuable services to teachers but have been dependent on unstable financing and generally have not been able to undertake systematic efforts at improving instructional practice in the schools. Partly for this reason, and partly because many teachers and administrators have felt that colleges and universities have not provided preservice and in-service training adequate to cope with the challenge in contemporary classrooms, the federal government is now financing the development of teacher centers in many parts of the country.[31]

Government funding

For the 1979–80 school year, 89 projects, including 29 new projects, were funded for a total of $12.65 million. Approximately another 50 teacher centers were functioning without federal money. Both the National Education Association and the American Federation of Teachers supported the establishment and expansion of the teacher center program, with teachers in the above centers having a major and sometimes predominant voice in their operation.

Once established, a teacher center is supposed to function and evolve in accordance with local needs. Some of the federally funded centers serve a single school district, but others serve a region or an entire state. For example, the center in Waitsfield, Vermont, serves seven school districts and offers a variety of services including recertification courses, graduate level courses for college credit, community education workshops, and small grants up to $500 for development of instructional projects in the classroom. The New York City Teacher Center, by way of contrast, not only includes the entire city but in so doing serves teachers who work with approximately 1 million public school students and a third of a million

Both regional and city teacher centers

31   Harry Bell and John Peightel, *Teacher Centers and Inservice Education* (Bloomington, Ind.: *Phi Delta Kappan*, 1976); Kathleen Devaney, "Surveying Teachers' Centers," *Teachers' Centers Exchange* (April 1977), pp. 1–8; Sharon Feiman, ed., *Teacher Centers: What Place in Education* (Chicago: University of Chicago for Policy Study, 1978).

private school students. Governed by a 28-member policy board that represents the teachers' union, board of education members, the supervisors'
council, the United Parents Association and other community groups, and
the deans of education from Fordham University and the City University,
the New York City Teacher Center coordinates the work of 29 higher education institutions in attempting to provide practical in-service training
for area teachers.[32] One can anticipate that federally-funded teacher centers will become increasingly important in the 1980s, at least until such
time as systematic evaluation indicates whether they are making important contributions in improving education in the field.

MEDIATED ENTRY   Mediated entry refers to the practice of
inducting persons into a profession through carefully supervised stages
that provide them with assistance in learning how to apply professional
knowledge successfully in a concrete situation. One good example is in the
profession of medicine, in which aspiring physicians serve one or more
years as an intern and then as a resident before being considered a full-
fledged professional.

**Supervised
stages of
assistance**

Dan Lortie has studied the job of the teacher from a sociological
perspective and concluded that in terms of sequenced professional entry,
teaching ranks in between occupations characterized by "casual" entry
and those that place protracted and difficult demands on would-be members.[33] The lack of more carefully mediated entry has profound consequences, because it means that there is relatively little chance to include
empirically derived and rigorously grounded principles and practices of
pedagogy. Teachers too frequently report that their main teacher has been
experience, and that they learned to teach through trial and error in the
classroom.

**Trial and error
in the
classroom**

Although efforts have been made to provide for more effective induc-
tion of new teachers into the profession, in general these efforts have been
neither widespread nor systematic enough to ensure their success in practice. Most school districts, for example, now require a probationary period
for new teachers, but in too many cases relatively little concrete assistance
is provided in developing and refining skills needed for effective performance. Many school districts and a few states require a fifth year of preparation beyond the traditional bachelor's degree and initial certificate, but
too often this requirement is implemented in a way that allows new
teachers to take a few more courses that may or may not help them im-

32 The functioning of teacher centers is described in Kathleen Devaney, ed., *Building a
Teachers' Center* (New York: Teachers College Press, Columbia University, 1979). Several
specific centers are described in some detail in Charlotte K. Hoffman, "Teacher Training Inside
Out," *American Education* (August–September 1979), pp. 6–17.

33 Lortie, *Schoolteacher*.

prove professionally.[34] As a rule, most new teachers are still largely on their own in their first professional position.

One major reason why greater emphasis is being placed on mediated entry is because school district officials no longer feel they must immediately accept and put new teachers to work as was done during the teacher shortage of the 1960s. With many applicants vying for a limited number of teaching jobs, school officials can make probationary requirements stronger and more meaningful than they were during the teacher shortage. The trend toward more carefully mediated entry will probably continue at least as long as the current oversupply of teachers applying for jobs in the nation's elementary and secondary schools.

Stronger probationary requirements

SUMMING UP

1. During the past few decades teachers have become better organized than they were and have moved significantly toward acquiring the status of a professional.

2. The AFT and the NEA now represent the large majority of classroom teachers; these organizations have enabled teachers to improve their salaries and gain a greater voice in decisions involving teaching and learning in the schools.

3. Professional practice commissions also are enabling teachers to participate in setting and interpreting criteria for entering and remaining in the teaching profession.

4. Other trends in education also are operating to increase the status and professionalism of the teacher. For example, teacher centers, partly governed by teachers, are beginning to play a significant part in professional training and development. Continuation of these trends should result in additional movement toward more professionalization of the teacher's job in the future.

---

34 Gallegos, "Politics and Realities of Staff Development."

DISCUSSION QUESTIONS

1. Is teaching a profession? Defend your answer.

2. What are some similarities and differences between the NEA and the AFT? Is a merger desirable? Defend your answer.

3. What kinds of issues do you think should be included in collective bargaining?

4. Does a teacher surplus tend to make teaching more or less of a full-fledged profession?

5. What are the trends that are making teaching a more full-fledged profession than it was in the past?

THINGS TO DO

1. Invite a representative from a local NEA or AFT chapter to your class to discuss major current issues.

2. Interview local school officials to determine the degree to which teachers play a part in setting educational policies.

3. Interview local teachers to determine what help they received as a new teacher. Are new teachers receiving more help today than in the past?

4. Visit or write to a teacher center and prepare a description of the services it provides for teachers.

5. Ask several experienced teachers to give their opinion on whether teaching is more of a profession today than in the past. What changes or developments do they believe are most needed to advance professionalism among teachers?

CHAPTER 4
TEACHER
EFFECTIVENESS
AND
ACCOUNTABILITY

Focusing questions

Can we define a "good" teacher?

What are "teachable" groups?

What does contemporary research say about effective teaching?

What practices are effective in classroom management?

Can we hold teachers accountable? For what and to whom?

What are the arguments and trends regarding minimum competency testing of teachers?

Over the years, thousands of studies have been conducted to identify the characteristics of effective teachers and effective teaching. However, teaching is a very complicated activity; what works in some situations with some students may not work elsewhere in differing school settings with different subjects and goals. It has been very difficult to determine just which teacher behaviors are associated with specific student behaviors and outcomes.

Nevertheless, much has been learned about effective teaching and, therefore, about ways to evaluate the performance of the teacher. The first part of this chapter summarizes both the problems and the results of research on effective teaching.

Despite uncertainties in defining good teaching, the public has been demanding greater accountability on the part of teachers and administrators. With high taxes and inflation a growing problem for most Americans, and with increasing concern about the adequacy of student performance and discipline, citizens and legislators have supported efforts to evaluate teachers in terms of student outcomes. Unfortunately, it is no easy task to develop a workable and equitable system for evaluating teachers according to the performance of their students. In the second part of this chapter, we describe both the gains that have been made in identifying the characteristics of effective teaching and the problems that have arisen as approaches to accountability are developed in elementary and secondary schools.

MEASURING TEACHER BEHAVIOR

Teaching is a complex art, and no single factor can entirely explain or describe the qualities of a good or effective teacher. In fact, it is questionable whether distinguishing between "good" and "bad" or "effective" and "ineffective" teaching is even possible. For example, some educational researchers maintain that "the problem of teacher effectiveness is so complex that no one today knows what the competent teacher is." They admit that they "do not know how to define, prepare for, or measure teacher competence," despite the urgent need for skilled teachers and for understanding teacher effectiveness.[1] They point out that confusion over terms and the complexity of the teacher act are major reasons for the negligible results in judging teacher behavior. Because we are unable to precisely define what a good teacher is, we "can define good teaching any way we like."[2]

Teacher effectiveness is complex

1 Bruce J. Biddle and William J. Ellena, "The Integration of Teacher Effectiveness," in B. J. Biddle and W. J. Ellena, eds., *Contemporary Research on Teacher Effectiveness* (New York: Holt, Rinehart, 1964), pp. 2-3.

2 Harry S. Broudy, "Can We Define Good Teaching?" *Teachers College Record* (April 1969), p. 583.

The following view on a good teacher comments in a lighter vein:

A good teacher can tell his students a lot of answers to a lot of questions. But the best teacher can play dumb while helping his students think out the answers for themselves.

A good teacher is an eager and enthusiastic talker. But the best teacher knows how to be quiet and patient while his students struggle to formulate their own thoughts in their own words.

A good teacher is humble; he naturally feels that the accumulated wisdom of his subjects is far more important than himself. But the best teacher is even humbler; for he respects the feeling of young people that they are naturally far more important than a silly old subject.

A good teacher knows that his students ought to be honest, responsible, and good citizens. But the best teacher knows that . . . [these qualities] are communicated through daily actions, not daily lectures.

The students of a good teacher pass their course, graduate and settle down with good jobs. But students of the best teacher go on receiving rewards every day of their lives for they have discovered that the life of the inquiring mind is exciting.[3]

True, these statements do not really define. It is almost like saying, "Happiness is a stroll in the woods." Nevertheless, you may find these simple definitions to be quite insightful in thinking about the qualities that go into effective teaching.

HISTORICAL BACKGROUND In a more serious vein, Harold Anderson and his associates laid the groundwork for classifying the process of what a teacher does in the classroom. Anderson's pioneer study of teacher-student behavior was the first systematic research concerning teaching styles and social climates of the classroom.[4] Based on behavior samplings of preschool and elementary school children with different teachers over a period of several years, teacher behavior was observed and classified as *dominative* as opposed to *integrative*. The dominative teacher used threats and shame and demanded conformity,

3 Fred H. Stocking, "Who Is the Best Teacher?" *Bennington Banner* (November 14, 1963), p. 4.
4 Harold H. Anderson, et al. "The Measurement of Domination and of Socially Integrative Behavior in Teachers' Contacts with Children," *Child Development* (June 1939), pp. 73–89.

whereas the integrative teacher exhibited approval for students' interests and was supportive and understanding. Dominative teachers produced dominative students, and integrative teachers stimulated further integration of students. Thus, the style and leadership of the teacher influenced classroom patterns.

Ronald Lippitt and his associates extended the general conclusions of Anderson.[5] Initially they developed an instrument for describing the "social atmosphere" of children's clubs and for quantifying the effects of group and individual behavior. Since the emphasis in the study was upon teaching style, the results have been generalized in numerous research studies and textbooks. The classic study used classifications of *authoritarian*, *democratic*, and *laissez-faire* styles of teaching as the basis for determining student performance. The authoritarian teacher directs all the activities of the program—a strong similarity to Anderson's dominative type of teacher. The democratic teacher encourages group participation and is willing to let students share in the decision-making process. This behavior is related to the integrative teacher. In the laissez-faire group climate, no (or few) goals and directions are provided for group or individual behavior. This is representative of the ineffective teacher.

The results of the Lippitt investigation indicated that children taught by the authoritarian teacher failed to initiate activity and became dependent upon the teacher; some of the authoritarian groups exhibited aggressive and rebellious behavior toward the leader. The democratic teacher generated a friendly and cooperative group atmosphere; students' output was the highest in this group and the students carried through work assignments without the aid of the teacher for periods of time. The laissez-faire style of leadership generated confusion and minimal student productivity.

Although these two investigations did not yield the only categories for defining teacher behavior, the dominative-integrative and authoritarian-democratic-laissez faire constructs led to hundreds of empirical studies that concentrated on the same or similar teacher behaviors, such as direct-indirect, teacher-centered–student-centered, and inclusive-conjunctive-preclusive.

Teaching styles

Different student behaviors

Ground work for future studies

TEACHER INFLUENCE AND STUDENT PERFORMANCE

One of the most ambitious attempts to study the social climate of the classroom was conducted by Ned Flanders and his

5 Ronald Lippitt and Ralph K. White, "The Social Climate of Children's Groups," in R. G. Barker, J. S. Kounin, and H. F. Wright, eds., *Child Behavior and Development* (New York: McGraw-Hill, 1943), pp. 485-508. Also see Kurt Lewin, Ronald Lippitt, and Ralph K. White, "Patterns of 'Aggressive' Behavior in Experimentally Created 'Social Climates,' "*Journal of Social Psychology* (May 1939), pp. 271-99.

TABLE 4.1
THE FLANDERS CLASSROOM
INTERACTION ANALYSIS SCALE

INDIRECT BEHAVIOR

1. ACCEPTS FEELING:
accepts and clarifies the tone of
feeling of the students in an
unthreatening manner. Feelings may
be positive or negative. Predicting or
recalling feelings are included.

2. PRAISES OR
ENCOURAGES: praises or
encourages student action or
behavior. Jokes that release tension,
but not at the expense of another
individual, nodding head or saying
"um hm?" or "go on" are included.

3. ACCEPTS OR USES IDEAS
OF STUDENT: clarifying, building,
or developing ideas suggested by a
student. As teacher brings more of
his [or her] own ideas into play, shift
to category 5.

4. ASKS QUESTIONS: asking a
question about content or procedure
with the intent that a student
answer.

DIRECT BEHAVIOR

5. LECTURING: giving facts or
opinions about content or procedure;
expressing one's own ideas, asking
rhetorical questions.

6. GIVING DIRECTIONS:
directions, commands, or orders with
which students are expected to
comply.

7. CRITICIZING OR
JUSTIFYING AUTHORITY:
statements intended to change
student behavior from unacceptable
to acceptable pattern; bawling
someone out; stating why the teacher
is doing what he [or she] is doing;
extreme self-reference.

Source: Ned Flanders, *Teacher Influence* (Washington D.C.: U.S. Government Printing Office, 1965), p. 20.

---

associates between 1954 and 1962.[6] The main focus of Flanders's research
concerned the development of an Interaction Analysis Scale for quantifying verbal communication in the classroom. Raters recorded teacher verbal behavior every three seconds into one of four categories representing
various degrees of *indirect* teacher behavior or one of three categories
representing *direct* teacher behavior. The seven categories are shown in
Table 4.1.

**Interaction
Analysis Scale**

    Based on Flanders's sampling, students in the indirect classrooms
learned more and exhibited more constructive and independent attitudes
than students in the classrooms of the direct teachers. All types of students in all types of subject classes learned more working with the indirect
(more flexible) teachers. In an interesting sidenote Flanders found that as
much as 80 percent of the classroom time is generally consumed in teacher
talk.

**Teachers talk
80% of the
time**

---

6 Ned A. Flanders, *Teacher Influence, Pupil Attitudes, and Achievement* (Washington,
D.C.: U.S. Government Printing Office, 1965).

COGNITIVE-ORIENTED STYLE   There are many teachers whose style is determined by cognitive operations in the classroom. Arno Bellack exemplifies this view of the classroom process.[7] Language becomes a function of the roles played by the teacher and students as well as of the nature of the content. Teacher behavior is defined by four basic verbal "moves" as teachers and students interact in the classroom—as they play the game of teaching and learning. The teacher's pedagogical moves are identified as:

> 1. *Structuring*. This begins or halts the interaction behavior between teacher and students. For example, the teacher begins the class period with a move to focus on the topic to be discussed in class.

> 2. *Soliciting*. Moves in this category are designed to elicit a verbal or physical response. For example, the teacher asks a question about the topic with the hope of encouraging a response from the students.

> 3. *Responding*. These moves occur in relation to and after the soliciting moves. Their ideal function is to fulfill the expectations of the soliciting moves.

> 4. *Reacting*. These moves are sometimes occasioned by one or more of the former moves, but are not directly elicited by them. Reacting moves serve to modify, clarify, or judge the structuring, soliciting, or responding moves.

Bellack found that certain rules prevailed as the teacher-learning game was played. The teacher was the major player—he or she spoke most often and for the longest time; in fact, he or she spoke three times as much as all the other players. About 50 percent of the time the teacher was speaking, his or her speech was designed to solicit responses from the other players. As compared with the teacher's role of soliciting, the students' primary role was that of respondents—devoting about two-thirds of their speech to responding to the teacher. For students, about 50 to 60 percent of their talk was devoted to fact stating and explaining; analytical and evaluative processes accounted for less than 10 percent of their total talk.

AFFECTIVE-ORIENTED STYLE   In the study by Donald Medley and Harold Mitzel, the affective dimension is considered as part of the teacher's behavior.[8] Instead of observing separate

Verbal moves determine classroom interaction

Teachers speak three times more than students

---

7   Arno Bellack et al., *The Language of the Classroom* (New York: Teachers College Press, Columbia University, 1965).

8   Donald Medley and Harold E. Mitzel, "A Technique for Measuring Classroom Behavior," *Journal of Educational Psychology* (April 1958), pp. 86–92; Medley, "Experience With the OScAR Technique," *Journal of Teacher Education* (September 1963), pp. 267–73.

behaviors, the researchers attempted to record the entire sequence of the lesson. The data of this study consisted of 216 twenty-five-minute films, four films each of 54 student teachers and 49 first-year teachers in grades three to six at nineteen schools in New York City.

The emotional climate of the classroom was measured by an instrument called OScAR (Observation Schedule and Record). The instrument contained about 170 items and three separate parts. One part contained 16 categories into which teacher statements were classified. The second part contained 12 teacher movements and 40 items describing incidents related to classroom management. The third section contained 100 items related to the teaching of the subject.

Emotional climate of the classroom

Typical items weighted positive were:

1. Teacher calls student "dear," etc.

2. Teacher exhibits affection toward student.

3. Student demonstrates affection for teacher.

4. Teacher makes supportive statements or gestures toward student.

Typical negative items were:

1. Teacher uses sarcasm.

2. Teacher frowns, glares, etc.

3. Student ignores teacher's questions.

4. Student scuffles or fights.

Typical items related to teaching included:

1. Student reads or studies at his seat.

2. Student writes at his seat.

3. Student (teacher) uses textbook.

4. Student (teacher) uses supplementary reading material.

Although the investigators were unable to identify and correlate any aspect of a teacher's behavior with student learning, teachers who expressed "warmth" were likely to be rated effective by both the trained observers and supervisors of teachers, and their rapport with students tended to be good. But there was no evidence that the students of these teachers learned more than those of the average teacher. Some later studies, however, have concluded that teachers who pay attention to students' feelings generate greater cognitive learning gains than teachers who do not.[9]

Warm teachers seem effective

9   David N. Aspy and Flora N. Roebuck, *A Lever Long Enough* (Dallas: National Consortium for Humanizing Learning, 1976); Aspy and Roebuck, "Teacher Education: A Response to Watts' Response to Combs," *Educational Leadership* (March 1980), pp. 507-10.

TEACHER
CHARACTERISTICS
Of the thousands of studies dealing with teacher behavior characteristics or lists of behaviors, the one by David Ryans is perhaps the most comprehensive.[10] More than 6,000 teachers and 1,700 schools were involved in the study over a six-year period. The objective was to identify through observation and self-ratings the teacher characteristics considered most desirable. A bipolar list of eighteen teacher behaviors (autocratic versus democratic, aloof versus responsive, disorganized versus systematic, and so on) was used to assess teacher characteristics and effectiveness.

These 18 behaviors were defined in detail and devised by a complex statistical procedure (factor analysis). Reliabilities of each behavior ranged between .50 and .70. The 18 teacher behaviors were further grouped and reduced to three patterns of teacher behavior. These primary teacher behaviors were designated as:

Teacher patterns

Pattern X, reflecting understanding, friendliness, and responsiveness v. aloof and egocentric teacher behavior . . .

Pattern Y, reflecting responsible, businesslike, systematic v. evading, unplanned, slipshod teacher behavior

Pattern Z, reflecting stimulating, imaginative, original v. dull, routine teacher behavior.[11]

Many interesting correlations were found. Elementary school teachers scored higher than secondary teachers on Pattern X. Differences between women and men teachers were insignificant in the elementary schools, but in the secondary schools differences were noted by subject type. For example, female science teachers were relatively high on Pattern Z and female English and female and male social studies teachers were relatively high on Pattern X. Younger teachers both at the elementary and secondary levels appeared to exhibit Patterns X and Z; older teachers (over 55) were observed to reflect Pattern Y. In general, the warm, systematic, stimulating teachers reflected the behavior considered most effective and desirable in most schools across the country.

TEACHABLE GROUPS As noted earlier, the analysis of teacher behavior and classroom operations eventually leads to research on teaching styles. Two questions arise: Is student learning affected by teachers' use of different approaches or styles? Does teacher behavior change when the teacher is confronted with different students? Assuming the answer is yes in both cases, the aim is to match the appropriate teacher style with the appropriate group of students in order to achieve the best teaching-learn-

Matching teachers and students

10 David G. Ryans, *Characteristics of Teachers* (Washington, D.C.: American Council on Education, 1960).

11 Ibid., p. 102.

ing situation. Herbert Thelen calls this the proper "fit."[12] He states that teachers recognize four kinds of students: good, bad, indifferent, and maladjusted. Each teacher places different students in these categories and teachable students for one teacher may be quite different for another. The proper fit between teacher and students results in the best kind of classroom. He contends that homogeneous grouping is essential for a group to become more "teachable." A teacher in such a group accomplishes more with students than would be the case where the range of ability and behavior is wide; moreover, it is easier to fit students and teachers together to achieve the best combinations. Any grouping that does not attempt to match students and teachers can have only "accidental success."

Homogeneous grouping

Of special interest to the concept of teaching style is the work of Louis Heil and his associates.[13] On the basis of observing fifth- and sixth-grade classrooms in New York City, four student types were categorized: (1) *conformers*—characterized by incorporation of school standards, high social orientation, and control over impulses; (2) *opposers*—conflict with authority relations, hostile or pessimistic tone, intolerant toward disappointment, easily frustrated; (3) *waverers*—anxious, ambivalent, fearful, and indecisive; and (4) *strivers*—showing marked drive for recognition, especially in school achievement and exhibitionistic activities. The teachers were divided into three personality types: *turbulent, self-controlling*, and *fearful*.

Student types

Neither the striving nor the conforming students were affected by the teacher type, but for the opposers and waverers, teaching style made a difference when controlling for student learning. For the last two groups, the self-controlling teachers (orderly, businesslike, organized, at the same time sensitive to the students' feelings) were the most effective. The turbulent teachers (sloppy, inconsistent, impatient) were least successful in teaching opposing students, who evidenced the highest intolerance of ambiguity. The fearful teachers (anxious, dependent on approval from students and supervisors, unable to bring structure and order to their teaching task) were the least effective with all kinds of students, especially the opposers and waverers.

Teacher types

In considering the problem of "teachable groups" and the different kinds of students and teachers, the discussion is reminiscent of some of the problems related to teaching many disadvantaged students. Thelen concludes that from 10 to 25 percent of the students in our schools are

---

12   Herbert A. Thelen, "Teachability Grouping" (mimeographed, 1961), pp. 220-21; Thelen, *Classroom Grouping for Teachability* (New York: Wiley, 1967).

13   Louis M. Heil, I. Feifer, and Marion Powell, "Characteristics of Teacher Behavior Related to Achievement of Children in Several Elementary Grades," (mimeographed, 1960). Also see Louis M. Heil and Carlton Washburne, "Brooklyn College Research on Teacher Effectiveness," *Journal of Educational Research* (May 1962), pp. 347-51.

considered unteachable by teachers, or at least very difficult to teach. In some inner-city schools, these percentages would be considered small. Similarly, Heil's opposers and to a lesser extent his waverers remind one of the behaviors exhibited by many disadvantaged children.

RECENT THEORY AND RESEARCH ON EFFECTIVENESS

In one of the more comprehensive surveys of teacher behavior research, Barak Rosenshine and Norma Furst found the field so confused that it was not unusual to find different institutions training teachers according to opposite criteria.[14] Thus the Far West Regional Laboratory uses minicourses to train teachers to repeat student answers *less* often, while the Northwest Regional Laboratory training program suggests *more* teacher repetition of student answers as a preferred measure of "indirect teaching." The researchers noted several other problems: (1) the difficulty in generalizing the research to actual classroom situations, (2) subjective factors related to observing and rating teachers, (3) the inability to translate actual teacher behaviors to paper-and-pencil items, and (4) the hazards of making causal inferences from correlational data. (For example, the conclusion that the more negative the teacher's comments, the less achievement on the part of the students makes good sense according to current fashion, but it may only reflect the likelihood that teachers with low-achieving classes have little to approve and much to criticize.)

Research difficulties

Despite these problems, Rosenshine and Furst were able to select 11 variables that they considered "most promising" for assessing teacher behavior with respect to student achievement. Their selections were based on 42 teacher behavior (process)–teacher effects (product) studies—what we might also call correlational studies. The 11 variables are: (1) clarity, (2) variability (variety of methods, approaches, etc.), (3) enthusiasm, (4) task-oriented or businesslike behaviors, (5) student opportunity to learn what is later tested, (6) use of student ideas, (7) praise, (8) structuring comments (summarizing, the use of verbal markers), (9) types of questions (though the best type is unclear), (10) probing, and (11) difficulty of instruction.

Promising variables

The rather manageable and solid list of variables gave cause for optimism. But in a more detailed examination of the same 42 studies and 11 variables by R. W. Heath and Mark Nielson our hopes are quickly dam-

---

14   Barak Rosenshine and Norma Furst, "Research in Teacher Performance Criteria," in B. O. Smith, ed., *Research in Teacher Education* (Englewood Cliffs, N.J.: Prentice-Hall, 1971), pp. 37–72; Rosenshine and Furst, "The Use of Direct Observation to Study Teaching," in R. M. W. Travers, ed., *Second Handbook of Research on Teaching* (Chicago: Rand McNally, 1973), pp. 122–83.

pened.[15] These investigators found that (1) a third of the 11 operational definitions did not correspond to the variables that later included them, (2) 78 studies formed the basis for the 11 variables, but only five citations were derived from random (well-controlled) assignments of students, (3) a majority (45-78) of the studies did not claim to find a significant relation between the variables cited and student achievement, and (4) the research procedures in all 42 studies suffered from numerous flaws, which they listed. Finally, Heath and Nielson argue, two important variables that could have affected the research were not controlled in any of the 42 studies: subject matter (teacher behavior and student achievement may be influenced by the content of what is being taught) and the students' age (the studies cited cover an age range from preschool to adulthood, yet teacher behavior and student achievement might vary for different age groups).[16]

Subject matter and students' age

ISSUES AND IMPEDIMENTS Although there are literally thousands of studies on the dynamics of teacher behavior, many theoretical and methodological problems remain unresolved.[17] It is questionable whether investigators can agree on a given method of quantifying behavior, much less on operational definitions. Take, for example, a single teacher trait such as "cheerful." It may be assumed that cheerful teachers have a distinctly different effect on students than do uncheerful teachers. But what do we mean by cheerful? Does it really mean the same thing to different investigators? And do cheerful teachers have the same effect on first graders and twelfth graders, on disadvantaged and advantaged learners? Is cheerfulness equally important in the classroom, the study hall, and the schoolyard?

Operationizing terms

A basic assumption of many investigations is that teacher behavior affects the social climate of the classroom; hence, the observers have focused mainly on classifying and analyzing the teacher's behavior with little consideration given to the behavioral patterns of the students. Although one can understand why the methodological approaches have focused on teachers, more emphasis should be given to student behaviors.

More emphasis on student behavior

15 R. W. Heath and Mark A. Nielson, "The Research Basis for Performance-Based Teacher Education," *Review of Educational Research* (Fall 1974), pp. 463-84.

16 For a supplementary review of the research on teacher behavior and student achievement, see Harry L. Miller, "Student Achievement, Teacher Behavior, and Accountability," in A. C. Ornstein and S. I. Miller, eds., *Policy Issues in Education* (Lexington, Mass.: Heath, 1976), pp. 69-82; Thomas Good, Bruce J. Biddle, and Jere E. Brophy, *Teachers Make a Difference* (New York: Holt, Rinehart 1975).

17 David C. Berliner, "Impediments to the Study of Teacher Effectiveness," *Journal of Teacher Education* (Spring 1976), pp. 5-13; N. L. Gage, *The Scientific Basis of the Art of Teaching* (New York: Teachers College Press, Columbia University, 1978); Allan C. Ornstein and Harry L. Miller, *Looking Into Teaching* (Chicago: Rand McNally, 1980); Travers, ed., *Second Handbook of Research on Teaching*.

Further attention should also be paid to whether significant teacher-student interaction patterns can be consistently obtained in successive studies.

Another shortcoming has been the emphasis on the teacher's verbal behavior while ignoring nonverbal behavior such as facial expressions and gestures. These nonverbal behaviors may very well affect the classroom climate and the behavior of learners. Still another problem of the research in this area has been the emphasis on method and design without a theoretical construct upon which to base studies. Many learning theories have been developed, but there are few, if any, teacher behavior theories. How do teachers behave under various conditions? How do teachers and students interact at different grade levels? While the research has been empirically based, the data have not always been related to actual classroom practice; often, teachers have commented that the research is *too* theoretical—not of practical value. On the other hand, theoretical constructs are needed that can identify existing teacher behaviors and their predictable effects on the learner.

More emphasis on nonverbal behavior

Apart from the problems noted above, which need further exploration, there are promising directions for research on teaching. These include the availability of tape-recording devices for recording classroom behavior in ways that make possible much more meticulous and repeated analysis of such behavior. Another promising approach is the analysis of much smaller time segments of teacher behavior, or micro-teaching. Perhaps the time is also ripe for a reexamination of what is desirable teacher behavior for specific groups of students. Careful analysis of who learns what from what type of instruction may reveal a great deal more about appropriate teacher-student behaviors.

Taping classrooms and micro-teaching

A look at the variety of teacher behaviors within a school cannot help but impress one with the variety of different teaching styles and behaviors considered effective in the classroom. Some of these successful styles and behaviors are not entirely democratic, indirect, warm, and so on. In fact, some of the most effective teachers break many of the rules of the book. Perhaps we will never agree upon a true classification of relevant teacher phenomena—what is "effective" and "ineffective" teacher behavior. There may be several different kinds of competencies found among teachers; fitting the right teacher for the right situation should be the ultimate aim.

Breaking the rules

After this overview of the complexity of the issue, you might now reassess the introductory comments on teacher behavior. Also, you might be impelled to ask, is there nothing that local schools can do to raise standards of teacher effectiveness? Is the research unrelated to practice? Is the field to be left only to "experts" who live in ivory towers? As a prospective (or new) teacher, a very important thing you can contribute is your cooperation with long-term, quality research conducted through a nearby university or other educational agencies. As a teacher, you can encourage your colleagues to adopt active and sensible approaches to educational experimentation—experimentation that may lead to an improved definition of good teacher behavior and teacher effectiveness, even if these characteristics cannot yet and may never be measured precisely.

PROSPECTS
AND PROGRESS

Despite the difficulties outlined above in determining what is effective teaching, educators nevertheless have been making substantial progress in relating teacher behaviors to classroom outcomes. Although there is considerable disagreement about the generalizability of any one set of findings to all classrooms and situations, a good deal has been learned about the characteristics of effective instruction.

Much of this knowledge has been summarized by Barak Rosenshine in a series of reviews of research dealing with the characteristics of effective teaching. In general, Rosenshine's work has delineated an approach that frequently is referred to as "direct instruction," which he defines as follows:

Direct instruction

. . . direct instruction refers to academically focused, teacher-directed classrooms using sequenced and structured materials. It refers to teaching activities where goals are clear to students, time allocated for instruction is sufficient and continuous, coverage of content is extensive, the performance of students is monitored, questions are at a low cognitive level so that students can produce many correct responses, and feedback to students is immediate and academically oriented. In direct instruction, the teacher controls instructional goals, chooses materials appropriate for the student's ability. . . . Interaction is characterized as structured but not authoritarian.[18]

Rosenshine's review of hundreds of research studies supported the conclusion that the direct instruction approach is more likely to produce gains in student achievement than are other types of approaches. "The message," he concluded, "is clear. What is not taught and attended to in academic areas is not learned."[19] Donald Medley also reviewed recent research on teacher effectiveness and came to essentially the same conclusion. After examining 289 studies, Medley concluded that the effective teacher places a direct emphasis on academic activities and devotes more class time to academic skills than does the ineffective teacher. Medley also concluded that the effective teacher maintains an orderly and psychologi-

Emphasis on academic activities

18 Barak Rosenshine, "Content, Time, and Direct Instruction," in P. L. Peterson and H. J. Walberg, eds., *Research on Teaching* (Berkeley, Calif.: McCutchan, 1979), p. 38.

19 Ibid., p. 36.

cally supportive classroom environment (in agreement with David Ryans's earlier findings) and that independent and small-group activity on the part of students is associated with low rather than high achievement.[20]

Much of the most important recent knowledge on teacher effectiveness has been provided as part of the Beginning Teacher Evaluation Study (BTES). The BTES was initiated in 1972 by the California Commission for Teacher Preparation and Licensing and has been disseminating regular research reports based on years of careful study in California schools. The most general finding of the study is that academic learning time (ALT) is the most important variable influencing student learning. Academic learning time, which some observers call "academically- (or student-) engaged learning time" is defined as "the amount of time a student spends attending to academic tasks, while also performing with a high success rate."[21] Students of teachers who rate high on ALT—which obviously is similar to direct instruction—learn more than students of teachers who provide relatively little ALT.[22]

Academic learning time

The importance of the BTES and other studies supporting direct instruction has not been in reaching conclusions that verify common sense—which they do—but in documenting the importance of variables one would expect to result in higher student achievement and in initiating efforts to bolster ALT in concrete classroom settings. Teachers, administrators, and researchers in California and other states now are searching for practical ways to increase ALT in the classroom.

Higher student achievement

Nevertheless, these recent conclusions about the value of direct instruction and ALT do not necessarily constitute complete or final knowledge of the characteristics of effective teaching. Questions that remain concerning the generalizability and utility of these conclusions in designing effective instruction include the following:

Important questions concerning ALT

1. Is direct instruction superior in accomplishing educational objectives other than those involving relatively simple cognitive skills that are easily tested?

2. To what degree are achievement gains made through direct instruction and ALT approaches retained by students in later years?

---

20 Donald M. Medley, "The Effectiveness of Teachers," in Peterson and Walberg, eds., *Research on Teaching*, pp. 11-27.

21 "An Overview and Future Activities," *Beginning Teacher Evaluation Study Newsletter* (October 1978), p. 1; Connie S. Cookson, "The Effects of Content and Structure in Teacher Behavior and Student-Engaged Time." Paper presented at the Annual Meeting of the American Educational Research Association, Boston, April 1980.

22 Some of the major findings of the BTES have been summarized in an article by Pamela Noli, "A Principal Implements BTES," *Beginning Teacher Evaluation Study Newsletter* (November 1979), pp. 10-14.

3. To what degree are direct instruction and ALT approaches inadequate because they fail to take into account time needed to learn as contrasted with time devoted to learning?

4. How can small-group work and independent or individualized study or seatwork be effectively incorporated into direct instruction and ALT approaches?

CLASSROOM MANAGEMENT AND STUDENT PERFORMANCE Much of the research on teacher effectiveness deals with differing approaches to classroom management. The teacher must make a number of choices involving management of the social and physical environment in the classroom and the procedures in implementing the instructional program. These decisions generally have important implications for student behavior, learning, and discipline.

We cannot summarize all of the thousands of studies on these topics. Many of the studies and theories on classroom management contradict each other, are concerned primarily with education in a particular setting or classroom, or support a variety of interpretations and inferences. We will summarize conclusions from recent reviews of research on these topics, but the reader should keep in mind that this section touches only very lightly on a vast literature; it would not be hard to find studies and theories to counter any particular conclusion.

Contradictory studies

DISCIPLINE Discipline in the schools is of great concern both to educators and to parents. It has been cited as the number-one problem in the schools by citizens responding to the educational Gallup poll in 11 of the 12 years between 1969 and 1980. Teachers, of course, also are concerned as the persons whose lives are made most difficult when discipline problems appear in the schools.

From one point of view, orderly classrooms are attained partly through the teacher's efforts at managing interaction in a way that reduces the occurrence and effects of student disruptions. Over the years, educators have identified a number of approaches that can help reduce disruption. No single managerial strategy or tactic is appropriate or effective with all students in all classrooms, but some of the approaches that frequently are effective in reducing or eliminating disruption include the following: *signal interference*—eye contact, hand gestures, and other teacher behaviors that reduce inattentive behavior; *proximity control*—touching or standing near the disruptive student while communicating that you are concerned but not upset; *tension release*—humor that reduces tension in the classroom; *lesson restructuring*—changing a lesson that is not working; *support from routine*—schedules, assignments, and

Reducing student disruptions

general class practices that provide a clear routine; *removing seductive materials*—removal of athletic equipment, outside reading, or other materials that encourage inattentive or disruptive behavior; and *antiseptic removal*—asking a child who is having trouble to get a drink of water or pick up papers from the office.[23]

Other characteristics of teacher behavior associated with student behavior outcomes in the classroom include *clarity, firmness,* and *roughness.* Clarity refers to the precision with which teachers communicate their expectations regarding student behavior. Firmness refers to the teacher's success in communicating definite expectations. Roughness refers to expression of anger or frustration. Research on these characteristics indicates that the teacher's actions in controlling a particular child affects other students in the classroom. Clarity and firmness help induce orderly behavior, but roughness seems to produce anxiety and disruptive behavior.[24]

In considering the goals of discipline, it should be kept in mind that the importance of orderly behavior is in making learning possible rather than as an end in itself. Teachers also should realize that ultimately the value of external control is in providing an environment in which students develop internal control. Over time, the ideal is to replace an external control system (discipline) with an internal control system (self-discipline) to the greatest extent possible.[25] We also should emphasize that the most effective way to deal with classroom management problems is to prevent them in the first place by advance planning and preparation of the classroom as a suitable environment for individual and group functioning.[26] Research indicates that the important differences between successful and unsuccessful teachers with respect to discipline are not in responding to student misbehavior but in planning and preparation that prevent or minimize inattention and disruption.[27] Research also supports the conclusion that "withitness" (being continuously aware of all that is going on in the classroom), "overlapping" (doing several things at once, such as monitoring the classroom while teaching a small group), "signal continuity" (for example, calling on students in a predictable pattern), and

Clarity and firmness are recommended

External control vs. internal control

Planning and preparation

23 Nicholas J. Long et al., "Conflict in the Classroom" in E. R. House and S. D. Lapan, eds., *Survival in the Classroom* (Boston: Allyn & Bacon, 1978), pp. 352–62.

24 Ira J. Gordon and R. Emile Jester, "Techniques of Observing Teaching in Early Childhood and Outcomes of Particular Procedures" in Travers, ed., *Second Handbook of Research on Teaching*, pp. 184–217.

25 David A. Welton, *Realms of Teaching* (Chicago: Rand McNally, 1979); Vernon F. Jones, *Adolescents with Behavior Problems* (Boston: Allyn & Bacon, 1980).

26 Jere E. Brophy and Joyce G. Putnam, "Classroom Management in the Elementary Grades," in D. L. Duke, ed., *Classroom Management*, National Society for the Study of Education, Part II (Chicago: University of Chicago Press, 1978), pp. 182–216.

27 Jacob S. Kounin, *Discipline and Group Management in Classrooms* (New York: Holt, Rinehart, 1970); Thomas L. Good, "Teacher Effectiveness in the Elementary School," *Journal of Teacher Education* (March–April 1979), pp. 52–64.

Young students may perceive the teacher as an authority figure who curtails their freedom.

variety and challenge in seatwork all contribute to positive student behavior and achievement.[28]

Discipline seems to be particularly troublesome at the secondary level, where students are older, stronger, and more capable of physical disruption. In addition, the relative impersonality of secondary schools and the tendency for more students to perceive schools as irrelevant as they proceed through the grades frequently lead to a greater incidence of overt behavior problems at the secondary level than at the elementary. Research on discipline at the secondary level has concentrated on two distinct approaches to classroom management: *behavior modification* approaches, which use principles of reward and reinforcement to encourage positive behavior, and *humanistic* approaches, which encourage expression and acceptance of students' feelings and creation of a nurturing

**Behavior
modification
vs.
humanistic
approaches**

28 Good, "Teacher Effectiveness in the Elementary School"; Jere E. Brophy, *Advances in Teacher Effectiveness Research* (East Lansing, Mich.: Michigan State University Institute for Research on Teaching, 1979).

school climate to eliminate the frustrations that cause disruptive behavior.[29] Research on these two approaches at the secondary level has supported the following conclusions:

> Those principals who feel most comfortable with behavior modification approaches will encourage teachers to use these programs or will institute their own reward systems with chronically disruptive students. One hazard with such approaches is the institution of inconsistent or poorly thought-out programs based on superficial understanding of behavioral principles. For the best results, both teachers and administrators must be carefully trained in behavioral theories and techniques.

Reward systems

> Those principals who are frightened by the implications of behavior modification and who accept the more humanistic approaches will treat students as young adults rather than as children and encourage teachers to do the same. Inservice training for them will focus on learning to communicate acceptance of students and their feelings. Principals may want to divide a large and impersonal school into several intimate schools-within-a-school that stress informality and personal contact between students and teachers.[30]

Feelings and personal contact

TEACHER PRAISE   Praise can be an important positive reinforcer for students. It also can have neutral or negative effects in cases where other considerations limit its utility. For example, praising a student may have little or no impact if the student feels it is underserved or if the teacher's actions are vastly different from his or her words. Jere Brophy has reviewed the research on the use of teacher praise to reinforce good behavior and academic performance, and has concluded that this strategy has been seriously oversold. Brophy found that praise frequently fails to reinforce behavior or increase achievement and that it actually can be harmful in some situations, particularly when it replaces accurate feedback about the quality of poor performance. His overall conclusion was that, "In view of . . . the weakness of praise as a reinforcer . . . and the difficulties of praising effectively, perhaps it is time to deemphasize praise. Instead, teachers can be encouraged to help their students learn to set appropriate goals and to evaluate their own performance."[31]

Overselling praise as a teacher strategy

29   William Glasser, *Schools Without Failure* (New York: Harper & Row, 1969). Glasser believes that corporal punishment should be abolished and that students should participate in managing the classroom. He advocates holding regular class meetings in which teachers and students discuss their problems openly and identify ways to solve them.

30   "Classroom Discipline," *ERIC Clearinghouse on Educational Management, Research Action Brief* (August 1979), p. 4.

31   Jere E. Brophy, "Praise Oversold as Teaching Strategy," *IRT Communication Quarterly* (Fall 1979), p. 3; also see Brophy, "Teacher Praise: A Functional Analysis." Paper presented at the Annual Meeting of the American Educational Research Association, Boston, April 1980.

Praise obviously is likely to have different effects with different students. Two scholars summarized the current research on this topic, generalizing that teacher praise is positively correlated with academic achievement for students low in socioeconomic status but has either no relationship or negative correlations with achievement for high-status students. They speculated that this pattern may mean that students who receive a lot of praise for successful performance then take it for granted, while students who have not been performing at a high level are impressed by a positive evaluation.[32]

Different effects on different students

PHYSICAL ENVIRONMENT Citizens as well as educators have many opinions concerning the effects of physical environment, such as classroom seating arrangements, the presence of decoration and bulletin boards, and the degree of crowding among students. Research on these and other environmental factors in the 1970s has been carefully reviewed, and the conclusion is as follows:

Seating arrangements and bulletin boards

> Although "solid proof" remains a distant goal, a picture of the environment's role in the educational process is gradually taking shape. It is a picture that is likely to please neither those who advocate minimally decorated, no-nonsense classrooms, nor those who call for "softer," more "humane" educational settings.

> Despite the objections by many . . . to the hard, "tight spaces" . . . characteristic of our schools . . . it would seem that the physical environment of the conventional classroom has little impact on achievement. When classrooms varying in terms of furniture arrangements, aesthetic appeal, and the presence or absence of windows are compared, differences in achievement are nonsignificant. Likewise, short-term exposure to typical school noise appears to have no effect on performance. . . . The only physical variable which has been linked to differences in school achievement is seating location . . .[33]

In regard to the effects of seat location, research supports the conclusion that students near the front of the room are more attentive and engage more in on-task behavior than do those in the back of the room. However, it is not certain whether this phenomenon is due more to seat location itself or to self-selection on the part of students, and it also is

Front of the room

---

32 Marilyn M. Kash and Gary D. Borich, *Teacher Behavior and Pupil Self-Concept* (Reading, Mass.: Addison-Wesley, 1978); Borich and Kash, "Teaching Personnel: Review and Discussion." Paper presented for the State of Georgia Department of Education, 1979.

33 Carol S. Weinstein, "The Physical Environment of the School: A Review of the Research," *Review of Educational Research* (Fall 1979), p. 598.

unclear exactly how front location facilitates achievement in studies where a significant effect has been reported.[34]

Some physical environment variables such as privacy, circular arrangements as opposed to rows, and noise level have not been studied very thoroughly. In addition, little research has been conducted relating physical environment to educational program. For example, traditional row patterns may be most appropriate for lectures, but small-group work probably is facilitated through cluster arrangements. These types of interactions between environment and program deserve additional study in the future.[35]

Row vs. cluster arrangements

The preceding section has summarized current knowledge regarding relationships between several aspects of classroom management and student behaviors and performance. This review of research was highly selective, inasmuch as many other aspects of teaching also might be considered an important part of classroom management. In addition, dimensions of teacher effectiveness presented in the first part of this chapter (for example, Ryans's characteristics of effective teachers and emerging definitions of academic learning time) also can be viewed as classroom management practices that have important implications for student behavior and performance. Much remains to be learned about ways in which teachers can be most effective in managing their classrooms, but research already has established a number of general conclusions that are useful both for practicing teachers and individuals preparing to be teachers in the future.

**TEACHER
ACCOUNTABILITY**

We now turn to a very different method for determining teacher success—the concept of accountability. Accountability is a concept borrowed from management. When applied to education, it means that some people (teachers or administrators), some agency (board of education or state department of education), or some organization (professional organization or private organization) is to be held responsible for performing according to agreed-upon terms. In the past, the students have been held accountable for their school performance. Now the finger is beginning to point in other directions, and the concept is taking on different forms and gaining in popularity.

Borrowed from management

Holding teachers accountable for specific agreed-upon objectives relating to student achievement is perhaps the most commonly advocated

---

34 Weinstein, "The Physical Environment of the School"; A. J. Schwebel and D. L. Cherlin, "Physical and Social Distancing in Teacher-Pupil Relationships," *Journal of Educational Psychology* (December 1972), pp. 543–50.

35 Weinstein, "The Physical Environment of the School."

form. In the traditional methods of evaluating teacher behavior, evaluation of performance is an end in itself, and, this method has proved to be inadequate and confusing. With accountability, the stress is not on the *process* of teaching but on the *effects* of the teacher upon student performance.[36] In short, the aim is no longer to estimate "good" or "successful" teacher behavior, but rather to estimate the teacher's ability to produce behavioral change in a group of students.

From
process
to
effects

DEMANDS FOR   The strongest case for accountability can
ACCOUNTABILITY   be found in the works of Leon Lessinger, often considered the "father" of the movement; in the writings of some educational reformers who wish to make teachers more responsible for student failure; and in the demands of budget-minded critics and taxpayers who wish to cut expenses and relate dollars to the results in student accomplishment. These demands can be summarized as follows:

1. An increasing number of parents realize that schooling is important for success and that their children are not learning. They have begun to blame the school and teachers for Johnny's failure. The outraged parent is saying, "If you cannot teach my child, I am going to have you fired."

2. The public has the impression that teachers are accountable to no one but themselves. This is leading some citizens to demand a new governance system of education.

3. The public feels overtaxed and wants to know where its dollars are being spent. Taxpayers are beginning to say to teachers: "You are paid to teach; you demand higher salaries; and we have a right to know what we are getting for this money."

Taxpayers

4. Some educators and policy makers claim that we need to develop an information system, including data gathering and input/output activities, to find effectiveness indicators and the means of obtaining them. Instead of equating the quality of school resources in the form of inputs, the important criterion should be output, or student results.

5. Some educators are saying that modes of proof can be established for assessment purposes. Instead of vague promises to increase student learning, precise objectives should be stated as to what students are expected to gain from their educational experiences. Instead of subjective assessments of teacher effectiveness and program effec-

Precise
objectives
and exact
outcomes

36   W. James Popham, "Found: A Practical Procedure to Appraise Teacher Achievement in the Classroom," *Nation's Schools* (May 1972), pp. 59–60; Popham, "Normative Data for Criterion-Referenced Tests?" *Phi Delta Kappan* (May 1976), pp. 593–94.

tiveness, we should concentrate on the exact outcomes of instruction and consequences of any given program.[37]

The concept of accountability has become linked to many evolving educational trends; in fact, it has become a unifying theme related to management by objectives, cost-effectiveness audits, systems analysis, performance contracting, voucher plans, community participation and community control, consumer education, criterion-referenced testing, competency-based teacher education, assessment of teacher performance, bilingual and bicultural education, program evaluation, and a host of other trends. While this "umbrella" aspect of accountability makes it difficult to provide a clear, agreed-upon definition of the term, it is this same broad entity that makes it acceptable to many reformers in education of various political orientations. Indeed, the fact that accountability means different things for different people is one reason for its easy acceptance.[38]

Dimensions of accountability   Where does accountability begin and end? Who should be held accountable? And for what, and to whom? Who determines who will be held accountable? Also, who determines the responsibilities or criteria of effectiveness, and who evaluates these criteria? Will the evaluators be too concerned with politics, ideology, or conclusions that will secure them next year's evaluation contract? How are the results to be measured and each participant's contribution to be determined?

Surely most people agree that everyone, including teachers and administrators, should be held accountable for their work. But what many educators object to, even fear, is the oversimplified concept that defines accountability as the sole responsibility of the teacher or principal. As Robert Havighurst points out, numerous other people bear some responsibility for student performance, and they should also be held accountable if we are going to employ a constructive model.[39] These include parents, community residents, school board members, taxpayers, and, most important, the students themselves—for the learner's state of health, cognitive abilities, motivation, self-concept, family background, and even age, all affect learning. With the teacher shortage at an end, however, Havighurst fears the development of a "simple system of accountability" that may put the total responsibility on the teacher and tie teacher jobs and pay to stu-

Who should be accountable?

37 Leon M. Lessinger, *Every Kid a Winner: Accountability in Education* (New York: Simon & Schuster, 1970); Henry M. Levin, "Conceptual Framework for Accountability in Education," *School Review* (May 1974), pp. 363–91; William A. Volk, "Educational Accountability: The New Jersey Model." Paper presented at the Annual Meeting of the American Educational Research Association, Boston, April 1980.

38 John E. Coons and Stephen D. Sugarman, *Education by Choice: The Case for Family Control* (Los Angeles: University of California, 1978); Myron Lieberman, "An Overview of Accountability," *Phi Delta Kappan* (December 1970), pp. 194–95; Allan C. Ornstein, *Accountability for Teachers and School Administrators* (Belmont, Calif.: Fearon, 1973).

39 Robert J. Havighurst, "Joint Accountability: A Constructive Response to Consumer Demands," *Nation's Schools* (May 1972), pp. 46–47.

dent achievement, while ignoring the realities and responsibilities of other groups who influence student learning.

Reservations among educators   With this in mind, it is understandable that most teachers and teaching organizations tend to have reservations about accountability. According to the NEA Research Division, teachers with negative views on accountability outnumber those with positive views by eleven to one. The National Commission on Teacher Education and Professional Standards (TEPS), a past NEA affiliate, contends that teachers must decide "matters that relate directly to teaching . . . and by what standards teachers shall be prepared . . . retained, dismissed, certified, and given tenure." It views the growing demands of accountability advocates "as infringing on the teachers' professionalism."[40] The NEA itself maintains that the accountability movement is a "warped attempt to apply business-industrial models to learning," and that it threatens "more and more students and teachers [with] punitive, ill conceived, and probably inoperable legislation and directives." Accountability misapplied, the organization continues, can lead to a "closed system—to educational fascism—compelling . . . educators and students to comply with inhumane, arbitrarily set requirements."[41] And the former president of the American Federation of Teachers strongly voices the view that "accountability offers ready teacher scapegoats to amateur and professional school-haters" and accountability advocates are approaching the idea "with all the insight of an irate viewer 'fixing' a television set: Give it a kick and see what happens."[42] Indeed, one does not have to agree with these fears to know they exist. A number of court cases in California and New York (which reaffirmed that schools are not responsible for student performance) and in Iowa (which reaffirmed that a teacher cannot be fired because her students fail to perform on tests) underscore these fears.

Teacher scapegoats

Despite the reservations and pitfalls of accountability, state legislatures and state offices of public instruction have moved forward with accountability plans of their own. According to the Cooperative Accountability Project (CAP), a seven-state repository for accountability projects, all the states will have enacted some type of legislation on accountability by the early 1980s.[43]

Evolving concepts of accountability   The majority of the states included in the CAP analysis have taken the position that accountability should be mandatory, leaving the specifics to the discretion of local states.

---

40 NEA National Commission on Teacher Education and Professional Standards, "The Meaning of Accountability: A Working Paper" (November 1970), p. 3.

41 *NEA Press Release* (January 4, 1973), p. 1.

42 David Selden, "Productivity, Yes. Accountability, No." *Nation's Schools* (May 1972), p. 50.

43 Cooperative Accountability Project, *Legislation by the States: Accountability and Assessment in Education* (Denver, Colo.: CAP, 1973); Cooperative Accountability Project, "Status of Accountability Legislation" (mimeographed, 1979).

The laws range in content, from definite and explicit to broad and vague. It is difficult to categorize these laws, and interpretation of the legislation is not always clear. Some call for the assessment of students, some require management goals and methods of evaluation, some require evaluation of professionals (with only two states giving personnel the right to appeal), and a few require citizen involvement.

Various
accountability
laws

The most comprehensive accountability legislation is included in California's Stull Act, the first law in the nation to require that competence of certified personnel be measured partly in terms of student performance.[44] The evaluation process in each school district must include (1) establishment of standards of expected student progress in each area of study and methods for assessing that progress, (2) assessment of personnel in relation to such standards of expected student progress, (3) assessment of personnel in their performance of other duties, and (4) assessment of personnel in their effectiveness in maintaining control and preserving a suitable learning environment. When a certified employee's performance is inconsistent with the standards prescribed by the school board, he or she must be told so in writing, and specific recommendations on improving performance must be made. The California Education Code also provides that any charges leading to dismissal procedures and revocation of certificates for incompetence or unprofessional conduct must be accompanied by an evaluation.

Teacher
dismissal
procedures

In one state (Michigan), statewide assessment and accountability plans have been tied to withholding of funds from the schools whose students were not meeting national or state norms—the very schools that most need the funds. Instead of clarifying educational issues, these programs clouded them with questions about comparative student and school district scores and about the definition of "minimum" objectives and performance standards, and with debate about whether test results are public information, and what to do with schools that fail to measure up.[45]

Debate over
test results

Various other states, such as Colorado, Florida, New Hampshire, New Jersey, and Oregon, have introduced statewide assessment plans in conjunction with some form of plan to improve the skills of students and management processes of schools as well as cost-effectiveness of teaching.[46] New York State has introduced the nation's toughest academic

44 Glen F. Ovard, "Teacher Effectiveness and Accountability," *National Association of Secondary School Principals* (January 1975), pp. 87–93; David W. Gordon, "An Approach to the Evaluation of State Initiatives in Staff Development." Paper presented at the Annual Meeting of the American Educational Research Association, Boston, April 1980.

45 Jerome T. Murphy and David K. Cohen, "Accountability in Education—The Michigan Experience," *Public Interest* (Summer 1974), pp. 53–81; "Michigan Association Battles Misuse of Competency Tests," *NEA Reporter* (January-February 1980), p. 5.

46 Michael J. Brophy and John L. Davy, "The New Hampshire Accountability Project: A Model for Local Accountability Planning." Paper presented at the Annual Meeting of the American Educational Research Association, Boston, April 1980). Ornstein, *Accountability for Teachers and School Administrators;* Volk, "Educational Accountability: The New Jersey Model."

standards (actual high-school level work), to take effect in 1981. Not only are thousands of students in danger of not graduating, but the state is linking student performance with teacher accountability.[47]

High-school
level standards

PROBLEMS IN
ACCOUNTABILITY
As we noted earlier, it is incorrect to conclude that teachers are solely responsible for student failure. We shall see in Chapter 10 that the most important variables associated with student learning are the family and peer group. Schools are responsible for only a small variation of the child's learning, and teachers represent a fraction of this variation. It follows, then, in all fairness that people cannot be held responsible for something they have little control over. To point the finger solely or mainly at the teacher reflects either extreme naiveté or a political motive.

Schools have
minimal
impact on
learning

Furthermore, the most important growing period for intellectual development and academic achievement takes place before the child enters school, and the most significant years—when change is more easily accomplished—are the early ones. Accountability advocates often fail to recognize that subsequent learning is determined by what the child has already learned. Hence, educators are working against overwhelming odds to effect changes with students who show deficits in learning, since much of the students' potential had been developed before they ever came to school. Also, effecting change becomes increasingly more difficult grade by grade. Thus, for example, a ninth-grade class with a two-year deficit in reading provides a more difficult change problem than does a sixth-grade class with the same reading deficit.

It should be understood by us all that the schools, especially the public schools, have been increasingly burdened with the tasks and responsibilities that other social institutions no longer do very well or do not care to undertake. The schools have been asked to develop the child's human potential regardless of background or ability, to educate him or her as well as possible, to mold a healthy and responsible citizen. Society, having directed to the schools the responsibility of educating the child, now envisions school people "as ideal agents to be made accountable to the rest of society for the quality and quantity of educational results."[48] But if the schools, and for that matter the teachers, do not have much influence on student learning, the most that school people can be reasonably held responsible for is continually trying to better the quality of education for all children in all schools, within the limits imposed by the abilities of the child and conditions of the school and community.

Overburdened
schools

---

47 "New York State Plans to Set Graduation Standards That Will Be the Nation's Toughest," *Phi Delta Kappan* (April 1979), p. 555; David S. Seeley, "Reducing Confrontation over Teacher Accountability," *Phi Delta Kappan* (December 1979), pp. 248–51.

48 Frank G. Jennings, "For the Record," *Teachers College Record* (February 1972), p. 333.

Few people would disagree with the notion of accountability. Teachers do not fear evaluation; in fact, most of them welcome it and prefer that supervisors observe, evaluate, and make recommendations in a constructive manner.[49] What they object to is any presumption of guilt or negative reasons for implementing an accountability system. What teachers want is a joint accountability plan that improves the overall educational delivery system.[50]

A joint
accountability
system

Another question that might be raised is: What consitutes malpractice in the classroom or school? This is a key to much of the legal aspect of the accountability movement. If a teacher is guilty of malpractice, then there are grounds for his or her removal. But the fact is that malpractice has never been determined in the field of education. Indeed, it is a controversial matter in other professions, too. We might also think about whether or not a school as an entity can be charged with malpractice and, if so, against which authorities the malpractice would be charged. The school board? The principal? On what basis? Several public school malpractice cases already have been argued in the courts. In a California case (*Peter W.* v. *San Francisco Unified School District*, 1976), a student was allowed to graduate from high school although he could not read at the sixth-grade level. Feeling that his job prospects were gravely damaged, he sued on the grounds that school officials had been negligent in failing to identify and correct his reading problem. A second case (*Donohue* v. *Copiague, New York Union Free School*, 1978) was one in which a student charged school officials with negligence in failing to adopt accepted professional methods and standards to cope with his learning problems. Both suits were rejected by the courts without reaching trial, primarily because the plaintiffs had not shown that the schools had acted in an illegal manner in fulfilling their duty to provide education.[51]

Educational
malpractice

Suing school
officials

In the face of such severe difficulties in trying to develop and obtain agreement on a system to hold the schools accountable for student outcomes, emphasis has been shifting toward minimum competency testing of students and teachers. In order to ensure that students learn to read, write, and compute at a minimally acceptable level, many state governments and school districts have started to administer tests for student promotion or graduation.[52] More recently, interest has been growing in administering minimum competency tests for teachers.

---

49 Myron Lieberman, "Against the Grain," *Phi Delta Kappan* (May 1980), pp. 635–37.

50 Doyle M. Bortner, "Coping with Demands for Instructional Accountability," *National Association of Secondary School Principals Bulletin* (May 1979), pp. 33–43.

51 Cynthia Kelly and Bernice McCarthy, "Educational Malpractice Worrying You?" *Update on Law-Related Education* (Winter 1980), pp. 16–20.

52 Joan C. Baratz, "Policy Implications of Minimum Competency Testing" in Richard M. Jaeger and C. K. Tittle, *Minimum Competency Achievement Testing* (Berkeley, Calif.: McCutchan, 1980), pp. 49–68.

MINIMUM
COMPETENCY TESTS
FOR TEACHERS

Along with efforts to hold teachers more accountable for the quality of their performance and with growing public dissatisfaction involving declining test scores of students, attention has been given to the possibility of instituting minimum competency tests for teachers. In most cases, advocates of testing of teachers are primarily concerned with screening out beginning teachers who may be poorly prepared to teach or may not possess minimum literacy skills in reading and math.

According to one educator, state testing of new teachers applying for certification became the "new, hot subject in education" in the late 1970s.[53] Florida gave impetus to the movement in 1978 when the legislature enacted a bill requiring applicants to pass a comprehensive written examination as a prerequisite to teach. Prior to this time, three states (Mississippi, North Carolina, and South Carolina) already were using the National Teacher Examination (NTE) in determining eligibility for a certificate. After the Supreme Court ruled in 1978 that use of the NTE was not discriminatory even though its use in South Carolina had disqualified 83 percent of black applicants as compared with 18 percent of white applicants, Louisiana, Tennessee, and West Virginia also began to administer the NTE for certification candidates. In addition, Georgia, New York, Wisconsin, and other states also began to develop plans for testing applicants for certification.[54] Altogether, eight states now require some form of competency testing prior to initial certification, and at least seven are considering similar requirements.[55] These developments were stimulated by studies such as a 1977 survey in which school superintendents and school district personnel directors estimated that from 5 to 15 percent of teachers were not performing adequately on the job. However, less than one-half of one percent were dismissed that year for incompetence.[56]

Some individual school districts also have been administering or developing minimum competency tests for teachers. For example, the Prince Georges County, Maryland, district has used pre-employment spelling and grammar tests since 1975 and a mathematics test since 1977. Approximately 20 percent of the applicants have been screened out by these tests.[57] Beginning in 1976, the Pinellas County School District in Florida

Screening out incompetent teachers

Increased use of the National Teacher Examination

Testing basic skills for employment

53 Russ Vlaanderen, *Trends in Competency-Based Teacher Certification* (Denver, Colo.: Education Commission of the States, 1979).

54 Walter E. Hathaway, "Testing Teachers to Ensure Competency: The State of the Art." Paper presented at the Annual Meeting of the American Educational Research Association, Boston, April 1980.

55 E. F. Nothern, "The Trend Toward Competency Testing of Teachers," *Phi Delta Kappan* (January 1980), p. 359.

56 *Staff Dismissal: Problems and Solutions* (Arlington, Va.: American School Boards Association, 1978).

57 Hathaway, "Testing Teachers to Ensure Competency."

has administered tests that require applicants for teaching jobs to attain an eighth-grade score in reading comprehension and a sixth-grade score in arithmetic; approximately 30 percent of the applicants have failed on the first try, but two additional opportunities are provided, which lower the failure rates to about 15 percent.[58]

Probably the best-known effort at minimum competency testing of new teachers has been in the Dallas Independent School District, where more than 50 percent of the candidates (the majority who were minority) failed tenth-grade level verbal and quantitative ability tests.[59] One can easily question whether candidates who score high on knowledge of education and instruction really are better teachers, potentially or in practice, than those who score low, but it is difficult to counteract the argument that teachers should be minimally literate in reading and math.

High failure rate among teacher candidates

To the surprise of many observers, AFT President Albert Shanker has been one of the advocates of tests for new teachers. In line with growing concern among educators regarding the need for greater professionalism, Shanker stated that "you have to take an examination to become a lawyer, and to get a driver's license, and to sell insurance"; exempting teachers from such a requirement is a "form of deprofessionalization."[60] However, Shanker does not support testing of teachers on the job, and in this regard stated that "there is no research to tell us which competencies are valid . . . [and] the selection of which competencies are to be required could change from year to year, depending on the political wishes and financial circumstances of the states and local school boards." The NEA also opposes testing of certified teachers, and its Director of Instruction and Professional Development has said that "There is no test conceived that would be helpful in determining whether teachers should continue to teach."[61]

AFT favors tests for new teachers

Minimum competency testing of teachers probably will become a topic of considerably greater interest and controversy in the 1980s. As efforts proceed to develop and validate tests for weeding out the most incompetent teachers, teachers' rights must be protected and the difficulty of equating test scores with performance in the classroom must be constantly kept in mind.

SUMMING UP

1. Although much remains to be learned about effective teaching, research has identified some of the teacher behaviors and related instructional approaches that influence the behavior and

58   Thomas S. Tocco and Jane K. Elligett, "On the Cutting Edge: The Pinellas County Teacher Applicant Screen Program," *The Board* (Winter 1980), p. 5.

59   William J. Webster, "The Validation of a Teacher Selection System." Paper presented at the Annual Meeting of the American Educational Research Association, Boston, April 1980.

60   *Education U.S.A.* (November 12, 1979), p. 85.

61   Ibid.

performance of students. In particular, direct instruction approaches, in which the teacher focuses instruction on specific goals and uses sequenced and structured materials, have been found to correlate with relatively high student achievement.

2. Research points toward teacher behaviors and approaches that result in effective classroom management. Planning, preparation, and judicious use of praise and evaluative feedback are among the teacher behaviors that influence the behavior and performance of students.

3. Even though much has been learned about effective teaching, not enough is known to allow for easy evaluation of teachers' performance in a manner that holds the teacher accountable for student outcomes.

4. During the past decade or so the public has been demanding accountability from the schools, but severe difficulties have prevented the development of workable arrangements.

5. Recent emphasis in accountability has shifted to minimum competency testing of students and teachers. Minimum competency tests for new teachers probably will be used more frequently in the next few years, but it is unlikely that tests will be widely used to assess the performance of tenured teachers.

DISCUSSION QUESTIONS

1. What is meant by the term "teachable groups"? What student and teacher learning styles might be considered in trying to form such groups?

2. What is direct instruction? What are its advantages and disadvantages?

3. What classroom management practices are most effective? How can new teachers learn to use these practices successfully?

4. Would you be willing to be held accountable for your teaching? What safeguards would you want to see established in a teacher accountability plan?

5. What are the pros and cons of using tests to select new teachers? What types of tests are most defensible for this purpose?

THINGS TO DO

1. Evaluate the teachers whom you know best in terms of the behaviorial characteristics detailed in this chapter. Try to discern whether their basic characteristics labelled "good" vary according to level of teaching, type of student, and sex and age of the teacher.

2. Volunteer to teach a lesson in class for about ten minutes. Use a simplified version of the Flanders Interaction Analysis Scale ("direct" versus "indirect" behavior) or Bellack's verbal "moves" (structuring, soliciting, responding, reacting). Note whether there is agreement among class members in categorizing your teacher behavior. (A majority opinion for a specific behavior should suffice.)

3. Observe three or four teachers at work in the classroom and analyze their performance with reference to use of direct instruction.

4. Interview several experienced teachers concerning their classroom management approaches. Which practices do they find to be effective, and which ineffective?

5. Survey several local school districts to find out if they make any use of applicants' test scores in selecting new teachers.

FOR PART I

Suggestions for Further Reading

Ronald G. Corwin, *A Sociology of Education* (New York: Appleton-Century-Crofts, 1965).

M. L. Cushman, *The Governance of Teacher Education* (Berkeley, Calif.: McCutchan, 1977).

Daniel L. Duke, ed., *Classroom Management,* National Society for the Study of Education, Part II (Chicago: University of Chicago Press, 1978).

N. L. Gage, *The Scientific Basis of the Art of Teaching* (New York: Teachers College Press, Columbia University, 1978).

Arthur T. Jersild, *When Teachers Face Themselves* (New York: Teachers College Press, Columbia University, 1955).

Allan C. Ornstein and Harry L. Miller, *Looking Into Teaching* (Chicago: Rand McNally, 1980).

Penelope L. Peterson and Herbert J. Walberg, eds., *Research on Teaching* (Berkeley, Calif.: McCutchan, 1979).

William A. Proefiedt, *The Teacher You Choose To Be* (New York: Holt, Rinehart, 1975).

Kevin Ryan, ed., *Teacher Education*, National Society for the Study of Education, Part II (Chicago: University of Chicago Press, 1975).

Charles E. Silberman, *Crisis in the Classroom* (New York: Random House, 1970).

PART TWO
HISTORICAL AND
PHILOSOPHICAL
FOUNDATIONS

Insight into the present and future rests upon the ability to understand the past and raise intelligent questions. An appreciation of historical trends and philosophical thought reveals the folly of attempting simple answers to complex problems. Schools do not exist in a vacuum; they are influenced by a changing society rooted in historical and philosophical foundations. The four chapters in Part Two examine the history and philosophy of education in this context.

In each chapter we learn that certain trends and lines of thought seem to have had a marked influence in shaping the character of American education. In Chapter 5, an analysis of its origins will help us understand that our education is rooted in European movements and people, and that it has been shaped by certain important periods—ancient Greek and Roman, medieval, Renaissance, etc. Next, in Chapter 6, we examine some educational ideas that have been developed and implemented by European thinkers. Eight leaders have been selected—Comenius, Locke, Rousseau, Pestalozzi, Froebel, Herbart, Spencer, and Montessori. The contributions of a number of American educational leaders are discussed also, including Washington, DuBois, Dewey, Counts, Holt, and Illich. Then, in Chapter 7 we look at the development of education in America, starting with the colonial period and ending with a discussion of some contemporary events. We see the complex interaction of schools and society as we learn how changing institutions and ideas of the nation influenced the development of American education. Chapter 8 shifts the discussion to some philosophical questions. First of all, what is philosophy? How does it influence human existence in society? Specifically, how does it relate to our view of schools? The philosophy we adopt interacts with historical events—and it is this relationship that affects our schools.

CHAPTER 5
ORIGINS OF OUR
EDUCATIONAL
HERITAGE

Focusing questions

Why should teachers study the history of education?

How did the leading educators of the past define knowledge, education, schooling, teaching, and learning?

What concepts of the educated person were dominant during the various periods of western history?

How have educational ideas changed over the course of time?

How have the educational theories of the leading educators of the western world contributed to modern education?

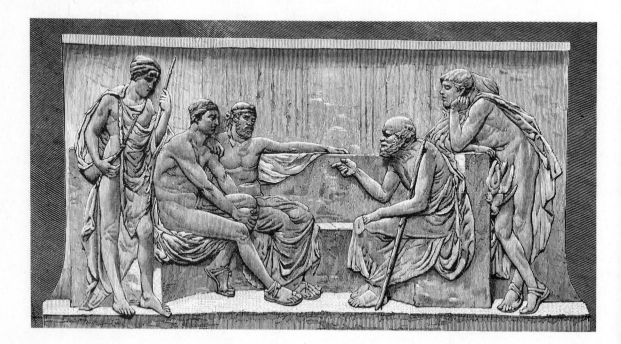

As a prospective teacher, you may seriously question the need to study the history of education. Why, you may ask, should I be concerned with the past when my main concern is what I will be doing in the classroom tomorrow? Is it not more worthwhile to spend my time trying to solve current educational problems? The next three chapters will attempt to answer these questions. Some new ones that may challenge you also will be raised.

The ideas of John Dewey suggest a rationale for historical study. As one of the world's leading thinkers on questions of philosophy, society, and education, Dewey developed his own educational philosophy, which he called Experimentalism. For Dewey, a genuine idea had to be an instrument that did something for us. A purely abstract idea that had no relevance to our personal or social life and no usefulness really had no practical meaning. Dewey also believed that what we do in our everyday life is not bound in time by the passing moment that dies when it is over. Rather, our practical everyday problems, decisions, and actions become a theory of experience that will help us in solving future problems.

Past experience helps solve future problems

In 1916 Dewey wrote a momentous book, *Democracy and Education*. It is useful to consider Dewey's ideas when we weigh the importance of studying education, because he was a theory builder who was also thoroughly practical. Dewey wrote:

> The past just as past is no longer our affair. If it were wholly gone and done with, there would be only one reasonable attitude toward it. Let the dead bury their dead. But knowledge of the past is the key to understanding the present. History deals with the past, but this past is the history of the present.[1]

Dewey is saying that whomever you are right now is a result of your past experience. Your personal hopes and problems are a product of your personal history. Your present social, political, and educational achievements, controversies, and problems are a result of what you have done as a member of the human group. Your history is a part of your present and, if handled intelligently, can be an instrument in shaping the future. As Dewey pointed out: ". . . past events cannot be separated from the living present and retain meaning. The true starting point of history is always some present situation with its problems."[2]

History can shape the future

In approaching the study of educational history from the perspective of your present concerns, it might be helpful to look to the experience of past educators for answers to questions that you will have to face as a teacher. The questions that will be put to these educators will be broad

1   John Dewey, *Democracy and Education: An Introduction to the Philosophy of Education* (New York: Macmillan, 1916), pp. 250–51.
2   Ibid.

ones, dealing with the very nature of teaching and learning. For example: What is knowledge? What is education? What is the purpose of the school? Who should attend school? How should teaching and learning be carried on?

EDUCATION IN ANCIENT GREECE

Historians of western civilization and education often look to the ancient Greek city states as the source of western culture. A number of small and often competing city states such as Athens, Sparta, and Thebes were noteworthy for a well-defined conception of civic duties, responsibilities, and rights. Athens, in particular, emphasized the humane, rational, and democratic form of social and political organization. Sparta, the chief adversary of Athens, was a military dictatorship. As each city state developed its own form of political organization, it also evolved an appropriate kind of education.

Source of western culture

For the Greeks, immersion and participation in the total culture were more important than formal schooling. Through *enculturation* the Greek youth became a citizen of his society. In most of the Greek city states, the formal educational process was reserved for boys. In Athens, for example, girls generally learned domestic skills at home. In contrast, Spartan girls received more public education, including a strenuous athletic training that prepared them to be healthy mothers of future Spartan soldiers.

More structured education began with the appearance of the Sophists. Following these teachers came Socrates and Plato, the moral philosophers; Aristotle, who attempted to formulate rational and systematic explanations of natural phenomena; and Isocrates, the educator and rhetorician.

THE SOPHISTS

The first professional educators were the Sophists, a group of wandering teachers who developed a variety of methods for instructing the rising commercial class of Athens and other Greek city states in needed intellectual and rhetorical skills.[3] By cultivating rhetoric—the art of persuasion—the students of the Sophists came to control the legal agencies of the city state. The Sophists claimed that they could teach any subject or skill to anyone who wished to learn it. While their pedagogical expertise often was exaggerated, they brought educational opportunities to more people than had previously enjoyed them and contributed to socioeconomic mobility.

Wandering teachers

The Sophists specialized in teaching grammar, logic, and rhetoric; these subjects later developed into the liberal arts. Logic, the rules of ar-

Grammar, logic and rhetoric

---

3 Gerald L. Gutek, *A History of the Western Educational Experience* (New York: Random House, 1972).

gument, aided students in clarifying their own thinking; grammar helped them express ideas clearly; rhetoric—the power of persuading others through speech—was considered most important. Essentially, the Sophists were concerned with developing the communication skills of their students so that they might become successful advocates and legislators. Regarding the power of communication:

> . . . in the middle of the fifth century B.C. there was a verbal
> explosion of unprecedented magnitude. . . . Men argued, debated,
> soliloquized, declaimed, contradicted, orated. In trade, in politics,
> in litigation, in estate management, in war, in courtship, in
> international relations, he who had the gift of words was victor.[4]

Some of the Sophists were excellent teachers who were well prepared to teach their subjects and skills. Unfortunately, others were fakes who offered instant success through tricks and gimmicks. Protagoras (485–415 B.C.) was one of the most effective teachers among the Sophists. His method involved: (1) the presentation of a simple lecture or declamation to his students to provide them with an excellent model of speech; (2) an examination of great orations that could be used as models of speech; (3) the study of rhetoric, grammar, and logic; (4) practice orations by the young orator, which were criticized by the teacher; and, finally, (5) a public oration delivered by the student. Protagoras believed it was possible for one to argue for or against any proposition and to win any kind of argument.

The Sophists were not particularly concerned with knowledge as a search for truth. Rather, they promised to provide their students with techniques needed to acquire wealth, political power, and social prestige. In ancient Athens, the key to power in the assembly and courts was the ability to attract people and to persuade them to follow you. For the Sophists, knowledge was more than speculation about abstract concepts of truth, beauty, and goodness. It was the ability to use information in such a way that you could motivate and persuade people to accept your point of view. It was not what you said but how you expressed yourself that won the argument or the case of law.

Information for persuasion

As itinerant or traveling teachers the Sophists did not establish schools in an institutional sense. They instructed anyone who could afford to pay them. Their students were ambitious young men who sought instant success. The teachers tried to give their students the image or appearance of confidence, skill, and talent. In one sense, the Sophists were democratic educators who did not restrict their teaching to an upper class or an hereditary aristocracy. In another sense, they contributed to the op-

---

4   James L. Jarrett, *The Educational Theories of the Sophists* (New York: Teachers College Press, Columbia University, 1969), p. 3.

portunistic attitude that stressed appearance and technique rather than truth and honesty. In some respects, the Sophists resembled the modern image makers, who try to "package" political candidates as if they were products that can be sold to voters. In fact, the word "sophistry," which means misleading but clever and subtle argument, is derived from the methods used by the ancient Greek Sophists.

Opportunistic attitude

SOCRATES: EDUCATION BY SELF-EXAMINATION

Unlike the Sophists, the Athenian philosopher Socrates (469–399 B.C.) sought to discover the universal principles of truth, beauty, and goodness, which he believed should govern human conduct. Socrates is important in western educational history because he firmly defended the freedom to think, to question, and to teach.[5]

Principles of truth, beauty, and goodness

Indeed, he died for academic freedom. He was also significant as the teacher of Plato, who later systematized many of Socrates' ideas. In fact, what we know about Socrates is known through the writings of Plato. Socrates also developed the methodology or dialogue of searching questions and answers that bears his name (Socratic method).

Socrates' philosophy was a simple ethic; it stated that a person ought to seek to live a life of moral excellence. Such an individual would live wisely and act rationally. A true education was one that aimed to cultivate morally excellent people. Socrates held moral excellence to be superior to technical or vocational training. Unlike the Sophists, Socrates did not believe that knowledge or wisdom could be transmitted from a teacher to a learner. He asserted that true knowledge existed within everyone and needed to be brought to consciousness. A liberating education would stimulate learners to discover ideas by bringing to consciousness the truth that was latently present in their minds.

Socrates' basic educational aim was that individuals should define themselves through self-examination and self-analysis. By self-examination each person should seek the truth that is universally present in all people. As a teacher Socrates used the method of asking probing questions that stimulated his students to investigate the perennial human concerns about the meaning of life, truth, and justice. As a result of the dialogue with the teacher, the student constructed, criticized, and reconstructed his basic conceptions.

Probing questions

Socrates frequented the Athenian marketplace, raising political, aesthetic, moral, and philosophical issues. As a social critic, he made powerful enemies. In 399 B.C. he was brought to trial on the charge of impiety to the gods and of corrupting Athens' youth. Found guilty, he was sentenced to death by his fellow Athenians.[6]

5 William K. Richmond, *Socrates and the Western World: An Essay in the Philosophy of Education* (London: Redman, 1954).

6 Henry J. Perkinson, *Since Socrates: Studies in the History of Western Educational Thought* (New York: Longmans, 1980).

PLATO: ETERNAL
TRUTHS AND VALUES
Socrates' educational efforts were continued by his pupil, Plato (429–347 B.C.).
A speculative philosopher, Plato founded the Academy in 387 B.C., and wrote *Protagoras*, a discourse on virtue, and the *Republic* and the *Laws*, treatises on political, legal, and educational theory. In general, Plato was a conservative social and educational philosopher who disliked the changes encouraged by the Sophists and held that reality consisted of an unchanging world of perfect ideas—universal concepts such as truth, goodness, justice, and beauty. As these images appear to our senses, however, individual examples are imperfect representations of these universal and eternal ideas. In structuring an unchanging order of reality, Plato challenged the Sophists' methodology of sense experience. In contrast, he asserted that human beings are good and honorable only when their behavior agrees with the ideal concepts of justice and goodness.[7]

Plato's theory of knowledge is based on the theory of "reminiscence," by which individuals recall the truths or ideas that are present in latent form in their minds. Reminiscence implies that the human soul, before birth, has lived in a spiritual world of ideas, which is the source of all truth and knowledge. With birth, this knowledge of truth is represented within one's subconscious mind. For Plato, learning was the rediscovery or recollection of this latent knowledge of perfect forms by bringing it to consciousness.[8] Since sense impressions, according to Plato, are distortions of reality, genuine knowledge is intellectual and not sensory. True knowledge, as contrasted with sensation, is changeless and eternal. There is but one idea of perfection that is common to all human beings regardless of their time and circumstances. Since truth is universal, education should also be universal and unchanging. Since reality can be apprehended only intellectually, education also should be intellectual.

Universal and unchanging education

Plato's ideal society　In the *Republic*, his most famous work, Plato fashioned a plan for a perfect state ruled by an intellectual elite of philosopher-kings. His ideal state and ideal educational system were based on the conception of unchanging truth and values. Plato's Republic, existing to cultivate truth and virtue in its inhabitants, rested on assumptions that only knowledgeable men should rule and that all inhabitants should contribute to the general welfare according to their particular aptitude. Education was the major agency for determining the social relations of the residents of Plato's Republic.[9]

Intellectual elite

In the *Republic* the inhabitants were divided into three major classes: the intellectual rulers or philosopher-kings; the auxiliaries and military defenders; and the workers who produced goods and services. Of

7　Adolphe E. Meyer, *Grandmasters of Educational Thought* (New York: McGraw-Hill, 1975).

8　Robin Barrow, *Plato and Education* (Boston: Routledge & Paul, 1976); Robert S. Brumbaugh, "Plato's Philosophy of Education: The Meno Experiment and the Republic Curriculum," *Educational Theory* (Summer 1970), pp. 207-28.

9　Plato, *The Republic of Plato*, trans. A. D. Lindsay (New York: Dutton, 1950).

which of the three classes of the Republic one became a member was determined by intellectual capacity, defined primarily in cognitive terms. The educational system played a selective role as it rated individual intellectual competencies and sorted people into categories. Once assigned to a class, individuals received the education appropriate to their assigned social role. Plato gave the philosopher-kings the task of selecting those who were intellectually able. Because of their intellectual expertise, the philosopher-kings were judged to be virtuous and intelligent men who possessed the capacity for leadership. The second class—auxiliaries (warriors)—were subordinate to the philosopher-kings. Strong of will, rather than intellectual, they were to defend the Republic. The lowest class, the workers, provided the needed economic products. For each class, there was an appropriate educational track to prepare them for their functions. Plato believed that each class would fulfill a necessary socioeconomic function as it contributed to the community. Such a society, he believed, would be harmonious.

Plato's educational curriculum   Since Plato believed that parents often passed on their prejudices and ignorance to their children, children were separated from their parents and reared in state nurseries in the Republic. The nurseries constituted a prepared environment, in which ideas and practices regarded as injurious to the child's proper development had been screened out. From ages six to eighteen, music and gymnastics were studied. Music included letters, reading, writing, choral singing, and dancing. After mastering reading and writing, the students read the classics, which had been censored carefully. Plato regarded literature as very important and chose worthy stories and poems that stressed truthfulness, obedience to authorities, and control of emotions. Plato considered literature to be a powerful force in shaping character. After mastering basic arithmetic, the students applied themselves to geometry and astronomy. Gymnastics consisted of functional exercises useful for military training, such as fencing, archery, javelin throwing, and horseback riding. Gymnastic exercises were considered essential for character building and physical development. Plato also included the rules of diet and hygiene in his curriculum.[10]

From 18 to 20, the students pursued intensive physical and military training. At twenty, the future philosopher-kings were selected for ten years of additional higher education in mathematics, geometry, astronomy, music, and science. At age 30, the less intellectually capable became civil servants; the most intellectually capable continued the higher studies of metaphysics and dialectic. In Platonic terms, intellectual capacity was related to a person's ability to reason in metaphysical terms. Since metaphysics dealt with questions of the nature of ultimate reality, those

State-run
schools

Athletics for
building
character

Metaphysic
and dialectic
studies

10 Barrow, *Plato and Education.*

who were to continue their education had to penetrate beyond the effects of immediate sense perception and grasp intellectually the ultimate cause of existence. The search for the ultimate cause of existence involved the process of *dialectic*, which was the procedure for logically arriving at the single principle upon which the hypotheses of all the sciences are based. For Plato, the dialectical process referred to the system by which all truth is held to derive from the single principle of the Form of the Good. When their studies were completed, the philosopher-kings began to direct the military and political affairs of the Republic. At age 50, the philospher-kings became the Republic's elder statesmen.

Concerned with questions of universal truth and virtue, Plato opposed the Sophists' stress on technique and method. For Plato, truth, learning, and education were intellectual, not technical. Hence, those who showed a propensity toward abstract thought were to be selected by teachers for studies that developed their reasoning powers. Individuals who were not suited to philosophical inquiry were given vocational training. Therefore, students who would be admitted to a Platonic school were a carefully selected intellectual elite. Educational opportunity was reserved only for those competent to master highly intellectual and abstract studies.

Focus on intellectual learning

ARISTOTLE: CULTIVATION OF RATIONALITY

Plato's student Aristotle (384–322 B.C.) was the tutor of Alexander the Great. He founded the Lyceum, an Athenian philosophical school, and wrote extensively on such subjects as physics, astronomy, zoology, botany, logic, ethics, and metaphysics. Aristotle's *Nicomachean Ethics* and *Politics* examined education in relation to society and government.[11]

As a philosophical realist, Aristotle held that reality was posited in an objective order. Objects, composed of form and matter, exist independently of our knowledge of them. Human beings are rational; therefore they have the ability to know and observe the natural laws that govern them. Aristotle also saw a basic duality in human nature. Human beings possess souls or minds and material bodies. Like the animals, people have appetites or physical needs, which must be satisfied for them to survive. Unlike the lower animals, men and women have intellect, which gives them the power to think. The good person has activated and fully uses this rational power. The truly educated person exercises reason in judging ethical and political behavior. Humankind's goal is happiness and the good life is one of moderation—an avoidance of extremes.[12]

Moderation

11   John H. Randall, *Aristotle* (New York: Columbia University Press, 1960).
12   Eva T. H. Brann, *Paradoxes of Education in a Republic* (Chicago: University of Chicago Press, 1979); Paul Nash, *Models of Man: Explorations in the Western Educational Tradition* (New York: Wiley, 1968).

For Aristotle, thinking and knowing begin with one's sensation of objects in the environment. From this sensory experience concepts are formed by extracting the forms or patterns of these objects from matter that appears to the senses. The Aristotelian emphasis on sensory experience as the beginning of knowing and of instruction later was stressed by educators in the eighteenth and nineteenth centuries. Aristotle's philosophical position was the historical predecessor of realism, also discussed in Chapter 8.

Aristotle on education   In *Politics* Aristotle set forth an educational theory that states that the good community is based on the cultivation of rationality. If education is neglected, then the community suffers. Aristotle gave education a major role in cultivating human and civic excellence or perfection. Like most of the Greek theorists, Aristotle made a distinction between liberal education and vocational training. Aristotle saw the liberal arts as a liberating factor, enlarging and expanding one's choices. Occupational and vocational training in trade, commerce, and farming were servile pursuits that interfered with intellectual pursuits. (Contemporary debates between liberal educators and career educators often reflect the same basic issues that were examined by Aristotle and the other Greek theorists.)

Cultivation of
rationality

Aristotle, who saw that education cultivated both the rational person and the rational society, recommended compulsory public schools. Infant schooling consisted of play, physical activity, and appropriate stories. Children from ages seven to fourteen were to develop proper habits by moral and physical education. They were to have gymnastic training or physical education. Music cultivated proper emotional dispositions. The basic skills needed for liberal education—reading and writing—were to be taught. From 15 through 21, youths were to study mathematics, geometry, astronomy, grammar, literature, poetry, rhetoric, ethics, and politics. At age 21, the students followed more theoretical subjects such as physics, cosmology, biology, psychology, logic, and metaphysics. Like many of the Greek theorists, Aristotle was concerned exclusively with the education of boys. Following the conventional mores of Athens, he believed women to be intellectually inferior to men.

Compulsory
schooling

Aristotle's theory of knowledge   For Aristotle, knowledge is always about an object. While cognition begins with sensory data about an object, knowledge is conceptual—it is based on the form of the object. Concepts are the generalized classes of objects. For example, if you walk through a forest, you might see such trees as pines, oaks, elms, and maples. While these trees vary in some aspects of their appearance, they are all similar in that they are members of a class. As trees, they share or participate in the form of "tree-ness." If a teacher of botany uses the Aristotelian method, he or she can teach about trees as a class or as a general category in botanical reality and can also teach about the particular trees that are members of the class. Since knowledge is always about an object, education and teaching are always about an object and should have a content. In the Aristotelian teaching act, the teacher instructs a learner about some object, some body of knowledge, or some discipline. Teaching and learning never represent merely an interpersonal relationship or the expression of feelings. They are always about disciplined inquiry into some aspect of reality.

The Aristotelian school was an institution for teaching and learning about knowledge. Instruction was both theoretical and practical. In fact, Aristotelians assert that theory is the best guide to conduct. The theory about reality is based on careful observation of objects as they occur in nature. The teacher can be called a demonstrator of theory. Since Aristotle defined human beings as rational, the school should cultivate and develop each person's rationality. A school, based on Aristotle's terms, would be a highly academic institution. It would offer a prescribed subject matter curriculum based on scholarly and scientific discipline. Within such a school, teachers would have expert knowledge of their subject and would be skilled in transmitting that knowledge to students who are motivated to learn it. Aristotle's philosophy became the foundation of medieval Scholastic education and is the basis of the educational philosophies of such modern humanist educators as Robert Hutchins and Mortimer Adler.

Focus on scholarship and science

ISOCRATES: ORATORY AND RHETORIC

The Greek rhetorician Isocrates (436–388 B.C.) is significant in western educational history because he developed a well-constructed educational theory based on rhetorical skills and knowledge.

Isocrates wrote *Against the Sophists* as a prospectus for his own school and method of instruction.[13] He denounced the Sophists for their superficiality, their stress on tricks and gimmicks, and their often exaggerated promises. In a more positive sense, Isocrates indicated that his major educational objective was to prepare rational men who would be rational speakers of the truth. Civic reform, he believed, could be secured only by educating virtuous leaders who could capably administer the state. Of the liberal studies, Isocrates held that rhetoric, the rational expression of thought, was most important in cultivating morality and political leadership.

Isocrates opposed those Sophists who taught rhetoric as a set of isolated persuasive routines or public relations techniques. Rather, he believed that rhetorical education was to be completely humanistic and cultural, including the tools and techniques of speech. The worthy orator should recognize and should serve those honorable causes that advance the public good. As a man above reproach, the orator would persuade men

Rhetorical education as humanistic

13 Perkinson, *Since Socrates: Studies in the History of Western Educational Thought.*

to follow good programs.[14] In this connection, Isocrates' students, who enrolled in his school for a term of three to four years, studied rhetoric, examined model orations, and practiced public speaking. To develop humanely educated men, Isocrates also taught politics, ethics, and history. The teacher was important in Isocrates' method of rhetorical education, since he had to be capable of influencing his students through his own demonstration of knowledge, skill, and ethical conduct.

An effective and methodological educator, Isocrates contributed to the rhetorical tradition in education. He had a direct influence on the Roman theorists Cicero and Quintilian. By recognizing the humanistic dimension of rhetorical study, Isocrates contributed to the ideal of the liberally educated man.

Influence on Roman education

EDUCATION IN ANCIENT ROME

While the Greeks were developing their concepts of culture and education in the eastern Mediterranean, the Romans were consolidating their political position on the Italian peninsula and throughout the western Mediterranean. In their drive from small republic to great empire, the Romans first were preoccupied with war and politics. After they had created their empire, they concentrated on the administration, law, and diplomacy needed to maintain it. The Greeks were concerned with speculative philosophy, but the Romans were most interested in educating the practical politician and able administrator.

War and politics

The Roman educational ideal was exemplified by a conception of oratory similar to that held by Isocrates. The Roman orator was the broadly and liberally educated man of public life—the senator, lawyer, teacher, civil servant, and politician. Cicero and Quintilian are important examples.

CICERO: MASTER ORATOR

The distinguished Roman senator Cicero (106-43 B.C.) had himself studied both Greek and Latin grammar and literature, history, and rhetoric. He appreciated both the old Roman stress on practicality and utility and the Greek emphasis on humanistic and liberal culture. His work *de Oratore* combined the Roman and Greek conceptions of the educated man.[15] In the Roman context, the practical results of oratory were winning debates and arguments in the Forum. Cicero added the Greek perspective of rhetorical education, which stressed broad and liberal culture, or *humanitas*. Cicero recommended that the orator, as a rational man, should be educated in the

Practical and liberal education

14 George Kennedy, *The Art of Persuasion in Greece* (Princeton, N.J.: Princeton University Press, 1963).

15 Aubrey Gwynn, *Roman Education from Cicero to Quintilian*, rev. ed. (New York: Teachers College Press, Columbia University, 1966).

liberal arts and should use his education in the public interest. Commenting on the education that was preparatory to rhetoric, Cicero also prescribed the role of the *grammaticus,* the secondary school teacher. The *grammaticus* was to comment on the poets, teach history, correct diction and delivery, and explain the meaning of language. Although Greek was the medium of instruction, the young Roman boy was also to be adept in using his own language, Latin.[16]

After the prospective orator had been prepared adequately in grammar, he went on to the higher studies. Like Isocrates, Cicero believed that the humanistically educated orator should be prepared thoroughly in the liberal arts—ethics, psychology, military science, medicine, natural science, geography, astronomy, history, law, and philosophy. In particular, Cicero believed that the great orator needed a knowledge of history. History would provide the young Roman with perspective into his own past and tradition. It would provide him with rhetorical illustrations and examples by examining the biographies of great Greeks and Romans. Students were to study the speeches of great statesmen and the ancient Roman Laws of the Twelve Tables. Effective speakers also needed to be versed in philosophy, which included psychology, ethics, politics, and logic.

Upon the broad framework of the liberal arts, the orator then studied rhetoric. As a public speaker, the orator had to select his words with care so that he could structure his arguments persuasively. He needed to use psychology to excite the emotions of his audience and to influence public affairs. The orator needed to be quick intellectually; he needed to be versatile in using a number of speaking styles and types of argument. Cicero also believed that oratory was a functional study which could actively influence public opinion and shape state policy. The word *humanitas,* which signifies all that is worthy in an individual as a humane and intelligent being, best expresses his ideal of the educated man.

Emphasis on rhetoric

QUINTILIAN: TEACHER OF RHETORIC

Marcus Fabius Quintilianus, or Quintilian (35–95 A.D.), worked in Rome as a legal assistant. It was as a teacher of rhetoric, however, that he gained the fame that led to his appointment to the first chair of Latin rhetoric. As the foremost Roman rhetorician, Quintilian served several emperors. Cicero had written when Rome was a republic; Quintilian's program of oratorical education reflected the political realities of imperial Rome, which was ruled by decree rather than by group decisions shaped by oratorical argument.[17] Unlike Cicero, who served in Rome's Senate, Quintilian was primarily a teacher, whose chief involvement was with education. Nevertheless, both Quintilian and Cicero

---

16   A. S. Wilkins, *Roman Education* (London: Cambridge University Press, 1931).
17   George Kennedy, *Quintilian* (New York: Twayne Publishers, 1969).

believed that the orator should be a man of *humanitas*, of liberal disposition and culture.

Quintilian's *Institutio Oratoria*, appearing in 94 A.D., was a systematic educational work that dealt with education preparatory to the study of rhetoric, rhetorical theories and studies, and the practice of public speaking or declamation. Quintilian recognized that instruction should be based on the stages of human growth and development. In the first stage, from birth until age seven, the child was impulsive and concerned with immediately satisfying needs and desires. Since the early childhood years established later attitudes and values, parents were to select well-trained nurses, pedagogues, and companions for their children. It was very important that the future orator should have a Greek nurse and pedagogue who used correct speech and pronunciation patterns so that good language usage became habitual to the student.

Stages of growth

In Quintilian's second stage of education, from seven to fourteen, the child learned from sense experiences, formed clear ideas, and exercised his memory. Now he wrote the languages that he already spoke. The reading and writing instructor, the *litterator*, was to be both of good character and a competent teacher. Instruction in reading and writing was to be slow but thorough. The school should include games and recreation. A set of ivory letters was to aid in learning the alphabet. By tracing the outline of the letters, the child learned writing.

In the third stage of education, Quintilian stressed the study of the liberal arts with the *grammaticus* in the secondary school. Both Greek and Latin grammars were to be studied concurrently. Grammar involved Greek and Roman literature, history, and mythology. Music, geometry, astronomy, and gymnastics also were studied. After grammar and the liberal arts, the prospective orator began rhetorical studies, which Quintilian identified as drama, poetry, history, law, philosophy, and rhetoric.[18]

Study of liberal arts

Declamations—systematic speaking exercises—were of great importance for the orator. The themes of the declamations were to be factual rather than fictitious. If students proved incapable of oratory they were dismissed, so as not to waste the teacher's time and energy. As soon as possible, the novice orator spoke in the Forum before an audience and then returned to the master rhetorician for expert criticism. The teacher was to correct the student's mistakes with a sense of authority but also with patience, tact, and consideration.

For Quintilian, oratorical perfection depended upon the speaker's own moral excellence.[19] To persuade, the orator had to be trustworthy. Quintilian's significance in western educational history lies in his atten-

18 E. Brandenburg, "Quintilian and the Good Orator," *Quarterly Journal of Speech* (February 1948). pp. 23–29.

19 William M. Smail, *Quintilian on Education*, rev. ed. (New York: Teachers College Press, Columbia University, 1966).

tion to the theory and practice of teaching and learning. In anticipating the modern teacher's concern for the learner's individual differences, he recommended that instruction be made appropriate to the learner's abilities and readiness. He also recommended that the teacher motivate students by making learning interesting and attractive.

Appropriate to the learner's abilities

MEDIEVAL CULTURE AND EDUCATION

The thousand years between the fall of Rome and the Renaissance (500 A.D.–1500 A.D.) have been labelled by historians as the Middle Ages, or the medieval period. This era of western culture and education began at the end of the ancient classical period of Greece and Rome and came to an end at the beginning of the modern era. The medieval period was characterized by a decline in learning at first, and then a revival by the Scholastic educators. In the absence of strong, centralized political authorities, the medieval order of life, society, and education was brought to a synthesis and unified by the Latin Catholic Church, headed by the Pope in Rome.

Decline, then revival, in learning

During this period the tradition of learning was carried on at elementary parish, chantry, and monastic schools conducted under Church auspices.[20] At the secondary level, both monastic and cathedral schools offered a curriculum of general studies. Schools that provided basic education as well as training for a trade were also maintained by the merchant and craft guilds. Knights received their training in military tactics and the chivalric code in the palaces.[21] In the development of educational institutions, the rise of the medieval university merits the most attention because together with the flowering of Scholastic education it was the major contribution to education during this period.

AQUINAS: SCHOLASTIC EDUCATION

By the eleventh century, medieval educators had developed Scholasticism as a method of inquiry, scholarship, and teaching. The Scholastics, as the teaching clerics were called, relied on faith and reason as complementary sources of truth. They accepted the sacred Scriptures and the writings of the Church Fathers as sources of God's revealed word and also trusted in human reason. The Scholastics believed that the human mind could deduce first principles which, when illuminated by Scriptural authority, were a source of truth.

A method of inquiry and teaching

Scholastic philosophy and education reached its zenith in the *Summa Theologiae* of Saint Thomas Aquinas (1225–1274), a Dominican

20 Frank P. Graves, *A History of Education During the Middle Ages and the Transition to Modern Times* (New York: Macmillan, 1922).

21 Donna R. Barnes, *For Court, Manor, and Church: Education in Medieval Europe* (Minneapolis: Burgess, 1971).

theologian who taught at the University of Paris.[22] Aquinas was primarily concerned with reconciling the authority of faith as represented by the Scriptures with the authority of Greek rationalism as represented by Aristotle. He used both faith and reason to answer basic questions dealing with the Christian conception of God, the nature of humankind and the universe, and the relationships between God and man. As a philosopher and a theologian, Aquinas knew both Christian doctrine and Aristotelian philosophy and sought to integrate these two important sources of the western intellectual and educational tradition into a coherent world view. In the Thomistic context, human beings possess a physical body and a spiritual soul. While living temporarily on earth, their ultimate purpose is to experience an eternity with God in heaven. Like Aristotle, Aquinas asserted that human knowledge of the world originates in sensation and is completed by abstraction or concept formation.

Relationship between God and man

In *De Magistro (Concerning the Teacher)*, Aquinas discussed the teacher's vocation as one that combines faith, love, and learning.[23] The teacher needs to be a contemplative scholar, an active agent of learning, a master of his discipline, and a lover of humanity. That is to say, the teacher needs to know his subject matter thoroughly and also to be expert in the method of teaching it. Aquinas and the other scholastic educators saw no conflict between research and teaching. The good teacher needs to do both and do them well so that teaching and scholarship are carefully blended.

Knowledge and schooling   Aquinas also recognized that informal education had to be related carefully to the discipline of formal schooling. Informal education, or *educatio*, involved *all* the agencies, such as family, friends, environment, etc., that developed a person's virtue or excellence. Schooling, or *disciplina*, was learning that was stimulated by formal teaching. Schooling was about bodies of knowledge and subject-matter disciplines, based on first principles and containing demonstrated conclusions. Such subject-matter disciplines formed the basis of formal instruction in schools. Scholastic teachers used the syllogism—a form of deductive reasoning—to accumulate an ordered body of demonstrated knowledge. The teacher aided the students in recognizing basic principles and in developing the implications of these principles. Aquinas held that the teacher had to select the language that effectively communicated the subject to the students. In curricular matters Aquinas followed the liberal arts tradition: logic, mathematics, natural and moral philosophy, metaphysics, and theology were the organized subject matters of the curriculum of higher education.[24]

Informal vs. formal education

22   Frank P. Cassidy, *Molders of the Medieval Mind: The Influence of the Fathers of the Church on the Medieval Schoolmen* (Port Washington, N.Y.: Kennikat Press, 1966).

23   John W. Donohue, *St. Thomas Aquinas and Education* (New York: Random House, 1968).

24   Donohue, *St. Thomas Aquinas and Education*.

Aquinas and the other Scholastics had definite ideas about the nature of knowledge, the meaning of education, and the purpose of schooling.[25] For the Scholastic, knowledge was derived from two complementary and mutually supporting sources: faith and reason. The Scholastic's faith, or belief system, was grounded on the assumption that God's truth came to the world through revelation. Certain divinely inspired men had recorded God's revealed word in the sacred Scripture of the books of the Bible. The medieval Church believed that it had a mission to teach God's revealed truth to people of all nations, and the Fathers of the Church and the Church Councils interpreted and explained the meaning of sacred Scriptures. For the medieval Scholastic, then, faith in the authority of the Scriptures and in the teaching of the Church was one component of knowledge; hence, the most important subjects in the medieval university were theological.

The medieval Scholastics also believed it was possible for people to use their rational potentiality, or power, to find truth. The Scholastic school was an institution that taught the principles of the Christian religion and of rational philosophy. Generally, it was governed and also protected by the Church. Its teachers were clerics who were under religious protection and governance. During the medieval period, schooling functioned to prepare priests, monks, court officials, scribes, and administrators. The serfs, the farmers bound to the soil, generally had no schooling in the formal sense.

The work of Aquinas and other Scholastic educators centered about the medieval university, the institution of higher education. An examination of the origins, development, and organization of the medieval university is useful to students of contemporary education, since the basic patterns of higher education were established in the medieval period.

MEDIEVAL
UNIVERSITIES

Such famous medieval seats of learning as the universities of Paris, Salerno, Bologna, Oxford, Cambridge, and Padua grew out of the intellectual revival of the twelfth and thirteenth centuries. It is generally believed that the major universities evolved from the expanding enrollments of the cathedral schools, which by the twelfth century were unable to accommodate the growing number of students. The universities evolved from associations, called *universitas*, which the students and teachers organized for their own protection and security.[26] Enrollment had increased because of the improved economic conditions stimulated by the Crusades. Crusaders had also come into contact with Byzantine Greek and

*Intellectual
revival*

25 Patrick McCormick, *History of Education* (Washington, D.C.: Catholic Education Press, 1953).
26 Charles H. Haskins, *The Rise of Universities* (New York: Holt, 1923).

Arabic scholarship, which was then brought back to western Europe. Through the Byzantine and Arab scholars, the medieval educators discovered the works of Aristotle, Euclid, Ptolemy, Galen, and Hippocrates. As indicated earlier, the works of Aristotle contributed to the development of the Scholastic philosophy of education. Theological interpretation and investigation of these newly discovered works were of major interest to the medieval Scholastics, especially at the University of Paris, where Thomas Aquinas attempted to reconcile Aristotle's rationalism with the Scriptures and doctrines of Christianity.

A high level of scholarship resulted from the rise and development of the medieval universities. The medieval universities established special- **Professional** ized professional schools of law, medicine, and theology in addition to the **schools** liberal arts curriculum.[27] The University of Bologna in Italy and the University of Paris in France represented two distinctive patterns of institutional organization in higher education; the former was shaped by students; the latter, by faculty.

Other universities were established throughout Europe between the twelfth and fifteenth centuries: in Italy, the University of Padua and the University of Naples; in France, the universities of Montpellier, Orleans, and Toulouse; in England, Oxford University, and Cambridge University a hundred years later. By the fourteenth century Europe had the Scottish universities of St. Andrew and Aberdeen, the Spanish university of Salamanca, and the German universities of Erfurt, Heidelberg, and Cologne. There were also universities in Vienna and Prague.[28]

RENAISSANCE CLASSICAL HUMANISM

The Renaissance began at the end of the fourteenth century and reached its height in the fifteenth century. It was a period in which there was a marked revival of interest in the humanistic aspects of the Greek and Latin classics. It was also a period of transition between **Revival in** the medieval and modern ages. The Renaissance classical humanist, like **Humanism** the medieval Scholastic, found his authorities in the past and stressed **and classics** classical manuscripts. Unlike the Scholastics, the humanist educators were interested more in the earthly experience of human beings than in a God-centered world view.[29]

The effects of the Renaissance were particularly noticeable in Italy, where the revival of commerce had produced a financial surplus that fos-

27 Pearl Kibre, *The Nations in the Medieval Universities* (Cambridge, Mass.: Medieval Academy of America, 1948); Hastings Rashdall, *The Universities of Europe in the Middle Ages* (London: Oxford University Press, 1936).

28 Charles H. Haskins, *The Renaissance of the Twelfth Century* (Cambridge, Mass.: Harvard University Press, 1927).

29 Emile Durkheim, *The Evolution of Educational Thought* (Boston: Routledge & Paul, 1977); Robert Beck, *A Social History of Education* (Englewood Cliffs, N.J.: Prentice-Hall, 1965).

tered art, literature, and architecture. Wealth, flowing into the prosperous Italian cities, supported humanist educators and schools. The Italian classical humanists, considering themselves an aristocratic literary elite, were self-proclaimed "custodians of knowledge." Coinciding with the spirit of the age, rulers in the Italian city states established court schools to prepare their children in the new learning.

The literary birth of the Italian Renaissance came with the works of Dante (1265-1321), Petrarch (1304-1374), and Boccaccio (1313-1375). Rejecting Scholastic techniques, the classical humanist writers and educators rediscovered Cicero and Quintilian. In the ancient classics of Greek and Rome, the humanist educators found models of literary excellence and style, the ideal of the educated man, and a portrayal of reality based on the wisdom of antiquity.

Classical humanist education produced a challenge to the older Scholastic model of education. The cleric, trained in Scholastic logic, was no longer the preferred model of the educated man. In the Renaissance, the courtier became the model. The courtier was a man of style and elegance; he was liberally educated in classical literature; he was a capable diplomat and could serve his ruler well in the affairs of state. Baldesar Castiglione (1478-1529) described the courtier and his education in a famous work, *The Book of the Courtier.*[30]

Challenge to Scholasticism

In northern Europe, also, classical humanist scholars began to critically examine the Scriptures and theological writing. They considered Scholastic education to be in a state of decay. Educators now sought to develop teaching methods and materials designed to produce the well-rounded, liberally educated courtier. The most suitable curriculum was classical Greek and Latin literature. The imitation of Cicero's style of writing would cultivate the elegance of style and expression needed by the cultured gentleman. An examination of the teaching styles of Erasmus of Rotterdam provides an example of the northern Renaissance humanist educator.

Educated courtier

ERASMUS: CRITIC AND REFORMER   Desiderius Erasmus (1465-1536) was born in the city of Rotterdam in the Netherlands. He was educated in the schools of the Brethren of the Common Life and studied scholastic philosophy at the University of Paris. *The Praise of Folly* is his best-known book of a general nature.[31] Erasmus' writings reveal his interest in literary criticism and social reform. His contribution to western education was that of a critic of contemporary institutions, a humanist educator, and an advocate of cosmopolitan humanism.

30 Baldesar Castiglione, *The Book of the Courtier,* trans. C. S. Singleton (New York: Doubleday, 1959).
31 William H. Woodward, *Desiderius Erasmus Concerning the Aim and Method of Education,* rev. ed. (New York: Teachers College Press, Columbia University, 1964).

The Praise of Folly shows Erasmus to be a biting and satirical commentator on the professions and institutions of his day. He criticized the teachers of grammar for their emphasis on trivial and obscure facts, and for ignoring the important aspects of learning while emphasizing unimportant matters that only confused students. Philosophers, Erasmus charged, were concerned only with the most abstract sort of speculations. Theologians, too, felt the jab of Erasmus's pen. Instead of examining the basic relationship of human beings with God, the doctors of theology were busily spinning subtle corollaries to demonstrate their own erudition. In some ways, Erasmus was like Socrates, who delighted in deflating the puffed-up egos of those who considered themselves to be exalted men of wisdom.

Erasmus was the leading classical scholar of the late Renaissance. Concerning the teaching of classical languages, he advised that the teacher should be well acquainted with archeology, astronomy, etymology, history, and Scripture since these areas were related to the study of classical literature. Recognizing the importance of early childhood, Erasmus recommended that the child's education begin as early as possible. Parents were to take their educational responsibilities seriously. Children should receive gentle instruction in good manners and hear stories that had a beneficial effect on the development of their character.

Early childhood education

Erasmus believed that understanding content was more important than mastering style and grammar. Students should understand the content thoroughly; conversation in the language would make learning interesting. Games and contests were also to be encouraged. Erasmus' concern for content and not just for style is clearly seen in his discussion of teaching methods. The teacher of language, he recommended, should: (1) present the author's biography, (2) examine the type of work under study, (3) discuss the basic plot, (4) analyze the author's style, (5) consider the moral implications of the work, and (6) explain the broader philosophical issues raised by the work.

Teaching methods

RENAISSANCE INFLUENCE ON EDUCATION

The Renaissance established some basic trends that were influential in the future development of western education. Most significant was the emphasis on the study of Latin as the hallmark of the educated person. (Until the end of the nineteenth century, knowledge of Latin was required for admission to many colleges and universities in both Europe and the United States.) Also significant was the class basis of secondary schooling; the humanist schools were primarily intended for the children of the nobility and the upper classes, while vernacular elementary schools attended to the needs of the commercial class and those of the lower classes who received little, if any, formal schooling. The aim of secondary education was to produce people skilled in languages. Learning at

Study of Latin

IMAGO·ERASMI·ROTERODA-
MI·AB·ALBERTO·DVRERO·AD·
VIVAM·EFFIGIEM·DELINIATA·

ΤΗΝ·ΚΡΕΙΤΤΩ·ΤΑ·ΣΥΓΓΡΑΜ
ΜΑΤΑ·ΔΙΞΕΙ

·MDXXVI·

*A humanist educator of the late Renaissance, Desiderius
Erasmus was a leading classical scholar concerned with the
content of education.*

this level was seen as the mastery of bodies of knowledge. The later pedagogical revolt and reforms of Rousseau, Comenius, Pestalozzi, Dewey, and
Kilpatrick (to be discussed in Chapters 7 and 9) were directed against
schools that gave exclusive emphasis to the study and mastery of literature, while neglecting experience.

The classical humanists' conceptions of knowledge, education, and
schooling established the outlines of secondary education that have persisted in many western countries. Erasmus and other Renaissance
humanist educators were moving slowly to a humanistic or human-cen-
tered conception of knowledge.[32] However, they did not approach their
human subject as an object of scientific inquiry. Rather than facing the

**Absence of
scientific
inquiry**

32 Charles D. Marler, *Philosophy and Schooling* (Boston: Allyn & Bacon, 1975); Meyer,
Grandmasters of Educational Thought.

human experience directly in biological or sociological terms, the humanist educators preferred to deal with it indirectly through literature. Although they created their own literature about humanity, they went about their task of human rediscovery by returning to the ancient literatures of classical Greece and Rome.

The Renaissance humanist educators were literary figures—writers, poets, and translators—as well as teachers. In many respects they were artist-teachers who approached learning through the medium of literature. To be educated meant to have read and mastered books and to have learned classical languages. For centuries these classical humanist preferences would both shape and confine secondary and higher education. The educated person would be defined as one who knew the classical languages and who had acquired that knowledge from books.

As artist-teachers the Renaissance humanists viewed their human subject with a sense of detachment and distance. They did not get close to their living and breathing human subject but kept a safe distance between themselves and the mass of humanity. They approached their subject through literature that had been written hundreds of years earlier. Their conception of human nature was distilled from a carefully aged literature in much the same way that a fine wine is carefully stored and aged. As a vintage wine is used to grace a carefully prepared dinner, the humanist education was reserved for the connoisseur. Humanist education was not given to everyone but was reserved for an elite who could appreciate and savour it.

Elitist
education

Finally, as an artist-teacher, the humanist educator was a critic of literature, of taste, and of society. Such a person brought a witty and penetrating mind and pen to his work as a critic. In broad terms the education advocated by the humanist was one that produced a critical person who challenged existing customs and mediocrity in literature and in life.

RELIGIOUS REFORMATION AND EDUCATION

The religious reformations of the sixteenth and seventeenth centuries were related to the northern European humanist criticism of institutional life and to the search for new authorities. The rise of the commerical middle classes and the concurrent rise of national states were also important factors. Primarily, however, the various Protestant religious reformers—such as John Calvin, Martin Luther, Philip Melanchthon, and Ulrich Zwingli—sought to free themselves and their followers from papal authority and to reconstruct religious doctrine and forms. These reformers, who were conversant with classical humanism, sought to develop educational philosophies and institutions that would support their religious reformations.

Rise of middle
class

The Protestant reformers significantly shaped the development of educational philosophies and institutions. The various religious sects developed their own educational theories, established their own denominational schools, structured their own curricula, and sought to convince their children of the rightness of the reformed gospels that were preached to them. The general impact of the Protestant Reformation on education was a push toward a general extension of literacy among the masses of the population. Most of the reformers insisted that the faithful should read the Bible in their own mother tongue. To do so the members of the various churches had to be made literate.

Extension of mass literacy

The commitment to defend the faith also led to the use of the catechetical method of religious instruction. The catechism was an elementary book that summarized the principles of the Christian religion, as interpreted by the various denominations, into systematic questions and answers. It was believed that as a result of memorizing the lessons in the catechism, the student would internalize the principles of his or her religious faith. While vernacular schools were used to make the lower classes literate, a variety of secondary schools were maintained to educate the upper classes in Latin and Greek. The gymnasium in Germany, the Latin grammar school in England, and the lycée in France were college preparatory schools that trained the leadership elite, particularly those who were to be clergymen, in the classical languages.

Although there were many strong personalities at work in the Protestant Reformation and Roman Catholic Counter-Reformation, special attention to the educational ideas of Martin Luther will exemplify the work of a major leader in the religious Reformation.

LUTHER: ADVOCATE OF REFORM   Of all the religious leaders of the era, Martin Luther (1483–1546) stands out as perhaps the most influential in shaping the history of western civilization. Luther was born and educated in Germany. He was awarded the Master of Arts in 1505 and then became an Augustinian monk. His intellectual brilliance brought him to the attention of the head of his religious order, and Luther was sent to Wittenberg to lecture on theology. In 1517 Luther nailed his famous "Ninety-five Theses" to the door of the castle church at Wittenberg. From this time on Luther was involved in a series of challenges to the Roman Catholic Church and the Pope on matters dealing with indulgences, the Sacraments, papal authority, and freedom of individual conscience. Luther's challenges stimulated great religious ferment and caused many others to preach religious reform. The culmination of this ferment was the Protestant Reformation, which spread through western and northern Europe.

Luther, who had been a university professor, recognized that educational reform was a potent ally of religious reformation. The church, state, family, and school were to be agents of reformation. The family, in particular, was an important agency in forming the character of children and in shaping values that were compatible with Christian life. He admonished

Educational and religious reformation

parents to teach their children reading and religion. Each family should pray together, read the Bible, study the catechism, and practice a useful trade. Once children had acquired the right values they were ready to benefit from a cognitive program of formal schooling. Luther believed that public officials needed to be made conscious of their educational responsibilities. His "Letter to the Mayors and Aldermen of All Cities of Germany in Behalf of Christian Schools" stressed the spiritual, material, and political benefits that come from schooling.[33] Schools were to produce literate citizens and members of the church. They would prepare trained ministers to lead their flocks in the Reformed religion.

In implementing his educational reforms, Luther was assisted by Philip Melanchthon (1497–1560). Both men wanted to end the monopoly of the Roman Catholic Church over formal schools. They looked to the state to supervise schools and to license teachers. In 1559 Melanchthon drafted the School Code of Würtemberg, which was a model for other German states. Vernacular schools were to be founded in every village to teach religion, reading, writing, arithmetic, and music. The classical secondary school, the gymnasium, was to provide instruction in the higher studies and the classical languages.

Vernacular schools

Even though Luther and Melanchthon argued for the establishment of elementary vernacular schools to teach reading, writing, and religion to the common people, they also strongly believed that the Latin and Greek language curriculum patterned in the Renaissance was most appropriate to prepare the leaders of the church and state. Thus, the German gymnasium followed the basic pattern of humanist education, with the addition of Lutheran theology. It is especially important to note that the general effect of the Protestant Reformation on educational institutions was to fix firmly the dual track system of schools, in which there was one set of schools for the common people and a second set of schools for the upper classes.

Reformation views on knowledge   Luther, Melanchthon, Calvin, and the other Protestant reformers had to concern themselves with questions of knowledge, education, and schooling because they wanted to use these powerful tools to advance the cause of the reformed theology.[34] While they differed in particular theological perspectives, these religious reformers shared a number of educational ideas. On the question of the nature of knowledge, they emphasized the authority of the Christian Bible. For them, individuals were to read the sacred Scriptures for themselves. Because they regarded Bible reading as necessary to gain salva-

Authority of the Bible

33   W. Baskin, ed., *Classics in Education* (New York: Philosophical Library, 1966); Raymond Holley, *Religious Education and Religious Understanding* (Boston: Routledge & Paul, 1978).

34   Frederick Mayer, *A History of Educational Thought* (Columbus, Ohio: Merrill, 1966); Elmer L. Towns, ed., *A History of Religious Educators* (Grand Rapids, Mich.: Baker Book House, 1975).

tion, the religious reformers emphasized literacy in the European vernacular languages. They favored universal schooling not only to enable
people to read the Bible but also to make them useful citizens of the nation
state.

Since the reformers were deeply religious men, they emphasized religious education and values. Schooling was a means of indoctrinating the
masses of the population with religious tenets and values. The sixteenth
and seventeenth centuries were times of fierce religious rivalries and contentions as the various Christian churches competed against each other
for adherents to their particular creeds. To achieve doctrinal conformity
through schooling, teachers used the official catechisms that were prepared for that purpose. Through a question-and-answer approach, the
teachers hoped to fix religious principles in the student's mind.

The Protestant reformers also were concerned with preparing an
educated elite who would become the ministers of the church and the
officials of the state. To prepare the elite, they retained the classical
humanist secondary school with its Latin and Greek language studies.
While this elite would share the Reformed religion with the masses of
people, their higher education would be based on those classical studies
that had identified the educated man in earlier periods of western European educational history.

**THE
ENLIGHTENMENT**

As we examine the eighteenth century
Age of Enlightenment (also called the
Age of Reason), we should keep in mind
that our own governmental institutions
as a republic are products of that era. The ideas of the Enlightenment
influenced such major educational reformers as Rousseau, Pestalozzi, and
Froebel. Although most of these reformers were European, their ideas
were transplanted to the New World. To the extent that American schools
cultivated the scientific method, they reflected the general influence of the
Enlightenment.

Foremost among the ideas of the Enlightenment was the supremacy
of reason. The philosophers, scientists, and scholars of the Enlightenment
clearly believed that it was possible for human beings to improve their
lives, their institutions, and their condition by using their minds to solve
problems.[35] Using the scientific method, scientists of the day formulated
"natural laws," which construed the universe as operating according to
orderly processes. And philosophers and social reformers developed social
theories as hypotheses for the investigation of society. The ideas underlying the American and French revolutions were designed to reconstruct the

*Transplanted
to the New
World*

*Reason and
the scientific
method*

35 Robert Anchor, *The Enlightenment Tradition* (New York: Harper & Row, 1967).

political order according to the dictates of reason. Clearly, these ideas implied that schools should seek to cultivate the reasoning powers of their students.

The learned men of the Enlightenment, such as Diderot, Rousseau, Franklin, and Jefferson, were committed to the view that mankind was progressing toward a new and a better world. No longer was it necessary to look backward to the "golden age" of Greece or Rome. If mankind followed reason and used the scientific method, it would be possible to have continual progress on this planet. Once again the work of the schools would be to cultivate a questioning attitude, which meant a willingness to use scientific and empirical methods. Further, these methods were to be applied to the problems of human society.

So it was the Enlightenment concepts of the scientific method, of reason, and of progress that formed the basis for the theories and practices that came from the educational reformers. As they sought to reform society, they tried to create a new kind of education and a new pattern of schooling based on equality, individualism, civic responsibility, and intellectual reasoning.[36] These efforts were to have a lasting influence on American education.

Reforming society

In the next chapter we turn to an examination of the educational contributions of the major pioneers of education—many from the Enlightenment era.

SUMMING UP

1. We have examined in historical context the questions dealing with the nature of teaching and learning that were formulated at the beginning of this chapter. What is knowledge? What is education? What is schooling? Who should attend school? How should teaching be carried on? Clearly, some of the answers to these questions given by educators in the past have influenced our own responses in the present. Often the historical responses to these questions were incomplete and ambiguous. Moreover, these answers varied from time to time and place to place. In many respects, contemporary educators still are attempting to answer these important but difficult questions.

2. The origins of American education are to be found in the European educational experience. In ancient Greece the concepts of the educated man, of rational inquiry, and of freedom of thought were enunciated by Socrates, Plato, and Aristotle. The idea of rhetorical education was developed by the Sophists, refined by Isocrates, and further elaborated by the Roman rhetoricians, Cicero and Quintilian.

36 J. J. Chambliss, ed., *Enlightenment and Social Progress: Education in the Nineteenth Century* (Minneapolis: Burgess, 1971); Durkheim, *The Evolution of Educational Thought.*

3. During the medieval period the foundations of the modern university were established at Bologna and Paris. The concept of the well-rounded, liberally educated man was developed by the classical humanist educators of the Renaissance. With its emphasis on literacy and vernacular education, the Protestant Reformation had a direct impact on the schools that were established in colonial America.

4. The birth of the United States as a republic was rooted in the political, social, and educational concepts of the Enlightenment.

DISCUSSION QUESTIONS

1. What is your definition of education? How does your definition agree or differ with that of the educational theorists discussed in this chapter?

2. Discuss five educators treated in this chapter on the basis of their contribution to modern educational theory.

3. How has the concept of the teacher changed through history? Use evidence from the chapter to support your argument.

4. What educational idea treated in this chapter is most relevant to your preparation for teaching? What educational idea is most irrelevant?

5. Describe a problem that you have experienced in your own education. Choose two educational theorists treated in this chapter and indicate how they would go about solving your problem.

THINGS TO DO

1. Read a biography of one of the educators treated in this chapter.

2. Write a short history of your own education. Identify causes, events, or teachers that had a pronounced influence on your educational ideas.

3. Attend a motion picture or watch a television program that portrays teaching in a fictional setting. What concept of teaching is portrayed? How does this portrayal relate to the theorists treated here?

4. Identify a course other than the one for which you are reading this book. Examine the historical origins of this course.

5. Choose one of the educators treated in this chapter. Present a lesson to the class based on this educator's method of instruction.

CHAPTER 6
PIONEERS IN EDUCATION

Focusing questions

What constitutes an educational pioneer?

What have been the major obstacles to change in education?

How did the pioneers modify the traditional concepts of the child and the curriculum? What major innovations in teaching and learning did they bring about?

How have the pioneers expanded the definitions of knowledge, education, schooling, teaching, and learning?

How do the educational models of the various pioneers contribute to contemporary educational reform?

Many distinguished individuals have contributed to educational theory and practice, but it is not possible to treat them all here. Therefore, judgment must be made on the basis of two criteria: How was the person a pioneer in education? What is the significance of the educator's work for you as a future teacher? Educational history provides the means for identifying those pioneers who were the first or earliest to work in the field of educational theory and practice and who succeeded in opening that field to further development by others.

But how significant are such pioneers for today's teachers? You can best answer that question by considering how these educational pioneers might have answered the global questions raised at the beginning of Chapter 5. By examining the contributions of these educational pioneers, we might gain further insights into such issues.

THE TRANS-ATLANTIC INFLUENCES

Before turning directly to the study of these educational pioneers, it is important to remember that education in the United States has been influenced by pedagogical developments that took place in Europe. While certain aspects of the American common school and high school movements are unique to historical, social, economic, and political developments in the United States, other aspects of the development of American education reveal a trans-Atlantic influence. By examining the educational contributions of such pedagogical pioneers as Comenius, Locke, Rousseau, Pestalozzi, Froebel, Herbart, Spencer, and Montessori, it is possible to appreciate the significance of this influx of educational theories and practices.

European
influence on
our schools

Although there were differences in the educational methods developed by these major European educational theorists, some parallel patterns can be identified. First of all, the work of such naturalistic educators as Comenius, Rousseau, Pestalozzi, and Spencer challenged the older view of child depravity and passive learning that had long dominated schooling. The theory of child depravity held the child to be evil at birth, and it stressed that corruptive weakness could be corrected by a strong teacher who used authoritarian teaching methods.

Child depravity
theory

In contrast, the naturalistic educators believed that the child was innately good. Concerned with examining the child's nature, they believed that the stages of human growth and development provided clues for the development of educational method. These pioneering educators came to be called "naturalistic" because they believed that children learn by working with and by examining the objects in their immediate natural environment. The stress on the educative impact of the environment was a theme that would be carried forward by such later American progressive educators as John Dewey and George Counts. Froebel's kindergarten and

Innate
goodness
theory

Montessori's prepared environment represent deliberate attempts to create learning situations that respect and utilize the child's own rate and pace of development.

These educational pioneers initiated instructional change. Others examined the social and political context of education. John Locke, Herbert Spencer, John Dewey, George Counts, Booker T. Washington, and W. E. B. Du Bois were concerned with the political, social, and economic relationships of education. Finally, critics such as John Holt and Ivan Illich provide a challenging look at a future in which schooling is divorced from humane education.

**Political, social
and economic
factors**

COMENIUS: THE SEARCH FOR A NEW METHOD

Jan Komensky (1592-1670), known as Comenius, was born in the Moravian town of Nivnitz. His family were members of the Moravian Brethren, a small, frequently persecuted sect of Protestants. Young Comenius attended the Brethren's vernacular school, where he studied the conventional elementary curriculum of reading, writing, singing, arithmetic, and catechism. He attended a Latin preparatory school and then went on to the University of Heidelberg in Germany. Upon completing his education, Comenius returned to his native province to pursue a career as a teacher and administrator in the Moravian schools, then later in Poland and the Netherlands. His educational theory contained pioneering ideas that stressed the establishment of a permissive school environment based on the natural principles of child growth and development.

**Permissive
school
environment**

As an educational reformer Comenius occupied a middle position between the humanist educators and the naturalistic reformers. While he still emphasized the teaching of Latin, he wanted it to be learned by natural means. Since language, especially Latin, was necessary to acquire universal knowledge, Comenius wanted to make language instruction both interesting and efficient. In his book *Gate of Tongues Unlocked,* he approached the study of Latin through the learner's own vernacular.[1] Beginning with short, simple phrases, the student gradually progressed toward more complicated sentences. He also prepared a picture book for the teaching of Latin, *The Visible World in Pictures,* consisting of pictures that designated objects in both their Latin and vernacular names.[2] The picture of the object combined language learning with sense perception. Note that Comenius was beginning to emphasize sensory experience in learning. This tendency toward sensory learning would grow and receive further emphasis in the work of Locke, Rousseau, and Pestalozzi.

**Language and
sensory
learning**

[1] See Jean Piaget, ed., *John Amos Comenius on Education* (New York: Teachers College Press, Columbia University, 1967); John Sadler, ed., *Comenius* (New York: Macmillan, 1969).

2 *The Orbis Pictus of John Amos Comenius* (Syracuse, N.Y.: Bardeen, 1887).

*PRINCIPLES
OF CHILD
DEVELOPMENT*   Comenius sought to develop an efficient method of instruction based on the principles of child growth.[3] He believed that nature revealed certain patterns of growth and development that should be followed in educational methodology. Teachers, he argued, should recognize that children have stages of readiness for specific kinds of learning. Materials and instruction should be based on these developmental stages. Since nature was orderly and gradual, instruction should be organized carefully into easily assimilated steps so that learning might be gradual, cumulative, and pleasant.

One of Comenius' most important methodological principles was his belief that instruction should parallel the appropriate stage of human development. Instruction should be arranged according to four six-year periods: (1) infancy, when education is informal and centered primarily in the home; (2) childhood, when learning takes place in the formal school; (3) adolescence, when the student is exposed to the learning of Latin; and (4) youth, when the student attends to the higher studies of the university.

Stages of growth and development

Among his pioneering contributions to education was his effort to develop teaching methods that paralleled inductive reasoning and the general pattern of human growth and development. His nine principles of teaching reflect his concern for the inductive method and for logical relationships: (1) teaching should involve presenting the object or idea in a concrete and direct way, not merely through symbols or concepts; (2) teaching should involve practical application to everyday life; (3) whatever is taught should be presented in a straightforward and uncomplicated way; (4) whatever is taught should be related to its true nature and origin; (5) general principles should be taught first; then details may be considered; (6) all things should be learned with reference to the whole and to how the parts are connected; (7) things should be taught in succession, and one thing at a time; (8) the teacher should not leave a specific subject until it is completely understood; and (9) differences among things should be taught so that the knowledge that is acquired may be clear.[4]

Principles of teaching

While many believed children were inherently bad and that strict corporal punishment was the best discipline to be used in managing schools, Comenius sought to enlist gentle and loving persons as teachers. He also argued that schools should be joyful and pleasant places.

Rejection of corporal punishment

Knowledge and school   For Comenius, education was to be carried on according to natural principles. Like other creatures in nature, human beings follow patterns of natural growth and development. Since natural development is slow and cumulative, education should be a slow

3 M. W. Keatinge, ed. and trans., *Comenius* (New York: McGraw-Hill, 1931); Keatinge, *The Great Didactic of John Amos Comenius* (London: Adam Black, 1896).
4 Edward J. Power, "Comenius: The Champion of Realism" in *Evolution of Educational Doctrine: Major Educational Theorists of the Western World* (New York: Appleton-Century-Crofts, 1969), pp. 238–41.

and gradual process. Comenius did not believe that the child should be hurried, coerced, or forced to learn before he or she was ready to do so.

In his own lifetime Comenius was a well-known and respected educator. He believed that teaching methods should emphasize the use of the child's interests and should actively involve the senses; in fact, he emphasized sensation as a basis of learning. The teacher should be a patient and permissive person who gently leads children to use and to understand the world in which they live. Such later educational theorists as Rousseau and Pestalozzi would follow Comenius' pioneering work in the field of naturalistic education.

Child's interest and senses

LOCKE: EMPIRICIST EDUCATOR

John Locke (1632–1704) was an English scholar, physician, scientist, and philosopher.[5] As a member of the Whig political party, Locke opposed the machinations of King James II to impose an absolute monarchy in England. After the Glorious Revolution of 1688, which exiled King James II, Locke gained prominence as the foremost philosophical champion of religious toleration and political liberalism. This section examines his ideas on knowledge, politics, and education.

Locke's major philosophical contribution, *An Essay Concerning Human Understanding*, published in 1690, examined the epistemological question of how we acquire ideas.[6] Locke held that at birth the human mind is a blank slate, a *tabula rasa*, empty of ideas. We acquire knowledge, he argued, from the information about the world that our senses bring to us. Through sensation, we learn about the objects in the environment. Simple ideas become more complex through comparison, reflection, and generalization. Locke was a pioneer of the inductive, or scientific, method. His empirical theory of knowledge had tremendous educational implications. He questioned the long-standing traditional view that knowledge came exclusively from literary sources, particularly the Greek and Latin classics. He also argued that learning was an active process that used the senses to investigate and acquire data about the world. Locke's stress on studying objects present in the environment was shared and developed further by Rousseau, Pestalozzi, and Dewey. Later educators would use Locke's pioneering ideas as they came to advocate the scientific method as the best approach for teaching and learning.

Blank slate

Inductive or scientific method

Locke's interests extended into political questions. His outstanding work on political philosophy was *Two Treatises of Government*, which

5 Robert Rusk and James Scotland, *Doctrines of the Great Educators* (New York: St. Martin's, 1979).

6 John Locke, *An Essay Concerning Human Understanding*, ed., R. Wilburn (New York: Dutton, 1947).

appeared in 1689. In it, he opposed the "divine right of kings" theory, which held that the monarch had the right to be an unquestioned and absolute ruler over his subjects. Locke argued that political order should be based on a contract between the people and the government, which ruled by the consent of those who had established it. He asserted that all human beings possessed inalienable rights of life, liberty, and property. **Inalienable rights** Locke's political philosophy contributed to the concept of representative government and to the system of checks and balances between the legislative, executive, and judicial branches of government that would later characterize the American political system. His theories inspired Thomas Jefferson and the other founders of the American republic.

Locke's political theory implied that the people were to establish their own government and select their own political leaders. No longer were aristocrats destined by birth to be rulers—the people were to elect their own leaders from among themselves. Locke's concept meant that the people should be educated to govern themselves intelligently and responsibly, which became a major theme in the nineteenth-century American common school movement and remains a major responsibility of American public schools.

Knowledge and school   In another treatise, *Some Thoughts Concerning Education*, written in 1697, Locke recommended utilitarian and practical learning.[7] Since it was a powerful force in shaping the course of a person's life, a good education, he reasoned, should cultivate the ability to manage social, economic, and political affairs in a practical manner. **Utilitarian and practical learning**

Specifically, Locke believed that a sound education began very early in a child's life. Stressing the maxim of a sound mind in a strong and healthy body, Locke directed attention to a child's physical environment, diet, and activities. Children should breathe fresh air, have plenty of sleep, eat light and plain food, bathe frequently, exercise regularly, and have time for play and recreation.

Learning, Locke insisted, should be a gradual process. The child's instruction in reading, writing, and arithmetic should be slow, gradual, and cumulative. Beyond the basics, Locke's curricular recommendations included conversational learning of foreign languages, especially French; mathematics; and the study of civil government through history. Physical education, games, and athletics were to be continued. Locke's educational goal was to cultivate the person who was ethical, would manage economic affairs prudently, and would participate in government effectively. **Slow and cumulative learning**

7   Peter Gay, *John Locke on Education* (New York: Teachers College Press, Columbia University, 1964); Adolphe E. Meyer, *Grandmasters of Educational Thought* (New York: McGraw-Hill, 1975).

**ROUSSEAU:
THE NATURAL
PERSON**

Jean Jacques Rousseau (1712-1778), a Swiss-born French theorist, profoundly influenced social, political, and educational ideas. Rousseau studied for a variety of careers but achieved fame as a social and educational philosopher. His works, *On the Origin of the Inequality of Mankind* and *The Social Contract*, state that the distinctions based on wealth, property, and prestige that give rise to social inequalities are artificial.[8] In the original state of nature, humankind had been free and uncorrupted but it was these artificialities of society that corrupted people. Property had produced inequalities, and government and other institutions had legitimized these artificial distinctions.

Rousseau's most famous educational treatise is his novel, *Emile*, written in 1762, which tells the story of the education of a boy from infancy to adulthood.[9] Rousseau's novel is an attack on the doctrine of child depravity and on exclusively verbal and literary education. Such doctrines and practices, he felt, ignored the child's natural interests and inclinations. Society has imprisoned us in a set of institutions. The child needs to be freed from one of the most coercive of these institutions—the school.

*The child's
natural
interests*

**PRINCIPLES
OF CHILD
DEVELOPMENT**

Like Comenius, Rousseau recognized stages of human growth and development. For Rousseau, there are five stages of growth: infancy, childhood, boyhood, adolescence, and youth. Each stage requires an appropriate kind of education to stimulate further development and growth. Most important, the early and formative stages of growth are to be free from the corruption of society. Emile, the subject of Rousseau's novel, was to be educated by a tutor on a country estate away from the blandishments and temptations of a ruinous society.

*Stages of
growth*

Rousseau's first stage, infancy (from birth to five), sees the human being as essentially helpless and dependent on others. The infant needs freedom to move and to exercise his body. He needs to make his first contacts with the objects of the environment. The infant's diet should be simple but nourishing.

During childhood (from five to twelve) the child is growing physically stronger. He is beginning to develop his own personality as he becomes aware that his actions have either painful or pleasurable consequences. During this stage the child is egotistical but also curious. He explores the environment and learns about the world through his senses. Rousseau calls the person's eyes, ears, hands, and feet the first teachers.

*Pain and
pleasure*

---

8   Jean Jacques Rousseau, *The First and Second Discourses*, ed., R. D. Masters (New York: St. Martin's, 1964): Rousseau, *The Social Contract*, rev. ed. (Baltimore: Penguin, 1969).

9   William Boyd, *The Emile of Jean Jacques Rousseau* (New York: Teachers College Press, Columbia University, 1962).

These natural teachers are far better and more efficient than the schoolmaster who teaches words that the learner does not comprehend; they are better than the silence of the schoolroom and the rod of the master. Emile's tutor did not attempt to introduce books at this stage. Reading was not substituted for the child's own direct experience with nature.

During boyhood, ages twelve to fifteen, the boy's bodily strength is still increasing. Nature, still the best teacher, gives instruction in science and geography. By watching the cycles of growth and development of plants and animals, Emile learned natural science. By exploring his surroundings, he learned geography far more realistically than he could have by the study of maps. Emile now read *Robinson Crusoe,* the story of a man marooned on an island who had to meet nature on its own terms. He also learned a manual trade so that he could understand the relationship between mental and physical work.

Nature as the best teacher

Next, in Rousseau's developmental schema, comes the years of adolescence, fifteen to eighteen. During these years Emile returned to society. Becoming aware of and interested in sex, he asked his tutor questions about human sexuality. His questions were to be answered honestly, directly, and sincerely by the tutor. Now that Emile had experienced a natural education, he was ready to cope with the outside world. He needed to be aware of society, government, economics, and business. His aesthetic tastes, too, were cultivated by visiting museums, art galleries and libraries and by attending the theatre. During the last stage of education, from eighteen to twenty, Emile traveled to Paris and to foreign countries to see different peoples and societies.

Interacting with society

Rousseau was a true pioneer; he challenged existing conventions and sought to destroy those that he felt impeded human freedom and progress. Rousseau was decidedly romantic and preferred the spontaneous, primitive, and emotional person to the rational and scientific individual. His personal bent was to demolish restrictive and coercive social institutions and customs.

Knowledge and school   For Rousseau, knowledge was based on sensations and feelings. Preferring the natural to the social, Rousseau stressed the human instincts as the means to knowledge. He was definitely opposed to relying on books as the pathways to truth. It was far better, he believed, to rely on direct and immediate experience with nature than to seek wisdom through the indirect source of the printed page.

Unlike the classical humanists, who equated education and schooling, Rousseau carefully separated the two. Like the contemporary advocates of deschooling, Rousseau believed that the school as an institution often interferes with and impedes learning. As a social institution the school puts the child into a social straightjacket that confines him to socially accepted customs, manners, and ideas. Rousseau wanted to liberate the child and adult from artificial social restrictions. His Emile was a child

Schools impede learning

of nature who followed his impulses and acted on them. If pleasure was the result, then Emile earned his own reward. If his actions brought pain, then Emile brought these consequences upon himself.

Rousseau's *Emile* exerted a strong influence on the development of western education. He directly influenced Johann, who put Rousseau's ideas into a more methodological and group-centered context. In the United States, Rousseau's impact was strong on such child-centered progressive educators as Francis Parker and Marietta Johnson, who elaborated a pedagogy based on the child's interests, needs, and inclinations.

Influential, progressive educators

PESTALOZZI: THEORETICIAN, EXPERIMENTER

The Swiss educator Johann Pestalozzi (1747–1827) had been an attentive reader of Rousseau's *Emile*. He agreed with Rousseau's basic contentions that human beings are naturally good but spoiled by the contagion of a corruptive society, that traditional schooling was a dull mess of deadening memorization and recitation, and that a pedagogical reformation could lead to social reform. A natural society could arise based upon the foundation created by a natural education.[10]

Natural education

Pestalozzi established an educational institute at Burgdorf to educate children and prepare teachers. Here he worked to devise a more efficient method of group instruction. He taught spelling by having the children begin with the shortest words and then proceed to longer ones by gradual and cumulative steps. Concrete objects, such as pebbles and beans, were used to teach counting. After becoming familiar with the basic mathematical processes, the children were introduced to the numbers that represented the quantities of the objects that they had counted earlier. The first writing exercises consisted of drawing lessons in which the children made a series of rising and falling strokes and open and closed curves. These exercises were intended to exercise the hand muscles and thus prepare the child for writing. The school's atmosphere was generally permissive and there were physical exercises, play activities, and nature study walks.[11]

Permissive school atmosphere

GENERAL AND SPECIAL METHODS

Pestalozzi's method of education can be divided into the "general" and the "special" methods. The general method is of great importance since it was used prior to the special method. In working with orphans, with the vic-

---

10 Robert B. Downs, *Heinrich Pestalozzi: Father of Modern Pedagogy* (Boston: Twayne Publishers, 1975); Gerald L. Gutek, *Pestalozzi and Education* (New York: Random House, 1968).

11 Johann Pestalozzi, *How Gertrude Teaches Her Children* (Syracuse, N.Y.: Bardeen, 1900).

tims of poverty and ignorance, and with those who might be called the
"disadvantaged" of the nineteenth century, Pestalozzi felt that—in order
to be effective—schools needed to be like secure and loving homes. The
general method called for educators who were loving persons, who were
emotionally secure, and who could contribute to the emotional health of
students by winning their trust and affection.

Warm and emotionally secure teachers

Once the general method had brought about the right emotional pre-
dispositions, then Pestalozzi used the special method. Since he believed
that all learning comes through the senses, all teaching should likewise be
sensory. To this end, Pestalozzi devised the object lesson. Children would
study the common objects found in their environment. They would study
the plants, rocks, artifacts, and objects which they saw and lived with in
their daily experience. The object lesson of the special method consisted of
three basic sorts of learnings: form, number, and sound. The children
would determine the form of the object and would draw and trace the form
or shape. They would count the objects and then name them.

Sensory learning

From the lessons in form, number, and sound came the more formal
exercises in drawing, writing, counting, adding, subtracting, multiply-
ing, dividing, and reading. The basic methodological innovation was that
Pestalozzi insisted that learning begin with the senses rather than with
words. Actually, he was following Rousseau's injunction that mere verbal
learning or abstract lessons are futile. Like Rousseau, Pestalozzi urged
that lessons be based on sense experience originating in the learner's
home and family life. This basic innovation became an important part of
progressive school reform in the twentieth century. It is also an obvious
part of the current school reforms based on the work of the British primary schools.

Pestalozzi was concerned that instruction should follow the ways of
nature. He developed a set of instructional strategies that are usually identified with Pestalozzian pedagogy. Instruction, he urged, should: (1) begin
with the concrete object before introducing abstract concepts; (2) begin
with the learner's immediate environment before dealing with that which
is distant and remote; (3) begin with easy exercises before introducing
complex ones; and (4) always proceed gradually, cumulatively, and
slowly.[12]

From concrete to abstract

Knowledge and school   As an educational pioneer, Rousseau had
attacked schools as social institutions that chained humankind to conventional thinking. Like Rousseau, Pestalozzi wanted to base learning on
natural principles and stressed the importance of the human emotions.
Unlike Rousseau, however, Pestalozzi did not abandon the school but
rather tried to reform it.

12   William H. Kilpatrick, *Johann Heinrich Pestalozzi: The Education of Man* (New York:
Philosophical Library, 1951); Mary R. Walch, *Pestalozzi and the Pestalozzian Theory of Education* (Washington, D.C.: Catholic University Press, 1952).

Rousseau and Pestalozzi were both naturalistic educators who believed that nature was the source of knowledge. To know, for Pestalozzi, meant to be involved with and to understand nature, its patterns, and its laws. Pestalozzi also had much in common with John Locke. Both stressed the empirical method of learning, through which human beings come to know their environment by actively using their senses in carefully observing natural phenomena.

Empirical
learning

Pestalozzi is significant to teachers also because he stressed methodology. Learning could be efficient and enjoyable if it were based on nature's own method. Like Comenius, Pestalozzi felt that the child should learn in a slow and precise manner, understanding thoroughly that which he or she was studying. Since nature appears to human perception in the form of objects, then Pestalozzi reasoned that the object lesson is the correct way to teach children about reality.

Devoted to
disadvantaged
learners

While Pestalozzi believed that all children should attend school, he was especially dedicated to those who were poor, hungry, and socially or psychologically maladjusted. If children were hungry, Pestalozzi fed them before he attempted to teach them. If they were frightened, Pestalozzi comforted and loved them. For him a teacher was not only a person who was skilled in instructional methodology but was also one who was capable of loving all children. In fact, Pestalozzi believed that love of mankind was necessary for successful teaching.

Impact on American education   Pestalozzi's ideas and methods had a great impact on the course of western and American education. William Maclure and Joseph Neef, in the early nineteenth century, and Henry Barnard, U.S. Commissioner of Education in the late nineteenth century, worked to introduce Pestalozzian ideas into the United States. Barnard's *Pestalozzi and Pestalozzianism* introduced American educators to the basic principles of the new method of instruction.[13] Edward Sheldon also was a major figure in introducing Pestalozzi's object lesson.[14] Horace Mann and William Woodward, who were among the leaders of the American common school movement, were familiar with Pestalozzianism and sought to incorporate its tenets into school practice. The impact of Pestalozzi has been a continuing one. Many of the educational reforms associated with the progressive movement in American education exhibit the Pestalozzian imprint. For example, the stress on the environment, the use of concrete objects, and the cultivation of sensory experience were all progressive emphases that had been anticipated by the Swiss pedagogue. When the focus of American educators came to center on the education of disadvantaged children, Pestalozzi's ideas took on a special relevance. His emphasis on emotional security as a precondition of skill learning bore a

Impact on
American
progressive
education

13   Henry Barnard, *Pestalozzi and Pestalozzianism* (New York: Brownell, 1862).

14   Ned H. Dearborn, *The Oswego Movement in American Education* (New York: Teachers College Press, Columbia University, 1925).

strong resemblance to the need for the close school-home relationships that many urban educators advocate.

FROEBEL: THE KINDERGARTEN MOVEMENT

Friedrich Froebel (1782–1852), a German educator, is known for his introduction of a school for early childhood education—the kindergarten, or child's garden.[15] Froebel, the son of a Lutheran minister, was born in the German state of Thuringia. His mother died when he was only nine months old. As a mature person, Froebel frequently reflected on his childhood and youth. He believed that those who were to be teachers should continually think back to the days of their own childhood to find insights that could be applied to their teaching. Like Pestalozzi, with whom he studied, Froebel was very shy as a child and highly introspective as an adult.

Student of Pestalozzi

He worked as a forester, a chemist's assistant, and a museum curator before turning to an educational career. His attraction to teaching led him to Pestalozzi's Institute at Yverdon, where he interned from 1808 to 1810. He accepted certain aspects of Pestalozzi's method: the reliance on nature as the chief educator, the permissive school atmosphere, and the object lesson. Froebel believed, however, that Pestalozzi had not established an adequate philosophical underpinning for his theory. Froebel gave the object lesson a more symbolic meaning in that the concrete object was to stimulate recall of a corresponding idea in the child's mind.

Like Pestalozzi, Froebel was determined to improve the educational methods of teaching. Both protested vigorously against teaching children ideas that they did not understand. They believed that the teacher must become an active instructor instead of a hearer and taskmaster of individual recitations.

Active teachers

THE KINDERGARTEN

In 1837 Froebel founded the kindergarten in the city of Blankenburg. It emphasized games, play, songs, and crafts, and subsequently attracted a number of visitors. Froebel's kindergarten was to be a prepared environment in which the first formal learning of the child would be based on self-activity. The kindergarten teacher was to be a moral and cultural model or exemplar who was worthy of the child's love and trust. Froebel readily accepted the Pestalozzian concept of the general method of emotional security for the child, but he raised it to a spiritual and highly symbolic level.[16]

Prepared environment

---

15 Irene M. Lilley, *Friedrich Froebel: A Selection from His Writings* (Cambridge, Mass.: Harvard University Press, 1967).

16 Robert B. Downs, *Friedrich Froebel* (Boston: Twayne Publishers, 1978).

The kindergarten curriculum had as its objective the cultivation of the child's self-development, self-activity, and socialization. It included songs, stories, games, "gifts," and "occupations." The songs, stories, and games, generally a part of early childhood education, were to stimulate the child's imagination and to introduce the child to the customs, heroes, and ideas of the cultural heritage. Games provided the cooperative activities that socialized children and developed their physical and motor skills. As the boys and girls played with other children, they became part of the group and were prepared for further group learning activities. As they played the various games, they also developed coordination and physical dexterity. Froebel's "gifts" consisted of objects whose form was fixed, such as spheres, cubes, and cylinders. The gifts were designed to stimulate children to bring to full consciousness the latent concept that was implied in the object. The kindergarten "occupations" consisted of materials that could be shaped by the children and used in designs and construction activity. For example, clay, sand, cardboard, and mud could be manipulated and shaped into castles, cities, and mountains.[17] Together these activities were to serve as the learning environment; they were to be the garden in which children could grow naturally and correctly in a prepared environment.

Gifts and occupations

Knowledge and school For most of us, the kindergarten class was our first introduction to school. First impressions of schools and of teachers were acquired there. We noted earlier that Froebel encouraged teachers to reflect on their early childhood experiences. Through this kind of introspection they would come to understand their own childhood, and thus could gain insights and perspectives that would help them to understand young children. According to Froebel, the personality of the kindergarten teacher is paramount. The teacher should be a person who respects the dignity of human personality and who embodies the highest cultural values, so that children can imitate the values that they see represented in the teacher's own personality. Above all, the kindergarten teacher should be an approachable and open person.

Dignity of the child

The kindergarten is now an established part of American education. Immigrants who fled from Germany after the Revolution of 1848 brought the concept of the kindergarten with them. The wife of the German-American patriot Carl Schurz established a kindergarten in Watertown, Wisconsin in 1855. Elizabeth Peabody founded the first English-language kindergarten and a training school for kindergarten teachers in Boston in 1860. The kindergarten was given great encouragement by William Harris, Superintendent of Schools in St. Louis, Missouri, and later U.S. Commissioner of Education. Harris believed that the kindergarten was an im-

Influence on American educators

17 Friedrich Froebel, *The Education of Man*, trans. W. Hailmann (New York: Appleton, 1889).

portant first stage of the school system because it prepared the child for the order and routine of the elementary school.[18]

HERBART: MORAL AND INTELLECTUAL DEVELOPMENT

Johann Herbart (1776–1841) was a German philosopher known for his contributions to moral development in education and for his creation of a methodology of instruction designed to establish a highly structured mode of teaching. Herbart attended the conventional German schools and then went on to study philosophy at the University of Jena, where he worked with the famous professor Gottlieb Fichte. Early in Herbart's career, while he was a tutor in Switzerland, he became interested in the educational theory of Pestalozzi. In 1809 Herbart was appointed to the chair of philosophy at the University of Konigsberg. He now turned to serious scholarship and conducted a seminar in the psychological and philosophical aspects of education.[19]

PURPOSE OF EDUCATION

For Herbart the chief aim of education was moral development; it was basic and necessary to all other educational goals or purposes. The chief objective of Herbartian education was to produce the good person who had many interests. Herbart argued that virtue is founded on knowledge and that human beings do not deliberately choose evil. Misconduct is the product of inadequate knowledge or of inferior education. Thus, he gave education a vital role in shaping moral character. For Herbart moral education involved the presentation of ethical ideas to the child's mind. In elaborating his work on moral education, Herbart specified five major kinds of ideas as the foundations of moral character: (1) the idea of inner freedom, which referred to action based on one's personal convictions; (2) the idea of perfection, which referred to the harmony and integration of behavior; (3) the idea of benevolence, by which a person was to be concerned with the social welfare of others; (4) the idea of justice, by which a person reconciled his or her individual behavior with that of the social group; and (5) the idea of retribution, which indicates that reward or punishment accrues to certain kinds of behavior.

> Moral development

> Convictions, harmony, social welfare, justice, retribution

Drawing from his ideas on moral education, Herbart also specified two major bodies of interests that should be included in education: knowledge interests and ethical interests. Knowledge interests involve empirical data, factual information, and also speculative ideas. Knowledge interests were broadly conceived to include logic, mathematics, literature, music,

> Knowledge and ethics

---

18 Daniel Tanner and Laurel N. Tanner, *Curriculum Development*, 2nd ed. (New York: Macmillan, 1980); Evelyn Weber, *The Kindergarten: Its Encounter with Educational Thought in America* (New York: Teachers College Press, Columbia University, 1969).

19 Harold B. Dunkel, *Herbart and Education* (New York: Random House, 1969).

and art. Ethical interests included sympathy for others, social relationships, and religious sentiments. Herbart's aim was to produce an educated individual who was also of good character and high morals. He believed that if your cognitive powers are properly exercised and if your mind is stocked with ideas, then you will use that knowledge to guide your behavior. The person who lives and acts according to knowledge will be a moral person.

Knowledge and school   In terms of organizing instruction, Herbart developed the concepts of curriculum correlation. These were to have a decided impact on education in the United States. According to the doctrine of correlation, each subject should be taught in such a way that it refers to and relates to other subjects. Knowledge would then appear to the learner as an integrated system of ideas that forms an apperceptive mass—the whole of a person's previous experience—into which new ideas could be related. Herbart believed that the subjects of history, geography, and literature were ideally suited as core subjects.

Integrating
ideas

In the United States Herbartian pedagogical principles were accepted enthusiastically. The American Herbartians were especially interested in the formal steps of instruction. Herbart developed: (1) clearness, or the careful analysis and comprehension of each single fact or element of the lessons; (2) association, the relating of the facts with each other and with previously acquired information; (3) system, the ordering of ideas into a coherent system; and (4) method, the development of projects by the student that would involve the learning acquired in the earlier steps.[20]

Herbart's followers revised the four original steps and developed the well-known five phases of the Herbartian method that came to be popular in the United States. These five steps are: (1) preparation, by which the teacher stimulates the readiness of the learner for the new lesson by referring to materials that were learned earlier; (2) presentation, in which the teacher presents the new lesson to the students; (3) association, in which the new lesson is deliberately related to ideas or materials that were studied earlier; (4) systematization, which involves the use of examples to illustrate the principles or generalizations to be mastered by the student; and (5) application, which involves the testing of the new ideas or the materials of the new lesson to determine if the students have understood and mastered them.

Herbartian
method

Formal steps of
instruction

Herbart's formal steps of instruction also were applied to teacher training. In theory, the teacher would prepare by thinking of the five steps, asking: What do my students know? What questions should I ask? What events should I relate? What conclusions should be reached? How can students apply what they have learned? To a large extent, these principles still serve as the guidelines for today's classroom developmental lesson.

20   Johann F. Herbart, *Textbook of Psychology* (New York: Appleton, 1894).

SPENCER: UTILITARIAN EDUCATION

Herbert Spencer (1820–1903) was an English social theorist who sought to fit Charles Darwin's theory of biological evolution into a comprehensive sociological and educational theory. Spencer believed that human development had gone through an evolutionary series of stages from the simple to the complex and from the uniform to the more specialized kind of activity.[21] Social development had also taken place according to an evolutionary process by which simple, homogeneous societies had evolved to more complex societal systems, characterized by an increasing variety of specialized tasks. Spencer's theory of "Social Darwinism" was developed in the last half of the nineteenth century, when industrialization was indeed transforming American and western European societies into more complicated social systems characterized by specialized professions and occupations. Industrialized society required vocational and professional education that was based on scientific and practical (utilitarian) objectives rather than on the very general educational goals associated with humanistic and classical education.

Evolutionary stages of human development

In arguing for social ethics based on competitive principles, Spencer asserted that the fittest individuals of each generation would survive because of their skill, intelligence, and propensity to adapt to environmental requirements. Because of this competition, the fittest would inherit the earth and populate it with their intelligent and productive offspring. Those individuals who were lazy, stupid, or weak would slowly disappear. Thus, the doctrine of the survival of the fittest postulated that individual competition would engender socio-economic progress.

Survival of the fittest

Knowledge and school   Spencer's Social Darwinism and his advocacy of industrial society influenced his educational theory.[22] Like such naturalistic educational theorists as Rousseau, Pestalozzi, and Herbart, Spencer opposed the excessively verbal, literary, and classical education associated with traditional schooling. He believed that the traditional schools of England were impractical and ornamental; they failed to meet the needs of a modern industrial society.

Spencer dealt with the social and political bases of modern education and featured a curriculum based on science and utility.[23] The most valuable education, in Spencer's view, was based on the physical, biological, and social sciences. Spencer influenced curriculum construction by classifying and arranging human activities according to their priorities for advancing human survival and progress. According to Spencer's curriculum rationale: (1) educational priorities should be based on those hu-

Stress on the sciences

---

21 Richard Hofstadter, *Social Darwinism in American Thought* (Boston: Beacon Press, 1955).
22 Andreas Kazamias, *Herbert Spencer on Education* (New York: Teachers College Press, Columbia University, 1966).
23 Herbert Spencer, *Education: Intellectual, Moral and Physical* (New York: Appleton, 1881).

man activities that sustain life; (2) education that is valuable should prepare men and women to perform these activities efficiently; and (3) science should have curricular priority since it aids in the effective performance of life activities.

Spencer gave highest priority to the activities that contributed to self-preservation, since those were basic to all other activities. Since physical health was needed to perform all the other human activities, a scientific education should include knowledge of human physiology and health in order to combat disease. Indirectly supporting self-preservation are the activities connected to one's economic occupation or profession. The basic skills of reading, writing, and arithmetic have immediate utility. The populace of an industrial society requires an education that contributes to technological, industrial, and scientific efficiency. Expertise in the physical and biological sciences, the social sciences, and the applied and technological sciences is needed.

Self-preservation as a priority

To prepare students for social and political participation, Spencer recommended the study of sociology. He was a pioneer figure in developing the sociological foundations of educational theory and practice. He was also a significant educational modernizer who stressed scientific and utilitarian education as essential to an industrial society. The educated members of modern societies needed knowledge of the science of society, of how social progress occurs, and of sociopolitical structures. They needed to be able to formulate scientific generalizations from masses of sociological data. Spencer relegated aesthetic and literary cultivation to the least important area of the curriculum. Such activities, he felt, were for leisure and did not directly relate to sustaining life or to earning a living. The defenders of the classical and literary curriculum attacked Spencer for neglecting the knowledge that developed one's artistic and literary nature.

Scientific and utilitarian education

A consideration of Herbert Spencer's educational theory provides a number of insights into questions about knowledge, education, and schooling. In replying to his own question, "What knowledge is of most worth?" Spencer argued that scientific knowledge was most useful in dealing with practical economic, social, and political problems. His educational ideas, which were readily accepted in the United States, influenced the NEA Committee that published the Seven Cardinal Principles of Education in 1918.

WASHINGTON: FROM SLAVERY TO FREEDOM

Booker T. Washington (1858–1915) was the leading educational spokesman for Black Americans in the half century after the Civil War. As he recounts in his autobiography, *Up From Slavery,* Washington was a transitional figure who was born a slave, experienced the hectic decades of Reconstruction, and painfully articulated the out-

The Tuskegee Normal School was established in 1881 by Booker T. Washington. This history class met at Tuskegee in 1902.

lines of a compromise with the White power establishment with which he had to deal.[24] Today, Washington is a controversial figure in educational history. Some say he made the best of a bad situation. Although he compromised on racial issues, they say, he can be viewed as one who preserved and slowly advanced the educational opportunities of Black Americans. Critics see Washington as an opportunist whose compromises restricted the progress of Black Americans. In any event, Booker T. Washington should be judged in terms of the realities in which he lived.

Advanced opportunities of Blacks

As a student at Hampton Institute, Washington had studied the educational ideas of General S. Armstrong, who had established the Institute to prepare Black youth for teaching, agriculture, and industry. Armstrong argued that industrial education was an important force in building character and economic competence for Blacks. Washington subscribed generally to Armstrong's philosophy of moral and economic "uplift" through work.

"Uplift" through work

24 Booker T. Washington, *Up From Slavery* (New York: Doubleday, 1938).

In 1881, Washington was named to head the institute that the Alabama legislature had established in Tuskegee. Washington shaped the Tuskegee curriculum according to his perceptions of the living and working conditions of southern Blacks. Basically, he felt that southern Blacks faced the problem of being a landless agricultural class. The remedy, he believed, consisted of creating an economic base—primarily in farming but also in occupational trades—that would provide southern Blacks with some degree of economic security. His curriculum stressed basic academic, agricultural, and occupational skills. The essential values emphasized were those of hard work and the dignity of labor. Although he encouraged his students to be elementary school teachers, farmers, and artisans, he discouraged them from careers in medicine, law, and politics. The pursuit of these fields, he believed, was premature and would result in strife with the dominant White power structure in the South.

Academic, agricultural, and vocational skills

Washington, a popular platform speaker, developed a theory of racial relations that argued that Blacks and Whites were mutually dependent economically but could remain separate socially. In 1885, Washington summed up his philosophy in an address at the Cotton Exposition in Atlanta, Georgia, when he said, "In all things that are purely social, we can be as separate as the fingers, yet one as the hand in all things essential to mutual progress."[25]

DU BOIS: CHALLENGER TO THE SYSTEM

W. E. B. Du Bois (1869–1963) was a sociological and educational pioneer who challenged the established system of education that tended to restrict rather than to advance the progress of Black Americans.[26] Du Bois challenged what was often called the "Tuskegee machine" of Booker T. Washington. A sociologist and historian, Du Bois called for a more determined and activist leadership than was being provided by Washington.

Unlike Washington, whose roots were in southern black agriculture, Du Bois's career spanned both sides of the Mason-Dixon Line. He was a native of Massachusetts, received his undergraduate education from Fisk University in Nashville, did his graduate study at Harvard University, and directed the Atlanta University Studies of Black American life in the South. Du Bois approached the problem of racial relations in the United States from two dimensions: as a scholarly researcher and as an activist for civil rights. Among his works was the famous empirical sociological study, *The Philadelphia Negro: A Social Study*, in which he examined

Scholar and activist

25 Booker T. Washington, *Selected Speeches of Booker T. Washington* (New York: Doubleday, 1932), p. 34.
26 Virginia Hamilton, *W. E. B. Du Bois: A Biography* (New York: Crowell, 1972).

Repetitive exercises developed sensory and muscular coordination. The formal skills and subjects included reading, writing, and arithmetic. Children were introduced to the alphabet through the use of unmounted, movable sandpaper letters. Reading was taught after writing. Colored rods of various sizes were used in teaching measuring and counting. **Sensory and muscular coordination**

The preplanned materials designed to develop the practical, sensory, and formal skills included lacing and buttoning frames, weights, and packets to be identified by their sound or smell. The use of these didactic materials was to follow a prescribed method so that the child would obtain the desired skill mastery, sensory experience, or intellectual outcome. The emphasis on the prepared environment and the use of didactic materials made the Montessori teacher a director of activities, rather than a teacher in the conventional sense. He or she was to be a trained observer of children. Since the child in the Montessori school is primarily involved in individualized activity, the activities of the director are geared to each child rather than to group-centered teaching and learning. **Didactic materials**

Montessori method in the United States   Montessori education has experienced two periods of interest in the United States. The early enthusiasm for Montessorianism took place just before World War I. Montessori visited the United States in 1913 and lectured on her method. However, the criticisms of William Kilpatrick and other progressive educators weakened the movement and it declined after an initial burst of popularity.[31] Since the 1950s there has been a marked revival of Montessorian pedagogy and Montessori schools in the United States, coinciding with the rise of preprimary and early childhood education. In addition, the growing interest in Head Start education for the disadvantaged has stimulated a renewed interest in the methods of the Italian educator. It is difficult to assess the long-range significance of Montessorianism in American education. While it has stimulated the rise of numerous private schools and current public and governmental early-childhood programs, the Montessori method has not yet made a pervasive impact on teacher education in the United States. **Decline and then revival of interest**

Maria Montessori was an early-childhood educator who concentrated her efforts on improving learning opportunities for children. She resembled Pestalozzi in that she initially was concerned with educating the disadvantaged child. Like Pestalozzi, her methods proved so successful that they were applied to all children. She was also like Froebel in that she created a special setting for the child's first learning experiences. She believed that she had discovered the laws of learning through her careful observation of children's work and play activities. Her method of instruction was a carefully organized one that followed her discovery of the patterns of human growth and development.

31 William H. Kilpatrick, *The Montessori System Examined* (Boston: Houghton Mifflin, 1914).

DEWEY: LEARNING THROUGH EXPERIENCE

An examination of leading educational pioneers would be incomplete without some comments on John Dewey (1859–1952), the American philosopher and educator. Dewey was a pioneer whose synthesis of Darwinism's evolutionary theory, Pragmatic philosophy, and the scientific method formed the basis for his work as an educational reformer. There is no doubt that Dewey's ideas influenced the course of educational development in the United States and throughout the world. His concepts of learning by experience and by problem solving were particularly influential in American teacher education. Viewing education as a process of social activity, Dewey recognized that the school was intimately related to the society that it served.

Education as a social activity

Dewey was born in Vermont. After receiving his doctoral degree in philosophy from Johns Hopkins University in 1884 he taught philosophy at several universities. Dewey's years at the University of Chicago, where he headed the combined departments of philosophy, psychology, and pedagogy, were important for the development of his educational theory. As the director of the University of Chicago's Laboratory School from 1896 until 1904, he tested his Pragmatic educational philosophy by using it as the basis of learning activities.[32]

Dewey's well-known work, *The Child and the Curriculum*, provides a guide to the ideas that he used at the laboratory school.[33] Viewing children as socially active human beings, Dewey believed that learners want to explore their environment and gain control over it. In exploring their world, learners encounter both personal and social problems. It is the problematic encounter that leads children to use their intelligence to solve the difficulty—to use the collected knowledge of the human race in an active and instrumental manner.

Laboratory school

Dewey outlined three levels of activity that would be used at the school.[34] The first level, for preschool children, involved exercise of the sensory organs and development of physical coordination. The second stage involved use of the materials and instruments found in the environment. The school was to be rich in the raw materials that excited children's interests and caused them to build, to experiment, and to create. Children in the third stage discovered new ideas, examined them, and used them. Now learning moved from simple impulse to careful observation, planning, and the conjecturing of the consequences of action.[35]

Learning through activity

---

32 R. S. Peters, ed., *John Dewey Reconsidered* (Boston: Routledge & Paul, 1977); Arthur G. Wirth, *John Dewey as Educator: His Design for Work in Education, 1894-1904* (New York: Wiley, 1966).

33 John Dewey, *The Child and the Curriculum* (Chicago: University of Chicago Press, 1902).

34 Wirth, *Dewey as Educator*.

35 Ibid.

EDUCATIONAL
PHILOSOPHY
Dewey conceived of education as the social process by which the immature members of the group, especially the children, are brought to participate in the society.[36] The school is a special environment, established by the members of society, for the purpose of simplifying, purifying, and integrating the social experience of the group so that it can be understood, examined, and used by its children.

For Dewey education's sole purpose is to contribute to the personal and social growth of individuals. Growth is that reconstruction of experience that adds to the learner's ability to direct and control the course of subsequent experience. Solving problems according to the scientific method is the process by which one comes to control one's experience. For Dewey the scientific method is the process by which human beings think reflectively and publicly, and it is also the method of intelligence in teaching and learning. The following steps of the scientific or reflective method are extremely important in Dewey's educational theory:

Personal and social growth

Scientific method

1. The learner has a "genuine situation of experience"—involvement in an activity in which he or she is interested.

2. Within this experience the learner has a "genuine problem" that stimulates thinking.

3. The learner possesses the information or does research to acquire the information needed to solve the problem.

4. The learner develops possible and tentative solutions that may solve the problem.

5. The learner tests the solutions by applying them to the problem. In this way one discovers their validity for oneself.[37]

Knowledge and school   For Dewey knowledge was not an inert body of information but was rather an instrument to solve problems. The funded knowledge of the human race—past ideas, discoveries, and inventions—were to be used as the materials for dealing with problems. This accumulated wisdom of the cultural heritage was to be tested. If it served human purposes, it became part of a reconstructed experience.

Schools translate the cultural heritage

Education was the process by which an immature human being was introduced to the cultural heritage and used this heritage in dealing with his or her problems. Since both human beings and their environment constantly were changing, knowledge was also continually being reconstructed or repatterned in the light of present needs. Each time a person solved a problem as an individual and as a member of the human group, he or she added to the store of experience that could be used in the future.

36   John Dewey, *Democracy and Education* (New York: Macmillan, 1916).
37   Ibid., p. 192.

Dewey's concept of the school was social, scientific, and democratic. The school introduced children to society and their heritage based on each child's own interests, needs, and problems. The school as a miniature society was the means of bringing children into social participation. The school was scientific in the sense that it was a social laboratory in which children and youth could test their ideas and values. It was also scientific in a methodological sense; the learner was to acquire the disposition and procedures associated with scientific, or reflective, thinking and acting.

School as a miniature society

Dewey was an advocate of democratic education and schooling. A democratic criterion of education meant that the learner is to be free to test all ideas, beliefs, and values. Cultural heritage, customs, and institutions are all to be subject to critical inquiry, investigation, and reconstruction. As a democratic institution the school should be open and used by all. He opposed barriers of custom or prejudice that segregate people from each other. People ought to live, share, and work together to solve common problems. He opposed the authoritarian or coercive style of administration and teaching that blocked genuine inquiry; his ideal school was a place where children and teachers together planned the curriculum and activities that they would pursue and where there was enjoyment in teaching and learning.

Children and teachers plan together

COUNTS: BUILDING A NEW SOCIAL ORDER

George Counts (1889–1974) was an educational pioneer who believed that education was not based on eternal truths but was relative to a particular society living at a given time and place. Counts asked the profound but still unanswered question: "Dare the school build a new social order?"[38] A professor of education at Columbia University Teachers College, Counts asked this question in 1932, when the United States was gripped by a severe economic depression. He believed that the American schools needed to identify with such progressive forces as the labor unions, the farmers' organizations, and disadvantaged minority groups. By allying themselves with groups that wanted to change or reconstruct society, the schools would become an instrument for social improvement rather than an agency for preserving the status quo.

Reconstructing society

EDUCATION IN A CHANGING SOCIETY

Counts believed that education is always conditioned by the particular culture of a given society. American education, as a whole, reflected the American historical experience and needed to be re-

---

38 George S. Counts, *Dare the School Build a New Social Order?* (New York: John Day, 1932).

constructed to meet the social, economic, political, and ethical needs of the people of the United States.[39] The Industrial Revolution, by uniting science and industry, had created a technological society.[40] Counts concluded that the democratic and equalitarian ethic of the American heritage was an appropriate cultural value that ought to be stressed in the schools. But it needed to be reconstructed so that it had meaning in this modern technological society. The schools, Counts said, should emphasize the dynamic forces of democracy and technology in their curriculum and methods of instruction.

Democracy and equalitarian ideas

Counts was concerned that a cultural lag had developed between our material progress and our social institutions and ethical values. Material inventions and discoveries were dynamic and had pronounced effects on many other areas of life. Unfortunately, organized education had not developed a method for planning the course of social change.

Lag between materialism and ethics

Knowledge and school   Counts wanted the schools to stress a planning attitude and an engineering mentality so that students could begin to understand and cope with the problems of social change that arose from technology. If you think about the awesome effects of the discovery of nuclear power, then Counts's argument for a planning education takes on a special relevance. If mankind does not develop constructive plans for the use of nuclear energy, then the spectre of nuclear war has the potential of destroying the human race.

Counts urged teachers to lead society rather than follow it. As leaders they were to be policy makers who would have to choose between conflicting goals and values. In the broadest sense of the term, educational statesmanship would not only be concerned with school matters but would also have to make important choices in the controversial areas of economics, politics, and morality.[41] For Counts each generation of educators would be called upon to make these choices. If they failed to do so, then others would make these decisions for them.

Teachers as agents of change

For Counts, the school was a social agency that was involved in society's politics, economics, art, religion, and ethics. Involvement meant that the school could either reflect the knowledge, beliefs, and values of the society, or it could seek to change them. When schools reflected society, they were simply acting like a mirror that reflected an image. If schools were to be socially reconstructive, their involvement would be an active attempt to solve problems and not merely to reflect the status quo. If school-

39   Gerald L. Gutek, *The Educational Theory of George S. Counts* (Columbus, Ohio: Ohio State University Press, 1970).

40   George S. Counts, *Secondary Education and Industrialism* (Cambridge, Mass.: Harvard University Press, 1929).

41   Raymond E. Callahan, "George S. Counts: Educational Statesman" in R. J. Havighurst, ed., *Leaders in American Education*, Part II, National Society for the Study of Education (Chicago: University of Chicago Press, 1971), pp. 177-87.

teachers were to act as statesmen, then the solving of major social issues would result in a new social order.

Counts saw the democratic ethic as an enduring value of the American heritage. For him it was based on the social equality of the American people. Therefore, everyone had the right to attend school. Further, schools ought to provide an education that afforded equal learning opportunities.

Equal
opportunity

Counts believed that instruction should combine content and problem solving. Its content should emphasize the democratic heritage, science, and technology. It should also involve students in defining and solving such important issues as the elimination of poverty and racial discrimination, the remediation of environmental pollution, and the prevention of war. Counts's contributions as an educational pioneer were the questions he posed that brought teachers and students to positions of leadership on new frontiers of education.

HOLT AND ILLICH: THE RADICAL CRITICS

Among those who might be called educational pioneers in the future are contemporary critics who have urged pervasive revolutionary changes in education and schooling. These critics range from those who seek to liberate childhood from the restrictions imposed by a prescribed curriculum to those who see no hope for reform and want to eliminate the institutionalization of learning in schools. Among the radical critics of contemporary education are Paul Goodman, Herbert Kohl, Jonathan Kozol, John Holt, and Ivan Illich.[42] The concluding section will discuss two of these critics: John Holt and Ivan Illich. Holt was a critic who in the 1960s urged a humanistic liberalization of schooling. Illich, a more recent critic, seeks to end what he calls the school's monopoly over education.

Liberalization
of schooling

John Holt (1923-   ) began his teaching career as an elementary teacher in large city school systems and in middle- and upper-middle-class private schools. He found his efforts at innovation were often limited and frustrated by "mindless" rules and regulations, by irrelevant traditions, and by inflexible administrators. Holt, in many respects a modern Rousseau, wanted to open the classrooms by creating a climate in which children were free to act on their own creative needs and impulses. His discontent with contemporary school structures led him to write such books as *How Children Fail, How Children Learn, The Underachieving School,* and *What Do I Do Monday?*

"Mindless"
rules and
regulations

42   For representative works, see Paul Goodman, *Growing Up Absurd* (New York: Random House, 1960); Herbert Kohl, *The Open Classroom* (New York: Random House, 1969); Jonathan Kozol, *Death at an Early Age* (Boston: Houghton Mifflin, 1967).

FAILING SCHOOLS　　　In *How Children Fail*, Holt identified a
CAN BE IMPROVED　　　number of obstacles that schools—as institutions—sometimes erect that impede the learning of children.[43] The
school's tendency to enforce rote learning and bureaucratic routine may
block, rather than stimulate, a child's creativity and curiosity. Often
teachers become guardians of knowledge who want the right answers
instead of stimulators of learning who pose open-ended questions. Holt
argued that schooling actually encourages *producers*—children whose
major goal is to please adults—rather than *thinkers* and problem solvers.
To Holt, many conventional schools force students into a prison-like existence where they follow meaningless procedures to answer meaningless
questions.

**Educating
thinkers, not
producers**

　　After trying for several years to reform American schools, Holt began to advocate a radical remaking of American education. Essentially, he
wanted to humanize schools. In *Freedom and Beyond*, Holt argued for an
open learning environment.[44] In such a free classroom climate, children
would create their own curriculum. Holt would discard a rigidly prescribed curriculum for an open classroom that provides children with a
wide range of options for alternative learning. To foster open environments for learning, Holt argued that for schools to be open environments for learning, they must cast off their functions of indoctrination
and selection. They must no longer function as sorting machines that
work in a factory-like way to force students to conform to prescribed
molds.

**Humanizing
schools**

DESCHOOLING　　　Ivan Illich (1926) is a radical educational
SOCIETY　　　critic who has gone beyond Holt in his
plans for the remaking of schools. Illich has argued that the creating of a
new society requires the prior deschooling of society.[45] Because of his
revolutionary proposal, Illich has become the center of controversy. He
differs from most of the educational pioneers discussed in this chapter
because he has rejected the school as an agency of education, while the
others have sought to reform the school so that it could educate more
effectively. Despite his rejection of the school, Illich may be considered a
pioneer in education because his theory has opened a new line of thought
that would bring about radical change if it were implemented. He is also a
leader in the sense that he has stimulated large numbers of disciples to
further the work of deschooling.[46]

**Eliminating
schools**

43　John Holt, *How Children Fail* (New York: Pitman, 1964).
44　John Holt, *Freedom and Beyond* (New York: Dutton, 1972).
45　Ivan Illich, *Deschooling Society* (New York: Harper & Row, 1970).
46　Alan Gartner, Colin Greer, and Frank Riessman, eds., *After Deschooling, What?* (New
York: Harper & Row, 1973).

Illich was born in Vienna. After ordination as a Roman Catholic priest and some years of advanced studies, he was assigned to do pastoral work in the Puerto Rican community in New York City.[47] For a time he was vice-chancellor of the Catholic University in Puerto Rico. His proposals for deschooling society were developed at the Center for Intercultural Documentation (CIDOC), which he established in Mexico.

Illich's basic thesis is that attempts to reform schools are futile and that schools should be abolished. (The school is seen as a coercive, discriminatory, and destructive agency of society.) The elimination of the schools, as institutions, would be the first step in operating a de-institutionalized social order. It is crucial, Illich asserts, that education be disengaged from schooling. If schools were eliminated, education could be open to all and could become a genuine instrument of human liberation. Learners would no longer have an obligatory curriculum imposed upon them; they would be liberated from institutionalized indoctrination. There would no longer be discrimination based on possession of a certificate or a diploma. Further, the public would no longer be forced to support a large bureaucratic school establishment through a system of regressive taxation.

Schools are coercive and discriminatory

Knowledge without skills   In attacking the myth of schooling, Illich asserts that learning is a continuous process; it occurs as people pursue their interests and seek to satisfy their needs and solve their problems; it is not confined to school walls. In fact, Illich argues that students do most of their real learning outside schools without and often in spite of teachers. What really happens in schools as a result of compulsory attendance laws is that students are indoctrinated to believe that they need to attend school; he affirms that schools should not be compulsory.

Real learning without teachers

Rather than equating schooling and learning, Illich defines learning as occurring when a person gains a new skill or insight. Instruction is viewed as the choice of circumstances that facilitates learning. In place of schools, Illich recommends the following four learning webs or networks to facilitate the public's access to educational objects, persons, and situations: (1) reference services to educational objects; (2) peer matching; (3) skill exchanges; and (4) reference services to "educators-at large." In other words, educational objects and persons should no longer be controlled by schools but should be available to learners in a public but noninstitutional way.

Learning networks to replace schools

Illich broadly defines *educational objects* to mean such things as tool shops, libraries, laboratories, print shops, museums, art galleries, and, in fact, any collection of places or tools that have learning possibilities in them. *Peer matching* would take place through a communications network in which persons wishing to engage in a particular learning

47   John Ohliger and Colleen McCarthy, *Lifelong Learning or Lifelong Schooling?* (Syracuse, N.Y.: Syracuse University Press, 1971).

activity would be identified and brought together to pursue it. The network would provide information regarding the activity and arrange the meeting time, place and facilities.[48]

The proposed *skill exchange* would enable interested learners to receive training in skills at public expense. Those who are competent in a particular skill such as foreign languages, swimming, computer programming, or automobile repair and who wish to teach that skill would be listed in the exchange. The individual wishing to learn the skill would make the specific arrangements with the skill teacher who provides the needed training.

Teaching what we know best

Illich's fourth learning network is that of *educators-at-large*. These are persons who have educational competency as administrators, pedagogical counselors, or intellectual initiators. The administrators are to create and operate educational exchanges or networks. Pedagogical counselors serve as advisers to parents and to students in that they provide assistance in using the networks. The educational initiator acts as a leader who points the way to major new ideas and who seeks to create new intellectual standards.

Educators as facilitators

SUMMING UP

1. The pioneers in education who are treated in this chapter made distinctive contributions to the development of education in their own countries and throughout the world.

2. In challenging the dogma of child depravity, Comenius, Locke, and Rousseau developed a method of education more closely based on the learner's natural growth and on the child's natural goodness.

3. The work of Pestalozzi led to a movement that helped to develop instructional methods based upon the use of the immediate environment and the objects within it. Throughout the nineteenth and early twentieth centuries, the Pestalozzian educational method was the basic strategy used in teacher education institutions and in schools throughout the United States. The theory of Froebel was used to develop the kindergarten movement in the United States. Both Pestalozzi's and Froebel's methods liberalized the American conception of early childhood education by making teachers more sensitive to the interests and needs of children. Herbart's principles of instruction and moral development have strongly influenced classroom teachers.

4. The concept of the sociological foundations of education developed by Spencer was a pioneer effort to relate the school to the broad currents of society. His theory of identifying social activities

48 Illich, *Deschooling Society*.

contributed to curriculum development based on social use and efficiency.

5. Booker T. Washington helped to ease the transition from slavery to freedom that most Black Americans experienced after the Civil War. W. E. B. Du Bois, through his penetrating sociological and educational analyses, helped to pave the way for the civil rights movement and for racial integration of the schools.

6. The impact of Maria Montessori currently is being felt in early childhood education. John Dewey's pioneering work at the University of Chicago Laboratory School pointed the way to progressive educational reform in the first half of the twentieth century.

7. George Counts's frontier ideas on the social and political role of the schools are still being debated by contemporary educators.

8. John Holt and Ivan Illich have presented a challenging vision of the purposes of education in the society of the future.

9. It is hoped that the study of the pedagogical pioneers discussed above will help teachers to examine and to illuminate their own educational ideas and practices.

DISCUSSION QUESTIONS

1. What are your conceptions of knowledge, education, and schooling? How do your conceptions agree or differ with those of the educators treated in this chapter?

2. Identify the various educational methods that were devised by the pioneer educators treated in this chapter. What are the strengths and weaknesses of these methods?

3. Of the pioneer educators discussed in this chapter, whose ideas are most relevant and most irrelevant to you as a prospective teacher?

4. Can you find any evidence of the influence of the pioneer educators mentioned here on your own education?

5. Identify a current educational controversy. How would the educators discussed in this chapter react to this controversy?

THINGS TO DO

1. Read a biography or autobiography of one of the educational pioneers discussed in this chapter. Analyze his or her life, ideas, and methods in a more detailed manner.

2. Volunteer to teach a lesson in class that is based on the method of one of these pioneers.

3. Examine a book on educational methods. Can you find evidence of the influence of any of the pioneers treated in this chapter?

4. Organize a debate on the topic, "Dare the school build a new social order?"

5. Organize a debate on the topic, "Society should be deschooled."

CHAPTER 7 HISTORICAL DEVELOPMENT OF AMERICAN EDUCATION

Focusing questions

What school of educational historiography do the authors of this text seem to represent? What about your professors?

How were European educational ideas and institutions modified in the American environment?

How did American democratic ideas contribute to the rise of public schooling in the United States?

How does the American educational ladder differ from the European dual system?

How was American education shaped by major historical forces?

What uniquely American problems of education have persisted over the course of time?

Chapter 7 provides a historical overview of the origins and development of American education. It traces the evolution of educational institutions and also identifies the contributions of leading individuals whose decisions shaped American education. The chapter begins by discussing educational historiography (the critical examination and interpretation of historical sources) and then examines: (1) the colonial period, when European educational ideas and institutions were transported to America; (2) the creation of a uniquely American educational system during the revolutionary and early national eras; (3) the development of secondary education from the Latin grammar school, through the academy, to today's comprehensive high school; and (4) the development of institutions of higher learning.[1]

AMERICAN EDUCATIONAL HISTORY

To understand American educational history, you also need to understand those who wrote it. While the historian's description of an event can be judged as either historically true or false, it is more difficult to appraise the point of view upon which the historian based his or her narrative and interpretation. To make judgments about historical writing, you should know the frame of reference that the historian used in selecting and interpreting evidence. To establish a perspective on American educational history, we will examine some of the schools of thought that have shaped educational historical scholarship.

Historical frame of reference

CELEBRATIONIST VIEW OF HISTORY

In the early twentieth century, American educational historians, such as Ellwood Cubberley and Paul Monroe, wrote detailed and thoroughly documented histories of public schooling.[2] Their professional backgrounds caused them to deal primarily with the evolution, structure, organization, law, and financing of public schools. By narrowly defining educational history as the history of public schooling, their interpretations often were isolated from the important social, political, and economic forces that were shaping American society.

Cubberley and Monroe have been called "celebrationists" since their histories celebrated the evolution of American public education as a popular victory won by crusade and struggle. They saw the common school, the high school, and the state college and university as rungs in an "educa-

Popular crusade

1 For an analysis of American educational historiography, see Sol Cohen, "History of Education as a Field of Study: An Essay on Recent Historiography of American Education" in D. R. Warren, ed., *History, Education and Public Policy* (Berkeley, Calif.: McCutchan, 1978), pp. 35–53.

2 For representative books of the "celebrationist" school, see Ellwood P. Cubberley, *The History of Education: Educational Practice and Progress Considered as a Phase of the Development and Spread of Western Civilization* (Boston: Houghton Mifflin, 1920); Paul Monroe, *A Brief Course in the History of Education* (New York: Macmillan, 1907).

tional ladder" that enabled Americans to obtain a complete public education and move upward in mobility. Minimizing the racial, ethnic, class, and social variables that limited educational opportunity, they believed that the public school system provided equality of educational opportunity to all Americans.

Equality of educational opportunity

These celebrationist historians believed that American civilization would improve progressively as it became more scientific, industrial, and technological. Public schools were seen to be institutions designed to ensure that progress would occur. Cubberley saw his writing as providing a proper historical setting for examining the "evolution of modern state school systems and the world-wide spread of Western civilization."[3]

Because of their desire to motivate and inspire teachers, celebrationist historians were often uncritical, laudatory, and exaggerated in their interpretation of America's educational past. For them, educational history was to prepare dedicated teachers who used the past for inspiration rather than to illuminate educational issues.

Uncritical portrayal

Celebrationist historians saw the public school as a conservative social institution designed to stabilize American life. Believing that public schooling should Americanize immigrants and other minority groups into a common mold, Cubberley narrowly stereotyped the American character in terms that were white, Anglo-Saxon, and Protestant. For him, immigrants, especially those from southern and eastern Europe, had little to contribute but much to learn from American culture.

Although contemporary revisionist critics have condemned celebrationist history as limited, insular, and parochial, the pioneer historians, such as Cubberley and Monroe, did establish a basic framework for American educational history by identifying its primary sources. They left a legacy of carefully compiled information on the origin and growth of the public schools, on school law and legislation, on the evolution of the curriculum, and on the contributions of educational leaders. Upon this historical legacy, later historians were able to develop more critical analyses of the American educational past.

Growth of public schools

A LIBERAL SHIFT IN EDUCATIONAL HISTORY

During the Depression of the 1930s, several significant developments occurred in educational history. American historical writing was influenced heavily by the "new history" of Charles Beard and Carl Becker, whose pragmatic progressivism asserted that each generation needed to reinterpret its past in terms of present social problems. From the publication of *An Economic Interpretation of the United States Constitution* in 1913 to the publication of *The Nature of the Social Studies* in 1934, Beard had been examining the effects of economic

3 Cubberley, *The History of Education*, p. viii.

forces and social change on American life and education.[4] During the Depression, with its severe economic dislocation and massive unemployment, an economic interpretation of history had a heightened significance.

Beard was a close friend and associate of George Counts, a leading proponent of the Social Reconstructionist educational philosophy. Counts adapted the "new history" into policy statements that suggested that the schools should be used as agencies for building a "new social order." Calling for a collective democracy, Counts argued that public schooling should deal with the problems of poverty, unemployment, and class conflict.

In the general historical framework with Counts and Beard, Merle Curti's *The Social Ideas of American Educators* examined the educational ideas of such major figures as Horace Mann, Henry Barnard, Booker T. Washington, William Harris, John Dewey, and others.[5] Although Curti's important contribution is often overlooked by current revisionist historians, it charted a new direction in educational historiography.

By the mid-1950s and early 1960s, American educational history experienced a marked revival. For example, the Committee on the Role of Education in American History encouraged historians to examine the significance of education in American life. Educational historians developed a cultural focus that examined the impact of political, economic, intellectual, and social forces on educational institutions and programs. Educational historians such as Archibald Anderson, R. Freeman Butts, Carl Gross, Adolphe Meyer, and others developed a broad vision of educational history. Butts, in particular, developed an exemplary and balanced rendition of educational history that located the school within its social, political, economic, and cultural context.[6]

In the early 1960s, educational historians were already moving to a broader perspective when the themes of Bernard Bailyn and Lawrence Cremin captured their attention. Bailyn's *Education in the Forming of American Society* and Cremin's *The Transformation of the School* argued that educational history, as a form of cultural history, should study informal educational agencies such as the family, media, library, press, and church, as well as the school.[7] Stimulating research and writing on a wide range of educational themes, the writings of Bailyn and Cremin

4   Charles A. Beard, *An Economic Interpretation of the United States Constitution* (New York: Macmillan, 1913); Beard, *The Nature of the Social Studies* (New York: Scribner, 1934).

5   Merle Curti, *The Social Ideas of American Educators* (New York: Scribner, 1935).

6   R. Freeman Butts, *The American Tradition in Religion and Education* (Boston: Beacon Press, 1950); R. Freeman Butts and Lawrence A. Cremin, *A History of Education in American Culture* (New York: Holt, Rinehart, 1953); Butts, *The Education of the West: A Formative Chapter in the History of Civilization* (New York: McGraw-Hill, 1973).

7   Bernard Bailyn, *Education in the Forming of American Society* (New York: Random House, 1960); Lawrence A. Cremin, *The Transformation of the School: Progressivism in American Education 1876-1957* (New York: Knopf, 1962).

caused a veritable renaissance in the history of education as historians examined a variety of formal and informal forces.[8]

THE REVISIONIST VIEW

In the late 1960s and 1970s, the revisionist school of educational historiography emerged. It should be pointed out that all historical writing involves a revision or reinterpretation of the past by giving it new or added meaning. In educational historiography, however, "revisionist" has been used to identify historians who have been critical of both the celebrationist history of Cubberley and Monroe and also the more liberal interpretation of historians such as Bailyn, Butts, and Cremin.

The appearance of revisionist historiography ran parallel to several social and educational trends of the late 1960s. It coincided with the mood of social protest and criticism that swept American colleges and universities in the late 1960s. Part of that climate of protest involved attacks on the "military-industrial complex" that was alleged to be directing the domestic and foreign policy of the United States, especially the military intervention in Viet Nam.[9] Some of the critics saw educational institutions as part of a corporate structure hostile to fundamental socioeconomic changes that would benefit disadvantaged minority groups. For many revisionists, the public school system was a mechanism by which the vested interests and upper socioeconomic classes exerted social control over lower socioeconomic classes, minorities, and immigrants.[10] The celebrationist view that public schooling has always been progressive, good, and ennobling has been rejected by revisionist historians as either simplistic or a carefully contrived apology for the status quo. Although more tolerant of Bailyn and Cremin's broad cultural perspective, revisionists prefer to investigate specific aspects of schooling that relate to social class, to student selection and retention, to employment, and to socioeconomic mobility. Revisionist historians, especially those influenced by Bowles, Gintis, and deLone, have focused their attention on the economic outcomes of schooling and frequently have used more quantitative research methods that earlier historians.[11] Until the 1960s, educational historians generally relied on documentary sources such as letters, manuscripts,

Critical of celebrationists and liberals

New mood of protest and criticism

Social class and mobility

8   H. Tsui Shapiro, "Society in the History of Educational Change: A Brief Review of Studies by Bernard Bailyn and Lawrence Cremin," *Educational Theory* (Summer 1978), pp. 186–93.

9   Michael W. Apple, *Ideology and Curriculum* (Boston: Routledge & Paul, 1979); Joel Spring, *The Sorting Machine: National Educational Policy Since 1945* (New York: McKay, 1976).

10   Examples of revisionist educational history are: Colin Greer, *The Great School Legend: A Revisionist Interpretation of American Public Education* (New York: Basic Books, 1972); Edgar B. Gumbert and Joel H. Spring, *The Superschool and the Superstate: American Education in the Twentieth Century, 1918-1970* (New York: Wiley, 1974); Clarence Karier, Paul Violas, and Joel Spring, *Roots of Crisis: American Education in the Twentieth Century* (Chicago: Rand McNally, 1973); Michael Katz, *Class, Bureaucracy, and Schools: The Illusion of Educational Change in America* (New York: Praeger, 1971); Katz, *School Reform: Past and Present* (Boston: Little, Brown, 1971).

11   Samuel Bowles and Herbert Gintis, *Schooling in Capitalist America* (New York: Basic Books, 1976); Richard H. deLone, *Small Futures: Children, Inequality, and the Limits of Liberal Reform* (New York: Harcourt Brace Jovanovich, 1979).

biographies, and government documents to supply the evidence for their writing and interpretation.

The revisionist criticism of earlier interpretations of American educational history has stimulated considerable controversy. For example, Diane Ravitch has attacked some of the revisionists for distorting the historical record.[12] She alleges that some revisionists have substituted radical political ideology for balanced historical scholarship. Most likely, the educational history that emerges in the future will incorporate some of the revisionist corrections of the American educational past.[13] As you read this chapter and the other chapters of this book, see if you can identify the school of thought to which the authors subscribe. Is it celebrationist, liberal, or revisionist? Or is it a synthesis of several points of view?

Distorting
history

THE COLONIAL PERIOD

The historical foundations of education in the United States were laid by colonists seeking to re-create in North America the patterns of British schools. The colonists were familiar with European institutional arrangements based on the dual track system of schools in which the lower socioeconomic classes attended elementary schools and the upper classes attended separate preparatory schools and colleges. The curriculum of the lower schools included the basic skills of reading, writing, arithmetic, and religious indoctrination. The chief preparatory school was the Latin grammar school, which stressed the Latin and Greek classics as the means to higher education. Education of the colonial upper classes was still heavily influenced by the Renaissance humanists, who believed that the classics contained the main body of wisdom that an educated man needed to know. The two kinds of schools—the elementary school and the Latin grammar school (precollege)—were separate systems. Neither the inherited European arrangements nor the social ideas of the British colonists in North America questioned the idea of class distinctions in education. The colonists also imported their Old World conceptions about the kind of education that was appropriate to males and females. Formal education, especially at the secondary and higher levels, was reserved for males. Although girls attended the elementary schools and the dame schools, they rarely attended Latin grammar schools and colleges during the colonial period of American history.

Influence of European schools

Different education for boys and girls

To the American colonist, a "public school" was not the same institution we are familiar with. In many cases the school was privately financed;

12 Diane Ravitch, *The Revisionists Revisited: A Critique of the Radical Attack on the Schools* (New York: Basic Books, 1978).

13 Donald R. Warren, "A Past for the Present: History, Education, and Public Policy," *Educational Theory* (Fall 1978), pp. 253–65; Warren, ed., *History, Education, and Public Policy.*

the term "public" distinguished it from a school catering exclusively to a special group—usually a religious group. The modern idea of public education—a local system of schools supported by taxes and administered by public officials certified by license, which compels attendance of all children up to a certain age (usually sixteen years), and which is separated from private interests—did not exist in the colonies. Granted, the colony sometimes organized the schools, but its role (outside of New England) was limited. Instead, several other agencies assumed the major responsibility of education—the family, the apprenticeship system, and private schools of various sorts. Of these agencies, the family carried the greatest burden; frequently, children had no formal learning or picked up only a little vocational training.

Limited role of government

The various colonies handled education matters differently. In New England the governing bodies exerted general authority over education and directly supported their schools. In the Middle Atlantic colonies, a tolerant policy toward religion fostered several different sects, each group wanting its own religious principles taught in its schools. Consequently, various schools with various policies emerged. The southern colonies did not pass laws requiring children to attend school. Individual parents educated their own children by arrangement with private tutors or by sending them to private schools.[14]

Regional differences on educational matters

NEW ENGLAND
COLONIES
The New England colonies of Massachusetts Bay, Connecticut, and New Hampshire were very important in the development of American educational ideas and institutions. The colony of Massachusetts, in particular, enacted the first laws that governed formal education in the British colonies of North America. Much of the history of education in early America can be generalized from the educational experiences of colonial Massachusetts.[15]

First education laws in Massachusetts

Massachusetts Bay Colony was settled mainly by the Puritans, a Protestant group that adhered to the theology of the Swiss religious reformer John Calvin. Unlike the contemporary situation in the United States, in which a strict separation between church and public school exists, the first schools established in New England were closely related to the Puritan church. As practiced by the Puritans, Calvinist theology had several significant implications for education. First, the doctrine of predestination held that those souls who were elected, or predestined, by God for salvation (others were damned to Hell) were to exhibit outward signs

14 R. Freeman Butts, "Search for Freedom: the Story of American Education," *NEA Journal* (March 1960), pp. 33–48; Butts, *Public Education in the United States* (New York: Holt, Rinehart, 1978).

15 Sheldon S. Cohen, *A History of Colonial Education, 1607-1776* (New York: Wiley, 1974).

of correct and religiously defined behavior. Second, the good person respected the sanctity of property and would prosper. As a steward of wealth, the good man would use his income wisely and for the enlightenment of his fellows. Third, educated persons who knew God's commandments, as revealed by Calvin and preached by the Puritan ministers, were likely to resist the temptations of the world, especially the flesh and the devil. The school's role in this society was seen as handmaiden of the Church. Schooling was intended to cultivate a respect for the laws of the theocratic state and for the sanctity of property. In Puritan New England education encouraged social conformity and religious commitment.

There was also an economic rationale for schooling in New England, which was reinforced by Puritan outlook. The good citizen of the Puritan commonwealth was to be an economically productive individual who would produce wealth by hard work in farming, manufacturing, and trade. It was further assumed that schooling would contribute to a person's economic and social usefulness by cultivating literacy, resourcefulness, enterprise, punctuality, and thrift.

Schooling for economic and social usefulness

Child depravity   The Puritan conception of the child was another important element in New England colonial education. The child was regarded as being naturally depraved—conceived in sin and born in corruption. Childish play was regarded as idleness, and child's talk was considered gibberish. In order to civilize the child, the Puritan teacher applied constant discipline. Over time childish ways would yield to the disciplined behavior that was regarded as the outward sign of the Elect. The good child appeared to be a miniature adult. A study of the Puritan child notes that the children of New England had always before them the vision of their own evil and of the punishment that they would receive in the hellfires of eternity.[16] The stories that they heard and the books that they read were designed to impress upon them the constant need for prayer and repentance. In their schools the New England children began to learn the alphabet with the rhyme: "In Adam's fall/we sinned all."

Harsh discipline

Religious rhymes

"Old Deluder Satan"   The Puritans of New England were a literate people. Their political ideas and their Congregational form of church governance made it necessary for them to train an educated leadership and a literate and disciplined followership. Even in the first years of their settlement of Massachusetts, the Puritans sought to establish schools for their children's education. In 1642, legislation of the Massachusetts General Court required parents and guardians of children to make certain that their charges could read and understand the principles of religion and the

16 Stanford Fleming, *Children and Puritanism: The Place of Children in the Life and Thought of the New England Churches* (New Haven, Conn.: Yale University Press, 1933); Ross W. Beales, "In Search of the Historical Child: Miniature Adulthood and Youth in Colonial New England," *American Quarterly* (October 1975), pp. 379–98.

laws of the Commonwealth. In 1647 the General Court enacted the "Old Deluder Satan" Act, which required every town of fifty or more families to appoint a reading and writing teacher. Towns of 100 or more families were to employ a teacher of Latin so that students could be prepared for entry to Harvard College.[17] The other New England colonies, except for Rhode Island, followed the Massachusetts example. These early laws indicated how important education was to the Puritan colonists of Massachusetts. Some historians have regarded these laws as the beginnings of American school law. It is clear that the Puritans did not want to see the growth of an illiterate class in North America. Such a class might be the beginning of a group of dependent poor as had existed in England. They also wanted to ensure that the children of the Commonwealth would grow up as adults who were committed to Puritan theology.

A literate citizenry

The town school   The New England town school was a locally controlled institution attended by both boys and girls of the community. They might range in age from five or six to thirteen or fourteen. Attendance was not always regular; it depended upon weather conditions and the need for the child's work on the farm.[18] The school's curriculum included reading, writing, arithmetic, catechism, and the singing of religious hymns. The child learned the alphabet, the syllables, words, and sentences by memorizing the hornbook, a single sheet of parchment covered by a transparent sheath made by flattening the horns of cattle. The older children read the *New England Primer*, which included more detailed materials of a religious and catechistic nature such as the Westminster catechism. Religion and reading were carefully integrated. Children combined memorization of the Ten Commandments, the Lord's Prayer, and the Creed with religion and reading. Arithmetic was primarily a matter of counting, adding, and subtracting.

The three R's

The New England town school was often a crude structure, dominated by the teacher's pulpit, located at the front of the single room. The students sat on benches. They studied their assignments until called before the schoolmaster to recite. The teachers were males. Some were persons who earned their living as teachers while preparing for the ministry. Others took the job to repay the passage money that had brought them to the North American colonies. Many, unfortunately, were incompetents who governed their charges by the use of the rod. Although there were undoubtedly some variations, the New England elementary school was characterized by rote learning, memorized responses, and corporal

Rote learning and corporal punishment

17   Nathaniel Shurtleff, ed., *Records of The Governor and Company of the Massachusetts Bay in New England*, vol. 2 (Boston: Order of the Legislature, 1853).

18   George H. Martin, *The Evolution of the Massachusetts Public School System* (New York: Appleton, 1894); S. Alexander Rippa, *Education in a Free Society: An American History* (New York: McKay, 1976).

punishment. It should be remembered that the children who attended town schools were often of the lower classes.

The Latin grammar school   The sons of the upper classes attended the Latin grammar school, which prepared them for entry to the colleges of Harvard or Yale. These children generally had learned to read and write English from private tutors. A boy would enter the Latin grammar school at the age of eight and remain there for eight years.[19] His lessons were based on such Latin authors as Cicero, Terence, Caesar, Livy, Vergil, and Horace. The Greek authors, such as Isocrates, Hesiod, and Homer, were read by the more advanced students who had already mastered Latin grammar and composition. Little or no attention was given to mathematics, science, history, or modern languages. The masters who taught in the Latin grammar schools possessed college degrees and were generally held in high esteem. The regimen of study in the Latin grammar school was exhausting and unexciting. As historian Samuel Morison points out, the Latin grammar school was one of colonial America's closest links to the European educational experience, resembling the classical humanist schools of the Renaissance.[20]

Classics

After completing the Latin grammar school, the student applied for admission to Harvard College, established in 1636. Harvard was based on the Puritan conception that those called to the ministry needed to be soundly educated in the classics and the Scriptures. The student had to demonstrate his competency in Latin and Greek to be admitted to Harvard. The Harvard curriculum consisted of grammar, logic, rhetoric, arithmetic, geometry, astronomy, ethics, metaphysics, and natural sciences. In addition, Hebrew, Greek, and ancient history were offered for their usefulness in Scriptural study.

MIDDLE ATLANTIC COLONIES   The Middle Atlantic colonies of New York, New Jersey, Delaware, and Pennsylvania differed markedly from the New England group. In contrast to New England, where a common language, religion, and value structure existed, the Middle Atlantic colonies were characterized by linguistic, religious, and cultural pluralism. Although English-speaking people were in the majority, there were the Dutch in New York, Swedes in Delaware, and Germans in Pennsylvania. In addition to linguistic pluralism, there was also religious diversity. The Dutch were members of the Dutch Reformed Church; the Quakers dominated Pennsylvania; the Germans might be Lutherans or members of small pietistic denominations; and there were also Baptists, Roman Catholics, and a small Jewish population.

Linguistic, religious, and cultural pluralism

19 Robert Middlekauff, *Ancients and Axioms: Secondary Education in Eighteenth-Century New England* (New Haven, Conn.: Yale University Press, 1963).

20 Samuel E. Morison, *The Intellectual Life of Colonial New England* (New York: New York University Press, 1956).

In such a situation, where there were divergent ideas and values, no single system of schools could be established. While New England created the town school, the Middle Atlantic colonies used parochial and independent schools that were closely related to the different churches.

New York   The colony of New York, which had first been under Dutch control, continued to operate the schools of the Dutch Reformed Church when it became a royal colony under English domination.[21] The Dutch parochial schools taught reading, writing, and religion. After the coming of English rule, a number of charity schools were established by a missionary society of the Church of England.

Since New York was a commercial colony, a number of private schools were established there to teach specific trades or skills. These private schools taught such subjects and skills as navigation, surveying, bookkeeping, Spanish, French, and geography. Some of them came to be known as "academies." These schools made education available to middle-class children whose parents could afford tuition. The idea soon spread to other colonies. One of the most famous of these private schools was the Philadelphia Academy, founded in 1751 by Benjamin Franklin. Others were the Newark Academy in Delaware and the Washington Academy in New Jersey.

Pennsylvania   The colony of Pennsylvania became a haven for Quakers under the leadership of William Penn. The Society of Friends, sometimes called Quakers, was a religious sect that rejected violence. The Friends refused to support war efforts or to serve in the military forces. They maintained a number of schools in Pennsylvania that were open to all children, including Blacks and Indians.[22] Their teachers, unlike those in New England, rejected corporal punishment. They respected the individual dignity of the child and opposed the view of child depravity that was common at that time. Like the other elementary schools of the colonial period, the Quaker schools taught reading, writing, arithmetic, and religion. In addition to these basic skills, a small amount of vocational training was given in the form of handicrafts, domestic science, and agriculture.[23]

Local control of schools

School for middle-class children

Schools for all children

SOUTHERN COLONIES   The southern colonies of Maryland, Virginia, the Carolinas, and Georgia represented still another pattern of colonial education. Unlike the New England and the Middle Atlantic colonies, where concentrations of popula-

---

21   William H. Kilpatrick, *The Dutch Schools of New Netherlands and Colonial New York* (Washington, D.C.: U.S. Government Printing Office, 1912).

22   James D. Hendricks, "Be Still and Know!: Quaker Silence and Dissenting Educational Ideals, 1740–1812," *Journal of the Midwest History of Education Society* (Annual Proceedings, 1975), pp. 14–40.

23   Thomas Woody, *Early Quaker Education in Pennsylvania* (New York: Teachers College Press, Columbia University, 1920).

tion had developed in cities and towns, the population of the southern
colonies was dispersed over a large land area. This made it difficult to
bring groups of children together in school classes. Those who could afford to do so resorted to tutorial education. Wealthy families engaged
private teachers to educate their children; a few families sent their children to private schools.

Effects of the plantation system   A second important characteristic of life and education in the South resulted from the unique agricultural economy that developed in that region. The plantations of the
South often produced a single, staple crop such as tobacco, cotton, or rice.
This type of agriculture became the mainstay of the economy. In an era
when mechanization was minimal or nonexistent, a large and cheap labor
force was needed to maintain this plantation economy. The African slave
trade provided large numbers of Black men and women, seized in their
native land and brought to the New World to work as unpaid labor.

The slave system of labor and the plantation system of land holding
and ownership contributed to a development of education in the South that
differed from that of both New England and the Middle Atlantic colonies.[24]
The children of the privileged class of White plantation owners had the
benefit of private tutors, who often lived on the plantation manor. Occasionally, the Anglican missionary society established a school for these
children. In the late colonial period boarding schools were established,
usually in towns such as Williamsburg or Charleston. As for the Black
slaves, they had been uprooted from their native Africa and brought to
work in the fields of the South. They were trained to be agricultural workers, field hands, craftsmen, or domestic servants, but generally were forbidden to learn to read or to write. For the poor Whites, who tilled the
infertile soils of the back country or the mountainous areas, formal education was nonexistent. The White children of the poor usually grew up to be
subsistence farmers like their parents before them. The unique situation
of the southern colonies tended to retard the development of a large-scale
system of schools. This educational retardation was felt long after the Civil
War period.

Despite these regional variations between the schools of New England, the Middle Atlantic colonies, and the South, certain parallels also
must be considered. All three sections were dominated largely by British
political rule. Moreover, despite the linguistic and religious variations
present, all three sections were heirs to the western European educational
tradition. There was similarity in the basic ideas and values that governed
individuals and groups.[25] Religion held a high priority in the value

*Tutorial and
private
education*

*No schooling
for Blacks and
poor Whites*

24   James C. Klotter, "The Black South and White Appalachia," *Journal of American History*
(March 1980), pp. 832–49.

25   Lawrence A. Cremin, *American Education: The Colonial Experience, 1607-1783* (New
York: Harper & Row, 1970).

structure, and the dual track system of education represented the social-class structure. Among informal sources of education, the family played a strong formative role as it shaped ideas, values, and skills.[26]

THE EARLY PERIOD OF NATIONHOOD The American Revolution of 1776 ended British rule in the thirteen colonies. A new government based on a system of checks and balances distributed political power among the executive, legislative, and judicial branches. Although the inherited vernacular and denominational elementary schools and Latin grammar schools continued for some time, the leaders of the new republic sought to create new patterns of education that would be suited to the self-governing citizens of the United States.[27]

Under the Articles of Confederation, Congress sought to administer the lands of the Northwest Territory. The first national educational legislation, included in the Northwest Ordinance of 1785, called for the surveying and division of the Northwest Territory into townships of six square miles. Each township was further divided into thirty-six sections, the sixteenth section of which was to be used for education. While the provisions of the Northwest Ordinance are no longer in effect, they established the pattern of the land grant, often used to finance education in the early nineteenth century.

Northwest Ordinance

The United States Constitution reserved education to each of the states, under the "reserved powers" clause of the Tenth Amendment. The colonial tradition of local school control and the opposiion to centralized political power contributed to a state rather than a national school system in the United States. Educational support and control became a state rather than a national function.

Education reserved to the states

Until the establishment of the common school system, leaders in the new republic grappled with the problem of designing an educational system that would serve the needs of a new political system and contribute to nation building. Numerous plans were put forth by such people as George Washington, Benjamin Rush, Robert Coram, Samuel Smith, and Noah Webster. These plans shared certain aims: (1) education should meet the needs of a self-governing polity; (2) education should reflect the needs of a developing nation that included vast expanses of frontier land and abundant supplies of natural resources; (3) education should be useful rather than classical or ornamental; and (4) education should be American rather

Rejection of European ideas

---

26 Bailyn, *Education in the Forming of American Society.*
27 Rush Welter, *Popular Education and Democratic Thought in America* (New York: Teachers College Press, Columbia University, 1962); David Madsen, *Early National Education: 1776–1830* (New York: Wiley, 1974).

than European.[28] To indicate the nature of the educational plans in the early days of the republic, special attention will be given to the educational proposals of Benjamin Franklin, Thomas Jefferson, and Noah Webster.

FRANKLIN:
THE ACADEMY

Benjamin Franklin (1706–1789) represented the rising American business class. His own formal education was brief, consisting of one year at the Boston grammar school, some writing and arithmetic lessons by private teachers, and experience as a printer's apprentice. He was a self-educated man who studied the major political and social tracts of his day. Franklin inaugurated several major scientific and educational organizations in Philadelphia, such as the Library Subscription Society, the Junto, and the American Philosophical Society. The proverbial folk wisdom of his *Poor Richard's Almanack* was very popular among the American middle classes, who readily accepted his emphasis on the virtues of frugality, diligence, thrift, hard work, and inventiveness.

Virtues of
thrift and hard
work

In 1749, Franklin wrote a treatise entitled "Proposals Relating to the Education of Youth in Pennsylvania." This work served as a basis for the academy that he founded. The academy offered a practical curriculum that included a variety of subjects and useful skills.[29] English grammar, classics, composition, rhetoric, and public speaking were to be the chief language studies rather than Latin and Greek. Students could also choose a second language based on their vocational interests. For example, prospective clergymen might study Latin and Greek; physicians could choose Latin, Greek, and French; businessmen might elect French, German, and Spanish. Mathematics was to be taught for its practical application to bookkeeping rather than as an abstract intellectual exercise. History would be the chief ethical study. By the study of the biographies of great men, students were to learn moral and ethical principles. Franklin's curricular proposal was especially noteworthy because it brought many practical skills into the formal school that hitherto had been ignored. It included such practical subjects and skills as carpentry, shipbuilding, engraving, printing, painting, cabinetmaking, farming, and carving. With a prophetic insight into the course of civilization and education, Franklin suggested that special attention be given to science, invention, and technology.

Practical
curriculum

JEFFERSON:
EDUCATION FOR
CITIZENSHIP

Thomas Jefferson (1743–1826) a leading statesman of the revolutionary and early republican periods, attended the local

28 David Nasaw, *Schooled to Order* (New York: Oxford University Press, 1979); Frederick Rudolph, *Essays on Education in the Early Republic* (Cambridge, Mass.: Harvard University Press, 1965).

29 John H. Best, *Benjamin Franklin on Education* (New York: Teachers College Press, Columbia University, 1962); Henry J. Perkinson, *Two Hundred Years of American Educational Thought* (New York: Longman, 1976).

English vernacular school and Latin grammar school near his home in Virginia. He also attended William and Mary College. Jefferson was a man of wide-ranging interests, embracing politics, philosophy, architecture, agriculture, and science. His political career was distinguished by his service as a member of the Virginia legislature and the Continental Congress, governor of Virginia, secretary of state, vice-president, and president of the United States. As the principal author of the Declaration of Independence, Jefferson stated his political belief that everyone is endowed with inalienable rights of "life, liberty, and the pursuit of happiness." Deeply involved in intellectual and educational affairs, he was a member of the American Academy of Arts and Sciences and was president of the American Philosophical Society.[30]

Jefferson's philosophy of education Jefferson's "Bill for the More General Diffusion of Knowledge" was introduced in the Virginia legislature in 1779. This legislation, expressing Jefferson's philosophy of republican education, assumed that the state had the responsibility to cultivate an educated and literate citizenry. The major purpose of education was to serve the general welfare of a democratic society by seeing to it that the knowledge and understanding necessary to exercise the responsibility of citizenship were made available to all. "If," said Jefferson, "a nation expects to be ignorant and free, in a state of civilization, it expects what never was and will never be." Hence, it was proper for the state to play an educational role and to provide the opportunities for the education of both the common people and the leaders of society "at the common expense of all."[31] To Jefferson formal education was largely a state or civic concern, rather than a matter reserved to religious denominations. Schools should be financed through public taxes.

> State
> responsibility
> for education

> Education as a
> civic concern

Jefferson's plan would have subdivided the counties of Virginia into wards, each of which would have had an elementary school to teach reading, writing, arithmetic, and history. All White children in Virginia were to attend the ward school for three years of elementary education supported by taxes. After the first three years the children would have been able to continue in the ward schools if their parents paid their tuitions. Jefferson's proposal also provided for the establishment in Virginia of twenty grammar schools at the secondary level. In each ward school the most academically gifted student who could not afford to pay tuition would have been awarded a scholarship to continue his education for three additional years in the grammar school. There he would have studied Latin, Greek, English, geography, and higher mathematics. Upon completing grammar school, half of the scholarship students would have been assigned positions as elementary or ward schoolteachers. The ten scholar-

> Scholarships
> based on merit

30 Roy J. Honeywell, *The Educational Work of Thomas Jefferson* (Cambridge, Mass.: Harvard University Press, 1931); Robert D. Heslep, *Thomas Jefferson and Education* (New York: Random House, 1969).

31 Thomas Jefferson, "A Bill for the More General Diffusion of Knowledge," in P. L. Ford, ed., *The Writings of Thomas Jefferson*, vol. 2 (New York: Putnam, 1893), p. 221.

ship students of highest academic achievement would have attended William and Mary College. Jefferson's plan used the school as a selective agency to identify and provide the most competent students with continuing education.

Although Jefferson's proposal was not enacted by the Virginia legislature, the bill reveals the educational theorizing in the early republic. It clearly demonstrates that a primary purpose of education was to promote good citizenship. It also shows that the earlier impact of the religious denominations was beginning to decline. Jefferson was concerned with the general education of the population and also with identifying individuals of superior ability who would exercise political leadership. The educational ideas of the leaders of the Revolutionary generation, such as Franklin and Jefferson, were to be defined and expressed by the proponents of the American common school in the nineteenth century.

Education to promote citizenship

WEBSTER: SCHOOLMASTER OF THE REPUBLIC

One of the leading cultural nationalists of the early republic was Noah Webster (1785–1843). A native of Connecticut and a Yale graduate, Webster was a lawyer, schoolmaster, politician, and writer.[32] His prominence in American intellectual and educational history rests on his writing of the *American Spelling Book* and the *American Dictionary*. Webster articulated a concept of cultural nationalism according to which nationality was based on and reflected the unique intellectual identity of a nation's citizens. For Webster, the major challenge was to create a sense of American cultural identity and unity.

In 1789 when the Constitution went into effect as the law of the land, Webster argued that the United States should have its own system of "language as well as government." The language of Great Britain, he reasoned, "should no longer be our standard; for the taste of her writers is already completed, and her language on the decline."[33] By the act of revolution, the American people had declared their political independence of England, and now they needed to declare their cultural independence as well. Realizing that a sense of national identity was conveyed through a distinctive national language and literature, Webster set out to reshape the English language used in the United States. He believed that a uniquely American language would: (1) eliminate the remains of European usage; (2) create a uniform American speech that would be free of localism and provincialism; and (3) promote self-conscious American cultural nationalism. The creation of an American language would become the linguistic mortar of national union.

Cultural independence from England

32   For biographies of Webster, see Harry R. Warfel, *Noah Webster: Schoolmaster to America* (New York: Octagon, 1936) and Ervin C. Shoemaker, *Noah Webster: Pioneer of Learning* (New York: Columbia University Press, 1936).

33   Noah Webster, *Dissertations on the English Language* (Boston: Isaiah Thomas, 1789).

Webster directly related the learning of language to organized education. As they learned the American language, children also would learn to think and act as Americans. The American language that Webster proposed would have to be taught deliberately and systematically to the young in the nation's schools. Since the curriculum of these Americanized schools would be shaped by the books that the students read, Webster spent much of his life writing spelling and reading books. His *Grammatical Institute of the English Language* was published in 1783. The first part of the *Institute* was later printed as *The American Spelling Book*, which was widely used throughout the United States in the first half of the nineteenth century.[34] Webster's *Spelling Book* went through many editions; it is estimated that 15 million copies had been sold by 1837. Webster's great work was *The American Dictionary*, which was completed in 1825 after twenty-five years of laborious research.[35] Often termed the "schoolmaster of the republic," Noah Webster was an educational statesman of the early national period whose work helped to create a sense of American language, identity, and nationality.

Specific American language

Spelling books and dictionaries

THE RISE OF UNIVERSAL EDUCATION

In the first two decades of the nineteenth century individuals and groups were seeking a new form of education, an institution of learning suited to the republican needs of a frontier society. Although they rejected the highly class-centered European model, proponents of a new form of American education experimented with selective borrowing from European educators. For example, Robert Owen's infant school, developed in the factory community of New Lanark, Scotland, gained some support.[36]

Education designed for frontier society.

In the infant school, young children from three to six were given both play activity and intellectual experiences. Although some infant schools were established, they were not widely instituted in the United States.

Like western Europe, early nineteenth-century America was undergoing the first phase of industrialization. Women and children worked in the factories of the industrial Northeast. To give the child factory workers some minimal learning, Sunday schools were opened in some of the larger cities such as New York and Philadelphia. The Sunday school concept was

34 Henry Steele Commager, ed., *Noah Webster's American Spelling Book* (New York: Teachers College Press, Columbia University, 1962).

35 Robert K. Leavitt, *Noah's Ark, New England Yankees and the Endless Quest* (Springfield, Mass.: Merriam, 1947); Richard M. Rollins, "Words as Social Control: Noah Webster and the Creation of *The American Dictionary,*" *American Quarterly* (Fall 1976), pp. 415-30.

36 Harold Silver, ed., *Robert Owen on Education* (Cambridge, Mass.: Harvard University Press, 1969); Gerald L. Gutek, "New Harmony: An Example of Communitarian Education," *Educational Theory* (Winter 1972), pp. 34-46.

developed by Robert Raikes, an English religious leader and publicist, who wanted to take children off the streets on the Lord's Day and give them some basic literary and religious instruction. In the United States, classes were conducted on the one day of the week when the factories were closed. Writing, reading, arithmetic, and religion were taught to those who attended.

The European method of instruction that received the most attention in the early nineteenth century was the monitorial method, promoted by two rival English educators, Andrew Bell, an Anglican churchman, and Joseph Lancaster, a Quaker teacher. The monitorial method, as the name implies, relied heavily on the use of student teachers, or monitors, who were trained by a master teacher in the rudiments of a subject.[37] It sought to cultivate basic literacy and arithmetic by having a master teacher train a number of student teachers, who then trained other students to act as monitors. The monitorial method attracted those who believed it possible to have a large system of education at very little cost.

Monitorial method utilized student teachers

At first, monitorial schools were very popular in the United States. In New York, Philadelphia, and elsewhere they were supported by private funds and by some state and city appropriations. When the New York Free School Society turned its property over to the public school system in 1853, over 600,000 children had been served in monitorial schools. By the early 1840s, however, interest faded when people realized that the monitorial approach provided only the barest minimum of learning. The following contributions of monitorial schools should be noted, however: (1) they made educational opportunities more easily available; (2) they acquainted parents with the concept of formal education for their children; (3) they demonstrated the possibility of mass education for most children; and (4) they demonstrated both the need and possibility for systematic teacher preparation.[38]

As the frontier was expanding, the northern states were experiencing the early stages of industrialization. The cities were growing into large urban centers with increasing populations of immigrants and needed a system of schools that would provide systematic elementary education in reading, writing, arithmetic, and citizenship. Both industrialization and the frontier movement produced a spirit of practicality that encouraged schools to cultivate basic skills as opposed to the traditional and classic subjects.

The need for basic skill learning was one of the early nineteenth-century arguments advocating schooling for all the people. There was also a strong conviction that the character and destiny of the United States required the participation of all citizens in the institutions of government. The advocates of popular education in both the West and North argued

---

37 David Salmon, *Joseph Lancaster* (London: Longman, Green, 1904).

38 John Reigart, *The Lancasterian System of Instruction in the Schools of New York City* (New York: Teachers College Press, Columbia University, 1916).

that in a democratic, self-governing society citizens needed to be able to intelligently elect competent officials to conduct the affairs of state. Thus a mixture of political, social, and economic motivations characterized the demand for universal schooling that culminated in the common school movement.

THE COMMON SCHOOL   While the major thrust of the American common school movement of the first half of the nineteenth century was to win popular support in publicly financed elementary education, it also had broad social, political, intellectual, and economic ramifications. The common school may be defined as an institution devoted to elementary education in the basic tool skills of reading, writing, and arithmetic. It was common in that it was open to the children of all social and economic classes. Through a common or a shared program of civic education, it was to cultivate a sense of American identity and loyalty.[39] Its major social purpose was to integrate children of various social, economic, and ethnic backgrounds into the broad American community. The political objective of common schooling had been enunciated earlier by such leaders as Jefferson. It was to educate the future citizens of a country with self-governing political institutions.

Melting pot theme

Intellectually, the common school curriculum was to cultivate the basic tools of literacy that could be used in everyday life and for ongoing practical education. It was not intended to teach the traditional classical curriculum. Economically, the common school was seen as a place to learn the skills and the attitudes that made one into a competent shopkeeper, merchant, artisan, and worker. It was an agency to develop the practical economic competencies that facilitated upward mobility and occupational choice.

Practical education

Since the Tenth Amendment of the U. S. Constitution reserved powers over education to each state, the patterns of common school establishment varied considerably from state to state. As noted earlier, the American educational system really was a decentralized system rather than a centralized one as was found in the continental nations of Europe. Even within a given state, especially in the frontier areas where a number of small school districts emerged, there might be significant variations in school support and organization from one local district to another.

State and local variations among school districts

The basic roots of the common school movement were established prior to the Civil War—actually between 1820 and 1850. Common schools generally were established first in the New England states, where Massachusetts and then Connecticut provided the leading examples.[40] The

39   Frederick M. Binder, *The Age of the Common School, 1830–1865* (New York: Wiley, 1974).

40   In 1826 Massachusetts passed a law that required every town to choose a school committee that would be responsible for all the schools in the local area. Thus began the policy of organizing public schools into a school system under a single authority. Eleven years later the Massachusetts legislature established the first state board of education. Connecticut quickly followed the example of its neighbor. See Lawrence A. Cremin, *The American Common School, A Historical Conception* (New York: Teachers College Press, Columbia University, 1951).

northern states generally followed the common school model of New England. As the frontier expanded, and as new states entered the Union, they too adopted the model and enacted the necessary provisions for inaugurating a common or public elementary system of schools. In the South the establishment of common schools was generally delayed until after the Civil War.

Although the pattern for establishing a common school varied from state to state, a general set of procedures occurred in the process of establishing elementary public education systems. Three legislative stages have been identified: *permissive, encouraging,* and *compulsory.* In the permissive stage the state legislature gave permission for the organization of each local school district subject to the approval of the majority of voters in the given school district. In the second stage the state legislature deliberately encouraged the establishment of school districts, the election of school boards, and the raising of tax revenues for school support. In this second stage, however, the state did not compel or require the establishment of common schools; rather, the states encouraged such institutions by providing funds. In the third stage the state compelled the establishment of school districts, the election of school boards, and the tax support of common schools by the setting of a minimum tax rate. The state also might specify in the common school code the minimum curriculum and specification requirements governing school construction, lighting, and maintenance.

Three stages of legislation

Tax support of common schools

Since the amount of taxation varied considerably from school district to school district, the quantity and quality of the education provided were uneven. For a considerable period of time, many districts also charged a tuition payment per child, called a rate bill. With the coming of the common school, the foundation of the American public school system was established. Later in the nineteenth century the public high school would be fashioned to complete the educational ladder that led to the state college and university. Perhaps the most prominent American educator who worked in establishing the foundation of the common school system was Horace Mann.

Foundation of the American public school

MANN: THE FIGHT FOR FREE SCHOOLS   Horace Mann (1796–1859) was born in Massachusetts, attended Brown University, and prepared for a legal career. He was elected to the Massachusetts legislature in 1827, where he became a proponent of the common school cause. When the legislature created a state board of education, Mann was appointed secretary. His *Annual Reports* contain his philosophy of education and his surveys of the condition of common schooling in Massachusetts. As editor of the *Common School Journal,* Mann gained a nationwide audience for his arguments advocating popular elementary education. When he retired from the Massachusetts Board of Education in

1849, Mann was elected to Congress. Later, he served as president of Antioch College.[41]

Horace Mann skillfully executed a consensus style of leadership and administration to gain support for the common school cause. He had to convince several major segments of the Massachusetts population. First, taxpayers had to be shown that it was in their interest to support public schools. To enlist the support of the business community, Mann developed the stewardship theory. He argued that wealthy people have a special responsibility in providing public education. Those who have prospered, Mann asserted, are the guardians or stewards of wealth. Their support of public education actually would create an industrious class of men and women who would obey the law, be diligent in their work, and add to the state's economic well-being. Tax support of education was really an investment that would yield high dividends of public safety, progress, and prosperity. To the workers and farmers of Massachusetts, Mann argued that the common school would be a great social equalizer. It would be the means by which the children of a lower socioeconomic class could gain the necessary skills and knowledge to achieve a higher status. Common schooling would be the instrument of social and economic mobility; it would open the doors to greater opportunities.

Enlisting support of the common schools

A social equalizer

As an administrator Mann realized that he had to have the support of the common school teachers. He sought to improve teacher preparation by encouraging normal schools to professionalize teaching and to secure higher salaries for teachers. His efforts generally were supported although some teachers opposed his liberal views on discipline and classroom management.

In addition to being a wise and effective administrator, Mann was an educational statesman. He clearly recognized the relationship between the common school and the political climate of a democratic society. Citizens in our society needed to be prepared to study the issues of the day and to vote intelligently. The United States was different from the more homogeneous nations of western Europe; it was composed of people of different religious beliefs and of varying ethnic origins and languages, crosscut by special and often conflicting interests. If the United States was to develop the unifying bond of a common culture, there needed to be a common basic education that developed a sense of national identity and purpose. Mann was convinced that common schooling was a national necessity. His quest was for a new public philosophy and a sense of community to be shared by Americans of all backgrounds—and the instrument would be the common school.[42]

A unifying bond of common culture

41 Jonathan Messerli, *Horace Mann: A Biography* (New York: Knopf, 1972).
42 Lawrence A. Cremin, ed., *The Republic and the School: Horace Mann on the Education of Free Man* (New York: Teachers College Press, Columbia University, 1957).

The school would be part of the birthright of every child, financed by the state and local community. It would be for rich and poor alike; it would not only be free, but also as good in quality as any private school; it would be nonsectarian, receiving children of all religions and classes. Through state legislatures and local boards, popularly elected officials rather than professional educators would exercise ultimate control and authority. Mann reasoned that the public, to support the schools, should govern them.[43] Thus he set in motion the built-in dynamism that characterizes today's public schools and the underlying ideals of universal education.

THE ONE-ROOM SCHOOL

The one-room school, often referred to as the district school, was often a rather homely building. In rural areas it was usually small and plain, housing children of many different ages. Rural schools were governed by an elected board of trustees, who levied the taxation rate and employed the teacher. The interior of one of these small country schools was described at the turn of the twentieth century as follows:

A homely building

> A door on the left admits us to the school-room. Here is a space about twenty feet long and ten wide, the reading and spelling parade. At the south end of it, at the left as you enter, was one seat and writing bench, making a right angle with the rest of the seats. This was occupied in the winter by two of the oldest males in the school. At the opposite end was the magisterial desk, raised upon a platform a foot from the floor. The fire-place was on the right, halfway between the door of entrance and another door leading into a dark closet, where the girls put their outside garments and their dinner baskets. This also served as a fearful dungeon for the immuring of offenders. Directly opposite the fire-place was an aisle, two feet and a half wide, running up an inclined floor to the opposite side of the room. On each side of this were five or six long seats and writing benches, for the accommodation of the students at their studies.[44]

The simplicity of the "little red schoolhouse," which was established in almost every rural community, especially throughout the West, eventually led to one of the nation's most lasting, sentimental pictures. The schoolhouse not only symbolized the local commitment to schooling—meager in outlook and facilities though it was—it coincided with the conditions and spirit of the age. In the classroom the basic skills of reading, writing, arithmetic, spelling, geography, and history were taught. An

The "little red schoolhouse"

43   Horace Mann, *Lectures and Annual Reports on Education* (Cambridge, Mass.: Cornhill Press, 1867).

44   Warren Burton, *The District School as It Was* (Boston: Lee & Shepard, 1897), p. 4.

This one-room schoolhouse in Massachusetts symbolizes the local committment to schooling.

important element was the cultivation of the virtues of punctuality, honesty, and hard work.

THE MCGUFFEY The simple ideals of literacy, hard work,
READERS diligence, and virtuous living that characterized nineteenth-century American public schools were epitomized by McGuffey and his readers. William Holmes McGuffey (1800–1873), clergyman, professor, and college president, is best known for the series of readers that bears his name. It is estimated that over 120 million copies of McGuffey's *Readers* were sold between 1836 and 1920.[45] McGuffey, himself, was nurtured in the theology and values of Scotch Presbyterianism, and his readers emphasized the importance of individual virtue and goodness.

120 million copies sold

Stressing the basic moral outlook of White, Anglo-Saxon, Protestant, rural America, the McGuffey readers also emphasized patriotism and heroism. Among the selections included as representative of American

Morality, patriotism, and heroism

45 John H. Westerhoff, *McGuffey and His Readers: Piety, Morality, and Education in Nineteenth-Century America* (Nashville: Abingdon, 1978).

literature were the orations of Patrick Henry, Daniel Webster, and George Washington. Through his readers, McGuffey, in many ways, was a teacher to several generations of Americans. McGuffey also provided the first graded readers for our school systems and paved the way for a totally graded system, which had its beginnings in the 1840s.

THE SECONDARY SCHOOL MOVEMENT

The establishment of the common school created the framework for a tax-supported and locally controlled public elementary school education in the United States. It was upon this base that the public high school would be created—the institution that linked the elementary school with the state colleges and universities. With the creation of public secondary schooling, the institutional links of the American educational ladder were forged.

As the common school movement expanded, the ideal was to provide as much education as possible for all children and youth. The keynote to the late nineteenth century became "more education for more people." While there were setbacks and criticism, the surge toward greater educational opportunity for more and more students continued. By 1900 the majority of children aged six to thirteen were enrolled in elementary schools. By 1980, the percentage had climbed to 99 percent. More remarkable was the expansion of secondary enrollments. At the turn of the century about 10 percent of the youth aged fourteen to seventeen were in school; in 1930 the figure was 50 percent; by 1980 as many as 93 percent were attending and 75 percent were graduating. The concept of universal education had been achieved—something of which few countries could boast.[46]

Increasing enrollments

THE ACADEMY: FORERUNNER OF THE HIGH SCHOOL

In the early nineteenth century the Latin grammar school of the colonial period declined and was replaced by the academy. The academy was the dominant institution of secondary education during the first half of the nineteenth century. Serving the educational needs of the middle classes, it offered a wide range of curricula and subject matter.[47] By 1855 there were more than 6,000 academies in the United States, with an enrollment of 263,000 students. These academies served the needs of both college preparatory and terminal students.

Decline of Latin grammar school

46 *Digest of Educational Statistics, 1980* (Washington, D.C.: U.S. Government Printing Office, 1980), pp. 36–37 Table 29; *Statistics of Public Elementary and Secondary Day School: 1977–1978 School Year* (Washington, D.C.: U.S. Government Printing Office, 1978), p. 32, Table 11. Also see Allan C. Ornstein and Harry L. Miller, *Looking into Teaching* (Chicago: Rand McNally, 1980), p. 403, Table 12.3.

47 Nasaw, *Schooled to Order;* Theodore R. Sizer, *The Age of Academies* (New York: Teachers College Press, Columbia University, 1964).

The academy was characterized by loose organization and ill-defined programs of instruction. The quality and the quantity of these programs varied considerably from academy to academy. Despite the wide range of curricula, three basic patterns were discernible: (1) the traditional college preparatory curriculum; (2) the English language course, which was the general curriculum for those who were completing their formal education; and (3) the normal course, which was intended for prospective common school teachers. In addition, there were also some specialized military academies.

The range of curriculum alternatives, however, was not a sure guide to the quality of instruction. There were great variations in the degree of competency of the instructors and a wide range in the aptitude of the students. Uniformity in accreditation was lacking. The length of the courses also varied considerably. Some courses might be the so-called short courses, which were taught for a few weeks or months, while others might require a semester or a year of study. **Variations in quality**

The academies were generally under the control of private boards of trustees or governing bodies. Occasionally, they might be semipublic and receive some support from cities or states. The era of the academies extended to the 1870s, when they declined in numbers and in popularity and were replaced by the public high school. A few private academies still exist in the United States and continue to provide secondary education for a small percentage of the population.

THE HIGH SCHOOL   Although a small number of high schools had existed in the United States since the founding of the English Classical School of Boston in 1821, the high school did not become the major institution of American secondary education until the second half of the nineteenth century, when it gradually replaced the academy. In the 1870s the courts ruled in a series of cases (especially the Kalamazoo, Michigan case in 1874) that the people of the states could establish and support public high schools with tax funds if they desired. After that, the public high school movement spread rapidly. By 1890 the 2,526 public high schools in the United States were enrolling more than 200,000 students. This can be contrasted to the 1,600 private secondary schools and academies that enrolled at that time fewer than 95,000 students.[48] **Taxes for public high school**

Eventually, the states passed compulsory school laws. Provision of public secondary schools thereafter became an obligation of the states, rather than a voluntary matter for parents of the local district to decide. Children were permitted to attend approved nonpublic schools, but the states had the right to supervise and set minimum standards for *all* schools.

48 Edward A. Krug, *The Shaping of the American High School, 1880-1920*, vol. 1 (New York: Harper & Row, 1964).

Urbanization and the high school   The rise of the high school as the dominant institution of secondary education in the United States was the result of a variety of socioeconomic forces. The United States in the mid-nineteenth century experienced a great transition from an agricultural and rural society to an industrial and urban nation. For example, New York City's population grew from 1,174,779 in 1860 to 4,766,833 in 1910. By 1930 more than 25 percent of all Americans lived in seven great urban areas: New York, Chicago, Philadelphia, Boston, Detroit, Los Angeles, and Cleveland. This rapid urbanization also brought with it a growing need for specialization of occupations, professions, and services, and the high school was seen as the major institution for meeting this need.[49]

As an educational agency of an urban and industrialized society, the high school provided a more intensive and specialized education for more and more people who were continuing their formal education beyond the eight years of elementary schooling. It served the needs of the so-called terminal students who would complete their formal schooling in the high school, and it continued to provide college preparatory schooling for those who were bound for institutions of higher education.[50] In the late nineteenth and early twentieth centuries, it began to include career or vocational courses such as home economics, manual training, industrial and shop training, and clerical-commercial preparation. In these ways the high school was an institutional response to the socioeconomic needs of a society that was becoming increasingly industrialized, urbanized, and specialized.

Academic and vocational courses

The popularization of secondary schools   As a school for students from varying social, economic, racial, religious, and ethnic backgrounds, the high school represented a new kind of secondary institution. In contrast to the European track system of secondary education, which rigidly separated the academic students from the terminal students, the American high school evolved into a democratic and comprehensive institution, which aimed at social integration while providing simultaneously some degree of curricular differentiation. As a school for adolescents, the American high school was a product of a society that was becoming increasingly affluent. It was a society that could afford the financial costs of educating large numbers of fourteen- to eighteen-year-olds. In contrast, poorer nations are unable to provide large systems of secondary education for the general adolescent population. In such countries, where the economy is underdeveloped, people usually go immediately from childhood to adulthood without the benefit of an education designed for the middle years of adolescence.

Social integration

---

49 Edward A. Krug, *The Shaping of the American High School: 1920–1941*, vol. 2 (Madison, Wis.: University of Wisconsin Press, 1972).

50 George S. Counts, *Secondary Education and Industrialism* (Cambridge, Mass.: Harvard University Press, 1929).

The American high school may be viewed as an institutional response to the pronounced social, economic, and educational changes in a nation that was becoming a modernized world power. When the high school became the dominant institution of American secondary education, it was possible for a student to attend an articulated sequence of publicly supported and controlled institutions that began with the kindergarten, extended to the elementary school, continued through high school, and reached the college and university. It was the high school that linked elementary and higher institutions of education and completed the American educational ladder. The creation of the high school also did away with the possibility that a dual system of educational institutions, similar to the European model, might be established in the United States.

Response to needs of society

Link between elementary and higher education

The Committee of Ten   The early years of the American high school witnessed some of the same confusion that had beset its institutional predecessor, the academy. Educators of the more traditional view defined the school as a college preparatory institution. Those who took a broader perspective saw the high school as a "people's school," which would offer a wide range of practical courses. In order to standardize the curricula of the high school, the National Education Association in 1892 established the Committee of Ten. This Committee was chaired by Charles Eliot, president of Harvard University and a major leader in higher education who had extended his interests to both elementary and secondary education. Eliot, a forceful chairman, guided the Committee to two major recommendations: earlier entry of several subjects, and uniform treatment in the teaching of subjects for both college and terminal students.[51]

Efforts to standardize curricula

The Committee recommended eight years of elementary and four years of secondary education. Four separate curricula were recommended as appropriate for the high school: classical, Latin-scientific, modern language, and English. Each curriculum included foreign languages, mathematics, sciences, English, and history—what we now call the basic academic courses. The first two options were more traditional in nature, and the latter two were considered more contemporary.

Subjects prescribed for the high school curriculum were Latin, Greek, English, German, French, and Spanish; algebra, geometry, and trigonometry; astronomy, meteorology, botany, zoology, physiology, geology, and physical geography; and physics and chemistry. History was to be studied by concentrating on well-defined historical periods.

The Committee of Ten structured the high school curriculum along the lines of the traditional college preparatory program. But its recommendations served to liberalize the school program by identifying alternatives to the prevalent Latin and Greek classical curriculum. The reasoning of the Committee was in part influenced by the popular educational psychology of the time, which stressed mental discipline. For example, the

51 National Education Association, *Report of the Committee on Secondary School Studies* (Washington, D.C.: U.S. Government Printing Office, 1893).

Committee concluded that the same subjects would be equally useful to both terminal and college preparatory students, since these subjects trained the mind in observation, memory, reasoning, and expression.

Still, the Committee of Ten had established a basically college preparatory orientation for the high school's program and curriculum; this view was soon challenged by a number of educators who believed that a truly comprehensive secondary institution had to provide a broader program and a larger number of educational alternatives. During the period from 1910 through 1930, several educators argued that the principle of social efficiency should be applied to high school education.[52] Social efficiency simply meant that each person should be prepared to contribute to his or her own personal well-being and the society's good. It represented a departure from the exclusively college preparatory point of view. Education was perceived as a rational and efficient mechanism that could cultivate an individual's capacities as a producer, as a citizen, and as a parent. While the social efficiency educators sought to broaden the context of the high school, they sometimes narrowly defined "useful" and "efficient" in challenging the humanistic aesthetic aspects of secondary education.

Broadened view of high school

In the early twentieth century, the numbers of high school students were growing larger. These students were no longer only the children of the professional and business classes. The population of the high school was coming from the adolescent population at large. The school, for some, was being viewed as the upward extension of the elementary school. This was clearly revealed by the enactment of compulsory school attendance laws in a majority of the states. By 1918 thirty states had laws that specified full-time attendance until age sixteen.[53]

Compulsory school attendance

The Commission on the Reorganization of Secondary Education The basic change in the high school from a college preparatory institution to a comprehensive institution was revealed clearly in the *Cardinal Principles of Secondary Education*, stated in 1918 by the National Education Association's Commission on the Reorganization of Secondary Education. In its statement of the need for reorganization the Commission was clearly aware of the pervasive social changes that had occurred in the United States:

> Secondary education should be determined by the needs of the society to be served, the character of the individuals to be educated, and the knowledge of educational theory and practice available. These factors are by no means static. . . . The evidence is strong that such a comprehensive reorganization of secondary education is imperative at the present time.[54]

52 Walter H. Drost, *David Snedden and Education for Social Efficiency* (Madison, Wis.: University of Wisconsin Press, 1967).

53 Krug, *The Shaping of the American High School, 1920-1941*, p. 7.

54 Commission on the Reorganization of Secondary Education, *Cardinal Principles of Secondary Education*, Bulletin No. 35 (Washington, D.C.: U.S. Government Printing Office, 1918), p. 1.

The Commission noted that:

1. The high school ought to be a truly comprehensive institution based on the various social groups that comprise the population of the United States.

Shift to
comprehensive
orientation

2. The high school curriculum could be differentiated to meet agricultural, business, commercial, industrial, and domestic as well as college preparatory needs without losing its integrative and comprehensive social character.

3. The results of educational theory, psychology of education, measurement, and evaluation should be applied to the programs and instruction of the high school.

4. American education comprises a set of articulated institutions that should function together rather than in isolation.

SECONDARY SCHOOL ORGANIZATION   As the high school assumed its institutional form, four basic curricular patterns could be identified: (1) the college preparatory or academic program, which included courses in English language and literature, foreign languages, mathematics, natural and physical sciences, and history and social sciences; (2) the commercial or business program, which offered courses in bookkeeping, shorthand, and typing; (3) industrial, vocational, home economics, and agricultural programs; and (4) a modified academic program for terminal students who planned to complete their formal education upon high school graduation.

Different
programs for
various
students

Despite some regional variations, the usual high school pattern followed a four-year attendance sequence that encompassed grades nine, ten, eleven, and twelve and was generally attended by the age group from fourteen to eighteen. There were exceptions, however, in that some reorganized six-year institutions could be found in which students attended a combined junior-senior high school after completing a six-year elementary school. The junior high school of three years, seventh, eighth, and ninth grades, combined with the senior school of tenth, eleventh, and twelfth grades, also began to appear in some large school districts in the 1920s.

The rise of
junior high
schools

The junior high school concept grew out of the Committee of Ten's suggestion that secondary education begin two years earlier to reduce the elementary school from eight years to six years.[55] In many instances, the junior high school was initially the first three years of a six-year school. As it developed in the 1920s and 1930s, the junior high school often became a separate facility housing grades seven, eight, and nine. Today, the junior high school has become part of the pattern of school organization for many districts; it represents 31 percent of all secondary schools, com-

---

55 Nelson Bossing and Roscoe Cramer, *The Junior High School* (Boston: Houghton Mifflin, 1965).

pared with 27 percent traditional high school (four years), 23 percent junior-senior school, and 19 percent senior school (three years).[56]

During the 1960s, the middle school appeared. The middle school generally includes students who are ordinarily enrolled in grades six, seven, and eight. The middle school concept was designed to meet the needs of preadolescents, usually ages eleven through thirteen, in an institution that is transitional between elementary and high school. It is intended to permit a gradual transition from childhood to adolescence by emphasizing special programs uniquely designed for preadolescents. Some educators classify the school as part of the elementary grade sequence.

Emergence of middle schools

The American high school today is a multipurpose institution: it provides a general education for all students; college preparation for those who wish to continue their formal schooling; and vocational and career preparation in agriculture, industry, and trade. It is comprehensive in the social sense, bringing together students of varying religions, social and economic classes, and ethnic and racial groups. Any institution that performs such varied social and educational services will necessarily be the scene of controversy and conflict. Despite disagreements about purposes, goals, and programs, the high school as an institution is a crucial component in the American educational ladder; in the 1980s, it will continue to serve as the main institution for achieving the notion of "equalization of opportunity" for most children and youth in our country.

THE AMERICAN COLLEGE AND UNIVERSITY

The colleges of the colonial period followed the British pattern of Oxford and Cambridge. In addition to preparing the scholar and theologian, the colleges in England sought to educate the well-rounded gentleman of upper socioeconomic class status. The essential curriculum was comprised of grammar, rhetoric, logic, music, astronomy, geometry, and mathematics.

The British model

The early colonial colleges were established under religious auspices. Believing that an educated ministry was needed to establish Christianity in the New World, the Massachusetts General Court created Harvard College in 1636. Yale was founded in 1701 as an alternative to Harvard, which some regarded as too liberal in theological matters. In 1693 Virginia's William and Mary College was granted a royal charter. Princeton, in New Jersey, was chartered in 1746 as a Presbyterian college, and King's College (later Columbia University) was chartered in 1754 to

Religious roots of colonial colleges

---

56 *Digest of Educational Statistics, 1977–78* (Washington, D.C.: U.S. Government Printing Office, 1978), p. 60, Table 60.

serve New York's Anglicans. Other colonial colleges were the University of Pennsylvania, Dartmouth in New Hampshire, Brown in Rhode Island, and Rutgers in New Jersey. Although there were curricular variations among these institutions, the general colonial college curriculum included: (1) Latin, Greek, Hebrew, rhetoric, and logic during the first year; (2) Greek, Hebrew, logic, and natural philosophy during the second year; (3) natural philosophy, metaphysics, and ethics during the third year; and (4) mathematics and a review in Greek, Latin, logic, and natural philosophy during the fourth year.[57]

LAND-GRANT COLLEGES

During the first half of the nineteenth century, the liberal federal land-grant policy encouraged the establishment of many of our state colleges and universities. In addition to state colleges, many religious denominations also founded their own private colleges as a wave of religious revivalism swept the country. These colleges offered liberal arts and frequently included seminaries for the training of ministers.

By the early 1850s critics of traditional liberal arts education were arguing that colleges for agricultural and mechanical science should be established with support from federal land grants.[58] Such institutions were deemed essential to further agricultural and industrial progress. Justin Morrill, a United States congressman from Vermont, sponsored a bill to use federal land grants for the support of agricultural and industrial education. The Morrill Act of 1862 granted each state 30,000 acres of public land for each senator and representative in Congress, based on the apportionment of 1860.[59] The income from this grant was to be used to support at least one state college for agricultural and mechanical instruction.

Agricultural and technical colleges

The effect of the Morrill Act was to bring higher education within reach of the masses. The general impact of land-grant colleges was to further agricultural education, engineering, and other applied sciences, as well as the more traditional liberal arts and professional education.

Higher education for more individuals

American higher education was influenced in the late nineteenth century by the importation of the German research model of scholarship to the United States. Many American professors went to Germany in the late nineteenth century to complete their doctoral studies. While at the German universities, they were engaged in research seminars with learned professors who investigated limited topics in the sciences and the

57 Frederick Rudolph, *The American College and University: A History* (New York: Knopf, 1962).

58 Allan Nevins, *The State Universities and Democracy* (Urbana, Ill.: University of Illinois Press, 1962).

59 Benjamin F. Andrews, *The Land Grant of 1862 and the Land-Grant College* (Washington, D.C.: U.S. Government Printing Office, 1918).

humanities. When they returned to the United States, they brought with them the German concepts of the seminar and the scholarly dissertation.

GROWTH OF
HIGHER EDUCATION

After World War II, American higher education experienced its greatest growth. From 1950 to 1965, college enrollments doubled from 2.4 million to 4.9 million students. By 1975, the number had almost doubled again to 9 million. By 1980, 12 million students were enrolled in institutions of higher education.[60] Whereas in 1910 about 5 percent of all youth aged 18–21 were attending college in a degree program, by 1960 the percentage was 36; by 1970 it was 52; by 1980, it was close to 60 percent.[61] Millions more were attending adult education classes offered by business, labor, armed services, and social agencies. Educational television and adult continuing education programs enrolled thousands of others. The concept of "equality of educational opportunity" had reached the institutions of higher learning.

Rising student enrollments

In the early 1970s, enrollment patterns in higher education began to change. Although the number of college students had grown slightly, the massive increases in student enrollments of the 1950s and 1960s had abated and apparently leveled off. While it is difficult to estimate future enrollment patterns, three implications of this trend can be considered: the enrollment or population of college age students, the planning of colleges and universities, and the degree of socioeconomic change.

Leveling-off period

1. *Enrollments.* The number of students who attend college depends on the size of the population in the eighteen-to-twenty-one age group. It is anticipated that this population will remain constant until the early 1980s and then decrease.[62]

2. *Planning.* During the 1950s and 1960s, colleges and universities expanded physical facilities, faculties, and supportive staff. The increasing costs of higher education placed tremendous financial burdens on lower- and middle-income students and their families. These costs may affect future student enrollments, especially at private colleges where tuition fees are higher than at public institutions.

Increasing financial burdens on students

3. *Socioeconomic Change.* The future of higher education in the United States is correlated to basic socioeconomic trends. The attraction of higher education to many college-age students depends on the national economy and the job outlook.

---

60 *Digest of Educational Statistics, 1980,* p. 102, Table 94; *Projections of Educational Statistics, 1986–87* (Washington, D.C.: U.S. Government Printing Office, 1978), p. 14, Table 2; p. 20, Table 5.

61 *Projections of Educational Statistics to 1983–84* (Washington, D.C.: U.S. Government Printing Office, 1974), p. 7, Figure 6; pp. 17–18, Table 2; *Projections of Educational Statistics to 1986–87,* p. 158, Table B-2.

62 *Projections of Educational Statistics to 1986–87,* p. 20, Table 5.

SUMMING UP

1. Development of the American system of public schools began in the colonial era, when European educational institutions such as the vernacular school and the Latin grammar school were transported to the New World.

2. With the founding of the United States as an independent sovereign nation, a new system of formal education was required for the American republic. Educational theorists such as Jefferson, Franklin, Webster, and Mann placed great emphasis on the role of free schools in cultivating the appropriate civic attitudes of a free people.

3. During the nineteenth century the American common school arose as the educational institution designed to supply basic civic and skill competencies. Near the end of the nineteenth century the public high school arose to link the common elementary schools with the colleges and universities.

4. At the beginning of the twentieth century an American public school system had been fashioned that embraced elementary, secondary, and higher institutions. The major educational problem of the present and the future is devising the ways these educational institutions will serve all Americans equally well, regardless of race, creed, or socioeconomic class.

DISCUSSION QUESTIONS

1. In terms of your reading of this chapter, indicate if the tone is celebrationist, liberal, or revisionist in interpretation. Explain your answer.

2. What has been the influence of the Puritan ethic on American culture and education?

3. Is Jefferson's concept of political education adequate for the needs of contemporary American society?

4. In terms of the history of American secondary education, why is the high school the frequent scene of controversy over its purposes?

5. In terms of the history of American education, what seems to be the American public school philosophy?

THINGS TO DO

1. Reflect upon your high school experience. Write a short history of your experience in relationship to the economic, social, and political trends of that period.

2. Interview your parents or grandparents regarding their school experience. Compare and contrast their educational experience with your experience.

3. Develop a collection of newspaper articles on education. Identify the major issues and attempt to trace their historical origins.

4. Request your professor to invite an experienced teacher or school administrator to speak to your class on the changes that have taken place in education during his or her career as an educator.

5. Request your professor to invite a college or university administrator to speak to the class on some of the problems confronting higher education.

CHAPTER 8
PHILOSOPHICAL IDEAS IN EDUCATION

Focusing questions

How do general philosophy and philosophy of education relate?

How do philosophers' conceptions of human nature influence their views of education?

How do philosophers of education treat the ethical or value dimension of education?

How does educational philosophy affect everyday school practice?

Is there a dominant American philosophy of education at this time?

How can teachers create their own philosophy of education?

Most speculative, reflective, and theoretical efforts to answer questions that concern the basic purposes of education are philosophical in nature. The same basic questions that were raised earlier in a historical context can now be examined in philosophical perspective. What is knowledge? What is education? What is schooling? Who should attend school? How should teaching be carried on? As a future teacher, you will be called upon to answer such questions. This chapter explores questions at the most abstract level. If an answer to a question is stated in its most abstract and general terms, it will be transferable to a wide variety of human situations. After discussing a particular school of educational philosophy, we can then suggest how the basic questions we have posed might be answered in the perspective of that philosophy.

As a teacher you will be involved in many immediate concerns—the day-to-day problems of preparing lessons and classroom management. These immediate concerns will seem to be very specific to a given day, time, or event, but how you deal with them will reveal your educational philosophy. Of necessity, as you examine yourself as a teacher you will be thinking about the purposes of education. You will be faced with the challenge of establishing your own meaning and significance in teaching. In essence, you will be creating your own philosophy of education. An examination of the systems of philosophy of education that have already been elaborated can help in your personal search for a philosophy of education.

The educational philosophies we shall examine have helped to shape American education. Idealism and Realism are early traditional philosophies that have long guided educational theory and practice in western culture. From Chapter 5, for example, you will recall that Plato espoused an Idealist philosophy and Aristotle a Realist. Closely related to these important traditional philosophies are the educational theories of Perennialism and Essentialism. In contrast to these more traditional philosophies, Pragmatism emphasizes the *process* of education. John Dewey, whose work as a pioneer in education was discussed in Chapter 6, stressed the processes of experience and problem solving in his work at the University of Chicago Laboratory School. The educational theories of Progressivism and Social Reconstructionism are closely related to Pragmatism and were derived from it. Most recently, Existentialism and Philosophical Analysis have emerged as new contributions to the philosophy of education.

We need to explore these varying and often conflicting approaches to education so that the different goals, purposes, curricula, and methodologies of teaching and learning can be viewed in philosophical perspective. Before we do so, however, certain terms and areas of philosophy need to be defined.

TERMINOLOGY In every field of disciplined inquiry, specialists develop a special terminology. In the philosophy of education the basic terms used are *metaphysics, epistemology, axiology,* and *logic.* Most succinctly, these terms have the following meanings: Metaphysics deals with the nature of reality. Epistemology deals with the nature of knowledge. Axiology deals with the nature of values. Logic deals with the nature of reasoning.

Metaphysics examines the nature of ultimate reality. In speculating about the nature of reality and existence, metaphysicians have not developed a single agreed-upon conclusion. Idealists see reality in nonmaterial, or spiritual, terms. Realists see it as an objective order that exists independently of humankind. For Pragmatists reality is a result of human experiences with the environment. In educational philosophy, metaphysics relates to the particular conception of reality reflected in the subjects, experiences, and skills of the curriculum. Much school learning represents the efforts of curriculum-makers, teachers, and textbook writers to describe reality to students. Such subject areas as the social and natural sciences attempt to describe certain dimensions of reality to the learner.

Reality and existence

Epistemology, which deals with knowledge and knowing, is closely related to methods of teaching and learning. Again, different philosophies hold different epistemological conceptions. Idealists see knowing, or cognition, as the recall of ideas that are latent in the mind. For them the Socratic dialogue is the most appropriate teaching method. In the Socratic method the teacher stimulates the student's consciousness by asking leading questions, which bring forth the ideas hidden in the learner's mind. For Realists knowledge begins with our sensations of objects. Through abstracting these sensory materials, we form concepts that correspond to the objects in reality. A teacher who uses the Realist formula of sensation and abstraction would develop classroom activities that utilize sensory stimuli. Pragmatists contend that we create knowledge by interacting with our environment; hence problem solving is the appropriate method of teaching and learning.

Knowledge and knowing

Axiology seeks to specify what is of value. Axiology is divided into *ethics* and *aesthetics.* Ethics examines moral values and the rules of right conduct; aesthetics deals with values in beauty and art. Teachers, concerned with forming values in students, encourage certain preferred behaviors. Parents, teachers, and society reward or punish behavior as it conforms to or deviates from their conceptions of what is right, good, and beautiful. Idealists and Realists subscribe to the objective theory of value, which asserts that the good, true, and beautiful are universally valid in all places and at all times. Pragmatists hold that values are culturally or ethically relative and depend on group or personal preferences that vary with the situation, time, and place.

What is of value?

Logic, concerned with the requirements of correct and valid thinking, examines the rules of inference that enable us to frame correctly our
propositions and arguments. Deductive logic, associated with Idealism
and Realism, moves from general statements to particular instances and
applications. Inductive logic, associated with Pragmatism, moves from the
particular instance to tentative generalizations that are subject to further
verification.

**Deductive and
inductive
thinking**

For the philosophies discussed in this chapter we also will present a
number of "basic questions," which are designed to focus your thinking
about philosophical issues about the nature of schooling, the theoretical
base of the curriculum, and the relationships between the teacher and the
learner.

IDEALISM

Idealism is among the oldest of the traditional philosophies. Plato usually is identified as giving classic formulation to
Idealist philosophical principles. The German philosopher Hegel created a
comprehensive philosophical and historical world view based on Idealism.
In the United States, the Transcendentalist philosophers Ralph Waldo
Emerson and Henry David Thoreau elaborated on the Idealist conception
of reality. In educational theory the founder of the kindergarten, Friedrich Froebel, was an exponent of Idealist pedagogy. William Harris, an
historically significant American educational leader, used Idealism as a
rationale for his administration as a U.S. Commissioner of Education at
the end of the nineteenth century. The leading contemporary proponent of
Idealist education is J. Donald Butler.[1]

**From Hegel to
Butler**

Metaphysics   To the Idealists, only the mental or the spiritual
ultimately is real. For them the universe is an expression of a highly
generalized intelligence and will—a universal mind. The individual's
spiritual essence, or soul, is durable and permanent. One's mind, or life
force, gives one vitality and dynamism. This world of mind and ideas is
eternal, permanent, regular, and orderly. Representing a perfect order,
the eternal ideas are unalterable, and truth and values are absolute and
universal.

Idealists, such as the Transcendentalists, have used the concepts of
the macrocosm and the microcosm to explain their version of reality. *Macrocosm* refers to the universal mind, the first cause, or God. Regardless of
the particular name used, the macrocosmic mind is the whole of existence.
It is the one, all-inclusive, and complete self of which the lesser selves are
parts. The universal, macrocosmic mind is continually thinking and valuing. The *microcosm* is a limited part of the whole—an individual and
lesser self. But the microcosm is of the same spiritual substance as the

1   J. Donald Butler, *Idealism in Education* (New York: Harper & Row, 1966); John P. Strain,
"Idealism: A Clarification of an Educational Philosophy," *Educational Theory* (Summer 1975),
pp. 263–71.

macrocosm. In educational terms the student can be conceived of as a spiritual entity, which is also a part of the larger spiritual universe. Although there are metaphysical differences among the various Idealists, they agree that the universe is made up of spiritual realities that are personal, and the individual or microcosmic selves are part of the one comprehensive and universal whole.

Epistemology   Idealist knowledge is based on the recognition or reminiscence of latent ideas that are already present in the mind. Through introspection the individual examines his or her own mind and finds a copy of the macrocosmic mind. What is to be known is already present in the mind. The teacher's task is to bring this latent knowledge to consciousness.[2] Through learning the student comes into a gradually larger apprehension of mental awareness. As a primarily intellectual process, learning involves recalling and working with ideas. Since reality is mental, education is properly concerned with conceptual matters. The learner seeks a broad and general perspective of his or her universe.

Latent
knowledge

The Idealist educator prefers the order and pattern of a subject-matter curriculum that relates ideas and concepts to each other. Throughout history conceptual systems such as those of language, mathematics, and aesthetics have been interrelated into a synthesis that represents the varying dimensions of the absolute. For example, the liberal arts embrace many conceptual systems, or learned disciplines, such as language, history, mathematics, chemistry, and philosophy. The highest level of knowledge recognizes the relationships and integrates these subject matters.

The Idealist curriculum, constituting the cultural heritage of humankind, is hierarchical. At the top are the most general disciplines, philosophy and theology. These more general subjects are abstract; they transcend the limitations of time, place, and circumstance, and they have the power to transfer to a wide range of situations. Mathematics is especially valuable because it cultivates the power to deal with abstractions. History and literature also rank high since they are sources of moral and cultural models, exemplars, and heroes. Somewhat lower in curricular priority are the natural and physical sciences, which deal with particular cause and effect relationships. Since it is necessary for communication, language is an essential tool at all levels of learning.

The hierarchy
of subjects

Axiology   To the Idealist, values are a reflection of the good inherent in the universe. They are absolute, eternal, and universal. Ethical conduct grows out of the permanent aspects of our cultural heritage. Since the ethical core is contained within and transmitted by this heritage, it is maintained that philosophy, theology, history, literature, and art are rich

Absolute,
eternal, and
universal
values

2   Van Cleve Morris and Young Pai, *Philosophy and The American School: An Introduction to the Philosophy of Education*, 2d ed. (Boston: Houghton Mifflin, 1976); Howard Ozman and Sam Craver, *Philosophical Foundations of Education* (Columbus, Ohio: Merrill, 1976).

value sources. Value education requires that the student be exposed to worthy models, especially the classics, which are regarded as the great works of the human race that have endured over time.

THE BASIC
QUESTIONS

If you were to ask an Idealist teacher, "What is knowledge?" he or she would likely reply that knowledge concerns the spiritual principles that are the base of reality. This knowledge of reality takes the form of ideas. If knowledge is about transcendent and universal ideas, then education is the intellectual process of bringing ideas to the learner's consciousness.

In answering the question, "What is schooling?" the Idealist educator would say that the school is a social agency where students seek to discover and pursue truth. It is an intellectual institution where teachers and students deal with the basic ideas that provide answers to the questions Socrates and Plato first asked: What is truth? What is beauty? What is the good life? These answers are present in our minds, though hidden, and we need to reflect deeply to bring them forth. Nothing should be allowed to distract us from the intellectual pursuit of truth.

Intellectual pursuit of truth

Who should attend school? To this question the Idealist would say everyone. Not all students will demonstrate the same intellectual aptitude, but all of them need to cultivate their minds to the limits of their capacities. The brightest students will need the greatest intellectual challenges that the teacher can provide. The goal of learning is the creative person.

How should teaching be carried on? The Idealist would say that thinking and learning are names for the same process of bringing ideas to consciousness. The Socratic dialogue, a process by which the teacher stimulates the learner's awareness of ideas, is appropriate to Idealist teaching and learning. The use of this method requires skillful questioning on the part of the teacher. Another important aspect of Idealist methodology is the role of imitation. The teacher is to be a person who has wide knowledge of the cultural heritage, who leads a well-ordered life, and who is a model worthy of imitation by the students.

Socratic dialogue

REALISM

Realism stresses objective knowledge and values as does Idealism, but the Realist view of metaphysics and epistemology is different. A basic definition describes the essential doctrines of Realism as follows: (1) there is a world of real existence which human beings have not made or constructed, (2) this real existence can be known by the human mind, and (3) such knowledge is the only reliable guide to human conduct, individual and social.[3] This definition provides a conven-

3 P. H. Hirst and R. S. Peters, *Education and the Development of Reason* (Boston: Routledge & Paul, 1975); John Wild, *Introduction to Realist Philosophy* (New York: Harper & Row, 1948).

ient starting point for considering the educational implications of Realist metaphysics, epistemology, and axiology.

Metaphysics and epistemology   For the Realist there is a material world that exists independently and externally to the mind of the knower. The basis for understanding reality is found in a world of objects and in the perceptions of these objects. All objects are composed of matter. Matter must be encased in a form and has to assume the structure of a particular object.

Human beings can *know* these objects through their senses and their reason. Knowing is a process that involves two stages: sensation and abstraction. First, the knower sees an object and records the sensory data about it such as color, size, weight, smell, or sound. These sensory data are sorted out in the mind into those qualities that are always present in the object and those qualities that are sometimes present in the object. Upon the abstraction of the necessary qualities of an object (those that are always present), the learner comes to a concept of the object. Conceptualization results when the mind has abstracted the form of an object and has recognized the object as belonging to a class. Objects are classified when they are recognized as having qualities that they share with other members of the same class but not with objects that belong to a different class.[4]

Knowing
involves
sensation and
abstraction

The Realist theory of knowledge has also been referred to as a "spectator theory." This simply means that people are spectators or onlookers in the world. In their experience people see many objects. Some of them are two-legged creatures like themselves, others are four-legged, or other forms of the animal kingdom, and still other objects are plants or minerals. As spectators of reality, men and women engage in a process of sorting out these objects according to their form or structure. They classify those objects that are alike into related classifications. Again as spectators their conception of an object is accurate when it corresponds with the structure of an object in reality.[5]

Sorting and
classifying
objects

Like the Idealist, the Realist believes that a curriculum consisting of organized, separate subject matters is the most effective and efficient way of learning about the reality of the objective order. Organizing subject matter, as scientists and scholars do, is simply a sophisticated method of classifying objects. For example, the past experiences of humankind can be organized into history. Plants can be studied in a systematic way according to their classifications in the subject matter of botany. Animals can be studied in the subject of zoology. Units of political organization such as nations, governments, legislatures, and judicial systems can be organized into the study of political science. For the Realist the way to

4 Harry S. Broudy, *Building a Philosophy of Education* (Englewood Cliffs, N.J.: Prentice-Hall, 1961).
5 William H. Howick, *Philosophies of Western Education* (Danville, Ill.: Interstate, 1971); Harry J. Perkinson, *Since Socrates: Studies in the History of Educational Thought* (New York: Longman, 1980).

gain knowledge of reality is to pursue ordered and disciplined inquiry through these compartmentalized bodies of knowledge or subject matters.

Axiology Based upon the Realist's conception of knowledge, certain prescriptions can be identified to govern intelligent behavior. For example, human beings ought to behave in a rational way; behavior is rational when it conforms to the way in which objects behave in reality. From their study of the subjects that explain reality, men and women can arrive at theories that are based on natural, physical, and social laws. The rational person governs his or her behavior in the light of such tested theory.

*Rational
behavior*

THOMISM Thomistic philosophy, named after Saint Thomas Aquinas, has been identified with Roman Catholic educational institutions.[6] As an offshoot of Realism, Thomism accepts many of Aristotle's basic principles. Its epistemology is much like that of Realism. It also embraces Christian theology from a Roman Catholic perspective. Thomism embraces supernaturalism in that it accepts revelation as a source of divinely-inspired truth.

*Realist
philosophy and
Christian
theology*

In Thomistic metaphysics, reality is viewed as both spiritual and material. Possessing both a soul and a body, the human person is best guided by faith and reason.[7] An educational philosophy based on supernaturalism, Thomists argue, can specify educational aims in terms of the human being's origin, nature, and destiny.

*Faith and
reason*

In the Thomistic conception of curriculum, the most general, abstract, and transferable subjects are located at the top of the curricular hierarchy, while particular, specific, and transitory subjects have a lower order of priority. Religious studies that cultivate spiritual growth and formation also receive emphasis. Logic and lessons designed to cultivate rationality are emphasized. Knowledge and skill that enable people to learn about the ethical, legal, political, and economic systems that contribute to their personal and social welfare are included in the curriculum. Reading, speaking, and writing are necessary in a person's basic education.

*THE BASIC
QUESTIONS* To begin our philosophical cross-examination, we again ask, What is knowledge? In line with their metaphysics, Realists would reply that knowledge concerns the physical world in which we live. An objective order of reality exists. When we know something, our knowledge is always about an object. The concepts that we have in our minds are true when they correspond to those objects as they really exist in the world.

6   John W. Donohue, *St. Thomas Aquinas and Education* (New York: Random House, 1968); John W. Donohue, *Catholicism and Education* (New York: Harper & Row, 1973).

7   William F. Cunningham, *Pivotal Problems in Education* (New York: Macmillan, 1940); Neil G. McCluskey, *Catholic Viewpoint on Education* (New York: Doubleday, 1962).

Education, the Realists would say, is the study of the subject-matter disciplines into which knowledge has been sorted and classified. History, language, science, mathematics—these are organized bodies of knowledge. If we know them, we will know something about the world in which we live. This knowledge is also our best guide in conducting our daily affairs.

Organized bodies of knowledge

The school is the institution that has been established to teach students about the objective world. The instruction that takes place in school should impart a body of knowledge. Students should learn subjects that will aid them in understanding their world so that they can live full and satisfying lives. The Realist teacher needs to be able to recognize the basic concepts in the subject and the generalizations that explain their interactions, and to render these into a teachable and learnable order that meets the needs of the learner. The teacher is to be an authority in both the knowledge of the subject and in the methods of teaching it.[8]

PERENNIALISM

Perennialism is an educational theory that draws heavily on the principles of Realism. It presents a conservative or traditional view of human nature and education. Agreeing with Aristotle's statement that human beings are rational, Perennialists see the school as an institution designed to cultivate human intelligence.[9]

Schools cultivate human intelligence

The Perennialists see the universal aim of education as the search for and the dissemination of truth. Since truth is universal and unchanging, a genuine education is also universal and constant. The school's curriculum should emphasize the recurrent themes of human life. It should contain cognitive subjects that cultivate rationality and the study of moral, aesthetic, and religious principles to cultivate the attitudinal dimension. Like the Idealists and Realists, the Perennialists prefer a subject-matter curriculum. The Perennialist curriculum includes history, language, mathematics, logic, literature, the humanities, and science. The content of these subjects should come from the great books of western civilization and from the classical works of literature and art. Mastering the subject matter of these learned disciplines is regarded as essential for training the intellect.

Great books of western civilization

One of the most articulate of the Perennialist spokesmen has been Robert Hutchins, former president of the University of Chicago. Hutchins has long argued that education ought to cultivate the intellect along with the harmonious development of all human faculties.[10] The central aim of education should be the development of the power of thought. Whereas

8 William O. Martin, *Realism in Education* (New York: Harper & Row, 1969).

9 Eva T. Brann, *Paradoxes of Education in a Republic* (Chicago: University of Chicago Press, 1979); John Stoops, *Philosophy and Education in Western Civilization* (Danville, Ill.: Interstate, 1971).

10 Robert M. Hutchins, *The Learning Society* (New York: Praeger, 1968).

most educators justify the emphasis on thought because it organizes and enriches life experiences, Hutchins derives it from a definition of the fixed and essential nature of human beings. Hutchins has described the ideal education as

> . . . one that develops intellectual power. I arrive at this conclusion by a process of elimination. Educational institutions are the only institutions that can develop intellectual power. The ideal education is not an *ad hoc* education, not an education directed to immediate needs; it is not a specialized education, or a pre-professional education; it is not a utilitarian education. It is an education calculated to develop the mind.[11]

Hutchins bases his educational philosophy on two major premises: human nature is rational and knowledge resides in unchanging, absolute, and universal truths. Since the rationality of human nature is universal, Hutchins stresses that education must also be universal.[12] Since reason is our highest power, the development of the intellect should be education's highest priority. Hutchins advocates a curriculum that consists of permanent, or perennial, studies. He particularly recommends the study of the classics or the great works of western civilization. Reading and discussing great books will cultivate the intellect and will prepare students to think carefully and critically. In addition to these classics, he urges the study of grammar, rhetoric, logic, mathematics, and philosophy.

In general, Perennialism represents a conservative theoretical position centered on the authority of tradition and the classics. Among its major educational principles are: (1) truth is universal and does not depend on the circumstances of places, time, or persons; (2) a good education involves a search for and an understanding of the truth; (3) truth can be found in the great works of civilization; and (4) education is a liberal exercise that develops the intellect.

Education for truth

ESSENTIALISM   Essentialism is a conservative educational theory that arose as a response to progressive education. Essentialism is basically a position that emphasizes the authority of the teacher and the value of the subject-matter curriculum. For the Essentialists, education involves the learning of the basic skills, arts, and sciences that have been developed in the past. These essential skills—reading, writing, and arithmetic—are to be found in every sound elementary school curriculum.[13] At

Basic skills and academic subjects

11 Robert M. Hutchins, *A Conversation on Education* (Santa Barbara, Calif.: The Fund for the Republic, 1963), p. 1.

12 Robert M. Hutchins, *The Higher Learning in America* (New Haven: Yale University Press, 1962).

13 William C. Bagley, "Just What Is the Crux of the Conflict Between the Progressives and the Essentialists?" *Educational Administration and Supervision* (September 1940), pp. 508–11; Gurney Chambers, "Educational Essentialism Thirty Years After," *School and Society* (January 1969), pp. 14–16.

the secondary level the basic curriculum consists of academic subjects in the arts and sciences. Mastering these skills and subjects prepares the student to function as a member of a civilized society. In addition, the student also should acquire the behavior needed for successful living. The learning of the essential curriculum requires discipline and hard work. Those who aspire to be teachers should be skilled professionals both in subject matter and in teaching.

Discipline and hard work

Arthur Bestor, an advocate of contemporary Essentialism, sees the liberal arts and sciences as the core of a general education that will enable all men and women to function intelligently. Bestor and the members of the Council on Basic Education have argued that the intellectual quality of American education has been weakened by those professional educators who have stressed life adjustment and other nonessentials. Bestor's book, *The Restoration of Learning*, argues that a good education should provide "... sound training in the fundamental ways of thinking represented by history, science, mathematics, literature, language, art and other disciplines evolved in the course of mankind's long quest for usable knowledge, cultural understanding, and intellectual power."[14]

Essentialists hold that these intellectual disciplines should be basic in the school curriculum since they are the necessary foundations of modern life. In the elementary school curriculum, reading, writing, arithmetic, and research skills are the indispensable studies. The high school curriculum should consist of science, mathematics, history, English, and foreign languages. These are the tools of a liberal education and the most reliable aids in meeting the requirements of both personal and social life. It is the task of the school to channel the accumulated experience of humankind into the organized, coherent, and differentiated disciplines. Only after mastering these basic disciplines can the student be expected to use them to solve personal, social, and civic problems.

Liberal education

Certain common themes can be found in the Essentialist position. Among them are: (1) the elementary school curriculum should aim to cultivate basic tool skills that contribute to literacy and mastery of arithmetical computation; (2) the secondary curriculum should cultivate competencies in history, mathematics, science, English, and foreign languages; (3) schooling requires discipline and a respect for legitimate authority; and (4) learning requires hard work and disciplined attention.

BASIC EDUCATION   Since the 1970s, the United States has experienced a revival of Essentialism with the "back-to-basics" movement. Since the movement has been a grassroots rather than professional one, it does not yet have a coherent philosophical rationale.[15]

Revival of Essentialism

14 Arthur E. Bestor, *The Restoration of Learning* (New York: Knopf, 1955), p. 7.

15 Ben Brodinsky, "Back to the Basics: The Movement and Its Meaning," *Phi Delta Kappan* (March 1977), pp. 523–27; William G. Huitt and Eui-Do Rim, "A Basic Skills Instructional Improvement Program: Utilization of Research to Improve Classroom Practice." Paper presented at Annual Meeting of American Educational Research Association, Boston, April 1980.

Back-to-basics proponents contend that social experimentation and untested innovations have lowered academic standards. They charge that many children have not mastered basic literary and computational skills. Also contributing to the academic weaknesses of American education at the secondary level has been a rejection of prescribed courses for electives and minicourses. The back-to-basics position is that schools should concentrate on the essential skills and subjects that contribute to literacy and to social and intellectual efficiency.

In this view teachers should be restored to instructional authority. They must be well-prepared and accountable for children's failure to learn. Instruction should be geared to organized learning, often in the form of textbooks. The method of instruction should center on regular assignments, homework, recitations, and frequent testing and evaluation. Chapter 16 discusses other aspects of the back-to-basics movement.

Homework and testing

THE BASIC QUESTIONS Since the Perennialists and Essentialists share many ideas about knowledge, education, schooling, and instruction, their views can be examined as a defense of educational traditionalism or conservatism in a cultural sense. They see historical experience as the surest guide to questions about educational issues. For them, the school is concerned with ideas, knowledge, the cultivation of human intellectuality, and the cultural heritage. The school's task, then, is to civilize human beings.

Traditional-conservative view of education

Based upon their traditional and culturally conservative perspective, Perennialists and Essentialists are suspicious of the argument that the school should be an agency of socialization, of life adjustment, or of vocationalism. They claim that such nonintellectual activities detract from and will ultimately destroy the school's intellectual and cultural civilizing role.

Perennialists and Essentialists are also suspicious of educational change for the sake of change. They see the teaching-learning relationship as centered on the transmission and mastering of academic subject matter.

PRAGMATISM In contrast to the traditional views of education discussed thus far, John Dewey's Pragmatism (or Experimentalism) represents a philosophy of education that is based on change, process, relativity, and the reconstruction of experience.[16] Dewey's work as an educational pioneer was examined in Chapter 6. In this chapter the focus will be directed to his Pragmatic philosophy.

---

16 R. S. Peter, *John Dewey Reconsidered* (Boston: Routledge & Paul, 1977); Arthur G. Wirth, *John Dewey as Educator: His Design for Work in Education 1894-1904* (New York: Wiley, 1966).

Dewey was a commanding figure in the field and wrote extensively on the subject.[17] Charles Darwin's theory of evolution had a marked impact upon his work. Dewey applied the terms "organism" and "environment" to education. The human being is a biological and sociological organism possessing drives or impulses that function to sustain life and to further growth and development. Every organism lives in a habitat or environment. In the process of living the human organism experiences problematic situations that threaten his or her continued existence or that interfere with ongoing activities. The successful human being can solve these problems and add the details of the particular problem-solving episode to his or her general stock of experiences.[18] In Dewey's philosophy of education, experience is the key word. Experience can be defined simply as the interaction of the human organism with its environment. Since living depends on the ability to solve problems, then education becomes that which cultivates the problem-solving skills and method.

Cultivating problem-solving skills

While Idealism, Realism, Perennialism, and Essentialism all emphasized bodies of substantive knowledge or subject-matter disciplines, Dewey stressed the methodology or the process of problem solving. According to Dewey, learning occurs as the person engages in problem solving. In Dewey's Experimental epistemology, the learner, as an individual or as a member of a group, utilizes the scientific method to solve both personal and social problems. For Dewey the problem-solving method can be developed into a habit that is transferable to a wide variety of situations.[19]

Metaphysics and epistemology   Based on the importance Dewey ascribes to the organism, the environment, experience, and problem solving, it is possible to establish some generalizations regarding the Pragmatic or Experimentalist philosophy of education. While the more traditional philosophies of Idealism and Realism had a carefully separated metaphysics and epistemology, Pragmatism or Experimentalism construes epistemology as a process in which reality is constantly changing.

The epistemological or knowing situation involves a person, an organism, and an environment. The person interacts with the environment in order to live, grow, and develop. This interaction may alter or change the environment and it may also alter or change the person. Knowing is thus a *transaction* between the learner and the environment. Basic to this interaction is the concept of change. Each interaction may have some generalizable aspects or features that can be carried to the next interaction, but each episode is somewhat different. Thus, the person is con-

Environmental interaction and change

---

17   John Dewey, *The Child and the Curriculum* (Chicago: University of Chicago Press, 1902); Dewey, *Democracy and Education* (New York: Macmillan, 1906); Dewey, *The School and Society* (Chicago: University of Chicago Press, 1923); Dewey, *Experience and Education* (New York: Macmillan, 1938).

18   John L. Childs, *American Pragmatism and Education* (New York: Holt, Rinehart, 1956).

19   Henry W. Hodysh, "Historical Theory and Social Change in John Dewey's Philosophy," *Educational Theory* (Summer 1970), pp. 245-52.

stantly changing, the environment is constantly changing, and the experiences or transactions are also changing.

If reality is continually changing, then a curriculum based on permanent realities such as that of the Perennialists or the Essentialists cannot be acceptable for the Pragmatists. What is needed is a method for dealing with change in an intelligent manner. Since reality is a process of transformation or reconstruction of both the person and the environment, how can the course of change be directed toward desired outcomes? The Deweyites stress problem solving as the most effective and efficient method for dealing with the direction or course of change. Concepts of unchanging or universal truth, such as the Realists and Idealists suggest, become untenable. The only guides that human beings have in their interaction with the environment are established generalizations or tentative assertions that are subject to further research and verification. Each time that human experience is reconstructed to solve a problem, a new contribution is added to humanity's fund of experience.

Dealing with change

Axiology and Logic   Based upon this concept of tentative truth, it can be seen that the Pragmatic conceptions of axiology are also highly situational. Values are relative to time, place, and circumstances. That which contributes to human and social growth and development is regarded as valuable, and that which restricts or contracts experience is unworthy. It is necessary to test and reexamine value assumptions in the same way that scientific claims are subjected to verification. Knowledge and values are subject to further experimentation and reconstruction.

The logic used in Experimentalist education is inductive and based on the scientific method. Tentative assertions are based on empirical experience and must be tested. Experimentalist logic is suspicious of a priori truths and deductions based on them.

Scientific method

THE BASIC QUESTIONS   The Pragmatist answers to questions about knowledge, education, schooling, and instruction are very different from those of the more traditional schools of educational philosophy. For the Pragmatists, knowledge is tentative and subject to revision. They are more concerned with the process of using knowledge than with truth as a body of knowledge. In contrast, the traditional philosophers tend to emphasize truth as a body of knowledge that is permanent rather than tentative.

For the Pragmatist education is an experimental process; it is a method of dealing with and solving problematic situations that arise as people interact with their world. Dewey argued that human beings experience the greatest personal and social growth when they interact with the environment in an intelligent and reflective manner. The most intelligent way of solving problems is to use the scientific method.[20] When you face a

20 Alan Lawson, "John Dewey and the Hope for Reform," *History of Education Quarterly* (Spring 1975), pp. 31-66.

problem, the information needed to solve the problem comes from many sources. It is interdisciplinary, rather than located within a single discipline or academic subject matter. For example, the information needed to define the problem of pollution of the physical environment and to suggest ways of solving it comes from many different sources. The factors that must be considered are historical, political, sociological, scientific, technological, and international. An educated person, in the Pragmatic sense, knows how to take information from various sources and disciplines and use that knowledge in an instrumental manner. The more traditional philosophical perspectives represented by Idealism, Realism, Perennialism, and Essentialism are suspicious of the interdisciplinary approach in education because they believe that a student must first master organized subject matter before attempting to solve problems.

Pragmatists, such as Dewey, see the school as a specialized environment that is continuous with the more general social environment. For them, no demarcation exists between school and society. The school is society's agency for selecting and simplifying the cultural elements that an individual needs to participate in social life. As a specialized environment, the school deliberately brings the young into cultural participation. As a selective agency, it transmits part of the cultural heritage and seeks to reconstruct other aspects of the culture. The school's threefold functions are simplifying, purifying, and balancing the cultural heritage. To simplify, the school selects elements of the heritage and reduces their complexity into appropriate units for learning. To purify, the school selects worthy elements of the cultural heritage and eliminates unworthy ones that limit human interaction and growth. To balance, the school integrates the selected and purified experiences into a harmony. Since many different groups participate in society, the school assists the children of one group in understanding members of other social groups. As a genuinely integrated and democratic learning community, the school should be open to all.

School as an agency of society

Transmitting the cultural heritage

Pragmatists consider teaching and learning to be processes of reconstructing experience according to the scientific method. Learning takes place in an active way as the learners, either individually or in groups, solve problems. These problems will vary in response to changing circumstances and environments. The important objective is that the learner will acquire the method or process of solving problems in an intelligent manner. Most significant, the teacher does not attempt to dominate learning but rather seeks to guide it by acting as a director or facilitator of the student's research.

PROGRESSIVISM

Although progressive education, or Progressivism, is often associated with John Dewey's Pragmatism or Experimentalism, the progressive education movement wove together a number of diverse strands. In its origins the progressive education movement was part of the larger sociopolitical movement of general reform that characterized American life in the late nineteenth and early twentieth centuries. The political progressives such as Robert La Follette and Woodrow Wilson wanted to curb powerful trusts and monopolies and to make the system of political democracy truly operative; Jane Addams and other progressives worked in the settlement house movement to improve social welfare in Chicago and in other urban areas. Progressive education was part of this general movement to reform American life and institutions.[21]

Part of a larger reform movement

By the 1920s the general reform currents had ebbed, but progressive education continued to flourish. Although there was no central dogma, Progressive educators stressed the view that all learning should center in the child's interests and needs. One described the principles of organic education as follows:

Child's interests and needs

> We believe the educational program should aim to meet the needs of the growing child. We believe that childhood is for itself and not a preparation for adult life. Therefore, the school program must answer the following questions: What does the child of any particular age need to minister to the health of his body, to preserve the integrity of the intellect, and to keep him sincere and unselfconscious of spirit?
>
> The answers to these questions will constitute the curriculum of the school, and as we grow in understanding of the nature and needs of childhood, the curriculum will change.[22]

Others stressed as well the need to make school a pleasant place for learning.

School as a pleasant place

> Every child has the right to live naturally, happily, and fully as a child. . . . Childhood in itself is a beautiful section of life, and children should be given a chance for free, full living.
>
> We try to make the schools happy, attractive places for children to be in. . . . We believe in colorfulness, coziness, hominess in our classrooms; in an opportunity for spontaneity. We want children to *want* to come to school.[23]

---

21 For the history of the general progressive movement in American life, see J. Leonard Bates, *The United States 1898-1928: Progressivism and a Society in Transition* (New York: McGraw-Hill, 1976). The progressive movement in education has been given an excellent treatment in Lawrence A. Cremin, *The Transformation of the School* (New York: Random House, 1961).

22 Marietta Johnson, "The Educational Principles of the School of Organic Education, Fairhope, Alabama," in H. Rugg, ed., *The Foundations and Technique for the Study of Education*, National Society for the Study of Education, Part I (Bloomington, Ind.: Public School Publishing Co., 1926), p. 349.

23 Carleton Washburne, "The Philosophy of the Winnetka Curriculum," in Rugg, ed., *The Foundations and Technique of Curriculum Construction*, pp. 222-23.

PROGRESSIVE PRINCIPLES The loosely structured Progressive Education Association, organized in 1919, was not united by a single comprehensive philosophy of education. The Progressives differed in many of their theories and practices, but they were united in their opposition to certain traditional school practices. They generally condemned the following: (1) the authoritarian teacher, (2) exclusive reliance on bookish methods of instruction or on the textbook, (3) passive learning by memorization of factual data, (4) the four-walls philosophy of education that attempted to isolate education from social reality, and (5) the use of fear or physical punishment as a form of discipline.

Criticized traditional school practices

The Progressive Education Association refused to proclaim a philosophy of education but did announce certain unifying principles. Among them were the following: (1) the child should be free to develop naturally; (2) interest, stimulated by direct experience, is the best stimulus for learning; (3) the teacher should be a research person and a guide to learning activities; (4) there should be close cooperation between the school and the home; and (5) the progressive school should be a laboratory for pedagogical reform and experimentation.[24]

Progressive education was both a movement within the broad framework of American education and a theory that urged the liberation of the child from the traditional emphasis on rote learning, lesson recitations, and textbook authority. In opposition to the conventional subject matter of the traditional curriculum, Progressives experimented with alternative modes of curricular organization—utilizing activities, experiences, problem solving, and the project method. Progressive education focused on the child as the learner rather than on the subject; emphasized activities and experiences rather than verbal and literary skills; and encouraged cooperative group learning activities rather than competitive individualized lesson learning. The use of democratic school procedures was seen as a prelude to community and social reform. Progressivism also cultivated a cultural relativism that critically appraised and often rejected traditional value commitments.

Focus on learner, not the subject

Although the major thrust of progressive education waned in the 1940s and came to an end in the 1950s, it did leave its imprint on education and the schools of today. Contemporary child-centered Progressivism is expressed in humanistic education and in the open educational arrangements based on the British Primary School.

THE BASIC QUESTIONS Since the Progressives were not of a single mind, they gave a variety of responses to questions about the nature of education, the school, teaching,

24 Patricia A. Graham, *Progressive Education: From Arcady to Academe* (New York: Teachers College Press, Columbia University, 1967).

*The elementary school children in this "open" classroom
situation are engaged in a self-teaching lesson that explores
the solar system.*

and learning. However, they were able to agree on their opposition to
traditionalism and authoritarianism. While some Progressives believed
that education was a process intended to liberate children, others were
more concerned with social reform.

**Liberating
children and
social reform**

Child-centered Progressives saw the school as a place where children
would be free to experiment, to play, and to express themselves. Those
inclined to a more societal perspective saw the school as a community
center or as an agency of social reform.

Progressives generally were not interested in using the curriculum
to transmit subjects to students. Rather, the curriculum was to come from
the child. Learning could take a variety of forms such as problem solving,
field trips, creative artistic expression, and projects. Above all, Progressives saw the teaching-learning process as active, exciting, and ever-
changing.

SOCIAL RECONSTRUCTIONISM

While the Deweyite practitioner and the project-method, child-centered, and creative-oriented educators were Progressive educators who emphasized the individuality of the child, there were also Progressives who were vitally concerned with social change. These Progressives, called Social Reconstructionists, argued that Progressive education should do more than reform the social and educational status quo; it should seek to create a new society. Social Reconstructionism will be examined here as a separate school of educational philosophy; its origins, however, were originally part of the Progressive movement in education.

Creation of a new society

Social Reconstructionism is a philosophy of education that postulates that humankind is in a state of profound cultural crisis. If schools reflect the dominant social values, as the traditional educational theorists suggest, then, according to the Reconstructionists, organized education will merely transmit the social ills that are symptoms of the pervasive problems and afflictions that beset humankind. The Reconstructionists generally assert that the only legitimate goal of a truly humane education is to create a world order in which people are in control of their own destiny. In an era of nuclear weapons, there is an urgent need that society reconstruct itself before it destroys itself.

In analyzing the cultural crisis, the Reconstructionists contend that while humankind has moved from an agricultural and rural society to an urban and technological society at the level of invention and scientific discovery, there is a serious lag in cultural adaptation to the realities of a technological society. Humankind has yet to reconstruct its values in order to catch up with the changes in the technological order, and organized education has a major role to play in reducing the gap between the values of the culture and technology.[25]

Lag in cutural adaptation

RECONSTRUCTIONIST THINKING

The Reconstructionists recommend that teachers and schools embark on a critical examination of the culture in which they live. They should seek to identify the major areas of controversy, conflict, and inconsistency and seek to explore and to resolve them. For example, certain nations enjoy plenty while other peoples live with the constant threat of starvation. While a few people enjoy luxury, many are victims of disease and poverty. Although the social and economic gap is not as wide in the United States as in other countries, it is still evident and a cause of many of our present problems. Education should expose these social inconsistencies and seek to resolve

Social and economic problems

---

25 Theodore Brameld, *Toward a Reconstructed Philosophy of Education* (New York: Dryden, 1965).

them in such a way that the common people can determine the distribution and control of the resources of the planet.

The Reconstructionists believe, further, that the technological era is one of tremendous interdependence. Events in one area of the globe will have their impact on other areas. For example, the pollution of the environment is a global problem that is not restricted to a single place or to a single people. In such an interdependent world the old forms of education that stressed either isolationism or nationalism are obsolete. The new education for the reconstructed society must recognize the reality of an interdependent world that is international in scope. In an era when nuclear weapons are proliferating, a war or conflict in any area of the globe can be a potential threat to all of humankind. Therefore, the Reconstructionist generally would seek to internationalize the curriculum so that men and women would learn that they live in a global village.

The Social Reconstructionists share a common concern that human survival and education are reciprocally related. To ensure the continuation of our species on this planet, we must become social engineers, plotting our course of change and then using our scientific and technological expertise to arrive at the defined goal. A Reconstructionist program of education will be one that: (1) critically examines the cultural heritage; (2) does not fear to examine the most controversial of social issues; (3) is deliberately committed to bring about social (and constructive) change; (4) will cultivate a planning attitude; and (5) will enlist students and teachers in definite programs of social, educational, political, and economic change as a means of total cultural renewal.

Human survival depends on education

Concern with social issues has led Reconstructionist philosophers to propose educational policies that are related to important national and world problems. They have encouraged policies designed to alleviate racial discrimination and poverty. A Reconstructionist orientation is compatible with programs of compensatory education, school integration, and bilingual and bicultural education. Reconstructionists have encouraged international education as a means of reducing world conflict. Since they are interested in policy formulation, Reconstructionists are interested in examining the ideas of the great utopian thinkers and in conducting futuristic studies that serve to predict the course of things to come.

Futuristic studies

THE BASIC QUESTIONS The Social Reconstructionists are convinced that a new social order will come about only as educators challenge obsolete conceptions of knowledge, education, schooling, and instruction and initiate carefully planned and directed educational change that will lead to social change. Like the Experimentalists, the Social Reconstructionists see knowledge in instrumental terms. The knowledge areas that are particularly useful are the social sciences such as anthropology, economics, sociology, political science, and psychology. These social sciences provide insights, information, and methods that can be used in devising strategies for planned social change in contemporary society.[26]

Education, for the Social Reconstructionists, is designed to awaken the students' consciousness about social problems and to engage them actively in the solving of problems. To awaken social consciousness, students are encouraged to question the status quo and to investigate controversial issues in religion, economics, politics, and education. It is by examining controversial issues that the student will develop alternatives to the conventional wisdom.

**Active
problem-solving**

The school, as a social agency, is an institution where divergent thinking and new suggestions for changing society are to be emphasized and encouraged. Divergent thinking is not regarded as a purely intellectual exercise, however. It is rather an instrument for creating alternative political, social, and economic forms, institutions, and processes. Since it is on the cutting edge of change, the school will be in the center of controversy.

EXISTENTIALISM

Rather than constituting a systematic philosophy as do Idealism and Realism, Existentialism is a way of examining life in a very personal manner. It became popular in the post World War II period.[27] In some ways Existentialism represents a feeling of desperation, but it also contains a spirit of hope. An education that follows the Existentialist orientation will emphasize deep personal reflection on one's commitments and choices.

**Self-
examination**

According to the Existentialist writer Jean-Paul Sartre, "Existence precedes Essence." This means that human beings are born into the world entirely without volition. They simply are here in the world. As people live, they are thrust into a number of choice-making situations. Some choices are minute and trivial ones. Other choices, however, deal with the purpose of life. These are decisions that lead to personal self-definition. A person creates his or her own definition and makes his or her own essence. You are what you choose to be.

The Existentialist conception of a human being as the creator of his or her own essence differs substantially from the Idealists and Realists, who see the person as a universal category. While the Idealist or Realist sees the individual as an inhabitant of a meaningful and explainable

26 William O. Stanley, *Education and Social Integration* (New York: Teachers College Press, Columbia University, 1952).

27 George F. Kneller, *Existentialism and Education* (New York: Wiley, 1958).

world, the Existentialist believes that the universe is indifferent to human wishes, desires, and plans. Human freedom is total, say the Existentialists, who also hold that one's responsibility for choice is total.

Total responsibility for choices

Another important concept in Existentialism is that of the sense of *Angst*, or dread. Each person knows that his or her destiny is death and ultimate disappearance and that his or her presence in the world is only temporary. As a conscious being, the individual must carry the knowledge of ultimate demise every day of life. It is with this sense of philosophical dread that each person must make choices about freedom and slavery, love and hate, and peace and war. As one makes these choices, the question is always present—What difference does it make that I am here and that I have chosen to be what I am?

As was stated earlier, Existentialism carries feelings of both desperation and hope. Human beings are indeed desperate creatures who realize that life is temporary. They live in a world where others—persons, institutions, and agencies—are constantly seeking to impinge upon and violate their choice-making freedom. One's response to life has to be based on an answer to the question—Do I choose to be a self-determined person or do I choose to be defined by others? At the same time that men and women are desperate, they also have the possibilities of loving, creating, and being. One has the possibility of being an inner-directed and authentic person. An authentic person is one who is free and aware of his or her freedom.[28] Such a person knows that every choice is really an act of personal value creation. The authentic person is his or her own definer and is aware that self-definition is a personal responsibility.

Desperation and hope

Since Existentialists have deliberately avoided systematization of their philosophy, it is difficult to categorize its metaphysical, epistemological, axiological, and logical positions. However, some comments on these areas will serve to illustrate the Existentialist point of view. The person creates his or her own metaphysical position, which is the being or essence created by individual choice. Epistemologically, the individual chooses the knowledge that he or she wishes to possess. It is axiology that is most important for Existentialists, since human beings create their own values through the choices that they make. Finally, the logic to which a person subscribes is a matter of individual preference.

Essence and values

THE BASIC QUESTIONS   The educational implications of Existentialism are many. The Existentialist realizes that we live in a world of physical realities and that we have

---

28 Maxine Greene, *Landscapes of Learning* (New York: Teachers College Press, Columbia University, 1978); Van Cleve Morris, *Existentialism in Education* (New York: Harper & Row, 1966).

developed a useful and scientific knowledge about these realities. However, the most significant aspects of our lives are personal and nonscientific. So to the questions we have asked about knowledge and education, Existentialists would say that the most important kind of knowledge is about the human condition and the choices that each person has to make, and that education is a process of developing consciousness about the freedom to choose, and the meaning of and responsibility for one's choices.[29] It is designed to create in us a sense of self-awareness and hopefully will contribute to our authenticity as human beings.

Meaning of life, love and death

An Existentialist educator would encourage students to engage in philosophizing about the meaning of the human experiences of life, love, and death. An Existentialist teacher would also raise these questions and put them before the students. The questioning process would grow into a dialogue between the members of the learning groups. It should be remembered that the answers to these questions would be personal and subjective for each individual. They would not be items to be measured on standardized tests.

An Existentialist curriculum would consist of the experiences and subjects that lend themselves to philosophic dialogue. They would be subjects that vividly portray individual men and women in the act of choice making. Since Existentialist choice making is so personal and subjective, those subjects that are emotional, aesthetic, and poetic are appropriate to an Existentialist curriculum.[30] Literature and biography are important sources for revealing choice-making conditions. Drama and film that vividly portray the human condition and human decision making ought to be seen and discussed by students. In addition to the literary, dramatic, and biographical subjects, students also need to find modes of self-expression. They should be free to experiment with artistic media, to dramatize or make concrete their emotions, feelings, and insights. The Existentialist classroom should be rich in the materials that lend themselves to self-expression.

Modes of self-expression

The school, for the Existentialist educator, is a place where individuals can meet to pursue dialogue and discussion about their own lives and choices. It is a place where subjects can be pursued that will illuminate choice making by examining the human condition as it is presented in literary, dramatic, and other aesthetic forms. Since every person is in the same predicament and has the same possibilities, every individual should have opportunities for schooling. In the school both teachers and students should have the opportunity to ask questions, to suggest answers, and to engage in dialogue.

29 Harold Soderquist, *The Person and Education* (Columbus, Ohio: Merrill, 1966).
30 Maxine Greene, *Existential Encounters for Teachers* (New York: Random House, 1967).

PHILOSOPHICAL ANALYSIS

Philosophical Analysis, or language analysis, is one of the newer approaches to issues in educational philosophy.[31] Basically, it is a method of examining the language used in making statements about knowledge, education, and schooling, and of seeking to clarify it by establishing its meaning. Philosophical Analysis has gained prominence among educational philosophers who believe that our communications about educational matters have grown increasingly confused and obscure. To establish meaning, the Philosophical Analysts also seek to reduce statements about education to empirical terms for those who participate in educational discussion and decision making.

Philosophical Analysis does not pretend to be creating or establishing a school of educational philosophy. To understand more clearly the Analytical view of the philosophy of education, it can be examined in reference to the educational philosophies already treated in this chapter. The Idealists, Realists, and Perennialists describe their philosophies in terms of a world view or a total philosophical system.[32] For these more traditional educational philosophies, humankind is part of this universal system. The Philosophical Analysts reject cosmic system building as a purely speculative exercise that has no real meaning for educators. The Analysts assert that the metaphysical basis of cosmic philosophies cannot be verified in human experience. They also would find the expressions of the Existentialists to be primarily poetic and emotional. While the Existentialists may be expressing personal feelings, the Analysts would find them sorely deficient in supplying empirical data that could be used to establish meaning in educational issues. Since the Pragmatists rely on the use of the scientific method in education, they are agreeable to the Analytical view. But even the Pragmatists have failed to use language with precise meaning. For example, Dewey's use of terms such as "democracy," "growth," "interests," and "experience" has caused much debate among philosophers of education.

It was this dissatisfaction with the schools of philosophy that led a number of philosophers to develop a new way of working with ideas and their expression in language. Two major philosophers who led the movement of language analysis were G. E. Moore and Bertrand Russell.[33] Russell in particular sought to identify the logical structure that underlies

Language analyses

Empirical analyses

Establishing precise meaning

31 D. J. O'Connor, *An Introduction to the Philosophy of Education* (New York: Random House, 1957); Israel Schaeffer, *Philosophy of Education* (Boston: Allyn & Bacon, 1966).

32 Adrian Dupuis, *Philosophy of Education in Historical Perspective* (Chicago: Rand McNally, 1966).

33 Barry Gross, *Analytical Philosophy: An Historical Introduction* (New York: Western, 1970); Jonas F. Soltis, *An Introduction to the Analysis of Education Concepts* (Reading, Mass.: Addison-Wesley, 1966).

language usage. For him philosophy's function is to formulate the logical rules that are the basis of language.

CONTRIBUTION TO EDUCATIONAL PHILOSOPHY

Although operational differences exist among the various Analysts, a few generalizations can be made to illustrate their contributions to educational philosophy. For example, we express ourselves in terms of sentences that attempt to convey propositions about reality. For the Analysts, only some of these sentences are meaningful communications between persons. Meaningful sentences are either analytically true or empirically true.[34] If we say that 2 + 2 = 4, we have expressed a mathematical statement that is analytically true because the 4 is analyzed out of and means the same as 2 + 2. The statement can be reversed and can be stated as 4 = 2 + 2. Other statements are true in that they can be verified in empirical terms. For example, the statement that water boils at 212° Fahrenheit can be tested and verified empirically. If meaningful statements are those that are either analytically or empirically true, this means that many other statements are meaningless in scientific communication since they cannot be examined by these two methods. For example, the Idealist proposition that "World is Mind" cannot be tested. Neither can the Existentialist statement that "Existence precedes Essence" be verified empirically. However, it is possible to examine and find meaning in the Experimentalist proposition that "Experience is the interaction of the human organism with the environment." To verify this statement, it would be necessary to render the words, "experience," "human organism," "interaction," and "environment" in terms that can be measured and verified empirically or analyzed logically.

Verifiable propositions

In many respects Philosophical Analysis is a response to the condition of knowledge in the twentieth century. The lives of men and women, their occupations, and their areas of knowledge competency have grown increasingly complicated and specialized as technology advanced and institutions were modernized. Each area of specialization has developed its own highly specialized language that is used by and is particular to the experts who work within it. The growing use of highly specialized terminologies has made it difficult for those in a given field to communicate with each other across their specialties. By explaining the language used in a complex technological society, the Philosophical Analyst can contribute to more meaningful communication.

Growing specialization

In addition to specialization, modern society is now characterized by the mass media of communications. More people than ever before in hu-

---

34 Albert J. Taylor, *An Introduction to the Philosophy of Education* (Dubuque, Iowa: Kendall/Hunt, 1978).

man history are receiving the same message via the press, radio, and television. We are beset by all sorts of communications that range greatly in their truthfulness, reliability, and validity. By analyzing the language used in these messages, Philosophical Analysts can help us to distinguish myth from truth and perhaps find meaning in an increasingly strident environment.

THE BASIC QUESTIONS

In dealing with questions regarding knowledge, education, schooling, and instruction, the Philosophical Analysts have not attempted to provide answers that are broad in scope as have the other philosophers of education treated in this chapter. Quite the contrary, they have tried to narrow these questions to specifics concerned with our speaking and writing about educational issues. In dealing with problems of knowledge, they have focused their interest on those knowledge claims and propositions that can be verified empirically. In education the Philosophical Analysts have not created new curricular proposals but have rather examined educational theories, programs, and practices in terms that can be evaluated empirically. They certainly have deflated many grandiose educational claims that cannot be put to the test of experience. In matters that concern teaching and learning, the Philosophical Analysts have given their careful attention to the language transactions that take place between the teacher and the learner in the classroom.

Concern with educational issues

SUMMING UP

1. Chapter 8 has attempted to put into perspective traditional philosophies of education such as Idealism and Realism and traditional theories of education such as Perennialism and Essentialism. The more contemporary, process-oriented philosophy of Pragmatism, or Experimentalism, and the theories of Progressivism and Social Reconstructionism have been discussed, too. The chapter concluded with a treatment of two newer schools or approaches to contemporary philosophy of education: Existentialism and Philosophical Analysis.

2. The major concepts of these philosophies and theories are summarized in Table 8.1. The study of these philosophies and theories of education reveals how varied are the goals and objectives of education.

3. By studying these various philosophical approaches to education, you can appreciate the rich complexity of educational theorizing, and can work toward formulating your own philosophy of education.

TABLE 8.1
PHILOSOPHIES AND THEORIES
OF EDUCATION

PHILOSOPHIES	METAPHYSICS	EPISTEMOLOGY	AXIOLOGY	PROPONENTS
Idealism	Reality is spiritual or mental	Knowing is the rethinking of latent ideas	Values are absolute and eternal	**Berkeley** **Butler** **Froebel** **Hegel** **Plato**
Realism	Reality is objective and is composed of matter and form	Knowing consists of sensation and abstraction	Values are absolute and eternal, based on nature's laws	Aquinas Aristotle Broudy Martin Pestalozzi
Pragmatism (Experimentalism)	Reality is the interaction of an individual with environment or experience	Knowing results from experiencing use of scientific method	Values are situational or relative	Childs Dewey James Peirce
Existentialism	Existence precedes Essence	Knowledge for personal choice	Freely chosen values	Sartre Marcel Morris Soderquist
Philosophical Analysis	Rejected as nonverifiable	Empirical verification or logical analysis of language	Regarded as emotional feelings	Soltis Russell Moore

THEORIES	GOALS	CURRICULUM	PROPONENTS
Perennialism (rooted in Realism)	To educate the rational person	Subject matter that is hierarchically arranged to cultivate the intellect (Great Books, etc.)	Adler Hutchins Maritain
Essentialism (rooted in Idealism and Realism)	To educate the useful and competent person	Basic education: reading, writing, arithmetic, history, English, science, foreign languages	Bagley Bestor Conant Morrison
Progressivism (rooted in Pragmatism)	To educate the individual according to his or her interests and needs	Activities and projects	Dewey Johnson Kilpatrick Parker Washburne
Reconstructionism (rooted in Pragmatism)	To reconstruct society	Social sciences used as reconstructive tools	Brameld Counts Stanley

DISCUSSION QUESTIONS

1. How would you answer the basic philosophical questions about knowledge, education, and schooling? How does your philosophy of education reflect or differ from the philosophies of education treated in this chapter?

2. Suppose you are a Realist. How would you assess Pragmatism and Progressivism?

3. Which of the philosophies of education treated in this chapter has had the greatest impact on American education? Why?

4. Suppose you are a Social Reconstructionist. Identify the major problems facing American society, construct an educational agenda, and devise a teaching strategy designed to promote the solution of these problems.

5. Which of the philosophies treated in this chapter is most relevant to contemporary education and which is most irrelevant? Why?

THINGS TO DO

1. Select and read a book on the philosophy of education of your choice. Identify the author's philosophical orientation and try to relate the book's thesis to the various schools of educational philsophy treated in this chapter.

2. Incorporate your ideas about knowledge, education, and schooling into a statement of your own philosophy of education. Include your beliefs concerning metaphysics, epistemology, axiology, and logic.

3. Volunteer to teach a class that follows the perspective of one of the philosophies of education examined here.

4. Using the techniques recommended by the Philosophical Analysts, analyze an article that has appeared in a recent journal in professional education. Is there difficulty in understanding the language used in the article? Discuss the meaning of the language used.

5. Read a novel or watch a motion picture or a television program that deals with an educational situation. Identify the philosophy of education that underlies the portrayal of this situation.

FOR PART II
SUGGESTIONS FOR FURTHER READING

R. Freeman Butts, *The Education of the West: A Formative Chapter in the History of Civilization* (New York: McGraw-Hill, 1973).

Lawrence Cremin, *Public Education* (New York: Basic Books, 1976).

John Dewey, *Democracy and Education* (New York: Macmillan, 1916).

Gerald L. Gutek, *Philosophical Alternatives in Education* (Columbus, Ohio: Merrill, 1974).

Erwin V. Johanningmeier, *Americans and Their Schools* (Chicago: Rand McNally, 1980).

Adolphe E. Meyer, *Grandmasters of Educational Thought* (New York: McGraw-Hill, 1975).

Henry J. Perkinson, *Since Socrates: Studies in the History of Western Educational Thought* (New York: Longman, 1980).

Richard Pratte, *Ideology and Education* (New York: Wiley, 1977).

Robert R. Rusk and James Scotland, *Doctrines of the Great Educators* (New York: St. Martin's Press, 1979).

Donald R. Warren, ed., *History, Education, and Public Policy* (Berkeley, California: McCutchan, 1978).

PART THREE
SOCIAL
FOUNDATIONS

Part Three is concerned with the influences of cultural milieu and social class upon learning. Educational institutions do not exist in a vacuum; they interact with the society of which they are a part. The cultural patterns of identifiable groups of people are reflected in their perception of the role and function of education; in turn, these cultural patterns (which rapidly change in contemporary society) have an effect on learning and the acquisition of skills important to survival and self-fulfillment. Most important to educators is an understanding of the influence that subcultures and social classes have on the socialization and education of their members. Social groups, based on status, prestige, power, or common interests, exist within a given society. These groups form the basis of stratification, of group identity, and of differences in education.

Chapter 9 deals with the nature of culture, how it is learned, how it shapes the child, and how the process of education varies in different kinds of cultures: traditional-inner-other directed; folk-urban-suburban, and preindustrial-postindustrial (nuclear). The nature of sex roles, the concept of cultural pluralism, and the effects of culture on personal development also are considered. The "culturally literate" educator needs to be aware of these sociopsychological growth patterns so as to provide experiences that are related to his or her students' interests and needs.

Chapter 10 concerns the relationship to education of social class and race. Particular attention is paid to the classic studies, starting with the 1940s when stratification theory, analysis of empirical data, and methodology evolved as scientific constructs. In this same period the studies of social-class and race differences—and of the difficulties of minority groups in adjusting to the dominant cultural group—began to have practical application and political significance in promoting change. From a study of class and race, we move to a discussion of stratification versus equality, to significant current research findings on the disadvantaged, and then to several equal educational opportunity reports.

Chapter 11 deals with the impact of student culture and peer conformity upon learning. We analyze the social climate of various classrooms and the nature of student behavior, with special emphasis on the use of drugs and alcohol. Student disruptions, disciplinary codes, and legal rights and responsibilities of students are also treated. Then we venture some hypotheses about the causes and directions of student activism and unrest. These phenomena are relatively new; in part they reflect the changing nature of society in general and of youth society in particular.

The methodological approach to data is minimized in this section. The focus here is on a descriptive, conceptual, and historical treatment of the major theories and thinkers in the field. Finally, let us remember that the findings about class, race, and ethnicity are intended merely as guidelines to aid in the diagnosis of individual problems of adaptation to the dominant culture. Within each group there is tremendous individual variation. There is no "typical" rural or urban child; lower-class or upper-class child; black, brown, red, yellow, or white child.

CHAPTER 9
CULTURE,
SOCIALIZATION,
AND EDUCATION

Focusing questions

How does culture influence human growth and development?

How do sex roles and sex differences influence learning and behavior?

How do schools socialize the young?

How have television and mass communication affected students today?

In what ways is the larger American culture changing?

In what ways has the youth culture changed?

Culture is the means of ensuring the unity and survival of a society. It provides patterns for the behavior of individuals and groups within the society, means of teaching its members to behave according to the norms and mores or the "rules of the game," and means of enforcing behaviors. The culture of a society is reflected in its institutions and ideas, and it is culture that influences human growth and development. In the United States the school serves as perhaps the major institution and source of knowledge devised by the adult generation for maintaining and perpetuating the culture; it imparts the tools necessary for survival and insures the transmission of values to future generations. In effect, the school provides us with a sense of the continuity and experience of our culture; it is a highly formal system for educating the young, an institution children are required to attend in order to be socialized and enculturated into the larger society and common culture.

Schools socialize and enculturate

To clarify this relationship, this chapter is divided into a discussion of the individual and culture, of sex roles and differences, of socialization agents, of American culture, and of adolescent culture—all with reference to education.

CULTURE AND THE INDIVIDUAL

Culture not only provides the lens through which individuals perceive the world, it also guides people in responding to what they perceive. Language is perhaps the clearest illustration of communicating shared meanings. Cultural meanings are also infused into nonverbal behavior and physical objects. For example, materials found in ancient ruins by archeologists help us learn about the people who once lived in that time and place. Culture is a way of thinking and behaving; it is a group's knowledge and customs in memories, written records, and objects for present and future use and example.

In a widely used definition, culture has been characterized as "continually changing . . . patterns . . . of learned behavior . . . transmitted among . . . members of society."[1] Anthropologist Ruth Benedict provided us with a similar definition when she said, "Culture is that which binds men together."[2] Individuals learn to conform to the cultural patterns that prevail in their societies. While it is true that genetic inheritance plays a part in our unique development and individual abilities, culture can explain certain racial, national, and ethnic differences. It is the major reason humankind has moved from the stone age to the nuclear age.

Culture binds us together

---

[1] John Cuber, *Sociology: A Synopsis of Principles*, 4th ed. (New York: Appleton-Century-Crofts, 1959), p. 60.
[2] Ruth Benedict, *Patterns of Culture* (Boston: Houghton Mifflin, 1934), p. 14.

DIFFERENT
CULTURES
If we lived in a different place and time, we would live in a different culture and we would think and behave differently than we do. So it is difficult for us objectively to evaluate cultures other than our own. Different cultures achieve specific benefits for their members relative to place and time. Because we are bound up in our own culture, we tend to overlook different perspectives and alternative strategies in dealing with the world around us. As we examine this relationship of individual, society, and culture, you might ask yourself where you fit in. What would life be like if there were no existing rules of society for playing the game? How are you shaped by society? How do you think you influence society? How do schools shape society? How do they mirror it?

**Evaluating
other cultures**

Neither a single individual, nor a group, nor an entire society can be understood without reference to culture. To know the meaning of culture for various groups is to discern the relativity of values, of what is "right" and "wrong," "good" and "bad," and why human beings behave the way they do. As anthropologist Clyde Kluckhohn points out, even those of us who pride ourselves on our individualistic behavior follow the customs of our culture most of the time.[3] The fact that we brush our teeth, eat three meals a day (not four or five), and sleep in a bed (not on the floor or on a sheep's pelt) reflects our culture. The individual's fate is inextricably bound up with that of the group to which he or she belongs, says Ralph Linton in a work on personality.[4] The individual cannot survive infancy or satisfy his or her adult needs without the aid and cooperation of others who work as functional and operative units of an entire group. The interests of the individual are subordinated to those of the larger group (even in the United States, which ideologically supports the individual's rights to life, liberty, and the pursuit of happiness). Societies do not hesitate to eliminate an individual who is a threat to the whole.

As individuals from different cultures mingle and interact with one another in a society, the various cultural patterns adjust to each other. (Linton's exposition supports the rationale for the recently disputed concept of the "melting pot" and the thrust behind integration of schools and society.)

PERSONALITY
AND CULTURE
A number of social scientists have pointed out the link between individual personality and culture. Most noted among this group is Erik Erikson, whose major work is a probing study of the pervasive influence of cultural

---

3 Clyde Kluckhohn, *Mirror for Man* (New York: McGraw-Hill, 1949).
4 Ralph J. Linton, *Cultural Background of Personality* (New York: Appleton-Century-Crofts, 1945).

institutions on the sociopsychological growth and development of the individual from childhood to adulthood.[5] He describes the critical periods of human maturing and the ego qualities that must emerge for a successful integration of the individual's needs and experience with the cultural demands of the society. The child is carefully nurtured in the societal values, beliefs, and norms, so that he or she will be able to find a meaningful role within the culture. Thus the child becomes a bearer of the parent tradition and an instrument of societal stability. This is an important step in personal integration or what is defined as ego development. This development of a person's social and psychological health finds its ultimate expression in eight maturing stages which are vital for personal and cultural fulfillment. These eight stages are:

Critical periods of human development

Eight maturing stages

1. *Trust versus mistrust.* This is the stage of the infant's initial and continuing sensuous experiences. The sameness of familiar, comfortable experience provides a rudimentary sense of ego development.

2. *Autonomy versus shame and doubt.* This is the period of muscular maturation, of the "holding on" and "letting go" decisions of early childhood. The child who loses self-control or is subject to overcontrol may develop lasting shame or doubt.

3. *Initiative versus guilt.* In this stage the child is eager and able to work cooperatively and to combine with other children to construct. He or she is willing to profit from teachers and to emulate ideal prototypes.

4. *Industry versus inferiority.* Now the child learns to win recognition by producing things and by learning to use tools.

5. *Identity versus role confusion.* Childhood is now at an end; one's ego identity is the accrued confidence that the sameness and continuity of the self will be exemplified in the wider society, in one's sexual identity, and in the promise of a career.

6. *Intimacy versus isolation.* The young adult is willing to fuse his or her identity with others, to make a commitment or to enter into a partnership, and to cope with those sacrifices or compromises that must be made.

7. *Generativity versus stagnation.* The adult is concerned with establishing and guiding the next generation, preferably one's own offspring. These goals may also be achieved by leaving a productive or creative achievement behind to successors.

5   Erik H. Erikson, *Childhood and Society* (New York: Norton, 1950).

8. *Ego integrity versus despair.* This is the fruition of the previous seven stages. Ego integrity is the acceptance of one's life; despair is the lack of this accrued ego integration, and is signified by the fear of death.[6]

The underlying assumptions for charting the life cycle are: (1) human growth develops according to predetermined steps (eight stages), and (2) society encourages the proper rate and sequence of the life cycle. Each of the critical stages is systematically related to all others, and all depend on the proper development and sequence of the previous stage. While the tempo and intensity of each stage will vary, depending on the given culture, failure to integrate one of the eight stages will influence all later stages and may impair psychological development, although a person may overcome an early impairment by working at it in later life.

Predetermined, sequential stages

THE INDIVIDUAL IN MODERN SOCIETY

The destiny of the individual in modern society is deeply influenced by the bigness and complexity of contemporary life. Indeed, according to Max Weber, this influence may completely overwhelm the individual. According to Weber, bureaucracy is a rationalized form of organization that eventually replaced charismatic leadership and tradition.[7] Based on rules, regulations, specified roles for each individual in the organization, and hierarchy of authority, bureaucracy functions according to universal rules designed to treat people impersonally rather than according to their family background, political contacts, or other personal characteristics. However, bureaucracy often creates problems of its own, particularly in connection with its tendency to end up as mindless application of impersonal rules. Weber came to believe that bureaucracy, which he had thought to be the most efficient and rational type of organization for modern society, was now out of control.

Bigness and complexity

C. Wright Mills, evolving his theories fifty years after Weber, was also concerned with the individual in relation to the structure of mass society, which he saw as dominated by markets and machines.[8] Mass society creates the "science machine"; it destroys the individual; it manipulates and alienates men and women from themselves and their community. Mass society distorts reality and morality. Instead of true persons dedicated to the public good, we have "mass indifference" and "moral insensibility." Hiroshima and Auschwitz are extreme but significant examples of the outcomes of mass society.

---

6 The above summary and analysis are adapted from Allan C. Ornstein and W. Eugene Hedley, eds., *Analysis of Contemporary Education* (New York: Crowell, 1973), pp. 199–205.

7 Max Weber, *The Theory of Social and Economic Organization* (New York: Oxford University Press, 1947).

8 C. Wright Mills, *White Collar* (New York: Oxford University Press, 1951).

Mills was passionately concerned with the moral identity of people, and their responsibility to society. He called for political and intellectual responsibility to pit oneself against the false idols that were shaping people and society.[9] The individual was being overwhelmed by a new false consciousness and irresponsible ignorance—new mass powers were shaping our minds.

The individual, Mills wrote, is an agent of the transformation of society and must become aware of and participate in the public issues of the day. Men and women are both creators and creations of society; they must be made conscious of the human condition. They must become active agents in society, rather than mere spectators, or cogs in a vast machine. Today, inflation, the mass media, and complex social, political, and bureaucratic forces tend to make individuals feel powerless and ineffectual. Education can be a vital element in helping people learn to gain more control over their lives and their future in society.

Powerless individuals in mass society

EDUCATION AND CULTURE The ethical, social, and psychological issues examined above involve the essence and totality of the individual in relation to society. It is the educational process that equips people to cope with the forces that impinge on them and their world.

Education is neutral; it can be used for constructive or destructive ends. The kind of education our young receive determines the quality of our life. The transmission of culture is the primary task of the educational system of a society. The values, beliefs, and norms of a society are maintained and passed to the next generation not merely by teaching about them, but also by the embodiment of these elements of culture in the very operation of the educational system.

Education is neutral

Most Americans tend to regard education as synonymous with schooling. Actually, a culture may have no schools but it still educates its young through the family or special ritual and training. Schooling plays a major role in education in modern industrial cultures; it becomes increasingly important as cultures become more complex and the frontiers of knowledge expand. In simple, nontechnological societies, almost everyone becomes proficient over the whole range of knowledge necessary for survival. In complex societies people acquire different proficiencies and abilities; no individual can range over the entire body of complex knowledge or expect to be proficient in all areas of learning.

The techniques of education used by nonliterate peoples include overt training by elders, emulation of older children, attendance at ceremonies, observation of parents and elders doing daily tasks, and inculcation of proper values and conduct by codes of admonition and rewards. In

9 C. Wright Mills, *The Power Elite* (New York: Oxford University Press, 1956).

technological societies education begins at home, and school takes on greater importance as the child becomes older. The schools become the crucial facility for helping the young acquire an education, inculcating them with the ideas and institutions of the culture, and bridging the gap between generations. In contemporary life the mass media of communication also serve an educational function by redefining values and ideas.

Teachers and professional educators have a choice; it is a choice that has been offered them throughout the ages. Teachers may uncritically accept the tendencies of the times in which they find themselves and develop school programs that *mirror* current forces. Or teachers may appraise the tendencies of the times and help students to reflect upon and act to *shape* the world around them. Indeed, there is danger to individuals and to society in an education that accepts uncritically and acts unthinkingly. "The danger is," says one educator, "that some forces which mutually reinforce each other may take us down roads contrary to the American [ideal]," contrary to the ideal of the individual who is free, responsible, and important.[10] We can educate powerless people in a powerful society. Or we can educate people who can cope with and improve society. As the world around us becomes more complex and more burdened with problems, it becomes increasingly urgent to educate a new generation of students who are wiser and more humane than those who teach them.

Schools can mirror or shape society

SEX ROLES AND SEX DIFFERENCES

Not only does society demand conformity to its fundamental values and norms, it also assigns specific roles to each of its members, expecting them to conform to certain established behavioral patterns. A good example of this type of socialization is found in sex roles; that is, the ways boys and girls and men and women are "supposed" to act. Sex roles vary from culture to culture, but within a given culture they are rather well defined, and they are developed through an elaborate schedule of selective reinforcement. For example, the preschool boy is ridiculed for playing with dolls, and girls are supposed to be "feminine."

Sex roles vary with culture

An important contribution to the understanding of sex roles has been made by David Lynn, who differentiated between parental identification, by which the child internalizes the personality characteristics of his parents, and sex-role identification of a given sex in a specific culture.[11]

10 William Van Til, "In a Climate of Change" in R. R. Leeper, ed., *Role of Supervisor and Curriculum Director in a Climate of Change* (Washington, D.C.: Association for Supervision and Curriculum Development, 1965), p. 16. More recently, a prominent educator has argued that the schools should function as a "thermostat," aiming at bringing about change in times of too much stability and stability in times of rapid change. See Neil Postman, *Teaching as a Conserving Activity* (New York: Delacorte, 1979).

11 David B. Lynn, "Sex Role and Parental Identification," *Child Development* (March 1962), pp. 555–64; Lynn, "Divergent Feedback and Sex-Role Identification in Boys and Men," *Merrill Palmer Quarterly* (January 1964), pp. 17–23.

The initial parental identification of both male and female children is with the mother, but the boy must shift his original mother identification to establish the masculine role identity. At this period differences begin: a girl has the same-sex parental model for identification all hours of the day, but a boy sees the father only briefly. Besides, the father participates in some roles that until very recently have been defined in American society as feminine (washing dishes, cleaning), so that he must distinguish the masculine role from the stereotype spelled out for him by society through a system of reinforcements and rewards. As a result, the boy's identification with the mother role diminishes and is gradually replaced by a learned identification with a culturally defined masculine role. This is accomplished mainly through negative admonishments such as "Don't be a sissy." Such cautions, however, do not tell him what he should do instead.

Parental role models

The girl more directly learns the female identification, partly through imitation and partly through the mother's reinforcement and reward of selective behavior. The boy has the problem of making the proper sex-role identification in the partial absence of a male model, and this is even more difficult in a female-headed household where the father is completely absent. By contrast, the boy must define his goals, restructure some of his experiences, and abstract underlying principles. The result has been a greater frequency of problems in learning sex roles among boys and greater dependency on the part of girls.

PROBLEMS REFLECTED IN THE SCHOOLS
When children come of school age, they find that the schools are largely staffed by females, especially at the elementary level, a critical age in child development. The schools are dominated by female norms of politeness, cleanliness, and obedience. The curriculum, tests, and classroom activities are female oriented—safe, nice, antiseptic. The school frowns on vulgar language and fighting; it suppresses the boys' maleness and often fails to permit action-oriented, tough sports. Thus the disadvantage that the boy finds at home in developing his masculine identity is compounded by the schooling process.

Female-oriented schools

In this connection, Patricia Sexton has presented data showing that schools are feminizing institutions that discriminate against the male and subvert his identity.[12] Her data show that approximately three out of four students regarded as problems are boys, and since teachers tend to fail problem students, approximately two out of three students who fail are boys.

Sexton maintains that the schools' values and the resulting discrimination against boys, compounded by the mothers' inability to relate

---

12 Patricia C. Sexton, *The Feminized Male* (New York: Random House, 1969).

Role-playing adds to the pleasure of this young student as he mixes up a batch of brownies.

to sons in helping them establish a healthy male identification, are negative and cumulative. In part they explain why boys largely outnumber girls in school dropout rates, deviant and delinquent acts, and mental illnesses. Although Sexton's conclusions may be somewhat overgeneralized and extend beyond her data, there is no question that girls receive higher grades throughout elementary school, with the gap being gradually reduced in high school. More boys are nonreaders; more boys fail; more boys are disciplinary cases; and more boys drop out of school.

Recent data have further clarified the ways in which boys may be at a particular disadvantage in the elementary school. According to some researchers in neuropsychology, boys tend to learn through active manipulation of their environment, while girls tend to learn through verbal communication. One researcher has summarized several studies analyzing this difference as follows:

Different methods for learning

> By the time they are five or six, [all] children in . . . classrooms are expected to behave like girls. The system requires children to remain attentive to one task and stay seated in one place for a considerable period of time. . . . They must use fine motor systems in writing and drawing, and they must persevere at tasks that are largely linguistic or symbolic in nature. . . . Boys [usually] cannot sit still; they are distractible; they test the properties of objects. Such behavior interferes with the concentration they need to learn to read and write.[13]

By way of contrast, the problems that girls experience in the educational system generally reflect their socialization for dependency rather than contradictions in expectations between the school and the home. Relative to boys, girls have not been encouraged to prepare for or enter high-status occupations such as law or medicine, or high-paying occupations requiring technical skills and training beyond high school; instead they have been expected to prepare for roles as wives and homemakers.[14] Except for a few occupations such as elementary teacher, social worker, and nurse, girls traditionally were not expected to enter fields that require college preparation, and the channelling of women into a few professions meant that these occupations tended to have relatively low pay and low status. Because women were available to fill jobs as teachers, for example, and because women were thought to require or demand less status and pay than men, a cycle was created wherein prestigious jobs were defined as "masculine" and less prestigious jobs were defined as "feminine." This type of socialization arrangement in schools and society did not motivate girls to achieve much beyond high school or to acquire skills that might contribute to later success in the economy. Furthermore, verbal communication of the kind in which girls tend to excel has not provided them with skills that lead to success in mathematics and science. As girls enter the secondary school, this tendency has had the effect of excluding girls from many educational opportunities.[15]

In addition, the emphasis placed on dependency in socializing females meant that girls were expected to be cooperative and even docile. In contrast, boys were taught to be competitive and to exercise leadership in overcoming obstacles.[16] As mentioned above, socialization in the

Cooperative girls and competitive boys

13   Diane McGuiness, "How Schools Discriminate Against Boys," *Human Nature* (February 1979), pp. 87–88.
14   Leslie Aldridge Westoff, *Women in Search of Equality* (Princeton, N.J.: Educational Testing Service, 1979).
15   Ibid.
16   Frank L. Mott et al., *Women, Work, and Family* (Lexington, Mass.: Heath, 1978).

elementary school frequently tried to make boys obedient and cooperative, but by high-school age athletics were stressed and boys received more opportunities to learn leadership and competitive skills that would be important in later life. Until recently, girls had little encouragement or opportunity to learn these skills, and those who did were perceived as violating "proper" norms for female behavior in American society.

ARE DIFFERENCES IN LEARNING BIOLOGICAL?

Efforts to reduce sex-role limitations and stereotypes of girls and to improve their educational opportunities have raised important questions concerning whether there are biological differences that lead to differential learning patterns between boys and girls. As noted above, there is reason to believe that, compared with girls, boys tend to learn more through manipulation of the environment while girls tend to learn through verbal communication; this difference has important implications for instruction. Researchers disagree, however, on whether such differences are inborn or develop because of socialization in the early years of life. Those who believe that learning differences between the sexes are present at birth point to differences that have been found in the brain functioning of boys and girls. Measurement of brain activity, for example, indicates that boys engaged in tasks involving spatial concepts and problem solving consistently use their right hemisphere, while girls are more likely to activate both hemispheres; also, the left side connotes emotional feelings.[17] Related studies indicate that the right hemisphere of the female brain has more verbal capacity than that of the male, while the male right hemisphere is almost purely spatial and imagistic.[18] Laboratory research also suggests that sex hormones play a part in directly influencing the growth and development of the brain.[19]

Environmental manipulation vs. verbal communication

Other observers, however, emphasize differences in socialization from the first day of life (boys are placed in a blue blanket, girls in pink) and argue that differences in experience and expectations account for most of the learning differences between boys and girls. While not necessarily arguing that brain or other physiological differences affecting learning do not exist or are of no importance, these observers argue that socialization differences are the major reason boys and girls diverge in learning patterns and performance.[20] For example, one observer has reviewed evidence on sex differences in learning and concluded that, "When

Different expectations

17 Richard M. Restak, "The Other Difference Between Boys and Girls," *Educational Leadership* (December 1979), pp. 232–35.

18 "The Split Brain: Studies in Laterality and Asymmetry," *The University of Chicago Division of the Social Sciences Reports* (Autumn 1979), pp. 5–8.

19 C. Sue Carter and William T. Greenough, "Sending the Right Sex Messages," *Psychology Today* (September 1979), p. 112.

20 Gloria C. Fauth and Judith E. Jacobs, "Equity in Mathematics Education: The Educational Leader's Role," *Educational Leadership* (March 1980), pp. 485–89.

one examines the limited amount of the cognitive differences between the sexes, one is struck by their inconsequential nature, at least in terms of any kind of evidence that would warrant advising boys and girls to pursue different courses or careers on the basis of sex differentials in ability."[21]

Particular attention has been given in recent years to the possibility that women tend to perform poorly in math (and therefore in science and other fields dependent on math) because of socialization practices that make them anxious and fearful about mathematical analysis.[22] A related line of argument is that women fear success in traditionally male activities and occupation because succeeding would violate sex stereotypes and thereby cause them ridicule and identity problems.[23] Some scholars have supported these kinds of conclusions by arguing that sex differences in math achievement, which usually are evident for the first time in grades eight or nine, are largely a function of differential course taking rather than inability of women to learn mathematics. (By grade eight, boys begin to take more math courses on the average than do girls.) Thus it is argued that if girls' enrollment in mathematics could be increased, most of the sex differences in achievement could be eliminated.[24]

CHANGING SEX
ROLES AND THE
STATUS OF WOMEN

The past two decades have led to major changes in socializing youngsters for sex roles in the schools and later life. In part, at least, these changes involve larger social changes that have been modifying the traditional roles of women as wives and homemakers. During the past few decades, the following trends have been both a cause and a result of changes in attitudes regarding sex roles and in changes in women's status and expectations in the schools and other social institutions:

Modifying
traditional
roles

Increase in working women. In 1979, just over half of the female population sixteen years or older was working for pay. The trend toward women entering the labor market is expected to continue so that by 1990 only one-quarter of the adult female population will fit the traditional stereotype of a wife who stays home to take care of her children.[25]

21 Julia A. Sherman, "Sex-Related Cognitive Differences: A Summary of Theory and Evidence," *Integrateducation* (January-February 1978), p. 40.

22 Sheila Tobias and Carol S. Weisslrod, "Anxiety and Mathematics: An Update," *Harvard Educational Review* (February 1980), pp. 63-70.

23 Georgia Sassen, "Success Anxiety in Women," *Harvard Educational Review* (February 1980), pp. 13-24.

24 Elizabeth Fennema, "Influences of Selected Cognitive, Affective, and Educational Variables on Sex-Related Differences in Mathematics Learning and Studying" in *Women and Mathematics: Research Perspectives for Change* (Washington, D.C.: National Institute of Education, 1977), pp. 79-135.

25 Ralph E. Smith, ed., *The Subtle Revolution: Women at Work* (Washington, D.C.: The Urban Institute, 1979).

Increase in educational attainment of women. Until recently, women completed fewer years of schooling than did men. This difference has been diminishing, however, and by 1977 the average years of education completed for both men and women was 12.6.[26] In 1979 females outnumbered males among college freshmen for the first time. Since women with more education are more likely to seek paid employment than women with less education, this trend will increase the number of working women in the future.

Declining fertility rates and family size. The birthrate in the United States and other western societies has been falling for decades.[27] The total fertility rate (the number of children under 5 years old per 1,000 women) fell from 704 in 1800 to 248 in 1970 and 186 in 1975, below the population "replacement" level of 211. As a result, the average number of children per family also has declined markedly, thereby making it easier for families to devote resources to the education of girls and for mothers to seek employment outside the home.

Partly as a result of these and other related trends, attitudes regarding sex roles changed substantially in the 1960s and 1970s. In particular, women's attitudes regarding sex roles became much less traditional, as they developed increasingly favorable attitudes toward equal home and work roles for men and women, equal decision making in the home, and fewer limitations on the activities of mothers outside the home. A 1977 survey showed that the women most likely to have adopted egalitarian sex role attitudes were younger women, those with more education, those with better educated husbands, and those who were working in 1962.[28] This trend is likely to continue in the future: American society, including males, will increasingly realize that women are one of the nation's greatest untapped natural resources. The social revolution involving the role of women is still in its early stages.

Equal work roles for men and women

Much progress has been made in equalizing educational, economic, and social opportunities for females, but much remains to be done before opportunities will be truly equal. Affirmative action in employment and education, encouraging girls to attend college and prepare for the professions, efforts to eliminate sexism from curriculum materials in the schools, and other actions to equalize opportunity are having an impact in the schools and the wider society.

26 "20 Facts on Women Workers," Bulletin published by the U.S. Department of Labor Women's Bureau, August 1979.

27 William P. Butz and Michael P. Ward, "Baby Boom and Baby Bust: A New View," *American Demographics* (September 1979), pp. 11–18.

28 "Fifteen-Year Study Documents Tremendous Change in Women's Sex-Role Attitudes," *ISR Newsletter* (Winter 1980), p. 3.

AGENTS OF SOCIALIZATION   Societies include a number of important institutions for transmitting their culture to children and youth. Historically, the most important of these institutions in many societies have been the church, the peer group, the school, and, of course, the family. Some institutions such as the church have become less influential in socialization for modern society than was true in the past, but others such as the mass media have emerged to play a major part in socialization.

Decline of church influence

THE FAMILY AS A SOCIALIZING AGENT   Though family organization varies from one society to another, the family is the major socializing agent in each one; as such, it is the first medium for transmitting the culture to the child. Because the family is the whole world to the very young child, its members teach children what matters in life, often without realizing the impact they are making. The desire to achieve the need for popularity, the belief that a girl should be docile, and other beliefs and values are passed from parent to child. The behaviors adults encourage and discourage and the ways in which they discipline the child also affect his or her basic orientation toward the world. Nevertheless, values and child-rearing styles are not uniform from family to family, even within a single culture.

Interclass differences   The traditional middle-class family is comprised of both a husband and a wife and two or three children. The husband/father is traditionally seen as the major provider and head of the family, and the wife/mother is seen as responsible for overseeing the development of values and emotions in the children. Although these roles are changing, partly because of the increasing number of middle-class, educated, working women and new perceptions of sex roles associated with the women's liberation movement, there is still stress on the children's achievement in school and, in general, on accomplishment and work.

In lower-class or poor families, parent roles and behavior are different from those in the middle class. Bernard Berelson and Gary Steiner, without reporting on the magnitude of the differences, summarize variations in child behavior expectations in lower-class as compared to middle-class families as follows:

Variation of parental roles by social class

> . . . lower-class infants and children are subject to less parental supervision but more parental authority, to more physical punishment and less use of reasoning as a disciplinary measure, to less control of sexual and other impulses, to more freedom to express aggression (except against the parent) and to engage in violence, to earlier sex typing of behavior, . . . to less development

of conscience, to less stress toward achievement, to less equalitarian treatment vis-à-vis the parents, and to less permissive upbringing than their middle-class contemporaries.[29]

Berelson and Steiner represent the current majority view of family and social-class differences and child-rearing techniques. However, this view is criticized by some social scientists as being culturally biased and anti-lower class.

Families with fathers absent   One important development regarding the family's socializing function involves the current increase in father-absent families. Much of this change has been due to an increase in divorce and separation, which leave many children in single-parent families headed by the mother. The results of the increase were made clear in a study that shows that the percentage of children growing up in "disrupted" families rose rapidly among both White and Black families between 1960 and 1975. Among five-year-old Whites, for example, 14 percent of youngsters born in the 1968–70 period had experienced disruption (divorce), as compared with 9 percent of those born in the 1956–58 period. Comparable figures for Black youngsters were 42 percent for youngsters born in the 1968–70 period as compared with 22 percent for the earlier period.[30]

Research on the impact of marital disruption on children reports conflicting results. Some studies conclude that there is little measurable impact on children,[31] but others see a variety of negative impacts, including a greater likelihood of falling into poverty and severe emotional problems among many children.[32]

Educators have been primarily concerned that father absence may lead to psychological and behavior problems in the school and may also detract from students' achievement. Their concern became a matter of national importance and controversy after Daniel Moynihan's 1965 pamphlet in which he pointed out that a large and growing percentage of Black children were in female-headed families and concluded that this trend represented a form of "social pathology" that seriously harmed the children involved.[33] Data analyzed by Moynihan, Martin Deutsch, and others indicate that children (whether Black or White) in father-absent

Increased behavior problems, decline in achievement

29   Bernard Berelson and Gary A. Steiner, *Human Behavior* (New York: Harcourt, Brace, 1964), pp. 479–80. See also James D. Wright and Sonia R. Wright, "Social Class and Parental Values for Children: A Partial Replication and Extension of the Kohn Thesis," *American Sociological Review* (June 1976), pp. 527–37.

30   Larry Bumpass and Ronald R. Rindfuss, "Children's Experience of Marital Disruption," *American Journal of Sociology* (July 1979), pp. 49–65.

31   Jessie Bernard, *Remarriage* (New York: Russell & Russell, 1971).

32   Lee Rainwater and William L. Yancey, *The Moynihan Report and the Politics of Controversy* (Cambridge, Mass.: MIT Press, 1967).

33   Daniel P. Moynihan, *The Negro Family: The Case for National Action* (Washington, D.C.: U.S. Government Printing Office, 1965).

families have lower IQs than children in intact families.[34] More recently, a 1980 study conducted by the National Association of Secondary School Principals indicated that students from one-parent families are lower in achievement and more frequently are tardy, truant, and suspended from school than are students from two-parent families, even after taking into account differences in family income.[35]

THE PEER GROUP AS A SOCIALIZING AGENT

While the family is the first and therefore the most basic of the primary groups with which the child is associated, interactions soon become frequent in the peer group—the play group for the small child and the teen-age clique for the adolescent. The peer group provides significant learning experiences in how to interact with others, how to be accepted by others, and how to achieve status in a circle of friends.

Significant learning experiences

Peers are relatively equal, as contrasted with the power structure in the family and the school. Parents and teachers can force children to obey rules they neither understand nor like, but peers do not have this type of authority, and thus the true meaning of exchange, cooperation, and equity can be learned more easily in this setting. Peer groups increase in importance over the years, reaching maximum influence in adolescence, when they in part dictate behavior in school.

Whereas once youth generally wanted to hurry their childhood to arrive at adulthood, this is no longer true for many young people. Once they are in their own subculture, many youth are reluctant to leave it and become a part of the adult culture. In effect, many students become alienated from the adult world because of the way the schools are organized. The importance of the peer group in socialization and education is discussed at greater length in Chapter 11.

Youth alienated from adult world

THE SCHOOL AS A SOCIALIZING AGENT

The avowed purpose of education is to teach children the information and skills they need to become productive members of their society. In traditional society, the family was the major educational agent for children and young people. In modern societies, including the United States, the school serves as the major institution devised by the adult generation to maintain and perpetuate the culture. It imparts the knowledge and tools necessary for survival and ensures the transmission of values to future generations. In short, the school provides a sense of continuity and past experience of the culture; it is a highly formal system

Transmission of values to future generations

---

34 Daniel P. Moynihan, "Sources of Resistance to the Coleman Report," *Harvard Educational Review* (Winter 1968), pp. 23-36; Martin Deutsch and Bert Brown, "Social Differences in Negro-White Intelligence Differences," *Journal of Social Issues* (April 1964), pp. 24-35.

35 B. Frank Brown, "A Study of the School Needs of Children from One-Parent Families," *Phi Delta Kappan* (April 1980), pp. 537-40.

for educating the young, an institution children are required to attend in order to be socialized and enculturated into the larger society.

The purposes of schools are basically twofold: to enhance the potential of the individual and to perpetuate society. The specific purposes of schools have changed over time, but generally they include the teaching of basic skills in reading, writing, and arithmetic, and the development of good citizens and productive workers. In addition, the schools have tended to take on more functions as the family and other institutions have found it difficult to provide children with as much guidance and assistance as in previous years. For example, schools have established arrangements to care for youngsters after school in recognition of the increased percentage of working mothers. Many school districts now provide students with supportive counseling of the kind formerly offered by local ministers and priests. Mental health workers, juvenile court personnel, and other human service professionals also provide children with assistance formerly offered by members of the family or other adults in the neighborhood.

Some observers believe that this shift in socialization responsibilities from the family to other institutions has had the effect of reducing parents' authority and capacity to raise their children in accordance with traditional standards for performance and behavior. Some eminent sociologists argue that this trend is making it difficult or impossible to develop effective internal controls (superego) among children and youth,[36] and Kenneth Keniston, speaking for the Carnegie Council on Children, has called for a national effort to improve public services for children in such a way as to support and strengthen rather than replace the child-raising efforts of parents.[37]

The culture of the school   The school has a subculture of its own—a set of values and behaviors that it reinforces and rewards. Education in school, compared with that in the family or peer group, is carried on in relatively formal ways. Groupings are formed not by voluntary choice but in terms of age, aptitudes, and sometimes sex. Students are tested and evaluated; they are told when to sit, when to stand, how to walk through hallways, and so on. There are many rules, rituals, and ceremonies that enhance group conformity. These include student codes, disciplinary procedures, and awards for attendance, achievement, conduct, or service to the school. In addition, school assemblies, athletic events, and graduation ceremonies—as well as the school insignia, songs, and cheers—all enhance the culture of the school and socialize the students.[38]

School rituals and rules

36   Christopher Lasch, *Haven in a Heartless World: The Family Besieged* (New York: Basic Books, 1977).

37   Kenneth Keniston et al., *All Our Children: The American Family Under Pressure* (New York: Harcourt Brace Jovanovich, 1977).

38   Edgar Z. Friedenberg, *Coming of Age in America* (New York: Random House, 1965); Jules Henry, *Culture Against Man* (New York: Random House, 1963); Edward Wynne, *Growing Up Suburban* (Austin: University of Texas Press, 1977).

It is generally accepted that the orientation of the school is funda-mentally middle class. The strong emphasis on punctuality, responsibil-ity, hard work, honesty, and achievement are middle-class values. Simi-larly, the language spoken by teachers is middle class, and the curriculum and tests tend to coincide with middle-class culture. Students from lower-status backgrounds are at a disadvantage; they frequently are not pre-pared to engage in self-directed learning; they often speak a different language than the formal one spoken by their teachers, and many lack the academic skills necessary for school success. In general, their socializa-tion experience is significantly different from the kind of middle-class socialization that teachers expect students already to have acquired in their family environment. As a result they experience cultural shock when they begin school, and they are at a disadvantage throughout most, if not all, of their school careers.[39]

Schools are middle-class institutions

TELEVISION AND THE MASS MEDIA

Other formal agencies share in socializ-ing the child, but their influence today generally is much less than that of family, peer group, and school. Among these are the church, scouting groups, and similar character-building organizations. However, the mass media, especially television, are ex-tremely influential in shaping the attitudes and behaviors of children as well as those of adults.

Recent evidence makes it clear that television has become "a second school system," as children sit entranced for hours in front of the televi-sion set. Children under five years old watch TV for an average of 24 hours a week, or about one-fifth of their waking hours. By the time a child graduates from high school, he or she will have spent 15,000 to 20,000 hours watching television as compared with 11,000 to 12,000 hours in school.[40] Before children reach eighteen, they will "have seen 350,000 commercials urging them to want, want, want."[41] Clearly, television is an important influence in the lives of children and youth.

"A second school system"

Rather than viewing television as a second school system, Neil Post-man views it and the other mass media (for example, radio, comic books, movies) as the "first curriculum" because it appears to be affecting the way children develop learning skills and orient themselves toward the acquisition of knowledge and understanding.[42] According to Postman and some other observers, television's curriculum is designed largely to main-tain interest; the school's curriculum must accomplish other purposes,

39 Allison Davis, *Social-Class Influences upon Learning* (Cambridge, Mass.: Harvard University Press, 1948); Sandra A. Warden, *The Leftouts: Disadvantaged Children in Heterogeneous Schools* (New York: Holt, Rinehart, 1968); Richard H. deLone, *Small Futures* (New York: Harcourt Brace Jovanovich, 1979).

40 Postman, *Teaching as a Conserving Activity.*

41 Evelyn Kaye, *The Family Guide to Children's Television: What to Watch, What to Miss, What to Change, and How to Do It* (New York: Pantheon, 1974), p. 7.

42 Postman, *Teaching as a Conserving Activity.*

such as moral development and mastery of abstract thinking skills that may not be very interesting to children. In addition, watching television requires little effort and skills of the viewer.[43] Children develop the bad habit of not having to think or solve problems; rather, they are entertained and become accustomed to instant stimuli and responses. In this context, teachers as well as parents have trouble competing with the media to gain children's attention. Educators face a formidable challenge in attempting to develop and maintain interest and motivation in schoolwork.

Educators and others who work with children also are concerned with media effects on the development of children's values and behaviors. For example, many adults are particularly worried that television and other media may encourage aggressive or violent behavior. A review of research on this issue concluded that effects of television on children's aggression are largely dependent on situational factors like the child's degree of frustration or anger, similarities between the available target and the target in the television portrayal, potential consequences such as pain or punishment, and opportunity to perform an act of violence.[44]

TV and aggressive behavior

It also is true, however, that television can be an important force for positive socialization. This conclusion has been supported by research indicating that the "Sesame Street" program has been helpful for both middle-class and lower-status youth,[45] and that children can become more cooperative and nurturant after viewing programs emphasizing these behaviors.[46] Recognizing both the good and the damaging effects that the media can have on children and youth, many individuals and groups have been working to bring about improvements in media to which young people are exposed. The Parent Teachers Association has made reform in television—particularly reduction in sex and violence during prime time—one of its major national goals, and organizations such as the National Citizens Committee for Broadcasting have been established to collect information and lobby for change.

THE CHANGING AMERICAN CULTURE

Although all cultures change, we find that American culture is changing more rapidly than in the past because of the acceleration of trends, the explosion of knowledge, the influence of mass communication, and the rise in gross national product. It is important, then, to point out the direction of the shift in values in American culture in order to see how schools fit into this drama of cultural transformation.

43 Neal J. Gordon, "Television and Learning" in H. J. Walberg, ed., *Educational Environment and Effects* (Berkeley, Calif.: McCutchan, 1979), pp. 57-76.

44 George A. Comstock, "Types of Portrayal and Aggressive Behavior," *Journal of Communication* (Summer 1977), pp. 189-98.

45 Aimee D. Leifer, Neal J. Gordon, and Sherryl B. Graves, "Children's Television: More Than Mere Entertainment," *Harvard Educational Review* (Autumn 1975), pp. 90-97.

46 Rita W. Poulos, Eli A. Rubenstein, and Robert M. Leibert, "Positive Social Learning," *Journal of Communication* (Autumn 1975), pp. 90-97.

*TRADITION-
INNER-OTHER-
DIRECTED*

David Riesman's *The Lonely Crowd*, which first appeared in 1950, had a tremendous impact on both laypersons and academicians.[47] It was Riesman's thesis that a shift had taken place in the character and orientation of the people of the western world and of the United States in particular.

Shift in
American
character

He formulated three major classifications of society in terms of how people were directed—tradition-, inner-, and other-directed. The *tradition-directed* character prevailed in a folk, rural, agrarian society. Primitive tribes, feudal-era Europeans, and present-day isolated villagers in Asia, Africa, and Latin America are examples. Although the societies varied, they shared common characteristics. They were dominated by centuries-old tradition. Little energy was directed toward finding new solutions to age-old problems. Almost every task, occupation, and role was substantially the same as it had been for countless generations, even centuries past; and each was so explicit and obvious that it was understood by all. Each person knew his or her station in life, and each played according to "the rules." The individual was obedient to tradition: in most cases he or she was not highly prized, and in many instances the individual was not encouraged to develop capabilities and use initiative beyond the limits and defined position of the society.

The Renaissance, the Reformation, and the commercial and industrial revolutions were brought on by a torrent of discovery, change, and innovation. This dynamism led to the landing of the Pilgrims and characterized American nineteenth-century westward expansion and early twentieth-century colonial expansion. Progress disrupted the tradition-directed character of western society; the conformity to the past no longer predetermined the behavior of men and women; experimentation and progress became important patterns of conduct and values. With this shift came an *inner-directed* society, characterized by population growth, increased personal mobility, accumulation of wealth, constant expansion of goods, and exploration and colonization. Tradition thus gave way, and individual initiative increased.

Commercial
and industrial
revolutions

Although an individualist, the inner-directed person is not quite independent. His or her values and behavior are rooted in those of the parents; moreover, the person is forced to cope with rapid change and sometimes violent upheaval, which makes him or her an easy victim of mass movements and group ideologies. This stage of society has been long drawn out and painful in western Europe and Russia. For the United States, Canada, and Australia, the transition has been short and relatively easy because of the benefits derived from European technology and discoveries.

47 David Riesman (with Nathan Glazer and Reuel Denney), *The Lonely Crowd* (Garden City, N.Y.: Doubleday, 1953).

Finally, *other-directedness* is the emergent character of American society. It is the product of a socioeconomic climate that has come to support and encourage teamwork, group integration, and gregariousness— and to disparage the individualism and independence of inner-directed virtues. The other-directed psyche aspires to fit and belong to the group, to be accepted by one's peers. Conformity is exacted from peers by mass media and the popular culture. Parents have less influence over their offspring than they did in the inner-directed society, and adult wisdom has much less influence over the young than it did in the tradition-directed society.

As a result, we have a breakdown of the extended family and of esteem for the wisdom of the elderly; the old must now make way for the young. Conspicuous consumption and the display of wealth are important to the other-directed person, a quite different individual from the inner-directed person, who saved money and was more concerned with succeeding. Education, leisure services, and entertainment go together with increased consumption of words and images from the new mass media of communications. Increasingly, relations with the outer world and with subcultures are mediated by the flow of ideas in urban centers, resulting in rapid synthesizing and changing of trends and fads. The individual is atomized and depersonalized. Recent writers have described this shift in culture in terms of the "organization man," "new middle class," "future shock," and the "greening of America."

FOLK-URBAN-SUBURBAN CULTURE

The folk-urban-suburban reference is not so much a geographical classification as a cultural concept. It is more abstract than concrete and represents a synthesis of social and historical situations. People need not necessarily dwell in rural areas to have a "folk" culture, nor do they have to live in suburbia to share the values and lifestyles that are labeled "suburban." Several models have been proposed to illustrate cultural populations: organic-mechanical, sacred-secular, folk-urban, rural-suburban, and communal-associational. The conceptual typology we shall explore has been developed by Harold Hodges; it combines American folk-urban-suburban living.[48]

The "folk" reference in the United States connotes the lifestyles of American-born farmers and villagers in rural areas, and of first-generation European immigrants in large cities. Their orientation is to the past, to tradition, and to communal ties. The urban reference represents a shift away from an "old-fashioned" lifestyle, away from the elderly, to an orientation toward the future. Urban cultural patterns are typified among

48 Harold M. Hodges, "The Folk-Urban-Suburban Continuum: A Conceptual Overview of America Yesterday, Today, and Tomorrow," in W. W. Kallenbach and H. M. Hodges, eds., *Education and Society* (Columbus, Ohio: Merrill, 1963), pp. 50–59; Hodges, *Social Stratification: Class in America* (Cambridge, Mass.: Schenkman, 1964).

the children of rural America who have moved to the cities, and among second-generation ethnic Americans who have no memories of the old country. Many of these offspring consider their parents either hopelessly out of date or embarrassingly foreign; the Americanization process has roundly rejected their parents' way of life. The suburban reference illustrates the cultural milieu of Americans who have rejected the ills of urbanization for suburban living. They are mobile, middle-class, and oriented toward conformity; they have gone full circle and re-entered the homogeneous society that characterizes folk living.

It is important to note that any modern industrial society will contain all three cultures; the boundaries that separate folk, urban, and suburban categories overlap and are fluid. It is also important to note that the qualities we attach to the various categories are basically hypothetical, and the "within and among" boundaries are blurred. Riesman's tradition-directed culture tends to correspond with Hodges's folk culture. Inner-directedness and urban culture are related. Similarly, the other-directed and suburban boundaries are related.

ETHNICITY AND
ASSIMILATION
The rise of racial pride on the part of Blacks caught most Americans by surprise in the late 1960s. Today, sparked by an economic situation that is no longer booming and by the feeling of having been overlooked and ignored by both the establishment and reform movements of the last decade, there is a growing consciousness of group cohesion among White ethnics. Whereas the social problems of American society were defined during the 1960s almost entirely within the context of poverty and race, ethnicity in relation to public policy became an important factor in the 1970s.

Overlooked and ignored by reform movements

With a few notable exceptions, there had been a strong reluctance up to the mid-1970s to admit to the persistence of an ethnic factor in American culture.[49] The idea of a common community, common interest, and common faith has characterized the sociological and educational literature; indeed, the public schools have always been viewed as the institution to assimilate subgroups and "foreign" groups—to promote the common culture.[50]

The ethnic factor and the assimilation process can be viewed in the perspective of three ideologies.

49   Nathan Glazer and Daniel P. Moynihan, *Beyond the Melting Pot*, 2nd ed. (Cambridge, Mass.: MIT Press, 1970); Milton M. Gordon, *Assimilation in American Life* (New York: Oxford University Press, 1964); Andrew M. Greeley, *Why They Can't Be Like Us* (New York: Institute of Human Relations, 1969); Oscar Handlin, *The Newcomers* (Garden City, N.Y.: Doubleday, 1962); Michael Novak, *Further Reflections on Ethnicity* (Middletown, Penn.: EMPAC, 1977).

50   This idea is embedded in the public school movement from its inception to the present; it has been promoted by Horace Mann, the most influential nineteenth-century American educator, and by John Dewey and James Conant, the most influential twentieth-century American educators. The writings of Jane Addams, who was sensitive to ethnic culture, presented a contrast to the writings of Mann, Dewey, and Conant, and were not typical of the age.

1. *Anglo-conformity*. This is a broad term used to describe a variety of viewpoints about immigration and assimilation—how approximately thirty to forty million foreign-born ethnics have been Americanized. Its negative aspects range from the discredited notion of White, Anglo-Saxon superiority and exclusionary immigration policies to the Japanese-American relocation camps during World War II. All of these actions reflect a highly ethnocentric view of the American majority culture. On the other hand, this ideology is the basis of our democratic institutions and is illustrated by the symbols of individualism and technological progress.

Ethnocentric
view of
American
culture

2. *Melting pot*. This term has idealistic overtones as it is used to describe the evolving American society—a nation of many nations. As early as the eighteenth century, America was depicted as the place where "individuals of all nations are melted into a new race of men."[51] The melting pot theme, which competed with the concept of Anglo-conformity, envisions Americans as a new blend of people, fused together in a great crucible of universal brotherhood.

3. *Cultural pluralism*. This term signifies that different ethnic groups can keep their identity and still work together; they can maintain both their own group interests and those of the nation. The concept promotes the legitimacy of ethnic politics and cultural enclaves. Cultural pluralism was a fact of life in American society long before it became a theory—that is, an accepted theory with explicit relevance for the nation as a whole. Only recently has it been discussed and advanced in American intellectual life.

With different ethnic groups and racial minorities competing for political gains and economic benefits, those who work to improve intergroup relations need to understand ethnics' concerns. A myopic view that ignores the reality of urban ethnic interests or promotes the interests of one group at the expense of another is naive and dangerous.[52] Moreover, at the point where each ethnic (and racial) group claims its interests deserve priority in future public policy, attitudes become highly polarized.[53] While every ethnic group has the right to advance its interests and protect its rights, the greater good of the country must prevail.[54] Recent trends

Group
interests vs.
nationwide
interests

51 Hector St. John de Crèvecoeur, *Letters from an American Farmer*, rev. ed. (New York: Albert and Boni, 1925), p. 55.

52 Richard Polenberg, *One Nation Divisible: Class, Race, and Ethnicity in the United States* (New York: Viking, 1979).

53 Michael Novak, *The Rise of the Unmeltable Ethnics* (New York: Macmillan, 1972); Novak, *Further Reflections on Ethnicity*; Robert A. Dahl, *Democracy in the United States*, 3rd ed. (Chicago: Rand McNally, 1975).

54 Nathan Glazer, *Affirmative Discrimination: Ethnic Inequality and Public Policy* (New York: Praeger, 1975); Allan C. Ornstein, *Race and Politics in School/Community Organizations* (Pacific Palisades, Calif.: Goodyear, 1974).

involving cultural pluralism and education are discussed further in Chapter 16.

**ADOLESCENT AND
YOUTH CULTURE**

Unfortunately, much of the literature on adolescent culture is negative. A young person who disturbs the larger society by overt acts or emotional conduct is looked upon with great disapproval and suspicion. Young people are products of the larger society in which they live; however, their assertions of individuality and discontent with the adult world are as much a part of the culture as are their approved actions.

Products of the larger society

In one sense the reference to youth culture can be viewed as a result of the breakdown of the process of socialization of the total culture. The problem of youth, especially in American society, is one that to some extent has been generated by the failure of the processes of enculturation. This failure is attributable to the fact that children and adolescents have been excluded from almost every responsible activity with the adults of the community. Youth are thrown back into their own peer group, which has formed what we commonly call "youth culture."

*ADOLESCENCE
AND ADULT
SOCIETY*

In primitive and traditional cultures, the young are usually initiated into adult life after puberty. This initiation is sometimes done through special rites and rituals that are designed to test and prove the young person's worth to assume adult roles. In such societies one is either a child or an adult; there is only a brief gap between the two—if it occurs at all. In modern societies the young are forced to postpone their adulthood, and the period is labeled adolescence or youth.

Postponement of adulthood

A major reason for this postponement is that modern society, particularly in the United States, no longer has an economic need or a viable social role for this age group to perform. We often tell adolescents to "grow up," "leave us alone," "play with friends," or "finish school."

Adolescent "apartheid"   An extensive study of youth groups in different cultures is S. N. Eisenstadt's comparison of a massive amount of anthropological and sociological data from primitive to modern societies. In all societies, there is some grouping of *children* apart from adults— with various types of cooperative behavior and acceptable norms.[55] However, it is mainly in western civilizations that *youth* are distinctly separated from adults. In such cases, the peer group or adolescent group becomes an important bridge between the home and adult society. At the same time, the peer group becomes more and more isolated from the rest of society. This adolescent isolation from the rest of society, according to

[55] S. N. Eisenstadt, *From Generation to Generation* (New York: Free Press, 1956).

Eisenstadt, also explains the strong emotional interdependence and intensive mutual identification of the peer group. For this reason, too, youth groups are susceptible to becoming the nuclei of various deviant movements and of activities that tend to resist authority.

In the same vein, Kingsley Davis contends that adolescence is the time when the individual is attaining physical maturity without attaining equal social maturity.[56] Full growth, strength, and mental capacity are reached shortly after puberty, but the adolescent still has a long way to go, in most societies, before full social status is reached.

While earlier physical than social maturity is most pronounced in modern societies, it is a condition inherent in all human societies. In most cultures, Davis points out, power and advantage have come to be dependent on social position, experience, and reputation rather than on brute strength or physical prowess. Insofar as these attributes have anything to do with age, they are more likely to come with middle age, or in some societies even old age. Thus, adolescents find themselves in a socially subordinate position despite their physical equality or superiority to older persons. Even an army, which presumably depends on physical excellence and strength, is controlled by elderly generals; government machinery, likewise, is run by middle-aged and elderly people.

Actually, the adolescent in modern society must keep on learning after the capacity to do so has already begun to decline. Even though one's mental potential has reached its peak during postadolescence, one is still required to gain experience, judgment, and wisdom—which come with age. Despite achievements in sports, in the arts, or even on the battlefield, the adolescent is forced to defer to older people whose biological capacities may have declined to less than his or her own.

It is clear, therefore, that the principle of seniority is no accident, no empty form. The charge is frequently made that the old hang on to their vested interests, and that this is the explanation of the subordination of youth. That older people do generally seek to hold the power they have is basically true, but this desire does not explain the fact that they are able to do so. They are able to retain their power because they have a kind of superiority—a superiority developed and supported by an organized society in which the rules and norms favor adults. To some degree, then, adult society has created a socially disadvantaged group of adolescents who have a secondary status in society.[57] This phenomenon is more obvious (and perhaps necessary) in modern societies; as society becomes more complex the lag between physical and social development becomes greater, and adolescence, as socially defined, extends farther into organic adulthood.

Experience, wisdom, and power with age

56 Kingsley Davis, "The Child and the Social Structure," *Journal of Educational Sociology* (December 1940), pp. 217-29; Davis, *Human Society* (New York: Macmillan, 1949).

57 Edgar Z. Friedenberg, *The Vanishing Adolescent* (Boston: Beacon, 1959); Margaret Mead, *Coming of Age in Samoa* (New York: Morrow, 1928).

*YOUTH AND
THE NUCLEAR
GENERATION*

Youth as a new
stage

For a broad sociopsychological explanation of why students and young adults seem willing to crusade against schools and society, Kenneth Keniston has provided a model of youth as a new stage in development in between adolescence and adulthood.[58] Adolescence describes behavior for older children and teen-agers, but the description of adolescence does not seem operational today for many young men and women, and this may be one reason why we are unable to understand them or are confused by their sometimes dissenting and militant behavior. Our anxiety is no longer focused on teen-agers or delinquents, but rather on postadolescents who cannot seem to "settle down." What characterizes a growing number of postadolescents today is that they have not resolved the questions whose answers once defined adulthood—questions of who they are, of vocation, of social role, and of their relationship to the existing society. In youth, society's definitions are questioned and there is *pervasive ambivalence* toward both self and society. This ambivalence, according to Keniston, leads to such behaviors as meditation, religious conversion, introspection, drug abuse, psychoanalysis, political activism, and rebellion. In regard to the relationship between self and society, the adolescent struggles for emancipation from external family control. With youth the focus of conflict shifts to society.

Questions
related to self
and society

While attending college seems to intensify the stage of youth, it is not a necessary factor in prolonging this transformation. For some youth the beginning of the stage may start in high school, and for some it may extend beyond their thirtieth birthday. Youth, then, is a state of mind, a transformation or maturing process that is more psychological than physical. It is not a definite rejection of society or the existing system, as some claim; rather, it is a time of tension when the relationship between self and society must be worked out.

Youth as a
state of mind

Today's youth has grown up in a society characterized by rapid social change, violence, and the bomb.[59] Keniston sees the new styles of dissent and unrest of the late 1960s as a reaction to the history of the past two and a half decades. The radical groups viewed themselves more as part of a generation rather than as part of an organization or ideology. Among dissenters there was a strong feeling that the older generation and the older ideologies were exhausted and irrelevant, including "old liberals" and members of the "Old Left." Young people became aware they were affected by developments in all parts of the world. The earth had become a global village; a conflict in a far-off country could change the status of the draft; changes in the foreign exchange rate in Europe or Japan were reflected in declining opportunities for employment at home. Most impor-

58 Kenneth Keniston, *Youth and Dissent: The Rise of a New Opposition* (New York: Harcourt Brace Jovanovich, 1971).

59 Kenneth Keniston, *Young Radicals: Notes on Committed Youth* (New York: Harcourt, Brace & World, 1968).

tant, the threat of nuclear annihilation was always present. Youth grew up in a world that has experienced violent upheaval and the unrelenting possibility of nuclear disaster. In this view, the primary tasks for youth were to develop a new social and political order that would solve our social ills and curtail the dangers of an impending holocaust.[60]

Adolescent obsolescence   Another interpretation for youth dissonance is that the young have been rendered obsolete by society. According to this view, advanced by Bruno Bettelheim, their prolonged education has made them relatively useless and impotent.[61] In addition, modern technology seems to have robbed them of any place in the real world of work. There are no frontiers to conquer, and adolescents have no way of proving themselves real adults. Youth are in a desperate search for therapeutic experiences which will help them feel they have at long last come of age. Rebellion offers this shortcut to a sense of adulthood; it provides meaning to existence. If there were no war, no poverty, no race problem, no bomb, youth would still rebel. These are only "screens" for what really ails them; they feel "socially irrelevant and, as persons, insignificant." They rebel not because of social injustice, urban decay, or because of nuclear holocaust, but because they feel that "society can do nicely without them." This is an even bleaker existence—a "feeling that youth has no future."[62] Bettelheim argues that the anxiety of youth is not about the future of society or their mission to build a new social order. Rather, it reflects their fear that society has no use for their present existence. They are rejecting the system because they feel "they have been classified as 'waste materials' by the system."[63]

Useless and impotent

Ideology of the counterculture   The concept of counterculture was popularized by Theodore Roszak.[64] While it is not strictly a youth movement, the ranks of the counterculture are populated primarily by young people from middle-class and surburban backgrounds. On college campuses the counterculture students tend to enroll in the humanities and social sciences. Off campus, the movement is popular among young artists and professionals—many of the older radicals of the 1960s. Alternative strategies, such as free schools, communes, and encounter groups, which connote personalized and retreatist behavior, are common. Drugs, the Jesus Movement, and various religious, demonic, and witchcraft cults also characterize the counterculture community—augmented by rural communes and segments of academic communities.

Primarily a middle-class culture

60   A similar view on youth's reaction to history and the post-World War II decades is presented by Robert J. Lifton, "The Young and the Old: Notes on a New History," *Atlantic* (October 1969), pp. 83–93.
61   Bruno Bettelheim, "Student Revolt." Statement before the House Special Committee on Education, March 20, 1969, in *Vital Speeches* (April 15, 1969), pp. 405–10; Bettelheim, "Obsolete Youth," *Encounter* (September 1969), pp. 29–42.
62   Ibid., p. 31.
63   Ibid.
64   Theodore Roszak, *The Making of a Counterculture* (New York: Viking Press, 1969).

The counterculture was born out of dissatisfaction with the kinds of lifestyles and options offered by contemporary society. The ideology of the counterculture, according to Charles Reich, is based on a new humanism. He calls it "Consciousness III."[65] "Consciousness I," with its emphasis on hard work, sexual morality, and material accomplishment and with its negative correlates of dogma and prejudice, is rejected. Also rejected is "Consciousness II," the impersonal efficiency of the technocratic and bureaucratic society. In short, the counterculture movement opposes the materialistic, puritanical values of American society; it draws on the romantic naturalism of Rousseau from western philosophy and the popularized version of Zen Buddhism from the East. The movement is an extension of the "flower children" phenomenon and an expression of the "make love, not war" slogan of the 1960s. The stress is on the goodness of men and women rather than on evil or destructive traits.

People rather than machines; peace rather than war; love rather than hatred; cooperation rather than conflict; truth rather than hypocrisy; good rather than bad. These are the beliefs of the counterculture. Few would quarrel with them; the Judeo-Christian belief in humankind and search for truth and serenity are not altogether different. What was new, however, was the widespread cynicism of our young and the irrational belief that machines, war, and all other evils of today can be wished away. If great numbers of middle-class young people do "cop out" of leadership roles in our society and choose "not to play the game," there will be many members of working-class and minority groups to take their place. A period of hard times—and through most of the 1970s the economy was straining—helped bring about a change in the attitudes of many of those who were part of the counterculture. The counterculture is much less important today than it was ten years ago.

CHANGING
YOUTH ATTITUDES
IN THE 1970s
Interest in political activism and social reform was high in the late 1960s and early 1970s. The counterculture still was prominent in the first part of the decade, and the New Left, though not widely embraced, enjoyed great credibility on college campuses and even in high schools. By the end of the decade, however, both movements had waned, and young people seemed to be more "tranquil" and conservative then their immediate predecessors.

Tranquility and conservatism   As the decade progressed, the end of the Vietnam War and difficult economic conditions had the effect (among other developments) of reducing support for the counterculture, the New Left, and other aspects of the youth culture that had emerged in the 1960s. Social scientists are now reviewing the developments of the last

65   Charles A. Reich, *The Greening of America* (New York: Random House, 1970).

two decades and trying to figure out what occurred and what implications can be identified for the future.

On the basis of extensive data collected between 1967 and 1973, Daniel Yankelovich has concluded that, first, there was a revolution in moral and social values that continued through the 1960s; largely achieved among college students, it was adopted by some noncollege youth in the 1970s. Second, there was a "political revolution," associated with the civil rights movement and the war in Vietnam. According to Yankelovich the latter has more or less ceased in terms of overt action, but the revolution in moral and social thinking still affects today's youth, representing new values, which he calls a "new naturalism."[66]

Moral and social revolution

Yankelovich found that young people today generally question the institutions of marriage, the nuclear family, sexual morality, hard work, excessive materialism, and religion. But the most dissatisfied young people now are not college students but high school students who have gone directly into the work force. Dissatisfaction among this younger working force, who make up about 75 percent of the present youth population, has greatly increased.

Related studies of high school graduates and college youth tend to confirm the Yankelovich findings; moreover, the new research indicates that youth today is concerned with school grades and career opportunities—perhaps reflecting the tightening job market and the decreasing number of good jobs available for graduates. Furthermore, they seem to be becoming increasingly materialistic and surprisingly conservative politically.[67] This represents a shift in the pendulum, in some respects back toward the 1950s.

Tightening job market

Jacob Getzels also has reviewed the data available on changing youth attitudes and reached the conclusion that values have evolved toward an emphasis on greater social and personal responsibility.[68] Traditional values changed during a transitional period in the late 1940s and mid-1950s and were further modified in the 1960s. Although it is difficult to characterize the seemingly rapid changes of the past decade, overall youth values still are less traditional than they were before 1970.

In particular, a series of recent studies of high school seniors (college-bound and others) indicates that youth today show considerable tolerance for "unconventional" behavior such as cohabitation and use of marijuana. Their views on racial and sexual equality are more liberal than those of their elders and pre-1960 youth. The studies also found that youth

66 Daniel Yankelovich, *The Changing Values on Campus* (New York: Washington Square Press, 1972); Yankelovich, *The New Morality* (New York: McGraw-Hill, 1974).

67 Brigitte Berger, "The Coming Age of People Work," *Change* (May 1976), pp. 24–30; Martin Mayer, *Today and Tomorrow in America* (New York: Harper & Row, 1976); James O'Toole, "The Reserve Army of the Unemployed," *Change* (May 1975), pp. 26–33 ff.

68 Jacob W. Getzels, "The School and the Acquisition of Values" in R. W. Tyler, ed., *From Youth to Constructive Adult Life: The Role of the Public School* (Berkeley, Calif.: McCutchan, 1978), pp. 43–66.

became more pessimistic about the state of the nation during the 1970s. Like earlier generations, however, they continue to rate "a good marriage and family life" as being their highest priority personal goal for the future.[69] A related study indicated that 63 percent of freshmen entering college in 1979 said that "being well off financially" is an important life goal, as compared with 44 percent in 1967.[70]

Priority on marriage and family life

A GLIMPSE INTO THE FUTURE   The most important factor related to the turbulence of the 1960s may have been the size of the youth population. Between 1960 and 1970 the size of this subgroup of the American population increased by unprecedented numbers, and it may never again grow by such a percentage.

If you look back from 1900 to 1960, you will find that the size of the subgroup age 14 to 24 in each succeeding decade never grew by more than 10 percent and sometimes by less than 1 percent. In the whole of these sixty years the total increase in the population of that age group was less than 12 million. Similarly, the number of high school enrollments increased from 915,000 to 8.5 million, an average of 125,000 per year. Then, during the 1960s, the youth population increased by some 13.8 million persons; high school enrollments, likewise, soared from 8.5 million to 15 million—an increase of 750,000 per year.

Dramatic increase of youth population

Youth grew by 13.8 million persons in the 1960s; it grew by 600,000 during the 1970s; it will decline in the 1980s. "It's all over, it happened once," writes Daniel Moynihan; "it will never happen again."[71] After a 54 percent increase in the 1960s, dropping to a 10-12 percent increase in the 1970s, we shall see a 7-10 percent decrease in the 1980s.

In terms of what we call a dependency ratio—that is, the number of young people compared to the number of older people who look after the young people, pay their bills and tell them how to behave—the ratio of persons aged 14-24 to persons aged 25-65 increased 40 percent in the 1960s, after either zero growth or a decline in every decade from 1900. The ratio of high school students to persons older than twenty increased even more dramatically. What happened? A new social group was created in the United States, so large in its number that in effect it was isolated from the rest of the society; it was isolated in the schools (and colleges); it was isolated in the slums; it was isolated in the armed forces; it was isolated in its treatment by the mass media. It was part of the rest of society—but it had its own culture, its own way of thinking and behaving. During this

69 Jerald G. Bachman and Lloyd D. Johnson, "The Freshman, 1979," *Psychology Today* (September 1979), pp. 29–87.

70 "College Freshmen More Materialistic, Study Finds," *Report on Education Research* (February 6, 1980), p. 5.

71 Daniel P. Moynihan, *Coping: On the Practice of Government* (New York: Random House, Vintage Books, 1975), p. 425.

ten-year period, the number of high school students increased by 45 percent, but the number of such persons who were employed grew by only 10 percent. The unemployment rates for teen-agers went up enormously, as did all other manifestations of dislocation and alienation. Youth acquired its own form of dress, music and entertainment and its own attitudes about drugs and sex. Attitudes changed toward authority figures (including teachers), toward patriotism, and toward big business.

Its own form
of dress,
music, and
entertainment

But the soaring growth of the youth population is all over now. By the end of the 1970s, additional teachers were no longer needed to maintain our present teacher/student ratio, and in the 1980s we shall probably not need more professors either. Many schools and colleges will probably close down. Our students are more docile again, and we are becoming a society of aged people. Unless something happens to increase the birth rate and the death rate, we are headed for a society in which the young will play a minor role. Have you noticed that in recent commercials on television and in magazines the advertisers are taking off the smiles and putting on the wrinkles? The "Coca-Cola generation" is fast disappearing, and those who "deserve a break" at MacDonald's seem older. In the future the school may cater to the old as much as it has catered to the young in the past. Hence, teachers may find adult education to have a more viable future than elementary or secondary education.

From smiles to
wrinkles in
advertising

SUMMING UP

1. A society is an organized group of individuals, and a culture is an organized pattern of learned behaviors and attitudes characteristic of a particular society. Societies, ranging from primitive to modern, can be defined in terms of culture.

2. There are general configurations in our society that illustrate and define the uniqueness as well as the meaning of our group relationships. As with all societies, these relationships change over time and thus our culture is in flux.

3. Although an adolescent subculture exists in American society, and some of the value systems are in conflict with the larger overarching culture, much of the value system of teen-agers is still shared with parents, teachers, and other adults.

4. The culture of a given society is dependent on education; through education society perpetuates its culture and teaches its young the skills required to function in society. In modern society schools play the most important role in the education of youth, as contrasted with more informal methods of education. As a prospective teacher, you too are involved in the climate of change—in the shifts and trends of the times.

DISCUSSION QUESTIONS

1. How does membership in society (or a subgroup) help the individual find answers to the question "Who am I?" Give several examples.

2. Compare and contrast the socialization experience of the average American male and female adolescent with the socialization experiences of Asian or Arab youth living in a rural or non-Western culture.

3. Recently, social scientists have pointed out several reasons why different ethnic groups would not quite blend into a homogeneous end product, and why the thesis of the "melting pot" has outlived its usefulness. Discuss why you feel this thesis is right or wrong. Based on your reasons for supporting or opposing this thesis, can you predict the rise or decline of "cultural pluralism" for the future?

4. How do value changes affect the role of schools?

5. Compare the youth generation of the 1960s with that of the 1970s. Which group will the youth of the 1980s more closely resemble? Why?

THINGS TO DO

1. How does bigness affect the individual in modern society? Debate this question in terms of bureaucracy, mass media, and political mass movements.

2. Consider your own experiences and explain how you have been discriminated against in the past on a sexual basis.

3. Interview some elderly people about how they were brought up. Compare their socialization process to your own.

4. Obtain a recent issue of an elementary school textbook and an issue about twenty-five years old. Compare and contrast value judgments and methods of the authors' socialization efforts in the two texts.

5. Invite someone who claims to be part of or was once part of the counterculture movement to speak to the class.

CHAPTER 10
SOCIAL CLASS, RACE, AND EDUCATIONAL ACHIEVEMENT

Focusing questions

How does the class structure in our society handicap children in school?

How are education and mobility related in American society?

How do excellence and equality result in conflicts within schools and society?

How have legislation and court decisions altered race relations?

In what sense is the study of the disadvantaged a study of poor and minority groups?

What are the implications of the equal opportunity studies of disadvantaged children?

The American social-class system is now generally understood to consist of three classes—lower, middle, and upper. It is well known that in American society there is a high correlation between social class and educational achievement. Traditionally, lower-class students have not performed as well as middle- and upper-class students in school. To be sure, teachers have been told over and over again that they are middle-class oriented, as are the institutions in which they teach. As you read this chapter you might ask yourself whether schools can be neutral or culture-free. Is it possible for a school in American society, or any society, to be oriented to any social class other than the dominant one? If so, what class orientation should the schools have? Given these questions, what is the significance of the relationship between schooling and social class for the teacher?

While social class is an important predictor for explaining differences in educational achievement, this chapter also deals with the study of race and educational achievement, as well as the study of the education of the disadvantaged. As you read the material on racial and ethnic groups, you might ask: Given the fact that there are educational differences among these groups, what are the political implications of such differences? To what extent are these differences related to social class, discrimination, and failure of teachers and schools to understand and respond to different cultures? Also, to what extent are these differences related to home and family characteristics?

When we discuss the disadvantaged, we shall be referring mainly to lower-class and minority groups, since class and race are considered important variables in examining school performance. We must be careful, however, not to overgeneralize from the available data and force evidence into these two categories.

HISTORICAL STUDIES OF SOCIAL CLASS

Prior to the 1960s interest in the relation between social class and education was limited mainly to the academic community. The descriptions were nonpolitical and based primarily on observations of community life and/or comparative statistical patterns among groups. Recent literature, which is political in nature, if not in tone, is sometimes used to justify policy, and is based on multiple correlations and more sophisticated statistical designs.

Early studies were nonpolitical

MIDDLETOWN, ELMTOWN, AND RIVER CITY

Classic studies of social class and education were conducted by the Lynds, Lloyd Warner, Allison Davis, August Hollingshead, and Robert Havighurst. As we shall see, these social scientists drew educators into a debate about the existence of social differentiation and its influence on our schools. The debate continues today. Although few deny

Social class and educational achievement

the existence of some social stratification within American society, there is still disagreement as to the effects social class has upon educational achievement.

The Lynds, in their extensive study of "Middletown," concluded that parents, regardless of social-class level, recognize the importance of education for their children; however, lower-class children are penalized within the school system because they do not come to school academically equipped to deal with the verbal symbols and behavioral traits most valued by the dominant middle-class groups.[1] In short, the schools reflect a middle-class ethos and consequently discriminate against lower-class students.

The Lynds' judgment of the schools was repeated in a series of studies of communities in New England, the Deep South, and the Midwest by W. Lloyd Warner and his associates at the University of Chicago.[2] The main function of school seemed to be sorting out students according to their potential for upward mobility, a process that tended to doom lower-class students to remain lower class. The schools served the middle class, and especially the upper class, well by teaching those skills that are essential for college preparation and high-status occupations. But the lower-class child, who is not prepared to conform to the school's middle-class standards and expectations, is handicapped in the school system. "One group" [the lower class], they reported, "is almost immediately brushed off into a bin labeled 'nonreaders,' 'first-grade repeaters,' or 'opportunity class,' where they stay for eight or ten years and are then released through a chute to the outside world to become 'hewers of wood and drawers of water.'"[3]

Sorting out students

In another study Warner identified six variables (occupation, amount of income, source of income, house type, dwelling area, and level of education) that in combination produced an index for measuring social status.[4] Other researchers have tested combinations of these and other indices and have found that they correlate with measures of attitudes and behaviors that reflect different social-class patterns. In general, occupation, education, and income have been found to be three important components of social status.

Allison Davis, who summarized Warner's data on middle-class and lower-class subcultures, argued that schools have a built-in bias in curriculum, teaching methods, and testing based on linguistic aptitudes that favor middle-class children and discriminate against lower-class chil-

1 Robert S. Lynd and Helen M. Lynd, *Middletown: A Study in American Culture* (New York: Harcourt, Brace & World, 1929).
2 W. Lloyd Warner, Robert J. Havighurst, and Martin B. Loeb, *Who Shall Be Educated?* (New York: Harper & Row, 1944).
3 Warner, Havighurst, and Loeb, *Who Shall Be Educated?*, p. 38.
4 W. Lloyd Warner, Marcia Meeker, and Kenneth Eells, *Social Class in America* (Chicago: Science Research Associates, 1949).

dren.[5] In addition, middle-class children are provided with more parental and home assistance in almost all social and cognitive learning situations and with more emotional and psychological support than lower-class children. These cultural factors result in middle-class children coming to school prepared to display appropriate behaviors and necessary learning modes for school achievement, as opposed to lower-class children coming to school unprepared to learn.

In a more sophisticated analysis of social class and school achievement, August Hollingshead divided social class into five categories ranging from upper-upper to lower-lower class, and contended that while lower-class family life and culture did not prepare students to adjust to the school, neither did the school adjust itself to the needs of lower-class children.[6] (See Table 10.1 and Table 10.2.) The result was that as many as two-thirds of the students from the two upper social classes were in the college preparatory curriculum, and less than 15 percent from the lower classes were in the college track. Not one student from the upper classes (whereas more than two-thirds from the two lower classes) was enrolled in the commercial track—which is the least prestigious and easiest track. More than half of the students in the top two social classes had mean grade scores of 85 to 100, and the others had mean grade scores of 70 to 84. Less than 25 percent of the two lower social classes had mean scores of 85 to 100, whereas two-thirds had averages of 70 to 84, and 20 percent had averages of 50 to 69. Table 10.1 indicates the correlation between social-class position and curricula, and Table 10.2 shows the relationship of mean grade scores.

As you examine these two tables, you might ask what is it about social class in our society that distinguishes between the groups who do or do not receive good grades and go or do not go to college. We must note in

Social class correlation with curriculum tracks

TABLE 10.1
SOCIAL CLASS DIFFERENCES AND
TYPE OF EDUCATION

SOCIAL CLASS	PERCENTAGE OF STUDENTS IN CURRICULUM		
	COLLEGE PREPARATORY	GENERAL	COMMERCIAL
1–2 (Upper-upper and upper)	64	36	0
3 (Middle)	27	51	21
4 (Upper-lower)	9	58	33
5 (Lower-lower)	4	58	38

Source: August B. Hollingshead, *Elmtown's Youth* (New York: Wiley, 1949), p. 462.

5 Allison Davis, *Social Class Influences Upon Learning* (Cambridge, Mass.: Harvard University Press, 1949).
6 August B. Hollingshead, *Elmtown's Youth* (New York: Wiley, 1949).

TABLE 10.2
SOCIAL CLASS DIFFERENCES AND
SCHOOL ACHIEVEMENT

	PERCENTAGE OF STUDENTS WITH MEAN GRADE OF		
SOCIAL CLASS	85–100	70–84	50–69
1–2 (Upper-upper and upper)	51	49	0
3 (Middle)	36	63	1
4 (Upper-lower)	18	69	13
5 (Lower-lower)	8	67	25

Source: Hollingshead, *Elmtown's Youth*, p. 172.

defense of the schools that they attempt to educate *all* children in a pluralistic society while retaining a tradition of localism and a considerable variety of systems. Schooling is an assortive process and it does make distinctions among students. But, as in virtually all comparable processes, attributable factors (family background) as well as achieved factors (individual ability) heavily influence the outcomes. Hence what the school does is at best secondary.

Influence of family and individual ability

Robert Havighurst and his colleagues, in the study of a midwest community called "River City," also showed the relationship between social class and the child's progress through school.[7] As reported in a companion source and shown in Table 10.3, nearly 90 percent of the dropouts

TABLE 10.3
HIGHEST EDUCATIONAL LEVEL OF
RIVER CITY YOUTH BY SOCIAL CLASS

	PERCENTAGE OF TOTAL STUDENT POPULATION		
SOCIAL CLASS	HIGH SCHOOL DROPOUTS	HIGH SCHOOL GRADUATES	COLLEGE ENTRANTS
Upper and upper-middle	0.5	1.5	7.5
Lower-middle	3.5	12.5	11.5
Upper-lower	15.0	15.5	8.0
Lower-lower	16.5	7.5	0.5
All classes	35.5	37.0	27.5

Source: Robert J. Havighurst, "Social Class Influences on American Education," in N. Henry, ed., *Social Forces Influencing American Education*, Part II, National Society for the Study of Education (Chicago: University of Chicago Press, 1961), p. 122.

7   Robert J. Havighurst et al., *Growing Up in River City* (New York: Wiley, 1962).

were from lower-class families, and less than one-third of the 27.5 percent who entered college came from such families. (It should be noted, however, the proportion attaining higher levels of education has increased in recent years, and most of the increase has come from lower-class families.)

Although the data show that children from higher social classes do indeed receive better grades and go further in school than children from lower social classes, it is simplistic to conclude that education merely perpetuates the status quo. Education is the means by which academically inclined boys from the lower class achieve upward mobility. For girls the same trend was apparent, but to a lesser extent, because mobility patterns were complicated by whom they married and at what age they married.

Although, of course, actual entry into college does not come until graduation from high school, the main dividing line is between those who are and those who are not enrolled in a college preparatory course in high school. According to the Havighurst studies cited, there is only a small amount of shifting either way after about the ninth grade, when the decision is normally made. But when the elementary school records are evaluated—and student grades, attendance, and discipline are considered—it is not stretching the evidence too far to say that, broadly speaking, the primary selective process occurs through differential school performance in elementary school and that the "seal" is put on it in junior high school.

To summarize, one can say that the kind of education an American child gets and the extent of the child's preparation for academic learning depend very much on the social-class position of his or her family. To categorize youth according to social class is to rank them in an order on the extent of their "success" in the American educational system. Social-class position predicts grades, achievement, intelligence test scores, course failure, truancy, suspension, retention rates, and plans for college. Although there is room for individual variation within groups, social class and education are related.

What, then, can be gleaned from these studies about the importance of social class as a factor related to school achievement? It may be said that the most important predispositional factor with which the child enters the school is probably social class. But each person is an individual, and is able to shape his or her own behavior. The student has a capacity to make his or her own decisions in coping with new situations: to work hard or take it easy, to overcome difficulties or to give up. Inevitably, there are differences in performance among groups, but there are usually greater differences within groups, and these differences are relative to the character formation of the individual.

The charge is frequently made that teachers and schools are middle-class caretakers of the system, and that they discriminate against other than middle-class students. Consider, however, that we live in a techno-

Upward mobility for lower-class children

The selective process starts in elementary school

Individual behavior and capacity

logical society in which reading and writing with some degree of facility
are not necessarily middle-class values, but are learning outcomes important for functioning in our society. Coming to school on time, sitting in
one's seat, and listening to the teacher are all part of the rules of the game;
they are basically the same rules that adults must learn in work situations
and in dealing with other institutions of our society. Members of the
larger society do not have to learn to function according to the norms of
various subcultures (be they based on class, race, or ethnicity); rather,
members of the subcultures must learn to function in the larger society in
order to achieve psychological health and economic well-being. Thus, as a
teacher, you ought to be aware of the possibility that your own middle-
class values may influence your acceptance of students who hold a different set of values stemming from their own background. At the same
time, you need to teach these students the skills required to function
within the larger society.

**Learning to
function
within the
larger society**

**STRATIFICATION
VERSUS EQUALITY**
The past decade has brought a host of
reevaluations of the role and effects of
schooling in American society. Some revisionist scholars have suggested that
the expansion of schooling has *not* been the story of the unfolding of a
humanitarian dream of equality and democratic participation. Rather,
they have argued, schools have prepared young people for roles in a
stratified, technological, corporate-dominated society.[8]

TRADITIONAL VIEW The traditional notion about the value of
public schooling and its connection with mobility and equality of opportunity is still supported by the majority of educators.[9] The traditional
American commitment to education places primary emphasis on the overall betterment of society and measures school success in terms of conventional statistical indices such as occupations, income levels, average
literacy, and improved living standards. Individual variation from the
general pattern is not a cause for surprise or concern. As long as schooling seems to maintain social values, improve society, and lead to higher

8   David K. Cohen, "Immigrants and the Schools," *Review of Educational Research* (February 1970), pp. 13–28; Colin Greer, *The Great School Legend: A Revisionist Interpretation
of American Public Education* (New York: Basic Books, 1972); Clarence Karier, Paul Violas,
and Joel Spring, *Roots of Crisis: American Education in the Twentieth Century* (Chicago:
Rand McNally, 1973); Michael Katz, *Class, Bureaucracy, and the Schools: The Illusion of
Educational Change in America* (New York: Praeger, 1972); Paul Violas, *The Training of the
Urban Working Class* (Chicago: Rand McNally, 1978).
9   Peter M. Blau and Otis D. Duncan, *The American Occupational Structure* (New York:
Wiley, 1967); Robert J. Havighurst and Bernice L. Neugarten, *Society and Education*, 4th ed.,
(Boston: Allyn & Bacon, 1975); Harry L. Miller, *Social Foundations of Education*, 3rd ed. (New
York: Holt, Rinehart 1978); Frederick Mosteller and Daniel P. Moynihan, eds., *On Equality of
Educational Opportunity* (New York: Random House, 1972); William H. Sewell and Robert M.
Hauser, *Education, Occupation and Earnings* (New York: Academic Press, 1975).

paying jobs for most of its products, a degree of individual failure is acceptable.

The traditional view admits that schools serve as a screening device to sort out different individuals into different jobs. But this screening process is not on the basis of race, ethnic origin, religion, or income, as the revisionists contend. Along with recognizing marked differences in individual abilities, the traditional view recognizes that certain qualities lead to success in school and asserts that these are related to qualities that make the individual more productive on the job. Although these correlations may be imperfect, competitive firms can use this information and offer the better jobs to individuals who complete more schooling and do well in school. Put another way, the more educated get the better jobs because they have been made more productive by the schools. Additional years of schooling constitute a signal or indication of this greater productivity. So long as the schools are permitted to test students, they can determine the individual's abilities and provide appropriate education. This process suggests the use of IQ tests, homogeneous grouping, and the tracking of students into special programs—all of which the revisionists condemn.

So long as jobs are based on competition and merit, those with greater abilities and better schooling will get the better jobs. The employer has to use some criteria to decide whom to hire; in a democratic society in which there is unimpeded mobility and equal opportunity, it is largely the amount and quality of education that counts—not the applicant's family connections, race, ethnic origin, or religion. Some observers contend that the more educated are selected not because they are more productive, but simply because education is a convenient criterion that most people regard as fair.[10] Nevertheless, even these scholars view education as the principal avenue of opportunity in American society; this proposition is indeed supported by massive empirical data.

REVISIONIST VIEW   The revisionists, on the other hand, accept the view that education, occupation, and income are related, but they tell us the data are incomplete. They contend the White, upper-middle class has successfully conspired to enhance its own power and prestige relative to lower-class and minority groups, both immigrants and native-born Americans.[11] By controlling the schools, the elite groups admitted

---

10 Daniel Bell, *Coming of Post-Industrial Society: A Venture in Social Forecasting* (New York: Basic Books, 1973); Bell, *Cultural Contradictions of Capitalism* (New York: Basic Books, 1976); Ivar Berg, *Education and Jobs: The Great Training Robbery* (New York: Praeger, 1970); Martin Carnoy, ed., *Schooling in a Corporate Society: The Political Economy of Education in America* (New York: McKay, 1975); Martin Carnoy and Henry M. Levin, *The Limits of Educational Reform* (New York: McKay, 1976); Randall Collins, *The Credential Society: An Historical Sociology of Education and Stratification* (New York: Academic Press, 1979).

11 Richard H. deLone, *Small Futures* (New York: Harcourt Brace Jovanovich, 1979).

few poor and minority youth into high school academic programs and institutions of higher learning; they channeled this "underclass" into second-rate programs, third-rate secondary schools, and fourth-rate jobs. In support of their thesis, the revisionists argue that White ethnics and particular minority groups have always had a tough time in school. The curriculum discriminates against them, the IQ tests discriminate against them, their teachers discriminate against them, and so do their vocational guidance counselors.[12] The success of many White ethnics, as well as Jews, Japanese- and Chinese-Americans, in our schools and society is ignored or minimized in this argument. The problem of institutional social class and race prejudice as it pertains to education is more subtle and complex, and some of these issues will be discussed later in this chapter.

EXCELLENCE AND EQUALITY	The traditional view, it must be noted, claims that it is the responsibility of soci-

ety to provide equal educational opportunity; it is not, however, the responsibility of society to equalize school results. In this framework, inequality in the outcomes of schooling is a function of the natural inequality of talent among people. The commitment to educational opportunity is satisfied by furnishing equality of access to a common set of experiences. Special help may be provided to disadvantaged populations, but the notion of equal results of schooling for all groups is considered impracticable, and the parallel notion of equal results of income for all groups is rejected as a form of reverse discrimination at the expense of merit.

This view is very individualistic and tends to coincide with the pursuit of *excellence*; however, each individual is afforded the opportunity to go to college. The system is designed to allow the individual more chances to attend college than do the educational systems of most other countries. The student is not confronted with an examination at age 11 that shunts him or her into one of several tracks from which a shift is virtually impossible. Even if a student does poorly in high school, he or she can go to a community college and subsequently transfer to a university. Furthermore, there are now relaxed admission standards at many four-year colleges, which permit open enrollment of any high school graduate. Ours is a flexible system with the focus on individual achievement.[13]

The objection to this traditional view focuses not on individuals but on groups, and tends to coincide with the pursuit of *equalitarianism*. Observably, children coming from poverty and from particular minority

---

12 Violas, *The Training of the Urban Working Class.*

13 John Gardner, *Excellence: Can We Be Equal and Excellent Too?* (New York: Harper & Row, 1961); James W. Guthrie et al., *Schools and Inequality* (Cambridge, Mass.: MIT Press, 1971); Richard A. Lester, "The Fallacies of Numerical Goals," *Educational Record* (Winter 1976), pp. 58–64; Robert Nisbet, "The Pursuit of Equality," *Public Interest* (Spring 1974), pp. 101–120; John Rawls, *A Theory of Justice* (Cambridge, Mass.: Harvard University Press, 1971).

groups do not avail themselves of educational opportunities as much as do children of the middle class or of other minority groups. Whatever the causes may be, it is the group outcome that counts. And it is the responsibility of schools and society to compensate for these unsatisfactory results. But whether schools can compensate for these deficiencies in the absence of a revolution is highly debatable. In this regard, some revisionists argue that disadvantaged groups will not succeed in school until they have better opportunities in the economy, even if this means a quota system. Finally, which groups are designated for preferential treatment becomes a political rather than a moral issue.

Group outcome

AFFIRMATIVE ACTION

Changes in admissions policies have helped make a college education available to members of minority groups. Along with provision of scholarships and systematic recruitment of minority students in higher education, there also has been an emphasis on recruiting more minority teachers at all levels of the educational system and on increasing the percentage of minority students in graduate and professional schools. Affirmative action to accomplish these goals has been required by the federal government, which has designated a number of minority groups for this purpose including American Indians, Asian Americans, Blacks, Hispanics, and women.

Minorities defined by the government

One of the most common affirmative action approaches was to set a quota for minority students, often at about 10 percent of enrollment of graduate and professional schools. Other approaches involved awarding admissions points to candidates from racially or economically disadvantaged backgrounds and accepting lower aptitude scores from minority candidates in recognition of possible cultural bias in the tests. In some cases, these policies resulted in admission of minority candidates whose aptitude scores were lower than nearly all nonminority applicants.

Affirmative action practices were initiated as a way to overcome the effects of past discrimination and were intended partly to increase the number of teachers, doctors, lawyers, and other professionals available in minority communities. They also raised questions, however, involving equity for nonminority candidates. If a minority candidate with a low test score is admitted while nonminority candidates with high scores are rejected, the latter are likely to perceive the situation as involving "reverse discrimination," which unfairly limits their opportunity to pursue a career of their choice. Grievances are particularly likely to be raised in view of the importance of professional training in modern societies and the fact that much professional preparation is a publicly subsidized activity to which all taxpayers contribute.

Limiting opportunities of nonminorities

THE ROLE
OF THE COURTS
Resistance was inevitable, especially as the competition for places in some professional schools became more intense in the 1970s. Controversy regarding affirmative action in schools and other institutions reached a peak in 1977 and 1978 when the U.S. Supreme Court heard arguments in the case of *Regents of the University of California* v. *Alan Bakke*. Bakke, a White candidate, had been rejected by the medical school at the University's Davis campus. The school, which had only two Black students and one Hispanic student in its 1968 and 1969 entering classes, set aside 16 out of 100 slots for minority students in subsequent classes. Pointing to the fact that the 16 special admissions students in 1973 had average percentile scores of 35 in science and 46 in verbal skills, Bakke—who had scores of 97 and 96—filed a suit charging that the admissions policy was racially discriminatory. The California Supreme Court concluded that Bakke's exclusion was unconstitutionally discriminatory under Fourteenth Amendment guarantees of equal protection of the laws. The case was appealed to the U.S. Supreme Court.

In 1978 the Supreme Court decided in a five-to-four vote that Bakke should be admitted to the Davis Medical School because its policies had violated the Fourteenth Amendment as well as Title VI of the Civil Rights Act of 1964, which states that "No person in the United States shall, on the ground of race, color, or national origin, be excluded from participation in . . . any program or activity receiving Federal financial assistance." School admissions policies setting aside places for minority students were viewed as violating the Fourteenth Amendment in the absence of a showing that members of the group had been intentionally excluded in a discriminatory manner in the past.

Bakke wins his suit

However, the Court also stated that institutions can give consideration to race or other background factors in making admissions decisions. A majority of the Court thus upheld this approach to affirmative action in stating that "The central meaning of today's opinions . . . [is that] Government can take race into account when it acts not to demean or insult any racial group but to remedy disadvantages cast on minorities by past racial prejudice." The decision declared illegal only those plans that rely on precise racial quotas in a manner that prevents admission of individual nonminority applicants. Instead, colleges and universities were encouraged to devise an admissions system that might give points toward admission on the basis of minority group membership, economically disadvantaged background, rural origins, or other characteristics that an institution might want to encourage in its student body.[14]

Eliminating precise racial quotas

14 John Sexton, "Minority-Admissions Programs after Bakke," *Harvard Educational Review* (August 1979), pp. 313-39.

The Bakke case did not directly address the important issue of affirmative action in employment and promotions. This latter topic was considered by the Supreme Court in the case of *Steelworkers* v. *Weber*. The suit was brought by Brian Weber, whose application for training at a Kaiser factory in Louisiana was rejected in accordance with the company's affirmative action agreement to make half of the training slots available to Black applicants. In 1979 the Court upheld the legality of the company's training program, which had been worked out jointly with the United Steelworkers of America. The Court's decision meant that employers are free to establish affirmative action programs in employment and that the federal government can continue to press employers to develop such programs to overcome the effects of past discrimination against minority groups and women.

Affirmative action upheld in employment

WHO GETS WHAT JOBS?   Affirmative action in employment raises the particularly difficult question of how one ensures that minority citizens are "adequately" represented in the labor force of a given employer. One can argue that disadvantaged groups should be represented in accordance with their overall percentage in the population, and that a disproportion between this percentage and the percent of employees in a given institution is due to discrimination. The issue is far more complicated, however, because for various reasons a suitable proportion of qualified minority candidates may not be available to fill a particular type of job. Consider, for example, the employment situation in a department of a university. If only 5 percent of the faculty are Blacks and 3 percent are Hispanics, can it be inferred that discrimination is being practiced? This conclusion would be difficult to support in a field in which few minority candidates are available.

One of the relevant criteria for hiring professors is the applicant's possession of a doctorate degree. In many fields, however, minority persons have earned very few doctorates. Although there has been an increase since 1973 in doctorate degrees received by Blacks and Hispanics, this still comes nowhere near providing a sufficient pool for most fields in which there are few minority candidates.[15] Thus it is not possible to expect that minority employees can be quickly added in accordance with their proportion in the population.[16]

Considering the pool of qualified candidates

15   Before 1973, fewer than 2,500 doctorate degrees had been awarded to Black students in all fields combined, and approximately half of these 2,500 degrees were in education. See William F. Brazziel, "Affirmative Action: Snail's Pace Gained," *Phi Delta Kappan* (December 1975), p. 492.

16   Essentially the same situation exists with respect to affirmative action for women. Between 1961 and 1973, for example, less than ten women received doctorates in fields such as pharmacy, theoretical chemistry, and civil engineering. See Commission on Human Resources, National Research Council, *Summary Reports, 1967–1973: Doctorate Recipients from United States Universities* (Washington, D.C.: National Academy of Sciences, 1974).

SOME SENSITIVE ISSUES   One important question raised by affirmative action approaches is whether they lower the quality of performance and result in deflated certificates for minority persons who are admitted to schools or employment on the basis of reduced standards. It is possible that some candidates admitted under lowered standards may perform more poorly than those admitted or employed under previous policies; in any case, such persons may be viewed by some people as less competent than other students or employees in the same institution.

Considering quality of performance

We do not argue that there has been no past discrimination in our society, but rather that affirmative action practices frequently are difficult to implement with due concern for equity and organizational effectiveness. Federal guidelines suggest that employment percentages disproportionate to those in the general population represent discrimination. Based on these guidelines, goals and timetables have been established that give preferential treatment to selected groups; in the process, nonminority applicants may be virtually excluded. One of the best-known critics of current affirmative action programs has summarized this and other objections to such programs as follows:

> I argue against the use of goals and quotas based on a statistical mirroring of the population as a policy to deal with what is admittedly a serious problem . . . on many grounds: the difficulty of determining the line between what groups should benefit and what groups should be penalized, the difficulty of assigning individuals to given racial and ethnic categories, the political and moral repugnance at doing so, the danger that more and more groups would demand consideration in receiving benefits, and the danger that group membership would become ever more salient and group conflict increase.[17]

What groups should benefit

Somehow a way must be found to overcome the effects of past and present discrimination without violating the rights of individuals or damaging the capacity of institutions to achieve their foremost goals. What is needed is a policy that provides individuals with the opportunity to fulfill their human potential: compensatory opportunities to overcome the effect of disadvantaged background, remedial help for people with limited skills, rewards for people who work hard and are competent, and mobility between social classes. From this point of view, compensatory education for the disadvantaged represents a central strategy for overcoming the effects of discrimination. To the extent that improved educational opportunities result in higher educational and social achievement

17   Nathan Glazer, "Comments on Duster's Review of Affirmative Discrimination," *American Journal of Sociology* (January 1979), p. 992.

and aspirations among disadvantaged ethnic minority groups and women, affirmative action may be less needed and less difficult to implement in the future.

STUDY OF THE DISADVANTAGED

Prior to the civil rights movement and President Johnson's War on Poverty in the early 1960s, interest in the twin subjects of class and caste was limited mainly to academic circles. Since then educators, along with interested laymen and political groups, have become increasingly concerned with the need to study the problems of the poor, especially the Black poor, in order to remedy their plight. The term "disadvantaged," and its derivative terms "deprived" and "underprivileged," began to appear with reference to the children and youth of lower-class and minority groups.

"Disadvantaged" replaces "class" and "caste"

Illustrating this new interest among educators, the classification *cultural deprivation* was added to the Educational Index. Beginning with 21 entries in 1962-63, the number by 1964-65 had increased to 122 entries. By 1968-69 the number was 370, with several other related headings such as *city schools, cultural differences, poverty,* etc.[18] Throughout the 1970s, there was a leveling off in the number of cultural deprivation entries, but additional related headings appeared.

THE EARLY BELL IS SOUNDED

The forerunners with the greatest impact in the field were social writer Michael Harrington and educators James Conant, Frank Riessman, and Patricia Sexton. Harrington's book helped spark the War on Poverty.[19] Subsequently, billions of dollars in federal programs were spent on educating the disadvantaged, along with funding for health and community programs. A much-needed popularization of governmental and scholarly reports, Harrington's book jolted many policy makers and moved educators to take a deeper look at the relationship between poverty, education, and social policy.

Relationship between poverty and social policy

Harrington estimated that between 40 and 50 million Americans lived in poverty (almost one-quarter of the population). In this category he put the needy, aged, and sick; the workers rendered useless by technology; the workers exempt from minimum wage protection; the uprooted migrant farm worker; the ghetto dweller who is the victim of racial discrimination; the uneducated youth; and other economic outcasts. Not since Dickens had anyone captured so vividly the problems and lifestyles of the poor—but this time the poor were Americans. Moreover, Harrington ar-

18 Allan C. Ornstein, "An Overview of the Disadvantaged: 1900-1970," in A. Kopan and H. Walberg, eds., *Rethinking Educational Equality* (Berkeley, Calif.: McCutchan, 1974), pp. 1-10.
19 Michael Harrington, *The Other America* (Baltimore: Penguin Books, 1963).

gued that poverty in America is no longer "cyclical"—that is, it is no longer temporary as in the Depression; rather, it is becoming "structural"—meaning there are few chances to escape from it and it is becoming an inherited curse for part of the young generation. He spoke of "an enormous concentration of young people who, if they do not receive immediate help, may well be the source of a kind of hereditary poverty new to America."[20]

Although the number of poor was challenged by numerous authorities and councils—including the government, which put the figure of poverty in America at between 30 and 35 million—Harrington's point was that a piecemeal, individual case approach could not solve the problem; massive funds and a full-scale program were needed. The poverty group was not limited to Blacks; it also included poor Whites; in fact, as much as 70 percent of the poor were White, he contended. Because they were White, they had low visibility; nobody paid much attention to them.

Low visibility of poor whites

Harrington blamed the system for creating and maintaining poverty; our affluent industrial society victimizes the poor. He struck at the American conscience by declaring that for the first time society had the material ability to end poverty but lacked the will to do it.

In a 1961 comparison of slum schools and slum students with their respective counterparts in suburbia, James Conant pointed out that half the children in slum neighborhoods dropped out of school in grades nine, ten, and eleven; that the per-pupil expenditure in disadvantaged schools was less than half the expenditure in the privileged schools of suburbia; and that there were 70 professionals per 1,000 pupils in privileged schools and 40 professionals per 1,000 in inner-city schools.[21] Conant coined the term "social dynamite" and warned that conditions were reaching an explosive point in the ghettoes of the cities. Dropout rates, lack of vocational skills, and soaring unemployment rates at that time among Black youth were leading to serious frustration in the American ghettoes. Five years later Conant's warnings were to echo loudly in many urban areas across the country.

"Social dynamite" building up

It should be noted that Conant was referring to the wealthiest suburbs, not to the average suburban schools. Per pupil expenditures and teacher costs in many less affluent suburbs parallel expenses for city schools. Also, pupil expenditures in recent years have shifted to favor disadvantaged populations, as a result of the funding program of the states and federal government and the general concern for educating the disadvantaged. Today, the inner-city schools obtain more money and teacher positions than the outer-city schools and are almost at parity with the mean suburban per pupil expenditures and teacher/student ratios. In

20 Ibid., p. 183.
21 James B. Conant, *Slums and Suburbs* (New York: McGraw-Hill, 1961).

any event, because of Conant's prestige and reputation as a leading educator, his book was extensively reviewed and widely read by policy makers as well as educators, who, in turn, helped clarify many issues related to educating the disadvantaged and set in motion the needed funds for inner-city schools.

Ranking 43 Detroit schools by the average family income of children attending those schools, Patricia Sexton in a 1961 study found that for several important school characteristics the advantages correlated with the higher-income ranked schools: experienced teachers, educational facilities and materials, and educational standards. With regard to favorable attendance, club activities, school achievement, and low dropout rates, the advantages similarly correlated with the higher-income schools.[22]

Advantages of high-income schools

The correlational techniques used by Sexton were certainly not new, nor were her results earthshaking. Rather, they were a confirmation of the sociological "wisdom" of the 1940s, supported by similar techniques and results that go back still farther to the Lynds' classic study, *Middletown*. What Sexton managed to do, however, was to report the data at an opportune time—when educators, governmental officials, and citizens were willing to listen. Thus, by the end of the 1960s, most of the low-income schools, because of extra state and federal money and special programs, were equal or almost equal to middle-income schools with regard to most of the school input characteristics described in the study.

In a brief book on the disadvantaged, Frank Riessman in 1962 popularized the idea (originally referred to in a Ford Foundation study) that as many as 1 in 3 children in the nation's 14 largest cities could be described as "disadvantaged."[23] It was estimated that by 1970 the number would soar to 1 out of 2. Riessman described the disadvantaged as having a number of positive characteristics that have been overlooked: exceptional physical orientation, hidden verbal ability, creative potential, group cohesiveness, informality, sense of humor, frankness, ability to manipulate others, and so on. He agreed with Allison Davis that the disadvantaged had their own culture and that this culture was in conflict with the schools.[24] But by using the words "deprived" and "disadvantaged" in his writings to describe these positive characteristics and culture, Riessman unintentionally endorsed the contrasting standards of middle-class school and society. Perhaps for this reason, in subsequent writings on the subject Riessman used the term "poor" youth in the mistaken conviction that it is a more positive term.

Positive cultural characteristics

22 Patricia C. Sexton, *Education and Income* (New York: Viking Press, 1961).

23 Frank Riessman, *The Culturally Deprived Child* (New York: Harper & Row, 1962). Also see *The Great Cities School Improvement Studies* (New York: Ford Foundation, 1960).

24 Davis, *Social Class Influences Upon Learning.*

But by the mid-sixties interest in the disadvantaged had reached "bandwagon" status, and articles, books, research studies, and workshops appeared in an endless stream. Only gradually, as the decade came to a close, did we come to the first stage of wisdom: humble confession of how little we knew about educating the disadvantaged.

THE ROLE OF ENVIRONMENT The importance of environment in the early years of child development is basic to the concepts of deprivation and modern compensatory education programs. Underlying the studies of J. McVicker Hunt and Martin Deutsch is Jean Piaget's theory that the child who is deprived of appropriate environmental stimuli will lack sufficient experiences for adequate development of the mental processes necessary for acquiring intellectual skills and abilities. It is assumed that the slum environment has less systematic ordering of environmental stimulation and variety than do other social-class environments, and this in turn is less useful to the growth and activation of cognitive potential.

Hunt summarizes thousands of studies related to intellectual growth.[25] He outlines various schools of thought and beliefs relating to intelligence and concludes that while heredity sets the limits on individual potential for intellectual growth, the role of environment is extremely important for improving cognition. Educators need to devise experiences that counteract deprivation and improve intellectual potential and achievement levels in schools. Preschool enrichment programs were strongly recommended as antidotes to cultural deprivation. Hunt, along with Deutsch, was instrumental in the trend toward compensatory education. According to the theory, it can do the most good at an early age, since the cognitive abilities of the child are still developing.

Heredity sets the limits

Martin Deutsch has outlined the main factors that affect the disadvantaged child's readiness to learn.[26] One such factor he cites is the lack of variety of visual, tactile, and auditory stimulation in the lower-class home. He explores the interrelations between social class, race, grade in school, and language skills. The language variables of abstraction, verbalization, and vocabulary are found to be correlated significantly with social class, race, and grade level. In other words, language ability is associated with class factors; when class is controlled, however, Black children are more handicapped than White; and with the increase in age, language deficiencies tend to increase. This coincides with conventional data findings that

Language handicaps

25 J. McVicker Hunt, *Intelligence and Experience* (New York: Ronald Press, 1961); Hunt, "Psychological Development: Early Experience," *Annual Review of Psychology* (1979), pp. 103-43.

26 Martin Deutsch, "The Role of Social Class in Language Development and Cognition" in A. H. Passow, M. L. Goldberg, and A. J. Tannenbaum, eds., *Education of the Disadvantaged* (New York: Holt, Rinehart 1967), pp. 214-24.

With a native teacher, these Objiway Indian children enjoy a book in their Ontario, Canada, school.

cultural deprivation becomes cumulative as students are passed from grade to grade and is more pronounced among Blacks than Whites.

In a companion study, a Deprivation Index was developed that has a higher correlation with IQ, language skills, and concept formation than social class has with these abilities.[27] This suggests that the Deprivation Index may be a more accurate predictor of school success than are the social-class indicators. It also suggests that social class/educational studies could be supplemented by another set of variables, such as the Deprivation Index provides. The seven components on the index included social background, economic background, motivation, family setting, parental interaction, adult-child activities, and school experiences.

Importance of early environment   The deprivation theory also holds that early years of development are more important than later years. Although not all human characteristics reveal the same patterns of development, the most rapid period of development of human characteristics, including cognitive skills, is during the preschool years. For example, Benjamin Bloom presents longitudinal data (extending over a

27   Martin Whiteman and Martin Deutsch, "Social Disadvantage as Related to Intellective and Language Development," Research Grant No. MH1098-3. Paper presented at the Conference of Cultural Deprivation and Enrichment Programs (New York: Yeshiva University, April 1965). Later published in M. Deutsch et al., eds., *The Disadvantaged Child* (New York: Basic Books, 1967), pp. 337-56.

period of several years) that strongly suggest that from birth to four years of age an individual develops 50 percent of his or her potential intelligence; from ages four to eight another 30 percent develops; and between ages eight and seventeen the remaining 20 percent develops.[28] Supplementary evidence suggests that 33 percent of learning potential takes place by the time the child is six years old—before entering first grade; another 17 percent takes place between ages six and nine. The potential for learning is cumulative. As much as 50 percent of learning potential is developed by the age of nine, 75 percent by the age of thirteen, and 100 percent by the age of seventeen.

Learning is cumulative

Based on the above estimates for intelligence and learning, home environment is crucial, according to Bloom, because of the large amount of cognitive development that has already taken place before the child enters the first grade. These estimates also suggest the very rapid cognitive growth in the early years and the great influence of the early environment (largely home environment) on cognitive development, and that *all* subsequent learning "is affected and in a large part determined by what the child has [previously] learned."[29] Furthermore, what the child learns in the early and most important years is shaped by what the child has experienced at home. (Even the prenatal stages affect the child's intellectual development, that is, the mother's general health, her diet, her alcohol intake and smoking habits, and biochemical changes related to stress and other emotional factors. And, in this regard, substantially more lower-income mothers than middle- and upper-income mothers, and more Black mothers than White mothers, suffer from poor physical and mental health as well as from poor diet.)

This does not mean that once a learning deficit occurs, remediation is impossible. But it does clearly imply that it is more difficult to effect changes for older children, and that a more powerful environment is needed to effect these changes.[30] Bloom reports, however, that learning differences can be reduced over time with appropriate environmental and training conditions. In short, our information on the extent to which intellectual deficits of one maturation period or age can be made up in another is limited and contradictory. We cannot now precisely equate differences in difficulty in reversing deficits at different stages of cognitive development.

Overcoming learning deficits

The theory of deprivation also coincides with the research findings that a child of low-income status will often suffer from a deprived environment or limited stimuli, which, in turn, negatively affects the child's

28 Benjamin S. Bloom, *Stability and Change in Human Characteristics* (New York: Wiley, 1964), p. 88. See also Moshe Smilansky, *Priorities in Education: Pre-School; Evidence and Conclusions* (Washington, D.C.: World Bank, 1979).

29 Bloom, *Stability and Change in Human Characteristics*, p. 110

30 Bloom, *Human Characteristics and School Learning* (New York: McGraw-Hill, 1976).

opportunities for adequate development within four cognitive areas of development. Conversely, a child of middle- or upper-socioeconomic status usually has an enriched environment of a sufficient quantity of high-quality stimuli, which affect positively his or her opportunities for adequate development within and among the cognitive referents. Thus, the child's social class is related to his or her environmental experiences, which subsequently influence the child's learning capabilities and academic development.

Since the relationships are group patterns, there is room for individual differences among children in both deprived and enriched environments. It cannot be emphasized too strongly, for example, that a lower-class child may have an enriched home environment and the child's middle-class counterpart may have a deprived home environment. Similarly, all children from deprived environments do not necessarily have limited school abilities, while all children from enriched environments do not have academic success; rather, social class and home environment will handicap or assist children in developing their mental capabilities.

TWO VIEWS OF INTELLIGENCE

During the past century there has been heated controversy concerning the extent to which intelligence is determined primarily by heredity or environment. When IQ tests were undergoing rapid development early in the twentieth century, many psychologists believed that intelligence was determined primarily by heredity. They thought they were learning to assess innate differences in people's capacity through IQ tests and other measures of cognitive development. Since economically disadvantaged populations and some minority groups such as Blacks scored considerably below middle-income populations and nonminority groups, these *hereditarians* believed that working-class populations and minority groups were innately inferior in intellectual capacity.

Role of heredity

By the 1950s, most social scientists took the *environmentalist* position that environment is more important than heredity in determining intelligence. Earlier sections of this chapter discussed the views of some noted environmentalists—J. McVicker Hunt, Martin Deutsch, and Benjamin Bloom. Environmentalists stress the great importance of environment as it impinges upon growth and development and the need for compensatory programs on a continuous basis beginning in infancy. They also criticize the use of IQ tests because these tests are seen as culturally biased. The differences in IQ scores between controlled groups of Blacks and Whites are attributed by the environmentalists to social-class differences and to racial prejudices existing in our society.

Environmentalists are continuing to conduct research and report data they believe indicate that environment is much more important than heredity in determining intelligence. Sandra Scarr and Richard Weinberg, for example, have been studying differences between Black children

Environmental factors

growing up in biological families and children growing up in adopted families, and concluded that the effects of environment outweigh the effects of heredity.[31] Thomas Sowell has been studying IQ scores collected for various ethnic groups between 1920 and 1970, and has found that the scores of some groups such as Italian Americans and Polish Americans have substantially improved. He also has found that neither the patterns nor the levels of Black mental test scores have been unique and that these scores "have risen by larger increments than have scores in the general population in response to such environmental improvements as better teaching or better test familiarity and test environment."[32]

The hereditarian point of view underwent a major revival in the 1960s and 1970s, however, based particularly on the writings of Arthur Jensen, William Shockley, and Richard Herrnstein. All three of these authors rekindled the emotional issues surrounding the relationship between race, heredity, and intelligence. Basing their data on a review and reanalysis of previous research, as well as their own studies, they each concluded independently that heredity is the major factor in determining intelligence—up to 80 percent of the variance.

The Jensen furor   Jensen, one of the nation's leading educational psychologists, published a lengthy article in the Winter 1969 issue of the *Harvard Educational Review*, which presented the following conclusions:

Jensen's conclusions

> 1. Blacks average about 15 points below the White average on IQ tests; this is due to the genetic difference between the two races in learning abilities and patterns.

> 2. Blacks as a group and "disadvantaged" children have more difficulty than do others in abstract reasoning—the basis for IQ measurements and for higher mental skills; unfortunately, the schools have assumed that all children can master higher cognitive skills.

> 3. Conversely, Blacks and "disadvantaged" children tend to do well in tasks involving rote learning—memorizing mainly through repetition; these aptitudes can be used to help raise their scholastic achievement up to a point.

> 4. Compensatory education, which is costing taxpayers hundreds of millions of dollars a year (actually billions), has failed and will continue to fail because it is trying to compensate children of limited intellectual talents with learning processes and concepts that are really geared to students of average or above average talent.[33]

31 Sandra Scarr and Richard A. Weinberg, "I.Q. Test Performance of Black Children Adopted by White Families," *American Psychologist* (July 1976), pp. 726–39.

32 Thomas Sowell, "Race and IQ Reconsidered," in T. Sowell, ed., *American Ethnic Groups* (Washington, D.C.: Urban Institute, 1978), p. 229.

33 Arthur R. Jensen, "How Much Can We Boost IQ and Scholastic Achievement?" *Harvard Educational Review* (Winter 1969), pp. 1–123.

Jensen made it clear that his data provide no basis for judging the intellectual capacity of any given individual but were based on group averages. He pointed out that the nature of the differences in intellectual skills between Blacks and Whites as groups and the role of genetics in these differences have not been fully explored; indeed, the subject has almost been tabooed. He strongly attacked those who argued that, with very few exceptions, children have the same potential for developing the same mental abilities, and who also claimed that most differences in IQ scores are the result of social, psychological, and economic deprivation. Alluding to the overwhelming failures in compensatory education, he pointed out that in other fields when things go wrong, when machines fail or when treatments do not cure, people question their assumptions and theories. A fresh look at classroom and school failure is in order, and it should start, he declared, with a re-examination of the nature of intelligence.

Tabooed research

The most comprehensive critical analysis of Jensen's conclusions appeared as a response in the next issue of the *Review*. The authors were fellow psychologists who support the view that environment plays the major role in IQ scores. Their main points are summarized below:

Criticism of Jensen

1. Jensen's research is based on relatively small samples.

2. The environment-heredity interaction is impossible to separate and measure.

3. IQ outcomes are affected by a host of environmental variables, such as malnutrition and prenatal care, which are difficult to measure.

4. Racial prejudice could account for any differences in IQ that might exist between Blacks and Whites.

5. IQ tests are biased and the scores do not necessarily measure intelligence.

6. Granted, billions of dollars have been spent on compensatory education and the results have not been impressive, but it is possible that we have not reached the threshold where the amount of money per child makes an impact.[34]

Since publication of the article, Jensen has been under severe criticism in the professional literature; his classes have been disrupted and his colleagues at the University of California at Berkeley made an unsuccessful effort to censure him. He and his family have been threatened and he has frequently needed police protection; he has been denied the opportunity to address many professional audiences, and on some occasions he has been prevented from finishing his lectures. He has been labeled "rac-

---

34 "How Much Can We Boost IQ and Scholastic Achievement: A Discussion," *Harvard Educational Review* (Spring 1969), pp. 273-356. Contributors were Jerome S. Kagan, J. McV. Hunt, James F. Crow, Carl Bereiter, David Elkind, Lee J. Cronbach, and William F. Brazziel.

ist," "Aryan propagandist," and "Hitlerite." Attacks on Jensen continued after his recent book, *Bias in Mental Testing,* in which he rejected the
conclusion that differences in teacher expectations, test administration,
cultural fairness of tests, and coaching are responsible for the average
difference of 15 points in Black and White IQ scores. He attributed at least
50 percent and perhaps as much as 75 percent of this difference to heredity.[35]

**Jensen updates
his position**

IQ and Meritocracy   Two years after Jensen's 1969 study,
Richard Herrnstein delved into the history and implications of IQ scores
and intelligence.[36] Herrnstein's article touched only lightly on the racial
issue. "Although there are some scraps of evidence for a genetic component in the black-white difference," he wrote, "the overwhelming case is
for believing that American blacks have been at an environmental disadvantage."[37] He contended that a neutral commentator (which one would be
hard-pressed to find) would probably say that there is insufficient evidence
to support an environmental or genetic hypothesis for racial differences in
intelligence.

Instead, Herrnstein charged boldly into another part of the heredity
versus environment battlefield. His argument on the importance of heredity in determining intelligence was made in the form of a syllogism. "(1) If
differences in mental abilities are inherited, and (2) if success requires
these abilities, and (3) if earnings and prestige depend on success, then
(4) social standing will be based to some extent on the inherited differences
among people."[38] His syllogism was sprinkled with "ifs," and the data on
which his article was based were drawn *entirely* from the study of Whites.
Nevertheless, he, too, was called a racist, an elitist, and a defender of
human exploitation, and was physically harassed.

The implication of his premise, further developed in a more recent
work, is that as society comes closer to the ideal of equality of opportunity
it also comes closer to "meritocracy," a system in which the ablest rise to
the top.[39] The syllogism implies that social classes are genetically distinct,
since the criteria for class membership tend to correlate with intelligence.
It follows that equality of opportunity—while unquestionably desirable on
both moral and practical grounds—can lead to an increasing genetic gap
between the classes. If IQ is inherited and social inequalities are removed,
then genetics will determine who achieves the more prestigious roles in
society. The less intelligent will be able to compete only if they are given
more than an equal opportunity. Note that the corollary of the syllogism is
concerned with schooling. Educational success is highly dependent on

"Meritocracy"

35 Arthur R. Jensen, *Bias in Mental Testing* (New York: Free Press, 1979).
36 Richard J. Herrnstein, "IQ," *Atlantic* (September 1971), pp. 43–64.
37 Ibid., p. 57.
38 Ibid., p. 58.
39 Richard J. Herrnstein, *IQ in the Meritocracy* (Boston: Little, Brown, 1973).

mental abilities measured by IQ scores. Intelligence influences school success, and success in school correlates with social class. If 80 percent of intelligence is related to heritability, then this helps explain why compensatory programs have limited educational value. Herrnstein's thesis ran counter to the traditional liberal and equalitarian stance that poverty, school failure, and intelligence result from the conditions of society—not from the individual's genetic background.

Threatening
the equilitarian
interpretation

THE SYNTHESIZERS   Thus the debate still continues as to the extent that intelligence is inborn (hereditary) or acquired (environmental). Although thousands of studies addressing this issue have been conducted, scientists still disagree vigorously on their interpretation. Some have concluded that intelligence is as much as 80 percent or more inherited, but others have concluded that it is 80 percent or more acquired.[40]

Meanwhile, however, a number of social scientists have taken a middle or "synthesizing" position in the controversy. The synthesizers point out that both heredity and environment contribute to differences in measured intelligence.[41] For example, Christopher Jencks and his colleagues reviewed a large amount of data on the issue and divided the IQ variance into .45 due to heredity, .35 due to environment, and .20 due to interaction between the two (abilities particulary thrive or wither in a specific environment).[42] Robert Nichols reviewed all these and other data and concluded that the true value may be anywhere between .40 and .80 but that the exact value has little importance for policy.[43] Nichols and other synthesizers maintain that the best way to conceptualize the contribution of heredity to a trait such as intelligence is to think of heredity as determining the fixed limits of a range. Within this range, sometimes referred to as the *genotype*, are the possible environmental ranges of an individual, sometimes referred to as the *phenotype*. The interaction effect of both ranges results in an IQ potential that can vary in either direction from the genotype limits. Hence, how much specific variance is due to heredity and how much is due to environment are not considered useful questions; the key consideration, rather, is the interaction effect (of both components)

Interaction
effects are
crucial

40   For a review of some of these studies, see Anne Anastasi, *Psychological Testing*, 3rd. ed. (New York: Macmillan, 1968); N. Bloch and Gerald Dworkin, eds., *The IQ Controversy: Critical Readings* (New York: Pantheon, 1976); Robert Cancro, ed., *Intelligence: Genetic and Environmental Influences* (New York: Grune & Stratton, 1971); Herrnstein, *IQ in the Meritocracy*; Robert C. Nichols, "Policy Implications of the IQ Controversy" in L. S. Shulman, ed., *Review of Research in Education*, vol. 6 (Itasca, Ill.: Peacock, 1978); Arthur W. Staats, *Child Learning, Intelligence, and Personality* (New York: Harper & Row, 1971).

41   Theodosius Dobzhansky, "Genetics of Race Equality," *Eugenics Quarterly* (December 1964), pp. 151–60; I. I. Gottesman, "Biogenetics of Race and Class," in M. Deutsch, I. Katz, and A. R. Jensen, eds., *Social Class, Race, and Psychological Development* (New York: Holt, Rinehart, 1968), pp. 11–51; Ronald S. Wilson, "Twins: Patterns of Cognitive Development as Measured on the Wechsler Preschool and Primary Scale of Intelligence," *Developmental Psychology* (March 1975), pp. 126–34.

42   Christopher Jencks, et al., *Inequality: A Reassessment of the Effect of Family and Schooling in America* (New York: Basic Books, 1972).

43   Nichols, "Policy Implications of the IQ Controversy."

that yields the individual's measured intelligence. Educators want to identify which educational environments will help each student live up to his or her innate potential and how much it may cost to do this.

IMPLICATIONS
FOR EDUCATION
The hereditarians have argued that the formation of socioeconomic classes is primarily a function of inherited genes, and only secondarily a function of family property and wealth. People of similar intelligence tend to marry; their offspring inherit better genes so far as intelligence goes, and this is reflected in intelligence tests. The environmentalists have argued that social mobility is related to education (not intelligence), and differences in intelligence of the children are basically environmental—primarily due to differences in home background.

The truth probably lies somewhere between these two views. To a point, very able people do migrate upward socially and economically, and less capable people are pushed downward in their job opportunities. The more democratic a society, the greater the chance that merit and intelligence will determine occupational class differences; however, luck, temperament, who you know or don't know, and prejudice are also factors; all of these have occupational impact. Adults tend to find their marriage partners within their own socioeconomic class, and they pass on their genetic makeup to their children. Those at the bottom of the socioeconomic scale as a group provide fewer opportunities to their children and create a less stimulating home environment than those with more money and leisure time. To the present day, breaking this cycle has proved too difficult for educational and social reformers, suggesting that human cognitive growth and development and social-class differences cannot easily be changed through educational and social programs. These facts may also suggest that social scientists do not have all the answers, a thought that some are just beginning to entertain in public and in print.

Breaking the cycle is difficult

Although we cannot precisely say how much of the child's intelligence is the result of environmental factors, teachers (and parents) need to provide each child with a psychologically productive environment in which to realize maximum potential. On the other hand, as a teacher you should be cautioned that applying pressures to make a child perform like a genius when he or she was never intended to be one can be counterproductive. You must assume there are limitations in intelligence, as there are limitations in the ability to run, to throw a ball, and to draw a lifelike figure.

You need to recognize that there are students who score low on IQ tests, yet manage to perform well in school, and vice versa. Because intelligence tests are loaded with verbal and academic content, differences in schooling *can* produce changes in IQ. Group scores differ on IQ tests, as well as in academic subjects; the reasons are open to debate. Note, how-

IQ tests and academic content

ever, that the cognitive domain is only one area of learning, and students with low IQ test scores and/or low school grades still can be quite successful in other domains of learning and in job performance. Perhaps educators themselves make too much fuss about low IQ test scores or low school grades, although it must be said in their defense that their job requires them to deal with and interpret such data.

EQUAL EDUCATIONAL OPPORTUNITY

The subject of equal educational opportunity has taken on great importance since the 1960s, coinciding with the study of the disadvantaged in education and the civil rights and poverty movements impacting on society in general. How do we define equal educational opportunity? (In terms of equal costs? Equal results?) What policy changes are needed to implement educational equality? Who should benefit by the policy changes? Will other groups suffer reverse discrimination? Some heated debates and controversial reports have emerged over time in connection with implementing educational opportunity for disadvantaged groups. The two most controversial people in this field are James Coleman and Christopher Jencks.

IMPORTANCE OF HOME AND FAMILY CHARACTERISTICS

To help increase the federal commitment to education, the Johnson administration commissioned James Coleman to conduct a nationwide study on the state of equal educational opportunity for minorities.[44] It was the most massive educational research enterprise ever conducted, consisting of about 1,300 pages, including 548 pages of statistics.

Coleman report

When the results were in from the 600,000 children and 4,000 schools, Coleman found that the effects of home environment far outweighed any effects the school program had on achievement. The Report analyzed the results of testing at the beginning of Grades 1, 3, 6, 9, and 12. Achievement of the average Mexican American, Puerto Rican, American Indian, and Black was much lower than that of the average Oriental or White at all grade levels. Moreover, the differences widened at higher grades. Teacher and school characteristics could not account for all the reasons why Blacks, who started only six months behind in reading at the first grade, ended up three-and-a-half years behind Whites in reading at the twelfth grade.[45]

Having established the substantive and consistent test score differences among various ethnic and racial groups, Coleman and his col-

44 James S. Coleman et al., *Equality of Educational Opportunity* (Washington, D.C.: U.S. Government Printing Office, 1966).
45 Ibid., p. 21.

leagues turned to the task of accounting for these differences. Coleman found that the most important variable in or out of school remains the educational and social background of the child's family. The second most important factor is the educational and social-class background of the other children in the school. Both of these elements outweigh any physical attributes of the school. The most logical method for improving the education of the disadvantaged, according to Coleman, was to integrate the schools and classrooms on a social-class basis so as to change the peer group influences. For some this meant racial integration of lower-class Blacks into largely middle-class White student bodies.

Accounting for text score differences

The Office of Education realized how startling the data were. The Report was stating that schools in general have little impact on learning; moreover, that schools among different minority and majority groups were not all that different. (The school variables that *were* associated with learning, such as the teacher's verbal scores by standardized tests, were difficult to change.) Rather, the data showed that home characteristics and peer group influences were in that order the two major variables associated with academic achievement. Compensatory advocates were being told that the amount of school monies available made little difference; in fact, it did not correlate with student achievement. Little wonder that the Office of Education allowed the Coleman Report to go out of print.

Other analyses of the Coleman data, and additional large-scale statistical studies of the determinants of student achievement, show the same results.[46] A large fraction of variation in student performance levels is accounted for by out-of-school variables, such as the students' home characteristics. Another large fraction is attributable to the so-called peer group effect, that is, the characteristics of the students' classmates. Of the variation that is explained by school factors (about 30 percent), only part can be attributed to teachers.

School variables have less impact

In a four-year study reanalyzing the U.S. census figures, the Coleman Report, and a national longitudinal study of more than one hundred high schools (Project Talent), plus many smaller studies, Christopher Jencks and his associates, using highly sophisticated statistical procedures, concluded that:

1. The schools do very little to close the gap between the rich and the poor, the disadvantaged and the advantaged learner.

2. The quality of education has little effect on what happens to students (future income) after they graduate.

46 George W. Mayeske et al., *A Study of Our Nation's Schools* (Washington, D.C.: U.S. Government Printing Office, 1966); Mosteller and Moynihan, eds., *On Equality of Educational Opportunity*, Harvey Averch et al., *How Effective Is Schooling? A Critical Review and Synthesis of Research Findings* (Santa Monica, Calif.: Rand Corporation, 1972); Raymond Boudon, *Education, Opportunity, and Social Inequality* (New York: Wiley, 1973); Herbert J. Kiesling, *The Relationship of School Inputs to Public School Performance in New York State* (Washington, D.C.: Rand Corporation, 1969).

3. School achievement depends largely on a single input, that is, the family characteristics of the students—and all other variables are either secondary or irrelevant.

4. There is little evidence that school reform (such as compensatory spending or racial or social-class integration) can substantially reduce cognitive inequality among students.

5. Hence, the achievement of complete economic equality regardless of ability would require actual redistribution of income.[47]

Jencks and his colleagues continued to study these issues and proceeded to devote several more years to analysis of the best available data on the relationships between family background, education, and later occupational status and income. To do this they utilized information from eleven major research studies that collected data on U.S. males aged 25 to 64. The results of this analysis did little to change Jencks's previous conclusions: He and his colleagues reported that family background accounted for about 48 percent of the variation in occupational status and from 15 to 35 percent of the variation in income. They also found that educational attainment accounted for about 55 percent of the variation in occupational status and about 20 percent of the variance in income, but since family background is highly correlated with educational attainment, amount of education is not much related to occupational status and income after taking account of family background.[48] Jencks's overall conclusion in 1979 was essentially the same as it had been in 1973: Past compensatory education efforts at equalizing personal characteristics such as educational attainment have been "relatively ineffective. . . . Thus, if we want to equalize income, the most effective strategy is probably still to redistribute income."[49]

*Jencks's
conclusions*

*LARGE-SCALE
INTERNATIONAL
STUDIES*
In the 1950s researchers from a dozen countries of the International Association for the Evaluation of Educational Achievement (IEA) decided to assess children's achievement on a cross-national basis. The first major survey was in the area of mathematics, involving 133,000 elementary and secondary students, 13,500 teachers, and 5,450 schools in twelve technologically advanced countries, including the United States. After the mathematics survey the research institutions embarked on a six-subject survey: science, literature, reading comprehen-

*Cross-cultural
research*

47 Jencks et al., *Inequality: A Reassessment of the Effect of Family and Schooling in America.* In response to criticism of the study, see Christopher Jencks et al., "Inequality in Retrospect," *Harvard Educational Review* (February 1973), pp. 102-28.
48 Jencks et al., *Who Gets Ahead? The Determinants of Economic Success in America* (New York: Basic Books, 1979).
49 Ibid., p. 311.

sion, English and French as foreign languages, and civic education. Together with mathematics, these subjects cover practically all the principal subjects in the secondary curriculum. In this latter study, 258,000 secondary students and 50,000 teachers from 9,700 schools in nineteen countries (four of them underdeveloped countries) were involved. Administratively and technically the task was complex. The first phase took place between 1966 and 1969. The second phase comprised the field testing and analysis of data and took place between 1970 and 1973.

In the mathematics study, especially noticeable were the overall good showings of Japan and Israel and the poor showing of the United States.[50] The range of difference between high- and low-performance countries decreased when the most able students were compared; this tends to support the proposition that countries differ considerably in the proportions of students talented in math, but that the "cream" of mathematical talent is distributed equally over various countries.

The data analysis, although complicated, tended to show that teacher and school characteristics are relatively unimportant in determining math achievement. Student characteristics highly correlated with achievement, and the child's social class accounted for the greatest share of variation in learning. The study also shows that at every age level and in most countries boys outperformed girls.

The six-subject survey was reported in nine scheduled volumes beginning in 1973. The reading survey is of most interest, at least to Americans. The conventional view regarding socioeconomic level and reading scores—students from higher socioeconomic backgrounds have higher reading scores than students from lower socioeconomic backgrounds—apparently holds true. The general belief in the universal superiority of girls' reading does not hold up in the study, however; age seems to be a factor with reading scores, and at the secondary school level reading scores between teen-age boys and girls are similar. The relatively low scores of the Americans, compared to the European scores, support the general view that many of our students are disadvantaged and have basic reading problems.[51]

The data from the subject areas tend to confirm the importance of the student's culture, and particularly the home, in differences in achievement. The total effect of home background is considerably greater than the direct effect of school variables.[52] The data are also sufficiently detailed to conclude, as the science report does, that "learning is a continuous and

Poor showing of U.S. students in math

Americans scored low in reading

50 Torsten Husen, *International Study of Achievement in Mathematics: A Comparison of Twelve Countries*, vols. 1 and 2 (New York: Wiley, 1967).

51 Robert L. Thorndike, *Reading Comprehension Education in Fifteen Countries* (New York: Wiley, 1973).

52 James S. Coleman, "Methods and Results in the IEA Studies of Effects of School on Learning," *Review of Educational Research* (Summer 1975), pp. 335–86; Torsten Husen, "An International Research Venture in Retrospect: The IEA Surveys," *Comparative Education Review* (October 1979), pp. 371–85.

cumulative process over generations."[53] Human beings learn during all their waking hours, most of which are spent at home and not in school; moreover, each generation provides the intellectual capital for the next to rise to higher and higher educational achievements. Significantly, the impact of schooling within a particular culture is shown to be generally more important for science and foreign language than for other areas.[54] Since the Coleman and Jencks data are based on reading and mathematical scores in the United States, the suggestion that certain subjects might be more amenable to school influences is encouraging to those who feel that schools should have a significant effect on learning.

School impact on selected subject areas

Of course, there are many limitations to such a large-scale study. There is the question of common content across countries; of age differences at school levels across countries (that is, not all thirteen-year-olds have had or are supposed to have had the same amount of schooling cross-nationally); of translation of content; and of the sheer magnitude of the data. Also, because of the size of the population, there are numerous variables possibly not accounted for which may have affected the scores. The investigators are well aware of these problems; they merely claim that their statistical models provide a method for obtaining comparative information in selected subject areas and countries. The studies still constitute the best models in existence for cross-national research on student achievement and schooling.

SCHOOLING CAN MAKE A DIFFERENCE

A number of recent studies regarding school effects on students tend to contradict the Coleman and Jencks conclusions in the continuing debate about the impact of schooling.[55] One researcher who analyzed 178 school districts in Colorado found that the following characteristics do have an effect on student performance: (1) district student-teacher ratios, (2) administrative ratios, and (3) staff qualifications.[56] (Surprisingly, per student expenditures and racial composition had no significant effect.)

School effects

Another group of researchers who believe that schools have an effect on pupil performance argue that most of the analysis on student achievement has been done at a given grade level, while their study emphasizes

53 L. C. Comber and J. P. Keeves, *Science Education in Nineteen Countries* (New York: Wiley, 1973), p. 298.

54 William E. Coffman, and Lai-min P. Lee, "Cross-National Assessment of Educational Achievement: A Review," *Educational Researcher* (June 1974), pp. 13–16.

55 Coleman and Jencks frequently have been misinterpreted as concluding that students do not learn in school. Instead, what they argued is that the schools do little to change students' initial disadvantages and advantages. Nor did they conclude that schools cannot make a difference, but only that few schools have been very successful in overcoming the effects of disadvantaged background in the past.

56 Charles E. Bidwell, "Nations, School Districts and the Schools: Are There Schooling Effects Anywhere?" *Journal of Research and Development in Education* (Fall 1975), pp. 57–69; Charles E. Bidwell and John D. Kasarda, "School District Organization and Student Achievement," *American Sociological Review* (February 1975), pp. 55–70.

that the number of years of schooling is related to the acquisition and quality of one's knowledge.[57] They base their conclusions on secondary analysis of 54 surveys of the national adult population between ages 25 and 72 in the years between 1948 and 1971; the sample of the people surveyed totaled over 76,000. After controlling for background variables such as age, sex, religion, place of residence, and occupation, the study concludes that with increased education (divided into three levels: elementary graduation, secondary graduation, and college graduation), there is increased awareness of domestic issues, foreign events, and popular culture. People with more formal education read more newspapers, magazines, and books; in effect, they have learned how to learn. The differential effects of education continue to be large even with the older groups; they begin to diminish only after age 60.

Learning how to learn

The main criticism of the findings is that differences in knowledge observed among the educational levels may be a result of other variables related to the sorting out process of who stops or continues with schooling. For example, part of the difference in knowledge of those with a college education may be due to the socioeconomic status of their parents and their own enriched childhood environments. Large differences in knowledge observed among the educational levels may be directly related to intelligence as well as to motivation to learn. Those with natural ability and desire to learn are more apt to participate in the rigors of formal education without giving up; moreover, they may read more in adulthood. In other words, levels of education may be associated with other variables that cause differences in knowledge found between groups. Levels of education cannot explain all of the large differences in knowledge as the research purports to do; other variables count and when you add them up, they seriously distort the effects of education.

Still, even with these problems, this study represents a good argument for those who wish to stress the "human-capital benefits" of education as opposed to the "economic benefits" of education. In an era when college graduates are having difficulty finding suitable jobs, the intrinsic value of education becomes more important while the extrinsic (monetary) value becomes less important.

"Human benefits" of education

Still other researchers have found that a careful search for unusually successful schools results in the identification of a few that have a much greater impact on student performance than most others with a similar student body, even in the case of inner-city schools. Thus one study of inner-city schools in London found that those that were well run and organized had a much more positive impact than those that were not.[58]

Well-organized schools and leadership count

57 Herbert H. Hyman and Charles R. Wright, *Education's Lasting Influence on Values* (Chicago: University of Chicago Press, 1979).

58 Michael Rutter et al., *Fifteen Thousand Hours: Secondary Schools and Their Effects on Children* (Cambridge, Mass.: Harvard University Press, 1979).

Similarly, a review of the research on successful urban elementary schools in the United States concluded that those with outstanding leadership and focused goals had achievement levels superior to otherwise similar schools.[59] (These two studies are described in more detail at the conclusion of Chapter 14.) Similarly, researchers in Ireland have reported that some schools are much more effective than others, after taking account of students' social class. This latter study was particularly important because it showed that school effects are much more apparent when student achievement is measured with criterion-referenced tests related to the curriculum rather than with general standardized tests. That is, differences show up when one uses tests that are based on what is actually taught in the school rather than on general examinations produced by testing agencies.[60] Taken together, these and other studies have provided encouraging indications that outstanding schools can make a difference in terms of improving the achievement of disadvantaged students.

SUMMING UP

1. Some scholarly critics seem to be saying that education cannot serve the purpose of mobility. Americans in general are beginning to doubt that the goals of equal educational opportunity can be achieved through the schools.

2. Starting in the mid-1960s, a number of studies have shown that school reform has very little effect on reducing achievement differences associated with social background. These studies have now been challenged by other scholars.

3. The studies have helped to dispel some of the myths about what schooling can and cannot achieve. One writer sums up this school of thought as follows: "The education community has often claimed more than it was prepared to deliver, and a more realistic appraisal of what we can expect will be healthy."[61]

4. Recent studies have indicated that schools can be effective in working with disadvantaged students, provided they have outstanding leadership and steps are taken to make them unusually successful.

5. Nevertheless, simply throwing money at the problem—for example, by reducing class size without making fundamental changes in curriculum and instruction—will probably repeat the mistakes of

59 David L. Clark, Linda S. Lotto, and Martha M. McCarthy, "Factors Associated with Success in Urban Elementary Schools," *Phi Delta Kappan* (March 1980), pp. 467-70.

60 George A. Madaus, "The Sensitivity of Measures of School Effectiveness," *Harvard Educational Review* (May 1979), pp. 207-30.

61 James Cass, "Where Are We Today?" *Saturday Review/World* (October 9, 1973), p. 43.

the past and reinforce the conclusions of those who argue that the schools perpetuate the existing social class structure. Efforts to reform the schools will have to be systematic and long-lasting if the schools are to provide more effective educational opportunities for disadvantaged students.

DISCUSSION QUESTIONS

1. How does social class influence school performance? Discuss several different kinds of school performance.

2. What are the functions of social class in American society? What are the functions of social mobility in American society?

3. Some people who could be upwardly mobile decide not to be. What are some of the reasons for such a decision?

4. If intelligence is mainly inherited, explain why compensatory education has limited educational value. If intelligence is mainly related to environment, explain why schools have failed to serve the needs of *all* children.

5. Discuss the implications of the statement, "The closer society comes to the idea of equal opportunity, the more it will increase income gaps among people."

THINGS TO DO

1. Visit a city council meeting or a similar civic or governmental office where the public is invited. Cite examples of any appearance of vested interests that might be class-related.

2. Visit two areas in your community that differ greatly in social class. Record material objects, styles of dress, and brand names in the local stores. Cite differences.

3. Evaluate the position of the individual who meets the definition of a member of a minority as expressed by affirmative action policies. What advantages and disadvantages do minorities have today in terms of schooling and jobs?

4. Organize a debate on the topic: "Given, as environmental influences become more similar for everyone, social mobility will become more rigid, with certain able families perpetually at the top and certain less able ones at the bottom."

5. Examine the relationship between family factors, peer group influence, and school conditions and their effects on academic performance. Which of the three variables—family, peer groups, or school—seems to have the greatest impact on cognitive outcomes?

CHAPTER 11
STUDENT SOCIETY AND PEER GROUP INFLUENCES UPON LEARNING

Focusing questions

How do classroom dynamics differ in inner-city and suburban classrooms?

Can we define an "average" or "typical" classroom?

What are the effects of participation in extracurricular activities?

How does student culture influence school behavior?

What is the nature of debate on the differences between teen-age drug use and teen-age drinking?

Why has student unrest declined?

How have the courts influenced student behavior, student discipline, and student rights?

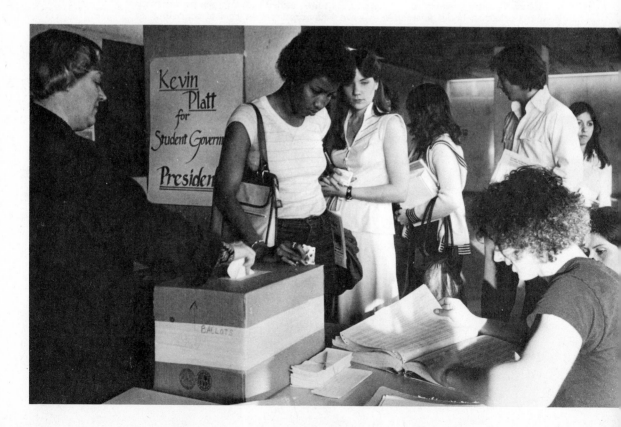

The classroom and school climate reflect the norms that children and teachers learn in their culture. In particular, students bring with them a predisposition to behave in groups as they do. The teacher is affected by these student behavior patterns and, in turn, his or her attitudes and behaviors vary in different learning climates. Some students are boisterous, aggressive, constantly fighting with one another, or directing their hostility toward authority figures. Other children are passive before adults, sit quietly, and take instructions and the teacher's explanation without question. Some students find status in drugs and violence, while others find reward in grades.

In general, schools are middle-class institutions, where middle-class teachers and administrators help perpetuate middle-class values. Hence, schools tend to favor those students who are middle class or who easily fit into the school mold. There is nothing startling about this analysis; to some extent you yourself are a product of this molding process—even if you are from a lower- or lower-middle-class background. In short, you have learned appropriate behaviors to function in school. Regardless of your background, by virtue of entering college in order to obtain the "proper credentials" deemed necessary by middle-class society, you have demonstrated the success of the molding process.

On many occasions, however, the school and its teachers and administrators find themselves in conflict with the students. This is true not only in elementary school settings where the lower-class children first encounter a middle-class culture of different norms that sometimes discriminates against them, but also in secondary school settings generally. As was pointed out in Chapter 9, the youth culture is often in conflict with adult culture even in middle- and upper-middle-class schools. In any case, the school's social setting is crucial in influencing the future of children and youth.

In this chapter, then, we shall explore the dynamics of the classroom, student culture—including drugs and drinking, student disruptions, and student rights. While we examine student society and social influence on learning, we should also keep in mind that the primary goal of the classroom and school is learning.

SOCIAL CLIMATE OF THE CLASSROOM

The social-emotional tone of the classroom, usually described as the social climate, manifests itself in the daily student-teacher interaction and the interpersonal relations that exist between the teacher and her students. In Chapter 4 we discussed the theory and research for measuring teacher behavior, where student-teacher interaction was considered as one source of the research. In this chapter we shall examine the inner-city and suburban classroom climate, in addition to the "average" or "typical" classroom.

INNER-CITY   In the 1960s and 1970s a wealth of litera-
CLASSROOMS   ture came out on inner-city schools and
teachers, coinciding with the nation's concern for the war on poverty and
the civil rights movement. The general classroom situation was described
as one where very little learning takes place, and where feelings and attitudes between the students and teacher were in conflict. An example of
miseducation in inner-city classrooms is found in the following report on a
confused and chaotic fourth grade class in New York City's Harlem section.[1] The children are not learning, not growing; they are being
shortchanged. The teachers seem either incompetent, indifferent, or just
unable to cope with the situation. One cannot help feeling that these children are doomed—victims of their own home circumstances and of the
school, which is unable to provide appropriate social, psychological, and
educational help. The first description takes place outside the office of
Assistant Principal Zang, and the second and third descriptions take place
in the classroom.

**Miseducation
in inner-city
classrooms**

> Edith, a beautiful woman of thirty-five from Barbados, is washing
> "pussy" and "f___ you" from the wall. . . . Two policemen are
> knocking at Zang's door. I too have to see Zang this morning
> about Danny Aquilez, an eleven-year-old who carries a . . . com-
> pass that he uses on children and on Wednesday told me to f___
> myself and threw a chair. With the help of a guard, Danny was
> dragged down to the office on Wednesday, where he repeated it,
> "f___ing bitch" in front of Zang and four others. Zang had heard
> of this kid before—Danny had been around the school for four
> years, progressively growing sicker. Zang said, "Can't we handle
> this tomorrow? . . ." But tomorrow never came for Mr. Zang.[2]

* * *

> Luce, who's found the right beginning page, is called on first to-
> day. . . . "Here is Ted, here is Sally," she begins. Mutterings start
> at once. Hands in the air.
>   "You will not rudely interrupt Luce while she is reading."
>   "Aw, she can' read." "You can' read neither." "Lemme
> read." "Mis Burke, I don' know what page we on." "I can' keep
> place, she read too fas'." "Someone stole my book, it's gone." A
> book is slammed shut. One kid gets up and walks out.[3]

* * *

> "Now we'll report on our library books. Manuel." Manuel jumps
> up, dropping his book with a loud crash, on purpose. "Mis' Burke,

1 Mary F. Greene and Orletta Ryan, *The Schoolchildren: Growing Up in the Slums* (New
York: Random House, 1965).
2 Ibid., p. 3.
3 Ibid., pp. 11–12.

Marshall cursed my mother.'' ''Man, whut I say was. . .'' A fight starts, kicking off noisy smaller fights across the room, where children had been working quietly on their own. . . .[4]

These are the kinds of descriptions reported in a diary of a Harlem elementary school. One begins to get an idea of the difficult situation that teachers face in these schools, the frustrations with which students and teachers are confronted, and some of the reasons why students and teachers fail in these schools.

Frustration
and failure

The situation does not improve in the secondary schools. One description of an English lesson presents us with an indifferent, sullen group of ''scholars'' who spend most of their class time slouching over their desks, sleeping and snoring, tapping on their desks, reading comic books, ridiculing themselves and their teachers, and sometimes fighting among themselves and harassing their teachers.[5] The attempt to teach vocabulary in the first few days of school is described as follows:

Sleeping,
tapping, and
comic books

''Quiet, please. Take out your notebooks. . .'' I pointed to the word at the top of the list. ''Can anyone pronounce this word?''

The boy in the last seat in the second row stretched his arms above his head, yawned deeply, closed his eyes, and sank back upon his spine.

''Does anyone know what the word means?'' One boy hissed at another, ''Wha' time?'' and got the leisurely answer, ''Nine oh tree. Half hour to go.'' The questioner started tapping on his desk with a key.

''Stop the noise, Medina.'' Medina exhaled loudly. ''Does anyone *care* what the word means?'' Louis grinned. ''Do you care, Marvin?'' ''Wa?''

''Wake up, Marvin, and tell what you think about the word up there. Are you awake?'' ''Yea.'' ''All right. What about the word?'' ''Where?'' ''There.'' ''That woid? Nuttin?'' ''That isn't the word.'' ''Yeah. I know, that's what I think.''[6]

Problems in inner-city schools occur not just in the classroom but also in the corridors and other parts of the school, particularly at the high school level. The situation in the corridors of one inner-city high school has been described by an observer in Chicago as follows:

Corridor
control

Life in many of Westside's classrooms may be a continued struggle for control, but there is normally little that one could honestly term a contest for control of the corridors. The students simply

4 Ibid., p. 13.
5 Joan Dunn, *Retreat from Learning* (New York: McKay, 1955).
6 Ibid., pp. 100–101.

run them. . . . They manage to make the hallways an extension of the streetcorner. They may smoke cigarettes or more exotic things, sit down and start a card game, play radios, work on their dance steps, or do some impromptu choral singing. A few are prone to setting off fire alarms from time to time.[7]

Some readers might say that these overwhelmingly negative descriptions are not a true picture of the inner-city school. Although we can argue about what the norm is, there is no question that most educators in inner-city schools report these types of descriptions, and some much worse—more hostile, more dismal, more threatening to life and limb.[8] As to who is to blame, pointing to one group and ignoring the interaction effects of all the groups would be misleading and unfair. Research indicates that teachers and administrators are overwhelmed by the learning and behavioral problems that arise in inner-city schools. Where a teacher in a suburban school may deal effectively with two or three students with serious learning problems, the same teacher in an inner-city school may have ten or twelve problem students and may be unable to provide sufficient help either to them or to other students in the class. The result is that both students and teachers become increasingly frustrated and apathetic, thus setting off a vicious circle of low achievement, frustration, and hostility. The underlying problem appears to be that schools with a substantial concentration of low-achieving poverty students generally do not function successfully.[9] Regardless of who if anyone should be "blamed," little learning goes on in many inner-city schools; too many students are failing in the classroom.

Teachers are overwhelmed

SUBURBAN CLASSROOMS

In the suburban classroom the underlying stress seems to be on conformity—and the students learn to acquire the habit of giving their teachers the answers expected of them. The emphasis is on being correct, not on thinking. Middle-class suburban children in elementary schools, contends one observer, learn to be docile in class and to behave mostly according to the wishes of others.[10] The first example is from the second grade.

Conformity and docility

The children have been shown movies of birds. The first film ended with a picture of a baby bluebird.
    Teacher: Did the last bird *ever* look as if he would be blue?
        (The children did not seem to understand the slant

7 Charles M. Payne, "Who Runs This Chicago High School?" *Integrateducation* (January–April 1979), p. 9.

8 Roland Betts, *Acting Out: Coping with Big City Schools* (Boston: Little, Brown, 1978).

9 Robert J. Havighurst and Daniel U. Levine, *Society and Education*, 5th ed. (Boston: Allyn & Bacon, 1979).

10 Jules Henry, "Docility, Or Giving Teacher What She Wants," *Journal of Social Issues* (April 1955), pp. 33–41.

of the question and answered somewhat hesitantly):
Yes.
Teacher: I think he looked more like a robin, didn't he?
Children (in chorus): Yes.[11]

In this example the teacher's stress on the word "ever" did not come through as a clear stimulus. It did not create the doubt in the minds of the children that would have brought the right answer, "No." Because the stimulus was unclear to the students, the teacher made it crystal clear the second time and got the "right" unanimous response.

In the next two examples we see the relation of stimulus to cultural values; a fourth-grade art lesson is in progress.

Teacher holds up a picture.
Teacher: Isn't Bobby getting a nice effect of mass and trees?
(Ecstatic *Oh's* and *Ah's* from the children.)

* * *

The art lesson is over.
Teacher: How many enjoyed this?
(Many hands go up.)
Teacher: How many learned something?
(Quite a number of hands come down.)
Teacher: How many will do better next time?
(Many hands go up.)[12]

The word "nice" led to a docile response, as did the word "enjoyed." The words "learned something" did not produce the desired unanimity. However, the teacher's follow-up signal, "better next time" evoked a response similar to the response evoked by "enjoyed." The teacher was satisfied and went on to the next activity.

When the children did not give the desired response on the first stimulus, the teacher provided assistance, gave additional cues, or reworded the question—leading to the conclusion that children in middle-class suburban schools are taught to give the answer the teacher wants. While in the inner-city classroom, the student's hostility is often directed at the teacher, in suburbia the teacher manages to direct existing student hostility toward other students (particularly in the form of peer criticism) and away from herself.[13]

Give teachers what they want

An account of how the middle-class child's intelligence, creativity, and interest in learning are discouraged and stunted by the classroom process is provided in John Holt's *How Children Fail*.[14] Holt describes Emily, a student who sounds like so many we know or remember.

11 Ibid., p. 34.
12 Ibid., p. 35.
13 Jules Henry, *Culture Against Man* (New York: Random House, 1963).
14 John Holt, *How Children Fail* (New York: Pitman, 1964).

This child must be right. She cannot bear to be wrong, or even to imagine that she might be wrong. When she is wrong, as she often is, the only thing to do is to forget it as quickly as possible. Naturally she will not tell herself that she is wrong; it is bad enough when others tell her. . . [S]he. . . awaits the magic words, "right," or "wrong." If the word is "right" she does not have to think about the problem anymore; if the word is "wrong" she does not want to, and cannot bring herself to think about it.[15]

Emily has adopted several strategies so as not to have to think. When someone else answers correctly she nods in agreement. She may add a comment, although her tone of voice is low and she feels this is risky. She does not raise her hand unless there are at least half a dozen other hands up, "since she knows that the teacher usually calls on nonvolunteers."[16]

Raising one's hand when it's safe

Emily is also good at bluffing answers. This strategy often pays off, because "a teacher who asks a question is tuned to the right answer, ready to hear it, eager to hear it, since it will tell her that her teaching is good and that she can go on to the next topic." Anything that sounds close to the answer is often accepted as the "right" answer. The mumble strategy is effective in language classes. Just mumble an answer, "and the teacher . . . will give the correct answer" and go on to the next student. Similarly, when a word "is spelled with an *a* or an *o*, . . . write a letter that could be either one of them"[17]

The mumble strategy

Concrete and specific examples are cited of how children learn to be stupid, how they learn not to learn, how they adopt strategies of fear and failure to please their teachers, and how teachers reinforce these sad practices. It is a personal and subjective account, however, which is difficult to substantiate by empirical data.

"AVERAGE" CLASSROOMS

Bearing in mind that the word "average" is sometimes misleading and almost impossible to agree on, a typical classroom has been described as a place:

> . . . where tests are failed and passed, where amusing things happen, where new insights are stumbled upon, and skills acquired. But it is also a place in which people sit, and listen, and wait, and raise their hands, and pass out paper, and stand in line, and sharpen pencils. [Here] we encounter both friends and foes, where imagination is unleashed and misunderstanding brought to ground. But it is also a place in which yawns are stifled and initials scratched on desktops, where milk money is collected and recess lines are formed.[18]

15 Ibid., p. 12.
16 Ibid.
17 Ibid., pp. 12–13.
18 Philip W. Jackson, *Life in Classrooms* (New York: Holt, Rinehart, 1968), p. 4.

Both aspects of life, the celebrated and the unnoticed, are important to all of us, but the everyday occurrences, routine events, and trivial acts repeated innumerable times often are neglected in the literature because they are bland and unsensational, and they often go unnoticed even by the teacher.

Often, when teachers are asked to define what happens in their own classrooms, they are at best vague. They lack a technical vocabulary, unlike other professionals, to describe the classroom social interaction process. They often simplify the complexity of the classroom into one or two underlying events. When called upon to justify their professional decisions, many admit that their behavior is "based more on impulse and feeling than on reflection and thought." They are more likely to describe their behavior and defend their actions by pointing to hunches or because an action "felt like the right thing to do, rather than claiming that they knew" the right answer.[19] Of course, it should be noted that these intuitive hunches are often seasoned by years of practical experience. Thus, their bases for behavior actually may be more rational than their own self-reports would lead us to believe. In addition, events in the classroom occur at the rate of about 200 to 300 interpersonal interchanges every classroom hour, and the content and sequences of these interchanges cannot be predicted, preplanned, or described with any exactitude. Moreover, the observer in the back of the room cannot separate or measure all of these interchanges. In short, classrooms "are not neat and orderly places even though some educational theories make them sound as if they are. . . ."[20]

Lack of technical vocabulary

Classrooms are not neat and orderly

Despite the continuous contact with children in the classroom, teaching is in many ways a lonely profession. Teachers rarely have the opportunity to discuss their problems or their successes with other colleagues, nor do they, as a rule, receive adequate help from their supervisors. Even the beginning teacher generally is unobserved and unassisted, and the shock of the initial year of teaching becomes his or her own private struggle.

In particular, teachers often are judged not by the way they teach but by their ability to manage or discipline their students. The stress on control is evident, and schools often are described as "jails" and "prisons."[21] But if schools are repressive, the blame certainly should not fall upon teachers or administrators alone. The role of the taskmaster is thrust upon the teacher partly from tradition and partly because parents and students themselves prefer that teachers maintain authority and control over students. The yearly *Phi Delta Kappan* polls, taken among parents between 1969 and 1980, list student discipline as the major school problem eleven of the twelve times.

Teachers judged by their disciplinary abilities

19 Ibid., p. 145.
20 Ibid., p. 149.
21 Charles E. Silberman, *Crisis in the Classroom* (New York: Random House, 1971).

Teacher-student interaction   A study of 158 classrooms in 67 elementary schools in thirteen states by John Goodlad and M. Frances Klein shows that reading is the most frequent activity.[22] In terms of teacher involvement, there were no marked differences between teachers in suburban and those in inner-city classes. Teachers exhibited positive attitudes toward children in the classroom in about 40 percent of the cases, with the words "supportive" and "warm" accounting for 20 percent of the descriptions. Negative attitudes accounted for 20 percent of the attitudes, and the remaining tended to exhibit neutral feelings, such as "formal," "directive," and "demanding." Student involvement generally coincided with the degree of teacher involvement, with one out of five classes exhibiting high involvement and one out of four exhibiting low involvement. About 60 percent of the classes showed average involvement.

The most frequent methods for disciplining and controlling students were praise and verbal rewards, reminders of "appropriate" behavior, commands and directives, and avoiding or ignoring the behavior deliberately. Threats accounted for only a small percentage of the total. Negative recognition occasionally took such forms as moving children from one seat to another, requiring that children place their hands on the desk or sit in a corner, sending children outside or to the principal, or using sarcasm. Concerning social-instructional interaction, it was stated:

Praise and rewards as control mechanisms

> At all grade levels, the teacher-to-child pattern of interaction overwhelmingly pervaded. This was one of the most monotonously recurring pieces of data. The teachers asked questions and the children responded, usually in a few words and phrases and usually correctly—that is, with the response approved or acknowledged as correct by the teacher. It is fair to say that teacher-to-child interaction was the mode in all but about 5 percent of the classes.[23]

Furthermore, when the children interacted with each other, it was usually outside the regular process of instruction and represented a few moments of distraction. Individual teacher tolerance determined the length of time that this diversion was permitted to continue. Whatever the type of interaction in the classroom—teacher to child, child to teacher, or child to child—it was dominated by the teacher. This pattern seems consistent in most grade levels.

Teachers dominate classroom interaction

"Accidental" nature of the classroom   Regardless of the type of school, the classroom is an "accidental" group as far as its participants are concerned. They are brought together by accident of birth, residence,

---

22   John I. Goodlad and M. Frances Klein, *Behind the Classroom Door* (Worthington, Ohio: Jones, 1970).

23   Ibid., p. 51.

and role, rather than by choice. The students of the different classrooms we have examined are participants in a miniature society because they all happen to have been born about the same time, live in the same area, and were assigned to a particular room. The teacher may not be in this particular classroom entirely by choice; however, she had the opportunity to choose her profession and school system. The students have no choice in whether they participate; they are compelled to attend school. The classroom lacks the characteristics of voluntary groups, which are held together by free choice of association and by mutual goals. We see the task of the teacher in a better perspective when we remember the accidental and mandatory nature of the classroom.

In a classic text on the sociology of teaching, Willard Waller discusses the authority given to the teacher by both law and custom.[24] Because of changing authority patterns throughout our society, the teacher's word is less authoritative than it was formerly, and the leadership role of the teacher and the social climate of the classroom have changed as well.

In describing the teacher's role, Waller says that "conflict is in the role, for the wishes of the teacher and the student are necessarily divergent, and will conflict because the teacher must protect himself from the possible destruction of his authority that might arise from this divergence of motives."[25] Do you agree that "the wishes of the teacher and student are necessarily divergent"? Can you think of ways in which a teacher protects "himself from the possible destruction of his authority"? Finally, how can the social climate of the classroom be improved when youth and adult society are becoming increasingly divergent?

Role conflicts

STUDENT CULTURE

Status-seeking by students brings with it strong pressure to conform. As one student said: "We have to be like everybody else to be accepted. Aren't most adults that way?"[26] The need to be "in," to be "with it," to display the proper symbols creates within adolescents conforming attitudes and behaviors. Even the leaders of student groups are subject to the sanctions of the group and maintain their status within its rules. The models of conduct are influenced by movies, magazines, television, radio, and phonograph records.[27] Boys and girls are influenced by a common ritual of dating, riding in cars, attending sports events, and expressing a common vocabulary of popular phrases. The emphasis on the peer group persists; adolescent culture largely dictates behavior in school.

Adolescent culture dictates school behavior

24 Willard Waller, *The Sociology of Teaching*, rev. ed. (New York: Wiley, 1965).
25 Ibid., p. 383.
26 "The High School," *Life*, October 11, 1963, p. 73.
27 Harold Taylor, "The Understood Child," *Saturday Review*, May 20, 1961, pp. 47–49, 66.

Peer group influence can promote or inhibit learning—or turn a fad into a craze. Were you ever a "Trekkie"?

STUDENT ACHIEVEMENT AND PEER CONFORMITY

A 1961 landmark study on adolescent society by James Coleman concluded that there exists a strong student culture in the schools, one that is different from adult culture.[28] Coleman and his team visited ten schools and examined the students' frame of reference and informal social system. They found that, in terms of reaction to disap-

28 James S. Coleman, *The Adolescent Society* (New York: The Free Press, 1961).

proval, 54 percent of the boys and 52 percent of the girls indicated that
parental disapproval was the hardest to accept, 43 percent of both sexes
were most concerned with peer group disapproval, and teacher disapproval got a very slight reaction. Coleman interpreted these data to mean
that the balance between parents and peers reflected the transitional experiences of adolescents, that is, the importance of family and friends.
Favored activities among students included dating, talking on the telephone, being in the same class, eating together with friends in school,
"hanging around together," or just "being with the group" outside of
school. Esteem was gained by a combination of friendliness and popularity, an attractive appearance and personality, and possession of skills and
objects (cars, clothes, records) valued by the culture. The image of the
athletic star for boys and the image of the activities leader for girls were
most esteemed, and the brilliant student per se was one of the less esteemed images. (Parallel data revealed that the brilliant student, especially
the brilliant girl student, fared poorly as a dating choice from the outset,
and declined even farther from the freshman to senior year.)

**Importance of
family and
friends**

No matter what the unique climate of the school or the parents'
socioeconomic status, the most popular male student was oriented to the
athletic image, although the athlete-scholar usually received the highest
sociometric status, and the scholar who was not an athlete had higher
status than the student who was neither a scholar nor an athlete. For girls
good grades were relatively unimportant, and in most schools were even
considered a detracting factor; it was important for girls not to appear
smarter than boys. In general, the highly esteemed students were less
favorable to the scholarly student than were the less esteemed students,
although at the same time the highly esteemed students tended to have
higher grades than the student body as a whole. The students with the
highest status were also less adult-oriented (less concerned about parental
or teacher approval) than the rest of the students. They were more concerned about school functions and were more likely to attend a school rally
than go riding with friends. Coleman concluded that the socially elite
students were "selective" in their choice of school-related activities.

While most data on family status and peer status point to the fact
that students from middle-class, relatively well-educated families tend to
have the most prestige in the schools, Coleman found that the correlation
between the student's family status and school status was modified by the
total social-class composition of the school. "The leading crowd of a
school, and thus the norms which the crowd sets, tend to accentuate these
very background characteristics already dominant, whether they are up-
per- or lower-class."[29] Students, then, were governed by the dominant
socioeconomic group, although the middle-class student had the best

**Norms set by
dominant
group**

29 Ibid., p. 109.

chance to be accepted in most schools. Similarly, Coleman showed that students within a given school grouped themselves into subgroups varying in status and favored activities. The elite students represented the dominant social background of the school's student body and performed well the activities most favored by the students as a whole.

Coleman's basic themes of the underlying values of student culture still remain strong, although some changes have recently occurred reflecting a new freedom and drug culture.

A "REPRESENTATIVE"
HIGH SCHOOL
A more recent in-depth study of a single "representative" high school in the midwest, drawing a student population of lower to middle class from small towns and suburban areas, is also illustrative of similar values of the student culture.[30] The three prestige groups are the boys who are athletes (or "jocks"), the "good-looking, personable" girls who dominate the extracurricular activities (especially the cheerleaders), and members of the music-drama group (who participate in the school band, plan school parties, decorate the halls prior to a big game or dance, and are in charge of the senior prom). The three groups, consisting of a core of about 25 out of 400 seniors, comprise the "power clique" and represent the most highly esteemed boys and girls; they get elected to almost all school offices and are actively engaged in all the major student activities. Compared to the top 25, the "brains" of the school have little power and esteem. They join the Math Club, Science Club, Latin Club, and Chess Club. These groups meet infrequently, and are often discontinued by midyear. Similarly, membership in the Honor Society demands little active involvement.

Three prestige groups

Although considerable resentment of those who ran the school did exist among the less esteemed and noninvolved students, these feelings were suppressed in class and only made known to their own friends. For example, "No student ever challenged the right of the central fifteen . . . students or the football players to run whatever activities there were."[31] All the students, regardless of their sociometric status, had their own group of friends and in truth each group paid little attention to others. It was extremely important to have friends; in fact, this "may have been the single most important thing in the school." Not to have friends meant having no one to be with in the hallways or classrooms, no one to walk with to class, no one to talk to, no one to eat with. As one student said, "When I didn't have any friends, I hated this place." Said another, "In school we groove with our friends." And still another stated, "You can't go to high school without friends."[32]

30   Philip A. Cusick, *Inside High School* (New York: Holt, Rinehart, 1973).
31   Ibid., p. 74.
32   Ibid., p. 66.

Friendship patterns were rigidly bounded. One did not "hang around" with just anyone. The student walked, talked, ate with, and spent most of his or her time with a few friends; this was particularly noticeable in the cafeteria. It was more important to sit with friends than to satisfy one's hunger. It was more important to have friends and be accepted by at least one group than to have good grades. When given a choice between failing a test or sitting alone in the cafeteria, most students indicated a preference for flunking the examination. The worst thing that could happen, according to one student, was to "walk around the halls alone."[33]

Friendships were more important than grades

The students who did not receive adequate attention were not necessarily the lower-class students; rather, it was those who did not take an active role in student activities who were left to their own devices. The study concludes that the school does not reward teachers for reaching students on an individual basis; those students who stand outside the power clique and high-esteem areas receive few rewards and often fail to receive remedial attention (even when needed). The most important influence on student behavior is not the teacher but fellow students. The implications of this conclusion are extremely important: in order to change student performance, perhaps more attention should be devoted to the student's relationship to classmates rather than to examining teacher attitudes or behavior.

PARTICIPATION IN EXTRACURRICULAR ACTIVITIES Investigators have had difficulty determining whether participation in extracurricular activities benefits students in other aspects of their personal and academic development. The basic reason for this difficulty is the problem of determining whether participation is a cause or an effect. It is known, for example, that students who have a high level of participation generally have higher grades, other things equal, than those who do not participate. It may also be true, however, that students who have higher grades are more likely to participate for various reasons in school-sponsored extracurricular activities than those with low grades. Thus it is necessary to take account of the possibility that high grades and participation go together initially if one wants to determine whether participation has a positive effect on grades. In addition, it also is desirable to know *how* participation results in higher grades, if it does. Do students who begin to participate come under the influence of highly motivated peers who provide a good academic model, or are the effects of participation transmitted in some other way?

Correlation between school participation and grades

Research on the effects of participation in extracurricular activities was not very extensive until the 1970s, when researchers began to give more adequate attention to this topic. Much of the research concentrates

33 Ibid., p. 67.

on the effects of participation in athletics, probably because interscholastic athletics has been of particular concern to parents and educators. Major conclusions from the research are as follows: (1) there is very little solid evidence that participation in athletics improves academic performance; (2) there is considerable evidence that participation in extracurricular activities affects a number of social and behavioral outcomes; and (3) in particular, participation in extracurricular activity, especially athletics, service and leadership activities, and music, contributes to the development of higher levels of educational and occupational aspirations and attainments (for example, more years of school completed later).[34] Increased educational and occupational aspirations in turn contribute to higher levels of income as an adult. The research also suggested that these effects probably are transmitted through peer associations, contacts with teachers, and encouragement from parents.

Social
outcomes and
occupational
aspirations

These conclusions regarding the effects of extracurricular activities may have great importance for educators. One reason is because participation outside the curriculum probably is more "manipulable" than most other factors that are related to educational outcomes.[35] For example, Chapter 10 pointed out that home environment of students is related to students' aspirations, but it is difficult for educators to change the home environment of students with low or unrealistic aspirations. Encouraging or facilitating appropriate student participation in extracurricular activities may be one of the most effective things teachers and administrators can do to help improve students' aspirations and attainments.

STUDENT ALIENATION

According to many investigators, schools and society have fostered a generation of alienated students who manifest their alienation through drugs, conflict, unrest, and withdrawal (a rejection of the goals and rules of the culture). Many contemporary adolescents have demanded that the school curriculum help them deal with the realities of modern life. A range of appeals has been made: from Blacks and other minorities for ethnic studies, and from middle-class, suburban students for a more expansive and psychologically oriented curriculum. In addition, many students reject the institutional controls of the schools and general orientation of the programs; they question whether one can achieve a comfortable, recognized position in the occupational and social structure of today's society without sacrificing one's individuality and integrity.

Questioning
today's society

34 Duane F. Alvin and David L. Morgan, "Extracurricular Activities: Review and Discussion of the Research on Educational Practices." Paper prepared for the State of Georgia Department of Education, 1979.

35 Luther B. Otto, "Extracurricular Activities and Aspirations in the Status Attainment Process," *Rural Sociology* (Summer 1976), pp. 217–33; Luther B. Otto and Duane F. Alvin, "Athletics, Aspirations, and Attainments," *Sociology of Education* (April 1977), pp. 102–13.

An interesting view is put forth by the Presidential Panel on Youth, chaired by James Coleman.[36] He points out that extended schooling in our society accentuates the self-consciousness of youth and renders the transition to adulthood more difficult. Schools have the paradoxical effect of creating a substantial group of young people who have a preference for continuing irresponsible and even deviant behavior.

Prolonged schooling, by isolating young people from adults, tends to shift socialization from the family to the peer group. Excluded from the major institutions of our society, young people are "outsiders," and have as a result the political and social views of outsiders. An outsider, according to Coleman, has no stake in the existing system. Whereas once youth wanted to hurry their childhood to arrive at adulthood, the opposite has begun to occur. "Having been forced to create and live with a youth subculture, an alternative subculture, many youth are reluctant to leave it, reluctant to become assimilated into adult culture, from which they have so long been segregated."[37] In effect, many students become alienated from the adult world. The Coleman Panel concludes that the schools must transform unsocialized adolescents into responsible adults and teach them the principles of self-management and adjustment to existing institutions.

Youth as "outsiders"

DRUGS AND DRINKING

In the last decade most forms of antisocial behavior in adolescents and youth have increased alarmingly, and this increase has been paralleled by the rise of illegal drug use among students. In the search for new experiences, coupled with demands for peer group conformity, young people have found several ways to achieve their aim, ranging from banana peel to cocaine and STP. Even nutmeg, cinnamon, and other condiments have been used. Cough medicine and other chemicals and drugs have been introduced into the body along with glue sniffing and lighter-fluid inhaling.

Both the inner-city and suburban student (and rural youth to a lesser extent because of the relative unavailability of drugs compared with other areas) is attracted to *marijuana*, and this has become the most popular drug among adolescents (even among a large percentage of adults). Inner-city youth who graduate from marijuana frequently are attracted to hard drugs such as *heroin;* suburban youth have tended to experiment with other hallucinogenics.

Marijuana

1. *Marijuana (cannabis sativa)* is a hallucinogenic drug. Its effects appear quickly and last from two to four hours. Depending on the

36   James S. Coleman et al., *Youth: Transition to Adulthood,* Report of the Panel on Youth of the President's Science Advisory Committee (Chicago: University of Chicago Press, 1974).
37   Ibid., p. 125.

individual and the dosage, the following symptoms may be manifested: sense of euphoria or exhilaration, free flow of ideas and imagery, intensified perceptions and sense feelings, relaxation and relief of anxieties, release of inhibitions, feelings of lightness, disconnected ideas, disorganized associations, distortion of body images, impairment of bodily and sexual functions, and hallucinations. The user may also exhibit lethargic behavior, slowed speech, giddiness, aggressive behavior, overt or covert hostility, depersonalization, introvertedness, depression, confusion, panic, and/or paranoia.[38] Virtually all studies of a person's performance while high on marijuana support the view that it interferes with immediate memory and other intellectual processes such as reading comprehension and arithmetic computation.[39]

A great range of symptoms

Marijuana is usually converted into cigarettes and smoked alone or in combination with tobacco. At times it may be boiled down, sniffed, or chewed and ingested as food. Marijuana is sometimes combined or used in conjunction with more potent drugs such as hashish, mescaline, peyote, or LSD—all of which are also hallucinogenics. There are few, if any, American reports of chronic serious effects resulting from prolonged use of marijuana; however, there is evidence that it has serious effects on hormonal development in children, on fetal chromosome development, and on lung capacity and other biological functions.[40]

It is difficult to find out the number of marijuana users; estimates indicate that more than 43 million Americans have tried marijuana, and half this number may be regular users.[41] The cost of marijuana is small compared with other illegal drugs and it is within easy financial reach for most young people. Depending on the local supply, marijuana usually costs about forty to fifty dollars per ounce. Marijuana itself does not lead to addiction to other drugs but numerous studies indicate that a majority of heroin users began by smoking marijuana.[42]

Millions of users

2. *Heroin (diacetylmorphine)* is produced by mixing morphine with acetic acid, and it is sometimes referred to as "H," "horse," or "white stuff."

38 James L. Chapel and Daniel W. Taylor, "Drugs for Kicks," *Crime and Delinquency* (January 1970), pp. 1–35.

39 Harold Schmeck, "More Potent Pot Has Health Experts Worried," *Chicago Tribune*, October 14, 1979, pp. 6–7.

40 Gabriel Nahas, "Current Status of Marijuana Research," *Journal of the American Medical Association* (December 21, 1979), p. 2725.

41 Schmeck, "More Potent Pot Has Health Experts Worried."

42 National Institute on Drug Abuse, *Let's Talk About Drug Abuse: Some Questions and Answers* (Washington, D.C.: U.S. Government Printing Office, 1979).

About 85 percent of all known drug addicts are heroin users. The laws against the use of this narcotic are administered by the federal government, unlike the varied marijuana laws of the states. Heroin effects can be relaxation, euphoria, increased self-confidence, feeling of physical power, relief from anxiety, apathy, depression, inability to concentrate, reduction of sex drive, hunger and other primary drives, impotence, reduction of or increased respiratory rate, blood pressure and temperature, chills, hot flashes, running nose, reddening of the eyes, constriction of pupils, stomach pains, loss of weight, vomiting, and diarrhea. A number of variables, including the situation in which the drug is taken, combine to determine the effects of the drug.[43]

Numerous possible effects

The addiction probability for heroin is almost 100 percent. Tolerance develops rapidly, followed by withdrawal symptoms. Addiction occurs in a short period—even within one or two weeks. The usual cost of a "fix" is ten to twenty dollars, depending on quality and location. The addict often lives in fear of not finding a "connection" when he or she is "coming down." As the habit becomes more expensive (the average addict spends from fifty two to five hundred dollars a day), the addict is usually forced to steal or turn to prostitution to obtain the money for the next "fix."[44] Sometimes assaults and killings are involved. Treatment programs have had mixed results; adolescents have a better chance than adults for recovery. After withdrawal, the final goal is to relieve the patient of his or her dependence on the drug through psychological and social counseling.

Psychological and social counseling

The laws concerning marijuana are becoming less stringent, while those dealing with heroin are becoming more stringent. The fastest growing use of drugs taken intravenously has been among suburban and nonminority groups, although there is still a much higher rate of use among minorities and the poor.[45] Of the heroin addicts, the majority are adults but the number of student addicts is significant. In some schools it is alleged that heroin is sold on school premises, and that students "shoot" heroin in the hallways, lavatories, and schoolyards. It is also reported that heroin sales and addiction are reaching the pupils in some inner-city elementary schools; in fact, children less than fourteen years old constitute the fastest growing group of drug users.[46]

43 Ibid.

44 *Drug Abuse: Escape to Nowhere* (Philadelphia: Smith, Kline, and French Laboratories,

45 Martin Kasindorf, "By the Time It Gets to Phoenix," *New York Times Magazine* (October 26, 1975), pp. 18-20, 24ff.

46 "Drug Pushers Go For Even Younger Prey," *U.S. News and World Report*, August 31, 1979, p. 31.

INCREASE   Marijuana is still the most popular drug
IN DRUG USE   among our children and youth, and it became increasingly popular during most of the 1970s. Sixty percent of
high-school seniors in 1979 had tried marijuana and daily or near-daily
use nearly doubled between 1975 and 1979, rising from 6 percent to 11
percent. However, this rise halted in 1979.[47] At the same time, there was a
three-fold increase (from 2 percent to 6 percent) in seniors who had used   **Increase in**
cocaine during the previous month, and use of amphetamines and inhal-   **cocaine**
ants also increased. On the other hand, use of sedatives, tranquilizers, and
heroin declined slightly. The overall percentage of seniors who had tried
illicit drugs other than marijuana increased from 26 percent in 1975 to 28
percent in 1979.[48]

The schools have responded to the growing student drug problem
with crash programs. These include informal sessions with ex-addicts,
guest speakers on the dangers of drug use, in-service teacher training,
films and pamphlets, curriculum revisions in health science, and meetings with teachers, parents, and students. Most of these programs have
been singularly unsuccessful in coping with the growing use of drugs   **Unsuccessful**
among our school youth. They have been found to be outdated, inaccurate,   **programs**
and distorted; moreover, these programs often reflect the biases of the
adult world, thereby setting up a vicious cycle that contributes to the
generation gap and greater drug use.

TEEN-AGE DRINKING   Recent data indicate that alcohol is now
an important mood-changing drug for the young. It is cheap in comparison to other drugs, easily obtained, and relatively more socially acceptable
than narcotics or other illegal drugs. The abuse of alcohol by adolescents
appears to have reached serious proportions in some parts of the country.
For example, a 1974 report shows that 60 percent of New York City's
youngsters between twelve and eighteen years of age drink on a frequent
basis and that 12 percent of them appear to display symptoms of alcoholism.[49] Research conducted between 1941 and 1975 indicated that 70   **Student**
percent of teenagers in 1975 had tried alcoholic beverages, as compared   **alcoholism on**
with 41 percent in 1941.[50] In 1974, 93 percent of high school senior boys   **the rise**
had consumed alcoholic beverages. One out of seven got drunk weekly.[51] A

47 New Light on What Marijuana Does, and How," *U.S. News and World Report* November
26, 1979, p. 72.

48 Lloyd D. Johnston, Jerald G. Bachman, and Patrick M. O'Malley, *1979 Highlights: Drugs
and the Nation's High School Students* (Washington, D.C.: National Clearinghouse for Drug
Abuse Information, 1980).

49 *New York Times*, August 15, 1974, sect. 4, p. 2.

50 "Teenage Drinking Almost Universal," *Adolescent Medicine* (July 1974), pp. 56–68.

51 *Alcohol Use and Abuse Among Youth* (Washington, D.C.: National Institution on Alcohol
Abuse and Alcoholism, 1978).

1979 survey of seniors indicated that 41 percent had taken five or more drinks in a row during the previous two weeks.[52]

Problems involving alcohol in the schools seem to be increasing: in 1979, 39 percent of 1,466 high school students in North Carolina who responded to the question "What do you think are the biggest problems, if any, with the public schools in this community?" answered "drinking" or "alcoholism."[53] Across the country teachers are taking away bottles of cheap wine and other sources of alcohol from eleven- and twelve-year-old children in school playgrounds, hallways, and lavatories of the inner city; students are also coming to class under the influence of alcohol.[54] In the surrounding suburbs, counseling sessions on the effects of alcohol are being given in the schools, and there is an increasing number of teenagers being arrested on drinking charges and drunk driving. Between 1951 and 1979 arrests of youth under eighteen for drunk driving increased 450 percent.[55] Furthermore, almost 40 percent of youth under eighteen report drinking "while driving around or sitting in a car."[56]

As the foregoing data make clear, there is a crying need for educational and health institutions, working in concert with the liquor, entertainment, advertising, and insurance industries, to formulate and publicize responsible guidelines and informational material about dangerous drinking practices among teen-agers.

STUDENT DISRUPTIONS

The student unrest of the late 1960s and early 1970s—the boycotts, demonstrations, sit-ins, picketing, vandalism, and violence—has declined considerably. In its wake came a flood of studies, polls, and surveys analyzing the disturbances.[57]

Although several factors were related to student unrest in the high schools, racial issues led the list.[58] Protests frequently involved demands for greater recognition of Black identity and for minority participation in

Causes of
student unrest

---

52 Johnston, Bachman, and O'Malley, *1979 Highlights: Drugs and the Nation's High School Students.*

53 Robert B. Pittman and Lewis E. Cloud, "Major Problems in Public Education From the Students' Perspective," *Phi Delta Kappan* (February 1980), p. 425.

54 *New York Times,* September 14, 1979, sect. 4, p. 3.

55 *Chicago Tribune,* March 14, 1980, p. 5.

56 *Summary of Final Report,* p. 154.

57 *The Gallup Polls of Attitudes Toward Education 1969–73* (Bloomington, Ind.: Phi Delta Kappan, 1973); Robert J. Havighurst, Frank L. Smith, and David E. Wilder, *A Profile of the Large-City High School* (Washington, D.C.: National Association of Secondary School Principals, 1970); Alan F. Westin, John De Cecco, and Arlene Richards, *Civic Education for the Seventies* (New York: Teachers College, Columbia University Press, 1970).

58 *Education, U.S.A.* (April 1969), p. 7; *New York Times,* May 9, 1969, p. 14; Westin, De Cecco, and Richards, *Civic Education for the Seventies.*

extracurricular activities in desegregated schools. Disruptions based on racial considerations continued to impact some schools in the mid- and late 1970s, as court orders desegregated a number of northern school districts.

Student protest also has occurred over school regulations dealing with dress and grooming, smoking, grades and examinations, assembly programs, censorship of school newspapers, the need for a "relevant" curriculum, and dissatisfaction with school personnel. These disruptions can be summed up as a desire for a greater student voice in rule making, or "student power." The students contended that lack of communication **Desire for** between students and school authorities was a major cause for student **"student** activism. More than 50 percent believed disruptions were an effective tac- **power"** tic in bringing about change. On a nationwide basis, a Harris poll of 100 schools revealed that more than 50 percent of the students were unhappy with their limited part in school decisions.[59] More than 60 percent wanted greater decision making powers. Conflict arose, however, when it was pointed out that only 20 percent of the parents and 35 percent of the teachers believed that students should participate in decision making. A survey of 512 high schools in thirty states revealed that more than 90 percent of the students believed the schools were "unsatisfactory."[60] **Irrelevance and** Overwhelmingly, the students maintained that courses were irrelevant, **incompetence** teachers were incompetent, too much stress was placed on grades, and school was boring. Themes of frustration, estrangement, powerlessness, and injustice also evoked sympathetic responses among students. These feelings, in conjunction with the Vietnam War, left a residue of resentment and hostility among many of our high school youth.

This brief description of forms and reasons for protest does not, of course, exhaust the list. It does suggest, however, that student protest was not limited to one or two issues and that there was a great difference of opinion between the school and its clients about the function and responsibilities of schools. You might think of other issues, and you might consider how various institutions (for example, schools, citizens groups, law enforcement agencies, and the courts) were caught in the cross-fire. You might also focus on the impact of the mass media on activism in student life.

DECLINE OF
ORGANIZED PROTEST

Although several reports and studies hypothesized that the disruptions would continue and even get worse in the 1970s, there has been a marked reduction in wide-scale student disruptions. Authorities differ on the reasons for this decline. Some authorities have linked it to the change in tactics

---

59 "What People Think About Their High Schools," *Life*, May 16, 1969, pp. 23–41.
60 Don H. Parker, *Schooling for What?* (New York: McGraw-Hill, 1970).

and status of the Black Power movement, the decline in influence of radical groups at nearby colleges, and the end of American involvement in the war in Vietnam. Some other authorities have speculated that the disruptions were just a "fad." Still others claim that the reasons for protest have been rectified in the main, that many of the issues over Black studies and Black representation, over student dress codes, disciplinary matters, and the burdensome position of the school in the place of a parent (*in loco parentis*) have been resolved.

Many issues resolved

VIOLENCE AND VANDALISM

At the same time, individual and unorganized acts of vandalism and physical violence increased in the 1970s. According to a 1975 U.S. Senate Subcommittee Report on Juvenile Delinquency, "violence and vandalism in the nation's schools has reached a crisis level and is worsening rapidly." Schools are experiencing serious "crimes of a felonious nature including brutal assaults on teachers and students as well as rapes, extortions, burglaries . . . and an unprecedented wave of wanton destruction."[61] In 1979, according to the National Education Association, the number of teachers assaulted by students on school property increased to more than 100,000.[62] School crimes in 1977 were costing the American taxpayer an estimated $600 million a year; this sum exceeds the total annual amount spent on school textbooks.[63] Furthermore, the above figures are based on reported incidents; there is good reason to believe that many school authorities are reluctant to report incidents, fearing a blot on their records or a mark against the school.

Rising level of school violence and vandalism

In particular, inner-city schools have become the victims of increasing acts of student violence and delinquency. The result is, according to several news accounts, that many teachers are afraid of their students and incapable of imposing discipline needed for teaching.[64] Such violence no doubt reflects to a large extent the conditions in the urban slums of America. It is here that youthful drug addicts are dangerously concentrated in large numbers, that gang fights spill over into school buildings, and that guns are easily available.[65] It is also where we compel many

Urban slum conditions

---

61   Senate Subcommittee Report on Juvenile Delinquency, U.S. Congress, April 9, 1975, quote in *Chicago Sun-Times*, April 10, 1975 p. 14; *Losses Due to Vandalism, Arson, and Theft in Public Schools* (Arlington, Va.: Educational Research Services, 1974).

62   Laurel Leff, "In Inner-City Schools, Getting an Education Is Often a Difficult Job," *Wall Street Journal*, February 5, 1980, pp. 1, 18.

63   Birch Bayh, "Seeking Solutions to School Violence and Vandalism," *Phi Delta Kappan* (January 1978), pp. 299-302.

64   "Blackboard Battlefield: A Question of Survival," *Time*, February 19, 1973, p. 14; Shirley B. Neill, "Violence and Vandalism: Dimensions and Correctives," *Phi Delta Kappan* (January 1978), pp. 302-307; *Chicago Tribune*, September 21, 1974; *New York Times*, November 5, 1972, p. 11; September 15, 1974, sect. 4, p. 8.

65   "Blackboard Battlefield," p. 14; *Challenge for the Third Century: Education in a Safe Environment* (Washington, D.C.: U.S. Government Printing Office, 1977); Neill, "Violence and Vandalism."

students to attend school who cannot cope with the curriculum and who in turn act out their frustrations. Solutions are hard to come by. It is a societal problem that will not go away until the causes are alleviated. Furthermore, affluent suburbs are beginning to report episodes and acts of vandalism that their residents once thought "could never happen here."

However, it also should be kept in mind that the majority of schools do not have serious problems regarding student violence; most of U.S. schools are in suburban and rural areas. In addition, violence has decreased in some schools as officials have moved to make their schools safer places in which to teach and learn. Steps taken to accomplish this have included: (1) provision of elaborate security systems and reduction of access to and entry from the street; (2) student and teacher identification cards; (3) provision of counseling services for students in trouble; (4) programs to improve students' basic skills in the classroom; (5) organizational modifications such as dividing a school into four or five independent communities; and (6) more police patrols when needed. Studies indicate that the overwhelming majority of school administrators who had initiated a combination of these six types of approaches felt that actions had been effective in reducing school violence.[66]

Most schools have minimal problems

STUDENT RIGHTS

Stiff regulations concerning student conduct in the schools have been justified in the past by the need to protect adolescents against their own immaturity. The assumption was twofold: adolescents in school were not entitled to their full rights as citizens until they could demonstrate their maturity, and the school served in place of the parents. It seems clear today that student regulations and student policies will be determined not by the whims of teachers and administrators, but rather by legal interpretations.

Legal precedents

Various civil rights and student agencies have brought to the attention of the courts the need for recognizing the rights of students. One of the first groups to issue a sophisticated policy statement on the subject of student rights and to support their views with legal precedents was the American Civil Liberties Union (ACLU). For example, the 1969 and the enlarged 1971 ACLU position affirmed that school personnel should recognize that:

> Freedom implies the right to make mistakes, and students must therefore sometimes be permitted to act in unwise ways so long as the consequences are not dangerous to life and property, and not

---

66 Francis A. J. Ianni, "A Positive Note on Schools and Discipline," *Educational Leadership* (March 1980), pp. 457–58; M. Martin et al., *Planning Assistance Programs to Reduce School Violence and Disruption* (Washington, D.C.: U.S. Department of Justice National Institute for Juvenile Justice and Delinquency Prevention, 1976).

seriously disruptive of the academic process. . . .Students in their schools should have the right to live under "rule by law" as opposed to "rule by personality." Students have the right to know the extent and limits of faculty authority, and the powers and responsibilities of students. . . . Deviation from the opinions and standards deemed desirable by the faculty is not *ipso facto* a danger to the educational process.[67]

Major constitutional rights of students were listed, as supported by recent court cases. These rights are summarized below:

1. *Freedom of expression and communication.* The school should not interfere with the students' expression and communication concerning controversial issues. "The students have the right to express publicly or to hear any opinion on any subject which they believe is worthy of consideration." They have the right to plan forums, select topics, and invite guest speakers. Student publications should be permitted and the context of the material should be based on the decision of the student editorial board. The students should be assured that they will be "free from coercion or improper disclosure which may have ill effects on [their] careers." Although the school may provide information about the students' character and academic performance to outside business or governmental agencies, it should not answer questions about the students' values and political opinions. Answers to such questions are an invasion of the students' privacy and academic freedom. Also, the students have the right to observe "their own religion or no religion." The recitation of a prayer, a Bible reading, or the use of public school facilities for religious instruction has been declared unconstitutional.

"Free from coercion"

2. *Freedom of assembly and the right to petition.* Students have the right to organize associations or clubs within the school for athletic, social, or political reasons, provided the organization does not deny membership to other students because of race or religion, or for any other reasons, unless they are related to the purposes of the organization. The forming of political organizations should be permitted, and the school administration should not discriminate against the organization. The students and/or student organizations should be permitted the right to assemble within the school or on school grounds. Peaceful demonstrations and picketing or the collection of signatures for petitions concerning nonschool or school issues (even for the dismissal of the principal) should be permitted and "subject only to reasonable restrictions of time and place."

67 *Academic Freedom in the Secondary Schools*, 2nd ed. (New York: American Civil Liberties Union, 1971), p. 10.

3. *Student government.* The organization and processes of the student government should be clearly specified by the school. All students should be allowed to vote. Similarly, they should have the right to run for and hold office, subject to the qualifications of the school's constitution. Candidates seeking office should be allowed to express their opinions and should have opportunity to campaign, subject to equally enforced rules. Vote counting should be scrutinized by representatives of the different candidates, and the winners of the election should be declared elected without a faculty veto.

No faculty veto

4. *Student discipline.* Students' lockers should not be opened without their consent, unless a warrant is presented. Corporal punishment should be severely restricted. Punishments should not affect students' grades, credits, or graduation, except when the infraction is related to academic dishonesty. Serious penalties (such as, possible suspension or expulsion from school) should be reached as a result of a formal hearing—where the student is presented in writing with the charges prior to the hearing, where the student's parents may be present, and where he or she may be advised by anyone of his or her choosing. Involvement with the police should not lead to harassment. A student who is questioned by the police should be advised of his or her rights, and the principal (or his representative) and the parents should be present.

Formal hearings and charges in writing

5. *Personal appearance.* Uniformity should not be equated with responsible citizenship. The students' appearance—their dress, length of hair, personal adornments, badges, or insignias—should not be restricted (so long as it does not disrupt the school); these personal belongings are a form of the students' freedom of expression and communication.

6. *Pregnant and/or married students.* Students' education should not be abrogated because of pregnancy or marriage. If temporary separation from school is warranted, "the education provided elsewhere should be as equal as possible to the regular school."[68]

STUDENT RESPONSIBILITIES   Much attention has been given in recent years to students' rights but relatively little has been done to develop a better understanding of their concomitant responsibilities. One of the few organizations that has attempted to delineate the basic responsibilities that every student assumes along with his or her rights is the National Council for Social Studies. The Council iden-

Responsibilities go hand in hand with rights

68 Ibid., pp. 11-12, 20. Also see Frank R. Kemerer and Kenneth L. Deutsch, *Constitutional Rights and Student Life* (St. Paul, Minn.: West, 1979).

tified students' basic responsibilities as follows, emphasizing that rights and responsibilities should be viewed as part of one large concept rather than separately:

1. *Regular school attendance.* Students should regularly attend their classes. This responsibility includes faithful execution of the terms of special contracts designed as part of an alternative school plan.

2. *Noninterference.* Students are responsible for observing the rights of others by refraining from actions that interfere with the education of fellow students, either inside or outside the classroom.

3. *Consequences of behavior.* Each student should know the rules and regulations of his or her school, and should consider the consequences of his or her own contemplated behaviors and be prepared to accept these consequences.

Accept the consequences of behavior

4. *Rights of others.* Students should respect the rights of others in the school. This includes, but is not limited to, (a) expressing one's opinions in a respectful manner so as not to offend, slander, libel, or show disregard for others; (b) assisting the school staff in running a safe and healthy school for all students; (c) avoiding libelous and obscene materials and other materials that would substantially interfere with classroom processes; (d) protecting the schools' property as well as the property of others; (e) dressing and grooming according to fair standards of health and safety; and (f) avoiding placing fellow students in positions that would cause them to engage in inappropriate behavior such as cheating or perjury.

5. *Climate for learning.* Students are responsible for cooperating with the faculty, administration, and community to establish a productive and beneficial learning climate. This includes, but is not limited to: (a) listening carefully to others; (b) carrying out individual responsibilities in committees or small groups; and (c) seeking improvement in the educational program, environment, and process.

Cooperating with faculty and administration

6. *Conscientious classroom work.* Students should give full effort to their studies. They should pursue and complete their courses; make all necessary arrangements for completing make-up work; and assist the teacher in making the class interesting and worthwhile.

7. *School rules and regulations.* Students should conform to fairly developed and enforced nondiscriminatory school rules and regulations. They should know these rules and be willing to participate in their development or revision when appropriate.

8. *Volunteer information.* Students have the responsibility to volunteer information in disciplinary cases when they have important knowledge concerning such cases.[69]

THE ROLE OF
THE COURTS
In general, the courts do not deny school authorities the power to discipline disorderly students, nor do they deny them the right to suspend or expel students so long as due process is followed. Students are not permitted to disrupt the educational process, nor are they to curtail the rights of others. However, it is becoming clear that it will be up to school authorities to prove disruptions when restricting the constitutional rights of students. In cases involving freedom of expression on serious social and political issues, school officials are asked to tolerate minor disruptions.[70] Although the courts are less inclined to help students who are seeking protection for expression in areas considered trivial or vulgar, they have allowed wide latitude in student newspapers, and have stated that the likelihood of disruption is not sufficient grounds for infringement upon freedom of expression.[71] The Supreme Court also takes the view that school people must afford students their rights regarding routine disciplinary actions.[72] Furthermore, school employees and school board members can be held personally liable for monetary damages if students are denied these rights, even by accident. Also, ignorance is no excuse.[73] A review of the recent court cases has made it clear that:

Tolerating minor disruptions

1. Schools are no longer regarded as sacred institutions.

2. Disciplinary codes and actions must meet the test of due process.

3. Accountability of school personnel in dealing with discipline problems is no longer limited to professional peers or superiors.

4. The Bill of Rights and the Fourteenth Amendment apply not only to adults but also to adolescents, particularly to those in secondary school.

69   "National Council for the Social Studies Position Statement on Student Rights and Responsibilities," *Social Education* (April 1975), pp. 240–45.

70   *Tinker* v. *Des Moines Independent School District* (1968).

71   *Scoville* v. *Joliet Township High School Board of Education* (1970). In this case the U.S. Court of Appeals ruled against school authorities and overturned the expulsion of two students who were responsible for an article in a student newspaper which named one member of the school staff as having a "sick mind," urged students to destroy information forms given to them by school officials, and stated that "oral sex may prevent tooth decay."

72   Surprisingly, the Court has also ruled that corporal punishment may be administered so long as certain procedural rules are followed: Students must be warned that specific misbehavior warrants a spanking; spanking may be administered only after other measures fail; and only in the company of another staff member; *Baker* v. *Owen* (1975). The Court later made it clear that paddling or other similar forms of corporal punishment are not unconstitutional under the Eighth Amendment's clause prohibiting "cruel and unusual" punishment; *Ingraham* v. *Wright* (1977).

73   *Wood* v. *Strickland* (1975).

5. Students have the right to express their opinions, even if these opinions may be held repugnant by school officials or local mores.

6. The school can no longer function *in loco parentis.*

7. Students are entitled to equal educational opportunity.

8. Public education is a guaranteed right, not a privilege.[74]

SCHOOL OFFICIALS
AND THE LAW

The *Goss* and the *Wood* decisions spell the end of the educators' almost total control over the disciplinary process. Since the *Goss* decision school people must now know what a student's constitutional rights are; it formalizes the suspension process and complicates it as well; some say it now becomes too costly and time consuming to pursue suspension as part of the disciplinary process when dealing with disruptive students. The *Wood* decision establishes personal liability; henceforth, most educators will be reluctant to act without checking the looming legal thicket. Many observers feel that these and other changes have all but destroyed the traditional authority of the classroom teacher.[75]

The "good old
days" are over

In addition to these Court rulings, the federal government has amended the Elementary and Secondary Education Act (ESEA) and now allows parents and students age 18 and over to examine the student's educational records and to challenge anything in them that may be construed as detrimental. The law, referred to as the Buckley Amendment (after its sponsor, former Senator James Buckley of New York), also prohibits schools from transferring student record data to third parties without first announcing the intention, stating the purposes for which the data are being released, and obtaining the parents' or student's written consent for the release. Failure to comply with these requirements may lead to withdrawal of all federal funds provided to the institution by the Department of Education.[76]

Students can
examine their
own records

All of these trends have caused educators to envision all sorts of horrors; the list of what educators must now do to ensure student rights precludes many discretionary decisions the schools used to make regarding discipline. Teachers and school administrators will be handcuffed by the letter of the law and, assuredly, some students will be ready, able, and willing to take advantage of it. Furthermore, the decision that educators are liable in money damages for violating students' rights is seen by many as indefensible. In effect, teachers and administrators are potentially liable

74 *Goss* v. *Lopez* (1975) Kern Alexander, *School Law,* 5th ed. (St. Paul, Minn.: West, 1980).
75 Jackson Toby, "Crime in American Public Schools," *Public Interest* (Winter 1980), pp. 18–42.
76 Martha L. Ware and Madaline K. Remmlein, *School Law,* 4th ed. (Danville, Ill., 1979).

for exercising their professional discretion. In addition, and most important, teachers and administrators are going to be extremely careful about putting any substantive information into student records (especially if it may be construed as negative) since a parent or student might sue. For example, if a student had threatened to rape or kill a teacher, but had not done so, it could be unwise for the principal to make any judgments about the student's personality. Unless there were witnesses who would testify in signed affidavits, it might even be best to omit the teacher's charges from the record. As for letters of recommendation, one must now read them with regard to what is omitted, not necessarily what is said. There is no guarantee that the letter of recommendation will be kept in confidence, and if the content is somewhat damaging, there is no guarantee that the student will not file a lawsuit.

**Omissions
from letters of
recommendation**

Nevertheless, there is no need to panic. The courts and the federal government merely are insisting that students have some of the rights of adults. In several court cases school authorities have had to learn, sometimes with embarrassment, that students do not surrender their rights upon entering a schoolhouse. The courts have reaffirmed the rights of students and are requiring strict adherence to these rights. As we noted earlier, the courts do not deny to schools the power to suspend or expel disruptive students; they simply require evidence and step-by-step due process. While personal liability is certainly a factor, it cannot be an overriding consideration lest it be construed as a form of rationalization to avoid the issue of disciplining a student. The courts require that educators act in "good faith," and define good faith as knowing, within the bounds of reasonableness, what a student's constitutional rights are. While this clearly leads to some homework for school people, it does not necessarily portend disaster. It merely suggests that educators should have some knowledge of the laws that affect schooling. Finally, the Supreme Court rulings usually contain a clause or statement presuming that student rights will not endanger the health and safety of the student population or disrupt the educational process. If the exercise of any of the students' rights does lead to such problems, school officials usually have the right to intervene and sometimes even to suspend these rights.

SUMMING UP

1. Every teacher should be aware of the social climate of the classroom.

2. In order to channel classroom behavior into constructive learning, the effective teacher creates a wholesome climate, recognizing individual differences and group dynamics among students.

3. Similarly, every teacher needs to cope with peer groups and peer behavior, which in turn are based upon the students' adolescent and

class culture. The school must use the culture of the students to promote rather than inhibit good learning.

4. The root causes and true character of student protest and dissent are not totally clear, although somewhat related to factors of race relations and student culture.

5. While organized protest on the part of the students has declined considerably, the rise of individual acts of student delinquency is worth noting. Both overt and covert forms of individual student disruptions and antisocial behavior are becoming institutionalized within the schools. Moreover, they have become more difficult to deal with in light of court decisions on student rights.

DISCUSSION QUESTIONS

1. How do adolescents gain high status within their peer group? What types of students are most popular? Why? How does the social composition of the school affect the status positions of peer groups?

2. What type of program should be implemented to succeed in rehabilitating heroin addicts? Explain why you think it would be effective. Is the program practical? Will it succeed in the short run? In the long run?

3. What changes in adolescent culture would support the statement, "The new teacher should be 'a new breed of cat.'" In what way do you agree or disagree with this statement? What kind of teacher would help reduce student unrest in school?

4. What is the nature and extent of student alienation in the schools of the communities with which you are most familiar?

5. What advantages and disadvantages do you see evolving from recent court decisions concerning student rights? Advantages to whom? Disadvantages to whom?

THINGS TO DO

1. Develop and plan trips to two schools. One should focus on an inner-city classroom, the other on a suburban classroom. Be prepared to compare similarities and differences when you return to your own class.

2. Volunteer your services to the administration of a school a few hours weekly if you have the time. Divide the year into two segments, devoting half time to an inner-city school and the other half to a suburban school.

3. Conduct an anonymous survey of class members to determine the percentage and frequency of drug users (soft and hard). Tabulate the data and discuss the implications.

4. Invite a representative from a drug prevention agency or youth-serving agency to talk to the class about the growing trend of drug use and/or alcohol use among teen-agers.

5. Invite a representative from a local student activist group or civil rights group to discuss student unrest and/or student rights.

FOR PART III

SUGGESTIONS FOR FURTHER READING

Ivar Berg, *Education and Jobs: The Great Training Robbery* (Boston: Beacon, 1970).

James S. Coleman et al., *Youth: Transition to Adulthood.* Report of the Panel on Youth of the President's Advisory Committee (Chicago: University of Chicago Press, 1974).

Erik H. Erikson, *Childhood and Society,* 2nd ed. (New York: Norton, 1963).

Herbert Gans, *More Equality* (New York: Random House, 1974).

Nathan Glazer and Daniel P. Moynihan, *Beyond the Melting Pot,* 2nd ed. (Cambridge, Mass.: MIT Press, 1970).

August Hollingshead, *Elmtown's Youth* (New York: Wiley, 1949).

Christopher Jencks et al., *Who Gets Ahead? The Determinants of Economic Success in America* (New York: Basic Books, 1979).

Margaret Mead, *Culture and Commitment* (New York: Doubleday, 1970).

John U. Ogbu, *Minority Education and Caste* (New York: Harcourt Brace Jovanovich, 1978).

Theodore Roszak, *The Making of a Counter Culture* (Garden City, N.Y.: Doubleday, 1969).

PART FOUR
SCHOOLS IN A
CHANGING
SOCIETY

Part Three examined the close relationship between the schools and total culture. Here we are concerned with how schools function in changing times and settings and with the major issues and problems that confront elementary and secondary education in the United States.

The first chapter in this section deals with the changing aims of education under the assumption that the schools serve the needs of both the individual and the society. Whereas the individual should be educated to his or her fullest potential, the dynamics of society must also be considered in formulating our educational aims. The implications of major policy reports throughout the twentieth century are examined, as are the differences between broad aims and specific objectives.

Chapter 13 focuses on the historical influences on school curriculum, various approaches to organizing curriculum, and recent innovations and future trends in curriculum.

The next chapter examines various organizational descriptions of schools; it attempts to categorize the existing large number of schools and diverse student populations into grade levels, size and distribution, and geographical settings. Strategies for reforming schools are outlined.

Chapter 15 is concerned with three major reform movements in American education: desegregation, decentralization, and compensatory education. All three of these movements aim in part to equalize and improve educational opportunities for disadvantaged students.

The final chapter delineates some of the most important educational trends and issues that will receive a great deal of attention in the 1980s. Among the topics considered are multicultural education, mastery learning, "back-to-the basics" and minimum competency testing, school finance arrangements and reform, and the increasing role of the courts and the federal government in education. The book concludes with a brief discussion of the future of education.

CHAPTER 12
AIMS OF
EDUCATION

Focusing questions

What should the schools teach?

How are aims formulated? How are objectives formulated?

What are the major differences between aims and objectives?

In what way does the social order affect educational priorities?

What groups of students have been targeted for special treatment in the 1950s, 1960s, and 1970s? What emphasis has there been on the academically talented and on the economically disadvantaged?

What are the major themes of recent policy reports on education? What aims will be most important in the future?

Few educators would dare talk about reform of schools without some mention of the aims they have in mind. All that is to be done in schools, it is usually asserted, is to be done with the aims of schooling in mind. Schooling is, the argument goes, a rational process directed at achieving some end. However, stating aims is often either mere ritual or a process that remains unclear.

Aims are often used interchangeably with the terms *goals, purposes, ultimate objectives*, and *broad objectives*. While aims are important guides in education, they cannot be directly observed or evaluated; they are statements that connote a desired and valued competency, a theme or concern that applies to education in general. Aims are usually formulated on a national or state level by prestigious commissions or professional groups; they are intended to guide schools in defining the nature of their subject matter and student activities. Examples of aims might be: "Preparing students for democratic citizenship," or "Preparing students for a vocation."

ESTABLISHING AIMS

Contemporary society changes fundamentally and rapidly. As it changes, we must fit ourselves into the present and project ourselves into the future. We look to the schools to help us cope with the climate of change. As a society, we react to change and social pressures by revising the aims of education, and, in turn, the schools respond by changing their programs. It would be nice to maintain that educators appraise the tendencies of the times and develop aims to help shape social forces. This approach conceives of schools as an instrument for change, but this has rarely been the case. Educators usually react to the times and change the aims to meet the new social pressures and forces. This approach conceives of the school as a mirror of society.

Schools as a mirror of society

When we examine the aims of society, we must take into account not only the forces of change and social pressures but also existing philosophies. People react differently to the same events: they appraise, reflect, and react to the tendencies of the times according to their biases and values. In short, the aims we advocate are based not only on social forces impinging on society but also on our philosophy of education. Historically, according to R. Freeman Butts and Lawrence Cremin, that philosophy in America has been rooted in the democratic way of life and in the search for freedom.[1]

Without philosophy we lack a framework for developing our aims. What is the point of seeking answers if one has not asked the right ques-

---

1 R. Freeman Butts and Lawrence A. Cremin, *A History of Education in American Culture* (New York: Holt, Rinehart, 1953); Butts, *Public Education in the United States: From Revolution to Reform* (New York: Holt, Rinehart, 1978).

tions—if one has no framework or philosophy to guide the inquiry? The crux of the issue today is whether, given current trends and social forces, educators can develop aims to fit the problems that confront society; each generation must find its own way.

It also seems that in many cases when we speak of aims, the language is so general that we cannot agree on the intent. For example, what does the phrase "Preparing students for democratic citizenship" mean? What do people have in mind when they claim that the schools should stress citizenship preparation? We simply do not know what the phrase means descriptively, in spite of its common use; hence, to say that people agree on or share an educational aim is often misleading. We must recognize that aims are general statements that only suggest a direction for people to follow. They are too vague for parents to know what the schools are attempting to accomplish and for teachers to know what they are expected to teach or what their students are expected to learn. In communicating aims, what the schools need to do is to translate them into statements that will make clear to those concerned with education what is intended.[2] These translations correspond to what educators call objectives. Without this translation of aims into objectives, it is difficult to make accurate judgments about planning curriculum and instruction strategies, or to evaluate what we have planned.

MOVING FROM AIMS TO OBJECTIVES

Aims are too broad and cannot be specifically applied to a particular curriculum or instructional procedure. In distinguishing between aims and objectives, Ralph Tyler's outline has become a model for curriculum planners.[3] Tyler identified four fundamental questions in developing aims:

1. What educational aims should the school seek to attain?

2. What educational experiences can be provided to help attain these aims?

3. How can these educational experiences be effectively organized?

4. How can we determine whether the aims have been attained? (And to what extent?)

Based on these questions, Tyler listed and discussed the information sources needed for looking at our aims and moving in the direction of formulating objectives. Five information sources were examined: (1) studies of learners themselves as a source of educational objectives; (2) studies of contemporary society outside of school; (3) suggestions from

2 Jack R. Frymier, *A School For Tomorrow* (Berkeley, Calif.: McCutchan, 1973); Jon Wiles and Joseph Bondi, *Curriculum Development: A Guide to Practice* (Columbus, Ohio: Merrill, 1979).

3 Ralph W. Tyler, *Basic Principles of Curriculum and Instruction* (Chicago: University of Chicago Press, 1950).

subject specialists, teachers, administrators, and parents; (4) the use of a philosophy in selecting objectives; and (5) the use of psychology of learning in selecting objectives.

While other useful model systems for planning aims and objectives are available, Tyler's concepts have influenced others in the field and these concepts can serve as a starting point for moving from aims to objectives.

When translating aims into objectives, many educators first formulate intermediate objectives, and then formulate specific or instructional objectives. Intermediate objectives are usually nonbehavioral and are written in terms of grade levels or subjects; for example, "The development of reading skills" or "The appreciation of art." These objectives are usually incorporated into state and local school guidelines; they describe what the schools intend to accomplish and provide general direction. But they are still too vague for teachers and students to know exactly what is intended. The need, then, is to be more precise in our wording of objectives or to state them as instructional objectives.

INSTRUCTIONAL OBJECTIVES   Instructional objectives are stated in behavioral terms, that is, terms that can be observed or measured. They are formulated to help teachers and students know if they are achieving the intermediate objectives, that is, the objectives of the grade level or subject. They are intended to direct student activity toward acquiring specific skills. For example, an intermediate objective might be:

Behavioral terms

1. The students will understand mathematical computations.
   Making it specific, we might state:

2. The students will be able to add two-digit numbers.
   Making it more specific, we might then state:

3. The students will be able to add 10 + 15 + 36.
   Making it still more specific, we might state:

4. The students are to add 10 + 15 + 36 in 30 seconds.
   And making it perhaps as specific as possible, we might state:

5. The students will be able to add 10 + 15 + 36 without the use of any book, slide rule, or mechanical device. They will use paper and pencil, show all the work on the spaces provided, and finish within 30 seconds.

Some educators, such as Robert Mager, advocate a very specific approach, similar to the fifth part of our example.[4] They contend that an instructional objective must describe (1) the *behavior* of the learner when demonstrating his or her achievement of the objective, (2) the *conditions* imposed upon the learner when demonstrating the mastery of the objec-

4 Robert F. Mager, *Preparing Instructional Objectives* (Palo Alto, Calif.: Fearon, 1962).

tive, and (3) the *minimum proficiency* level that will be acceptable. Writing a behavioral objective in American history and using the Magerian approach, we might state:

> The student is to read the biography of Benjamin Franklin. He or she is then to prepare a one-thousand-word oral statement combining three or more important facets of the man's life in a five-minute presentation to the class to be judged successful by at least three out of five students who have also read the biography.

One more example should suffice, this time in science:

> After studying the unit, the student must be able to complete a 100-item multiple-choice examination on the subject of pollution. Acceptable performance will be 80 items answered correctly within an examination period of 60 minutes.

Some educators strongly advocate this specific approach, claiming that it helps us define exactly what we mean, provides a method for arranging sequences of content, promotes direction for teachers and students, provides a guide for determining teaching methods, materials, and activities, and provides a guide for constructing tests and other measurements.[5] Other educators advocate a less specific approach, but one that is still behavioral and measurable.[6] They contend that the Magerian method for stating instructional objectives produces an unmanageable number of objectives, leads to trivia, and wastes a lot of time; they also contend that it is difficult to know or prescribe all of our objectives in advance. The entire procedure becomes too mechanistic and rigid.

TAXONOMY   Another way of translating aims into instructional objectives is to categorize the desired outcomes into a classification system analogous to classifying books in a library, chemical elements in a periodic table, or the divisions of the animal kingdom. Through this system, known as a taxonomy, standards for classifying our aims and objectives have been established and educators are now better able to communicate and add precision to their language.

The educational taxonomy calls for the classification of three domains of learning—cognitive, affective, and psychomotor. The *Taxonomy of Educational Objectives, Handbook I: Cognitive Domain* was developed by a committee of 36 AERA members headed by Benjamin Bloom.

Three domains of learning

5   Robert Kibler, Larry L. Baker, and David T. Miles, *Behavioral Objectives and Instruction* (Boston: Allyn & Bacon, 1970); W. James Popham, *The Uses of Instructional Objectives* (Palo Alto, Calif.: Fearon, 1973).

6   Robert L. Ebel, "Some Comments about Educational Objectives," *School Review* (Autumn 1967), pp. 261–66; Norman E. Gronlund, *Stating Behavioral Objectives for Classroom Instruction*, 2nd ed. (New York: Macmillan, 1978); Bruce J. Tuckman, *Evaluating Instructional Programs*, rev. ed. (Boston: Allyn & Bacon, 1979).

The cognitive domain includes objectives that are related to recall or recognition of knowledge and the development of higher intellectual skills and abilities.[7] The *Taxonomy of Educational Objectives, Handbook II: Affective Domain* by David Krathwohl and his associates is concerned with aims and objectives related to interests, attitudes, and feelings.[8] The psychomotor domain, dealing with manipulative and motor skills, was never completed by the original group of educators. A classification of psychomotor objectives by Anita Harlow closely resembles the intent of the original group and also is based on hierarchical levels.[9]

Below is a brief listing, along with illustrative examples, of the types of objectives of the three domains of learning.

The Cognitive Domain

1. *Knowledge*. Included at this level are objectives related to (1) knowledge of specifics such as terminology and facts; (2) knowledge of ways and means of dealing with specifics such as conventions, trends and sequences, classifications and categories, criteria, and methodologies; and (3) knowledge of universals and abstractions such as principles, generations, theories, and structures. Example: To identify the capital of France.

2. *Comprehension*. Objectives at this level include (1) translation, (2) interpretation, and (3) extrapolation of materials. Example: To interpret a table showing the population density of the world.

3. *Application*. Objectives at this level are related to the use of abstractions in particular situations. Example: To predict the probable effect of a change in temperature on a chemical.

4. *Analysis*. This includes objectives related to breaking a whole into parts and distinguishing (1) elements, (2) relationships, and (3) organizational principles. Example: To deduce facts from a hypothesis.

5. *Synthesis*. This includes objectives related to putting parts together in a new form such as (1) a unique communication, (2) a plan for operation, and (3) a set of abstract relations. Example: To produce an original piece of art.

6. *Evaluation*. This is the highest level of complexity and includes objectives related to judging in terms of (1) internal evidence or logi-

Cognitive objectives

7 Benjamin S. Bloom et al., *Taxonomy of Educational Objectives, Handbook I: Cognitive Domain* (New York: McKay, 1956).

8 David R. Krathwohl, Benjamin S. Bloom, and Bertram Masia, *Taxonomy of Educational Objectives, Handbook II: Affective Domain* (New York: McKay, 1964).

9 Anita J. Harlow, *Taxonomy of the Psychomotor Domain: A Guide for Developing Behavioral Objectives* (New York: McKay, 1972).

cal consistency and (2) external evidence or consistency with facts developed elsewhere. Example: To appraise fallacies in an argument.

The Affective Domain

1. *Receiving.* This objective is indicative of the learners' sensitivity to the existence of stimuli and includes (1) awareness, (2) willingness to receive, and (3) selected attention. Example: To recognize musical instruments played in a musical score.

2. *Responding.* This includes active attention to stimuli such as (1) acquiescence, (2) willing responses, and (3) feelings of satisfaction. Example: To contribute to group discussions by asking questions.

3. *Valuing.* Included in this objective are beliefs and attitudes of worth in the form of (1) acceptance, (2) preference, and (3) commitment. Example: To argue over an issue involving health care.

4. *Organization.* This level of internalization involves (1) conceptualization of values and (2) organization of a value system. Example: To organize a meeting concerning the women's liberation movement.

5. *Characterization.* This is the highest level of internalization and includes behavior related to (1) a generalized set of values and (2) a characterization or philosophy of life. Example: To wage war in order to preserve a way of life.

The Psychomotor Domain

1. *Reflex movements.* These objectives include (1) segmental reflexes (involving one spinal segment) and (2) intersegmental reflexes (involving more than one spinal segment). Example: To contract a muscle.

2. *Fundamental movements.* Included in these objectives are behaviors related to (1) walking, (2) running, (3) jumping, (4) pushing, (5) pulling, and (6) manipulating. Example: To run a 100-yard dash.

3. *Perceptual abilities.* These objectives include (1) kinesthetic, (2) visual, (3) auditory, (4) tactile, and (5) coordination abilities. Example: To distinguish distant and close sounds.

4. *Physical abilities.* Included at this level are objectives related to (1) endurance, (2) strength, (3) flexibility, (4) agility, (5) reaction-response time, and (6) dexterity. Example: To do five sit-ups.

5. *Skilled movements.* This includes objectives concerning (1) games, (2) sports, (3) dances, and (4) the arts. Example: To dance the basic steps of the waltz.

6. *Nondiscursive communication.* This level includes objectives related to expressive movement through (1) posture, (2) gestures, (3) facial expressions, and (4) creative movements. Example: To act a part in a play.

The categories of the three taxonomies are each related to levels of complexity from the simple to the more advanced. Each level is built upon and assumes acquisition of the previous skill. One must have knowledge of facts, for example, before he or she can comprehend material. The taxonomy as a whole is a useful source for developing educational objectives and for categorizing and grouping existing sets of objectives. Perhaps the greatest difficulty in using the taxonomy arises in making decisions between adjacent categories, particularly if the objectives have not been clearly stated. To avoid the frustration of categorizing objectives into appropriate categories, it is best for the classroom teacher to work in groups and share opinions. By studying and using the taxonomy, you may eventually appreciate it as a valuable tool in implementing objectives and formulating test items.

**Assumes
knowledge of
previous skills**

**TRENDS IN
INSTRUCTIONAL
OBJECTIVES**
Emphasis on stating learning objectives in a precise and measurable form grew out of *operant psychology* (also called associationist psychology and behavioral psychology) and related theories that analyze learning primarily in terms of organisms' responses to specific stimuli. Experiments running rats through mazes and teaching pigeons to play ping pong by controlling their rewards are frequently used to illustrate the basic principles of operant psychology. By way of contrast, *cognitive psychology* emphasizes complex intellectual processes that cannot be understood based on a simple stimulus-response (S-R) analysis of behavior. Cognitive psychologies have become a much more important element in the study of learning during the past twenty years, but psychologists and educators are still working out the implications of this shift for the construction of learning objectives and other aspects of instructional planning. The situation has been summarized by Robert Glaser as follows:

**Rooted in
animal
psychology**

In psychological research, at the present time, modern cognitive psychology is the dominant theoretical force. This is in contrast to the first half of this century when behavioristic S-R theories of learning were in ascendance. In contrast to this scientific shift, much of the application of psychological theory currently going on in schools represents the earlier behavioristic approach. The concepts of behavioral objectives and behavior modification, for example, now pervade all levels of education, including special education, elementary school instruction in basic literacy skills, and personalized systems of instruction in the university. There is a lag between research and application which is the normal condition of science. While older theory is a focus of activity in applied contexts, work on new theoretical developments is proceeding in experimental settings. However, relative to the experience of older theories, such as operant psychology, the new cognitive psychology is a fledgling with respect to the application of its findings and techniques to practical human endeavors.[10]

Thus many of the fundamental questions addressed by cognitive psychology are just beginning to be translated into practical instructional objectives and methods. What instructional approaches should be used with students who have different learning styles? How and to what degree should teachers emphasize improving students' attitudes in order to increase their time on tasks in the classroom? How should concepts be taught to students who are at different stages of development in abstract reasoning? These are the questions being asked by those who construct instructional programs designed to enhance students' learning through taking account of their unique learning styles and previous intellectual development.

Cognitive psychology

BASIC GUIDELINES   Some basic guidelines can be set for formulating your instructional objectives regardless of which approach you use.

1. Objectives should be related to aims.

2. Objectives should be appropriate to the subject and the academic level of your students.

3. Objectives should describe behaviors that you actually intend to bring about in class.

4. Objectives should be stated in the form of expected learning outcomes. (We must know precisely what is expected of students.)

5. Objectives should be stated in behavioral terms, that is, they should be observable and/or measurable.

6. Objectives should be stated through action verbs (such as, "to identify" or "to compare") so as to note finitely observable, measurable behavior.

7. Objectives should be brief, trimmed of excessive wordiness.

8. Objectives should be grouped logically so as to make sense in determining units of instruction and evaluation.

10 Robert Glaser, "Trends and Research Questions in Psychological Research on Learning and Schooling," *Educational Researcher* (November 1979), p. 12.

9. Objectives should be periodically revised.

10. In developing objectives, you should feel free to consult other sources for help.[11]

While these approaches sound very logical and appealing in designing aims and objectives, several questions come to mind. For example, whose values should be embodied in formulating the aims of the schools? Should the federal government be involved? Should state officials? Should teacher organizations or teacher representatives? And how should these groups be involved? When we move to objectives, how can both teacher and local community prerogatives be preserved and enhanced? How can communication between educators and parents be improved in the process of formulating objectives?

Other problems also arise. It is a great leap from general aims to behaviorally stated objectives. What evidence is there that those behaviors that are measured bear a reasonably close relationship to these aims? According to one observer, "The enthusiast, sometimes quite unwittingly, still confuses the technical process of stating objectives with the empirical one of establishing real rather than merely assumed relationships between a specific performance measured and a [general aim] desired."[12] The absence of adequate evidence does not destroy the validity of the above approach, but it does raise serious questions about the wisdom of forcing this approach on teachers, as some educators advocate.

Questioned relationship between aims and objectives

Whether the performances we stress and reward in school add up to our expressed aims is a difficult question to answer; in fact, many experienced educators avoid the issue. Admittedly, we lack an educational science that can derive properly inferred objectives from our stated aims even though we have the techniques for stating the objectives rather precisely. But there is no need for disillusionment—only caution. We can now move on to an examination of some of the major aims of American education.

MENTAL DISCIPLINE OR LIFE NEEDS

Prior to the twentieth century, subject matter was organized and presented as a mere accounting of information. Improvements were made largely within the broad framework of existing subjects to improve reasoning and mental faculties. It was believed that the strengthening of the mind is enhanced through mental exercises, just as the body is strengthened by exercising. Social and psychological concerns

Value of the mental discipline approach

11   Gronlund, *Stating Behavioral Objectives;* Kibler et al., *Behavioral Objectives;* David A. Payne, *The Assessment of Learning* (Lexington, Mass.: Heath, 1974); Bruce W. Tuckman, *Measuring Educational Outcomes* (New York: Harcourt Brace Jovanovich, 1975).

12   John I. Goodlad, "A Perspective on Accountability," *Phi Delta Kappan* (October 1975), p. 109.

of the learner were largely ignored. Traditional subjects, such as Latin and geometry, were valued for their cultivation of the intellect; the more difficult the subject and the more the student had to exercise the mind, the greater the value of the subject. A critic of the doctrine provided this outline of what three decades of mental discipline had produced:

> A twelve-grade scheme of housing children from the ages of six to eighteen divided into eight elementary and four secondary grades. Public secondary instruction, an accepted American doctrine, organized about a dozen or more school "subjects," and based essentially on the reading and memorizing of textbooks. The textbook in each subject, a morphological compendium . . . of facts. Mental discipline and knowledge for knowledge's sake, the dominant purposes of the school. Growth—physical, mental, and cultural development—although already . . . the basis of the reform ideas of Francis Parker, William James, and John Dewey—was totally missing from the educational philosophy of the collegiate and administrative rulers of our schools.[13]

Gradually, however, demands were made for various changes in the school to meet the needs of a changing social order. The pace of immigration and industrial development led a growing number of educators to question the classical curriculum and the constant emphasis on mental discipline and to oppose the methods of incessant drill. The adherents of the new pedagogy represented the growing and influential progressive voice in education. They emphasized schoolwork and school subjects designed to meet the needs of everyday life for *all* children.

Progressive education as a new pedagogy

This new impetus to study life needs and student needs was strongly influenced by Herbert Spencer, who argued that the principal goal of education was preparation for "complete living."[14] He advocated a curriculum based upon basic human needs—health, vocation, family, citizenship, and leisure. (See fuller discussion in Chapter 6.) Although these needs may seem obvious to most educators today, his ideas were considered a radical departure from the dogma of the advocates of mental discipline, who stressed the classical studies as well as the cultivation of the intellect over practical studies and the cultivation of the whole person. Spencer's criterion for utility and function was indeed upsetting to the advocates of literary and classic studies. He wrote:

> So terribly in our education does the ornamental override the useful [that] men who would blush if caught saying Iph-i-ǵe-nia in-

13 Harold Rugg, "Three Decades of Mental Discipline" in G. M. Whipple, ed., *The Foundations and Techniques of Curriculum Construction*, Part I, National Society for the Study of Education (Bloomington, Ill.: Public School Publishing Co., 1926), p. 33.

14 Herbert Spencer, *Education: Intellectual, Moral and Physical* (New York: Appleton, 1881).

stead of Iph-i-ge-ñia . . . show not the slightest shame in confessing that they do not know where the Eustachian tubes are.[15]

Gradually, the adherents of new educational ideals prevailed; by 1890, the movement toward reforming the schools along more progressive lines was moving into full swing. Out of this came a number of committees and organized groups whose new educational aims have been influential to the present.

CARDINAL   Perhaps the most widely accepted list of
PRINCIPLES   educational aims in the past was compiled by the Commission on the Reorganization of Secondary Education in 1918. Its influential bulletin entitled *Cardinal Principles of Secondary Education* was based on Herbert Spencer's approach. The seven areas of life or aims of secondary education designated by the commission are discussed below.

Aims during the World War I period

1. *Health.* The secondary school should . . . provide health instruction, inculcate health habits, organize an effective program of physical activities, regard health needs in planning work and play, and co-operate with home and community in safeguarding and promoting health interests. . . .

2. *Command of fundamental processes.* The facility that a child of twelve or fourteen years may acquire . . . is not sufficient for the needs of modern life. [Further instruction in the fundamentals is urged.]

Broadened aims of education

3. *Worthy home membership.* Worthy home membership as an objective calls for the development of those qualities that make the individual a worthy member of a family, both contributing to and deriving benefit from that membership. . . .

4. *Vocation.* Vocational education should equip the individual to secure a livelihood for himself and those dependent on him, to serve society well through his vocation, to maintain the right relationships toward his fellow workers and society, and, as far as possible, to find in that vocation his own best development. . . .

5. *Civic education.* Civic education should develop in the individual those qualities whereby he will act well his part as a member of neighborhood, town or city, state, and nation, and give him a basis for understanding international problems. . . .

6. *Worthy use of leisure.* Education should equip the individual to secure from his leisure the recreation of body, mind, and spirit, and the enrichment and enlargement of his personality. . . .

15   Ibid., p. 43.

7. *Ethical character.* In a democratic society ethical character becomes paramount among the objectives of the secondary school. Among the means for developing ethical character may be mentioned the wise selection of content and methods of instruction in all subjects of study and the social contacts of pupils with one another and with their teachers.[16]

The goals cited in 1918 are still to be found in one form or another in statements of major goals of contemporary education, as may be noted by the discussion to follow. The most important aspect of the document is that it emphasizes the aim of secondary schools to educate *all* youth for "complete living," not just college-bound youth for mental vigor. The commission noted that more than two-thirds of entering high school students dropped out prior to graduation. It endorsed the concept of meeting the various and diverse needs of students, while providing a common ground for teaching and enhancing American ideals and educating all citizens to function in a democratic society.

Educate all youth for "complete living"

PURPOSES OF EDUCATION IN AMERICAN DEMOCRACY Twenty years later the Educational Policies Commission of the NEA, which included the presidents of Harvard and Cornell, the Commissioner of Education, and a number of progressive pedagogical specialists, issued a report in 1938 entitled *The Purposes of Education in American Democracy.*[17]

Concerned with the problems of out-of-school youth and unemployment resulting from the Great Depression and the general need to adjust to daily life patterns, these educators put forth a comprehensive set of four aims (which they called objectives): (1) self-realization, (2) human relations, (3) economic efficiency, and (4) civil responsibility. The objectives of *self-realization* included the inquiring mind, speech, reading, writing, numbers, sight and hearing, health knowledge, health habits, public health, recreation, intellectual interests, aesthetic interests, and character formation. The objectives of *human relationships* included respect for humanity, friendships, cooperation with others, courtesy, appreciation of the home, conservation of the home, homemaking, and, democracy in the home. The objectives of *economic efficiency* included work, occupational information, occupational choice, occupational efficiency, occupational appreciation, personal economics, consumer judgment, efficiency in buying, and consumer protection. The objectives of *civic responsibility* included social justice, social activity, social understanding, critical

Aims in the 1930s

16 Commission on the Reorganization of Secondary Education, *Cardinal Principles of Secondary Education*, Bulletin no. 35 (Washington, D.C.: U.S. Government Printing Office, 1918), pp. 11–15.
17 Educational Policies Commission, *The Purposes of Education in American Democracy* (Washington, D.C.: National Education Association, 1938).

Young children need a teacher's understanding and empathy in order to feel that education is a positive force in their lives.

judgment, tolerance, conservation of resources, social applications of science, world citizenship, law observance, economic literacy, political citizenship, and devotion to democracy.

EDUCATION FOR ALL
AMERICAN YOUTH

During the mid-1940s the Educational Policies Commission continued to modify and formulate the aims of education. Influenced by World War II, they subsequently stressed aims related to democracy and world citizenship, as well as those related to the general needs of children and youth. Their most influential report, *Education for All American Youth* listed "Ten Imperative Needs of Youth." All youth need to:

Aims in the 1940s

1. Develop salable skills and those understandings and attitudes that make the worker an intelligent and productive participant in economic life. To this end, most youth need supervised work experience as well as education in the skills and knowledge of their occupations.

2. Develop and maintain good health and physical fitness.

3. Understand the rights and duties of a citizen of a democratic society and be diligent and competent in the performance of their obligations as members of the community and citizens of the state and nation and of the world.

4. Understand the significance of the family for the individual and society and the conditions conducive to successful family life.

5. Know how to purchase and use goods and services intelligently, understanding both the value received by the consumer and the economic consequence of their acts.

6. Understand the methods of science, the influence of science on human life, and the main scientific facts concerning the nature of the world and man.

7. Have opportunities to develop their capacities to appreciate beauty in literature, art, music, and nature.

8. Be able to use their leisure time well and budget it wisely, balancing activities that yield satisfaction to the individual with those that are socially useful.

9. Develop respect for other persons, grow in their insight into ethical values and principles, and be able to live and work cooperatively with others.

10. Grow in their ability to think rationally, express their thoughts clearly, and read and listen with understanding.[18]

From the 1918 Seven Cardinal Principles to the 1944 Ten Imperative Needs, the aims are representative of an era dominated by the philosophy of Progressivism and by the offshoot science of child psychology. During this period, emphasis was placed on the "whole child" and life adjustment; hence, these aims stressed social, psychological, vocational, moral, and civic responsibilities. The whole-child concept and the corresponding growth of child psychology had a tremendous impact on the schools. Underlying this movement was the view that schools had to be concerned with the growth and development of the entire child, not just with certain selected mental aspects of the child's growth. In any learning situation the total organism responds; the whole child learns. When a child is involved in intellectual pursuits, his or her whole being is involved; the child cannot disengage the emotions, feelings, and social and physical competencies.

"Whole-child" concept

Aims related to cognitive or mental growth were not considered preeminent at this time. They were on a par with other important aims of education. To be sure, the traditional emphasis on the "three Rs" and mental discipline faded into the background as observers of education interpreted and commented on the expanding functions of the schools. Most educators viewed these broad aims as an inevitable and undirected

The three Rs fade into the background

18 Educational Policies Commission, *Education for All American Youth* (Washington, D.C.: National Education Association, 1944), pp. 225-26.

expansion of the schools—a kind of residual growth—resulting from the schools' inherited responsibility for meeting the needs and problems of students that the family and other social agencies failed or declined to meet. Others, primarily critics, viewed these expanding functions of the school as a move on the part of educators to usurp responsibilities belonging to other segments of the society and to divorce the schools from the primary aim of teaching children how to think. Among some groups the pendulum was beginning to swing back to an emphasis on cognitive processes.

FOCUS ON THE ACADEMICALLY TALENTED

None of the aforementioned aims seems controversial. But after World War II, during the era of the Cold War and the Soviet Sputnik flight, these aims became a target of criticism. The critics claimed that there was too much stress on the "whole child" and general education at the expense of schooling for intellectual rigor. On the other hand, the influential Harvard Report, published at the end of World War II, looked forward optimistically to an era of educating the whole person. This was seen as the means for developing the understanding that all citizens in a free society must have in common despite their intellectual differences. According to the Report, education must aim at producing good and useful citizens through a general broad education.[19]

Effects of Cold War and Sputnik era

But powerful forces called for a return to academic essentials and mental discipline. "Concern with the personal problems of adolescents [had] grown so excessive as to push into the background what should be the school's central concern, the intellectual development of its students," stated noted historian Arthur Bestor.[20] Admiral Hyman Rickover questioned why Johnny could not read while Ivan could and did. He demanded that in the national interest, there be a return to the basics, a beefing up of our science and mathematics courses, and a "de-emphasis of life-adjustment schools and progressive educationalists."[21]

Return to academic essentials

Werner von Braun, the German-educated missile expert, testified before a U.S. Senate Committee in 1958 in the same vein. He urged the adoption of the European system of education, which emphasized academic excellence. Then he went on to reminisce about his own education:

I do not remember that I ever attended any classes in Europe on "family life" or "human relations," or subjects like "boy-girl rela-

19 Report of the Harvard Committee, *General Education in a Free Society* (Cambridge, Mass.: Harvard University Press, 1945).
20 Arthur Bestor, *The Restoration of Learning* (New York: Knopf, 1956), p. 120.
21 Hyman G. Rickover, *Education and Freedom* (New York: Dutton, 1959), p. 190.

tions at college." We just learned reading, writing, and arithmetic in the lower schools. Later on they taught us technical and scientific subjects, *but nothing else* [italics added].[22]

Testifying before the same committee on the same day, Lee Du-Bridge, then president of the California Institute of Technology, recommended that curriculum areas of science and mathematics be "singled out for federal support." DuBridge urged that schools recognize, encourage, and provide special programs for students who are "unusually gifted and ambitious." The pursuit of excellence was stressed, perhaps even overstressed, with this comment:

The pursuit of excellence

> The right of a student to an education is a right which persists as far as his intellectual capacities and his ambitions should take him. This might be the sixth grade in the case of an unfortunate individual, and it might be the doctor of philosophy degree for someone favored by intellectual capabilities.[23]

Unfortunately, the senators did not ask von Braun or DuBridge what schools or society should do with the intellectually less able student. These positions regarding the pursuit of excellence were characteristic of many scientists and mathematicians, as well as of many conservative critics of the day. A relatively more moderate position, but one that still emphasized the gifted and intelligent student, was evidenced by a number of other well-known educators.

John Gardner, the president of the Carnegie Corporation, expressed the crucial need of the day in his 1956 annual report:

> It is not just technologists and scientists that we need, though they rank high in priority. We desperately need our gifted teachers, our professional men, our scholars, our critics, and our seers. . . . As the cradle of our national leadership, their vitality and excellence become a matter of critical importance.
>
> Concern for the full use of human capacities will produce intensive efforts to salvage the able youngsters who are now lost to higher education.[24]

Shift in emphasis to the gifted

In 1952, as Chairman of the Educational Policies Commission, James Conant had endorsed a progressive policy document that urged a student-centered, whole-child approach to schooling. By 1959 Conant's vision was still to "provide a good general education for *all* the pupils," but

22 *Science and Education for National Defense*, Hearings before the Committee of Labor and Public Welfare, United States Senate, Eighty-Eighth Congress (Washington, D.C.: U.S. Government Printing Office, 1958), p. 65.

23 Ibid., pp. 39, 54.

24 John W. Gardner, "The Great Talent Hunt," in the *Annual Report for the Fiscal Year Ended September 30, 1956* (New York: Carnegie Corporation, 1956), pp. 12, 20.

there was also an emphasis now on "educating adequately those with a talent for handling advanced subjects."[25] After visiting fifty-five high schools across the country, he concluded:

> If the fifty-five schools I have visited, all of which have a good reputation, are at all representative of American public high schools, I think one general criticism would be in order: The academically talented student, as a rule, is not being sufficiently challenged, does not work hard enough, and his program of academic subjects is not of sufficient range.[26]

Although Conant gave some consideration to slow learners, his major emphasis for reform was related to ability grouping and serving the needs of the highly gifted (the intellectually highest 3 percent of the student population on a national basis), and the academically talented (the next 20 percent in terms of scholastic aptitude). **Ability grouping**

A number of policy statements focused on the academically bright student during this period, although each expressed concern for every child, whatever his or her capabilities. Various aims were listed, but great emphasis was placed on identifying and developing the abilities of the talented, as well as on the three Rs and on academic subjects such as English, foreign languages, science, and mathematics.

For example, the White House Conference on Education in 1955 stressed the theme of quality and proposed that "educational programs [must] fully exercise and develop the abilities of especially bright students."[27] Five years later the President's Commission on National Goals gave top priority to science, mathematics, and foreign languages and called for "a testing program beginning in grade one if not before . . . and ability grouping from the earliest years of school. Every effort [was to be] made in and out of school to provide enrichment for the gifted student."[28] **Priority to academic subjects and testing**

FOCUS ON DISADVANTAGED STUDENTS During the aforementioned era, student financial aid and college scholarship programs were mainly provided for students who evidenced academic merit and ability. But the 1960s ushered in a period in which the social conscience of America burst forth—coinciding with our concern over poverty, racial discrimination, and equal educational opportunity. Hence, new aims and educational priorities surfaced to meet

25 James B. Conant, *The American High School Today* (New York: McGraw-Hill, 1959), p. 15.

26 Ibid., p. 40.

27 *Proceedings, White House Conference on Education* (Washington, D.C.: U.S. Government Printing Office, 1955), p. 12.

28 *Goals for Americans*, The President's Commission on National Goals (Englewood Cliffs, N.J.: Prentice-Hall, 1960), p. 85.

the climate of change. With the majority of students not going on to college, and with a large percentage of students dropping out of school or graduating as functional illiterates, serious problems could be anticipated if our aims and priorities continued to be narrowly directed at our most able students. The shift to the problems of disadvantaged students gradually accelerated until this population became the number-one concern in education. The swing was exemplified by the changes in the writings of the same educators—John Gardner and James Conant—who previously had stressed the need to challenge the gifted student.

At first the shift was gradual, and this can be illustrated by John Gardner's concern for both the talented and underachieving child, for both excellence and equality. Questioning whether we can be equal and excellent too, he reviewed the problem in these terms:

> We might as well admit that it is not easy for us as believers in democracy to dwell on the differences in capacity between men. Democratic philosophy has tended to ignore such differences where possible, and to belittle them where it could not ignore them. And it has some grounds for doing so: the enemies of democracy have often cited the unequal capacities of man as an excuse for institutions which violate our most deeply held beliefs. [But] extreme equalitarianism—or as I would prefer to say *equalitarianism wrongly conceived*—which ignores differences in native capacity and achievement, has not served democracy well. Carried far enough, it means the . . . end of that striving for excellence which has produced mankind's greatest achievement . . . no democracy can give itself over to extreme emphasis on individual performance and still remain a democracy—or to extreme equalitarianism and retain its vitality. . . .
>
> A society such as ours has no choice but to seek the development of human potentialities at all levels. It takes more than an educated elite to run a complex, technological society. Every modern, industrialized society is learning that hard lesson.[29]

The issues Gardner raised were those that directly affected the social fabric of the country; these issues later gave rise to equal opportunity legislation and affirmative action policies. Gardner noted that extreme forms of equalitarianism and proportional representation of groups in school or jobs tend to eliminate both excellence and merit, but that, on the other hand, extreme forms of elitism based on excellence and merit could create a permanent underclass among the less able. He tried to draw a middle position, sounding a note of urgency that other educators would soon note.

29   John W. Gardner, *Excellence: Can We Be Equal and Excellent Too?* (New York: Harper & Row, 1961), pp. 14–15, 74, 77.

The same year that John Gardner's book was published, James Conant wrote *Slums and Suburbs*. Only two years before, Conant had advocated academic rigor and upgraded academic subjects, as well as greater attention to the top 20 percent of the high school graduates. Now he was urging educators and policy makers to pay closer attention to the inner-city and disadvantaged child. He was urging that slum schools be upgraded and greater attention be given to the less able student. Conant wrote:

Closer attention to the disadvantaged child

> I am concerned we are allowing social dynamite to accumulate in our large cities. I am not nearly so concerned about the plight of the suburban parents [and their children] who have difficulty finding places in prestige colleges as I am about the plight of parents in the slums whose children either drop out or graduate from school without prospects of either future education or employment. . . . Leaving aside human tragedies, I submit that a continuation of this situation [youth out of school and out of work] is a menace to the social and political health of the large cities.
>
> The improvement of slum conditions is only in part a question of improving education. But the role of the schools is of utmost importance. . . . Added responsibility, however, requires additional funds. Indeed, the whole question of financing public education in the large cities is a major national concern.[30]

Conant's new position was a sign of the times—a shift in educational aims to focus on the disadvantaged. Historically a strong advocate of excellence, a former scientist who tried to combine academic rigor with the social development of the whole child, he was expressing a new viewpoint: one that would correct the educational discrepancies among students by placing greater emphasis on less able students.

Given the student unrest and urban riots of the 1960s, it was easy to accept the arguments of an impacted crisis in schools and society. The government reports that were published in the 1960s strongly suggested an impending social upheaval. The needs of disadvantaged groups were stressed, both in schools and society, and these needs were reflected in such reports as the 1967 National Advisory Commission on Civil Disorders, the 1969 National Advisory Council on the Education of Disadvantaged Children, the 1970 HEW Urban Task Force Report, the 1972 President's Commission on School Finance, and the 1973 Brookings Report on *Setting National Priorities*. A new political bias seemed to evolve; in education it overlooked the average and above-average student, and in social and economic arenas it overlooked what was later to be called "middle America." As a result of this "new politics," it sometimes was

Social upheaval of the 1960s

30   James B. Conant, *Slums and Suburbs* (New York: McGraw-Hill, 1961), p. 2.

viewed as meanspirited (and, by and large, it still is) to reject the social welfare reform strategies of the day.

Modifying our priorities As we enter the new decade we are still witnessing great concern for the disadvantaged student from prekindergarten to the university level, illustrated by large-scale funding and a host of programs. At the same time, we also are experiencing a renewed interest in the education of gifted and talented students. Concern for the gifted student reached a low point during the 1960s but began to increase again during the late 1970s.[31] Much of this renewed concern was due to initiatives undertaken by former U.S. Commissioner of Education Sidney Marland, who submitted a 1972 report to Congress recommending greater emphasis on education of gifted children and offering a broadened conception of giftedness defined as follows: "Children capable of high performance include those with demonstrated achievement and/or potential ability in any of the following areas: (a) general intellectual ability, (b) specific academic aptitude, (c) creative or productive thinking, (d) leadership ability, (e) visual and performing arts, and (f) psychomotor ability."[32]

Interest in the
gifted student
increases

The commitment to educating the gifted and talented child and the average child in the 1980s, however, still is slight compared to efforts directed at the disadvantaged. As two authorities stated, only "a very small percentage of the gifted and talented population [is] being serviced by existing programs, [about] 4 percent of the 1.5 to 2.5 million children."[33] A low funding priority and lack of trained personnel, coupled with the focus on the disadvantaged, result in few programs for these youth who in terms of numbers represent a real minority. Most of us just assume that talented and gifted students will all graduate from college and find good jobs.

As of fiscal year 1980, federal funding was $6.5 *million* for the gifted and talented, compared to $3.2 *billion* for the disadvantaged, and another billion or more in related programs. These include Bilingual Education, Right to Read, Follow-Through, Emergency School Assistance Act, Teacher Corps, Early Childhood Education, and a good share of the $2.1 billion for higher education in terms of scholarships and loans.

Discrepancies
in funding
student groups

And what about our aims and priorities for the average, ordinary student who is nonrich, nonpoor, and non-newsworthy? While the theme of "unmeltable ethnics" is beginning to evolve, there is still little today in the educational literature, especially in comparison to the "underdog"

31 Abraham J. Tannenbaum, "Pre-Sputnik to Post-Watergate Concern About the Gifted" in A. Harry Passow, ed., *The Gifted and the Talented: Their Education and Development* (Chicago: University of Chicago Press, 1979), pp. 5–27.

32 Sidney P. Marland, *Education of the Gifted and Talented* (Washington, D.C.: U.S. Government Printing Office, 1972), p. 2. Also see David Feldman, "Toward a Nonelitist Conception of Giftedness," *Phi Delta Kappan* (May 1979), pp. 660–63.

33 A. Harry Passow and Abraham J. Tannenbaum, "Education of the Gifted and Talented," *National Association of Secondary School Principals* (March 1976), pp. 4–5. Also see John C. Gowan, Joe Khatena, and E. Paul Torrance, *On the Education of Gifted Children* (Itasca, Ill.: Peacock, 1979).

literature of the disadvantaged and minority student, that notes the cultural and ethnic diversity of students of middle America—what it is like to grow up in Astoria, New York; Lombard, Illinois; Des Moines, Iowa; Whittier, California. There is little recognition that there are hundreds of thousands, actually millions, of students from working-class and middle-class families who are in desperate need of educational assistance. True, some assistance is available in their schools, but because educators are not focusing on them, the remedial programs for these students are minimal. Since the late 1970s some attention unwittingly has been devoted to them as a result of other trends, such as minimum competency testing and basic skills programs, but the programs for the average child per se are minimal and the funding is even less.

Minimal assistance for average student

EDUCATIONAL AIMS OF THE 1970s AND 1980s

Coinciding with concern for the disadvantaged, as well as with equalitarian movements in schools and society, some additional problems facing society began to emerge by the late 1960s and continued into the past decade. A frustrating war in Vietnam was dividing the nation at home, and a more militant civil rights movement was emerging. An era of minority and youth unrest descended on the schools, followed by dissatisfaction among female students concerning women's status and sex discrimination. Alienation and disillusionment with society and dissatisfaction with formal schooling were apparent. Crime and violence plagued our streets and schools. Then the economy went into a tailspin. High school and college graduates found themselves underemployed or unemployed. Prices soared, and working-class and middle-class wage earners felt new economic burdens. The ranks of the unemployed grew larger. Frustration and bitterness permeated the social order. With the new social discontent came new demands on schools and colleges and new priorities.

Several major policy reports and national commissions appeared, pointing out that the schools were in crisis and were in need of sweeping reform. The new aims and recommendations were hard-hitting. The traditional method of schooling was considered outdated, and there was recognition of the need to provide alternative modes of education. Some of the policy statements extended beyond the school walls and had political implications.

Schools in crisis

In its 1973 report entitled *The Reform of Secondary Education*, the National Commission on the Reform of Secondary Education (commonly called the Kettering Commission) observed that big-city high schools, which had once been the best in the nation, were now "on the verge of complete collapse."[34] The commission expressed concern that the schools

Predicament of big-city schools

34 National Commission on the Reform of Secondary Education, *The Reform of Secondary Education* (New York: McGraw-Hill, 1973).

seemed exhausted and irrelevant, unable to cope with the changes of society. It particularly noted that "crime [and drugs] had become part of the normal experience in many high schools" and fewer than half the enrolled students attended classes regularly in many schools.

The commission listed thirty-two recommendations for reforming schools. Several of them centered around racial and sexual biases in the curriculum, in counseling, and in the instructional and administrative process. Career education and career opportunities were stressed, along with a variety of alternative educational programs including credit for life experience. Security measures to combat growing school violence, along with student codes and rights, were listed. The schools were urged to realign the curricula to provide a broad range of activities and experiences; it was recommended that students receive a "global education," one that "is concerned with scientific, ecological, and economic issues which affect everyone."[35] The most controversial recommendation was to change the compulsory school-leaving age to fourteen years so as to alleviate the custodial nature of the schools. The commission members recognized the implications of this recommendation and urged that real alternatives for employment and other modes of education and job training be developed first.

The U.S. Office of Education, in a 1974 report, concluded that high schools have become inappropriate institutions for a growing number of students "who are either too old or too mature to live under the routine of controls and structures . . . without serious disturbances to them and to the school."[36] The USOE Panel recognized that we have nearly realized our equalitarian belief in universal education for all youth, that the high schools have a diversity of programs for their diverse student populations. Nonetheless, the panel pointed out, schools prolong adolescent dependency and isolate youth "from the reality of the community and the adult world."[37] The 1976 final report of the panel also criticized the high schools for "retaining controls and supervisory practices more in keeping with the costly custodial care of masses of children in large institutions than with developing the potentials and increasing maturity for self-direction of young adults."[38] Thus while the USOE Panel recognized that our society has nearly completed the monumental task of providing universal schooling at the secondary level, it was disturbed by the way we isolate youth and delay adult roles and work habits.

35 National Commission on the Reform of Secondary Education, *The Reform of Secondary Education*, p. 64.

36 U.S. Office of Education, *Report of the National Panel on High School and Adolescent Education* (Washington, D.C.: U.S. Government Printing Office, 1974), p. 7.

37 U.S. Office of Education, *Report of the National Panel on High School and Adolescent Education*, p. 47.

38 U.S. Office of Education, *The Education of Adolescents* (Washington, D.C.: U.S. Government Printing Office, 1976), p. 5.

The panel dealt with the question of aims in terms of five domains: (1) personal values, (2) citizenship education, (3) the arts, (4) the humanities, and (5) career education. It argued that the schools have focused primarily on cognitive skills and have failed two basic missions—citizenship and career education. To fulfill these latter missions, the panel urged the creation of community-based sites and programs for civic purposes and satellite centers to provide youth with the experience of work.

The 1974 Report of the Panel on Youth of the President's Science Advisory Committee, *Youth: Transition to Adulthood* (often referred to as the President's Panel, or Coleman II after its chairman, James Coleman), raised questions about the incomplete nature of schooling for the accomplishment of many important facets of youth maturation.[39] The President's Panel noted that students were bored with school, and that their peer culture was in conflict with the established process of schooling.

The President's Panel proposed sweeping organizational changes of the schools: limiting the student population to 500 per school, various alternative forms of education, and the simultaneous enrollment by students in more than one school at a time. Schools would be reconstructed around special talents and interests of youth, and all youth over age sixteen would be required to experience a wide range of skill and job training programs, using the community's resources for work and study. It also expressed concern over the point when societal controls over youth cease to be legitimate protections of the welfare of young people and become unwarranted restraints. How diverse must schools become to facilitate youth transition to adulthood? How should schools be organized to deal with the socialization and development of youth? These questions were raised; they were not fully answered.

How to facilitate youth to adult transition

The National Association of Secondary School Principals' report, *American Youth in the Mid-Seventies*, expressed concern that "formal schooling is doing nothing for a large part of the young adult population 16 through 20—they've dropped out—and it is not going very well for another larger group, those who stay on in school, graduate, but get little from it."[40] Even "successful" students, who receive good grades, are bored with school. The NASSP report discussed the financial plight of the schools, student disruptions, employment trends, integration and racial balance, and the need for school-community involvement. Its major recommendations revolved around fostering "action-learning" experiences outside school in paid or unpaid jobs or in personal performance that could be assessed and accredited by an educational institution. These action-

Learning experiences outside school

39   James S. Coleman et al., *Youth: Transition to Adulthood*, Report of the Panel on Youth of the President's Science Advisory Committee (Chicago: University of Chicago Press, 1974). Also see Chapter 9.

40   *American Youth in the Mid-Seventies* (Washington, D.C.: National Association of Secondary School Principals, 1973).

learning experiences were viewed as a desirable alternative to classroom study, as well as a complementary activity. Opportunities of this kind would be provided to all youth, for some on a part-time basis and for potential dropouts on a full-time basis.

The National Education Association, looking toward education in the 1980s and beyond, organized a panel to reexamine and update the 1918 Cardinal Principles of Secondary Education. The panel first acknowledged that the 1918 principles had provided a general statement of goals for all of U.S. education, not just the secondary schools, and proceeded to suggest modifications in line with developments of the recent past and emerging imperatives of the future. In a 1977 book, panel members made some broad observations concerning the context of curriculum goals for the future.[41] Among other things, panelists suggested that:

Goals for the future

(1) The 1918 goals did not sufficiently recognize that the schools do not educate in isolation but in conjunction with the home, the media, and other institutions. For this reason, educators should not "over-promise" what they can do, and must be sensible in deciding what schools can accomplish.

(2) Education must be viewed more as a total learning system extending beyond the school walls.

(3) More emphasis should be placed on problems caused by the growing importance of the mass media as an influence on students.

(4) More recognition must be given to the need for lifelong learning, from early childhood through old age.

(5) Social and academic goals of the school should not be completely separated. Youth need to be taught coping skills and technological skills as part of their academic preparation.

(6) Education must develop a spirit of "global" belonging in an interdependent world. This should include recognition of the need for multicultural and multilingual education in the U.S. and abroad.

A 1979 report by the prestigious Carnegie Council on Policy Studies in Higher Education came to many of the same conclusions as had the studies cited above. Concerned particularly with secondary education for the 1980s, the 332-page report concluded among other things that: (1) compulsory schooling should be ended at age 16 and a work-study program should be available to low-income youth; (2) juniors and seniors should attend regular classes three days a week and devote two other days a week to education-related work or community service; and (3) new ap-

Work or community service

41 Harold G. Shane, *Curriculum Change Toward the 21st Century* (Washington, D.C.: National Education Association, 1977).

prenticeship programs should be established for sixteen- and seventeen-year-olds. The council also recommended increased attention to teaching basic skills in high school and establishment of a national educational fund from which people could draw financial credits for schooling throughout their lives. Actions along these lines, the council said, would correct some of the serious inequities caused by the fact that U.S. society allocates increasing resources to young people enrolled in higher education while less adequate resources are allocated to those who do not enroll in college. Such action thereby also might counteract future trends toward the creation of a "permanent underclass and a self-perpetuating culture of poverty."[42]

All of the reports cited above were critical of American schools, particularly the secondary schools. Heavy emphasis was placed on creating and utilizing nonschool learning environments, as well as on greater linkages between social and community agencies and the school. The reports advocated curriculum changes to provide students with a greater range of experiences and options, and to permit them to take advantage of career opportunities. Questions of reform extending beyond the school walls and involving the larger society were examined, too, especially those concerning equal opportunity by race and sex and by social class.

Reform beyond school walls

CHANGING AIMS OF EDUCATION

The aims of education have been changing, reflecting an increase in criticism of the public schools. When the schools were attacked in the 1950s, voices of moderation invariably pointed out that the schools were doing a relatively good job and there was no need for a major change. Two years after the Russians launched Sputnik, James Conant provided educators with necessary recommendations for improving the schools, but assured us that "no radical alteration in the basic pattern of American education [was] necessary to improve our public high schools."[43] By the 1970s there was perhaps no one of similar stature in education assuring us that the schools were doing an adequate job.

Twenty-five years ago criticism and demands for reform came mainly from conservative voices. In the 1960s the pendulum had swung to the other side, and the criticism and cries for reform could be heard from the political left. By the 1970s it seemed that many groups along the entire political continuum had reached the conclusion that something was wrong with the educational process, and that more than bandages were

Many groups are criticizing the schools

42 Carnegie Council on Policy Studies in Higher Education, *Giving Youth a Better Chance: Options for Education, Work and Service. Summary of Concerns and Recommendations* (Washington, D.C.: Carnegie Council on Policy Studies in Higher Education, 1979), p. 4.

43 Conant, *The American High School Today*, p. 40.

needed to mend the cracks in the school wall (although there was disagreement on what was specifically wrong and needed).[44]

SWINGS OF THE PENDULUM

In examining the aims of education from the turn of the twentieth century until today, we see considerable reiteration, but we also note considerable evolvement: from education for mental discipline to individual enlightenment, from the emphasis on college-oriented students to non-college-oriented students. These aims appear to be linked to the sweep of social change. For example, the early twentieth-century adherents of mental discipline advocated rigorous intellectual training, as did the Essentialist critics and moderate reformers in the 1950s. At the turn of the century public schools stressed a college-oriented curriculum, and this curriculum priority reappeared during the era of the Cold War and space race. In the early 1900s progressive educators sought to broaden the aims of school to serve all children and youth, especially non-college and vocationally oriented students; beginning with the early 1960s and into the 1970s this priority reappeared with emphasis on poor and minority students. Although the label "career education" replaced vocational education, the functional value of schools in terms of jobs was again considered.

Old ideas with new labels

In looking at the broad sweep of American educational aims you may ask yourself the question: Are the schools expected to do more than is feasible? Increasingly, the schools are being burdened by the rest of society with roles and responsibilities that other agencies and institutions no longer do very well, or, for that matter, want to do.[45] The schools are seen as ideal agencies to solve the nation's problems. With this perspective, many people refuse to admit to their own responsibilities in helping children develop their capabilities and adjust to society. More and more, the schools are being told that they must educate *all* children, regardless of the initial input.

The importance of social pressure and various interest groups also needs to be stressed. As society changes, and as different groups seek to further their interests and promote their causes, the aims of education must change. Thus, rarely will there be complete agreement on the aims of education, much less on what the schools should teach. Popular rhetoric and slogans of the day, as well as the demands of interest groups, must be balanced by a consideration for the good of the general public.

Demands of interest groups

So long as society is dynamic and composed of a conglomeration of cultural and social groups, the debate over the means and ends of education will stir up controversy. Perhaps this is good; perhaps this is what makes a society viable and able to resist decay. Indeed, this controversy is

44 Mary Anne Raywid, "The Novel Character of Today's School Criticism," *Educational Leadership* (December 1979), pp. 200-03.

45 Mary Haywood Metz, *Classrooms and Corridors* (Berkeley, Calif.: University of California, 1978), John Henry Martin, "Reconsidering the Goals of High School Education," *Educational Leadership* (January 1980), pp. 278-85.

as old as western civilization itself. More than 2,000 years ago Aristotle wrote:

> As things are . . . mankind [is] by no means agreed about the existing things to be taught. The existing practice is perplexing, no one knowing on what principle we should proceed. . . . About the means there is no agreement; for different persons, starting with different ideas about the nature of virtue, naturally disagree about the practice of it.[46]

Unquestionably, aims of education must be relevant or meaningful to the times. If the schools are not adaptable to changing conditions and social forces, how can they expect to produce people who are? This issue is pointedly illustrated in a satire on education entitled *The Saber-Tooth Curriculum*.[47] It describes a society in which the major tasks for survival were catching fish to eat, clubbing horses, and frightening away saber-tooth tigers. The school in this society set up a curriculum to meet its needs: namely, teaching courses in these three areas of survival. Eventually conditions changed: the streams dried up, and the horses and tigers disappeared. Social change necessitated learning new tasks for survival, but the school curriculum continued to feature catching fish, clubbing horses and frightening saber-toothed tigers.

Education must be relevant

Today we live in a highly technical, automated, and bureaucratic society; we are faced with pressing social problems—racial polarization, economic inequality, and pollution of the physical environment. These forces and trends are highly interrelated, mutually reinforce each other, and occur with increasing acceleration. You will not have the luxury of leisurely contemplation. In an era of space technology and computers you cannot continue to advocate catching fish. Whether we allow the times to engulf us, or whether we can cope with our new environment will depend to a large extent on what kinds of skills are taught to our present-day students.

Coping with the times

SUMMING UP

1. We must learn to live with some disagreement about what the schools are all about and what the aims of education should be.

2. We must remember that as society changes so do the needs of education.

3. We should keep in mind the many achievements and positive aspects of the educational system in the United States. One of the major accomplishments includes the fact that education through the sec-

---

46 *The Works of Aristotle, Politics*, Book VIII, trans. B. Jowett (Oxford: Clarendon Press, 1921), p. 1338.

47 Harold Benjamin, *The Saber-Tooth Curriculum* (New York: McGraw-Hill, 1939).

ondary level has been made available to the vast majority of students.

4. But it also is important that educators do not allow the changes to merely "happen" or to occur by default. Aims of education must be planned—and made to happen—if they are to result in appropriate improvements in education and abilities to cope with changes in society.

5. As we enter the 1980s, one of the chief aims of society seems to be that the schools become a key instrument for solving our social ills. The years ahead will severely test this aim.

6. We have plenty of debaters, critics, and extremists; what we need are more problem solvers who are responsible and committed to the values we profess to cherish as a nation. We need educators who are aware of social, economic, and political trends and who are able to work with others in developing and continuously modifying the aims of education to prepare youth and our future leaders for life in a rapidly changing world.

DISCUSSION QUESTIONS

1. In terms of aims and objectives, why is the question "What are schools for?" so complex?

2. Why is the bulletin *Cardinal Principles of Secondary Education* such an important milestone in American education? How did it differ from later approaches or reports? Do the seven principles seem valid today?

3. Are the proposed objectives of the Educational Policies Commission, set forth in *The Purpose of Education in American Democracy* and *Education for all American Youth*, desirable objectives for education today? How might you modify them?

4. Who should have educational priority: underachievers, average students, or above-average students?

5. Why is it important for the aims of education to change as society changes?

THINGS TO DO

1. Set forth your own statement of the central aims of education appropriate for today. How important are your own values in formulating these aims?

2. Write five behavioral objectives according to the Mager approach. Then categorize each one according to an appropriate cognitive and affective level within the taxonomy.

3. Develop a panel to debate the question: "Can a society stress equality and excellence?"

4. Given a school of 1,000 students with one third of the student body as disadvantaged learners, one third as average learners, and one third as gifted learners, how would you allocate—if you had the authority—$200,000 for special programs?

5. Visit one or two schools to observe in actual teaching practice the pursuit of the aims of education and/or policy recommendations about which you have read in this chapter. Talk to teachers involved in instruction about what they are attempting to do. Summarize what you have observed and compare the professor's views in your class.

CHAPTER 13
CURRICULUM FOR
THE SCHOOLS

Focusing questions

How does curriculum content reflect changes in society?

What forces affect curriculum change?

How might your work as a teacher be different in a school that utilizes team teaching? flexible scheduling? computerized instruction?

Why are matters of content change more often controversial than matters of instructional change?

What are some emerging and future trends affecting curriculum?

Americans—perhaps more than citizens of any other country—have demanded the utmost from their schools. We ask the schools to teach children to think, to socialize them, to alleviate poverty and inequality, to reduce crime, to perpetuate our cultural heritage, and to produce intelligent, patriotic citizens. Inevitably, American schools have been unable to meet all of these obligations. Nonetheless, the American public continues to demand much from its schools, and it is the curriculum—the planned experiences provided through instruction—which is the focal point of these demands. Consequently, the curriculum is continuously being modified as the goals and objectives of the schools are revised, as student populations change, as issues are debated, as interest groups are activated, and as society changes in general. Keep these concepts in mind as we sweep through time in this chapter to note the shifts in curriculum and to put our curricular heritage in perspective in order to better understand the present and envisage the future.

**HISTORICAL
INFLUENCES**

Part Two examined the historical development of the American schools. Here we will briefly summarize the historical factors that shaped curriculum. A changing society demands changes in education, which, in turn, require changes in the curriculum. That is to say, as the role of schools changes, the aims and objectives are modified and so is the curriculum. By analyzing the historical trends in curriculum, we may better understand the themes that pervade curriculum today.

A changing society requires curriculum changes

As noted in Chapter 7, three different regional attitudes toward the functions of education arose during colonial times. In the New England colonies education was considered to be the responsibility of the commonwealth. The middle Atlantic colonies tended to keep education as a function of the local community, or more precisely, the local religious denominational group. In the southern colonies, responsibility for education was left to the family. With the exception of the rich, who could afford private education, parental neglect of children's education was evident in the South. In general, the major purpose of education during the colonial years was to meet the needs of religion; the learning of the catechism and various prayers was a part of the reading program. As the schools evolved, the three Rs were stressed, and the practical values of reading, writing, and doing simple mathematical sums were associated with the new occupations and apprenticeship programs.

Early religious and three R emphasis

Instruction was usually inadequate; it consisted mostly of rote recitations and oral readings. Attitudes toward children were steeped in Calvinist traditions. Children were born in sin, and it was the function of the teacher (and other adults) to beat the sin out of them.[1] The famous *New*

1 Ellwood P. Cubberly, *Public Education in the United States* (Boston: Houghton Mifflin, 1934).

England Primer was the most used book in colonial schools for more than a hundred years; all the editions contained the alphabet, some sounds and syllables. The content was of a religious nature. It has been estimated that more than 3 million copies of the *Primer* were sold.[2] In 1740 Thomas Dilworth published *A New Guide to the English Tongue,* which contained a mixture of grammar, spelling, and religious material, followed a few years later by the *Schoolmaster's Assistant,* a widely used mathematics text. Noah Webster's spellers first appeared in 1783; they were continuously revised and set the standard for spelling until midway in the nineteenth century.[3]

Only a small percentage of colonial youth took advantage of secondary schooling. The Latin grammar school continued to be the main instrument of schooling for the privileged class in the early colonial period, while the academy was designed to offer a more practical curriculum for future tradesmen and workers. The academy eventually became academically oriented, included the classics in its curriculum, and drove the Latin school out of existence. However, the new academies did offer a larger variety of courses. Among the course offerings could be found Latin, Greek, English, oratory, composition, literature, accounting, surveying, geography, ancient history, American history, mental philosophy, logic, astronomy, chemistry, geology, biology, needlework, optics, bookkeeping, botany, and agriculture.[4]

Academy replaces the Latin grammar school

From the time of the American Revolution to approximately 1840, great uniformity prevailed and very little change in the elementary school curriculum occurred. Reading, spelling, writing, and arithmetic continued to be stressed in the elementary schools, along with good manners and morals, and the *McGuffey Readers,* first published in 1836, were used in most elementary school districts throughout the nineteenth century. But curricular changes and the inclusion of more and more subjects were gradually being made. Between 1840 and 1875 penmanship, advanced mathematics and science, music, art, and physical education were added to the list.

In the meantime the common schools, which evolved in Boston in the 1820s, became popular, particularly on the frontier; and in 1874 the concept of free public schooling was extended to the high school level. Thereafter the academy dwindled in importance. Although many of the new high school students had no intention of going to college, the high school curriculum concentrated on academic and college preparatory subjects, thus illustrating the pervasive influence of the ideals of mental discipline.[5]

Common schools and free public high schools

2   John A. Nietz, *Old Textbooks* (Pittsburgh: University of Pittsburgh Press, 1961).

3   R. Freeman Butts and Lawrence Cremin, *A History of Education in American Culture* (New York: Holt, Rinehart, 1953).

4   See Merle Curti, *The Social Ideas of American Educators* (New York: Scribners, 1935); I. L. Kandel, *History of Secondary Education* (Boston: Houghton Mifflin, 1930).

5   Merle Curti, *The Growth of American Thought,* 2nd ed. (New York: Harper & Row, 1951); David Nasaw, *Schooled to Order: A Social History of Public Schooling in the United States* (New York: Oxford University Press, 1979).

As the scientific and industrial revolution shaped the United States from the second half of the nineteenth century to the present, a companion movement for social reform of schools evolved. There was increased recognition of the relationship between school and society—and of the need to reform both. The purposes of schools gradually were broadened to meet the new demands of society. Social problems relating to unemployment, poverty, urbanization, and the Americanization of immigrants who did not speak English became associated with the responsibilities of the schools. The curriculum was broadened to meet the diverse needs of *all* children and youth.[6] And a companion shift occurred in school curriculum and teaching methods from a complete disregard for the learner, accompanied by respect for the subject matter only, to a strong regard for the child's interests, motives, and abilities. Much of the impetus for change came from the Progressive movement in education, especially at the University of Chicago and Columbia University; in fact, education in the twentieth century "may be characterized by the rise and fall of the Progressive Education Movement."[7]

Progressive education

On a general level there was gradual movement away from traditional subjects and teaching techniques toward utility in subject matter and toward student interests and self-expression, but changes were gradual and peripheral. Robert and Helen Lynd's description of Middletown schools illustrates the normal, regimented world of schooling in the mid-1920s.

Immovable seats in orderly rows fix the sphere of activity of each child. For all, from the timid six-year-old entering for the first time to the most assured high school senior, the general routine is much the same. Bells divide the day into periods. For the six-year-olds the periods are short (fifteen to twenty-five minutes) and varied; in some they leave their seats, play games, and act out make-believe stories, although in "recitation periods" all movement is prohibited. As they grow older the taboo upon physical activity becomes stricter, until by the third or fourth year practically all movement is forbidden except the marching from one set of seats to another between periods, a brief interval of prescribed exercise daily, and periods of manual training or home economics once or twice a week. There are "study periods" in which children learn "lessons" from "textbooks" prescribed by the state and "recitation periods" in which they tell an adult teacher what the book has said. With high school come some differences; more

Regimented classrooms

6 Butts and Cremin, *A History of Education in American Culture;* Lawrence A. Cremin, *The Transformation of the School* (New York: Random House, 1961).

7 George A. Beauchamp, *The Curriculum of the Elementary School* (Boston: Allyn & Bacon, 1964), p. 45.

"vocational" and "laboratory" work varies the periods. But here again the lesson-textbook-recitation method is the chief characteristic of education.[8]

In many ways the description of the Middletown schools indicates that Progressive education did not carry over in mass scale beyond the universities and their campus laboratory schools. The same sort of mechanical bureaucracy that infected Middletown characterized most of the schools in Boston, Chicago, and New York. While there were shining examples like the Dalton, Massachusetts and Winnetka, Illinois schools, some school systems still used *McGuffey* into the 1930s. Yet, this Progressivism did leave its mark, helping to increase educational opportunity for all students in a number of ways: (1) school organization shifted from eight-year elementary schools and four-year high schools to three-year junior high and senior high schools to give greater attention to the requirements of pubescent children; (2) the curriculum was reorganized and extended to areas such as vocational education, agriculture, home economics, physical education, and the arts; (3) extracurricular activities expanded; (4) students were grouped with greater flexibility to meet varying needs; (5) students and teachers tended to be more active and more informal in their relationships with one another; (6) innumerable materials and media were introduced into the classroom; and (7) certification of teachers required more education.[9]

Looking back at the schools since the colonial period, the curriculum can be viewed as an evolutionary process of course offerings in more and more subjects. In brief, the seventeenth- and eighteenth-century schools put emphasis on the three Rs at the elementary school level and emphasis on Greek, Latin, and higher mathematics at the secondary school level. The nineteenth century witnessed additional course offerings, especially in history, science and mathematics. The twentieth century saw the development of a general and diversified curriculum to fit the needs of a diversified student population.

The curriculum as an evolutionary process

ORGANIZING THE CURRICULUM

The shifts and changes in organizing curriculum that resulted from the increased complexity of the American schools during the present century can be viewed in terms of two basic schools of thought. One emphasizes the *learner;* the other emphasizes the *subject.* In the first case, the curriculum is viewed in terms of learning experiences based on the needs of the student; there is an attempt to categorize the personal and social life

Learner v. subject emphasis

8 Robert S. Lynd and Helen M. Lynd, *Middletown* (New York: Harcourt, Brace and World, 1929), p. 188.
9 Cremin, *The Transformation of the School.*

Informal curriculum gives children a chance to experiment with their creative abilities, as well as fulfill formal learning requirements.

functions or needs of the learner and to adjust the curriculum to these needs. In the second view, the curriculum is defined in terms of subject matter such as the "science curriculum" or "English curriculum," and sometimes in terms of grade levels, too, such as the "elementary school curriculum" or "secondary school curriculum." Limits are put on the activities and experiences that take place in teaching the learner; these limits are often based on subject matter.

CHILD-CENTERED CURRICULUM

The child-centered approach to organizing curriculum coincides with the reforms of those who tried to implement the philosophy of Rousseau in a pure, undiluted form. That is to say, allow the child to develop his or her capacity for individual self-expression, and develop a curriculum around the needs and experiences of the child; in fact, the child becomes the source for curriculum construction.

Implied in this theory of curriculum was the necessity of leaving the child to his or her own devices; creativity and freedom were considered important for children's growth. Furthermore, the child would be a happier personality if he or she were free of teacher domination and free from the demands of subject matter and adult-imposed curriculum aims. The new hands-off policy was a reaction to the domineering teacher of the traditional school, whose sole purpose was to drill facts into the child's brain. It was, in some aspects, the product of the radical wing of the new Progressive movement, by whom the theories of John Dewey were misunderstood and misapplied.

Creativity and freedom for children

Although Dewey was one of the chief advocates of meeting the needs of children in school, and established an experimental school at the University of Chicago in 1896 to organize a new curriculum around the Progressive philosophy, he criticized educators who overlooked the importance of subject matter. Dewey's intention was to establish a balanced view of the curriculum. As early as 1902 he pointed out the fallacies assumed by both educational camps—the subject-centered or mental discipline proponents who regarded the learner as "a docile recipient of facts" and the child-centered proponents who regarded the child as "the starting point, the center, and the end" of school activity.[10] More than thirty years later Dewey was still criticizing educators who were overly permissive toward students and provided little direction under the guise of meeting the expressed and impulsive needs of the child. With unusual sharpness, he commented: "Such a method is really stupid. For it attempts the impossible, which is always stupid; and it misconceives the conditions of independent thinking." Freedom, he warned, is not given at birth, nor is it developed by planlessness and nondirection of adults. "It is something that must be taught by experienced teachers; the child does not know best."[11] Dewey also criticized those who felt subject matter was contrary to the needs of children or who held that it inhibits the child's individuality. He made it clear that he did not advocate the doctrines of permissiveness and watered-down subject matter attributed to the Progressive movement in education.[12]

A balance between learner and subject

10 John Dewey, *The Child and the Curriculum* (Chicago: University of Chicago Press, 1902), pp. 8–9.
11 John Dewey, *Art and Experience* (New York: Capricorn Books, 1934), pp. 32, 40.
12 John Dewey, *Experience and Education* (New York: Macmillan, 1938).

The focus on children and their individual needs led the way to the founding of a number of new schools—play schools, day schools, activity schools, which had been established specifically as part of the new pedagogical movement—such as the Fairhope School in Alabama, the Francis Parker School in Chicago, and the Lincoln School and Henry Street Settlement in New York City. The common denominator of these schools is that they were typically organized by parents and teachers who were dissatisfied with the public schools. George Dennison's alternative school in New York City and Jonathan Kozol's description of one free school in Boston are good examples of modern child-centered schools. A. S. Neill's Summerhill school in Suffolk, England, which he organized in 1939 and which is still in existence, is perhaps the most prominent of all the contemporary child-centered and unstructured schools.[13]

Organized by dissatisfied parents

ACTIVITY-CENTERED CURRICULUM The activity movement grew out of the child-centered movement and particularly changed the elementary school curriculum. The movement was led by William Kilpatrick, who was Dewey's student at Columbia University. In 1918 Kilpatrick wrote a theoretical article on "the project method" that catapulted him to national prominence.[14] Kilpatrick emphasized *purposeful activity*, coinciding with Dewey's concern for the child's needs and purposes. He extended Dewey's concept of the child's social and physical environment, and claimed that desirable learning could be produced by active participation of the individual within his or her environment.

In developing his activity-centered idea, Kilpatrick pointed out that he differed with Dewey's child-centered view that the interests and needs of children cannot be anticipated and that therefore no preplanned curriculum framework can be agreed upon.[15] Actually, the child-centered program, as envisioned by Dewey, did plan child activities and content, but Kilpatrick wished to detail projects and procedures. He attacked the curriculum of his day as being unrelated to real problems of life and advocated purposeful activities as "life-like" as possible. Such activities, he explained, proceeded through four steps: purposing, planning, executing, and judging.

Purposeful activities

During the 1920s and 1930s many elementary schools adopted some of the ideas of the activity movement. From this movement emerged a host of pedagogical concepts that were associated with activity learning, such as life experiences, units, projects, social enterprises, field trips, and cen-

13 George Dennison, *The Lives of Children: The Story of the First Street School* (New York: Random House, 1969); Jonathan Kozol, *Free Schools* (Boston: Houghton Mifflin, 1972); A. S. Neill, *Summerhill: A Radical Approach to Child Rearing* (New York: Hart, 1960).

14 William H. Kilpatrick, "The Project Method," *Teachers College Record* (September 1918), pp. 319–35.

15 William H. Kilpatrick, *Foundations of Method* (New York: Macmillan, 1925).

ters of interest. All of these activities involved the notion of problem solving and active participation on the part of students, socialization of students to the world around them, and greater school-community linkages.

Recent educational reformers have associated the activities approach with community action and citizenship education of the student. For example, "learners [are] given opportunities in real life situations. . . . This means that students . . . work with poverty agencies, early childhood units, governmental institutions, hospitals, old age homes, etc.[16]

In general, an activity-centered curriculum organizes elements of the curriculum in a cluster of activities or problems. Ideally, activities deal with problem areas or "realities," are community-oriented, and require extensive student participation in their design and conduct.

Community-oriented activities

SUBJECT-MATTER CURRICULUM

Subject matter always has been the first basis for curriculum organization and is still the most popular method, primarily because of educational convenience. Emphasis is placed on separate academic areas, an approach that is rooted in the philosophy of Plato and Aristotle, who stressed certain basic disciplines for transmitting the wisdom of the ages to the young. In this approach, curriculum is organized around a discipline or body of knowledge. Extreme advocates of this position emphasize the mastery of various subjects and de-emphasize the sociopsychological factors, that is, the student's personal needs. The arguments in favor of this type of curriculum include: (1) the subjects constitute a logical method for organizing and interpreting learning; (2) the approach is based on tradition, which adds to its status; (3) teachers have been trained in subject curriculum and better understand it; and (4) planning is easier. Criticisms raised are: (1) the curriculum is fragmented, (2) life experiences are de-emphasized, and (3) the curriculum tends to relegate teaching to knowledge and recall of subject matter.[17]

Pros and cons of subject matter curriculum

In response to the growing proliferation of academic subjects, and the failure of students to relate one subject matter to another, various modifications of the traditional subject-curriculum have been attempted. In general, these modifications have tried to integrate subject matter to make it more manageable for the learners and to allow students more opportunity to pursue activities that are interesting and motivating.

Coinciding with the influence of the Educational Policies Commission and its emphasis on personal and social needs of youth, the core program became popular in the junior high schools in the 1930s and

---

16 Mario D. Fantini, *The Reform of Urban Schools* (Washington, D.C.: National Education Association, 1970), p. 45.

17 David Pratt, *Curriculum: Design and Development* (New York: Harcourt Brace Jovanovich, 1980); Daniel Tanner and Laurel N. Tanner, *Curriculum Development*, 2nd ed. (New York: Macmillan, 1980).

1940s. The approach draws on social issues, moral content, and demo-cratic values, coinciding with the issues of pre- and post-World War II. The advocates of this approach pointed out that the core curriculum combined subject matter with the realities and challenges of the day.[18] Although this approach drew heavily on subject matter, the purpose was to integrate knowledge of various subjects for studying social issues and problem areas related to the individual student as well as to society.

With the core approach the social issues and problem areas are pre-planned by the teacher and students, and in some cases the teachers plan them grade level by grade level. In theory it allows great freedom and flexibility, and pays close attention to students' needs and interests, as well as to content. It attempts to combine the child-centered approach with the subject-centered approach. The core curriculum directly coincides with the rise and fall of Progressive educational philosophy. While the adherents of the core emphasized critical thinking and problem solving in the literature, post-World War II critics (mentioned in Chapter 12) con-demned it on the ground that it was socially oriented rather than cogni-tively oriented.

THE STRUCTURE OF A SUBJECT   Recent developments stemming from the Sputnik era and the demands for intellec-tual rigor led to another way of organizing curriculum—teaching the structure of a subject or discipline. By structure we mean the broad uni-fying concepts, rules, and principles that define and delimit a given sub-ject matter and control research and method of inquiry. The structure binds a field of knowledge into a whole, organizes this knowledge, suggests its limits, and provides the basis for discovering what else exists within the field.

A major impetus for curriculum organization based on structure was Jerome Bruner's *The Process of Education.*[19] Bruner contended that the school curriculum should emphasize the structure of knowlege, rather than the details. Given the limited time for schooling and the amount of information and data available to be learned, the most practical way of proceeding is to focus curriculum and instruction upon the structure of various disciplines. Equipped with structural insight, the student will be able to efficiently and effectively utilize whatever specific information is at hand. As Bruner wrote later: "The merit of a structure depends upon its power for simplifying information, for generating new propositions, and for increasing the manipulability of a body of knowledge."[20]

18 Roland C. Faunce and Nelson L. Bossing, *Developing the Core Curriculum,* 2nd ed. (Englewood Cliffs, N.J.: Prentice-Hall, 1958).

19 Jerome S. Bruner, *The Process of Education* (Cambridge, Mass.: Harvard University Press, 1960).

20 Jerome S. Bruner, *Toward a Theory of Instruction* (Cambridge, Mass.: Harvard Univer-sity Press, 1966), p. 41.

The emphasis on structure led to emphasis on methods of inquiry. Each discipline has its own unifying concepts, principles, and methods of inquiry. Learning by the "discovery method" in chemistry is different from learning in physics. Each subject needs to be taught by its own methods. As curriculum planners attempted to put this theory into practice, however, there was little agreement on how the theory applied to history and English, or how structure was to be taught to students. Science and mathematics programs have offered the most promising examples of teaching the structure of a subject, and most of the curricula in these two areas were updated in the early 1960s along the lines of this theory. Critics of reorganizing the subject around its structure point out that the new curriculum projects fail to demonstrate the validity of structure of a discipline as a unifying principle. If curriculum is to be organized according to the structure of a discipline for each subject, the problem of growing multiplicity of subjects, characteristic of the traditional subject curriculum, remains unresolved.

RENEWED SEARCH FOR RELEVANCY

There is a renewed concern today that a school curriculum should not be simply compartmentalized into subjects or structure. The demand for "relevancy" comes from both students and educators. In fact, the student disruptions of the late 1960s and early 1970s were related in part to the demand by students for a relevant curriculum. The belief is that schools insist on creating artificial boundaries between subjects and are more concerned with content within these boundaries than with what the student is interested in learning.[21]

Representative educators who stress the need for relevance contend that "most schools and school systems have become anachronistic. They are out of phase with everyday realities of their students' lives. They do not illuminate the concerns of youngsters. They are irrelevant."[22] The trouble is "either the teacher does not recognize that the subject matter is irrelevant, if ever it was relevant, or he is unwilling to change, discard, or restructure his materials and procedure as relevance demands."[23] These educators would like to introduce new experiences, develop small-step skill sequences, make the content more functional and immediate to student interests and more reality-oriented, and move from a less cognitive to a more affective curriculum. It should be noted, however, that many of the educators who stressed relevancy and advocated returning to a student-

---

21 Ralph J. Kane, "The Mindless Box: The Case Against the American Classroom," *Phi Delta Kappan* (March 1979), p. 501.

22 Mark Shedd, "The Kinds of Educational Programs We Need—for Later Adolescent Years" in J. G. Saylor, ed., *The School of the Future—Now* (Washington, D.C.: Association for Supervision and Curriculum Development, 1972), p. 57.

23 Carlton E. Beck et al., *Education for Relevance: The Schools and Social Change* (Boston: Houghton Mifflin, 1968), p. 238.

oriented curriculum were writing in an era of student protests, and they were influenced by this activism. The students were particularly concerned with the allocation of our resources toward military and technological ends rather than social and human ends. They attacked mathematicians and scientists who worked for the government as part of the war machine, and criticized mathematical and scientific subjects as irrelevant to the spirit of solving social issues.

In response to the demands for curriculum relevance, many schools and colleges have added courses in Black studies, urban studies, sex education, drug education, and environmental education. In addition, content designed to stress cognitive skills and intellectual rigor has been supplemented with content that stresses feelings and attitudes. Spin-off trends of the search for relevance now include values education and affective or "humane" education. Value building often appears in courses or discussions involving pluralism in our society, and in content areas that focus on morals and aesthetics.[24]

Value building and "humane" education

The attempt to humanize the schools and curriculum is not new; it is rooted in the Progressive thought of the 1920s and 1930s which sought to reform the schools with a new visionary social outlook.[25] Advocates of humane education today believe that motivating learners through high-interest materials they select themselves is more important than making sure that everyone learns the same material, which a teacher or a curriculum specialist has chosen as indispensable in a given subject.[26] Many of them have tended to de-emphasize subject matter and academic rigor in favor of affective processes and value clarification in the curriculum.

The major controversy of the twentieth century with respect to the various ways of organizing curriculum revolves around whether the child or the subject matter ought to be the base. Regardless of your approach, however, decisions on *what* you teach constitute a related issue and are based on the aims and objectives of the school system.

PAST
CURRICULAR
INNOVATIONS

The search for new programs and methods of instruction is a continuing one. The era of the 1950s and 1960s saw a large and sustained effort to reform curriculum and instruction. It was regarded by many educators as an era that would transform the schools.

High hopes for the 1950s and 1960s

24 Michael W. Apple, *Ideology and Curriculum* (Boston: Routledge & Paul, 1979); Louis E. Raths et al., *Values and Teaching: Working With Values in the Classroom* 2nd ed. (Columbus, Ohio: Merrill, 1978); Sidney B. Simon et al., *Values Clarification: A Handbook of Practical Strategies for Teachers and Students* (New York: Hart, 1972).

25 Boyd H. Bode, *Modern Educational Theories* (New York: Macmillan, 1927); George S. Counts, *Dare the Schools Build a New Social Order?* (New York: John Day, 1932).

26 Gerald Weinstein and Mario D. Fantini, *Toward Humanistic Education: A Curriculum of Affect* (New York: Praeger, 1970); Jon Schaffarzick and Gary Syker, eds., *Value Conflicts and Curriculum Issues* (Berkeley, Calif.: McCutchan, 1979).

These twenty years, said one educator, would be considered "one of the major turning points in American public education."[27] Similarly, the New York State Commissioner of Education wrote in 1960:

> Never before have so many new approaches developed in such a relatively short period . . . we are learning that many of the old ways of operating our schools are not necessarily the best ways. New methods of organization, the use of new technological devices and new concepts of the role of the teacher provide answers that numbers alone cannot provide.[28]

TEAM TEACHING   The team teaching approach is rooted in the early organizational plans of the twentieth century, particularly the Gary Plan and Batavia Plan. It was reintroduced and modernized in 1957 at the Franklin School in Lexington, Massachusetts, under the directorship of Robert Anderson and with the assistance of the Harvard Graduate School of Education. From this experiment the team teaching approach became one of the most widely discussed and frequently adopted organizational programs.

Team teaching is an arrangement where two or more teachers combine their abilities and interests to complement each other, and assume joint responsibility in teaching students.[29] In the original experiment by Robert Anderson there were both large teams, composed of five or six teachers, and small teams, composed of three teachers. The titles "team leader" and "senior teacher" were used to designate teachers who had responsibility for leadership in the teams. Each team was assigned a part-time clerical aide, and the two large teams also were assigned a quarter-time teaching assistant.

Teachers combine their abilities and interests

As various schools across the country have adopted the team concept, the team patterns have varied. Most of the present plans provide for a learning situation where the master teacher or teacher with the most knowledge of the subject instructs a large group and where there is opportunity for students to work in small groups with other teachers and to do individual work as well. An experienced or master teacher is usually teamed with less experienced teachers, student teachers, and a teacher aide.

The teacher designated as a team leader is sometimes paid an additional remuneration for his or her increased responsibilities. This is supposed to serve as a means of holding able teachers in the classroom, rather

Renumeration for increased responsibilities

27   Robert H. Anderson, "Team Teaching in the Elementary and Secondary Schools," in A. de Grazia and D. A. Sohn, eds., *Revolution in Teaching* (New York: Bantam, 1964), p. 127.

28   James E. Allen, "Forward," in Arthur D. Morse, *Schools of Tomorrow—Today* (Garden City, N.Y.: Doubleday, 1960), p. 6.

29   Robert H. Anderson, Ellis A. Hagstrom, and Wade M. Robinson, "Team Teaching in an Elementary School," *School Review* (Spring 1960), pp. 71–84.

than losing them to administration. In most cases, however, the schools using the team approach do not distinguish either the role or salary of various team teaching members. Rarely does the team have an aide or clerical assistant. Cooperative planning of curriculum and instruction is essential; however, in some instances there may be conflict over the inadequate performance of team members and there may also be little time for planning. Charles Silberman's description of team planning seems to be characteristic of most schools.

> An elementary school in one of the wealthiest suburbs in the
> United States claims to be using team teaching in its fifth grade.
> What this means is that some teachers are handling math and sci-
> ence, others English and social studies. It is called team teaching
> because the teachers allegedly "get together and discuss all the
> children." "Isn't that kind of conference difficult to fit into a full
> teaching schedule?" a visitor asks with feigned innocence. "Well,
> you know how it is," comes the reply. "We fit it in during lunch
> hour, or we stay around after three for a few minutes."[30]

The team approach has been successfully adopted in some form by many school systems, but it seems to have failed to achieve its intended successes in many other places. Educators are still in the process of learning how to make team teaching work effectively in the classroom.[31]

TEACHER AIDES   Teacher aides, sometimes called para-professionals or auxiliary personnel, often are required to perform the tasks assigned to the educational assistant under differential staffing. However, the case for teacher aides can be considered independently of any particular model of faculty utilization.

Teacher aides were originally used to offset the shortage of classroom teachers in the early 1950s. The idea of using teacher aides on a system-wide basis was first tried in the Bay City, Michigan schools in 1953, from where it quickly spread across the country. In 1967 the results of a nationwide NEA survey showed that almost one in five schoolteachers, or 19 percent, had assistants of some kind.[32] About 14 percent shared the services of one or more aides with other teachers, and 5 percent had one or more aides of their own. Twice as many elementary school teachers as high school teachers reported having aides. The typical aide at that time earned about $2 per hour. Job qualifications varied among school systems. Most of them required at least a high school diploma.

30   Charles E. Silberman, *Crisis in the Classroom* (New York: Random House, 1971), p. 162.

31   Mary Saily, "Teachers Team to Cope With Complex Materials," *Educational R & D Report* (Winter 1979), pp. 1–5.

32   "How Paraprofessionals Feel About Teacher Aides," *NEA Journal* (November 1967), pp. 16–17.

A massive program to train several hundred thousand auxiliary personnel was funded by the federal government in the late 1960s. This resulted from the increasing impetus to train minority teachers, to provide jobs in ghetto areas, and to fight the War on Poverty, coupled with the advent of Headstart and Follow-Through programs. Thus the ranks of teacher aides had swelled to 200,000 by 1970, and it was estimated that by 1975 the number was 400,000.[33] This expanding trend came to a halt, however, as federal spending decreased in the Nixon-Ford administration and as the demand for teachers waned in the 1970s.

Jobs for minorities

Trend has now diminished

At present New York City is one of the few school systems that is still committed to teacher aides, who are referred to as paraprofessionals. The school system employs twice as many paraprofessionals as any other school system—about 10,000. They have permanent status and are unionized with the teachers. They have full medical and hospital coverage, obtain free schooling at the colleges, and in 1980 generally earned between $3.50 and $7.00 per hour depending on their education and experience. Most important, a career ladder program has been developed for them; they may improve their education and job opportunities and move up the ladder to become regular teachers.

FLEXIBLE SCHEDULING

Although there are literally hundreds of different methods for grouping students and teachers, one of the most widely discussed proposals, which was introduced in the 1950s, is the concept of modular scheduling—a popular example of flexible scheduling. The idea, proposed by J. Lloyd Trump, is to organize the school around large-group instruction, small-group discussion, and independent study.[34] About 15- to 20-minute units of time replace the regular bell schedule and permit greater flexibility and variations in scheduling.

Large-group instruction includes activities carried out in groups of 100 or more students, and occupies about 40 percent of the time. Instruction is carried out by a particularly competent teacher, and he or she is provided with additional time for preparation. Small-group instruction consists of 12 to 15 students and occupies about 20 percent of the students' time. Most of this activity is related to the large-group instruction, with the teacher serving as a consultant or counselor. Independent study consists of students in small groups of two or three, or as individuals, engaging in independent work on projects and research in laboratories, resource centers, libraries, and outside school. This occupies 40 percent of

Organizing large, small, and independent groups

33 Allan C. Ornstein, Harriet Talmadge, and Anne W. Juhasz, *The Paraprofessional's Handbook* (Belmont, Calif.: Fearon, 1975); Stanley S. Robin and Martin O. Wagenfeld, *Paraprofessionals in the Human Services* (New York: Human Sciences Press, 1980).

34 J. Lloyd Trump, *Images of the Future* (Washington, D.C.: National Association of Secondary School Principals, 1959); J. Lloyd Trump and Dorsey Baynham, *Focus on Change* (Chicago: Rand McNally, 1961).

the students' time. Teachers and other personnel serve as consultants, and greater responsibility is afforded to the students.

Periodically the students are regrouped in order to cope with differences in student abilities and interests. Flexibility of grouping is a key concept. Teachers work ten to twenty hours and have more time for professional preparation and professional conferences. More time also is devoted to student conferences. The plan relies on a team teaching approach where high salaries are paid to team leaders and commensurately higher salaries to master teachers. A few schools have introduced the concept of the modular or some sort of flexible scheduling. Most schools, however, still maintain the older daily schedule.

INDIVIDUALIZED INSTRUCTION The 1950s and 1960s saw a renewed stress on individualized learning, with new content and materials designed for individual learning, new instructional activities to provide a one-to-one teacher-student relationship, new machines to aid in this process, and a new philosophy that advocated that students proceed at their own rate of comprehension. In the early 1960s several educational yearbooks devoted their entire issues to this subject.[35] By 1968 a supporter of the individualized approach noted: "For half a century we have been committed to individualized instruction. . . . Yet only now have [we] been able . . . to act on our conviction with the prospect of success."[36] With the advent of team teaching, teacher aides, flexible scheduling, and independent study, he concluded that education was ready to assume responsibility for preplanned individualized learning programs.

One of the best known individualized programs of the late 1950s and early 1960s was the Project on Individually Prescribed Instruction (IPI) which was developed at the University of Pittsburgh and later became known as Adaptable Environments for Learning (AEL). IPI was an application of the principles of programmed instruction and behavioral instruction. The curriculum was stated in behavioral objectives with proficiency levels; each student was diagnosed, and an individual plan was developed for each subject; several materials were introduced to provide a variety of paths for mastery of any given objective; learning tasks were individualized for each student; and there was continuous evaluation.

Other systems for delivering individualized instruction in elementary and secondary schools that appeared in the late 1960s are the Univer-

Principles of programmed and behavioral instruction

35 The 1962 Yearbook of the National Society for the Study of Education, the 1963 Yearbook of the Association for Student Teaching, and the 1964 Yearbook of the Association for Supervision of Curriculum Development.

36 Alexander Frazier, "Individualized Instructions," Paper presented at the Annual Meeting of the Association for Supervision of Curriculum Development, Los Angeles, November 1968, p. 1. Also see Alexander Frazier, "Individualized Instruction," *Educational Leadership* (April 1968), p. 616.

sity of Wisconsin's Individually Guided Education (IGE), and the Program for Learning in Accordance with Needs (PLAN). IGE is a total educational system for formulating and carrying out instructional programs for individual students in which planned variations are made in what each student learns, in how he or she goes about learning, and how rapidly he or she learns. Instructional objectives are developed for each student; the student participates in a one-to-one relation with the teacher, teacher aide, or another student; and included are independent study, small-group instruction, large-group instruction, and various classroom activities. The actual mix of these activities for each student is dependent on the abilities of the student, the objectives to be attained, and the costs involved.[37] IGE was developed as an alternative to age-graded education and to unstructured open education, but it can be implemented in either age-graded or ungraded schools and in either self-contained or departmentalized classrooms.

Individualized objectives and rates of learning

The five components of the PLAN system are as follows: (1) a set of educational objectives, (2) related teaching-learning units, (3) a set of tests, (4) guidance activities to enhance self-understanding, and (5) an evaluation system. Individualization is essentially accomplished by (a) ungraded materials appropriate to the student level of achievement, (b) alternative sets of materials for each unit of instruction, and (c) two-week modules, arranged according to each student's level of achievement.[38]

All three individualized systems IPI, IGE, and PLAN, have been field tested and are in existence today, and there have been various reports of success and significant gains in student achievement and comparative skills. They have not been implemented on a mass scale because of funding costs and administrative obstacles. Of the three, IGE seems to be the most popular. It has been introduced in several thousand schools and a network of participating resource persons now exists to help school officials learn to implement it effectively.[39] Nevertheless, the majority of schools today remain geared to group instruction, group norms, and group expectations, rather than individual student differences.[40]

Funding costs and administrative obstacles

37 Herbert J. Klausmier, "The Wisconsin Research and Development Center for Cognitive Learning," in H. J. Klausmier and G. T. O'Hearn, eds., *Research and Development Toward the Improvement of Education* (Madison, Wis.: Dembar Educational Research Services, 1968), pp. 146–56; Herbert J. Klausmier and Richard E. Ripple, *Learning and Human Abilities*, 3rd ed. (New York: Harper & Row, 1971).

38 John C. Flanagan, "Program for Learning in Accordance with Needs," Paper presented at the Annual Conference of the American Educational Research Association, Chicago, February 1968).

39 Herbert J. Klausmeier and Patricia S. Allen, *Cognitive Development of Children and Youth* (New York: Academic Press, 1978).

40 John I. Goodlad and M. Frances Klein, *Behind the Classroom Door* (Worthington, Ohio: Jones, 1970); Harriet Talmadge, ed., *Systems of Individualized Education* (Berkeley, Calif.: McCutchan, 1975); J. Lloyd Trump and Delmas F. Miller, *Secondary School Curriculum Improvement*, 3rd ed. (Boston: Allyn & Bacon, 1979).

INSTRUCTIONAL
TELEVISION
In the late 1950s a great many educators saw the new medium as a panacea for many educational ills. Instructional television (ITV) was expected to solve the teacher shortage, enable master teachers to reach more students, and make it possible to substantially increase class size. In addition, television was expected to reduce some of the inequalities of educational resources, enable students in rural and small schools to receive high quality instruction, and make available instruction in specialized subjects. It also was supposed to provide a library of tapes and kinescopes that would be reused like library books.

Both the Ford Foundation and the federal government poured hundreds of millions of dollars into a variety of ITV experiments to assess the new potential. In Hagerstown, Maryland more than one hundred live programs were transmitted each week from five studios to 37 elementary and secondary schools, containing 90 percent of the 18,000 students of Washington County schools. In Southwest Indiana, lessons were transmitted to more than 23,000 students in 108 schools. These experiments served as models for guiding other school systems in adopting educational television.[41]

The experiments were initially perceived to be making a real contribution to education and they became a vital part of many school systems; eventually, however, educational television was criticized for fragmenting learning and impersonalizing and standardizing it into mere information acquisition. Television failed to consider individual interests and learning rates; the costs were high; there were technical difficulties—and the effort was not considered worthwhile, since ITV mainly served as low-level occasional enrichment.

Criticisms
of ITV

After a decade of intensive effort and expenditures, its most ardent advocates had to admit that ITV had not made a decisive impact on the schools.[42] A recent review of the research on instructional television indicated that although it is known children can learn from TV in the classroom, little is known concerning the ways in which it should be used to be most effective.[43] The question that needs to be explored today, however, is why the new medium proved so disappointing. Even "Sesame Street," which reached more than eight million children regularly and was originally intended partly to help disadvantaged children catch up with other students, had to be reassessed. "Sesame Street" did improve the learning of disadvantaged children, but it also helped more nondisadvantaged

41 Morse, *Schools of Tomorrow—Today;* Alexander J. Stoddard, *Schools for Tomorrow* (New York: Fund for the Advancement of Education, 1957).

42 Alvin C. Eurich, *Reforming American Education* (New York: Harper & Row, 1969).

43 Gretchen S. Barbatsis, "The Nature of Inquiry and Analysis of Theoretical Progress in Instructional Television from 1950-1970," *Review of Educational Research* (Summer 1978), pp. 399-434.

youngsters, and thus did little or nothing to close the gap between the two groups.[44]

The current status of instructional television has been portrayed in a recent report by the Corporation for Public Broadcasting. The report indicated that approximately one of every three teachers uses ITV "regularly" but only 17 percent of teachers have received training in how to use it. There is some indication that students react positively to the use of ITV in the elementary schools, but the history of ITV in high schools has been one of "many unproductive experiments and unfulfilled promises."[45]

Unfulfilled
promises

PROGRAMMED INSTRUCTION   Although a number of auto-instructional devices were developed during the 1920s, their impact was inconsequential.[46] Except for sporadic use mainly during World War II, such devices were virtually forgotten until B. F. Skinner stimulated a new surge of interest in 1954.[47]

The principles of programmed instruction were derived from Skinner's principles of operant conditioning, which were based on the laboratory work he did with animals. A relatively small unit of information called a frame is presented to the learner as a *stimulus*. The learner is required to make a *response* by completing the statement or answering a statement. By a feedback system, the learner is informed if the response is correct or wrong. If wrong, he or she is told why. If correct, the response is *reinforced*. The learner is then presented with another frame, and the stimulus-response-reinforcement cycle is repeated until a series of hundreds or thousands of frames is presented and the program is completed in a logical sequence of information. The instructional sequences are simplified to such a degree that if the percentage of errors of the average learner is more than 10 percent, the program usually is considered to be in need of revision.

Stimulus-
response
reinforcement
cycle

Skinner called the device a "teaching machine." Since more attention was focused on the machine than on the instructional program, more machines than programs were produced during the first years of the movement, and many commercial companies produced them in ranges of $20 to $2,000.

The concept caught on but as criticism toward programmed instruction snowballed, the "boom" turned into a "bust." Even one of the re-

44   P. M. Almeida, "Children's Television and the Modeling of Prosocial Behavior," *Education and Urban Society* (November 1977), pp. 55-66; Gerald S. Lesser, *Children and Television: Lessons from Sesame Street* (New York: Random House, 1974).

45   "Instructional Television: A History of 'Unfulfilled Promises'?" *Education USA* (March 31, 1980), pp. 1, 4.

46   Sidney L. Pressey, "A Third and Fourth Contribution Toward the Coming 'Industrial Revolution' in Education," *School and Society* (November 19, 1932), pp. 668-72.

47   B. F. Skinner, "The Science of Learning and the Art of Teaching," Paper presented at a Conference on Current Trends in Psychology, University of Pittsburgh, March 1954. For a current description of his approach to programmed instruction, see B. F. Skinner, "The Steep and Thorny Way to a Science of Behavior," *American Psychologist* (January 1975), pp. 42-49.

searchers who had worked with auto-instruction in the 1920s attacked the current procedures as based on "a false premise that the important features of human learning are to be found in animals." The current animal-devised procedures fragmented learning and replaced "processes of cognitive classification with largely rote reinforcings of bit learning."[48]

COMPUTER-ASSISTED INSTRUCTION The application of computer technology has increased steadily since the first commercial computer began operation in 1951. In education the computer is capable, first of all, of presenting individualized lesson material almost simultaneously with feedback and correction. A second approach between student and computer is the tutorial system, which takes over the responsibility of presenting inquiry learning. As soon as the student manifests a clear understanding of the concept or problem, as with programmed instruction, he or she moves to the next exercise. The third and most sophisticated level of student-teacher interaction is the dialogue system, which permits the student to conduct a genuine dialogue with and ask questions of the computer. By 1968 there were more than 300 computer-instructional programs of the first two types being used in the United States.[49]

Three different types of instruction

There are several advantages to using the computer for instruction: the current emphasis on individualized instruction, the increasing amount of new knowledge to be learned, the growing need for periodic upgrading of one's education, and the unlimited diversity it presents for curriculum and teaching. A prominent educator in the field of computer-assisted education sees the day when a large computer with as many as 1,000 terminals will handle more than 30,000 students at the same time. Each student will be at a different point in the curriculum, since the computer will provide instruction to students working at different rates.[50]

Critics point out that the use of the computer limits human interaction in teaching and learning, that it leaves the role of the teacher unspecified, and that it provides little insight into student purposes, motives, or feelings. Most important, the values of individuality and human freedom are considered by some to be threatened by the widespread use of technology in education. Most of these same fears have been raised traditionally over the years with the introduction of other types of educational machines—a perceived conflict between humanism and technology—but

Criticisms of computerized instruction

48 Sidney L. Pressey, "Teaching Machine (and Learning Theory) Crisis," *Journal of Applied Psychology* (February 1963), p. 5.

49 A. Hickey, ed., *Computer-Assisted Instruction: A Survey of the Literature*, 3rd ed. (Newburyport, Mass.: Enteleck, 1968).

50 Patrick Suppes, "Computer Technology and the Future of Education," *Phi Delta Kappan* (April 1968), pp. 420–23; Suppes, "The School of the Future: Technological Possibilities," in L. Rubin, ed., *The Future of Education: Perspectives on Tomorrow's Schooling* (Boston: Allyn & Bacon, 1975), pp. 145–57.

they remain an important factor to consider. To this date, computer-assisted programs are just beginning to play a role in instruction. A minicomputer can now be purchased for $500, and a small computer system costs only $2,500. Lowered computer costs mean that computers may be more widely used in the future.[51]

ADDITIONAL INNOVATIONS In addition to the aforementioned major innovations of the 1950s and 1960s (team teaching, teacher aides, flexible scheduling, individualized instruction, instructional television, programmed instruction, teaching machines, and computerized instruction), there are many other innovations in curriculum and instruction to consider, many of which have been adopted only on a piecemeal basis. The following are representative innovations of the period between the 1950s and the 1970s:

More innovations between 1950s and 1970s

1. *Resource center.* A specialized center with learning materials specially selected to meet the needs of the students and staffed with teachers, teacher aides, and other special personnel.

2. *School-within-school.* A large school organized into smaller units for administrative and/or instructional purposes.

3. *Open space.* Classrooms and/or schools organized to permit students and teachers to move about and share space in various ways, ranging in size and purpose, but suggesting flexibility.

4. *Language laboratories.* Equipment used to present recorded voices as part of the audiolingual approach to learning a language.

5. *Telephone amplification.* Long-distance discussions held by students and/or the teacher with persons from outside the school, with amplification for the entire classroom to hear.

6. *Simulation or gaming.* An experience used to create a problematic situation, usually logical or reality-oriented, involving students in role playing and/or decision making.

7. *Pass-fail.* Students are given the option of taking a specified number of courses, usually elective courses and no more than one course per term, on a pass-fail basis instead of for traditional grades.

8. *Nongraded programs.* A series of programs open to students without regard to grade level and/or sequence of courses. The students usually work at their own pace.

---

51 "Classrooms Make Friends with Computers," *Instructor* (February 1980), pp. 52–58; Lee Marvin Joiner, Sidney R. Miller, and Burton J. Silverstein, "Potential and Limits of Computers in Schools," *Educational Leadership* (March 1980), pp. 498–501.

9. *Continuous progress*. Students are provided special units of instruction and materials to work on at their own pace. The course may or may not have a completion date.

10. *Independent study*. The student conducts work on a topic of interest and uses school or nonschool resources with the teacher serving as a resource agent or guide.

11. *Directed study*. The students complete work for credit independent of the group but under the supervision of a specific teacher.

12. *Instructional materials center*. A center that houses a variety of printed and audiovisual materials for direct student use.[52]

WHAT WENT WRONG?   Hopes for the innovations of the last three decades never really came to fruition. Most of the promising plans were tried for a short time and then dropped or modified. In short, curriculum and instruction remained about the same. The following description of a Massachusetts school system in 1967, which still could apply to most schools in the United States today, seems to closely resemble the aforementioned Middletown schools of nearly forty years earlier. It is almost as if the average school had not changed.

Hopes not realized

> Watertown's young people do not find school an intellectually exciting place . . . the student is not encouraged to explore, to stretch his thinking, to pursue an independent line of inquiry. The program of studies is defined by the school, and the student is expected to learn what the school decides he should learn.
>
> The pervasive method of instruction consists of lectures and teacher-dominated activities. The teacher talks; the students are expected to listen or recite in response to the teacher's cues. The emphasis is on the acquisition of factual information untempered by reflective thought.
>
> Textbooks determine course content and organization, and many courses are untouched by current thought in curriculum development. In Watertown, the student succeeds by being quiet, by following directions, and by memorizing the information the teacher doles out. The teacher succeeds by following textbook instructions.[53]

52 Lyn S. Martin and Barbara N. Pavan, "Current Research on Open Space, Nongrading, Vertical Grouping, and Team Teaching," *Phi Delta Kappan* (January 1976), pp. 310–15; John U. Michaelis, Ruth H. Grossman, and Lloyd F. Scott, *New Designs for Elementary Curriculum and Instruction* (New York: McGraw-Hill, 1975); Margaret Nelson and Sam D. Sieber, "Innovations in Urban Secondary Schools," *School Review* (February 1976), pp. 213-31; Donald C. Orlich, et al., *Teaching Strategies: A Guide to Better Instruction* (Lexington, Mass.: Heath, 1980); John Wiles and Joseph Bond, *Curriculum Development: A Guide to Practice* (Columbus, Ohio: Merrill, 1979).

53 *Watertown: The Education of Its Children* (Cambridge, Mass.: Harvard Graduate School of Education, 1967), p. 34.

At about the same time an educator who recorded observations in more than one thousand high school classrooms arrived at a similar conclusion:

> I found the words *inquiry* and *process* being espoused all over the land. But, let me give you my data: 90 percent of the teachers in the eleventh and twelfth grade lectured 90 percent of the time, 80 percent of the teachers in the tenth grade lectured 80 percent of the time. They were all teaching through "inquiry." We defraud ourselves by using new words.[54]

Other observers, too, arrived at similar conclusions. After visiting some 260 kindergarten and first-grade classrooms in one hundred schools in thirteen states during the 1960s, John Goodlad indicated in 1969 that things were much the same as they had been twenty years previously:

Not much
change in
20 years

> Teaching was predominantly telling and questioning by the teacher, with children responding one by one or occasionally in chorus. In all of this, the textbook was the most highly visible instrument of learning and teaching . . . Rarely did we find small groups intensely in pursuit of knowledge; rarely did we find individual pupils at work in self-sustaining inquiry . . . we are forced to conclude that much of the so-called educational reform movement has been blunted on the classroom door.[55]

Ten years later, the situation still was basically unchanged. Goodlad and his colleagues now were completing a major national project titled a Study of Schooling. In 1979 they reported preliminary data indicating that "in the academic subjects there is a lot of telling and questioning of students and a heavy reliance on textbooks and workbooks." There was also considerable emphasis on teacher talk and group instruction "at the expense of student interaction and individualized learning."[56]

The reform movement of the 1950s, 1960s, and 1970s was summed up by Charles Silberman as "techniques to increase efficiency which left the content of curriculum and the process of instruction untouched." The reformers were mainly university scholars "with little contact with public schools . . . and they also tended to ignore the harsh realities of classroom and school organization."[57] To a large extent, the reformers' expectations were unrealistic. They expected that all students would want to learn and know how to learn; they expected unfailingly dedicated and competent

Ignoring the
classroom
realities

---

54 Paul F. Brandwein, "The Role of the Teacher," Proceedings at the Abington Conference, Abington, Pa., 1968, p. 59.

55 John I. Goodlad, "The Schools vs. Education," *Saturday Review* (April 19, 1969), p. 60.

56 "A Conversation with John I. Goodlad," *Educational Leadership* (December 1979), p. 226. Also see John I. Goodlad, et al., *A Study of Schooling* (Los Angeles: Institute for Development of Educational Activities, 1979).

57 Silberman, *Crisis in the Classroom*, pp. 160, 180.

teachers. They failed to consider that teachers perceived their problems differently and frequently did not see the reformers' answers as if relevant, however elegantly packaged. In their view all that was needed was to show teachers the new material, and by its very nature students would learn it in the prescribed way—a highly idealistic view of the educational process.

John Goodlad has pointed out that innovative projects frequently failed because they did not take much account of the tendency for schools and other institutions to continue established practices. It is very difficult to change the "regularities" that exist in a school and to convince teachers that different practices are necessary or possible. National innovation priorities were set for curriculum improvement, but relatively few projects gave much attention to working intensively with the teachers who were to implement change.[58]

Frequently little progress was made in changing the schools. "Surface changes, small and isolated innovations, lack of comprehensive approaches to changes, and research based on weak assumptions seemed to say that the need for innovation was not taken seriously enough. Even the small innovations were not widespread."[59] Most often, whatever innovations were made were mainly in suburban areas where most people assumed that there was nothing really wrong with the schools. In inner-city schools, where change and reform were needed most, there were too many political and social problems to cope with to be systematically concerned with innovation.[60]

In addition, many of the innovations of the past three decades were considered to be "teacher proof," that is, they would work whether teachers were good or bad. With this patronizing view of teachers, the reform effort could not succeed. The failure to involve the classroom teacher in all phases of developing new curricula tended to inhibit—even destroy—the effectiveness of the innovations that were designed in this era. Indeed, if there is a lesson to be learned, it is that curriculum and instructional programs need to include classroom teachers at all phases of planning, development, implementation, and evaluation.

Isolated innovations and weak assumptions

SUBJECT-AREA CURRICULAR TRENDS TODAY

In addition to those areas already discussed, the school curriculum is considerably influenced by certain persuasive emergent trends in subject areas. These areas of curriculum are affected by the movement to break away from traditional disciplines to more interdisci-

58 John I. Goodlad, *The Dynamics of Educational Change* (New York: McGraw-Hill, 1975).
59 Glenys G. Unruh and William M. Alexander, *Innovations in Secondary Education*, 2nd ed. (New York: Holt, Rinehart, 1974), p. 2.
60 David Bresnick, Seymour Lachman, and Murray Polner, *Black White Green Red* (New York: Longman, 1978).

plinary and multidisciplinary approaches. They are also affected by the thrust toward greater individualization and the desire to implement relevant curriculum.

Current subject trends may be categorized in the following areas:

1. *Career education.* There is a widespread reform of vocational education and, indeed, the functional value of education in general, with an emphasis for all students on career education. The long-standing discontent with vocational education, especially with its stepchild status, has finally led to the development of work motivation programs for *all* youth. Characteristic of these career programs is the extension of career guidance activities, the involvement of community groups and business groups, and the increased provision of career information and occupational training at the high school level.[61]

Reform of vocational education

2. *Environmental education.* Mounting concern over such problems as pollution, overpopulation, and depletion of food and natural resources has created demands for more knowledge and new programs in ecology and environmental education. Much of the relevant content has long been included in traditional earth science, biology, and geography courses and in conservation programs. But the new demand calls for a more meaningful and better coordinated program, coupled with a theme of crisis and the possibility that the worldwide ecosystem is in jeopardy and can no longer support the growing world population.[62]

3. *Ethnic education and cultural pluralism.* That a rapid growth of curriculum offerings in various ethnic studies came on the heels of Black studies is not surprising. The sense of being neglected and overlooked, the need for identity and recognition, and the need for heroes and jobs are by no means limited to Blacks. There are several ways to look at the rise of ethnic consciousness. On the positive side is the fact that these related programs will lead to greater understanding of various groups and will enhance the concepts of cultural richness and diversity and of ethnic self-esteem. On the negative side is the possible divisive effect these programs may have on the body politic, loosening the ties that bind together our society.

Pros and cons of ethnic consciousness

The focus varies from state to state, ranging from little interest whatsoever in ethnic studies to considerable legislation instituting various programs. In some cases, even though no laws or defined policy have been established on the state level, there is considerable

61 David Savage, "Career Education Programs Expose Students to World of Work," *Educational R & D Report* (Winter 1979), pp. 5-10.
62 Robert U. Ayres, *Uncertain Futures* (New York: Wiley, 1979).

local activity. In total, nearly forty states have published materials and media on the subject of ethnicity, nearly thirty states have formed policy statements on ethnic studies, and nearly twenty states have mandated ethnic studies in school curriculum.[63]

4. *Drug abuse education.* Critical social problems related to drug abuse and drug addiction among many children and youth from all parts of the country and all social classes have resulted in national concern and expansion of educational programs. Traditionally, drug abuse education in the United States has been in the form of teaching units about drugs in science classes or the scheduling of an occasional assembly program. Now there are coordinated programs with former drug abusers and community and health groups, as well as extensive counseling and even school-community therapy programs.

A nationwide
problem

5. *Metric education and calculators.* Two important factors have affected the mathematics curriculum: the metric conversion and the calculator boom. Corresponding with the conviction of business and industry that adopting the metric system would be an advantage to the United States, a number of school systems have introduced the metric system of measurement at various elementary school levels. While the changeover to the metric system is still voluntary, the conversion is growing. The U.S. Department of Education, the newly created National Institute of Education of HHS, and the National Science Foundation are cooperating with the National Bureau of Standards in assessing the national needs of metric education and related curricula and educational materials for the school systems of the country. "Think metric" has become a popular catchword.

At the same time, handheld calculators are blinking away in more and more schools. Four years after the introduction of the calculator in 1972, one out of ten Americans owned one. The price of a calculator has plummeted to as low as five dollars, putting it within reach of most students. Minicalculators are in wide use in high school and college mathematics classrooms, and regardless of any "official" stance on calculators, young children have taken to them as readily as they have to other kinds of gadgetry.[64] At what age level children receive the most advantages (and the least harm) from a

Handheld
calculators are
blinking away

63   Mario D. Fantini and René Cardenas, *Parenting in a Multicultural Society* (New York: Longman, 1980); Wilma S. Longstreet, Aspects of Ethnicity (New York: Teachers College Press, Columbia University, 1978).

64   Ty Harrington, "Those Hand-Held Calculators Could Be a Blinking Useful Tool for Schools," *American School Board Journal* (April 1976), pp. 44–46; Donald R. Quinn, "Calculators in the Classroom," *National Association of Secondary School Principals* (January 1976), pp. 77–80; Gary G. Bitter and Jerald L. M. Kessell, *Activities for Teaching with the Hand-Held Calculator* (Boston: Allyn & Bacon, 1980).

65   Dennis M. Roberts, "The Impact of Electronic Calculators on Educational Performance," *Review of Educational Research* (Spring 1980), pp. 71–98.

"calculator curriculum" is an unresolved question.[65] If introduced too early, it may prevent the establishment of the student's foundation in mathematics; moreover, if relied on excessively, it may lead to the student forgetting the fundamentals.

6. *Sex education.* Despite objections from some community groups and even sporadic controversy after programs are introduced, sex education has become increasingly accepted and is filtering down to the elementary school curriculum. Because of mounting divorce rates, illegitimacy, and venereal disease among our youth, many educators and citizen groups have deemed sex education to be essential. Traditional instructional units in hygiene, home economics, and family living have been supplemented with comprehensive explanations and prescriptions about dating, marriage, parenthood, and health problems.[66] In total, the U.S. Department of Education is presently funding more than one thousand school districts in "Education for Parenthood," a common euphemism for sex education.

7. *Nonsexist curriculum.* Curriculum and instruction also are being influenced by Title IX of the Education Amendments of 1972 and by other laws and forces that aim to reduce sexism in education. Curriculum efforts in elementary, secondary, and postsecondary schools include a requirement that institutions develop programs to meet the athletic needs and interests of both sexes. Schools thus are required to provide equal opportunity in athletic offerings, facilities, and equipment. In addition, government is attempting to encourage development of materials that reduce sexual stereotyping and other forms of sexism in textbooks and other instructional materials.[67]

Athletic needs of both sexes

8. *Consumer education.* Most school districts have provided some form of consumer education as part of their social studies curriculum, but consumer education has been expanding and now frequently is offered as a subject in its own right or as an important component in career education or economics or as preparation for required state examinations.[68] Given serious national problems regarding energy costs and general inflation, the trend toward expanded emphasis on consumer education is likely to continue in the future.

66   Anne M. Juhasz, "A Chain of Sexual Decision-Making," *Family Coordinator* (January 1975), pp. 43–49; Anne M. Juhasz and Mary Sonenshein Schneider, "Responsibility and Control: The Basis of Sexual Decision Making," *Personnel and Guidance Journal* (November 1979), pp. 181–85.

67   Robert J. Havighurst and Daniel U. Levine, *Society and Education*, 5th ed. (Boston: Allyn & Bacon, 1979).

68   John E. Clow, Michael A. MacDowell, and L. Gayle Royer, "How Are Career, Consumer, and Economic Education Related?" *Educational Leadership* (March 1980), pp. 518–22.

**CURRICULUM
FOR THE FUTURE**

Material in this chapter and the preceding chapter has indicated that instructional goals and curriculum have changed but that new approaches in curriculum and instruction do not seem to have been implemented successfully on a widespread basis. We will consider the problem of bringing about change and improvement at some length in the next chapter, but at this point it is appropriate to discuss some of the major changes in society and education that are likely to affect curriculum in the future.

There are many different opinions concerning the directions in which education should or will evolve in the future, and library shelves are filled with volumes describing current and anticipated changes in society and education. Despite disagreements, however, considerable consensus exists on several broad trends that are likely to have a major impact on curriculum planning in the educational system. Some of the most important of these trends are the following:

Considerable consensus with some trends

1. *Communication.* Technology will make it possible to revolutionize the communication of information and understanding in the classroom. The technological revolution in communications has been proceeding for many years, but most observers agree that there is no real end in sight and that substantial improvements in communications capacity will continue to occur at an accelerating rate in the next few decades. Predictable and envisioned improvements in technology lead to such scenarios as the following description of the way in which much student learning may take place in the future:

Consider each student of school age having at his disposal a television receiver, either in his home or in a publicly supported neighborhood center. Assume also that each student has available a dial-access facility which permits him access, via laser, to a central learning center equipped with a large, high-speed computer plugged into . . . knowledge that is programmed into any learning resource center anywhere in the world.[69]

2. *Lifelong learning.* In line with the growing complexity of modern society and the corresponding need for people to have access to a greater variety of educational resources at differing stages of their lives, education will continue to become more a "lifelong" enterprise and increasingly will take place outside the confines of the traditional school.[70] The trend toward lifelong learning is occurring in all

69   Glen G. Eye, et al., "Instructional Technology Reshapes the School: Its Impact on Faculty and Administrators" in R. W. Hostrop, ed., *Education Beyond Tomorrow* (Homewood, Ill.: 1975), pp. 25-26.

70   Michael G. Bruce, "Notes on European Education," *Phi Delta Kappan* (December 1979), pp. 281-83.

modern societies in accordance with the explosion of knowledge and rapid social, technological, and economic changes that persuade or force people to prepare for second or third careers and to keep themselves updated on new developments that affect their personal and social goals. Taking note of these trends, the Carnegie Commission has developed the concept of a "step-in, step-out" educational system for lifelong learning. This means that people could move in and out of educational programs throughout their lives.[71]

Second or third careers

Some observers, in addition, believe that much of the learning that in the past has been provided by elementary, secondary, and postsecondary schools may be provided by business and industry in the future.[72] Still other versions of the future envision educating adolescents and adults through establishing a network of community resources and individually appropriate learning opportunities.[73]

Learning sponsored by industry and community centers

3. *International cooperation.* In accordance with the growing interdependence of nations made possible by improved technology, education will place a greater emphasis on understanding of other nations and cultures than it has in the past. The advent of telecommunications satellites, the energy crisis, supersonic airliners, multinational corporations, and other forces have had the combined effect of making the peoples of the world even more dependent on one another than they have been in the past. Although historically the United States frequently has taken a relatively isolationist position related to its geographical separation from most of the world, interdependence among nations no longer allows Americans to ignore what happens elsewhere or to remain ignorant about developments in countries with unfamiliar traditions or cultures. One concerned observer has spelled out some of the implications of this change for school curricula as follows:

In the area of *content* of schooling, multicultural experiences —as a means of coping with our ever-increasing global interdependence—are a pressing need. For instance, more than 50% of the business of Midwestern farmers is export-related. Japan has 400 international salespeople, all of whom speak English; the U.S. has 1,000 international salespeople, none of whom speaks Japanese. Who do you suppose drives the better bargain?

Need for studying foreign languages

---

71 Jim Bowman et al., *The Far Side of the Future: Social Problems and Educational Reconstruction* (Washington, D.C.: World Future Society, 1978).

72 Russell C. Doll, "Speculations on the Meaning of the Trend Toward Corporate Education," *Phi Delta Kappan* (January 1980), pp. 333–37. Other articles in this issue also deal with the role of business and industry in the future of education.

73 Mario Fantini, "From School System to Educational System," in Wagschal, ed., *Learning Tomorrows*, pp. 109–117.

All of this indicates that innovative learning in today's schools must be widely multicultural if a nation is to participate effectively in the world. We must revive our dying foreign language programs. We must expand our travel exchange programs and make study *in* another culture a requirement for graduation, certainly from college, possibly even from secondary school.[74]

Expanding travel-exchange programs

4. *Values*. The greatest danger in planning future curriculum is the subordination of human values to technological advances. Worthwhile human goals ought not be replaced by computerized and mechanized techniques that may do more harm than good. For example, it may be undesirable to teach more facts about history if students are unable to use these facts to better understand the people they interact with and world in which they live. Similarly, drug education programs may succeed only in stimulating drug abuse unless students also understand the ways in which dangerous drugs are abused in everyday life. In short, when we plan curriculum, we need to be aware of the byproducts—both intended and unintended—and to weigh our immediate gains against the consequences of these gains. Apparent success could turn into disaster if the technological experts of tomorrow rush pell-mell into curriculum planning without knowledge of the effects of the new learning on the social and psychological development of the child, as well as on the attitudes and behaviors of teachers, parents, and community groups. The questions that we must always keep in mind as we move into the future are: "What kinds of people do we wish to produce?" and "What kinds of human behavior do we wish to encourage?"

What kinds of people we wish to produce

SUMMING UP

1. Curriculum revision in the past was uniform and slow to change because the society was slow to change. Today the social changes are swift and curriculum modification must keep pace.

2. Once the future was foreshadowed in the past—in decisions and traditions that society transmitted to its young through the home, the church, and the school. Now we find that we are unable to predict the nature of things to come by analyzing the past or even the present. We must rely on new guides and new projections to help us cope with the future.

3. While there are indeed many sensitive and frightening questions that must be resolved in the future—the possibility of nuclear war-

74 Judith M. Barnet, "Learning in Crisis The World Over," *Phi Delta Kappan* (October 1979), pp. 113-14. Also see James M. Becker, *Schooling for a Global Age* (New York: McGraw-Hill, 1979).

fare, pollution of the atmosphere, fuel scarcity, racial polarization, poverty—the basic curriculum questions remain the same. We ask ourselves: How can the schools meet the new challenges? How can schools best serve both the individual and society? What should be taught and how? And, is it relevant now and in the future?

DISCUSSION QUESTIONS

1. Give a definition of curriculum and support it with at least three examples.

2. Describe a team-teaching program you would adopt for an elementary or secondary school. What problems might you encounter?

3. Summarize the rationale for flexible scheduling as it pertains to the learner and teacher.

4. Discuss the future possibilities of computerized learning.

5. Discuss the problems and prospects of the future trends in curriculum. What other trends can you foresee?

THINGS TO DO

1. Visit a school and observe a teacher in the classroom. Is the teacher student-centered or subject-centered? Compare your results with classmates who observed other teachers.

2. Interview a teacher at a local school concerning the value of team teaching, teacher aides, and programmed learning. What are the attitudes of the teacher toward these innovations? Can you venture a guess as to why he or she adopts these attitudes?

3. Invite a guest speaker from a local television station to speak to the class on the educational potential of television.

4. Invite a guest speaker to speak on any one of the subject trends discussed in this chapter.

5. Peruse some magazine and newspaper articles that speculate about the future classroom or school. Using these resources, organize a debate about what good curriculum and instruction will be like in the future.

CHAPTER 14
SCHOOL ORGANIZATION AND SCHOOL REFORM

Focusing questions

How are schools differentiated by grade level and size?

What is the role of school boards?

What are some of the implications of declining enrollment?

What are the major types of public schools?

What alternative school models are being tried?

Can schools be reformed? How? What approaches to reform are most promising?

This chapter is divided into three parts. The first part examines several different ways of organizing and grouping schools. A discussion of grade level units suggests a pattern within which schools operate. We then group schools according to diverse settings. In the last part of the chapter, we examine several reform strategies for schools and school systems. Together, these will provide the reader with a conceptual framework for analyzing the way in which schools are organized and the potential of proposals to improve and reform them.

ORGANIZATION OF SCHOOLS BY GRADES

In examining schools according to grade levels, keep in mind that the school unit came into being as a response to widely recognized needs, and that the manner in which the school is organized represents the way educators and the public meet these needs. Not only the children's needs are considered, but also enrollment pressures, existing buildings, state laws, and limited resources. As time passes and new needs and new methods arise, either the old grade level units are modified or new ones are established. What we describe below is generally typical. The units discussed may not precisely reflect a particular grade level pattern in any one school system, however, since the exact patterns vary from place to place.

A response to public needs

NURSERY SCHOOL AND HEAD START

Nursery school and Head Start are pre-kindergarten programs that enroll children of three, four, and five years of age. The first nursery school in the United States was for the children of poor working mothers, founded by a philanthropic workers' organization in New York City in 1854. Public support of nursery programs was provided during World Wars I and II, not primarily because of concern for the children's welfare, but mainly for reasons of national defense. At their peak in 1945, nursery schools, then called day care centers, enrolled 1.6 million children.[1] With the exception of California, all the states placed day care centers within the department of public welfare. California placed them under its department of education. At the same time that the day care centers operated, there was a steady growth of private nursery schools mainly for people who could afford the fees. These private schools were geared more toward play and cooperative social behavior than toward preschool learning.

Growth of private nursery schools

The nursery school (public and private), then, was not part of the school unit. However, the situation radically changed when the federal government, through the Economic Opportunity Act in 1964 and the

---

1 William Fowles, *Infant and Child Care* (Boston: Allyn & Bacon, 1980); Ruby Takanishi-Knowles, "Federal Involvement in Early Childhood Education, 1933–73: The Need for Historical Perspectives," Paper presented at the annual meeting of the American Educational Research Association, Chicago, April 1974.

Elementary and Secondary Education Act in 1965, made funds available for prekindergarten poor children.

Project Head Start, launched in the summer of 1965, expanded the prekindergarten movement, and eventually more and more schools integrated the program into their unit organization. Of the 1.8 million children enrolled at the nursery and prekindergarten level in school year 1978–79, about 33 percent were housed in public schools, whereas the remaining children were being taught in parochial schools, community action agencies, and voluntary and independent schools approved by the federal government.[2] The 1.8 million represented about 20 percent of the population of three- to five-year-olds; this compares with 10 percent in 1969. More than 67 percent of the children attended school for only part of the day.[3]

The main purpose of many preschool programs is to promote the optimal development of each child and especially to counteract the cognitive deprivation of children who come from homes that are environmentally impoverished. Instruction frequently is based partly on the methods used by Maria Montessori (see Chapter 6), who worked in the slum areas of Italian cities, and on various compensatory approaches to education.

To counteract cognitive deprivation

In recent years considerable attention has been given to the possibility of further expanding preschool education to serve a much higher proportion of the population of children under five. Historically, day care for young children has been provided primarily in the home or through relatives, friends, or the private markets, but many public officials and educators believe that the government should make preschool programs available to all children. Pointing to the large increase in working mothers and growing recognition of the educational importance of the child's early environment, they argue that licensed preschool centers meeting professional standards for the provision of day care and educational services should be funded by the federal government. Opponents fear that expansion of government-sponsored preschool programs will further reduce the family's role in raising children and will be an expensive and unnecessary burden on the taxpayer.

Working mothers

KINDERGARTEN Kindergarten education, traced to Friedrich Froebel's experimental school in Blankenburg, Germany, eventually spread to many European cities. In the United States, kindergarten education became a part of the St. Louis public school system in 1873. Within less than fifteen years kindergartens had been established in all of the

2 *Digest of Education Statistics, 1980* (Washington, D.C.: U.S. Government Printing Office, 1980), p. 48, Table 42.
3 *Digest of Education Statistics, 1979* (Washington, D.C.: U.S. Government Printing Office, 1979), p. 46, Figure 7; p. 9, Table 4.

major cities of the country. With the exception of St. Louis, however, all the kindergartens were under private auspices and available chiefly for the middle-class and upper-middle-class child until the turn of the century. Then kindergarten was slowly introduced into public school systems.

Not all communities provide kindergarten education, and since it is noncompulsory, not all parents send their children to kindergarten. To-day, however, more than two-thirds of the public school systems in the country, and all major cities, provide kindergarten education at which attendance is voluntary.[4] More than 2.7 million students were enrolled in kindergarten in the school year 1977–78. Five-year-olds accounted for 84 percent of this enrollment, and these five-year-olds represented 81 percent of the five-year-old population.[5]

Attendance is voluntary

The kindergarten is a more or less separate unit in the school system, fully integrated neither with the prekindergarten school program, where one exists, nor with the first grade. This separation usually is considered desirable on the ground that rapid growth and development take place between the ages of four and six and that different programs must be developed for each of these ages.

The major purpose of kindergarten is to facilitate the child's readiness to learn. Readiness to learn is characterized by sufficient maturity (mental, physical, social, and emotional), by appropriate visual and auditory experiences, and by adequate speech and vocabulary. Some children learn to read while in kindergarten, but many others who have had kindergarten experience are still not ready to begin reading when they enter first grade. Comparing both groups, however, the child who has had a year's kindergarten experience is better prepared than the child who has not had the experience.[6]

Facilitates readiness to learn

ELEMENTARY SCHOOL

The traditional grade school in early America enrolled children from grades one through eight. Students who finished elementary schooling transferred to a four-year high school. Since the turn of the century, there has been a move to reduce the elementary school unit from eight to six, five, or four grades. Estimated enrollments for public school students (grades one through eight) were 14.9 million in 1900 and 25.8 million in 1978–79, the latter figure accounting for 60 percent of the total public school enrollment.[7]

4 *Educational Directory: Public School Systems, 1977–78* (Washington, D.C.: U.S. Government Printing Office, 1978), p. xvii, Table 2.

5 *Digest of Education Statistics, 1979, 1980,* p. 51, Table 45; p. 48, Table 42.

6 Lucile Lindberg and Rita Swedlow, *Early Childhood Education* (Boston: Allyn & Bacon, 1980).

7 *Digest of Education Statistics, 1980,* p. 35, Table 28.

In the elementary school that has eight grades the first three are often called primary grades, four through six are often called intermediate grades, and seven and eight are often called upper grades. In the six-unit elementary school the grades one through three are also called primary grades and four through six often are called intermediate, middle, or upper grades. The elementary school usually follows a single or general curriculum, and the subject matter is modified to meet the needs of the children, who vary widely in both abilities and interests. In this respect, the elementary school is a comprehensive school.

The elementary school normally is organized around traditional self-contained classrooms. The furniture is movable in new schools so that it can be rearranged according to the activity or individual or group project. Under this arrangement one teacher, sometimes with the help of an aide, is responsible for the whole range of activities, and the classroom is supposed to be equipped with materials and media to meet this whole range of activities. Ideally, toilet and washroom facilities are also provided, as well as art equipment, a piano, and a record player.

Self-contained classrooms

The students usually leave the classroom for specialized instruction such as physical education, library work, and remedial reading, or a resource teacher takes over the classroom for one or two periods per week. The efforts of various specialists such as the school nurse, psychologist, and social worker are coordinated with those of the classroom teacher. In some elementary schools, especially where grades seven and eight are included in the same building, subject matter is departmentalized, and instruction is handled by various teachers. This type of arrangement is customary in some schools as far down as the fifth grade.

MIDDLE, INTERMEDIATE, AND JUNIOR HIGH SCHOOL

The school units between elementary and senior high school are the middle, intermediate, and junior high schools. These grade units vary according to state and local systems. In most school systems grades five through eight constitute a middle school, grades six through eight an intermediate school, and grades seven through nine a junior high school.

The move toward these in-between school units can be traced back to 1896, when the city of Richmond, Indiana, placed its seventh and eighth grades in a separate building and revised its curriculum. Seventh and eighth grades in this city, and subsequently in other cities, tended to be viewed as part of the secondary school rather than part of the elementary school. This is one reason why many elementary schools that still house the seventh and eighth grades provide for departmentalization at these two grade levels.

The reasons for the in-between units vary. In addition to the pressure of enrollments, age and condition of buildings, and changing state regulations, there is the prevailing educational philosophy that emphasizes the importance of putting together in one school unit an age group facing similar social, psychological, and physiological changes. Specialists then can be utilized to facilitate adjustment. Yet these in-between school units do not always fulfill this intended function. As James Conant pointed out after surveying the diversity of junior high schools, the placement of the grades and the rearrangement of the grade span are not as important as the quality of the program and personnel provided.[8]

Clustering age groups with similar needs

SENIOR HIGH SCHOOL

The senior high school embraces grades nine through twelve or ten through twelve, depending on the school system. The most common arrangement today is the three-year senior high school, that is, grades ten through twelve. At the beginning of the century about 520,000 students were enrolled in grades nine through twelve, with 8 percent of *all* American youth graduating from senior high school. By 1978–79, there were some 14.2 million students in public grades nine through twelve.[9] Approximately 75 percent were graduating—a higher percentage than in any other nation.[10]

Comprehensive high schools   The comprehensive high school is the most common type of high school, and it is aimed at meeting the needs of all youth enrolled in the school; in theory, special arrangements are also made to meet the needs of both slow and talented students. A comprehensive school drawing mostly middle-class students will tend to stress college preparatory work and may neglect the students who are terminating their education after graduating from high school. On the other hand, a school drawing mostly working-class students will tend to stress vocational courses, and may fail to provide adequate college preparation in foreign language, science, and mathematics.

Need for diversified programs

In his report on the American high schools Conant pointed out that in 1956 approximately 17,000 of the nation's 21,000 public high schools were too small (graduating less than one hundred students per year) to do an adequate job of offering a diversified program to meet the needs of all students.[11] Approximately two-thirds of the students attended high schools that were too small. Since his report there has been a trend toward consolidating small high schools, coinciding with the general trend toward consolidating school systems.

School consolidating

Vocational high schools   In most large school districts, there are one or more vocational high schools in which boys and girls may enroll.

8 James B. Conant, *Education in the Junior High School Years* (Princeton, N.J.: Educational Testing Service, 1960).

9 *Digest of Education Statistics, 1979, 1980*, p. 37, Table 30; p. 35, Table 28.

10 *The Condition of Education 1979* (Washington, D.C.: U.S. Government Printing Office, 1979), p. 182, Table 5.4.

11 James B. Conant, *The American High School Today* (New York: McGraw-Hill, 1959).

Smaller school districts generally send students to "area" vocational high schools designed to serve a group of contiguous school districts. Vocational schools until very recently usually separately enrolled boys or girls. They generally offer one or more of the following programs: trade and industrial, home economics, agriculture, practical nursing, office, and technical. The technical schools (also considered vocational schools) usually have selective academic requirements and offer a wide range of skilled and technical programs of study.[12] Two of the most prominent are Brooklyn Technical High School in New York City and Lane Technical High School in Chicago.

Separately enrolled boys and girls

From a standpoint of economy, the education of vocational and commercial students in separate schools is perhaps the most practical arrangement. School boards are either unable or unwilling to allocate sufficient money to purchase necessary equipment for a vocational program in every high school. On the other hand, there is some criticism that the vocational student (but not the technical school student) is stigmatized as second rate, and that vocational high schools in large cities predominantly enroll minority students and thus impede integration.

Specialized high schools   Besides the vocational schools, some large cities have specialized high schools for students with superior scholastic aptitude or specialized artistic talents. The size of the city is important because the nature of the specialization is often uncommon, and a large student population is needed to find sufficient students to warrant a special school. New York City, the largest school system in the country, has several specialized schools, including the Bronx High School of Science and Hunter High School—both of which stress academic excellence, the High School of the Performing Arts, and the High School of Music and Art. The question has been raised as to whether it would be better to develop more specialized high schools or to work toward making the high schools more comprehensive as far as the characteristics and abilities of the students are concerned.[13]

Limited to large cities

NONGRADED SCHOOL   The concept of the nongraded school was developed to help meet the limiting aspects of chronological-age education, which many educators claim is inflexible and lockstep-oriented. It came out of such programs as the Pueblo Plan, developed by Preston Search, superintendent of schools in Pueblo, Colorado, in 1885–94; the Platoon School, which is credited to Superintendent William Wirt, who initiated the program in Bluffton, Indiana, in 1900; the Burke Individual Plan, started by Frederick Burke in the ele-

12   John T. Grasso and John R. Shea, *Vocational Education and Training: Impact on Youth* (Berkeley, Calif.: Carnegie Council on Policy Studies in Higher Education, 1979).
13   Gordon I. Swanson, "High School Goals: Response to John Henry Martin," *Educational Leadership* (January 1980), pp. 288–89; Daniel Tanner, "Splitting Up the School System: Are Comprehensive High Schools Doomed?" *Phi Delta Kappan* (October 1979), pp. 92–97.

mentary school of San Francisco State Normal School in 1912; and the Winnetka Plan of Carlton Washburne, who brought Burke's plan to Winnetka, Illinois, and modified it when he became superintendent.

These plans were concerned basically with differentiating instruction to meet individual differences among students. The idea received support by early influential educators who emphasized individual diversity and advocated that the organization of the school must reflect this diversity.[14]

Meeting
student
differences

Nongraded elementary schools are much more common than nongraded secondary schools, with about 800,000 elementary students and 485,000 secondary students enrolled in some form of nongraded program.[15] The details of the plan vary from school to school. In general, the curriculum is planned around the individual's readiness for learning and interests. Students progress at their own rates and are classified on the basis of achievement rather than age. In its pure form, no grade designators are used. Levels of sequential content frequently are used as the organizational basis. For example, the student may be at an advanced level in mathematics but at a less advanced level in social studies. The student must complete a prescribed level before moving to the next level, and the amount of time it takes the student to complete a level in a subject will vary. The slow learner may take three years to complete what should normally be accomplished in two years; the rapid learner may accomplish three years' work in two or less.

ORGANIZATION OF SCHOOL SYSTEMS

School organization issues also involve questions as to how school districts are established and governed. How many school districts are there and how large are they? Who decides matters of educational policy in the schools? The following sections provide basic information dealing with these types of questions.

NUMBER OF SCHOOL SYSTEMS

The number of school systems in the United States continues to decline. In 1930, there were more than 130,000 school districts. By 1950 the numbers had shrunk to 83,718; by 1980 to 15,625. Figure 14.1 illustrates the declining number of school systems in ten-year intervals from 1930 to 1980, with projections for 1990.

Shrinking
number of
school districts

Between 1930 and 1970 the number of school districts decreased 86 percent, with the most noticeable decline occurring between 1950 and

---

14 See Charles W. Elliot, *Educational Reform: Essays and Addresses* (New York: Century, 1909); Charles H. Judd, *The Evolution of a Democratic School System* (Boston: Houghton Mifflin, 1918).

15 *Digest of Education Statistics, 1980*, p. 35, Table 28.

FIGURE 14.1
DECLINING NUMBER OF PUBLIC
SCHOOL SYSTEMS

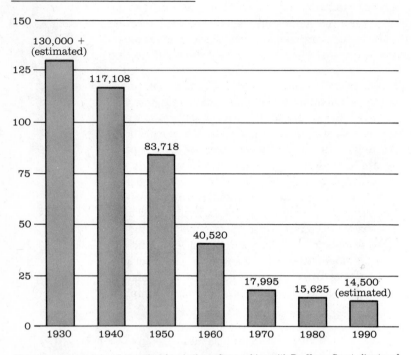

Note: 1990 estimate is based on authors' projections after speaking with Dr. Vance Grant, director of the National Center for Educational Statistics, May 29, 1980.

Source: *Digest of Education Statistics, 1979* (Washington, D.C.: U.S. Government Printing Office, 1979), p. 62, Figure 5; p. 61, Table 58; *Educational Directory: Public School Systems, 1980–81,* Advance Report (Washington, D.C.: U.S. Government Printing Office, 1980), Table 2, Manuscript form.

1970. Most of the shrinkage occurred in the Midwest, the region that still has close to one-half of the school districts in the country. The disproportionate numbers are illustrated by the fact that one school district, New York City, enrolled more students in 1953 than the total enrollment in each of forty states.[16] In the early 1960s Iowa, Nebraska, North Dakota, and South Dakota, which educated less than 5 percent of the children in the nation, had about 25 percent of the nation's school districts. Despite

16 Willard R. Lane, Ronald G. Corwin, and William G. Monahan, *Foundations of Educational Administration* (New York: Macmillan, 1967); Edgar L. Morphet, Roe L. Johns, and Theodore L. Reller, *Educational Organization and Administration* (Englewood Cliffs, N.J.: Prentice-Hall, 1974).

the continuing trend toward consolidation, as of 1980 there were still four states with over 1,000 districts: California, Illinois, Nebraska, and Texas.[17]

A great many of the reorganized school districts are still too small to provide a comprehensive educational program and adequate specialized personnel to meet the needs of all the students. While the trend toward consolidation continues in the rural and small school districts, there is a recent counter trend in city school districts to decentralize the large districts.

SIZE OF SCHOOL SYSTEMS What is the ideal size for a school district? In terms of minimum size, how **Ideal size for a school district** many students must be enrolled to justify offering the diversified programs, services and personnel needed to meet modern educational requirements? A 1934 study of city and county school systems concluded that a minimum of 10,000 to 12,000 students was needed to justify specialized and adequate staff size, as well as a varied program, in relationship to reasonable costs of the educational program.[18] At the time those numbers were criticized severely by many educators who believed that a district of that size was unattainable and impractical for most parts of the country.

Regarding maximum size, a research team headed by Paul Mort and Francis Cornell developed a method for measuring the effectiveness of a school system based around an adaptability index.[19] The index was correlated with school characteristics such as financial policies, curriculum innovation, community and staff participation, location, and size. These studies considered the maximally effective school district to comprise 100,000 students. This estimate was supported by other researchers,[20] but later was disputed by advocates of decentralization who put the figure between 12,000 and 40,000.[21] One view of the professional literature has concluded that the optimal size for a school district is between 10,000 and 50,000 pupils.[22]

17 *Digest of Education Statistics, 1979*, p. 13, Table 9; *Educational Directory: Public School Systems, 1980-81*, Advance Report (Washington, D.C.: U.S. Government Printing Office, 1980), Tables 1, 2, manuscript form.

18 Howard A. Dawson, *Satisfactory Local School Units*, Field Study No. 7 (Nashville, Tenn.: George Peabody College for Teachers, 1934).

19 Paul R. Mort and Francis G. Cornell, *American Schools in Transition* (New York: Teachers College Press, Columbia University, 1941); Paul R. Mort, William S. Vincent, and Clarence Newell, *The Growing Edge, An Instrument for Measuring the Adaptability of School Systems*, 2 vols. (New York: Teachers College Press, Columbia University, 1955).

20 Stanton F. Leggett and William S. Vincent, *A Program for Meeting the Needs of New York City Schools* (New York: Public Education Association, 1947); Donald H. Ross, ed., *Administration for Adaptability* (New York: Metropolitan School Study Council, 1958).

21 Mario D. Fantini, Marilyn Gittell, and Richard Magat, *Community Control and the Urban School* (New York: Praeger, 1970); A. Harry Passow, *Toward Creating a Model Urban School System* (New York: Teachers College Press, Columbia University, 1967).

22 *Summary of Research on Size of Schools and School Districts* (Arlington, Va.: Educational Research Service, 1974).

TABLE 14.1
DISTRIBUTION OF PUBLIC SCHOOL
SYSTEMS BY SIZE OF SYSTEM,
1980–81

SIZE OF SYSTEM	PUBLIC SCHOOL SYSTEMS		PUBLIC SCHOOL PUPILS	
	NUMBER	PERCENTAGE	NUMBER	PERCENTAGE
Total operating systems	15,625	100.0	42,851,396	100.0
Systems with 300 pupils or more	11,464	73.4	42,347,198	98.8
25,000 or more	183	1.2	11,907,985	27.8
10,000 to 24,999	511	3.3	7,434,630	17.3
5,000 to 9,999	1,106	7.1	7,705,372	18.0
2,500 to 4,999	2,065	13.2	7,181,460	16.8
1,000 to 2,499	3,457	22.1	5,665,386	13.2
600 to 999	1,820	11.7	1,437,725	3.4
300 to 599	2,316	14.8	1,014,640	2.4
Systems with less than 300 pupils	4,161	26.6	504,198	1.2

Source: *Educational Directory: Public School Systems, 1980–81*, Table 1, Manuscript form.

Among the approximately 15,625 public school systems that enrolled 42.8 million public school students in the 1980–81 school year, 183
school systems had enrollments of 25,000 or more students, and this accounted for 11.9 million students (28 percent of the total). At the base of
this school system pyramid there were 4,161 school systems with 300 or
fewer students. This represented 27 percent of the school systems but only
1.2 percent of the total student enrollment. Table 14.1 shows how school
systems are distributed according to enrollment size.

Most of the hundred largest school systems (50,000 or more students) are located in California, Florida, Texas, Ohio, and Maryland. In
most cases, the larger school systems are located in or near cities, the
largest being the New York City system with approximately 960,000 students as of 1980, followed by Los Angeles with 545,000 students and
Chicago with 475,000 students. (Two other large school systems, Puerto
Rico and Hawaii, span an entire territory and state, respectively.) The
medium-sized and smaller school systems have followed metropolitan
sprawl and tend to be located in the outer ring of the suburbs or in rural
areas.[23]

23   A list of the largest 753 school systems, enrolling 10,000 or more students, can be found in
the *Educational Directory: 1980–81.*

LOCAL
SCHOOL BOARDS
The local boards of education have been delegated powers and duties by the state for the purpose of assuring that the schools of their communities are operated properly. The schools are agencies of limited power and can exercise only those prerogatives specifically delegated to them by the state legislatures. Nevertheless, by law and custom, school boards have assumed significant decision-making responsibility. For the most part, the state sets up a framework of procedures with minimum requirements for operating local public schools and certain other restrictions for financial accounting. School boards are given the power to raise money through taxes with a debt limitation. They exercise power over personnel and school property. Some states leave curriculum and student policy pretty much in the hands of the school board, but others, by law, insist on specific requirements. In general, the school board conforms to state guidelines to qualify for state aid, as well as to federal guidelines where U.S. government monies are involved.

Delegated powers from the state

Methods of selecting board members are prescribed by state law. The two basic methods are by election and appointment. Election usually is thought to make for greater accountability to the public, but the appointment method sometimes is supported as leading to greater competence and less politics.[24] Popular election is the most common practice. In 1978, 86 percent of school board members were elected in nonpartisan elections, 10 percent were elected in partisan elections, and 4 percent were appointed. Appointment is more common in large urban districts than in suburban or small-town districts: 11 percent of urban board members in 1978 were appointed.[25]

Most school boards are elected

A few states specify a standard number of board members, still others specify a permissible range, and a few have no requirements. Most fall within a three-to-nine-member range, with the largest known having nineteen members. An optimum number for efficient school board operation has not been determined. In a 1980 survey of the largest school systems, comprising 50,000 or more students, numbers of school board members ranged from five to thirteen, with an average and majority of seven. The notion of an uneven number of board members suggests the need for a tie-breaking vote. Minority members comprise 29 percent of school board composition; women members make up 36 percent.[26] Some large city school boards have increased their size to defuse tension in the

24 "What Works Best? An Elected or an Appointed School Board?" *The American School Board Journal* (July 1972), pp. 21–23.

25 *NSBA Factsheet*, (Washington, D.C.: National School Boards Association, 1979).

26 Allan C. Ornstein, "Composition of Board Members of Big School Systems," Paper presented at the Annual Meeting of the American Educational Research Association, Los Angeles, April 1981.

community, to limit the effects of partisan politics, and to acquire a broader representation.[27]

There are three general types of board meetings: regular, special, and executive. The first two are usually open meetings and the public is invited. Open board meetings obviously are beneficial for enhancing school-community relations and allow parents to understand the problems of education as well as to air their concerns. The use of closed board meetings to reach major policy is generally disdained but is occasionally used by central school boards in some large cities as conflict and tensions increase.[28]

One of the most important responsibilities of a school board is to appoint a competent superintendent of schools. The superintendent is the executive officer of the school board, while the board is the legislative policy-making body. One of the major functions of the school superintendent is to gather and present data so that school board members can make intelligent policy decisions. Increasingly, reliance on the superintendent and his or her staff is evident in school systems that grow in size. The superintendent advises the school board and keeps members abreast of problems. It is recommended practice that the school board refrain from setting policy that does not have the recommendation of the school superintendent. It is common practice that when there is continuous disagreement or a major conflict over policy between the school board and superintendent, the latter is usually replaced.[29]

Open and closed board meetings

THINKING SMALL FOR THE FUTURE   One of the great problems facing the schools over the next decade or two is the probability of declining enrollments. This decline in total enrollments hit the grade schools in 1972 and has recently moved to high schools.[30] But we are very ill equipped for the management of a downward trend. For several generations we have enjoyed growth in almost all aspects of social and economic life—population, per capita real income, productivity, and gross national product. Almost all of our institutions, including our schools, have been geared to an age of accelerated growth.

Declining enrollments

27 Allan C. Ornstein, *Metropolitan Schools: Administrative Decentralization v. Community Control* (Metuchen, N.J.: Scarecrow Press, 1974); Ornstein, "Administrative Decentralization and Community Participation: Research with Policy Implications," *Viewpoints* (April 1980), pp 82–96; Richard W. Saxe, *Educational Administration Today* (Berkeley, Calif.: McCutchan, 1979).

28 Alfred Lightfoot, *Urban Education in Social Perspective* (Chicago: Rand McNally, 1978); Jay Scribner, and David O'Shea, "Political Developments in the Urban School Districts" in C. Wayne Gordon, ed., *Uses of the Sociology of Education*, Part II, National Society for the Study of Education (Chicago: University of Chicago Press, 1974), pp. 380–408.

29 Ronald F. Campbell, et al., *The Organization and Control of American Schools*, 4th ed. (Columbus, Ohio: Merrill, 1978); Saxe, *Educational Administration Today.*

30 "The Ups and Downs of Education," *American Demographics* (June 1979), pp. 9–11; "Schools Will Spend $11 Billion More This Year Than Last; Enrollment Down 1.2%," *Phi Delta Kappan* (November 1979), p. 156.

This age is coming to an end, not only with regard to our schools but for almost all of our social and economic institutions. The prospects for the next ten or twenty years, barring a major change in social trends, suggest that we are entering an age of slowdown and smallness. The rate of overall productivity is likely to decrease, along with a declining student population and school industry. An interesting analysis surrounding these kinds of changes in Colorado school districts between 1960 and 1970 was done by Kenneth Boulding.[31] Many superintendents were unaware that their own districts had experienced decline, especially in areas where the turnover of administrators was high. They were absorbed in current problems and not aware of what the system was like years ago. However, in declining school districts, and especially where superintendents were aware of these declines, there was a *higher* quality of education than in the expanding ones. This suggests, according to Boulding, that decline in enrollments may result in an opportunity for improving education, as measured by such crude indicators as class size, number of dropouts, performance on tests, and so on. A further conclusion was that the larger districts undergoing decline were able to make successful adjustments, probably because there were more material and people to move around. As a result of this trend, however, many smaller districts are likely to go under, and there may be a merger of small districts in the future with possibly less variety. In addition, existing school districts will continue to confront a need to close schools they now operate.[32] This does not seem too unreasonable; in fact, it coincides with present school consolidation trends, as well as with the experiences of small businesses that go under or merge during hard times and/or in a period of decline.

Age of slow down and smallness

Future school mergers

Maintenance and improvement of existing educational programs also have been hampered by the inflationary forces that characterized the 1970s and seem likely to continue in the 1980s. The consumer price index almost doubled between 1970 and 1980, so that goods and services that cost $1.16 in 1970 had risen to $2.30 by 1980. Teacher salaries and school budgets also increased, of course, but they generally did not keep pace with inflation, and rising prices made taxpayers less willing and able to increase expenditures in schools. Double-digit price increases (more than 10 percent a year) of the late 1970s probably will continue in the 1980s, thus making it still more likely that educators will have to think in terms of reducing expenditures, staff, and instructional programs.

We might also explore the question of local school spending in relationship to size. A demand for thrift has become apparent among school boards—cutting expenses, reducing budgets, and lowering tax rates. The

Demand for thrift

---

31   Kenneth E. Boulding, ''The Management of Decline,'' *Change* (June 1975), pp. 8-9, 64.
32   Doyle E. Winter, ''Public Schools Cut Their Costs,'' *American Demographics* (June 1979), pp. 31-33.

general need for conservation of resources has gained acceptability as a high priority aim. What is happening in the automobile and energy industries, and with food and other natural resources, may soon characterize schooling. We are going to have to think of trimming the fat if school districts are to survive.

1. *Size*. Classroom size, in the interest of economy, may increase. The data on classroom size and student achievement are somewhat contradictory, and many studies show no significant differences. When differences were found, they were about as likely to favor large classes as small. Some recent reviews of the research have shown that class size is related to pupil achievement, but only when the size of classes is reduced sufficiently (fifteen or fewer students) to result in altered teaching methods.[33] Thus educators should not be too quick to reduce class size without considering whether teachers can be helped to adapt appropriate methods utilized for small classes.

2. *Modernization.* Instead of building new schools, it is cheaper in many cases to maintain and modernize older schools. Older schools frequently were better constructed than the newer ones, and those not in distress should be saved in an era of declining birth rates. Moreover, many older buildings are not detrimental to student learning.

Opting for older schools

3. *New building.* Small schools can be cheaper than large schools, especially if they are well insulated and stress utilization of space. The increasing costs of fuel and light are factors to consider now. We no longer need to build big and expensive cafeterias, auditoriums, and gymnasiums. They add to construction costs, are unoccupied for a large portion of the day and year, and cost a great deal for maintenance, heating, and lighting. Educators are trying to reduce unnecessary energy costs and have succeeded in reducing energy use by 35 percent between 1974 and 1979.[34]

Building smaller schools

4. *Energy economies.* Related to the need for saving fuel, more and more schools will be reducing temperatures during vacation, delaying warming up the school before classes each morning, switching to the night heat cycle earlier in the day, reducing heat in the hallways and other specialized areas, scheduling custodial care during the day, insulating pipes, walls, and windows, preparing additional cold lunches, reducing lunch periods or activity periods, shortening

33   Gene V. Glass and Mary Lee Smith, *Meta-Analysis of Research on the Relationship of Class Size and Achievement* (Boulder, Colo.: University of Colorado Laboratory of Educational Research, 1978). See also Nicola Filby et al., "What Happens in Smaller Classes," Paper presented at the Annual Conference of the American Educational Research Association, Boston, April 1980.

34   "Schools Cut Energy Use by One-Third," *Phi Delta Kappan* (December 1979), pp. 234–35.

the school day and, if things really get rough, rescheduling holidays and even the school year to coincide with warmer seasons. Between 1973 and 1980 the total bill for heating schools in the U.S. tripled, despite reduced consumption. School officials have responded by looking for ways to reduce energy outlays and have identified a number of steps that can be taken to cut energy use.[35]

5. *School closings.* The closing of schools is fast becoming the focal act of this new era of retrenchment. One approach to this decline is for school districts to rent their closed schools to tenants; in most cases, they are service agencies themselves: churches, private schools, and community centers. In still other cases, schools can be sold. For example, in Ithaca, New York, a downtown high school was sold to private investors who converted it to a shopping mall. In Orlando, Florida, a school became a hotel; in Pittsburgh, a hospital; in Peoria, a bakery.[36] Both approaches (rental or sale) represent wise courses—bringing money to the school district, as opposed to mothballing a school, leaving it subject to vandalism, and standing as a blight on its neighborhood. As we enter the 1980s, we can expect increased school closings—we guess some 200 to 500 nationwide each year.

Renting or selling school property is wise

GEOGRAPHICAL TYPES OF SCHOOLS

Beside being organized into different grade span units, schools can be classified according to geographical characteristics. Below are a number of school groupings that cut across and include both elementary and secondary schools; they can apply to individual schools and in many cases to an entire school system.

1. *Rural schools.* About 30 percent of public school enrollments are located in rural (or nonurban) areas. These schools are often unable to offer a diversified program. Many of the students who attend these schools are from low-income families, especially in Appalachia and some parts of New England. Some educators believe these students do not receive their fair share of federal funding for the economically disadvantaged.[37]

Limited federal funding

2. *Suburban schools.* About 40 percent of the public school enrollments are located in suburban areas. While differences between

35   John Mulholland, "How to Save 117% in School Fuel," *Phi Delta Kappan* (May 1980), p. 639; David K. Wiles, *Energy, Winter, and Schools* (Lexington, Mass.: Heath, 1979).

36   Diane Devoky, "Burden of the Seventies: The Management of Decline," *Phi Delta Kappan* (October 1979), pp. 87–91.

37   Jonathan P. Sher, "A Proposal to End Federal Neglect of Rural Schools," *Phi Delta Kappan* (December 1978), pp. 280–82.

city and suburban schools are usually striking, the differences among suburban schools can be almost equally striking. (One reason that suburbs are incorrectly perceived as uniformly middle class is because they tend to be racially homogeneous. Nevertheless, the student population in each suburb can vary greatly in income.) Similarly, the schools in the suburbs vary in size; many are large and offer diversified programs; others are small and have limited programs.

**Suburban
schools are not
all alike**

3. *City schools*. About 30 percent of the public school enrollments are located in the cities, and the figure is decreasing in some cities with movement of middle-class families to the suburbs. City schools are often large, and some big cities still operate a number of schools that were built around 1900. As a group, city students perform below the national norm on reading and mathematical standardized tests. While comparisons are often made between city and suburban schools, there are differences between outer-city and inner-city schools.

Outer-city schools tend to be populated by working-class and/or lower-middle-class groups. Many of these schools are located in White ethnic neighborhoods and racially changing neighborhoods. There are also a small number of suburban-type, middle- and high-income neighborhoods within city limits.

Inner-city schools usually are located in Black or Hispanic neighborhoods. Most of the students are from low-income families. For the last fifteen years these city schools have been the focus of attention by the federal government and educational reformers.

4. *Metropolitan schools*. A few schools already draw on both city and suburban student populations. The Nashville-Davidson Metropolitan County school system in Tennessee is an example of a large city system that combined with a suburban system to form one metropolitan school system.

5. *County schools*. This type of school system usually cuts across city, suburban, and rural boundaries. Thus it draws on a diversified student population. There are several county school systems, such as Dade County (Miami), Florida; Montgomery County (Baltimore), Maryland; and Clark County (Las Vegas), Nevada.

6. *Regional schools*. This type of school system is formed when an appropriate state agency mandates establishment of one or more schools with specialized educational capability. Regional schools serve a group of school districts within a state. A good example is the St. Louis County Special School District, which operates special edu-

cation schools and provides audiovisual materials for suburban school districts in the St. Louis Metropolitan Area.

STRATEGIES FOR REFORMING SCHOOLS

Reform strategies designed to improve the quality of schools can take a number of forms. One form provides a conceptual framework of broad reform with many highly theoretical components. This approach sets up *alternative reform models* of schools and school systems for analysis and interpretation. A second approach deals with public schools as a system and attempts to bring about *systematic reform* throughout a school or school district. These strategies are not mutually exclusive because it is possible to use both at the same time. For example, an effort to bring about systematic reform in a school or school district can incorporate alternatives to the educational programs that have been provided in the past.

Alternative v. systematic reform

ALTERNATIVE SCHOOL MODELS

A number of models have been proposed for urban schools. The one developed by Kenneth Clark identified five alternatives to public schools.[38] Instead of working within the present educational system, these models establish new public options, to the extent of going outside the system. The first model consists of *regional schools* financed by federal or state funds. Those financed by the federal government could serve students from neighboring states; those financed by states could serve neighboring school systems. A second alternative, *college-oriented schools*, would be laboratory schools operated by colleges and universities and supported by public funds. *Industrial and business-sponsored schools,* a third choice, would be operated on contract by private industry or business in conjunction with a school district or governmental agency. Fourth, *labor-union-sponsored schools* would be operated on contract by a local or national labor union in conjunction with a school district or a governmental agency. Finally, *schools for dropouts* would be established that would be analogous to present Job Corps training programs.

Involving governments, college, industry, and labor

By contrast, the four models proposed by Ornstein suggest innovative approaches within the system.[39]

1. *Linear campus.* This includes a group of schools located on different sites within their respective communities, rather than on a single site. The schools are connected by a transportation line and share educational centers that offer special facilities and personnel.

Options within the system

---

38 Kenneth B. Clark, "Alternative Public School Systems," *Harvard Educational Review* (Winter 1968), pp. 100–113.

39 Allan C. Ornstein, *Urban Education* (Columbus, Ohio: Merrill, 1972).

Students are brought together for a few hours daily or one or more days weekly to supplement their studies.

2. *Joint occupancy*. This concept combines public and private financing and ownership of a multipurpose structure. The lower floors of the structure might be relegated to private business, and the upper floors might house the school. The plan would help to cope with diminishing land resources and increasing real estate costs for acquiring and building new businesses and school sites, and it yields revenues from land that would normally be tax-exempt.

3. *Open-air school*. This is sometimes called the "school without walls"; it is an attempt to go beyond the regular "four walls" school and convert the community or city into a classroom. Students can take full advantage of business and cultural resources of the surrounding area and many classes are held off the school site.

4. *Educational park*. This type of school is a clustering of elementary and secondary schools located on one site and housing 5,000 to 30,000 students. Schools share facilities (gym, library, pool, computers) and personnel (nurses, social workers, physicians, psychologists). The size of the school permits the most specialized facilities and personnel. The site is usually a racially "neutral" area, and quality offsets the problem of bigness. While a small community system may house its entire school system in such a setting, in its most imaginative use the educational park takes the form of a metropolitan school. Ideally, city and suburban communities would combine their resources to construct such a school at the city-suburb boundary.

MAGNET AND
ALTERNATIVE
SCHOOLS

A somewhat different approach to reforming education is frequently undertaken by establising *magnet* schools and *alternative* schools. Magnet schools are schools that attract enrollment on a voluntary basis by offering special instructional programs or curricula designed to appeal to students in more than one neighborhood attendance area. Most magnet schools attract students by providing either a special field of study (e.g., foreign languages, preparation in a career field such as health care) or a distinctive approach to instruction (e.g., "open" education, "traditional" education). Some magnet schools, such as the Bronx High School of Science in New York City, have existed for many years, but such schools usually were not called magnets until the 1970s, when many big-city districts established magnet schools to increase desegregation through voluntary methods. Daniel Levine and Connie Campbell have studied urban magnet schools and concluded that they

Special programs to attract different students

differ from magnets of previous decades in that they are designed to achieve a greater variety of goals (e.g., desegregation) and that they appeal to a much more diverse clientele than the selective schools that generally enrolled only high achieving students in the past.[40]

Growth of the magnet school movement has been greatly accelerated by passage in 1976 of an amendment to the Emergency School Aid Act (ESAA) providing for the funding of desegregated magnet schools. By 1980, hundreds of school districts had established one or more magnet schools, in many cases as part of court orders to reduce racial isolation of minority students. Magnet schools can include any number of grades from kindergarten through grade twelve, but most are organized as either elementary or secondary schools. A national survey of magnet schools in 1979 indicated that the largest number of magnets were elementary schools and that the most common magnet themes were fine arts and career/vocational education.[41]

Alternative schools are schools that provide alternatives to learning opportunities available in the average public school. From this point of view magnet schools are alternative schools, as are many parochial and other nonpublic schools, schools for special-needs students such as the physically handicapped or the emotionally disturbed, institutions such as "street academies," "storefront schools," high school "outposts" designed to make education more relevant for inner city students, and "schools without walls," which draw heavily on community resources for learning.[42] A recent survey of alternative schools indicated that alternative schools tend to have the following characteristics as compared with more traditional schools: enrollment of students who have not succeeded in traditional schools or want a different kind of education, greater individualization, ungraded learning experiences, more openness to the outside community, small size, and lack of formal accreditation.[43]

Alternative schools were established at a relatively rapid rate in the 1960s and 1970s. In addition to financial insecurity, which is particularly a problem for many alternative schools outside the public school system, such schools frequently face a number of special problems and needs. For example, the survey just cited identified the following major problems and challenges: lack of communication and mutual support; need for more evaluation; lack of accreditation; need to provide vocational counseling,

Financial
problems plus
other
challenges

40   Daniel U. Levine and Connie Campbell, "Developing and Implementing Big-City Magnet School Programs" in D. Levine and R. J. Havighurst, eds., *The Future of Big-City Schools* (Berkeley, Calif.: McCutchan, 1977), pp. 247-66.

41   Cheryl Stanley, "A National Survey of Magnet Schools Utilized for Voluntary Integration." Paper presented at the Annual Meeting of the American Educational Research Association, San Francisco, April 1979.

42   Daniel U. Levine, "Educating Alienated Inner City Youth: Lessons from the Street Academies," *Journal of Negro Education* (Spring 1975), pp. 139-48.

43   Greg Hodes, et al., *Alternative Education in the Metropolitan Kansas City Region* (Kansas City, Mo.: Teaching Assistance Organization, 1978).

skill training, and job placement; lack of long-range goals; and need to work with teacher training institutions.

Advocates of the alternative school movement point out that generally only one model of education is available to parents in any given public school system. Some argue for creating alternative schools within the system; some advocates argue for greater alternatives outside the system, contending that the only true alternatives *are* outside the system. Whether within or without the existing establishment, alternatives would permit a choice on the part of the parent and child of the school that best suits them. Developing alternatives within the school system can be done by uniting teachers and parents in pursuance of common goals in contrast to the cleavage between them now.[44] Developing alternatives outside the school system is more difficult because of limited financial resources.

Arguments against alternatives center on the fact that there is little convincing evidence, largely anecdotes and personal opinion, that alternatives do make a difference in achievement. Moreover, many of these alternative schools have the reputation of de-emphasizing cognitive skills while focusing mainly on affective education. Critics also point out that public education must serve society as a whole, not just individuals or subgroups. They worry that the proliferation of alternatives outside the system may increase divisiveness and polarization, including the encouragement of private all-White or all-Black schools.

Possibility of increasing segregation

SYSTEMATIC SCHOOL REFORM

In the previous chapter we pointed out that many knowledgeable observers believe there has been relatively little improvement in elementary and secondary schools in the United States. Despite the expenditure of billions of dollars on a host of innovations and highly publicized school reform efforts, it appears that relatively little was accomplished in bringing about fundamental improvements in teaching and learning or in introducing new system-wide approaches designed to make schools more effective and more humane. This is not to say that our schools generally are not worthwhile institutions or, as some critics would have it, are instruments of oppression that destroy the hearts and minds of children. What is clear, however, is that many expensive school reform efforts have not resulted in much noticeable or widespread improvement in schools.[45]

Experience in the 1960s and 1970s did show, however, that promulgating, legislating, and even packaging change is not the same as actually changing. Examination of this experience has resulted in a much better

44 Mario D. Fantini, *Public Schools of Choice: A Plan for the Reform of American Education* (New York: Simon & Schuster, 1973); Jonathan Kozol, *Free Schools* (Boston: Houghton Mifflin, 1972).

45 John I. Goodlad, *A Study of Schooling* (Los Angeles: Institute for Development of Educational Activities, 1979); Dale Mann, ed., *Making Change Happen?* (New York: Teachers College Press, Columbia University, 1978).

understanding of the steps that must be taken to ensure that school reform efforts have a significant and lasting impact. Among the lessons that can be deduced from innovative efforts of the past are the following:

1. Implementation of an innovation frequently either is not carried out successfully (i.e., the innovation is never truly implemented) or has little or no effect on students because a host of problems arise to stifle practical application. For example, experts may devise a wonderful new science curriculum for fourth graders and school districts may purchase large quantities of the new curriculum materials, but teachers may choose not to use the materials, may use them improperly because they do not fit the existing curriculum or schedule, or may not know how to use them. For this reason, innovations are not likely to be implemented successfully unless the organization introducing them is *adaptive* in the sense that it can identify and solve day-to-day implementation problems.[46]

2. Because the innovating organization must identify and solve day-to-day problems, the focus in bringing about change must be at the level of the individual school facility where many of the problems occur.

3. Implementation of a significant innovation requires change in a variety of interrelated institutional arrangements, including scheduling of staff and student time, selection and utilization of instructional methods and materials, development of new behaviors and attitudes on the part of teachers and students, mechanisms for making decisions, and many other aspects of school organization and operation. This in turn means that the building principal, who is fundamentally responsible for arrangements throughout the institution, is the key person in successfully implementing change.

4. Because people who are expected to change their working patterns will not cooperate fully unless they have a voice in designing and implementing an innovation, teachers who are to use innovative materials in the classroom must have an opportunity to help select and evaluate them.

5. Major changes require not only a good deal of time and resources but also a systematic examination of all their implications and a plan for overcoming the many obstacles that will arise in bringing them about; otherwise they will be "swallowed up" by forces that tend to maintain stability in an existing organization. In this regard, one observer has noted that, "Organizations legitimately seek a state of

46   Willis D. Hawley, "Horses Before Carts: Developing Adaptive Schools and the Limits of Innovation" in Mann, ed., *Making Change Happen?* pp. 224-53.

equilibrium in order to sustain themselves. . . . Schools can tolerate only so much change and still attend to the business of 'keeping school,' and planned change programs should be sensitive to that need."[47]

The preceding conclusions are supported in the findings of hundreds of studies that have examined the origins, characteristics, and impact of innovative educational projects carried out during the past twenty or thirty years. One reviewer who has systematically examined this literature on the process of innovation has concluded that we now know a tremendous amount about implementation and that recognition of the following principles (among others) would, if followed, lead to the successful implementation of any worthwhile innovation:[48] (1) the size of the project is unrelated to its success, (2) innovations that rely too heavily on technology will be short-lived, (3) successful implementation is directly related to immediate administrator support, (4) innovations in curriculum and instruction are easier to implement than those requiring changes in organization or administration, (5) implementation requires a critical mass of advocates, (6) directives are seldom effective in stimulating adoption or implementation, and (7) various sources of information tend to increase the likelihood of diffusion and adoption.

Studies of unusually successful schools also provide an indication of the factors that are needed to make educational programs—whether traditional or innovative—work effectively. (Since most schools are not unusually successful in the first place, unusually effective implementation of traditional or existing approaches is itself innovative.) In this regard, a U.S. Department of Education report stated that:

Effective approaches are innovative themselves

The findings of several studies of unusually effective school programs converge in stressing the importance of commitment and capacity at the individual school level. Particularly important . . . are such characteristics as strong and effective leadership (usually from the principal), the atmosphere of the school (including student-teacher rapport), high expectations for student achievement, small group and individualized instruction, exchange of ideas among staff, and a clear focus on objectives and priorities, including basic skills.[49]

47 Wayne J. Doyle, "A Solution in Search of a Problem: Comprehensive Change and the Jefferson Experimental Schools" in Mann, ed., *Making Change Happen?*, p. 97.
48 Donald C. Orlich, "Federal Educational Policy: The Paradox of Innovation and Centralization," *Educational Researcher* (July–August 1979), pp. 6–10.
49 *Progress of Education in the United States of America 1976-77 and 1977-78* (Washington, D.C.: U.S. Government Printing Office, 1979), p. 67.

Recently, parents and teachers have cooperated more fully in the conduct of schools. Here, a social studies teacher talks with seventh-grade parents at a Back-to-School Night.

WHAT MAKES A GOOD SCHOOL?

Possibilities involving the reform of instruction can also be understood better by identifying the characteristics of schools that are particularly effective in accomplishing their goals. To do this, researchers frequently define a "good" school by identifying those with higher achievement levels, lower absence rates, more productive educational climates, or other indicators of success as compared with schools of similar socioeconomic status and student body composition. Several such studies are summarized in this section.

One answer to the question of what is a good school has been provided by Edward Wynne, based on data on 140 Chicago metropolitan schools.[50] Wynne found that good schools have evolved over periods of time instead of being created *ab initio*. The staffs of these schools are comparatively stable. Evidently, it takes time for teachers and administrators to pull a school into shape.

Good schools evolve over time

There is a high level of communication among all staff members in these schools, via formal and informal meetings and written notices.

50 Edward A. Wynne, *Looking at Teaching* (Lexington, Mass.: Heath, 1980).

Morale is good, transfers from the school are minimal, and typically the policies are clearly written down and distributed to students, parents, teachers, and administrators. Rules and regulations are reviewed, updated, and complied with. The policies of the school regarding homework, attendance, lateness, grades, promotion, and discipline and punishment are well understood by all.

Good morale and communication

Students are safe in these schools, and so are teachers. While there is stress on the cognitive domain, the affective domain among students is not ignored. Students, parents, and staff trust one another. School spirit is high and extracurricular activities are important and supported by students and staff, and usually by parents. There are frequent assemblies and other such gatherings, and the walls of the classrooms and halls are filled with posters and announcements about awards for both academic and extracurricular achievements. At the high school level, there is a vital and informative student paper.

The principal runs the school with a firm hand, but he or she also engages in extensive consultation with teachers and parents and to a lesser extent with students. This type of principal has such traits as energy, intelligence, pride, moral courage (willingness to stand up for what one believes is right), and imagination. Salary has little to do with these traits.

Leadership characteristics of the principal

In any case, what Wynne has provided is a scorecard to help identify good schools. Once we identify and agree upon these elements—and what causes them—then we can attempt to duplicate them in other schools, either existing or newly created.

Other scholars also have been trying to identify the characteristics of a good school. The way a school is run, or how "good" it is, can make a difference in how much a child learns and how he or she behaves, according to a group of British researchers.[51] Michael Rutter and his colleagues contend that there are ways that the schools can be improved to make them more effective. The most important factor is what the researchers called the "ethos," or general tone, of the school.

After studying twelve low-income high schools in London for four years, the British research team reported that children in the bottom aptitude rank of the best school scored as well on standardized final examinations as did the children in the top of the worst school. In other words, a slow student entering one of the better schools had about the same chance to earn good grades as a bright student entering one of the worst schools.

In distinguishing between effective and ineffective schools, Rutter identified such factors as degree of academic emphasis, degree of teacher involvement in lessons, availability of rewards for students, and extent to which children were given responsibility. Children tended to do better in

Involvement, rewards, and responsibilities

51 Michael Rutter, et al., *Fifteen Thousand Hours: Secondary Schools and Their Effects on Children* (Cambridge, Mass.: Harvard University Press, 1979).

schools where classes began on time, where teachers gave immediate and frequent praise, and where students were made to feel that success was expected of them. The study found that it was easier to be a good teacher in some schools than in others. For example, student achievement was better in schools in which discipline policy was defined and worked out by teachers, rather than being ill-defined or imparted from above.

In schools in which children of average ability did better, more able children also tended to do better. Thus what seemed to work for average students also worked for bright students. (Well-educated parents constituted a built-in advantage.) Finally, a school that was effective in one area tended to be effective in others as well, reinforcing the theory that how the school is run makes a significant difference.

Also concerned with the question of identifying "good" schools, David Clark and his colleagues reviewed nearly 800 studies dealing with unusually successful elementary schools in urban areas and concluded that a few have been able to bring about substantial gains in students' learning. Factors associated with the success of these schools included the following: outstanding leadership, emphasis on staff development and in-service training, reduced child/adult ratios, clearly stated curricular goals and objectives, individualized instruction, and a high level of parental contact with the school.[52]

Staff development, small classes, and clear goals

Studies such as those reported by Wynne, Rutter, and Clark give hope to educators who have despaired of improving the quality and effectiveness of education in the public schools, particularly those in the inner city. None of these authors attempts to argue that the family or social-class characteristics of students are unimportant. Rather, they conclude that schools constitute an important influence on student performance and one that is susceptible to change as part of a systematic school reform effort.

SUMMING UP

1. The enterprise of elementary and secondary education is conducted through nearly 16,000 public school systems (plus thousands of private schools), 43 million students (public and private), and 2.4 million teachers, all operating under a widely accepted system of laws, regulations, and customs. Those who wish to reform the schools must either work to improve what we have now or work around the fringe of the system while reaching relatively small groups of students.

2. The existing schools can be improved internally, and whatever reforms are attempted should involve provisions for alternatives to

52 David L. Clark, Linda S. Lotto, and Martha M. McCarthy, "Factors Associated With Success in Urban Elementary Schools," *Phi Delta Kappan* (March 1980), pp. 467-70.

existing programs and for systematically reforming and improving instruction in the public schools.

3. Research during the past few years has shown that vigorous leadership, emphasis on staff development, focused instructional efforts, and other aspects of good administration can make schools more effective than most have been in the past.

4. One overriding challenge for educators in the future is to put these findings into practice in working to raise the general level of effectiveness of the public schools.

DISCUSSION QUESTIONS

1. Which secondary school grade organizational pattern do you advocate? Why?

2. Discuss the various geographical types of schools in terms of stereotyping. In which type of school (geographical) would you prefer to teach? Why?

3. What are the functions of the school board? How are responsibilities divided between the board and the superintendent of schools?

4. What are magnet schools and alternative schools? What are the major arguments for and against alternative schools?

5. What forces or conditions make it difficult to improve schools? What approaches to improvement and reform have the best chance to succeed?

THINGS TO DO

1. Invite a teacher or principal who works in a nongraded school to speak to the class.

2. Interview officials in a nearby school district to determine whether changes have been or may be made in grade organization. Has a middle school been established or considered? What changes may be made in the future? Why?

3. Invite several school board members to discuss the rewards and frustrations of the job. What changes would they like to see take place in the schools?

4. Visit an alternative school and analyze its methods of operation. How does it differ from more traditional schools?

5. Survey local school districts to determine whether systematic reform efforts have been made in one or more schools. Have these efforts succeeded? What obstacles have arisen in carrying them out?

does." Hence, *de jure* segregation, that is, segregation by government action, was ruled unconstitutional.

EARLY PERIOD   Many schools and communities in the border states, such as Delaware, Kentucky, Maryland, Missouri, Oklahoma, and West Virginia, responded positively and with "all deliberate speed," as required. Attempts to desegregate the school systems in the heart of the South were not easy and took more time. In several places violence accompanied the moves to achieve racial balance, and later a number of stall tactics, such as bureaucratic mishandling of transfer applications, were tried. Virginia even made it legal for the state to pay tuition of students in private schools where public schools did not exist, and Prince Edward County closed its public schools for two years. (Both of these measures were subsequently struck down by the Supreme Court.) Official opposition to desegregation ended in the South by the mid-1960s. To a significant degree, school desegregation is an accomplished fact below the Mason-Dixon line.

Private schools to resist desegregation

As the northern and western cities experienced a major influx of Blacks in the 1950s and 1960s, *de facto* school segregation (segregation based on residential patterns) became more and more apparent. Concern about school segregation in the North was mounting, and the New York City Board of Education took the lead in a 1954 statement of objectives to implement the spirit of the *Brown* decision. Attendance boundaries were modified and free transportation was given to students who wished to transfer to other schools; the total effect, however, was limited. The Cleveland and Detroit schools followed with similar statements and procedures in the late 1950s, but for the greater part, the official policy of the schools outside the South was "color blind."

"Color blind" school policies

Several court cases in the North were brought to force school boards to take active steps to reduce *de facto* segregation or "racial imbalance," as it was called. Decisions of the lower courts in the early 1960s (involving Boston; New Rochelle, New York; and Englewood and Teaneck, New Jersey) ordered school systems to abandon segregated education.

The desegregation movement initially was directed mainly at southern schools, however, by 1970 the once-segregated schools of the eleven southern states were more integrated than those in the rest of the country. In fact, this regional gap has steadily widened; thus, decreasing *de jure* segregation in the South has been offset by increasing *de facto* segregation in the North and West.

IMPORTANT
SUPREME COURT
DECISIONS

Selected Supreme Court decisions on the subject of school desegregation are noted below. Since 1972 there has been concern not only with schools outside the South but also with metropolitan (city and suburbs) desegregation.

1. *(1969) United States v. Montgomery County Board of Education, Alabama.* The Court ruled that a federal judge had the right to order school boards to integrate the schools' staffs according to specific ratios.

School staff ·
integration

2. *(1971) Swann v. Charlotte-Mecklenburg County, North Carolina.* The Court supported busing and other devices, such as racial quotas, pairing, and revision of attendance zones, to remove state-imposed school segregation.

3. *(1974) Bradley v. Milliken.* The remedy of metropolitan busing in the Detroit area was rejected on the basis that before separate and autonomous school districts may be set aside "it must be shown that there has been a constitutional violation within one district that produces a significant segregation effect in another district."

4. *(1974) Keyes v. School District No. 1, Denver, Colorado.* The Court ruled that if schools are racially segregated in a portion of a school district as a result of deliberate official acts, then the entire school district may have to be desegregated.

Deliberate
official acts

5. *(1974) Morgan v. Hennigan, Boston, Massachusetts.* Based on the Supreme Court decision in *Keyes*, the district court found that the entire school system in Boston had to be desegregated. The Supreme Court refused to hear the case, and by doing so confirmed the lower court's decision.

6. *(1975) Newburg Area Council of Board of Education of Jefferson County v. Board of Education of Louisville, Kentucky.* Black students in Jefferson County schools had been required to attend schools in Louisville in 1954. In accordance with *Milliken* standards the Court's judgment ordered implementation of a merger of the Louisville schools and the surrounding Jefferson County schools. The principal action, exemplifying interdistrict violation and justifying metropolitan desegregation, involved the fact that before 1954 Black students were bused across school district lines to attend segregated schools in Louisville.

7. *(1975) Evans v. Buchanan, Wilmington, Delaware.* As in *Louisville*, the case hinged on the fact that Black students had been required to cross district lines in 1954 to attend schools in the city of Wilmington. Desegregation relief embraced intradistrict and interdistrict action involving the Wilmington schools and the surrounding suburbs.

8. *(1976) Pasadena Board of Education v. Spangler.* After White enrollment fell from 17,859 to 11,188 in the first four years of de-

segregation, the Court held that a school board, having once reassigned students to achieve racial balance, does not have to do so every year, even if residential patterns have since resegregated some schools.[2]

9. *(1979) Columbus Board of Education* v. *Penick; Dayton Board of Education* v. *Brinkman.* The Columbus and Dayton school boards appealed district-wide desegregation orders on the grounds that they had not demonstrated ''discriminatory purpose'' and that prior segregative actions had not been shown to have caused unconstitutional segregation in all or most of their schools. The Supreme Court ruled that the existence of predominantly minority and nonminority schools is not in itself unconstitutional. In upholding lower-court desegregation orders, however, the Supreme Court stated that ''the systematic nature'' of earlier violations ''furnished *prima facie* proof that current segregation'' was caused at least in part by ''prior intentionally segregative official acts.'' In effect, the Supreme Court re-affirmed its decision in the *Keyes* case and indicated that system-wide desegregation plans might well be ordered in other districts that had not taken vigorous or successful steps to desegregate their schools.

Implications of the court decisions   The immediate effect of the *Detroit* decision ruled out the possibility of school desegregation in that city, but it still allowed for regional interdistrict remedies in other metropolitan areas in which state action could be shown to have caused significant segregation in city schools. Thus, the decision provided for interdistrict or metropolitan remedies in individual cases. The *Louisville* and *Wilmington* rulings illustrate that if plaintiffs can show interdistrict violation as prescribed by the U.S. Supreme Court in the Detroit case, the lower courts will rule in favor of desegregation of city schools with surrounding suburbs. This has obvious implications for all southern and border states as well as some metropolitan areas elsewhere in the country. Plaintiffs may match neighborhood census tracts with school enrollments to show that past segregation may have been established by assigning Black students to schools across the boundaries of White school districts.

The *Wilmington* case is also important because of the lower court's analysis of and emphasis on housing discrimination as one cause of segregation in city and suburban schools. (The *Wilmington* decision also hinged on the state's failure to desegregate Wilmington when it developed plans to reorganize school districts in Delaware.) Developing this prece-

---

2 Thomas H. Flygare, ''Can Federal Courts Control an Educational Program?'' *Phi Delta Kappan* (April 1976), pp. 550–51; ''Washington Report,'' *Phi Delta Kappan* (October 1976), p. 215.

dent, the Supreme Court in 1976 ruled that federal courts can (it doesn't mean they will) order that low-cost public housing be built in the suburbs if it is not being built on a nonsegregated basis within city limits. The Court advocated an integrated society, one in which relief should involve a comprehensive metropolitan plan.[3]

The *Pasadena* case may provide a way out for school boards, once they have implemented a desegregation plan; the Court was probably concerned with white withdrawal from the cities, and the fact that another desegregation move on the heels of one just a few years ago would only exacerbate the situation.

The precedent set in the *Denver* case, followed by *Columbus* and *Dayton*, also is of major importance. These cases set a precedent for district-wide reassignment and transportation of students, provided plaintiffs can show that segregation had been caused by "intentional" government action or inaction and that the scope of the violation requires a district-wide remedy. A number of lawsuits challenging segregation in the North and West have been filed in other cities, and the U.S. Departments of Education and Justice have initiated action to cut off federal funding to school districts that may be in violation of the *Keyes* decision. By 1980, court cases had resulted in district-wide desegregation orders in Cleveland, Detroit, San Francisco, and several other major cities, while the federal government was bringing pressure to bear to desegregate schools in Chicago, New York, and other large school districts.

"WHITE FLIGHT"   One of the prime movers of school desegregation, James Coleman, has now concluded that busing has been counter-productive because it has tended to cause the flight of White families to the suburbs.[4] While redrawing school attendance lines can and often does reduce segregation sharply in small cities, it cannot accomplish the same purpose in large cities, where large, racially homogeneous residential neighborhoods often include one or more ghetto areas. In the 125 largest cities he analyzed, there was a continuous loss of White students from the schools between 1968 and 1973. Although the evidence was inconclusive, the accelerated loss of Whites appeared to occur during the first and second year after desegregation, with a continuing but slower loss in subsequent years. Substantial desegregation seemed to have hastened the shift of the city and school system to becoming predominantly Black, thus resulting in resegregation.

Busing is counter-productive

Coleman's "White flight" thesis, a familiar one in parlor debates on the subject, was immediately attacked in educational journals and subsequently argued in the popular weekly news magazines and in public

A heated debate surfaces

3 *New York Times*, April 24, 1976, p. 13; Marian W. Edelman, "Winston and Dovie Hudson's Dream," *Harvard Educational Review* (November 1975), pp. 417–50.

4 James S. Coleman, Sara D. Kelley, and John Moore, *Trends in School Desegregation, 1968–1973* (Washington, D.C.: Urban Institute, 1975).

forums.[5] The critics charged that Coleman never interviewed a single set of White parents about why they left the city, that White flight to the suburbs had been going on at a rapid rate prior to busing, that his research design was inadequate, and that they could not replicate his study in nineteen selected cities. This set off a vigorous exchange of views, with Coleman defending his data and reporting that the loss of Whites in cities corresponded with forced desegregation. He explained that his critics did not replicate his data because they used a different set of cities and a cutoff of 1972 rather than 1973, which in turn obscured most of the White flight. Coleman also argued that the White loss rate from the cities in 1974 and 1975 had jumped even more than the 1973 rate, thus strengthening his original data.

To a degree, the White flight controversy was resolved when participants on both sides reached some agreement that White withdrawal from the public schools frequently had been accelerated by desegregation in large school districts with a high percentage of minority students surrounded by predominantly White suburbs. In smaller districts with relatively few minority students, however, and in some large county or regional districts in the South and Southwest, White withdrawal did not seem to increase much as a result of desegregation. Conclusions along these lines have been summarized by one social scientist who has concluded that "White flight from school desegregation is a reality. It is also apparent that most journalists and many partisans overemphasize its importance by quoting total enrollment declines rather than the increment due to desegregation. This increment averages out to be a doubling of the normal loss in northern school districts."[6]

NON-BLACK
MINORITIES

One other aspect of big-city segregation that deserves special attention involves the status of non-Black minority groups. Depending on regional and local circumstances and court precedents, some racial minority groups may or may not be counted as minority for purposes of school desegregation in a particular city.[7] For example, Mexican American students have been classified as unconstitutionally segregated in the Southwest and some other

5   James S. Coleman, "Racial Segregation in the Schools: New Research With New Policy Implications," *Phi Delta Kappan* (October 1975), pp. 75–78; Robert L. Green and Thomas F. Pettigrew, "Urban Desegregation and White Flight: A Response to Coleman," *Phi Delta Kappan* (February 1976), pp. 399–402; Thomas F. Pettigrew and Robert L. Green, "School Desegregation in Large Cities: A Critique of the Coleman 'White Flight' Thesis," *Harvard Educational Review* (February 1976), pp. 1–53; James S. Coleman, "A Reply to Green and Pettigrew," *Phi Delta Kappan* (March 1976), pp. 454–55; Robert L. Green and Thomas F. Pettigrew, "The Coleman Debate Continued," *Phi Delta Kappan* (April 1976), p. 555.

6   Christine H. Rossell, "Assessing the Unintended Impact of Public Policy: School Desegregation and Resegregation." Boston: Boston University Political Science Department (mimeograph, 1979), p. 72.

7   However, federal data collection activities are standardized and have required that student enrollments be reported separately for the following groups: "Black," "American Indian," "Spanish-Surnamed American," "Portuguese," "Oriental," "Alaskan Natives," "Hawaiian Natives," and "Non-Minority."

locations since the courts determined in the 1970s that they were victims of the same kinds of segregative discrimination as were Black students. In some northern cities such as Cleveland and Milwaukee, however, Mexican American and other Hispanic students have not been explicitly designated by the courts to participate as minorities in a desegregation plan, even though many or most attend predominantly minority schools.

Mexican
American
students as
minorities in
the Southwest

The situation is further complicated by the relatively large and growing number of Asian minority groups in many big cities. With rapid increases occurring in the numbers of Filipino, Korean, and Vietnamese students and the already substantial numbers of Chinese and Japanese students, many school districts face considerable uncertainty in trying to devise multiethnic desegregation plans. The court order for San Francisco, for example, has required multiethnic enrollment and busing of four groups (Asian American, Black, Hispanic, and non-Hispanic White), but Los Angeles is still considering whether or how Asian students should participate in desegregation plans in the future.

Questions involving the desegregation of non-Black minority groups obviously will become more important in the 1980s as Hispanic students become the plurality or majority group in Houston, Los Angeles, and other cities. Resolution of these issues will be difficult because bilingual services that tend to require some concentration of many of these students will conflict with desegregation goals emphasizing dispersal and multiethnic enrollment. In addition, parents of non-Black minority students tend to be more divided among themselves regarding the necessity for desegregation than are Black parents; thus demand and support for desegregation of non-Black minority students tend to vary greatly in accordance with local political circumstances. Many educators and lay leaders also are very uncertain concerning the question of whether or how to include middle-class Asian and Hispanic students in desegregation plans. Most of these students perform well academically, and many seem to be very well integrated into U.S. schools and society. Some concerned observers, such as Thomas Pettigrew, suggest that middle-class minority students should attend schools with low-income minority students in order to reduce economic isolation of the latter group in districts that have few nonminority students.[8]

OBSTACLES
TO DESEGREGATION

Given the fact that residential patterns are so highly segregated, a major stumbling block to desegregation of schools has been the preference of the majority of Whites and many minority parents for the maintenance of neighborhood schools. Added to this resistance to desegregation is the preference of a growing number of minority spokesmen for local control of

Maintaining
neighborhood
schools

[8] *Report of Dr. Thomas Pettigrew to the Superior Court of the State of California for the County of Los Angeles.* Case No. 822, 854, November 14, 1978.

their schools rather than for desegregation. In addition, opposition to desegregation has increased in school districts where a high percentage of minority students are from low-income families. Middle-class parents, whether nonminority or minority, are reluctant to send their children to schools with a high proportion of low-income students. They generally are quick to withdraw their children from schools in which desegregation has substantially increased the proportion of such students.

In addition to the attitudinal resistance that exists against desegregation, there are practical obstacles. Typically, the increasing concentrations of minority students in large cities have resegregated the neighborhoods to a greater extent than in previous generations. Under these conditions, attempts to integrate a decreasing number of White students with a stable or increasing number of minority students have only increased the movement of White families to the suburbs. Middle-class minority families also have been withdrawing their children from low-status schools in the cities and enrolling them in private schools or suburban schools. The net result is that city school districts have become increasingly low income and minority in their student composition, with a high proportion of minority students attending predominantly minority, poverty schools.

Another result is that some suburban public schools in metropolitan areas also are beginning to be resegregated as middle-class minority families move to suburbs next to the central city and then find that White enrollment falls because of White population decline and withdrawal. Growing segregation of minority students in the suburbs is illustrated in the Cleveland Metropolitan Area, where the East Cleveland suburban school district has become nearly all Black; in the Chicago Metropolitan Area, where the Harvey and Evanston Elementary Township school districts have become more than 50 percent Black; and in the St. Louis Metropolitan Area, where the University City public schools have become more than 70 percent Black. In the Los Angeles Metropolitan Area, similarly, a number of suburban school districts, including Baldwin Park, Duarte, Pasadena, and Pomona have enrollments now more than half minority.

Increasing
Black
suburban
student
population

Thus resistance to desegregation became more widespread in the 1970s as big-city school districts became increasingly low status and minority while the courts as well as state and federal executive agencies moved to desegregate public schools in the North and West. By the end of the decade, most big-city school districts had a large proportion of minority students, and widespread desegregation within their boundaries seemed attainable only by reassigning White students to sometimes distant minority schools that many were not willing to attend, or by moving minority students from one predominantly minority school to another. In this context, public opinion indicated that less than one-fifth of White Americans and one-half of Black Americans favored busing for purposes

of school desegregation, and a substantial majority of the public favored a
Constitutional amendment to prohibit it.[9] Furthermore, public statements
by President Ronald Reagan and the last three presidents before him, by
key officials of the Department of Education and Justice, and by the old
HEW have suggested limitations on busing orders and trying other alternatives instead.[10]

SOLUTIONS TO
BIG-CITY
DESEGREGATION

The above trends make it clear that
school desegregation problems are most
serious in the nation's large metropoli-
tan areas in which the central-city school population has become predominantly minority and low income. Desegregation is now an accomplished fact in much of the South and in many small towns and cities,
but larger cities tend to have a substantial proportion of minority students
attending racially isolated poverty schools, and suburban school districts
tend to be predominantly White and middle or mixed in social class. Some
suburbs have a desegregated student population, but many of these suburbs adjoin the central-city minority ghetto and are becoming resegregated as White families move farther out and are replaced by minority students from the city.

Faced with this situation, educators and the courts have tried to find
ways to reduce school segregation and otherwise to improve educational
and social opportunities for students in the big cities. Solutions involving
these goals have taken a variety of forms, such as those listed below.

1. Altering attendance areas.

2. Establishing magnet schools that incorporate specialized programs and personnel and tend to attract students from various parts
of the city's school system.

3. Changing elementary school feeder patterns to secondary
schools.

4. Permitting students to attend school outside their neighborhood
(free-choice transfer).

5. Busing students, involving two-way routes.

6. Busing students, involving one-way routes.

7. Offering open enrollment from predominantly non-White schools
to predominantly White schools so long as space is available.

8. Pairing schools, where two schools in adjacent areas are brought
together in one larger zone. For example, School A may enroll all

---

9   "Opposition to Busing Reaches Peak in Congress and Nation," *Phi Delta Kappan* (January
1976), p. 356.
10   "Opposition to Busing Reaches Peak," *Chicago Sun Times*, June 15, 1976, pp. 1, 14; *New
York Times*, June 6, 1971, sect. 4, p. 2; "Support for Busing to Achieve Racial Integration
Waning?" *Phi Delta Kappan* (January 1975), p. 287.

students from grades one through four; School B enrolls all students from grades five through eight (Princeton plan).

9. Bringing together three or more neighborhood schools to make one attendance zone, thereby increasing the pool of students and achieving better racial balance than with two schools (cluster plan).

10. Creating four to eight attendance zones, with the narrowest point of each located in the inner city and the broadest at the city's edge (pie-shaped plan).

11. Exchanging White and non-White students on a one-to-one voluntary basis.

12. Establishing educational parks, which provide for a large concentration of schools and facilities in a section of the city on a racially neutral site or at the edge of the city.

13. Merging the city and surrounding suburbs into a single school system (metropolitan complex).

A survey of superintendents of school systems enrolling 50,000 or more students (school systems that enroll about half of the minority student population) found that the first five approaches comprised 67 percent of the responses (used most often), and the last three represented only 2 percent of the responses. When the superintendents were asked to consider the most effective approaches from the above list, the five top choices, in descending order, were: (1) altering attendance areas, (2) two-way busing, (3) free-choice transfers, (4) magnet schools, and (5) one-way busing. These five approaches represented 64 percent of the responses.[11]

The most effective approaches

EFFECTS ON STUDENT
PERFORMANCE
AND ATTITUDES
Independent of the legal issues and lack of public support for busing, the question ultimately remains: To what extent do students benefit from integrated schools? Although there is voluminous research on this subject, it is inconsistent and contradictory. There is a body of data that shows a positive relationship between desegregation and academic achievement (although most of the differences in achievement have been attributed to socioeconomic integregation), but there is also evidence that shows no relationship, or even a negative relationship.[12]

Inconsistent and contradictory data

11 Allan C. Ornstein and Glen Thompson, "Desegregation of Schools Enrolling 50,000 Students: A Status Report," *Illinois Schools Journal* (Winter 1977-78), pp. 40-48.

12 Widely cited studies showing a positive relationship are the 1966 Coleman Report and the U.S. Commission on Civil Rights Report entitled *Racial Isolation in the Public Schools.* Widely cited to prove the opposite point are David J. Armor, "The Evidence on Bussing," *The Public Interest* (Summer, 1972), pp. 90-126 and Harold B. Gerard and Norman Miller, *School Desegregation* (New York: Plenum, 1975). For important reviews of the research that cites both positive and negative findings, see Nancy St. John, *School Desegregation: Outcomes for Children* (New York: Wiley, 1975) and L. A. Bradley and G. W. Bradley, "The Academic Achievement of Black Students in Desegregated Schools: A Critical Review," *Review of Educational Research* (Summer 1977), pp. 399-449.

Similarly, there are data showing that desegregation has positive effects on interracial attitudes, but some studies indicate no effect or a negative effect. The data on minority students' aspirations are somewhat more consistent in indicating that desegregation frequently improves the educational aspirations and college enrollment of minority students by making these aspirations more realistic and better informed. Several studies also indicate that desegregated schooling helps minority students enter the mainstream ''network'' of social and cultural aspirations and contacts needed for success in later life.[13]

One of the most influential documents reporting the positive effects of desegregation and Black achievement is the 1966 Coleman Report. The summary section of this report has been used by both DE and the Office of Civil Rights as a powerful weapon in the desegregation effort. By 1975, however, Coleman was taking a much less positive stand on the academic gains related to desegregation. He summarized his new findings as follows: ''The achievement benefits of integrated schools appeared substantial when I studied them in the middle 1960s. But subsequent studies . . . have found smaller effects, and in some cases none at all.''[14]

However, there are a few studies that focus on schools in which desegregation seems to have been carried out successfully and effectively. Studies focusing on this type of school avoid the problem typical in educational research of mixing well-implemented examples of an innovation with poorly-implemented ones, and then concluding that the innovation is universally unsuccessful. One of the most comprehensive studies of successful desegregated schools is a report evaluating the Emergency School Aid Act (ESSA), which has provided hundreds of millions of dollars since 1972 to facilitate desegregation. This study indicated that desegregation had a favorable impact on black achievement in schools that have the following characteristics: resources are focused on attaining goals, administrative leadership is stronger, classroom lessons are more highly structured, parents are more heavily involved in the classroom, and staff make greater efforts to promote positive interracial attitudes.[15]

**Successfully
desegregated
schools**

In general, the research on the effects of desegregation and integration is complicated by statistical and sampling problems: (1) the inability to set up control and experimental groups; (2) the varying definitions of social class and income; (3) the differing percentages of Blacks and Whites

13   Robert L. Crain and Rita E. Mahard, *The Influence of High School Racial Composition on Black College Attendance and Test Performance* (Washington, D.C.: National Center for Education Statistics Sponsored Reports Series NCES 78-212, January 1978); G. Forehand, M. Ragosta, and D. Rock, *Conditions and Processes of Effective School Desegregation* (Princeton, N.J.: Educational Testing Service, 1976); *Report of Dr. Thomas Pettigrew*, pp. 46, 61; Robert E. Slavin and Nancy A. Madden, ''School Practices that Improve Race Relations,'' *American Educational Research Journal* (Spring 1979), pp. 169–80.

14   Coleman, ''Racial Segregation in the Schools,'' p. 77.

15   J. E. Coulson, *National Evaluation of the Emergency School Aid Act (ESAA): Survey of the Second-Year Studies* (Washington, D.C.: System Development Corporation, 1976).

to define desegregation; (4) the fact that data are reported on a district- or school-wide basis, which often does not reflect the classroom racial mix; (5) the strong possibility that Blacks who attend desegregated schools tend to come from relatively more stable homes than those living in the core of the inner city, as well as the possibility that Whites who remain in desegregated and changing schools come from relatively less stable, low-income homes with less pressure for educational achievement; (6) the degree of disruption that may exist in schools that are in the process of desegregating or changing from predominantly White to Black; and (7) the lack of longitudinal data to show cumulative effects of desegregation at various grade levels. Finally, several variables influence the child's education, ranging from the number of siblings at home, number of books at home, whether the family is female-headed or husband-wife, and so on. Desegregation may be only one factor, and a small one at that, in the composite measure of school performance.

Despite the mixed evidence regarding academic achievement, aspirations, and interracial attitudes, perhaps the most compelling reasons for integration are political and moral. Politically, two separate societies cannot continue to exist in America without serious harm to the body politic. Morally, our national policy must reflect a commitment to American ideals of equality.

Political
and moral
reasons for
desegregation

**DECENTRALIZATION
AND COMMUNITY
INVOLVEMENT**

Increasing pressure from minority groups, accompanied by increasing pressure for reform from educators, has played a part in forcing school authorities in many large school systems to decentralize and increase community involvement in the schools. What has emerged are the following, not mutually exclusive, administrative-community alternatives for governing metropolitan schools: (1) administrative decentralization, (2) community participation, and (3) community control. Usually community involvement in the form of either alternative (2) or (3) accompanies decentralization.

Administrative decentralization is a process whereby the school system is divided into smaller units; the locus of power and authority remains with a single, central administration and board of education. Although decentralization need not necessarily lead to increased community involvement, it often occurs within the decentralized school boundaries. *Community participation* connotes the formation of advisory committees or groups beyond the usual parent/teacher associations. The committees that are formed may operate at various levels within the system—the local school, decentralized unit, or central level. The main function of these groups is to make recommendations (not policy) and to serve as a liaison between the schools and community. *Community control* connotes a legal provision for an elected community school board functioning under specific guidelines and in conjunction with the central school board. It means a sharing of decision-making authority and power between the local and central school boards; it also means that the powers of the professionals and central school board members are abridged and transferred to community groups.

We can telescope the three alternative models into two options: administrative decentralization and community participation, or administrative decentralization and community control. Most educators advocate the first option because it allows their decision-making influence to remain relatively intact. On the other hand, an increasing number of liberal and minority leaders favor the second option as a vehicle for transferring power to the community, or at least to people who claim they represent the community.

In reality there is little controversy over decentralization as such, because most people, including the defenders and critics of the system, accept this organizational model. Many professional educators see a need for it in terms of reducing school bureaucracy and accept it because they retain power; many critics accept it because they view it as a first step toward community control. The controversy concerns community control: which group—elected public officials and professional educators or community groups—will have the power and authority to run the schools. The main concern is not limited to education, which is commonly emphasized in the literature on community control, but extends to politics and related issues of self-interest and group ideology.

A 1980 nationwide survey on decentralization of school systems with 50,000 or more students was conducted.[16] The number of school systems falling into this category was 69, and data were obtained from 66 of these school systems (96 percent). Forty-two out of 66 school systems (64 percent) reported that they were decentralized, and they are listed in Table 15.1. Three school systems—Anne Arundel County (Maryland), Milwaukee, and Pittsburgh—had moved from decentralization to centralization since 1973, when an earlier nationwide study was conducted of school systems with 50,000 or more students.[17] On the other hand, six school systems not decentralized in 1973 had enacted such a policy (see Table 15.1, note b).

The larger school systems had decentralized more than the smaller ones. For example, 20 out of 22 (91 percent) of the school systems enrolling 100,000 or more students had decentralized, whereas 22 out of 44 (50 percent) of the school systems enrolling between 50,000 and 100,000 students had decentralized. The decentralized unit names were basically

16 Allan C. Ornstein, "Decentralization and Community Participation Policy of Big School Systems," *Phi Delta Kappan* (Decmeber 1980), in print.
17 Allan C. Ornstein, "Administrative/Community Organization of Metropolitan Schools," *Phi Delta Kappan* (June 1973), pp. 668-74.

confined to three terms: 28 school systems referred to areas (66.7 percent);
7 to districts (16.6 percent), including community districts and subdis-
tricts; 6 to regions (14.3 percent); and 1 to zones (2.2 percent). Such terms
as "clusters," "complexes," "pyramids," and "units" were no longer a
part of the decentralization vocabulary as they were 7 years ago. The
number of decentralized units varied from as little as 2 areas in Portland
and Oakland to as many as 32 community districts in New York City, with
4 decentralized units as the most frequent organizational plan in 14 school
systems (33 percent) and 3 decentralized units second most frequent in 10
school systems (24 percent). Larger school systems (with more than
100,000 students) averaged 7.7 decentralized units, while smaller ones
(with fewer than 100,000 students) averaged 3.9 decentralized units. The
approximate range of students per decentralized unit varied from as few
as 6,000 students in St. Louis to as many as 110,000 in Puerto Rico. The
variation was greater in 1973, from as few students as 2,500 in Milwaukee
to as many as 216,000 in Chicago. As a point of further comparison, the
most frequent range of students per decentralized unit was between
10,000 and 30,000 students—more than 70 percent of all school systems
falling in this range. The average number of students per decentralized
unit was 25,500 with larger school systems (with more than 100,000 students) averaging 33,000 students and smaller school systems (fewer than
100,000 students) averaging 19,000 students. These figures correspond
with the 1973 survey mentioned, when the most frequent size was between
15,000 and 25,000 students per decentralized unit, and with the ideal
figures recommended by Mario Fantini and Marilyn Gittell, 12,000 to
40,000; A. Harry Passow, 20,000; and Robert Havighurst and Daniel
Levine, 25,000 to 30,000.[18] In any event, these decentralized student numbers seem to represent the proper size to perform administrative functions
with relative efficiency and sufficient resources.

**Proper size to
perform
efficiently**

Seventeen reasons were given for decentralization. Among the top 8,
in order of priority and representing 79 percent of the responses, were:
(1) to enhance school-community relations, (2) to provide greater community input at the local level, (3) to provide local schools with more field and
resource personnel, (4) to provide efficient maintenance and support for
local schools, (5) to reduce administrative span of control, (6) to provide
greater linkages between local schools and the central school board, (7) to
redirect spending for local school needs, and (8) to provide greater curriculum continuity, from kindergarten through grade 12. These results
closely correspond with a 1974 case study that detailed the major reasons
for decentralization among 18 school systems.[19]

18 Mario D. Fantini and Marilyn Gittell, *Decentralization: Achieving Reform* (New York:
Praeger, 1973); A. Harry Passow, *Toward Creating a Model Urban School System* (New York:
Teachers College Press, Columbia University, 1973); Robert J. Havighurst and Daniel U. Levine,
Education in Metropolitan Areas, 2nd ed. (Boston: Allyn & Bacon, 1971).

19 Allan C. Ornstein, *Metropolitan Schools: Administrative Decentralization v. Community Control* (Metuchen, N.J.: Scarecrow Press, 1974).

TABLE 15.1
DECENTRALIZED SCHOOL SYSTEMS
WITH 50,000 OR MORE STUDENTS,
1980

SCHOOL SYSTEM	STUDENT ENROLLMENT (IN THOUSANDS)	DECENTRALIZED UNIT NUMBER	DECENTRALIZED UNIT NAME	STUDENTS/DECENTRALIZED UNIT RANGE (IN THOUSANDS)	STUDENTS/DECENTRALIZED UNIT AVERAGE (IN THOUSANDS)
New York City[a]	962	32	Community Districts	12–30	19
Puerto Rico[a]	721	7	Educational Regions	90–110	103
Los Angeles	545	10	Areas	42.5–65	54.5
Chicago	475	20	Districts	15–30	24
Philadelphia	235	8	Districts	17–40	30
Dade County, Fla.	226	4	Areas	40–80	56
Detroit[a]	216.5	8	Regions	8–36	27
Houston	194	6	Areas	30–36	32.5
Hawaii	168.5	7	Districts	7.5–41	24
Baltimore City	136	6	Regions	20–25	22.5
Broward County, Fla.	135.5	4	Areas	27.5–41.5	34
Dallas	130.5	6	Subdistricts	20.5–27.5	22
Fairfax County, Va.	127.5	4	Areas	30–34.5	32
Prince George's County, Md.	127	3	Areas	36–46	42.5
Memphis[a]	113.5	4	Areas	23.5–31.5	28.5
Washington, D.C.[b]	106	6	Regions	12–25	17.5
Jefferson County, Ky.[b]	103.5	4	Regions	20–30	26
Baltimore County, Md.	102.5	5	Areas	19.5–28	20.5
Duval County, Fla.[b]	102	4	Areas	22.5–30	25.5

Montgomery County, Md.	102	5	Areas	18–26	20.5
New Orleans	87	4	Districts	18.5–25.5	21.5
Albuquerque	81	3	Areas	23.5–29	27
Jefferson County, Colo.	81	4	Areas	19–24	20.5
DeKalb County, Ga.	78	3	Areas	23–29	26
Charlotte-MecKlenburg County, N.C.[b]	76	8	Areas	7.5–12	9.5
Palm Beach County, Fla.	73	5	Areas	14–20	14.5
Atlanta	72	3	Areas	21.5–27	24
Nashville-Davidson County, Tenn.	71.5	3	Districts	16.5–27	24
St. Louis	66	4	Areas	6–20.5	16.5
Mobile County, Ala.[b]	63.5	4	Areas	13–18	16
San Antonio	62	3	Areas	16–24	20
El Paso	60	3	Areas	17.5–23	20
Polk County, Fla.	60	4	Areas	9–23	15
Granite, Ut.	59.5	3	Areas	18–24	20
San Francisco	58.5	4	Areas	11–16	14.5
Tucson[b]	56.5	4	Regions	11.5–17	14
Cincinnati	55.5	4	Areas	10.5–15.5	13.5
Portland[a]	53.5	2	Areas	23.5–28.5	26.5
Greenville County, S.C.	53	5	Areas	9.5–13	10.5
Seattle	50.5	3	Zones	15–19	17
Oakland	50	2	Areas	23–26	25
Brevard County, Fla.	50	3	Areas	9–22	16.5

Note: a = School board operating at the decentralized level.

b = Decentralized since 1973.

Source: Allan C. Ornstein. "Decentralization and Community Participation Policy of Big School Systems." *Phi Delta Kappan* (December 1980), in print.

Oddly enough, little evidence has been found to support these generalizations about administrative decentralization and any concurrent plans for community involvement. Very few of the school systems indicate an evaluative procedure for their new organizational models, and very few point out the need for pilot testing some of the related assumptions, goals, and recommendations.

COMMUNITY
PARTICIPATION
AND CONTROL

In New York City and Detroit, administrative decentralization has led to some form of community control with elected school boards functioning in conjunction with the central school board. A far more frequent arrangement accompanying administrative decentralization has been the appointment of advisory committees at either the neighborhood school, decentralized unit, or central board levels. These committees are usually appointed by school officials; only in a few cases are the advisory groups elected by the community. Nevertheless, the committees are advisory, as their names suggest, and whenever guidelines are established, the school boards usually reaffirm their own authority and expectations that the advisory committees abide by the rules and regulations of the system.

In the main, school officials have been reluctant to transfer power to community groups; moreover, many school systems, such as Los Angeles, Philadelphia, and Portland have stated clearly in policy reports that community control has the potential for more harm than good. Although community control has the appeal of a viable alternative for involving community persons in the educational process, developments in New York City and Detroit indicate that disruptions and controversies among small local groups also can occur.[20]

For example, spin-off problems have erupted concerning the hiring and firing of personnel on the basis of race and ethnicity and the question of who represents the community.[21] Although it has been said that local units can more easily be made participatory, this clearly has not been the case, especially in New York City where voter turnout for the first two community school board elections has been 15 percent and 11 percent, respectively.[22] Moreover, many of those elected to local boards in both cities have not been well enough informed to function effectively on the school boards to which they have been elected. There are also reports that community school board members have been as susceptible to venality and nepotism as establishment-oriented school boards. While community

20 Harry L. Miller, *Social Foundations of Education*, 3rd ed. (New York: Holt, Rinehart, 1978); Allan C. Ornstein, Daniel U. Levine, and Doxey A. Wilkerson, *Reforming Metropolitan Schools* (Pacific Palisades, Calif.: Goodyear, 1975).

21 Bernard Bell, "The Battle for School Jobs: New York's Newest Agony," *Phi Delta Kappan* (May 1972), pp. 553–58; William R. Grant, "Community Control v. School Integration—The Detroit Case," *United Teacher Magazine*, November 7, 1971, pp. 1–4.

22 Ornstein, Levine, Wilkenson, *Reforming Metropolitan Schools*.

control does lessen the "heat" from the community,[23] it sometimes seems to be a strategy for accommodating the demands of a small number of militant groups in the hope of preventing an explosion. It can serve as a way to satisfy demands for change without having to invest enormous resources in schools, jobs, and housing—and it can promote further racial segregation.[24]

Militant groups

Because of these problems, some of the original advocates of community control have softened their position and are now opting for a strong stance on community participation. Marilyn Gittell, for example, still insists that parents and community members are usually powerless in their dealings with school boards, and that the only groups that have succeeded in offsetting the entrenched administrative and school board bureaucracies have been teacher groups. However, instead of outright community control, her earlier position, she advocates a school policy that includes public participation from the local school to central school board level.[25]

For the most part, school officials have been willing to encourage community participation but have resisted movement toward community control of schools. A recent survey of the 399 school systems that had more than 15,000 students in 1975 showed that superintendents were much more positive about community participation (defined as input involving advising on school policy) than about community control (defined as determining school policy).[26] They envisioned that community control entailed the forfeiture of their perceived or actual decision-making power; furthermore, they perceived community participation as beneficial and in line with traditional school-community relations and community control as disruptive with potential for overt hostility between different school-community factions. Upon surveying hundreds of examples of community participation, researchers at the Institute for Responsive Education found nine general areas in which citizen groups were providing advice and assistance to educators in many school districts: (1) identification of goals, priorities, and needs; (2) budget analysis; (3 and 4) selection and evaluation of teachers and principals; (5) development of curricula; (6) extracurricular programs; (7 and 8) community support and financing for schools; and (9) recruitment of volunteers.[27]

Areas of community involvement

23 George R. LaNoue and Bruce L. Smith, "The Political Evolution of School Decentralization," *American Behavioral Scientist* (September 1971), pp. 73-93; LaNoue and Smith, *The Politics of School Decentralization* (Lexington, Mass.: Heath, 1973); Martin Schiff, "The Educational Failure of Community Control in Inner-City New York," *Phi Delta Kappan* (February 1976), pp. 375-78.

24 LaNoue and Smith, "The Political Evolution of School Decentralization"; Schiff, "Educational Failure of Community Control in Inner-City New York."

25 Marilyn Gittell, "Critique of the Citizen Participation in Education," *Journal of Education* (February 1977), pp. 7-22.

26 Harriet Talmage and Allan C. Ornstein, "School Superintendents' Attitudes Toward Community Participation and Control," *Educational Research Quarterly* (Summer 1976), pp. 37-45.

27 Mary E. Stanwick, *Patterns of Participation* (Boston: Institute for Responsive Education, 1975).

To a significant degree, community participation in school district activities and decisions has been stimulated by changes in the policy of the national Parent Teacher Association (PTA). Membership in the PTA dropped from 12 million in the 1960s to 6.3 million in 1979, during which time parents were becoming more active in other organizations concerned with decisions about instruction in local schools. Responding to this and other factors, the national PTA has endorsed parent participation in local district policymaking.[28]

THE CHALLENGE   The question that must eventually be an-
FOR THE FUTURE   swered is whether administrative decen-
tralization accompanied by community participation or control improves the educational progress of students. Needless to say, very little empirical data are available on the effects of decentralization or community control. There is, however, a wealth of expository literature on these two organizational models, but the content is highly intuitive and anecdotal, and is presented in terms of a debate or a specific position (for or against). Although data are available suggesting that community participation in the traditional sense of involving parents in the school system has beneficial effects on student learning—and even this is limited—this should not be equated with the effects of community control or even community participation as it is presently evolving in some large urban school systems.[29]

Controversies involving decentralization and community control have been somewhat dormant in the past few years, but they may come into prominence again if a serious community effort is made to reform and improve U.S. public schools in the future. When school officials are forced to confront the problem of making classrooms and schools more effective, they may look for ways to locate more authority and responsibility for solving instructional problems at the local level where the problems are manifested. Considering this prospect, David Selden has summarized the situation in urban school districts as follows:

Any successful scheme of parent or community participation in school decision making must take into account . . . [that] most American cities are . . . becoming mainly black, Hispanic, and Oriental, and this shift will have lasting effects on the American political structure. . . .

Little empirical data

28 Lois S. Steinberg, "The Changing Role of Parent Groups in Educational Decision Making" in R. S. Brandt, ed., *Partners: Parents and Schools* (Alexandria, Va.: Association for Supervision and Curriculum Development, 1979), pp. 46–57.

29 J. Filipczak, "Parental Involvement in the Schools." Paper presented at the annual meeting of the American Educational Research Association, New York, April 1977; T. E. Wagennar, "School Achievement Level Vis-a-Vis Community Involvement and Support: An Empirical Assessment." Paper presented at the annual meeting of the American Sociological Association, Chicago, 1977.

The most notable change within the educational establishment is the rise of teacher power. . . . Teachers, through collective bargaining and political action, have achieved a large measure of autonomy and a greater share in decision making . . . it seems obvious that the future of both society and education can best be served by forming a new coalition, based on mutual respect, between teachers and leaders of the new urban power structures. . . .[30]

COMPENSATORY EDUCATION

The move toward compensatory education coincides with our concern for the disadvantaged child. Although these children exhibit lower achievement levels than middle-class children, most educational and social reformers presume that an improved school environment with remedial programs and special activities can compensate for many of their educational disadvantages.

Compensatory programs have been funded mainly by the federal government, although state and local money is also available for these programs. The Elementary and Secondary Education Act (ESEA) was passed in 1965 and immediately provided $1 billion in Title I funds to supplement and improve the education of poor and minority-group children. Ten years later ESEA money was totaling $2 billion per year or about $200 extra per disadvantaged child. (A disadvantaged child was defined in 1976 as a child from an urban family of four with an income of $5,200 or less.) By 1980, Title I expenditures were more than $3 billion per year, and other federal compensatory expenditures totaled over $2 billion more for a total of about $500 extra per disadvantaged child.

PROGRAMS AND PRACTICES

Although most programs for school-age children usually are funded with ESEA money, other federal sources of compensatory money are the Manpower Development and Training Act of 1962, the Vocational Education Act of 1963, the Civil Rights Act of 1964, the Economic Opportunity Act of 1964, the Higher Education Act of 1965, the Bilingual Education Act of 1968, and the Emergency School Aid Act of 1972. A variety of programs from preschool to higher education have been authorized, with emphasis on reducing class size and providing remedial programs, special personnel, and enrichment experiences. An overview of these programs includes the following:

---

30 David Selden, "The Future of Community Participation in Educational Policy Making" in C. A. Grant, ed., *Community Participation in Education* (Boston: Allyn & Bacon, 1979), pp. 67–77.

1. *Infant education and intervention in family life.* Research indicates that parent-child and family interactions are important influences on cognitive and school development of children. Programs of infant education and parental involvement range from helping the mother become a teacher of her child to improving family stability.

2. *Early childhood education.* Head Start and Follow-Through are the most common programs under this category. Whereas Head Start attempts to help disadvantaged children achieve "readiness" for the first grade, Follow-Through concentrates on sustaining readiness and supplementing in the early grades whatever gains are made by the children who have had a year's experience in Head Start.

Preschool
education

3. *Reading, language, and basic skills development.* Poor academic achievement is linked to abilities in basic reading and language areas. More than half of the ESEA projects deal directly with the improvement of reading and language through various materials, machines, and personnel.

4. *Bilingual education.* Emphasis and content of these programs vary, but they commonly focus on children whose mother tongue is not English. Hispanic children are the major target groups in these programs.

5. *Curriculum revision.* Curriculum efforts have involved different objectives and content to coincide with subject modifications or new subjects pertaining to Black, Hispanic-speaking, and American Indian identity and pride. These changes have included greater student and community involvement and a proliferation of ethnic studies.

6. *Instructional materials.* A flood of new materials has focused on disadvantaged and minority children. These range from simple printouts and changes in textbooks to sophisticated language laboratories and computers.

7. *Guidance and counseling programs.* Various social, psychological, and vocational services have been provided for the disadvantaged. Social workers and community aides have been involved to help bridge the gap between school and home.

8. *Tutoring programs.* Individual and small-group tutoring programs have been greatly augmented. These have involved both volunteer and paid student tutors, as well as volunteer and paid community people and aides. The programs at the public school level usually aim at also providing a positive older student or adult model.

Tutoring

*Children can learn to cooperate when they are motivated by a
group community project.*

9. *School organization.* Many schools serving the disadvantaged
have received funds for purposes of offering a variety of organizational plans ranging from extended school days and extended school
years to open classrooms and flexible schedules.

10. *Dropout prevention programs.* Along with vocational and
career education, a number of programs have aimed at preventing
students from dropping out of school. Numerous work-study programs, on-the-job training programs, and financial incentives have
been offered. Some of these programs have been incorporated into
the regular school program; others have been offered in special centers. Some are in the daytime, others are in the evening or summer.

11. *Personnel training.* A great many preservice and inservice training programs have been funded for beginning interns and
experienced educators (teachers and administrators) to gain insight
into teaching the disadvantaged.

**Teacher
training**

12. *Auxiliary school personnel.* The recruitment and training of teacher aides and paraprofessionals, along with nonpaid volunteers, have increased. Emphasis is on employing low-income workers from the local community for purposes of reducing the student-adult classroom ratio, enhancing school-community relations, and providing jobs to enhance the economy in low-income neighborhoods.

13. *School desegregation.* Money has been provided to aid schools and school personnel in dealing with desegregation problems and to provide technical assistance, grants to school boards, and workshops.

14. *Higher education.* Special programs in this area include the following: (a) identifying students of college potential early in the secondary schools and enriching their learning experience; (b) accepting special provisions and lower academic requirements for college admission; (c) using admission criteria that allow open enrollment, whereby every high school graduate has the opportunity to attend a two-year or four-year college, thus favoring low academic achievers who might not otherwise be granted admission; (d) transition programs to increase the probability of success for disadvantaged youth once admitted into college; and (e) special scholarships, loans, and jobs based solely on financial need and minority status.

15. *Adult education.* The most rapidly growing sector in education is adult education. Much of the focus is on adults who are illiterate and those who need training in basic job skills. Programs are usually offered at public schools, colleges, private industries, and special centers located in impoverished areas.[31]

Adult education

EVALUATION OF
PROGRAMS,
1965–1975

The overwhelming majority of compensatory efforts during the first decade of compensatory education emphasis were not shown to be effective in raising cognitive levels of target students. For example, according to Richard Fairley, the former Director of the Division of Compensatory Education of the U.S. Office of Education, of more than 1,200 educational projects evaluated between 1970 and 1972, only ten had solid data that unambiguously demonstrated their success.[32] Even Head Start, the best known and most heavily funded compensatory program, turned out to be ineffective according to the Westinghouse-Ohio Univer-

Unsuccessful programs

---

31 Allan C. Ornstein, *Education and Social Inquiry* (Itasca, Ill.: Peacock, 1978); A. Harry Passow, "Compensatory Instructional Intervention" in F. N. Kerlinger and J. B. Carroll, eds., *Review of Research in Education*, vol. 2 (Itasca, Ill.: Peacock, 1975), pp. 145–75.

32 Richard L. Fairley, "Accountability's New Test," *American Education* (June 1972), pp. 33–35. Also see *Compensatory Education and Other Alternatives in Urban Schools* (Washington, D.C.: U.S. Government Printing Office, 1972).

sity evaluation of 104 centers. The evaluation report indicated that there
was no significant difference in learning between Head Start children and
a matched control group, and that the program failed to help disadvantaged learners catch up to their middle-class counterparts or to alleviate
any of their cognitive deficiencies.[33] A Rand Corporation report concluded
that with regard to school financing and compensatory education, we have
been spending too much and not getting enough in return.[34] In the early
stages of compensatory programs, input increments had a high marginal
return; however, they gradually diminished until the point was reached
where input was wasted because there was virtually no increase in output.
It was concluded that we had reached a "flat area," less output in relation
to input, or even worse, no return.

Other studies also pointed to government's failure to secure objective, reliable measures of successful programs. The so-called "successes"
generally were based not on hard data but on impressions and testimonies
(in many cases bias); furthermore, lawmakers who allocate federal monies
for compensatory programs became increasingly concerned about putting
money into areas where little worth had been empirically shown.

**Inability to
pinpoint good
programs**

A number of reasons have been suggested for the disappointing record of compensatory education. A popular one is that as the program was
extended to larger numbers of children and the impact was watered down:
efforts were less intensive, teachers less well-trained, classes larger. However, there was little evidence that even intensive programs managed to
maintain more than moderate gains over a long period. It is likely that the
dramatic gains in early periods of some programs can be explained by the
"Hawthorne effect," the fact that students and teachers alike knew an
experiment was taking place and their behaviors changed for a short
period. Longitudinal studies of several compensatory programs also revealed a "fadeout" process, that is, the early gains made by these children
eventually level off and are equivalent to gains made by children without
such training after a few years of schooling.[35]

Advocates of compensatory education claim that the amount of
money usually earmarked for disadvantaged children is hardly enough to
make a difference. There is speculation that a threshold of several
thousand dollars extra per child may be needed before differences will be
noted.[36] Another proposal put this cost at $75 to $120 billion, or more than

**More money
needed**

---

33 Westinghouse Learning Corporation and Ohio University, *The Impact of Head Start*
(Washington, D.C.: U.S. Government Printing Office, 1969).

34 Harvey A. Averch et al., *How Effective Is Schooling? A Critical Review and Synthesis of
Research Findings* (Santa Monica, Calif.: Rand Corporation, 1972).

35 David J. Fox, *Expansion of the More Effective School Program* (New York: Center for
Urban Education, 1967); Harry L. Miller and Roger R. Woock, *Social Foundations of Urban
Education*, 2nd ed. (Hinsdale, Ill.: Dryden, 1974).

36 J. McVicker Hunt, "Has Compensatory Education Failed? Has It Been Achieved?" *Harvard
Educational Review* (May 1969), pp. 278-300.

half the total national budget in 1968, when these proposals were first considered.[37] However, there was little or no evidence that additional money would improve the outcome. Compensatory funding was criticized for "scattergun approaches, slipshod work, poor results or no results at all." The atmosphere was one "of giving away money without expecting real benefits." The evaluation data at best was suffused with technical errors and limitations, and in some cases testimonial and even empirical data were suspect.[38] The whole ESEA movement seemed to be undermining America's blind faith that educators could achieve their objectives.

In this connection compensatory education was and sometimes still is criticized for: (1) its piecemeal approach; (2) mismanagment and misappropriation of funds; (3) unethical methods of getting and awarding grants; (4) large consultant fees paid for work done poorly or not at all; (5) inadequately trained personnel at the state and local level; (6) high salaries for people at the administrative levels; (7) disregard for and lack of teacher participation; (8) vague objectives; (9) poor evaluation procedures; and (10) little change in the quality of content of the programs—only increased quantity of services.[39]

EVALUATION AFTER 1975

Recent data on compensatory education have justified a much more positive view concerning its potential and actual impact than was prevalent before 1975. In part, recent positive results can be traced to correction of some of the most serious mistakes of the first decade. In addition, data on some particularly outstanding efforts did not become available until the latter half of the 1970s. Important changes in the organization, operation, and evaluation of compensatory education leading to a more positive assessment of its effectiveness included the following: (1) the federal and state governments improved monitoring procedures and required local school districts to spend a "comparable" amount of funds on disadvantaged and nondisadvantaged students *before* the addition of compensatory funds; (2) some states such as California and Michigan began to provide additional money as part of a systematic plan to reduce scattershot spending; (3) the federal government required more adequate evaluation arrangements,

Improved monitoring procedures

37 Edmund W. Gordon, "Education of the Disadvantaged: A Problem of Human Diversity" in N. F. Ashline et al., ed., *Education, Inequality, and National Policy* (Lexington, Mass.: Heath, 1976), pp. 101-123. Edmund W. Gordon and Adelaide Jablonsky, "Compensatory Education in the Equalization of Educational Opportunity," *Journal of Negro Education* (Summer 1968), pp. 280-90.

38 Peter F. Drucker, "Rejoinder," *Saturday Review* (March 17, 1973), pp. 48, 53; Milbey W. McLaughlin, *Evaluation and Reform: The Elementary and Secondary Act of 1965/Title I* (Cambridge, Mass.: Ballinger, 1975); *New York Times*, January 27, 1973, p. 14.

39 Howard A. Glickstein, "Federal Education Programs and Minority Groups," *Journal of Negro Education* (Summer 1969), pp. 303-314; Edith Green, "The Educational Entrepreneur—A Portrait," *Public Interest* (Summer 1972), pp. 12-25; William W. Wayson, "ESEA: Decennial Views of the Revolution: The Negative Side," *Phi Delta Kappan* (November 1975), pp. 151-56.

provided technical assistance to make this possible, and initiated national studies designed to assess and improve compensatory education; and (4) many local school district officials and lay leaders learned how to avoid some of the mistakes of the first decade. By 1980, studies and data supporting the conclusion that compensatory education can and frequently does have relatively successful outcomes included:

1. Several big cities reported that student achievement in some low-income schools equaled or exceeded the national average through the second or third grades, indicating that preschool programs, Head Start, Follow-Through, and other early childhood compensatory education efforts were beginning to succeed.[40]

2. A 1976 national study of compensatory reading programs in grades two, four, and six identified schools in which these programs were successful and then identified some of the characteristics of the successful schools as follows: emphasis on reading as a priority goal and expenditure of more time on reading or improving reading resources, outstanding administrative leadership (usually provided by the principal) for the reading program, "careful attention" to basic skills, relative breadth of materials, and evidence of cross fertilization of ideas among teachers.[41]

Characteristics of successful programs

3. Several studies of outstanding early childhood education programs have shown that such efforts can have a long-lasting effect if they are well conceived and effectively implemented. For example, Francis Palmer's longitudinal study of working-class Black children who participated in a special preschool program in New York City showed that these children scored no higher than control group children in the first grade. When retested in the fifth grade, however, they scored nine points higher on IQ tests and three months higher in reading than did the control children.[42]

4. Some programs aimed at infant education and very early intervention in family life also have been found to have long-lasting and sometimes very significant effects. For example, the Milwaukee Project conducted by Rick Heber and his colleagues in the late 1960s involved 40 inner-city Black children whose mothers had IQ scores below 70. The Milwaukee project had two primary components: edu-

40 Irving Lazar et al., "Preliminary Findings of the Developmental Continuity Longitudinal Study." Paper presented at the Office of Child Development Conference on Parents, Children and Continuity, El Paso, May 1977; *Lasting Effects After Preschool* (Washington, D.C.: U.S. Government Printing Office, 1979).

41 George W. Mayeske, "Developmental Stages in a Quest for Successful Practices in Compensatory Education." Paper presented at the annual meeting of the American Educational Research Association, San Francisco, April 1979.

42 Francis H. Palmer, "The Effects of Minimal Early Intervention on Subsequent IQ Scores and Reading Achievement." Paper presented at the annual meeting of the American Psychological Association, Washington, D.C., September 1976.

cational and vocational rehabilitation of the *mothers*, as well as training in child care and home-making skills, and individualized enrichment for the *children* beginning in the first few months of life. The results were astounding: at age nine, the control children had average IQ scores less than 90, compared with a score of nearly 110 for children in the experimental group.[43]

5. Compensatory education programs that start at age three, according to a noted authority, "yield gains three times as great as those that start when the children are four."[44] Reviews of many Follow-Through evaluation studies indicated that instructional approaches based on a well-defined curriculum with emphasis on the development of basic skills generally produce meaningful gains over a variety of cognitive and affective outcome measures.[45] A national evaluation also provided some indication that "models that emphasize basic skills succeeded better than other models in helping children gain these skills."[46] (The term "basic" skills in this research referred particularly to relatively "mechanical" skills such as spelling, decoding of words, and simple arithmetic computation.) This finding has been widely publicized and has been interpreted as supporting the conclusion that "direct instruction"—highly structured instruction organized on a step-by-step basis—is the most effective way to teach basic skills to disadvantaged students in the primary grades.

Early intervention and basic skill emphasis

QUESTIONS ABOUT COMPENSATORY EDUCATION

Recent data indicating that compensatory education can be successful should not be viewed as proving that compensatory programs are equalizing or can equalize educational opportunity for disadvantaged students. These data have been encouraging but there still are many questions and problems concerning the status and effectiveness of compensatory education. Among the most central of these questions and problems are the following:

1. *Can compensatory education result in permanent meaningful gains for most disadvantaged students?* Students who make large gains frequently are dropped from Title I in order to make room for

Can cognitive gains be sustained?

43 Rick F. Heber, "Sociocultural Mental Retardation—A Longitudinal Study." Paper presented at the Vermont Conference on the Primary Prevention of Psychopathology (mimeograph), 1976.

44 Maya Pines, "Head Start in the Nursery," *Psychology Today* (September 1979), p. 64.

45 Eugene Tucker, "The Follow Through Planned Variation Experiment: What is the Payoff?" Paper presented at the annual meeting of the American Educational Research Association, New York, April 1977.

46 Linda B. Stebbins et al., *Education as Experimentation: A Planned Variation Model, Volume IV-A, An Evaluation of Follow Through* (Cambridge, Mass.: Abt Associates, 1977).

lower-achieving students, and the evidence indicates that the performance of many disadvantaged students entering secondary schools is unacceptably low regardless of whether they have been in Title I or other compensatory programs. In big cities, for example, the average reading score of ninth graders at inner-city schools generally still is about the sixth-grade level. This means in turn that 50 percent or more of these students are unable to read well enough to succeed in schools or rewarding jobs later in life. While there are some successes, in many programs, "the results . . . [are] either indistinguishable from or in some cases even worse than those for children in comparison schools."[47]

2. *What type of early instruction should be provided?* Much of the uncertainty regarding instruction for early compensatory education involves the issue of whether programs should utilize a behavioristic direct-instruction approach or should emphasize conceptual development and abstract thinking skills. Some direct instruction programs have had excellent results through the third grade, but performance levels fall when participating children enter the middle grades. Results in cognitive-oriented programs stressing conceptual development generally have not been as good in terms of mastery of "mechanical" skills in the primary grades, but some of the best cognitive approaches have resulted in gains that show up later in basic and conceptual skills.[48] The fall-off in scores frequently found as children enter the middle grades probably is due in part to inadequate conceptual development in the primary grades.

What instructional methods are best?

3. *What should be done at the secondary school level?* Although most sizable programs of compensatory education have been carried out at the elementary level, some efforts have been initiated in secondary schools and a few secondary programs have reported promising results. Some success has been achieved in individual classrooms, in "schools-within-a-school," and in "street academies" or store-front schools.[49] There also is reason to believe that direct-instruction approaches emphasizing structured learning and basic skills can help improve instruction in inner-city secondary schools.[50]

47   Carl E. Wisler, Gerald P. Burns, and David Iwamoto, "Follow Through Redux: A Response to the Critique by House, Glass, McLean, and Walker," *Harvard Educational Review* (May 1978), p. 179.

48   David P. Weikart, James T. Bond, and James McNeil, "Ypsilanti Perry Preschool Project: Preschool Years and Longitudinal Results Through Fourth Grade," *Monographs of the High-/Scope Educational Research Foundation* (Series No. 3, 1977).

49   Daniel U. Levine, "Educating Alienated Inner City Youth: Lessons from the Street Academies," *Journal of Negro Education* (Spring 1975), pp. 139–48.

50   Meredith A. Larson and Freya E. Dittman, *Compensatory Education and Early Adolescence: Reviewing Our National Strategy* (Menlo Park, Calif.: Stanford Research Institute, 1975).

4. *How can community resources be best utilized for compen-*
satory programs? One of the approaches that seems to be working
most successfully in some inner-city high schools is to emphasize
community resources in preparing students for jobs and to tie classroom instruction in with this type of career education focus. Following this approach, students spend part of their time learning
about jobs (often on a work-study basis) in a field that particularly
interests them, and much of the traditional subject matter is taught
in conjunction with activities involving occupational or related
studies outside the school. This general approach seems to be working well in Boston, New York City, and several other locations.

Another promising approach for improving inner-city schools
is the PUSH-Excel programs now being funded in Chicago, Los
Angeles, and several other cities. PUSH-Excel is the project organized by Rev. Jesse Jackson of the People United to Save Humanity
organization in Chicago. Aimed particularly at improving achievement in inner-city high schools with a predominantly Black student
body, the program encourages parents in poverty neighborhoods to
exercise more control over their children and to join together with
teachers, ministers, and the students' peer groups in stressing excellence and enforcing higher academic standards in inner city
classrooms.[51]

PUSH
programs

5. *Is it financially feasible to include most economically disadvan-*
taged students in effective compensatory education programs?
Research on early compensatory education has demonstrated that
important gains can be made in improving the performance of disadvantaged students, but effective programs tend to be expensive because they require massive and prolonged intervention in the child's
family environment. At present no one can say exactly what proportion of economically disadvantaged children requires this type of intervention, but the true percentage is likely to be high and per pupil
costs are likely to run several thousand dollars per year. Federal and
state funding per student in some elementary and secondary compensatory programs already approximates $3,000 per year or more,
yet many of these students continue to fail. Those who need help may
not participate for long enough periods and many programs do not
have adequate funding to accomplish their basic goals. Thus it is
clear that effective compensatory education on a national scale will
cost significantly more than is now available for this purpose, despite the fact that expenditures for compensatory education already
constitute 70 to 80 percent of U.S. Department of Education funds

Are the
programs
financially
feasible?

51 Eugene E. Eubanks and Daniel U. Levine, "The PUSH Program for Excellence in Big-City
Schools," *Phi Delta Kappan* (January 1977), pp. 383–88.

and 20 to 25 percent of the funds the federal government spends on a variety of education activities.[52] All this leads to a real question concerning the public's willingness and ability to spend additional money on compensatory education, as well as the cost-effectiveness ratio for success: Just how many dollars it takes to raise achievement levels one increment among disadvantaged students?

A NATIONAL ISSUE   The fundamental question concerning these and other educational reform efforts is whether they really can provide, particularly for minority students in concentrated poverty neighborhoods, a chance to succeed in the schools and later in life. There is great uncertainty concerning the possibility or likelihood that desegregation, decentralization, and/or compensatory education will provide meaningful opportunities for students in concentrated poverty neighborhoods in big cities. In recent years, for example, several forceful critics of U.S. schools and society have offered strong arguments concluding that public schools have failed and will fail in the future to provide equal opportunity for the poor unless fundamental reforms are made in U.S. society as a whole. Among the most prominent of these critics are Samuel Bowles and Herbert Gintis, whose book *Schooling in Capitalist America*[53] argued that hierarchical social relations in the schools correspond to the hierarchical division of labor in the economy (the "correspondence" principle) in order to prepare economically disadvantaged and working-class youth for menial and low paid jobs and to prepare middle-class youth for rewarding positions requiring independent thinking and advanced education. The public schools, according to Bowles and Gintis, are thus systematically organized to develop discipline among low status children and channel them into subservient jobs that perpetuate their low social status.

Another recent book representing this "neo-Marxist" point of view has been written by Richard deLone. DeLone's *Small Futures*, published for the Carnegie Council on Children, argues that there is little social mobility in the United States and that economically disadvantaged children do not have much opportunity to develop or demonstrate "meritocratic" abilities that would enable them to succeed later in the schools and society.[54] Part of his argument is that neighborhood, school, and other environmental conditions are such that children in poverty families develop or are taught feelings of futility and powerlessness that ensure they will fail in the classroom; for this reason, reform programs "such as Head Start or parent education may succeed briefly in making apparent

Can schools succeed in poverty neighborhoods?

Schools perpetuate social hierarchies

52 Estimates in this section depend on how one defines and classifies federal expenditures for education.

53 Samuel Bowles and Herbert Gintis, *Schooling in Capitalist America* (New York: Basic Books, 1976).

54 Richard H. deLone, *Small Futures: Children, Inequality, and the Limits of Liberal Reform* (New York: Harcourt Brace Jovanovich, 1979).

changes . . . [but] usually lack the historical scope to sustain the changes they induce.''[55] Only major social and economic changes in basic policies dealing with full employment, affirmative action, and income redistribution, he concludes, can give the poor a meaningful opportunity to improve their lot in U.S. society.

Similarly, Kenneth Keniston's *All Our Children: The American Family Under Pressure*[56] and John Ogbu's *Minority Education and Caste: The American System in Cross-Cultural Perspective*,[57] both published for the Carnegie Council on Children, also conclude that compensatory education is unlikely to prove effective in the absence of more fundamental changes in U.S. society. Keniston and the Council point out that parents have surrendered or lost much of their supervision over children to other institutions and conclude that tax policies to significantly redistribute income are required so that low-status parents can provide environmental conditions conducive to their children's success in school and society. Based on his studies of low-status Black communities, Ogbu argues that Black children in poverty communities are not likely to demonstrate adequate motivation and performance in school unless caste-type barriers to minority advancement are systematically eliminated in all aspects of U.S. society. Thus he attacks the assumption that ''improving black school performance and educational attainment is a prerequisite to increasing effectively their opportunities in society.'' Instead, he concludes, ''The present study suggests that the reverse may be the case, so that there is a need to plan the policies and programs dealing with social and occupational barriers in terms of their possible effects on black school performance.''[58]

Changing society before changing schools

Views such as those above naturally are subject to intense controversy and criticism. Some of the most important of the points made by critics are as follows:[59]

1. Immigrant groups in the United States historically have achieved a substantial amount of social and economic mobility, much of it through the public schools.

55 Ibid., p. 168

56 Kenneth Keniston et al., *All Our Children: The American Family Under Pressure* (New York: Harcourt Brace Jovanovich, 1977).

57 John U. Ogbu, *Minority Education and Caste: The American System in Cross-Cultural Perspective* (New York: Academic Press, 1978).

58 Ibid., p. 6.

59 Alice Kessler-Harris and Virginia Yans McLaughlin, ''European Ethnic Groups'' in T. Sowell, ed., *American Ethnic Groups* (Washington, D.C.: The Urban Institute, 1978), pp. 107–137; Robert J. Havighurst and Daniel U. Levine, *Society and Education*, 5th ed. (Boston: Allyn & Bacon, 1979); David H. Kamens, ''Book Reviews,'' *American Educational Research Journal* (Fall 1977), pp. 499–510; Diane Ravitch, ''The Revisionists Revised: Studies in the Historiography of American Education,'' *Proceedings of the National Academy of Education*, Vol. 4 (Palo Alto, California, 1977), pp. 1–84; Ravitch, ''Liberal Reforms and Radical Visions,'' *New York Times Book Review* (September 16, 1979), p. 3.

2. There is evidence indicating that the United States and other western societies are becoming more meritocratic (mobility is being attained through merit) and that education is accounting for an increasing share of mobility.

3. Many low-income and working-class students are *not* being shunted into vocational courses and programs to the degree claimed by some of the neo-Marxists.

4. Many low-income and working-class students do not attend predominantly low-status schools.

5. Recent data on compensatory education, desegregation, and other efforts to improve education for the disadvantaged indicate that some progress is being made in achieving this goal.

6. The schools can do only so much; other institutions of society, especially the family, must be held accountable and do their share in providing the best education for *all* children.

To a degree, the conclusions of many of the neo-Marxists or, at least, the relatively positive responses to their writing among many social scientists reflect the widespread pessimism concerning educational reform that was prevalent in the 1970s. It remains to be seen whether efforts to further improve education for disadvantaged students will become sufficiently effective on a national scale—expensive though this may prove—to belie the assertions of those who believe that basic changes in economy policy amounting to or approaching a social revolution are necessary if disadvantaged youngsters are to have a real chance to succeed in U.S. society.

**National
reforms**

SUMMING UP

1. Efforts to improve education for disadvantaged students have been manifested in movement toward desegregation, decentralization, and compensatory education.

2. Much desegregation has been accomplished in smaller school districts, but the concentration of minority students and economically disadvantaged students in big-city districts has made it difficult to bring about stable desegregation. School officials in many districts have achieved a substantial degree of desegregation, but many others have been unable or unwilling to do so.

3. In part because desegregation has not been accomplished and also, in part, as an independent attempt to improve public schooling for the disadvantaged, emphasis in city school districts has been placed on decentralization and community involvement and on com-

pensatory education. Most large school districts have decentralized to some degree, but problems have been encountered in districts where decentralization took the form of local community control.

4. Whether or to what degree education has been improved as a result of decentralization and community involvement is uncertain, but many observers believe that this approach has helped or can help improve the public schools.

5. Compensatory education seemed to be unsuccessful until evidence accumulating in the latter half of the 1970s began to justify a more positive conclusion. However, many serious questions remain concerning the degree to which compensatory education as well as desegregation and decentralization can have substantial and lasting results on a large scale.

6. Evidence bearing on these questions will play an important part in determining whether the United States does or can provide equal opportunity in schools and society for all its citizens.

DISCUSSION QUESTIONS

1. What are the pros and cons of desegregation and integration? (Be sure to include in the discussion academic learning, psychological factors, political factors, and moral factors.)

2. What is the difference between *de jure* and *de facto* segregation? What implications do these two types of segregation have for the North and South?

3. Why might administrative decentralization and community control impede school desegregation?

4. What is the current status of compensatory education? How have conclusions about compensatory education changed during the past decade?

5. Why is compensatory education an important national issue? What larger conclusions follow from one's viewpoint concerning its success or failure?

THINGS TO DO

1. Arrange a debate among members of your class concerning the advantages of compensatory education, desegregation, and administrative decentralization.

2. Visit a school that has desegregated on its own or has been forced to desegregate. Speak with as many of its students, teachers, and administrators as possible concerning the problems of desegregation and be prepared to discuss these problems in class.

3. Invite two or three individuals who represent different views concerning administrative decentralization, community participation, and community control to speak to the class.

4. Visit a school heavily funded with compensatory money and speak with as many of its teachers and administrators as possible. Discuss the school's programs and be prepared to describe these programs to your classmates.

5. Interview school district officials responsible for the conduct of Head Start, Follow-Through, or other compensatory education programs. What are the major problems they have encountered in carrying out their programs?

CHAPTER 16
TRENDS AND
ISSUES IN
THE 1980s

Focusing questions

What is multicultural education and what forms does it take in public schools? What are its major benefits and dangers?

What are the trends in educating handicapped children? What has been the influence of PL 94–142?

What is mastery learning? Can it improve students' academic performance?

Why have school districts instituted minimum competency testing? What problems are involved in competency testing?

How and why are school finance arrangements undergoing change?

Why and how have the courts and the federal government become more important in education?

What are likely to be some of the most important changes in education in the future?

It is difficult to predict the future, but probable trends can be gleaned by studying recent developments and identifying those that are most likely to receive attention and further development in the future. In this chapter we identify and analyze some of the most important trends and issues that have had a growing influence on education in the latter part of the 1970s and probably will become even more influential in the 1980s. The chapter concludes with a discussion of education and educational planning in the future.

No attempt has been made to identify and discuss all the important trends and issues that will preoccupy educators in the 1980s. Our primary intent in this concluding chapter is to call attention to developments that either have been emerging in full force only during the past few years or have not been delineated fully in earlier chapters; these trends and issues are related to multicultural education, education of the handicapped, mastery learning, minimum competency testing, school finances, the federal role in education, and educational futurism.

MULTICULTURAL EDUCATION

Concern with multicultural education grew throughout the 1970s and should continue to increase in the 1980s. This concern reflects the difficult problems regarding intergroup contact and individual and group opportunity that people encounter in a nation with many ethnic groups and subcultures. More than most other countries, the United States consists of a large number of ethnic groups with a diversity of distinctive cultural patterns and histories. Many individuals are severely disadvantaged in the larger society because their cultural patterns or physical characteristics set them apart from the "mainstream" or generate overt or covert forms of discrimination and inequality. Except for some groups of Native Americans (Indians and Eskimos), all groups in the United States have faced problems transplanting their cultural patterns from one location to another, and Native Americans have had to adjust to patterns that frequently include discrimination and oppression imposed by the newcomers.

A nation with many ethnic groups

FROM MELTING POT TO CULTURAL PLURALISM

Although the United States always has been pluralistic in its population composition, emphasis through much of our history has been on assimilation of subcultures into the national mainstream rather than on maintenance of group subcultures. Some groups such as Blacks, Hispanics, and Native Americans were systematically segregated from the national culture, but most had substantial opportunity to acquire cultural patterns required for success in the larger society. Of course, it should not be necessary to completely give up one's group identity in order to participate in the national culture, but for much of our history emphasis was placed on assimilation into national culture,

Assimilation of subcultures

perhaps because this may have seemed necessary in building a new nation of so many diverse groups.

Whatever the reasons, the emphasis was on assimilation, and as early as 1782 St. John de Crevecoeur commented that the colonists were being "melted" into a "new race" of men. Israel Zangwill's 1908 play "The Melting Pot" popularized this term and called attention to the challenge of "Americanizing" the large streams of immigrants who were entering the United States in the late nineteenth and early twentieth centuries. Zangwill and others believed that each group should be able to participate fully in American society and contribute to a melded culture without having to become uniform in all cultural patterns, but many other "established" citizens advocated a type of "Americanism" that insisted on conformity with prevailing "Anglo" influences in language, religion, attire, and other cultural patterns.

Except for the most segregated minorities, however, non-Anglo ethnic groups were able to achieve substantial mobility.[1] An expanding economy, cheap land on the frontier, the establishment of free public schools, availability of jobs in government and politics, and other opportunities made it possible for them to enter the mainstream of society, in the process acquiring many of the attitudes and behaviors of the typical American while also enriching the national culture with their contributions in language, music and the arts, food, sports, entertainment, scholarship, and other aspects of culture.[2]

Mobility among ethnics

Nevertheless, scholars and laypeople also began to realize that the melting pot had not melted its ingredients as fully as many had thought, and that ethnic identity not only was not being completely eliminated but seemed also to be undergoing a resurgence. Andrew Greeley, for example, described how the Irish in the United States maintained themes and practices from their traditional culture,[3] and Glazer and Moynihan's study of major ethnic groups in New York City found that ethnic identification was increasing as a result of down-grading of working-class occupational statuses, international events that served as stimulants to affirmation of ethnicity, and decline in traditional forms of patriotism.[4] Other observers pointed out that Blacks, Hispanics, American Indians, and European minorities had been systematically discriminated against to the extent that the shortcomings of the melting pot concept were apparent.[5]

1 Historical mobility data for a number of ethnic and racial groups in the U.S. are reviewed in Alice Kessler-Harris and Virginia Yans-McLaughlin, "European Immigrant Groups," in Thomas Sowell, ed., *American Ethnic Groups* (Washington, D.C.: Urban Institute, 1971), pp. 107-137.

2 Richard Pratte, *Pluralism in Education* (Springfield, Ill.: Thomas, 1979).

3 Andrew Greeley, *That Most Distressful Nation* (Chicago: Quadrangle, 1973).

4 Nathan Glazer and Daniel P. Moynihan, *Beyond the Melting Pot*, 2nd ed. (Cambridge, Mass.: MIT Press and Harvard University Press, 1970).

5 Howard Bahr, Bruce A. Chadwick, and Joseph H. Strauss, *American Ethnicity* (Lexington, Mass.: Heath, 1979); Michael Novak, *The Rise of the Unmeltable Ethnics* (New York: Macmillan, 1971).

In this context, the Civil Rights movement emerged and fought to reduce the exclusion of minority groups, and emphasis shifted (in some interpretations) from the melting pot's stress on uniformity to a stress on diversity and cultural pluralism. In place of the metaphor of the melting pot, the concept of cultural pluralism introduces new metaphors such as a "tossed salad" or a "mosaic" that allows or requires maintenance of distinctive group characteristics within a larger whole. The American Association of Colleges of Teacher Education (AACTE) has defined cultural pluralism as follows:

Shift to
cultural
pluralism

> To endorse cultural pluralism is to endorse the principle that there is no one model American. To endorse cultural pluralism is to understand and appreciate the differences that exist among the nation's citizens. It is to see these differences as a positive force in the continuing development of a society which professes a wholesome respect for the intrinsic worth of every individual. Cultural pluralism is more than a temporary accommodation to placate racial and ethnic minorities. It is a concept that aims toward a heightened sense of being and of wholeness of the entire society based on the unique strengths of each of its parts.[6]

It should be emphasized that acceptance of or stress on cultural pluralism does not mean that one supports a philosophy aiming at cultural, social, or economic separation. Depending on how cultural pluralism is defined, it may or may not stress integration in cultural, social, or economic matters, but generally it lies somewhere in between total assimilation of ethnic or racial groups into a uniform mass on the one hand and strict separation of groups from each other at the opposite pole.

Between
assimilation
and separation
of groups

CULTURAL PLURALISM
AND MULTICULTURAL
EDUCATION
Recognizing and responding to social trends emphasizing the desirability of cultural pluralism, educators have been examining and developing ways to build the goals of a constructive pluralism into the educational system of the United States. The AACTE views this goal as a major educational responsibility because of the fact that schools "play a major role in shaping the attitudes and beliefs of the nation's youth . . . [and in] preparing each generation to assume the rights and responsibilities of adult life."[7] The AACTE statement further spells out implications for providing this type of multicultural education as follows:

Multicultural
education as
a school
responsibility

> Multicultural education is education which values cultural pluralism [and] affirms that schools should be oriented toward

6 "No One Model American. A Statement of Multicultural Education." (Washington, D.C.: American Association of Colleges of Teacher Education, 1972), p. 9.
7 Ibid., p. 14.

the cultural enrichment of all children and youth through programs rooted to the preservation and extension of cultural alternatives. . . .

If cultural pluralism is so basic a quality of our culture, it must become an integral part of the educational process at every level. Education for cultural pluralism includes four major thrusts: (1) the teaching of values which support cultural diversity and individual uniqueness; (2) the encouragement of the qualitative expansion of existing ethnic cultures and their incorporation into the mainstream of American socioeconomic and political life; (3) the support of explorations in alternative and emerging life styles; and (4) the encouragement of multiculturalism, multilingualism, and multidialecticism. . . . In addition, special emphasis programs must be provided where all students are helped to understand that being different connotes neither superiority nor inferiority; programs where students of various social and ethnic backgrounds may learn freely from one another; programs that help different minority students understand who they are, where they are going, and how they can make their contribution to the society in which they live.[8]

School officials at every level of the educational system in the United States have been developing specific approaches for translating the goals of multicultural education into practice in the classroom. In particular, state departments of education, national professional organizations, local school district curriculum developers and supervisors, and colleges of teacher education have been introducing guidelines for providing constructive multicultural education for all students.

Translating into practice

MULTICULTURAL INSTRUCTION   One of the key areas in which educators are attempting to develop effective approaches for multicultural education involves the use of differential instructional approaches appropriate in teaching students with differing ethnic and racial backgrounds. Some of the most important and frequently discussed approaches have been concerned with student learning styles, dialect differences among ethnic and racial groups, and bilingual education.

Different instructional approaches with different ethnic groups

Student learning styles   A good example of a serious attempt to explore the possibility of differentiating instruction according to learning styles associated with students' background is the "bicognitive" approach described and advocated by Manuel Ramirez and Carlos Castañeda. After conducting preliminary research with Hispanic students, Ramirez and Castañeda concluded that Chicano children tend to be more "field sensi-

8 Ibid., p. 15.

tive" than nonminority children. Field-sensitive children are described as being more influenced by personal relationships and by praise or disapproval from authority figures than are "field-independent" students. Ramirez and Castañeda reviewed the implications of these findings for instruction and concluded that a "field-sensitive curriculum" should be "humanized through use of narration, humor, drama, and fantasy" and should emphasize "description of wholes and generalities" and be "structured in such a way that children work cooperatively with peers or with the teacher in a variety of activities."[9]

Although "bicognitive" instruction and similar approaches potentially may improve instruction for many minority students in the future, little research has yet been reported to indicate that these approaches are of proven value in improving the performance of disadvantaged students. It also should be noted that the learning styles of field-sensitive minority students may be associated as much or more with low socioeconomic status as with ethnicity or race per se.

Another example of an effort to identify instructional approaches uniquely suited to students' ethnic or racial background has been provided by Vera John-Steiner and Larry Smith, who have worked with Pueblo Indian children in the Southwest.[10] They concluded that schooling for these children would be more successful if it took better account of their "primary learning" patterns (learning outside the school) and organized classroom instruction in a manner more compatible with these patterns. These investigators point out that primary learning tends to take place in *personal* communication with emotionally significant individuals, in *tutorial* situations (face-to-face) in which learning is *pervasive* (not limited to a single setting) and highly *adaptive* (closely linked to the concerns and needs of the community).

In the case of Pueblo children, the researchers found that primary learning also emphasized verbal instruction, exploratory play, and monitoring of the complex activity of elders, and that children's observations centered on individuals—such as a favorite uncle—who were particularly important to a particular child. The researchers concluded that teachers should do more to "match their techniques with the previous learning of the child"—particularly in the middle and upper grades.[11] It should be noted, however, that the value of this approach is not well

Emphasis on
personal
relationships

Matching
teaching
activities with
children's
experiences

9   Manuel Ramirez and Carlos Castañeda, *Cultural Democracy, Bicognitive Development, and Education* (New York: Academic Press, 1974), p. 142. Also see James A. Vasquez, "Bilingual Education's Needed Third Dimension," *Educational Leadership* (November 1979), pp. 166–69.

10   Vera John-Steiner and Larry Smith, "The Educational Promise of Cultural Pluralism," Paper prepared for the National Conference on Urban Education, St. Louis, Missouri, 1978.

11   Ibid.

documented and its specific implications for classroom instruction have not been worked out in much detail.

Recognition of dialect differences   Many educators have become concerned with the problems of teaching students who speak nonstandard dialects that may hamper their progress in the traditional classroom. Historically, U.S. public schools have attempted to teach "proper" or standard English to students who speak nonstandard dialects, but simplistic insistence on proper English sometimes has caused students either to reject their own cultural background or to view teachers' efforts in this direction as demeaning and hostile.

In recent years educators have been particularly concerned with learning problems encountered by students who speak Black English. A number of scholars have been studying the Black English dialect and have succeeded in identifying its underlying grammatical forms and differences from standard English.[12] Because Black English seems to be the basic form of speech of many low income Black students who are not succeeding academically, some educators have proposed that the school teach such students in Black English until they learn to read. Other proposals and experiments have advocated teaching English as a foreign language to students who speak Black English or other nonstandard dialects, emphasizing students' personal experience in teaching language and a variety of other transitional techniques.

Research on teaching in Black English or other dialects has not provided much support for the conclusion that students will gain academically if initially taught in their own dialect. Thus one review of the research dealing with Black English has concluded that "there is, as yet, no conclusive empirical evidence in the literature supporting the belief that using any of the methods which purport to minimize the interference of Black English on reading performance . . . is more successful than the traditional standard instructional materials."[13] In addition, there usually is considerable disagreement among members of dialect communities concerning the way in which the school should teach English. In working-class Black communities, for example, many or most parents believe or insist that their children should be taught only in "proper" English in order to acquire language skills required for success in the larger society.

Black dialect v. "proper" English

Despite lack of research indicating the superiority of any particular method for teaching students with nonstandard dialects, educators still should seek constructive ways to overcome the learning problems many of these students encounter in standard English classrooms. This task

12   J. L. Dillard, *Black English* (New York: Random House, 1972).

13   J. R. Harber and D. N. Bryan, "Black English and the Teaching of Reading," *Review of Educational Research* (Summer 1976), pp. 397-98.

became particularly important when a federal judge ruled in 1979 that the Ann Arbor, Michigan, school district must recognize that students who speak Black English may need special help in learning standard English.[14] The court ordered the school district to submit a plan defining the steps it will take to identify children who speak Black English and then to take their dialect into consideration in teaching them to read. Although the decision is being appealed and is not binding on anyone outside the Ann Arbor schools, it may have an important future influence in many school districts struggling to provide effective multicultural education for students who speak nonstandard dialects.

Bilingual/bicultural education   Bilingual education, which provides instruction in their native language for non-English speaking students, has been an expanding activity in U.S. public schools. In 1968 Congress passed the Bilingual Education Act and in 1974 the Supreme Court ruled in *Lau* v. *Nichols* that the schools must take steps to help students who ''are certain to find their classroom experiences wholly incomprehensible'' because they do not understand English. Congressional appropriations for bilingual education increased from $7.5 million in 1969 to $158.6 million in 1979. Although the federal and state governments fund bilingual projects for more than 60 language groups speaking various Asian, Indo-European, and Native American languages, the large majority of children in these projects are Hispanic.

Bilingual education has been expanding partly because the federal Office of Civil Rights (OCR) has been insisting that educational opportunities be improved for limited-English-speaking (LES) and non-English-speaking (NES) students. The Supreme Court's unanimous decision in the *Lau* case involving Chinese children in San Francisco did not focus on bilingual education as the only remedy for teaching non-English-speaking students. Instead, the Court said ''Teaching English to the students of Chinese ancestry is one choice. Giving instruction to this group in Chinese is another. There may be others.'' However, in practice, federal regulations for implementing the *Lau* decision have tended to focus on bilingual education as the most common solution for helping LES and NES students, generally suggesting that school districts initiate bilingual programs if they enroll more than twenty students of a given language group at a particular grade level. Bilingual programs have proliferated accordingly, but there is considerable disagreement concerning the kinds of programs that can or should be offered.

Controversies over bilingual education have become somewhat embittered as federal and state actions have led to the establishment of addi-

Focus on Hispanic bilingual projects

14   ''Schools Must Help Break Down the 'Black English' Barrier,'' *Phi Delta Kappan* (October 1979), p. 144.

tional programs. As in the case of teaching through dialect, there are arguments between those who would "immerse" children in an English-language environment and those who believe initial instruction will be more effective in the native language. Divided on this issue, residents in some ethnic neighborhoods have engaged in bitter internal struggles over the establishment of bilingual programs in the public schools.

Educators and laypeople concerned with LES and NES students also argue over whether emphasis should be placed on teaching in the native language over a long period (maintenance) or proceeding to teach in English as soon as possible (transitional). On the one side, those who favor maintenance feel that this will help build or maintain a constructive sense of identity among ethnic or racial minorities.[15] On the other side are those who believe that cultural maintenance programs are harmful because they separate groups from one another or discourage students from mastering English well enough to function successfully in the larger society.[16]

Maintenance v. transitional programs

Adherents and opponents of bilingual education also differ on the related issues of whether bilingual programs sometimes or frequently are designed to provide teaching jobs for native language speakers and whether individuals who fill these jobs are competent in English. Observers who favor bilingual/bicultural maintenance tend to believe that the schools need many adults who can teach LES or NES students in their own language, while many observers who favor transitional programs feel that very few native language or bilingual speakers are required to staff a legitimate program.

cerned with the question of whether this approach is effective in improving the performance of low-achieving students. Most scholars who have examined the research agree that bilingual education has brought about little if any improvement in the performance of participating students. Other scholars partially disagree, arguing that programs which are implemented well can result in significant achievement gains. There is considerable agreement, however, that much more than bilingual/bicultural education is needed to improve the performance of economically disadvantaged LES and NES students. In this regard, Joshua Fishman has summarized the research literature by stating that "on the whole," bilingual education is "too frail a device in and of itself, to significantly alter the learning experiences of the minority-mother-tongue in general or their majority-language-learning success in particular . . . precisely because there are so many other pervasive reasons why such children achieve

Little improvement in academic outcomes

15 Leonard C. Pacheco, "Educational Renewal: A Bilingual/Bicultural Imperative," *Educational Horizons* (Summer 1977), pp. 168–76.

16 Noel Epstein, *Language, Ethnicity, and the Schools: Policy Alternatives for Bilingual-Bicultural Education* (Washington, D.C.: George Washington University Institute for Educational Leadership, 1977).

poorly; . . . removing the extra burden . . . does not usually do the trick."[17]

DANGERS IN
MULTICULTURAL
EDUCATION
Multicultural education can be indispensable in helping to achieve constructive cultural pluralism in a nation composed of diverse ethnic groups. At the same time, however, multicultural education potentially can be harmful or damaging. In general, the potential dangers of multicultural education are the same as those associated with the larger concept of cultural pluralism. Major dangers are that:

1. *Multicultural education can emphasize separatism in a way that is divisive and disunifying.* If too much emphasis in multicultural education is placed on differences and separation, educators may neglect unifying themes and similarities that are desirable in a society in which groups are interdependent. Emphasis on differences may lead to neglect of the need to develop citizens who understand and act on national and universal responsibilities of citizenship.

Too much
emphasis on
differences

In addition, educational arrangements for some aspects of multicultural education such as bilingualism may conflict with constitutional requirements for ethnic and racial desegregation. For example, bringing students from a particular ethnic group together in a bilingual program may increase their segregation within a school district or school.

2. *Multicultural education may be used to justify second-rate education for economically disadvantaged students or minority students.* Encouraging the separation of disadvantaged students in "remedial" education programs or of minority students in "ethnic studies" programs under the guise of cultural pluralism can result in the establishment or maintenance of programs that are widely viewed as second rate. Unless great efforts are made to maintain the quality and reputation of such programs, students who participate in them may find that the diplomas or degrees they receive are viewed as worthless or second class.[18]

3. *Multicultural education may lead to fragmentation of the school curriculum.* For example, to the extent that attempts are made to broaden the curriculum to achieve all the possible goals of cultural pluralism, attention may be diverted from other equally or

17   Joshua A. Fishman, "Bilingual Education—A Perspective," *IRCD Bulletin* (Spring 1977), p. 5.

18   These and other dangers in multicultural education are discussed in Thomas R. Lopez, "Toward Cultural Pluralism in Education: Some Caveats," *The University of Toledo College of Education 1979/Educational Comment,* pp. 101–108.

more important topics. In this regard, Harry Broudy has stated that cultural patterns that "do not enhance the potential of their members for human development and achievement may be interesting, if sufficiently quaint, but they are not worth disrupting the public schools for their preservation. . . . Ethnic identity by itself, a language, cuisine, folk costumes and customs, a geographical, historical, religious origin do not necessarily qualify a cultural pattern for preservation by publicly supported formal schooling."[19] Attempts to incorporate a large amount of material on ethnic diversity, according to another observer, may "trivialize rather than enrich the curriculum."[20]

Trivializing the curriculum

EDUCATION FOR ALL HANDICAPPED CHILDREN

One of the major trends in education in the 1970s and 1980s involves schooling for handicapped children. Large gains were made during the 1970s in providing and improving education for handicapped students. Approximate numbers and percentages of handicapped students now being served in or through public education are shown in Table 16.1. As indicated in the table, the percentage of students receiving educational services varies from about 90 percent in the case of mentally

TABLE 16.1
APPROXIMATE NUMBERS AND
PERCENTAGES OF STUDENTS
RECEIVING EDUCATIONAL SERVICES
BY TYPE OF HANDICAP

TYPE OF HANDICAP	NUMBER	PERCENTAGE
Speech impaired	2,000,000	90
Mentally retarded	1,350,000	90
Learning disabilities	275,000	15
Emotionally disturbed	275,000	20
Crippled and other health impaired	275,000	80
Deaf	50,000	92
Hard of hearing	70,000	25
Visually handicapped	45,000	70
Deaf-blind and other multihandicapped	20,000	45

Source: Authors' estimates based on data provided in B. Marian Swanson and Diane J. Willis, *Understanding Exceptional Children and Youth* (Chicago: Rand McNally, 1979), p. 11.

19 Harry S. Broudy, "Educational Unity in a Pluralistic Society," *School Review* (November 1977), p. 75.

20 Stanley D. Ivie, "Multicultural Education: Boon or Boondoggle?" *Journal of Teacher Education* (May–June 1979), p. 25.

retarded, speech impaired, and deaf students, to about 15 percent in the case of students with learning disabilities.

Much of the activity and improvement that have taken place with respect to the education of handicapped students can be attributed to two federal laws: Public Law 93-380 in 1974, and Public Law 94-142 (The Education for All Handicapped Children Act) in 1975. Public Law 93-380 authorized increased levels of aid to states for the implementation of special education services and set forth due process requirements to protect the rights of handicapped students and their families. Public Law 94-142 set forth as national policy the goal that "free appropriate public education . . . must be extended to handicapped persons as their fundamental right."

First priority under PL 94-142 was accorded to children not currently receiving needed special services, and second priority was given to children who are not adequately served. Other sections of the law include requirements that: (1) testing and assessment services will be fair and comprehensive (testing cannot be based on a single criterion such as an IQ score), (2) parents or guardians have access to information on diagnosis and may protest decisions made by school officials, (3) educational services will be provided in the least restrictive environment (exceptional children may be placed in special or separate classes only for the amount of time judged necessary for providing appropriate services), and (4) Individual Education Plans (IEPs) that include both long-range and short-range educational goals must be provided. These plans must include periodic review of the instructional goals and methods elected.[21]

Least
restrictive
environmental
conditions

Largely as a result of these federal mandates, special education expenditures rose steadily in the 1970s. According to a survey by the National School Boards Association, there now are more than four million handicapped students who comprise about 9 to 10 percent of public school enrollment. The average annual cost of educating handicapped students is twice the national average of nearly $2,000. However, although the federal government requires local school districts to provide free appropriate education for all students aged three to 21, it provides approximately $200 extra per child to help make this possible.[22] Federal expenditures for special education have increased from $75 million in 1969 to $1.2 billion in 1980; almost 75 percent of the nation's handicapped children now are receiving special services as compared with less than half in 1974; the number of special education teachers increased by 23,000 between 1977 and 1979; and nearly 40 percent of handicapped children previously confined to institutions now receive part of their education in public schools.[23]

Increased
funding and
personnel

21 B. Marian Swanson and Diane J. Willis, *Understanding Exceptional Children and Youth* (Chicago: Rand McNally, 1979).

22 "Handicapped Education Costs Rising," *Educational Leadership* (February 1980), p. 446.

23 "Update on Special Ed Successes by the Feds," *Phi Delta Kappan* (April 1980), p. 158.

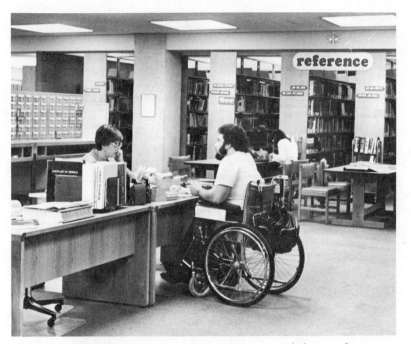

Only recently have educators become aware of the need to provide barrier-free buildings for handicapped students.

Nevertheless, much progress still needs to be made in many school districts that tend to have high percentages of mentally retarded, learning disabled, and emotionally disturbed students. For example, a 1980 report presented data indicating that thousands of handicapped children in many big cities are on waiting lists for placement in special education programs. The report further charges that the federal Bureau of Education for the Handicapped (BEH) has failed to monitor and enforce PL 94-142 effectively. According to this report, the BEH has the power to delay or withhold federal funds and to issue cease and desist orders to states that do not comply with the law, but it has failed to take these steps to ensure compliance.[24]

Waiting lists and poor enforcement policies

CLASSIFICATION AND LABELING OF STUDENTS   Many of the problems associated with improving education for handicapped children are related to difficulties in identifying and classifying students who require special education. It is very difficult to be sure, for example, whether a slow child is mentally retarded and could benefit from special educational services or is simply a

24 "BEH Fails to Enforce, Monitor Handicapped Law, Group Says," *Education Daily* (n.d.), pp. 7–8.

slow learner who requires more time and guidance to learn. Similarly, it is difficult to determine whether a child who is working below capacity has brain damage or some other learning disability, or is performing poorly because he or she is poorly motivated or poorly taught. (Of course, all three reasons may be operative for the same child.) Specialists in special education disagree among themselves on what constitutes a learning disability requiring special educational services, and what services should be provided for a particular disability. Similar problems are encountered in distinguishing between children who are severely versus mildly emotionally disturbed, partially deaf versus nonhearing, or close to some borderline (which may be very fuzzy and ill defined) on other aspects of handicapped status.

Defining what constitutes a learning disability

Uncertainty in accurately classifying students is connected with fundamental questions regarding appropriate treatment for a given child. Uncertainty about classification also raises issues involving the effects of "labeling" of handicapped students. As state government requirements to provide special services for handicapped students increased during the 1950s and 1960s, a higher percentage of students than in earlier decades was being labeled as handicapped and placed in special programs to improve their learning. This "special class" approach was an attempt to provide help to children who clearly needed it. During the 1960s, however, many educators and parents began to question the special-class approach, primarily on the grounds that it isolates mildly handicapped children from other students. In so doing, critics argue, it fails to prepare them to function in the larger society, and it generates feelings of inadequacy and inferiority among students who are shunted aside in classes organized under such labels as "emotionally disturbed" or "retarded." Critics also are concerned with the possibility that handicapped classification may generate a self-fulfilling prophecy: students labeled as disturbed, for example, may be more inclined to act in a disturbed manner because the label makes this acceptable and expected.[25]

Researchers concerned with the effects of labeling on handicapped students have tried to determine whether classification and placement in a special class or program really do have a detrimental effect on students. Among the variables they have considered are effects on self-concept, peer acceptance, and postschool outcomes. This type of research is very difficult to conduct because of problems involving definition of terms, the measurement of program effects, and the fact that differing students have different reactions to a given program or placement. Moreover, the likelihood that labeling may have a negative effect does not mean that placement in a nonlabeled (regular) class or setting necessarily will be more beneficial. Two researchers who reviewed studies on labeling thus were

Effects of placing students in special programs

25 Donald L. Macmillan and C. Edward Meyers, "Educational Labeling of Handicapped Learners" in D. C. Berliner, ed., *Review of Research in Education* vol. 7 (Washington, D.C.: American Educational Research Association, 1979), pp. 121–94.

forced to conclude that the allegedly overall negative effects of special or separate classes or programs for the handicapped were not well established. However, neither has it been proved that separate classes or programs for the handicapped are more beneficial, on the average, than is placement in regular or normal classes.[26]

MAINSTREAMING Despite the lack of conclusive data showing detrimental effects of labeling and special classes for the handicapped, some courts have weighed the evidence and concluded that special placement probably does have detrimental effects for many students, particularly for those who are or might be classified as only mildly handicapped. In addition, PL 94-142 now requires that handicapped students be placed in the "least restrictive environment"—the handicapped child should participate in regular or "normal" educational programming to the fullest extent possible. Efforts to place handicapped children in regular class settings generally are referred to as "mainstreaming" and have been encouraged and carried out in school districts throughout the country since the passage of PL 94-142.

Fundamentally, mainstreaming is the movement toward integrating handicapped children into regular schools and classrooms, providing maximum opportunities not only to join in usual school activities but also to be "counted in" among their nonhandicapped peers. It is not intended to be a wholesale elimination of special services, programs, or classes designed for children with exceptional needs. The mainstreaming philosophy requires that handicapped children still receive as much extra support from specialists as each requires. Extra professional support may include a wide range of services, including interpretation by specialists skilled in working with a particular handicap and provision of special equipment needed to help a child with a serious disability. But even if a disability is severe and a child needs to spend a relatively great amount of time away from the regular classroom, he or she can still be encouraged to take part in activities such as art, music, or shop that are open to other children.

Extra support from specialists

Research on mainstreaming has led to conclusions as ambiguous as the results of studies of labeling and special class placement. Three researchers who examined the literature on mainstreaming concluded that the data regarding effects on self-esteem are inconclusive. They did report, however, that mainstreaming can improve the social acceptance of handicapped students, provided that direct interventions are made to achieve this goal.[27] Their overall conclusion was as follows: "First and foremost,

26 Ibid.

27 Melvyn I. Semmel, Jay Gottlieb, and Nancy M. Robinson, "Mainstreaming: Perspectives on Educating Handicapped Children in Public Schools," in Berliner, ed., *Review of Research in Education*, vol. 7, pp. 223–79.

there is little evidence that mainstreaming practices result in superior performance among handicapped students.'' They went on to speculate that this general finding probably is related to difficulties in defining and measuring various mainstreaming approaches, as well as to the special placement settings with which they then are compared. Available evidence indicates that amount of time in regular classes, without considering the quality of instruction or the criteria employed to determine who gets mainstreamed and for how long, has little impact on social or academic outcomes. ''Until such time as the content, nature of instruction, and other process variables'' in mainstreaming are identified and measured, they concluded, it is useless to ask the general question whether mainstreaming is beneficial or detrimental.[28]

Identifying variables

Researchers who have reviewed the data on special class placement and mainstreaming thus seem to be in agreement that research has not provided conclusive support for either approach. In part, this can be attributed to the probability that neither approach is carried out very well in a large number of settings; in this case one would expect to find that both are ineffective and neither is superior to the other. The research indicates that regular classroom teachers have not been well prepared to work with handicapped students in their classes.[29]

However, these pessimistic observations should not be viewed as justifying despair concerning the future of mainstreaming or other efforts to improve education for handicapped students. Mainstreaming may prove to be a positive answer to the long tradition of isolating handicapped students, but in itself it is not a panacea. To be effective, mainstreaming requires a variety of special resources and educators who are skilled and dedicated in creating an effective learning environment and acceptance for handicapped students.[30] One of the nation's foremost educational goals in the 1980s will be to try to make the mainstreaming approach now mandated by the federal government more successful in the future than it has been in the past.

Improving mainstreaming efforts

MASTERY LEARNING

Mastery learning strategies are being developed at a variety of grade levels from preschool to postsecondary. The approach that is being used most widely in elementary and secondary schools is the LFM approach (Learning for Mastery) associated with Benjamin Bloom.[31] Bloom's mastery learning

28 Ibid., pp. 267-68.

29 Semmel, Gottlieb, and Robinson, ''Mainstreaming''; R. Bruce Baum, ''Educating the Exceptional Child in the Regular Classroom,'' *Journal of Teacher Education* (November-December 1979), pp. 20-22.

30 Thomas E. Linton and Kristen D. Juul, ''Mainstreaming: Time for Reassessment,'' *Educational Leadership* (February 1980), pp. 433-35.

31 Benjamin S. Bloom, *Human Characteristics and School Learning* (New York: McGraw-Hill, 1976); Bloom, *All Our Children Learning* (New York: McGraw-Hill, 1980).

ideas have been gaining supporters particularly in big-city school districts, where there is an obvious need to improve academic performance
among disadvantaged students. Chicago, New Orleans, New York, and
other big-city districts are launching major mastery learning projects to
improve the performance of students at both the elementary and secondary levels.[32]

Bloom's LFM approach is based on the central argument that 90
percent of public school students can learn much of the curriculum at
practically the same level of mastery, with the slower 20 percent of students in this 9/10s distribution needing 10–20 percent more time than the
faster 20 percent. Though the slower students require a longer period of
time, they can succeed if their initial level of knowledge is correctly diagnosed and they are taught with appropriate materials and methods in a
sequential manner, beginning with their initial level.

To accomplish this goal, attention must be focused on small units of
instruction, and criterion-referenced tests must be used to determine
whether a student possesses skills required for success in each step in the
learning sequence being taught. An entire course such as third grade
mathematics is too complex to be studied in large units. Instead, it should
be broken into smaller pieces following some of the principles of programmed instruction. Joan Hyman and S. Alan Cohen, who have been
developing ways to do this through LFM and other mastery learning approaches, have summarized some of the key steps in mastery learning as
follows: (1) define instructional objectives behaviorally so the teacher and
learner both know exactly where they are and what they must accomplish;
(2) teach the behavior or attitude sought in the objective directly rather
than "building" to or around it; (3) provide immediate feedback to all
learner responses; (4) set the level of instruction so that students are
maximally successful; (5) divide instruction into small, self-contained
modules; (6) control the stimulus so the teacher knows exactly what the
learner is responding to; and (7) provide positive feedback to reinforce the
learner's "critical" response (the response that corresponds to the instructional stimulus precisely defined by the instructional objective).[33]

**Key steps in
mastery
learning**

Educators are still working to identify the best methods for introducing mastery learning in the classroom.[34] But construction, testing,
and validation of mastery learning units and curricula generally take
years to accomplish and require the development of teacher and administrator training materials as well as the identification of which specific

32 Gene Geisert, "SCIP: A New Orleans Solution to a National Problem," *Educational
Leadership* (November 1979), pp. 128-35; Michael Katims, "The Chicago Plan: Mastery
Learning in the Chicago Public Schools," *Educational Leadership* (November 1979),
pp. 120-23.

33 Joan S. Hyman and S. Alan Cohen, "Learning for Mastery: Ten Conclusions After 15 Years
and 3,000 Schools," *Educational Leadership* (November 1979), pp. 104-09.

34 Hyman and Cohen, "Learning for Mastery"; James H. Bloch, *Schools, Society and Mastery Learning* (New York: Holt, Rinehart, 1974).

variations and practices work best in the classroom.[35] These variations include such approaches as DISTAR (developed by Bereiter and Engelmann) and other direct instruction programs—all of which stress teaching and learning basic skills in small steps, precise learning goals, drill and immediate feedback from the teacher, diagnostic tests, and reteaching exercises. A substantial body of data already available indicate that mastery learning can result in large learning gains for students. In this regard, one observer has reviewed more than a hundred studies on mastery learning and concluded that the results "indicate that mastery strategies do indeed have moderate to strong effects on student learning when compared to conventional methods of instruction."[36]

Data favorable to mastery learning do not mean that all the important questions have been answered or that mastery strategies do not have critics. We do not yet know, for example, how well differing mastery learning approaches can work for "higher-order" learning, for affective learning, or for different types of students (both high-aptitude and low-aptitude).[37] And a number of observers have criticized mastery learning for such reasons as its emphasis on narrowing rather than broadening achievement differences, its insistence that all students should be taught the same material at least part of the time, and its alleged focus on "behavioristic" rather than "humanistic" learning objectives and activities.[38] Skeptics also point out that there is still a long way to go in developing sophisticated diagnostic and assessment tests and instruments to make mastery learning a reality on a more widespread basis.[39]

Critical
questions and
criticisms

Answering the critics, mastery learning advocates have argued that its emphasis on motivating students through success is a basically humanistic approach in accord with sound psychological principles and that mastery approaches that bring nearly all students to a minimum level of performance leave plenty of room for accelerated or enriched learning among high-aptitude students. Supporters also argue that mastery learning in some ways resembles other "adaptive" instructional systems such as IGE and PLAN (see Chapter 13) that attempt to address students' individual learning needs while arranging for the accomplishment of specific behavioral objectives.[40] In addition, Hyman and Cohen as well as

35 Carol Barber, "Training Principals and Teachers for Mastery Learning," *Educational Leadership* (November 1979), pp. 126-27.

36 Robert B. Burns, "Mastery Learning: Does It Work?" *Educational Leadership* (November 1979), p. 112.

37 Ibid.

38 Carl D. Glickman, "Mastery Learning Stifles Individuality," *Educational Leadership* (November 1979), pp. 100-02; Lauren B. Resnick, "Assuming That Everyone Can Learn Everything, Will Some Learn Less?" *School Review* (May 1977), pp. 445-52.

39 Lowell Horton, "Mastery Learning: Sound in Theory, But . . . ," *Educational Leadership* (November 1979), pp. 154-56.

40 Lorin W. Anderson, "Adaptive Education," *Educational Leadership* (November 1979), pp. 140-43.

others also point out that the success of mastery learning is attributable to its effects on increasing the percentage of classroom time in which students participate in prescribed learning activities, and that this result agrees with a great deal of other research which has found "time on task," "academically engaged learning," and related measures of student perseverance in pertinent learning activities to be the central element in determining how much students learn.[41] Mastery learning approaches already are being used with more than one million students in the United States and are being introduced in many other parts of the world.[42] Given the encouraging results of research to date and the stress these days on learning basic skills, mastery learning is likely to become much more widespread in the 1980s.

Similarity to direct learning

MINIMUM COMPETENCY TESTING

Despite some progress in improving the teaching of basic skills through mastery learning and similar approaches, "back-to-basics" was a term frequently heard in the 1970s. The demand for stress on "basics" came about for a number of reasons, which brought together supporters with widely divergent viewpoints and concerns about public schools. Knowledgeable observers have cited the following considerations as being among the most important sources of demands for a return to emphasis on traditional values for mastery of fundamental skills in education: (1) a general swing toward conservatism in U.S. society and a feeling that the family, the schools, and other institutions had become too permissive; (2) an increase in the role of citizens in school affairs leading some participants to become disillusioned with what they saw in the schools; (3) growing demands of minority groups for improved academic achievement; (4) employer dissatisfaction with the reading and arithmetic skills of high school graduates; (5) complaints from college officials and business organizations concerning skill deficiencies of high school graduates; (6) declining test scores on college entrance tests and other examinations; and (7) a feeling that the schools were initiating many unsuccessful experiments and changes and were trying to accomplish too many purposes unrelated to academic performance.[43]

Reasons for basic skills trend

Arising from a variety of sources, insistence on return to the basics naturally meant different things to different people. Depending on who one listened to, "back to basics" included such demands as:

41 Hyman and Cohen, "Learning for Mastery."

42 Ron Brandt, "A Conversation with Benjamin Bloom," *Educational Leadership* (November 1979), pp. 157-61.

43 Ben Brodinsky, "Back to the Basics: The Movement and Its Meaning," *Phi Delta Kappan* (March 1977), pp. 522-27; R.P. Riegel and N.B. Lovell, *Minimum Competency Testing* (Bloomington, Ind.: Phi Delta Kappan, 1980).

1. Greater emphasis should be placed on reading, writing, and arithmetic in the elementary grades.

2. Secondary schools should concentrate more heavily on English, science, history, and math.

3. Learning activities should be more consistently teacher-directed.

4. More emphasis should be placed on drill, recitation, daily homework, and evaluation.

5. Discipline should be strict, and dress codes should regulate student appearance.

6. Promotion should be based on performance rather than age or time spent in class.

7. "Frills" should be eliminated from the curriculum of the public schools. Definitions of "frills" vary from citation of courses in use of leisure time to studies of human relations or major social problems.

8. Electives should be eliminated and courses in traditional categories such as U.S. history and English grammar should be required.

9. Innovations such as "new math" and linguistic approaches in reading should be abolished.

10. Patriotism should be a fundamental part of the curriculum.[44]

Demands for stress on the basics stimulated much debate and disagreement among educators. Some felt that attempts to place more stress on creativity and "humanization" in the schools had been only half-hearted and fragmented in the first place and that most U.S. schools never had retreated from a basic skills emphasis. Others felt that newer approaches were developing basic skills as well as had traditional approaches, and that substantial gains in student performance were more likely to be attained through new technologies or instructional arrangements emphasizing both affective and cognitive goals than through traditional stress on mechanical acquisition of cognitive skills. Many felt that emerging public demands for a return to the basics were simple-minded attempts to deal with complex problems and likely would have a detrimental effect on the public schools.[45]

Many educators also concluded that too much stress on these relatively mechanical skills was detracting from students' learning of

44 Ibid.
45 John I. Goodlad, *What Schools Are For* (Bloomington, Ind.: Phi Delta Kappa, 1979).

higher-order skills involving comprehension and reasoning. This point of view was expressed in 1979 by the president of the National Council of Teachers of Mathematics, who stated that her organization had been criticizing overly narrow emphasis on computation and rote learning since 1975. "What can be most easily tested and taught," she added, "is dictating the objectives of many schools. This is an educational world turned on its head . . . the means to the end have become the ends in themselves."[46] Similarly, the president of the Association for Supervision and Curriculum Development told a federal House of Representatives sub-committee that the national decline in math performance was due to an "over-emphasis on back-to-basics and rote computation." "We are committed," he concluded, "to the importance of basic skills. But we also believe in balanced education . . . that includes both computational skills and use of those skills in meaningful ways."[47]

Need for balanced education

Given its diversity of supporters and content, the back-to-basics movement took differing forms in various states and school districts. In many school districts, for example, so-called "new math" approaches, which emphasize the development of conceptual understanding, were cut back in favor of drill in mathematical operations and computations. The establishment of "fundamental" schools emphasizing whole-class grouping and traditional instructional methods such as drill and recitation also can be attributed partly to demands for increased emphasis on development of basic skills in the schools. The largest and most important manifestation of the movement toward greater emphasis on basics, however, involved the introduction of minimum competency testing programs, usually on a statewide basis, in schools and school districts throughout the United States.[48]

EVOLVING COMPETENCY PROGRAMS Minimum competency testing, which establishes scores a student must meet to advance in or graduate from an instructional program, has existed for many years in some locations. Denver, for example, has had minimum competency testing since 1960.[49] Most school districts, however, have not had such requirements. Fueled by concerns that students were graduating from high school unable to read or do simple arithmetic, the majority of state governments introduced some form of a minimum competency program during the latter part of the

46 Shirley Hill, Testimony presented at the U.S. House of Representatives Sub-Committee on Elementary, Secondary, and Vocational Education Hearing, Washington, D.C., April 1979, p. 4.

47 "Ebersole Tells House Subcommittee to Take a New Look at 'New Math,'" *ASCD News Exchange* (December 1979), p. 2.

48 Richard M. Jaeger and Carol K. Tittle, eds., *Minimum Competency Achievement Testing: Motives, Models, Measures, and Consequences* (Berkeley, Calif.: McCutchan, 1980).

49 Ibid.

1970s. By 1979, 39 states had established competency testing for elementary and/or secondary students, and the remaining thirteen were considering doing so or were examining alternate approaches to statewide testing. A large number of school districts also initiated their own competency programs during this period, either in conjunction with or as an alternative to state testing. Chicago, for example, introduced reading requirements for entrance into high school; as a result, more than 4,000 eighth graders who failed the test had to attend summer school in 1979 and then take another exam before entering high school.

Gary, Indiana, is a good example of a school district that is developing its own approach to minimum competency testing. Gary is an industrial city with a high proportion of working-class students and poverty students. In 1974 the board of education extended graduation requirements to include "demonstrated proficiency in reading, oral and written communications, and mathematics." School officials realized that such requirements cannot be established successfully simply by publishing them and holding students to them, but rather by requiring a systematic effort to ensure they will be attained. For this reason they initiated a district-wide effort to help low-achieving students at all levels, with attention concentrated at the beginning of the program on secondary students who would have to make the most progress to meet the new graduation requirements that became operational between 1977 and 1980.[50]

New graduation requirements

State-level minimum competency testing programs can be illustrated by developments in such states as Pennsylvania and Florida. Pennsylvania's program is called Project 81 and began in 1976 with completion scheduled in 1981. The State Board of Education has characterized Project 81 as involving a "redefinition of the purposes of public education in terms of the competencies that children and young people should be acquiring at various grade levels" and as requiring the "development of a plan for shifting state board curriculum and graduation requirements from their dependence on courses, credits, and Carnegie units to newly defined competencies."[51] To graduate from high school, students will be required to demonstrate competence in both *basic skills* (reading, writing, speaking, computation, physical dexterity, problem solving, interpersonal relations) and *life roles* (tentatively categorized as focusing on citizenship, work, leisure, and home life). Based on pilot development in twelve school districts and an elaborate state committee structure including citizens and educators, plans are being developed to introduce statewide and local testing programs.

From courses and credits to competencies

50 Donald J. Henderson, "Gary, Indiana: High School Diplomas with Meaning," *Phi Delta Kappan* (May 1978), pp. 613-16.

51 John H. Sandberg, "K-12 Competency-Based Education Comes to Pennsylvania," *Phi Delta Kappan* (October 1979), p. 119.

Florida has been a leader in developing minimum competency tests. Following years of legislative work on educational accountability systems, a 1976 state law established the Florida Statewide Assessment Program and directed that a minimum standards test would be required for graduation from high school beginning in 1979. The test was administered to eleventh graders in 1977 and was divided into two components respectively designed to provide screening information that school districts could use to identify students needing special help and to determine whether students possessed functional literacy skills required for graduation.[52] State failure rates were 36 percent in mathematics and 8 percent in communication, and some districts—particularly those with high proportions of disadvantaged minority students—had much higher percentages.

Although few public objections had been registered in Florida prior to pilot testing in 1977, release of the data generated widespread discussion and heated debate throughout the state, as well as other parts of the nation. Among the most vocal objections were that the tests were culturally biased against minority students and that it would be unfair to prevent students from graduating if their schools had not been able to develop adequate mastery of basic skills. Florida State Department of Education officials responded by calling together curriculum specialists and teachers who examined the tests for cultural bias but found none, and by pointing out that the state was providing school districts with $10 million each year in compensatory education funds.[53] The director of the State Department of Education's Student Assessment Section also responded to a *Time* magazine statement that "Florida Flunks" in an article in which he said that "it is unfortunate that some educators still feel it would be better to graduate a student without necessary skills than to 'upset' him. Is this preferable to placing the student in a job or in college work for which he does not possess the necessary skills? . . ."[54]

Such responses did not, of course, silence critics of minimum competency testing in Florida or elsewhere. For example, one respected educational researcher described Florida's functional literacy testing program as "bizarre" and concluded that such efforts to distinguish between passing and failing students necessarily will yield arbitrary and "potentially dangerous" results.[55] Many other researchers have similar reservations, and civil rights groups in Florida were particularly concerned about

52 Thomas H. Fisher, "The Florida Competency Testing Program" in Jaeger and Tittle, ed., *Minimum Competency Achievement Testing*, pp. 217-38.

53 Ibid.

54 Thomas H. Fisher, "Florida's Approach to Competency Testing," *Phi Delta Kappan* (May 1978), p. 601.

55 Gene V. Glass, "Minimal Competence and Incompetence in Florida," *Phi Delta Kappan* (May 1978), pp. 602-04.

Vocal
objections and
criticisms

potentially inequitable effects on minority students. In 1978 a class action suit was initiated on behalf of ten Black students who believed that the state test had discriminatory impact, and a 1979 court ruling prohibited Florida from using competency test scores as a requirement for graduation until at least 1983. Florida may not use the exams as an exit requirement, the judge ruled, until it "insures a necessary period of time to orient students and teachers to the new functional literacy objectives, and to eliminate the taint on educational development which accompanied segregation."[56]

ISSUES
TO BE RESOLVED
The competency testing movement probably will continue to expand in the 1980s, particularly at the individual school district level where many districts will introduce or refine systematic efforts to improve student performance by coordinating testing with compensatory education and general instructional reform. However, the impact and durability of the competency movement will be determined partly by the degree to which such efforts are able to solve practical problems that arise in implementation of the tests. Among the most central problems and questions that still plagued the minimum competency movement as it entered the 1980s were the following:

1. *What content should be measured on tests required for promotion or graduation?* There is general agreement that reading and computation should be measured, but opinions differ on whether writing and speaking should be included, and there is relatively little agreement concerning whether or how to measure such areas as health, citizenship, and use of leisure time. Should failure on tests of these latter "life-role" competencies prevent a student from graduating from high school?

Need to agree on content and measuring methods

2. *How should standards be set?* What level of test performance should a state or school district require for graduation? Experts tend to be pessimistic about the adequacy of present test-construction procedures for providing valid answers. Some experts believe that disagreements among educators and judges regarding level of performance defined as acceptable and the skills that are required for success in employment make any particular minimum cut-off point arbitrary and indefensible. Standard-setting methods "ultimately rely on human judgment, whether or not it is cloaked by sophisticated machinations."[57]

Need to agree on standards

56 "Federal Judge Postpones Use of Competency Tests for Graduation," *Phi Delta Kappan* (September 1979), p. 4.

57 "Minimum Competency Testing: Procedures, Impact and Legal Issues," *Clearinghouse for Applied Performance Testing Newsletter* (November 1977), p. 2.

3. *What will be the impact on school curricula?* Skeptics further point out that setting minimum scores so low that virtually everyone passes may make tests little more than a mockery while setting scores so high that there are many failures may lead teachers to spend inordinate amounts of time "teaching" the test. Even if standards are not set very high, some observers argue, competency testing is likely to divert instructional efforts from important goals such as creativity and affective learning to others such as computation that are more easily measured.[58]

4. *What are the legal obstacles, and how can they be overcome?* Lawyers have pointed to several important legal issues in addition to possible discriminatory impact of minimum competency tests. For example, students must be given sufficient prior notice so they can prepare for tests, test phase-in procedures must ensure that students have an opportunity to learn the material tested, and provision must be made to protect the rights of handicapped students.[59] Courts are just beginning to provide guidelines to resolve these and related issues.

5. *Can schools afford the expense of preparing students to pass tests in a variety of skill areas?* Do students retain the skills in which they are tested? One observer who has made a national study of minimum competency testing has pointed out that remedial programs to improve skills can be very expensive and that justification of large amounts of spending for this purpose depends on evaluation of their long-range impact. In this regard he also points out that some evidence indicates that students forget much of what they learned in school within a few years.[60] Research can provide answers that will help assess the worth of minimum competency testing, but little research specifically designed to relate costs to benefits is now available.

SCHOOL FINANCE REFORM

School finance reform has been spurred by a series of judicial and legislative actions that have fundamentally changed the financing of elementary and secondary schools in most of the states. The first landmark decision was in the 1971 *Serrano* v. *Priest* decision in California. California, like nearly all the states, depended on local property taxes to support the schools, and plaintiffs argued that this system of financing resulted in unconstitu-

Property taxes and schools

---

58 Ibid.
59 "Lawyers Look at Competency Testing," *NAEP Newsletter* (August 1979), pp. 1-2.
60 "Need 'Hard' Evidence to Judge Tests," *NAEP Newsletter* (August, 1979), p. 6.

tional disparities in expenditures between wealthy and poor school districts. The California Supreme Court agreed, stating the following: "We have determined that . . . [the California] funding scheme invidiously discriminates against the poor because it makes the quality of a child's education a function of the wealth of his parents and neighbors."

Following the *Serrano* decision, more than thirty similar cases were filed in other states. One of these, *San Antonio Independent School District* v. *Rodriquez*, was taken to the U.S. Supreme Court after a federal court ruled that school finance arrangements in Texas were unconstitutional. By a five-to-four vote, the Supreme Court ruled in 1973 that expenditure disparities based on differences in local property taxes between school districts in a state were not unconstitutional under the federal constitution but might be unconstitutional under state constitutions, depending on the situation and the wording of the laws in a given state. The *Rodriquez* decision had the effect of placing the issue of inequities in school finance in the hands of the state courts and legislatures.[61]

Since *Rodriquez*, a number of state courts have ruled that financial arrangements that result in large differences in per pupil expenditures based on wealth differences between school districts are unconstitutional, and state legislatures in these and other states have enacted new financial arrangements designed to reduce or eliminate such disparities. In 1976, for example, the California Supreme Court's *Serrano II* decision reaffirmed its earlier finding that large financial disparities between districts are unconstitutional under the equal protection clause of the state constitution. In doing so, the Court observed that "there is a distinct relationship between cost and the quality of educational opportunities afforded." In some other states such as Idaho and Oregon, however, the courts have ruled that large differences in school district expenditures are not unconstitutional, provided that state finance formulas yield sufficient funds independent of a district's wealth to provide an adequate education for each child.

States reduce financial disparities

In general, many state legislatures have moved to introduce "equal yield" or "fiscally neutral" arrangements wherein funds raised by the property tax are supplemented or replaced by other state or local taxes. Provided that voters in low-wealth districts tax themselves at a rate similar to that in high-wealth districts, state government funds will significantly reduce per pupil expenditure differentials between poor and wealthy districts. This "power equalization" approach thus is intended to give low-wealth districts power equal to that of wealthy districts in financing adequate elementary and secondary education. Between 1971 and 1975, eighteen states reformed their school finance laws in a way that increased

61   David C. Long, "Litigation Concerning Educational Finance" in C. P. Hooker and K. J. Rehage, eds. *The Courts and Education*, Part I, National Society for the Study of Education Yearbook (Chicago: University of Chicago Press, 1978), pp. 217–47.

the state share of public school expenditures from an average of 39 percent to an average of 51 percent.[62] For the nation as a whole, the percentage of school system funding drawn from local sources decreased from 52 percent in 1971 to 44 percent in 1979.

Nevertheless, state judicial and legislative decisions to reduce or eliminate district disparities do not automatically result in the establishment of equitable arrangements for financing education. Legislatures must develop formulas that ensure that local districts are encouraged to raise funds beyond the minimum needed for adequate education, and one must still ask whether new finance formulas are working as intended. In addition, defining "adequate education" raises questions that have resulted in a great deal of subsequent litigation and legislation, particularly with reference to urban school districts that have a high proportion of disadvantaged students for whom adequate schooling may require larger per pupil expenditures than the state or regional average. In the latter half of the 1970s, school finance reform activities dealing with these issues have been widespread, and more litigation and legislation can be expected in the 1980s.

Larger student expenditures for disadvantaged students

Much of the activity in this regard has been stimulated by the *Levittown* v. *Nyquist* decision in New York State. Initiated by Levittown and twenty-six other districts, the plaintiff's case described cost differential and "educational overburden" problems of city school districts due to "municipal overburden" and to "mismatch" between property wealth and actual taxing capacity.[63] Educational overburden is illustrated by high operation and maintenance cost of city schools due to age and vandalism, high instructional cost due to teacher seniority and unionization, and high proportions of disadvantaged students who require special assistance. Municipal overburden refers to the fact that city residents have relatively higher costs than taxpayers in most other school districts for police and fire protection, public health, social welfare, street repair, and other municipal functions; as a consequence voters are reluctant to raise school taxes because their overall tax bills already are very high. Mismatch between wealth and taxing capacity refers to the fact that though cities tend to have a relatively large amount of commercial and industrial property, voters in cities tend to be relatively unable or unwilling to approve school taxes because they include a relatively high proportion of low income individuals (particularly the elderly) and a relatively low proportion of persons with children in public schools. Plaintiffs also argued that existing school finance formulas based on the daily average of students in attendance also penalizes urban districts because they have a relatively

"Educational" and "municipal overburden"

---

62 *State School Finance Reform in the 1970s* (Excerpted from *School Finance Reform: A Legislators' Handbook* (Washington, D.C.: National Conference of State Legislatures, 1976).

63 Joan Scheuer, "Levittown v. Nyquist: A Dual Challenge," *Phi Delta Kappan* (February 1979), pp. 432-36.

high percentage of absent students for whom they still must arrange basic instructional services.

In 1978 the court issued a straightforward opinion affirming plaintiffs' arguments and concluding that New York's school finance system had failed to give "all the state's schoolchildren the opportunity to acquire at least those basic skills necessary to function in a democratic society. . . . Where it is demonstrated that there is a greater need, it follows that a greater amount of aid must be furnished if equal educational opportunity is to be available." The *Levittown* decision was still being appealed in 1980, but Michael Kirst, president of the California State Board of Education and a leading scholar in school finance, has reviewed its significance along with other developments such as California's 1978 Proposition 13 (drastically cutting the local property tax) and 1979 Proposition 4 (tying government spending increases to population and inflation), and concluded that:

Proposition 13 in California

> . . . the school finance reform movement has moved creatively in new directions. It went about as far as it could with the *Serrano* approach. The courts have given renewed life to educational need formulas after rejecting "need" as too complex in the 1960s. . . . Two rival political movements—school finance reform and spending/tax limitation—are going to confront each other in several states. This is a major development in the state politics of resource allocation.[64]

LARGER ROLE OF COURTS AND GOVERNMENT

Material in this chapter has illustrated the increasing initiative and role of the courts in determining practices and policies in the public schools. Bilingual education, how to teach Black students who speak non-standard English, school finance arrangements, education of the handicapped, and state or local minimum competency testing are but a few of the educational issues that are being governed or modified by decisions in the courts. As we saw in other chapters, desegregation, student and teacher rights, and a host of other topics and practices in the public schools also are receiving attention partly as a result of the decisions of local, state, and federal courts.

Increasingly active role of the courts

The growing role of the courts in general and the federal courts in particular is evident when one considers the total number of state and federal court cases in the United States between 1789 and 1971. In the 107

64 Michael W. Kirst, "The New Politics of State Education Finance," *Phi Delta Kappan* (February 1979), pp. 429, 431.

years from 1789 to 1896, there were only 3,096 such cases, and only 50 of them were federal. In the decade from 1947 to 1956, by way of contrast, there were 7,091 state and federal court cases, and 112 were federal. An increasing federal role, however, was even evident in the 1967–71 period, during which time there were 1,273 federal cases as compared with 964 state cases.[65] In the words of one veteran observer, the general increase in educational litigation and the growing role of the federal courts reflect the fact that "Education has assumed an importance in our society that it did not have just a few decades ago. Today, we are in a time of profound change. . . . It is natural that public education would be the subject of spirited community discussion and debate."[66]

Much of the control of education remains, as it always has, in the hands of states and local school districts, from whence come most of the revenues for education. Local school districts continue to exert the primary authority—delegated from the states—on personnel, curriculum, and instructional decisions affecting the day-to-day operation of the schools. State government has always had the power to rescind or modify the policies of the local district.

Control at local and state levels

But while local control and state powers over local districts are considered so well established as to be almost folklore, and while the federal government has traditionally been a distant third in directing the course of the public schools, the situation is changing.[67] The role of the federal government, according to the Department of Education, is to "provide encouragement, financial support, and leadership on educational issues of broad national concern, as appropriate within legislative mandates and constitutional constraints. It has the responsibility also of safeguarding the right of every citizen to access to free public education and to equality of educational opportunity."[68]

As education has become more important in national affairs, the federal government has played an increasingly larger role in financing the public schools and initiating programs to improve instruction in the classroom. After the Russians orbited their Sputnik space satellite, for example, Americans became more conscious of the importance of education in national defense and international affairs, and Congress responded by passing the National Defense Education Act of 1958. Similar federal initiatives regarding equal educational opportunity followed civil rights

Federal initiatives

65 John C. Hogan, *The Schools, The Courts, and the Public Interest* (Lexington, Mass.: Heath, 1974).

66 Thomas A. Shannon, *Current Trends in School Law* (Topeka, Kan.: National Organization in Legal Problems of Education, 1974), p. 5.

67 Arthur Wise, *Legislated Learning: The Bureaucratization of the American Classroom* (Berkeley, Calif.: University of California Press, 1979).

68 *Progress of Education in the United States of America 1976-77 and 1977-78* (Washington, D.C.: U.S. Government Printing Office, 1979), p. 8.

activities of the 1950s and 1960s and a string of court decisions delineating unequal opportunities available to minority groups and women in the 1960s and 1970s.

Federal funding has always meant some supervision to assure it was used for the purposes designated, but since the 1960s the concept of program purpose has been enlarged to mean that federal financing of one program subjects any other program or activity to regulation. In other words, by accepting federal money for any aspect of the school or college program, the recipient institution is open to federal regulation of its overall operation. Schools that receive federal funds to assist low income students, for example, must thereby meet detailed federal guidelines for the affirmative action employment of women and minorities. This developing set of regulations has extended the whole range of federal statutory requirements to schools and colleges both public and private. Local and state school officials now must prepare literally hundreds of federal forms and reports dealing with topics as diverse as student records and information, personnel recruitment, desegregation, school heating systems, and participation in athletic programs.[69] The federal government has made a concerted effort to simplify and reduce local school reporting requirements, but officials in most school districts still have an enormous workload in describing and justifying their efforts to meet the federal government's reporting and program implementation requirements.[70] As indicated in one national survey, by 1980 annual school district costs for providing federally mandated data were more than $230 million.[71]

The increasing role of the federal government in education also has been highlighted by the establishment in 1980 of a separate U.S. Department of Education. Formerly part of the Department of Health, Education, and Welfare, the Department of Education was established to achieve the following objectives: (1) strengthen federal commitment to ensure access to equal educational opportunity for every individual; (2) supplement and complement efforts by other institutions to improve the quality of education; (3) encourage increased involvement of the public, parents, and students in federal education programs; (4) improve the quality and usefulness of education through federally supported research, evaluation, and sharing of information; (5) improve coordination, management, and efficiency of federal education programs and activities; and (6) increase accountability to the President, the Congress, and the public.

**Establishment
of Department
of Education**

The Department of Education had a first-year budget of about $14 billion and had approximately 17,500 employees and 150 programs trans-

69 Allan C. Ornstein, *Education and Social Inquiry* (Itasca, Ill.: Peacock, 1978).

70 "Feds Promise Paperwork Cuts, But Don't Hold Your Breath Waiting," *American School Board Journal* (October 1979), pp. 26-27.

71 Stanley Pogrow, "Controlling the Paperwork Burden," *Phi Delta Kappan* (January 1980), pp. 345-46.

ferred from other federal agencies. Congressional legislation specifically stated that the "Department of Education shall not increase the authority of the Federal government over education or diminish the responsibility for education which is reserved to the States and the local school systems and other instrumentalities of the States." Proponents of the legislation included the National Education Association and more than 140 other organizations that argued that the Department would give education greater status and influence. Opponents included the American Federation of Teachers and other organizations that feared the Department would give the federal government greater control over education and would be dominated by interests representing elementary and secondary education.[72] Whichever side proves to be more nearly correct, there is little doubt that the new U.S. Department of Education will have an important impact on all aspects of education in the 1980s.

Support and opposition from other organizations

EDUCATION IN THE FUTURE

Professional educators are joining scholars in other fields in speculating about the American future. Futurist writings have a long tradition, from Plato's *Republic* to the despairing visions of George Orwell's *1984*, but futurists of today have better tools and more sophisticated statistical data from which to work and speculate than did those of the past. Although they are often charged with escapism and with dodging present problems, actually the opposite is more nearly true; the futurists study alternatives and clarify options available in the present and in the future.

Long tradition since Plato

Studying alternatives and options

Future trends (many of which are already becoming apparent), based on the combined assessments of three outstanding futurists in education are listed below:

1. The school curriculum will be extended downward and upward. Two-year-olds may start school in front of the television. Adults in their forties and fifties will return to college for retraining. Senior citizens will look at postcollege work as a form of leisure.

2. Educational experiences will extend throughout the year, eliminating the present standard summer vacation.

3. Standardized measures for assessing students in relation to a large group (*normative* measures) will be complemented by an evaluation of personalized growth patterns (*criterion* measures).

4. Fewer teachers will be employed. Some teachers will be replaced by machinery, part-time specialists, and teacher aides. We shall see an increase in the variety of teachers' roles and assignments.

72 "Support of Over 140 Organizations Gives Education Cabinet Status," *Department of Education Weekly* (October 17, 1979), pp. 7–8.

5. There will be fewer or no semester terms and less rigid class schedules; rather, there will be more mini-subjects for a few weeks or months and a much greater variety of subjects to choose from. Students will more readily exit and re-enter school so that their academic experiences will be coupled with the world of work and travel.

6. Subjects will be expanded to include materials and knowledge from new fields. Education will bring into its ranks many more people whose preparation combines educational and other academic backgrounds.

7. Human values will receive greater attention in the curriculum.

8. Self-realization and group therapy centers will be part of the school complex. Additional health, guidance, and psychological services will be administered by an educational center.

9. A host of chemicals and drugs and electrical current may be used in manipulating human behavior and accelerating learning.

10. Schools, as we know them, will be replaced by diversified learning environments. Greater utilization will be made of social and psychological centers, homes, parks, public buildings, and private industry.

11. Educational technology will expand, particularly computers and television. The role of industry in computer technology will be similar to the role of publishers in the production and marketing of textbooks. Big business, already involved in new ventures in educational material and technology, will expand its interests and production into the educational market.

12. Education will be more and more concerned with developing international understanding and with preparing students to live in an interdependent world. Schools will become more systematic in making sure that students understand the meaning and implications of trends and developments throughout the world.[73]

We have encountered such violent changes in the recent past that many of us are suffering from disorientation. The social and physical environment in which we find ourselves today is literally as strange, in many ways, as that in which a U.S. Peace Corps volunteer finds himself in a remote village in the Andes or on the Congo. We have encountered not only *cultural shock*—a new and partly incomprehensible way of life, a

73 Louis Rubin, ed., *The Future of Education: Perspectives on Tomorrow's Schooling* (Boston: Allyn & Bacon, 1975); Harold G. Shane, *Educational Significance of the Future* (Bloomington, Ind.: Phi Delta Kappa, 1973); Alvin Toffler, ed., *Learning for Tomorrow* (New York: Random House, Vintage Books, 1974).

new value system—but also *future shock*—in which we are so overwhelmed by numerous options and stimuli that our cognitive process breaks down, and there is a loss of ability to communicate ideas.[74]

Future-planning concepts will be needed in order to prevent future shock in education. In the past, future planning in education was linear and based on intuitive guesses or estimates as to the nature of tomorrow. Future planning of education will have to be based on multivariable possibilities and on scientific projection of data. Customary planning and intuitive guessing are being replaced by systematic analysis of the opportunities the future has to offer.[75]

Methods that are being developed or used to forecast the future include the *Delphi approach*, in which expert opinions are tabulated and refined into a prediction of the future; *trend extrapolation and modification*, in which past trends are extended into the future but modified according to predicted change caused by specific variables that are taken into consideration; *computer simulations*, in which a large number of complex forces are examined to see how they interact and influence the future; and *alternative scenarios*, in which one portrays and analyzes differing future possibilities to determine which is most desirable and how it can be attained.

Futuristic forecasting methods are designed to identify the perils of existing policies and the probable results of changes that might give us more control over our future. "Every society," according to Alvin Toffler, "faces not merely a succession of *probable* futures, but an array of *possible* futures, and a conflict over *preferable* futures. The management of change is the effort to convert certain possibles into probables, in pursuit of agreed-on preferables."[76] Futuristic forecasting in its various forms already has begun to be applied in shaping decisions regarding the public schools. For example, school districts all over the country are employing specialists in computers and statistics to predict future enrollment patterns. Schools are using these data to make decisions about how many teachers to hire and which schools to close. Future enrollment studies are being used to draw up desegregation plans that are reasonable and feasible for the future.

SUMMING UP

1. Developments in the future are foreshadowed by what has happened in the past. We have described some of the trends and issues that have become prominent in the 1970s and are likely to receive a great deal of attention in the 1980s.

---

74 Alvin Toffler, *Future Shock* (New York: Random House, 1970); Toffler, *The Third Wave* (New York: Morrow, 1980).

75 Jim Bowman, et al., *The Far Side of the Future: Social Problems and Educational Reconstruction* (Washington, D.C.: World Future Society, 1978).

76 Toffler, *Future Shock*, p. 460.

2. Various aspects of multicultural education will be further developed and argued over, education for the handicapped will continue to expand, mastery learning and related efforts to improve instruction in the classroom will be introduced more widely in the public schools, issues involving minimum competency testing will be resolved in the courts and the schools, state governments will provide a larger share of school taxes and will tie financing more closely to instructional reform, and the courts and the federal government will play a still more active role in elementary and secondary education. Planning of education for the future will attempt to relate education more closely to major changes and problems in U.S. society as a whole.

3. Previous chapters also discussed major contemporary educational problems including desegregation, the quest for equal opportunity, and tensions between cognitive and affective goals in education. Because these problems arise from larger issues that confront society as a whole, educators are forced to deal with them whether they want to or not. It is tempting to try to ignore larger social trends that impact on the public schools, but teachers and administrators are no longer allowed this luxury because the courts and the federal government reflect public concerns and demands that the educational system be responsive to current and emerging national problems.

4. Expenditures for education (elementary, secondary, and post-secondary, public and private) amounted to approximately $200 billion in 1980 and constituted about 7.5 percent of the gross national product, as compared with corresponding figures of $6.6 billion and 2.8 percent of GNP in 1947. These increases reflected education's growing importance in an increasingly complex and crisis-ridden modern society. In an era when crises in government and society occur with growing rapidity, education as an institution must help bring about planned change to ensure that the future will be livable and worthwhile.

DISCUSSION QUESTIONS

1. What do you think is the best definition of cultural pluralism? What implications does it have for education?

2. How have arrangements for educating handicapped children been changing? What are some of the most important problems and issues at the present time?

THINGS TO DO

1. Contact local public school officials and interview several teachers to determine what they are doing in multicultural education. Compare several schools or school districts to identify similarities and differences.

2. Organize a debate on the topic, "Advantages and Disadvantages of Main-

3. What are the major arguments for and against minimum competency testing of students?

4. For what reasons have the courts and the federal government become more involved in elementary and secondary education? What dangers are associated with federal involvement?

5. What are some of the probable future trends in education that you see taking shape in the 1980s? Try to add to the list cited in the chapter.

streaming Handicapped Children." Contact proponents and opponents to obtain information and points of view.

3. Find a school district that has tried to introduce mastery learning. Has the program succeeded? What problems have been encountered in implementing the program?

4. Collect data on minimum competency testing in a nearby school district. How many students are having problems passing? What do the tests measure? What problems has the district encountered?

5. Interview school officials who work with federally-funded programs in elementary or secondary schools? What restrictions are imposed? What changes seem to be needed in federal policy?

FOR PART IV
SUGGESTIONS FOR FURTHER READING

Benjamin S. Bloom, *All Our Children Learning* (New York: McGraw-Hill, 1980).

James B. Conant, *The American High School Today* (New York: McGraw-Hill, 1959).

Richard H. deLone, *Small Futures: Chidren, Inequality, and the Limits of Liberal Reform* (New York: Harcourt Brace Jovanovich, 1979).

Noel Epstein, *Language, Ethnicity, and the Schools: Policy Alternatives for Bilingual-Bicultural Education* (Washington, D.C.: George Washington Institute for Educational Leadership, 1977).

John I. Goodlad, *What Schools Are For* (Bloomington, Inc.: Phi Delta Kappa, 1979).

David R. Krathwohl et al., *Taxonomy of Educational Objectives, Handbook II: Affective Domain* (New York: McKay, 1964).

Harold G. Shane, *Curriculum Change Toward the 21st Century* (Washington, D.C.: National Educational Association, 1977).

Alvin Toffler, *The Third Wave* (New York: Morrow, 1980).

Paul C. Violas, *The Training of the Urban Working Class: A History of Twentieth-Century American Education* (Chicago: Rand McNally, 1978).

Arthur Wise, *The Bureaucratization of the American Classroom* (Berkeley, Calif.: University of California Press, 1979).

CREDITS

Acknowledgement is made to the following for their permission to reprint materials from copyrighted sources:

Page 7, Table 1.1, from *Status of the American Public School Teacher, 1970-71*, p. 54, Table 36, copyright 1972 by the National Education Association. Reprinted by permission of the publisher.

Page 9, Table 1.2, from Charles E. Hood, "Why 226 University Students Selected Teaching as a Career," *Clearing House* (December 1965), p. 228. Reprinted by permission of Heldref Publications.

Page 18, Table 1.3, from *Estimates of School Statistics, 1979-80*, p. 32, Table 7, copyright 1980 by the National Education Association. Reprinted by permission of the publisher.

Page 19, Table 1.4, from Frank S. Endicott, "Trends in Employment of College and University Graduates in Business and Industry," in Northwestern University *Annual Reports* (1965, 1966, 1970, 1971, 1975, 1976, 1979, 1980), p. 35, Table 32; reprinted by permission of the author. Also taken from *Economic Status of the Teaching Profession, 1972-73*, p. 35, Table 32, copyright 1973 by the National Education Association, and from *Prices, Budgets, Salaries, and Income*, p. 24-26, Tables 20-22, copyright 1980 by the National Education Association; both reprinted by permission of the publisher.

Page 260, Table 10.1, from August B. Hollingshead, *Elmtown's Youth*, p. 462, copyright 1949 by John Wiley & Sons, Inc. Reprinted by permission of the publisher.

Page 261, Table 10.2, from August B. Hollingshead, *Elmtown's Youth*, p. 172, copyright 1949 by John Wiley & Sons, Inc. Reprinted by permission of the publisher.

Page 261, Table 10.3, from Robert J. Havinghurst, "Social Class Influences on American Education," in N. Henry, ed., *Social Forces Influencing American Education, Part II*, p. 122, copyright 1961 by University of Chicago Press. Reprinted by permission of the National Society for the Study of Education.

PHOTOS

3 Joe Di Dio, National Education Association; 6 Joe Di Dio, National Education Association; 29 Miriam Reinhart/Photo Researchers, Inc.; 30 Michael Goss; 47 Raimondo Borea/Marilyn Gartman Agency; 51 Raimondo Borea/Marilyn Gartman Agency; 71 Dailo Nardi/Freelance Photographers Guild; 87 Michael Goss; 105 Historical Pictures Service, Inc., Chicago; 123 Historical Pictures Service, Inc., Chicago; 130 Historical Pictures Service, Inc., Chicago; 147 Library of Congress; 161 Historical Pictures Service, Inc., Chicago; 183 Old Sturbridge Village Photo by Donald F. Eaton; 194 Don Getsug/Rapho/Photo Researchers, Inc.; 211 Spencer Blank/Freelance Photographers Guild; 225 Nancy Hays/Monkmeyer Photo Service; 233 Fred Forbes/Humbird Hopkins, Inc.; 257 Rohn Engh/Freelance Photographers Guild; 274 Eric Kroll/Taurus Photos; 290 Sybil Shelton/Peter Arnold, Inc.; 300 Freelance Photographers Guild; 323 Sybil Shelton/Monkmeyer Press Photo Service; 335 Peter Karas/Freelance Photographers Guild; 351 Erika Stone/Peter Arnold, Inc.; 356 George Bellerose/Stock, Boston, Inc.; 382 James H. Karales/Peter Arnold, Inc.; 405 Sybil Shelton/Peter Arnold, Inc.; 409 Robert Llewellyn/Freelance Photographers Guild; 431 Nancy Hayes/Monkmeyer Press Photo Service; 443 Arthur Grace/Stock, Boston, Inc.; 455 Sybil Shelton/Peter Arnold, Inc.

AUTHOR INDEX

SUBJECT AND NAME INDEX